China Arbitration Yearbook

Series Editor

Yifei Lin, Shenzhen, Vatican City State

Yifei Lin

New Arbitration Law in China

Springer

Yifei Lin
Yi & Partners
Shenzhen, Guangdong, China

ISSN 2524-8618 ISSN 2524-8626 (electronic)
China Arbitration Yearbook
ISBN 978-981-92-0641-4 ISBN 978-981-92-0642-1 (eBook)
https://doi.org/10.1007/978-981-92-0642-1

This Springer imprint is published by the registered company Springer Nature Singapore Pte Ltd.
The registered company address is: 152 Beach Road, #21-01/04 Gateway East, Singapore 189721, Singapore

Preface

On September 12, 2025, the 17th Session of the Standing Committee of the 14th National People's Congress voted to adopt the newly revised Arbitration Law of the People's Republic of China (the New Arbitration Law), which became effective on March 1, 2026. Since the implementation of China's Arbitration Law on September 1, 1995, more than 30 years have passed, with two amendments made in 2009 and 2017, respectively. By the end of August 2025, China had established over 280 arbitration commissions, which had collectively handled more than 5 million arbitration cases involving over 9 trillion RMB in disputed amounts. In 2024, arbitration institutions nationwide accepted a total of more than 760,000 cases, with the total amount in dispute exceeding 1.2 trillion RMB. Parties involved in arbitration came from more than 100 countries and regions, and the disputes handled covered various fields such as trade, investment, finance, construction engineering, maritime, intellectual property, and supply chains. Arbitration is assuming growing importance within the diversified dispute resolution framework.

With the rapid development of China's economy and society and the continuous expansion of its opening-up, the arbitration system needs to address new situations and issues, adapt to the new landscape, and further refine the legal framework for arbitration. The New Arbitration Law represents the first major overhaul since the promulgation of the Arbitration Law (1994), signaling that China's arbitration system is gradually entering a new phase of systematic improvement, high-quality development, and deep international integration. The New Arbitration Law clarifies the overarching requirements for the development of arbitration endeavors and introduces a series of institutional arrangements in areas such as foreign-related arbitration mechanisms, arbitration institutions, arbitrator systems, and other systems aligned with international arbitration practices.

Regarding the improvement of the foreign-related arbitration system, firstly, the scope of foreign-related arbitration cases has been expanded. Secondly, the concept of seat of arbitration and *ad hoc* arbitration has been introduced, clarifying that for specific disputes, parties may choose to have their case heard by an arbitral tribunal composed of persons meeting statutory requirements, conducting the arbitration in accordance with agreed-upon arbitration rules, as an alternative to institutional arbitration.

With regard to improving the arbitration institution and arbitrator system, firstly, it clarifies that the nature of arbitration institutions is that of nonprofit legal persons serving the public interest. Secondly, it requires arbitration institutions to establish and improve their internal governance structures, strengthen supervision over the members and staff of arbitration institutions, as well as arbitrators, while authorizing the State Council to formulate specific measures for the registration and management of arbitration institutions, and standardize the registration procedures for modifications and deregistration of arbitration institutions. Thirdly, it standardizes the terms and reappointment of the members of arbitration institutions. Fourthly, it improves the qualifications for serving as an arbitrator and establishes disclosure systems for arbitration institutions and arbitrators.

Regarding the promotion of arbitration practices aligned with internationally accepted rules, it mainly includes: (1) explicitly emphasizing that arbitration shall adhere to the principle of good faith, while adding relevant provisions to prevent sham arbitration; (2) introducing an online arbitration system; (3) expanding the methods for recognizing arbitration agreements; (4) adding provisions on the service of arbitration documents; (5) broadening the methods for selecting the presiding arbitrator; (6) standardizing the procedural requirements for the designation of arbitrators by an arbitration institution; (7) shortening the time limit for applying to set aside an arbitral award; and (8) enhancing court support for arbitration in areas such as property preservation, conduct preservation, evidence preservation, and evidence collection; and so forth.

To facilitate readers from the arbitration, legal, and business communities in understanding and applying the New Arbitration Law, this book has been specifically prepared by integrating practices from arbitration in China. For each specific legal provision, in the form of Notes, we attempt to interpret the content of each clause from the perspective of arbitration law, modern commercial arbitration practice, and theoretical research. Additionally, for some provisions, we have listed some cases for reference. The cases involved are mostly guiding cases or typical cases used by the SPC of China and other courts at various levels to guide judicial review of arbitration. Of course, due to the interconnections between various specific systems of arbitration, cases may also overlap or cross-reference each other. For example, cases from the sections on the validity of arbitration agreements may also be applicable in chapters on setting aside or non-enforcement of awards.

This book aims to facilitate the understanding and application of the New Arbitration Law, striving to build a bridge between textual interpretation and practical operation. In doing so, it not only explains the legislative background, institutional logic, and connotations of the provisions of the new law but also explores its application paths and potential disputes in specific cases. It serves not only professionals such as lawyers, arbitrators, judges, and corporate legal counsel but also aims to provide references for academic research, policy formulation, and public awareness. New issues arising during the implementation of the New Arbitration Law, corresponding responses, and other matters not covered or involved in this volume will be further discussed in subsequent publications of this series based on practical needs.

In addition, it should be specially noted that nearly all the full texts of the cases and materials mentioned or contained in this book and all other books in this series, as well as more comprehensive data, commentaries, and academic debates, are available for access and reference via the **CNARB Arbitration Database**(www.cnarb.com). To provide the arbitration and commercial communities worldwide with the latest developments and insights on arbitration and dispute resolution, we have specially developed the **Cydeem APP**. On this APP, users can search for the most relevant cases, materials, and the latest developments in the arbitration and dispute resolution sectors, learn about the professional backgrounds of cross-industry arbitration and dispute resolution experts, and exchange views and information with peers in the arbitration and legal communities worldwide. You may download the **Cydeem APP** via www.cydeem.com.

I wish to express my sincere gratitude to my colleagues, especially Lulu CAI and Minyan LIANG, who devoted significant time to assisting me in the drafting of the initial manuscript, case research, and text proofreading. I also thank the publishing team of the press for their efficient work. I am committed to continuing my efforts in the research of arbitration law and practice. Dear readers and friends, should you have any suggestions or inquiries, please feel free to contact me at lyf@yipartners.com or follow me on the **Cydeem APP**.

Shenzhen, China Yifei Lin
May 7, 2026

Contents

Table of Abbreviations and Short Forms

AAA	American Arbitration Association
ACICA	Australian Centre for International Commercial Arbitration
Administrative Litigation Law	Administrative Litigation Law of the People's Republic of China
AFSA	Arbitration Foundation of Southern Africa
Arbitral Award Enforcement Provisions	Provisions of the Supreme People's Court on Several Issues concerning the Handling of Cases regarding Enforcement of Arbitral Award by the People's Courts
Arbitration Judicial Review Provisions	Provisions of the Supreme People's Court on Several Issues concerning Deciding Cases of Arbitration-Related Judicial Review
Arbitration Law (1994)	Arbitration Law of the People's Republic of China (adopted in 1994)
Arbitration Law (2017)	Arbitration Law of the People's Republic of China (amended in 2017)
Arbitration Law Interpretation	Interpretation of the Supreme People's Court on Certain Issues Concerning the Application of the Arbitration Law of the People's Republic of China
Arrangement Concerning Mutual Enforcement of Awards	Arrangement Concerning Mutual Enforcement of Arbitral Awards between the Mainland and the Hong Kong Special Administrative Region
ASA	Swiss Arbitration Association (Association Suisse de l'Arbitrage)
BAC	Beijing Arbitration Commission
Bankruptcy Law Interpretation (III)	Interpretation (III) of the Supreme People's Court on the Application of the Bankruptcy Law of the People's Republic of China
CCOIC	China Chamber of International Commerce
China	People's Republic of China
CIETAC	China International Economic and Trade Arbitration Commission
Civil Code	Civil Code of the People's Republic of China
Civil Procedure Law	Civil Procedure Law of the People's Republic of China

Civil Procedure Law Interpretation	Interpretation of the Supreme People's Court on the Application of the Civil Procedure Law of the People's Republic of China
CMAC	China Maritime Arbitration Commission
Choice of Law Interpretation	Interpretations of the Supreme People's Court on Several Issues Concerning Application of the Law of the People's Republic of China on Choice of Law for Foreign-Related Civil Relationships
Co.	Company
Company Law	Company Law of the People's Republic of China
Company Law Interpretation (II)	Interpretation II of the Supreme People's Court on Several Issues Concerning the Application of the "Company Law of the People's Republic of China"
Company Law Interpretation (IV)	Interpretation IV of the Supreme People's Court on Several Issues Concerning the Application of the "Company Law of the People's Republic of China"
Conference Minutes	The Minutes of the National Courts' Civil and Commercial Trial Work Conference
Construction Contracts Interpretation	Interpretation on Issues Concerning the Application of Law in the Trial of Cases Involving Disputes over Construction Contracts
Contract Law	Contract Law of the People's Republic of China
CPC	Communist Party of China
Corp.	Corporation
Criminal Law	Criminal Law of the People's Republic of China
ed.	Edition
Enterprise Bankruptcy Law	Enterprise Bankruptcy Law of the People's Republic of China
etc.	et cetera
FOSFA	The Federation of Oils, Seeds and Fats Association Ltd.
GAFTA	The Grain and Feed Trade Association
Geneva Protocol 1923	Protocol on Arbitration Clauses, signed at Geneva, September 24, 1923
HKIAC	Hong Kong International Arbitration Centre
Hong Kong	Hong Kong Special Administrative Region
IBA	International Bar Association
ICC	International Chamber of Commerce
ICC International Court of Arbitration	International Court of Arbitration of the International Chamber of Commerce
ICDR	International Centre for Dispute Resolution
ICSID	International Centre for Settlement of Investment Disputes
ICSID Convention	Convention on the Settlement of Investment Disputes Between States and Nationals of Other States
Insurance Law Interpretation (II)	Interpretation II of the Supreme People's Court on Several Issues Concerning the Application of the Insurance Law of the People's Republic of China
JCAA	Japan Commercial Arbitration Association

Judges Law	Judges Law of the People's Republic of China
KCAB	Korean Commercial Arbitration Board
Labor Dispute Mediation and Arbitration Law	Law of the People's Republic of China on Labor Dispute Mediation and Arbitration
Law of the Application of Law for Foreign-related Civil Relations	Law of the People's Republic of China on the Law Applicable to Foreign-Related Civil Relationships
Law on Choice of Law	Law of the People's Republic of China on Choice of Law for Foreign-Related Civil Relationships
LCIA	London Court of International Arbitration
L.P.	Limited Partnership
Ltd.	Limited
Macao	Macao Special Administrative Region
Minutes on Foreign-Related Commercial and Maritime Trial Work	Minutes of the National Courts' Symposium on Foreign-Related Commercial and Maritime Trial Work
Model Law	UNCITRAL Model Law on International Commercial Arbitration
NAI	Netherlands Arbitration Institute
New Arbitration Law	Arbitration Law of the People's Republic of China (amended in 2025)
New York Convention	Convention on the Recognition and Enforcement of Foreign Arbitral Awards
Ninth Conference Minutes	Minutes of the National Courts' Civil and Commercial Trial Work Conference
No.	Number
Notice on Issues Concerning Setting Aside of Foreign-Related Arbitral Award	Notice of the Supreme People's Court on Issues Concerning the People's Courts' Setting Aside of Foreign-Related Arbitral awards,
Notice on the Implementation of the New York Convention	Notice of the Supreme People's Court on Implementing the Convention on the Recognition and Enforcement of Foreign Arbitral Awards Acceded to by China
p./pp.	Page/Pages
Rural Land Contract Management Disputes Mediation and Arbitration Law	The Law of the People's Republic of China on Mediation and Arbitration of Rural Land Contract Management Disputes
SCC	Stockholm Chamber of Commerce
SCC Arbitration Institute	Arbitration Institute of the Stockholm Chamber of Commerce
SCIA	Shenzhen Court of International Arbitration
SHIAC	Shanghai International Arbitration Center
SIAC	Singapore International Arbitration Centre
SPC	Supreme People's Court of the People's Republic of China
Sports Law	Sports Law of the People's Republic of China
Supplemental Arrangement Concerning Mutual Enforcement of Awards	Supplemental Arrangement Concerning Mutual Enforcement of Arbitral Awards between the Mainland and the Hong Kong Special Administrative Region
Tort Liability Law	Tort Liability Law of the People's Republic of China

UK	United Kingdom
UNCITRAL	United Nations Commission on International Trade Law
U.S.	United States of America
v.	Versus (against)
WIPO	World Intellectual Property Organization

Competing Interests The author has no competing interests to declare that are relevant to the content of this manuscript.

Chapter 1
General Provisions

Article 1
This Law is formulated in order to ensure the impartial and expeditious arbitration of economic disputes, to protect the legitimate rights and interests of the parties and to safeguard the sound development of the socialist market economy.

Notes
This Article articulates the purpose of China's arbitration legislation and its arbitration system, defines the value orientation of the arbitration regime, and touches upon several of its fundamental concepts.

Impartiality and expeditiousness are the fundamental values of arbitration. Unlike litigation, which is an inherent public power of the state, arbitration stems from party autonomy and is a private procedure. However, its awards possess the effect of public power, and are enforceable in accordance with legal procedures. Arbitration has a quasi-judicial nature and must prioritize impartiality or fairness as its fundamental premise. This includes both substantive fairness, such as accurately ascertaining the facts and applying the law, and procedural fairness, such as safeguarding the parties' right to be informed and the right to present arguments. Expeditiousness is one of the core advantages that distinguish arbitration from other dispute resolution methods. The ordinary procedure in civil litigation has longer time limits and may be extended due to jurisdictional objections, expert evaluations, etc. In contrast, arbitration follows the principle of finality, with flexible procedures that can eliminate unnecessary steps.

Resolving economic disputes is the core purpose of arbitration. Under the framework of the New Arbitration Law, arbitration primarily applies to contract disputes and other disputes over property rights and interests between equal parties, excluding disputes such as marriage, inheritance, and administrative disputes. The New Arbitration Law also added provisions related to investment arbitration. Arbitration needs to resolve various commercial disputes, which also requires further

Y. Lin, *New Arbitration Law in China*, China Arbitration Yearbook,
https://doi.org/10.1007/978-981-92-0642-1_1

enhancing the professionalism and internationalization of the arbitration industry. For example, in response to the increase in cross-border economic disputes and new types of economic disputes, arbitration institutions need to strengthen the cultivation of professional talent, improve international arbitration rules, and enhance the international recognition of arbitration, making China's arbitration institutions an important platform for resolving international commercial disputes.

In traditional arbitration practice, the term "commercial disputes" is often used instead of "economic disputes." Most countries exclude certain disputes from the scope of arbitration jurisdiction, allowing only commercial disputes to be resolved through arbitration. Domestic laws or international conventions generally stipulate this. The Geneva Protocol 1923 stipulates that each contracting state shall recognize the validity of arbitration agreements relating to disputes arising from contracts "relating to commercial matters or to any other matter capable of settlement by arbitration." Furthermore, the Geneva Protocol 1923 also stipulates that each contracting state may limit its obligations to contracts "considered as commercial under its national law." The New York Convention, in Article 1(3), similarly allows contracting states to declare that "it will apply to the Convention only to differences arising out of legal relationships, whether contractual or not, which are considered as commercial under the national law of the State making such declaration. " Many countries, when acceding to the New York Convention, made a "commercial reservation," declaring that the contracting state would only recognize and enforce arbitral awards made in the territory of another contracting state that are considered commercial in nature, excluding awards of other natures. China also made such a reservation when joining the New York Convention. Therefore, determining whether a dispute is commercial in nature relates to whether the dispute can be resolved through arbitration and whether the award can be enforced by domestic or foreign courts after it is rendered.

As for whether a specific dispute falls within the commercial category, it is determined by domestic law, as there is no unified international definition. The commercial reservation in the aforementioned conventions also leaves this to each contracting state. The Model Law, in a footnote to Article 1(1), indicates that the term "commercial" should be given a wide interpretation so as to cover matters arising from all relationships of a commercial nature, whether contractual or not. Relationships of a commercial nature include, but are not limited to, the following transactions: any trade transaction for the supply or exchange of goods or services; distribution agreement; commercial representation or agency; factoring; leasing; construction of works; consulting; engineering; licensing; investment; financing; banking; insurance; exploitation agreement or concession; joint venture and other forms of industrial or business cooperation; carriage of goods or passengers by air, sea, rail or road.[1] China uses the term "contractual and non-contractual commercial legal relationships." In the Notice of the SPC on Implementing the Convention on

[1]Article 1(1) stipulates that the Model Law applies to "international commercial arbitration".

the Recognition and Enforcement of Foreign Arbitral Awards Acceded to by China,[2] the SPC pointed out the term "contractual and non-contractual commercial legal relationships" specifically refers to economic rights and obligations arising from contracts, torts, or relevant legal provisions, such as purchase and sale of goods, property leasing, project contracting, processing contracts, technology transfer, equity joint ventures, contractual joint ventures, exploration and development of natural resources, insurance, credit, labor services, agency, consulting services, passenger and cargo transport by sea, civil aviation, railway, and road, as well as product liability, environmental pollution, maritime accidents, and ownership disputes, but excludes disputes between foreign investors and host state governments.

Protecting the lawful rights and interests of the parties, as stipulated in this Article, is an important mission of commercial arbitration. The "legitimate rights and interests" protected by arbitration refer to the rights enjoyed by the parties according to law or contract, including property rights and interests and the proprietary aspects of personal rights and interests. Arbitration confirms rights and orders the performance of obligations through awards, which, upon becoming effective, may be applied to the court for compulsory enforcement. At the same time, claims for rights and interests that violate mandatory legal provisions or public order and good customs are not protected. Arbitration institutions need to substantively review the legality of the rights and interests, and the parties bear the burden of proof; failure to prove results in adverse consequences.

Safeguarding the sound development of the socialist market economy is the core function of arbitration in China. Parties can autonomously choose arbitration institutions and rules to resolve disputes efficiently, maintain a stable commercial order, and reduce transaction costs. In specific practice, by standardizing arbitration procedures, enhancing arbitration quality, and innovating arbitration services, arbitration institutions launch specialized arbitration services to elevate the professionalism and targeting of dispute resolution, thereby safeguarding the robust and sustainable development of the market economy in specific fields. Simultaneously, by constructing a diversified dispute resolution mechanism, arbitration institutions establish coordination mechanisms with people's courts, mediation organizations, industry associations, etc., forming a "unified force" for dispute resolution and improving the overall efficiency of dispute resolution. With the development of digital technology, arbitration institutions optimize arbitration procedures and adopt technical means, such as online arbitration and intelligent case handling assistance systems, to boost the convenience and efficiency of arbitration services, further ensuring the orderly development of the market economy.

Article 1, serving as the provision stating the legislative purpose of the entire law, retains its core substance compared to the original Arbitration Law (1994). Its enduring significance in the new era lies in upholding the stability and continuity of the arbitration system, thereby averting a potential crisis of confidence among market entities that could arise from changes to the legislative intent. Against the

---

[2] Dated April 10, 1987.

backdrop of a continuously improving market economy system and increasingly complex commercial disputes, a stable arbitration framework provides market participants with a predictable dispute resolution mechanism. This bolsters their confidence in commercial transactions and promotes the sustained development of the market economy.

The core elements established in this provision are important concepts and bases for the improvement and advancement of the arbitration system. With the internationalization and diversification of China's market economy, the arbitration system will face new opportunities and challenges. However, any reform and innovation of the arbitration system must be premised on adhering to these core elements, ensuring that the direction of reform does not deviate from the fundamental purpose of the arbitration system.

Article 2

The development of the arbitration industry implements the guidelines, principles, policies, decisions and plans of the Communist Party of China and the state, serves the country's high-quality development and high-level opening-up to the outside world, fosters a market-oriented, law-based, and international business environment, and plays a role in resolving economic disputes.

Notes

In the 30 years since the implementation of the Arbitration Law (1994), the cause of arbitration in China has undergone tremendous changes and plays an important role in social and economic life. With the further development of China's reform and opening-up, it can be anticipated that the direction of modernization and internationalization of arbitration will become increasingly clear. In this context, the addition of this Article in the New Arbitration Law proposes the overall guiding principles for the development of China's arbitration cause, clarifies the function and purpose of arbitration in national and social governance, and specifically points out the important role of arbitration in the country's economic development.

In 2014, the Fourth Plenary Session of the 18th Central Committee of the Communist Party of China put forward the reform task of "improving the arbitration system and enhancing the credibility of arbitration," marking the first time that the development of arbitration was included in the national development strategy. The 19th National Congress proposed to strengthen the construction of mechanisms for preventing and resolving social conflicts, opening a new journey for the development of the arbitration cause with Chinese characteristics. On December 31, 2019, the General Office of the CPC Central Committee and the General Office of the State Council issued the Several Opinions on Improving the Arbitration System to Strengthen the Credibility of Arbitration ("Several Opinions"), which put forward specific requirements for improving the arbitration system and proposed studying and amending the Arbitration Law.

The Several Opinions pointed out that arbitration is a dispute resolution system stipulated by Chinese law and an internationally accepted method of dispute resolution. Giving full play to the role of arbitration in respecting party autonomy, and resolving disputes conveniently and efficiently, is of great significance for improving the diversified dispute resolution mechanism, resolving conflicts fairly and promptly, properly settling disputes, maintaining social stability, promoting reform and opening- up, and ensuring the sustained and sound development of the economy and society.

The Several Opinions clarified that the legal system of arbitration must be strictly implemented by standardizing the establishment and succession of arbitration institutions, ensuring their independent work according to law, implementing the principle of party autonomy, and correcting behaviors that disrupt the order of arbitration development. It emphasized clarifying the public welfare and non-profit nature of arbitration commissions, strengthening their construction, reforming and improving their internal governance structures and management mechanisms, and enhancing the selection and management of arbitrators.

The Several Opinions also required that all departments in all regions, based on their actual conditions, study and propose specific implementation measures, plan carefully, arrange meticulously, assign responsibilities, and accelerate progress to strive for a new phase in the arbitration cause with Chinese characteristics in the new era. For violations of the New Arbitration Law and other relevant provisions, the municipal government that established the arbitration commission shall conduct a comprehensive review and reorganization in accordance with the principle of "who establishes, who is responsible, and who supervises."

This newly added Article defines the direction, service objectives, and core functions of the arbitration cause. These elements are interconnected and progressively layered, forming a complete guiding system for the development of the arbitration cause.

Implementing the lines, principles, and policies of the Communist Party of China and the state, along with their decisions, is not an abstract requirement but one with concrete practical implications. The arbitration sector must closely align with the state's concrete decision-making and deployments. In specific initiatives such as the Belt and Road Initiative, the development of pilot free trade zones, and digital economy innovation, arbitration institutions need to proactively adjust and innovate their service models to fulfill the requirements of the country's opening-up policy.

Serving the nation's high-quality development and high-level opening-up is one of the core objectives, clarifying the national strategic dimensions that the arbitration cause must align with. This is the core orientation for the function of arbitration. The essence of "high-quality development" is a shift from "prioritizing speed" to "prioritizing quality and efficiency." The arbitration cause serves this objective by, for example, formulating specialized arbitration rules or providing customized services in industrial upgrading sectors, such as strategic emerging industries like high-end manufacturing, new energy, and biomedicine, tailored to their dispute characteristics. Similarly, in regional coordinated development, arbitration institutions can break geographical restrictions and strengthen cross-regional collaboration. "High-level opening up" requires the arbitration cause to possess an "international perspective" and "international competitiveness." On the one hand, it must align with international commercial arbitration rules to enhance the international recognition of arbitration in China. On the other hand, with the deepening of opening up, disputes arising from new business forms such as cross-border e-commerce, offshore finance, and cross-border trade in services are increasing, necessitating targeted improvements in the service capabilities of arbitration institutions.

Creating a market-oriented, law-based, and internationalized business environment is the specific path for the arbitration cause to achieve its service objectives. The core of a market-oriented business environment is letting the market play a decisive role in resource allocation, where arbitration helps to reduce administrative intervention and respect the autonomy of market entities. The core of a law-based business environment is ensuring market order through legal thinking and legal methods, where arbitration aims to strictly adjudicate according to law and maintain legal authority. The core of an internationalized business environment is aligning with international rules and reducing institutional costs in international economic and trade activities, and the role of the arbitration cause is mainly reflected in connecting with international standards and eliminating barriers to cross-border dispute resolution.

Giving full play to its role in resolving economic disputes constitutes the fundamental function of the arbitration sector and provides the necessary support for achieving the aforementioned orientation, service objectives, and pathways. The "economic sphere" primarily encompasses dispute types directly related to economic activities, including but not limited to general commercial contract disputes (e.g., sales contracts, lease contracts), investment disputes (e.g., equity investment, foreign investment), intellectual property disputes (e.g., patent licensing, trademark assignment), and financial disputes (e.g., bank loans, securities transactions) and so on. These disputes are characterized by their involvement of property rights and interests, strong professional specificity, and high demand for efficiency. The professionalism, efficiency, and confidentiality inherent in arbitration precisely meet these requirements.

Article 3
Contractual disputes and other disputes over rights and interests in property between natural persons, legal persons and other unincorporated organizations that are equal subjects may be arbitrated.

The following disputes cannot be arbitrated:

(1) **Marital, adoption, guardianship, support and succession disputes;**
(2) **Administrative disputes that shall be handled by administrative bodies in accordance with law.**

Notes
Arbitrability, also known as the scope of arbitration, holds a pivotal position within the arbitration system, serving as a gateway to arbitration. Conceptually, arbitrability refers to which disputes can be resolved through arbitration and which are excluded from the arbitration path, as defined by national law. It constitutes a restriction on the autonomous will of the parties (primarily manifested through the

arbitration agreement), a restriction that permeates the entire arbitration process. From the initiation of arbitration proceedings to potential objections, defenses, and the stages of recognition and enforcement after the award is rendered, arbitrability is a key issue that must be considered. In practice, parties often raise defenses or challenges to the commencement of arbitration or the validity of an award on the grounds that the dispute is not capable of settlement by arbitration or is not arbitrable. With evolving times and the increasing complexity and diversity of economic activities, modern arbitration shows a trend towards expanding arbitrability, and the scope of matters that can be arbitrated is continuously broadening.

The arbitrability of a dispute primarily concerns what types of disputes can be resolved through arbitration and what types fall exclusively within the purview of courts or other institutions. Broadly speaking, the term "arbitrability" encompasses the following two meanings: firstly, matters not agreed upon by the parties cannot be arbitrated and hence lack arbitrability; secondly, matters agreed upon by the parties are not necessarily arbitrable or possess arbitrability. The former relates to the scope of the arbitration agreement and does not preclude the possibility of resolving the dispute through arbitration after the parties conclude a new arbitration agreement. The latter, however, constitutes a limitation on the system of resolving disputes through arbitration itself.

Arbitrability significantly restricts party autonomy. Although arbitration is based on party consent, initiated through an arbitration agreement, this consent is not without boundaries, and arbitrability is a key factor defining these boundaries. At the stage of initiating arbitration proceedings, if the subject matter of the dispute is determined to be non-arbitrable, the arbitration process cannot commence even if an arbitration agreement exists between the parties. Arbitrability also plays a crucial role in the post-award stage, including objections, defenses, recognition, and enforcement. After an arbitral award is rendered, if a party raises an objection or defense on the ground that the dispute was not arbitrable, and the court, upon review, finds the dispute indeed non-arbitrable, the award may be set aside, refused recognition, or refused enforcement.

In practice, it is not uncommon for parties to challenge the commencement of arbitration or the validity of an award based on non-arbitrability. Such challenges often stem from differing understandings of the arbitration system, considerations of self-interest, and varying interpretations of legal provisions. In complex commercial disputes involving areas such as antitrust or securities, where laws and regulations are intricate and grey areas may exist regarding the arbitrability of certain disputes, parties might raise non-arbitrability defenses based on their respective positions.

With the deepening of economic globalization, international commercial exchanges have become increasingly frequent and complex, leading to the emergence of various new types of commercial disputes, which demand higher efficiency and professionalism from dispute resolution mechanisms. Arbitration, with its advantages of efficiency, flexibility, and confidentiality, can better meet the parties' needs for rapid dispute resolution, reduced transaction costs, and preservation of business relationships. For instance, in cross-border e-commerce transactions involving parties from different countries and complex logistics and payment systems, traditional litigation might be protracted due to jurisdictional conflicts and complexities in applicable law. Arbitration, however, can resolve disputes promptly by allowing a flexible choice of seat of arbitration, rules, and arbitrators, thereby facilitating smooth cross-border e-commerce transactions. However, when choosing arbitration for these new types of commercial disputes, it is necessary to determine whether the issue of arbitrability might be challenged.

The arbitrability of the subject matter is a prerequisite for the validity of an arbitration agreement. If a national laws provide that certain disputes cannot be resolved through arbitration, the scope of the arbitration agreement is likewise limited. For example, Article 2 of the Geneva Protocol 1923 limited arbitration agreements to those "in connection with such contract relating to commercial matters or to any other matter capable of settlement by arbitration".[3] The New York Convention states that shall recognize an agreement in writing under which the parties undertake to submit to arbitration all or any differences which have arisen or which may arise between them in respect of a defined legal relationship, whether contractual or not, concerning a subject matter capable of settlement by arbitration."[4] The New York Convention also provides for a "commercial" reservation such that a contracting state may also declare that it will apply the New York Convention only to differences arising out of legal relationships, whether contractual or not, which are considered as commercial under the national law of the State making such declaration.[5] The Model Law provides grounds for refusing recognition or enforcement, including if: "(i) the subject-matter of the dispute is not capable of settlement by arbitration under the law of the State; or (ii) the recognition or enforcement of the arbitral award would be contrary to the public policy of the State."[6] These international legal instruments indicate that if the subject matter of the award is not arbitrable in the country where the award was made or is sought to be enforced, recognition and enforcement may be refused.

Theoretically, arbitrability can be divided into subjective arbitrability and objective arbitrability. The former typically refers to capacity, where a party might argue it lacks the capacity to arbitrate. The latter refers to the domain of arbitration, where a party might argue that, under the applicable law, the subject matter of the dispute falls outside the scope of arbitration. Subjective arbitrability addresses who can arbitrate, while objective arbitrability addresses what can be arbitrated. The term "arbitrability" commonly refers to objective arbitrability, i.e., disputes, according to legal provisions, can be resolved through arbitration and fall within the scope of arbitration.

---

[3] Article 1, Geneva Protocol 1923.

[4] Article II (1), New York Convention.

[5] Article I (3), New York Convention.

[6] Article 36(1)(b), UNCITRAL Model Law.

This Article combines Articles 2 and 3 of the Arbitration Law (1994). In defining the scope of arbitration, it primarily uses an affirmative generalization supplemented by a negative enumeration. The affirmative scope includes: contract disputes and other disputes over property rights and interests between equal subjects—citizens, legal persons, and other organizations. The negative enumeration includes: disputes concerning marriage, adoption, guardianship, support, and succession; and administrative disputes that by law shall be handled by administrative organs, which cannot be arbitrated. In modern commercial arbitration, there is a trend towards expanding arbitrability. The increasing respect for party autonomy is a significant factor driving this expansion. As the parties directly involved in the dispute, they often prefer to autonomously decide the method of dispute resolution and the decision-maker. Arbitration, initiated based on party agreement, grants parties greater autonomy, including the choice of arbitration institution, arbitrators, and procedures, making arbitration better able to reflect the parties' will and needs in resolving disputes. As long as the parties' choices do not violate mandatory legal provisions or public interest, the law should afford them full respect and protection.

In practice, arbitrability is one of the areas prone to dispute. For example, relevant Chinese laws and judicial interpretations do not clearly define the concept and scope of "administrative disputes that shall be handled by administrative bodies in accordance with law." A contract where an administrative body is one party is not necessarily an administrative agreement. Therefore, for contracts involving administrative bodies, it is necessary to consider factors such as the contract's purpose, the rights and obligations of both parties, and the administrative bodies' duties. If the contract is determined to be a civil or commercial contract and there are no grounds for invalidity, it is arbitrable, and the arbitration clause within it is valid.

Illustrative Cases

Case 1: *BO Company v. M Bureau and others*[7]

BO Company applied to an arbitration commission for arbitration, claiming a material misunderstanding regarding the provision in Article 9 of the Construction and Operation Contract that stipulated "each floor of the office building shall not be divided into more than 5 units," and requested the revocation of said provision. After the X Arbitration Commission accepted the case, M Bureau raised an objection to jurisdiction, arguing that the Land Grant Contract and the Construction and Operation Contract were administrative agreements falling outside the scope of the jurisdiction of arbitration. X Arbitration Commission dismissed the jurisdictional objection and issued an award.

M Bureau, and M Administrative Committee subsequently applied to the court to set aside the arbitral award. Their main facts and reasons were: firstly, the Land Grant Contract involved in the case constituted an administrative agreement, and the arbitral tribunal's characterization of it as a civil contract was erroneous. Secondly, the dispute in this case, arising from the performance of the Land Grant Contract, was an administrative dispute falling within the scope of administrative litigation.

[7] (2021) Zui Gao Fa Min Ta No. 97.

The arbitration commission lacked jurisdiction over such a dispute. Thirdly, the matters determined in the arbitral award fell outside the scope of the arbitration agreement. Article 40 of the Land Grant Contract stipulated that "disputes arising from the performance of this Contract shall be resolved through negotiation between the parties; if negotiation fails, the dispute shall be submitted to X Arbitration Commission for arbitration." According to this provision, the arbitration clause applied only to disputes concerning performance and did not extend to disputes regarding the validity of contract clauses. Finally, X Arbitration Commission's consolidation of the Land Grant Contract dispute and the Construction and Operation Contract dispute for joint adjudication violated procedural law. The Land Grant Contract was an administrative agreement concluded between the claimant and M Bureau in the exercise of land administration functions, while the Construction and Operation Contract was a separate administrative agreement concluded by the M Administrative Committee in performing its own duties. These two administrative agreements constituted independent contracts.

BO Company argued in its defense that both the Land Grant Contract and the Construction and Operation Contract constituted civil juristic acts between equal civil subjects, were civil agreements, and not administrative agreements. The dispute in this case arose from the performance of these civil agreements, fell within the scope of arbitrable matters, and the arbitration commission had jurisdiction to hear the case. Article 138(1) of the Property Rights Law stipulated: "where the right to use the land for construction is created by means of a grant such as a bid invitation, auction, or agreement, the parties concerned shall conclude a contract for the grant of the right to use the land for construction in written form." Therefore, contracts for the grant of the right to use land fell within the category of civil agreements governing property relations. The SPC's Interpretation on Issues Concerning the Application of Law in the Trial of Cases Involving Disputes over Contracts for the Right to Use State-owned Land addressed the applicable law for contracts for the grant of state-owned land use rights and characterized such contracts as civil agreements. The matters determined in the arbitral award fell within the scope of the arbitration agreement. Regarding Article 9 of the Construction and Operation Contract, a material misunderstanding had arisen during the performance of the contract and rendered continued performance according to the terms of that article impossible. The essence of the dispute was whether to continue performing the stipulations of that article or to rescind it, which constituted a "dispute arising from the performance of this Contract."

The High People's Court of Zhejiang Province held: Article 40 of the Land Grant Contract stipulated that disputes arising from the performance of the contract should be resolved through negotiation between the parties, and if negotiation failed, such disputes were to be submitted to a designated arbitration commission for arbitration. Subsequently, the grantee under the Land Grant Contract was amended to BO Company, and the rights and obligations specified in the original grant contract and land registration documents were assumed by BO Company. As both Article 45 of the Land Grant Contract and Article 11 of the Construction and Operation Contract stipulated that the Construction and Operation Contract was an annex to the Land Grant Contract and had the same legal effect, the rights and obligations under the Construction and Operation Contract were consequently also assumed by BO Company. Pursuant to Article 9 of the Arbitration Law Interpretation, the arbitration agreement should be binding on all parties, as BO Company, being the transferee, acknowledged its awareness of the arbitration agreement. Therefore, the lower court's denial of the claimant's right to challenge the validity of the arbitration agreement was improper.

The SPC held that: A contract for the grant of state-owned land use rights typically comprises clauses of both civil and administrative nature. In this case, the arbitration claim filed by BO Company sought to rescind the provision in Article 9 of the Construction and Operation Contract. Article 9 implemented and executed the decisions of a municipal government meeting minutes, reflecting the administrative organ's exercise of urban construction planning functions within its authority, thereby possessing an administrative management character. Consequently, the dispute constituted an administrative dispute. In accordance with Article 3(2) of the Arbitration Law (2017), which precluded the arbitrability of administrative disputes, the dispute in question was not capable of settlement by arbitration. As X Arbitration Commission adjudicated a dispute that was not arbitrable, the award in this case should therefore be set aside.

Case 2: *B Company v. A Company and others*[8]

M Company had multiple shareholders, among which both A Company and B Company were shareholders. A Company held a 60.3% equity stake, while B Company held 14.5%. B Company believed that A Company had directed and arranged for the staff of M Company to transfer over RMB 90 million of M Company's funds to A Company without resolutions from M Company's board of directors or shareholders' meeting and without informing other shareholders. Shortly after the funds were transferred to A Company, A Company filed for bankruptcy reorganization with the court. Therefore, B Company considered A Company's transfer of M Company's funds to be a withdrawal of registered capital.

[8] See the 9 Typical Cases on Judicial Review of Arbitration published by the Sichuan Province Chengdu Intermediate People's Court in May 2025. This case performs a dual function. First, it accurately interpretes that Article 27 of the Civil Procedure Law and Article 22 of the Civil Procedure Law Interpretation are intended to resolve issues of territorial jurisdiction within the court system when a case is accepted by the courts; they are not designed to exclude other forms of dispute resolution. The case thus strictly applies Article 2 of the Arbitration Law (2017), accurately establishing that shareholder capital contribution disputes are matters capable of settlement by arbitration. Second, the case serves to reaffirm the legal binding force of a company's articles of association upon the company, its shareholders, and its directors, supervisors, and senior management personnel. Importantly, it holds that the arbitration clause within the articles of association is legally effective against directors and senior managers, regardless of whether they personally signed the document.

Yin was the then-chairperson of the board of M Company, and Tang was a director at the time. B Company believed that Yin and Tang had failed to fulfill their obligations in accordance with the Company Law and M Company's articles of association, and had facilitated the aforementioned fund transfer for A Company, and thus should be held jointly and severally liable. Before initiating arbitration, B Company had sent a letter to M Company's board of supervisors requesting that the board of supervisors file a lawsuit, but the board of supervisors refused. As a result, B Company filed for arbitration with the Chengdu Arbitration Commission in accordance with the arbitration clause stipulated in M Company's articles of association, and the Chengdu Arbitration Commission accepted the case.

A Company, as well as Yin and Tang, argued that the dispute in question was a dispute between shareholders and fell outside the scope of the arbitration clause in M Company's articles of association. They also contended that Yin and Tang were not shareholders of M Company and had not signed the company's articles of association, and therefore were not bound by the arbitration clause. Consequently, B Company had no right to apply for arbitration.

The Sichuan Province Chengdu Intermediate People's Court held that, firstly, based on the arbitration claims filed by B Company, the dispute involved property interest disputes between shareholders and between shareholders and the company, arising from obligations stipulated by the Company Law and the company's articles of association. It constituted a property interest dispute between equal civil and commercial subjects and was therefore arbitrable. Secondly, pursuant to Article 5 of the Company Law, which states that the articles of association shall be binding on the company, shareholders, directors, supervisors, and senior management personnel, Yin and Tang served as the chairman and a director of M Company at the time, respectively. The articles of association, once registered and filed with the administrative authority, carried public effect. Whether they had signed the articles of association did not affect the legally binding force of the arbitration clause therein on them. Accordingly, the court dismissed the request filed by A Company A, Yin, and Tang.

Case 3: *Zhejiang M Company v. Ninghai N Company*[9]

Ninghai N Company and Zhejiang M Company signed an agreement, which stipulated that Ninghai N Company would lease land to Zhejiang M Company for a project construction, and any disputes arising therefrom were to be resolved by arbitration through X Arbitration Institution. Subsequently, Ninghai N Company filed for arbitration, while Zhejiang M Company applied for confirmation that the arbitration clause was invalid.

[9] See the 10 Typical Cases on Judicial Review of Commercial Arbitration published by Zhejiang Province Ningbo Intermediate People's Court in June 2024.

Zhejiang Province Ningbo Intermediate People's Court held the following: although Ninghai N Company was fully funded by state-owned assets and the agreement was reviewed and approved by the Management Committee, the Management Committee did not authorize Ninghai N Company to exercise administrative functions. The land use right involved in the agreement was part of a commercial legal act implemented through leasing, lacking the purpose element of an administrative agreement aimed at fulfilling administrative management or public service objectives. Meanwhile, the unilateral termination right of Ninghai N Company under the agreement was subject to certain constraints and did not constitute an administrative preferential right. The Court accordingly dismissed the application.

Case 4: *WMC v. Ruisu Company*[10]
The Winter Sports Management Center of the General Administration of Sport of China ("WMC") and Stellar Group entered into the Cooperation Agreement, stipulating that the WMC authorized Stellar Group to be responsible for the operation of the FIS Freestyle Ski Aerials World Cup China stop. It was also agreed that any disputes arising from the agreement could be submitted by either party to the CIETAC for resolution in accordance with CIETAC's then-effective arbitration rules. Ruisu Company joined the Cooperation Agreement, sharing corresponding rights and obligations under the agreement with Stellar Group. Subsequently, the three parties signed the Supplementary Agreement, stipulating that Ruisu Company would be solely responsible for organizing the event, with Stellar Group assisting Ruisu Company and bearing supplementary liability to the WMC regarding Ruisu Company's event organization work and the performance of the Supplementary Agreement. In 2019, the WMC, as the claimant, filed an arbitration application with CIETAC against Ruisu Company and Stellar Group as respondents. In January 2021, Ruisu Company applied to the Beijing No.4 Intermediate People's Court to confirm the arbitration clause invalid.

The Beijing No.4 Intermediate People's Court held that the WMC entered into the Supplementary Agreement regarding sports event operation cooperation with Stellar Group and Ruisu Company as equal subjects, rather than representing the government for a concession operation. Therefore, the dispute in this case constituted a commercial contract dispute between equal subjects and was arbitrable. The arbitration clause clearly designated the arbitration institution and was legally valid. As a party joining the Cooperation Agreement, Ruisu Company was aware of the

[10] See the 10 Typical Cases on the Construction of Pilot Free Trade Zones published by the SPC. This case affirms the arbitrability of international sports event operation cooperation agreements, demonstrating a judicial stance that supports sports arbitration. It creates a favorable legal environment for resolving commercial disputes arising from the sports industry operations through arbitration, and plays a positive role in promoting the healthy development of China's sports industry.

content and had indicated its adherence to all terms of the agreement. Thus, Ruisu Company should be bound by the arbitration clause within the Cooperation Agreement. The court hence ruled to dismiss Ruisu Company's application.

Case 5: *Shanghai M Company v. Guangzhou B Company and others*[11]

Shanghai M Company was a limited partner of Ningbo N Partnership. Ningbo N Partnership and Guangzhou G Company signed an agreement stipulating that disputes would be resolved by B Arbitration Institution. Subsequently, Shanghai M Company filed a limited partner derivative lawsuit against Guangzhou G Company as the defendant, and Guangzhou G Company raised a jurisdictional objection.

The Zhejiang Province Ningbo Intermediate People's Court held that although Shanghai M Company was not a party to the agreement, it filed the lawsuit against Guangzhou G Company in its own name for the benefit of Ningbo Partnership, based on the agreement signed between Ningbo N Partnership and Guangzhou G Company, and the outcome of the lawsuit would also accrue to Ningbo N Partnership. Therefore, the derivative lawsuit in this case violated the arbitration clause in the agreement, and the court accordingly dismissed the complaint.

Case 6: *FY Company v. CPC Company and others.*[12]

FY Company, CPC Company, and HD Company entered into the Warehousing Service Contract in November 2016. The contract stipulated that CPC Company would issue goods storage certificates to FY Company after the goods were delivered to the warehouse. CPC Company was only authorized to release goods to HD Company upon receiving formal proof of title transfer or delivery instructions from FY Company. It was also agreed that any disputes arising from or related to the contract should be submitted to an arbitration institution at the place of contract performance. Between 2017 and 2019, FY Company purchased over 110,000 tons of mixed aromatics and successively stored all the goods with CPC Company. Subsequently, FY Company discovered that a portion of the goods had been taken away without its consent. FY Company alleged that CPC Company and HD

---

[11] See the 10 Typical Cases on Judicial Review of Commercial Arbitration published by the Zhejiang Province Ningbo Intermediate People's Court in June 2024. The Partnership Enterprise Law only provides for derivative lawsuits by limited partners, but does not specify whether arbitration institutions have jurisdiction over limited partner derivative disputes. The Arbitration Law also contains no relevant provisions, leaving the jurisdiction over such derivative disputes ambiguous. This case clarifies that "derivation" means acting on behalf of the partnership enterprise in external matters, and therefore should be bound by the arbitration clause in the underlying legal relationship, reasonably defining the jurisdiction of arbitration institutions and courts over such disputes.

[12] (2022) Zhe 09 Min Chu No. 47;(2022) Zhe Min Zhong No. 1415; see also the 10 Typical Cases on Judicial Review of Commercial Arbitration published by the High People's Court of Zhejiang Province in November 2024. In situations where liability for breach of contract and tort liability concur, the aggrieved party's claim for tort liability to avoid submitting the dispute to arbitration as stipulated in the contract essentially constitutes a circumvention of the applicable arbitration clause. This case accurately identifies the scope of dispute resolution matters agreed upon in the arbitration agreement and legally determines that tort disputes arising during contract performance fall within the scope of the arbitration clause. It supports the resolution of the entire dispute through a "single arbitration proceeding."

Company had misappropriated the goods without authorization, resulting in the loss of the goods, and therefore filed a lawsuit with the Zhejiang Province Zhoushan Intermediate People's Court, seeking compensation for its cargo losses.

CPC Company raised a jurisdictional objection, arguing that the tripartite Warehousing Service Contract explicitly contained an arbitration clause, and the case should therefore be governed by arbitration as agreed. Additionally, FY Company had already initiated arbitration proceedings regarding a portion of the goods under the same Warehousing Service Contract based on claims of contractual breach.

The Zhejiang Province Zhoushan Intermediate People's Court held that this case involved a dispute arising from the execution of the Warehousing Service Contract among FY Company, CPC Company, and HD Company. The contract stipulated that relevant disputes should be submitted to an arbitration commission at the place of contract performance. There was a concurrence of claims in this case: where a party's breach of contract infringes upon the property rights of the other party, the aggrieved party has the right to choose to claim either liability for breach of contract or tort liability. Although FY Company filed this lawsuit based on tort liability, the tort dispute arose from the performance of obligations under the Warehousing Service Contract. Therefore, jurisdiction should still be subject to the arbitration clause in the Warehousing Service Contract. Accordingly, the case should fall under the jurisdiction of the arbitration commission at the place of contract performance, namely the Zhoushan Arbitration Commission.

Furthermore, while FY Company had initiated arbitration with the Zhoushan Arbitration Commission regarding a portion of the goods under the Warehousing Service Contract, it filed this lawsuit concerning over 50,000 tons of goods based on tort liability. FY Company refused to accept the court's legal explanation, which constituted a bad-faith evasion of the arbitration clause. The court therefore dismissed FY Company's complaint. FY Company appealed the decision, and the High People's Court of Zhejiang Province upheld the ruling by the Zhejiang Province Zhoushan Intermediate People's Court.

Article 4

Where the parties choose to resolve their dispute through arbitration, they should follow the principle of party autonomy and reach an arbitration agreement. If a party applies for arbitration in the absence of an arbitration agreement, the arbitration institution shall not accept the case.

Notes

Among modern diversified dispute resolution mechanisms, arbitration has long been one of the important ways for parties to resolve commercial disputes by virtue of its specific advantages. The most important characteristic of arbitration is party autonomy, which is often considered its primary advantage. Arbitration is premised on the parties' voluntariness, and the parties enjoy full autonomy of will. Party autonomy is also reflected specifically in the informal and flexible nature of the procedure. The principle of autonomy of will in arbitration, as the bedrock of the arbitration system, runs through the entire arbitration process and profoundly influences its nature, functions, and operation. It not only reflects the parties' autonomous disposition of their own rights but is also a key feature distinguishing arbitration from litigation and other dispute resolution methods.

The autonomy of the parties pervades every stage of the arbitral proceedings. From the initiation of the procedure, the parties must have concluded a valid arbitration agreement, which is a prerequisite for the arbitration institution in China to accept the case. An arbitration agreement is the written expression of the parties' voluntary submission of disputes to arbitration, specifying the intention to refer disputes to arbitration, the scope of arbitrable matters, and the selected arbitral institution. In selecting the arbitration institution, the parties may freely choose a competent arbitration institution within the limits permitted by law. Different arbitration institutions vary in their specialized fields, arbitration rules, and composition of arbitrators. Parties can select the most suitable arbitration institution based on factors such as the nature of the dispute, their own needs, and trust in the institution. Furthermore, the parties may autonomously agree on procedural matters such as the composition of the arbitral tribunal, the selection of arbitrators, the form of hearing, and the method of conducting sessions. For example, the parties may agree to form a tribunal of three arbitrators, each selecting one arbitrator and jointly selecting the presiding arbitrator; they may also agree to a hearing without oral sessions; or they may agree that the arbitration shall be conducted privately to protect commercial secrets or personal privacy. These agreements fully embody the principle of autonomy of will in arbitration, making the arbitration procedure better suited to the parties' individual needs and enhancing the efficiency and quality of dispute resolution. The terms of the arbitration agreement are freely agreed upon, but these terms may affect the determination of the arbitration agreement's validity. If the arbitration agreement is deemed invalid, the dispute cannot be submitted to arbitration.

1. **Voluntarily Concluded Arbitration Agreements**

This Article establishes the fundamental status of the principle of autonomy of will in the arbitration system, clarifies that an arbitration agreement is a necessary condition for an arbitration institution to accept a case, and emphasizes the importance of the parties' voluntary choice of arbitration. Other provisions of this Law further refine and implement this principle. For example, Article 43 of the New Arbitration Law regarding the selection of arbitrators reflects the parties' rights in the composition of the arbitral tribunal and the selection of arbitrators, ensuring that the tribunal's composition aligns with the parties' wishes and enhances their acceptance of the outcome.

The arbitration agreement is the primary manifestation of the principle of autonomy of will in arbitration. According to this Article, a dispute can only be submitted to arbitration if an arbitration agreement exists; without an arbitration agreement, the arbitration institution shall not accept the case. According to Article 27 of the New Arbitration Law, an arbitration agreement includes an arbitration clause stipulated in a contract, as well as an agreement to request arbitration concluded in another written form before or after the dispute arises. An arbitration clause in a contract is the most common form of arbitration agreement. It is embedded at the time of contract formation as part of the contract, stipulating that future related disputes shall be submitted to a specific arbitration institution for arbitration. Arbitration agreements concluded in other written forms are diverse, including separate arbitration agreements, correspondence, data messages (such as telegrams, telexes, facsimiles, electronic data interchange, and emails), etc. Despite the varied forms, their essence is the parties' written expression of their intention to submit disputes to arbitration. In modern commercial activities, with the development of information technology, electronic contracts and electronic transactions are increasingly prevalent, and arbitration agreements in the form of data messages are also becoming more common. For instance, if both parties reach a consensus on dispute resolution via email, clearly stating that disputes shall be submitted to a specific arbitration institution for arbitration, the content of that email constitutes a valid arbitration agreement.

The expression of intention to arbitrate reflects the parties' willingness to forgo litigation and choose arbitration to resolve disputes. It must be genuine, clear, and unambiguous. The matters for arbitration refer to the specific scope of disputes submitted to arbitration, determining the boundaries of the arbitral tribunal's review. They should be definite and capable of settlement by arbitration, i.e., matters permitted by law to be resolved through arbitration. The designated arbitration institution is one of the key contents of the arbitration agreement, identifying the specific arbitration commission responsible for hearing the case. The parties have the right to freely choose a suitable arbitration commission based on their own needs, degree of trust, and the professional advantages of the arbitration institution, among other factors. The selection must be clear, specific, and not ambiguous.

The validity of the arbitration agreement directly affects whether the arbitration procedure can be initiated and whether the award will be effective. A valid arbitration agreement has multiple legal effects, such as excluding court jurisdiction, conferring jurisdiction upon the arbitration institution, and binding the parties. Once the parties have reached a valid arbitration agreement, it signifies their voluntary grant of jurisdiction over the dispute to the arbitration institution, excluding the judicial jurisdiction of the courts. Simultaneously, the arbitration institution acquires jurisdiction based on the valid arbitration agreement, having the authority to hear and decide the dispute between the parties. The parties are also bound by the arbitration agreement and must comply with the arbitration procedure and the award.

However, not all arbitration agreements possess legal effect. Under specific circumstances, an arbitration agreement may be deemed invalid or voidable. Article 28 of the New Arbitration Law enumerates various situations where an arbitration agreement is invalid. Courts annually handle a significant number of judicial review cases involving the validity of arbitration agreements. For invalid arbitration agreements, the arbitration institution lacks the authority to accept the relevant case, and the parties can only seek other legal avenues to resolve the dispute.

In the process of concluding an arbitration agreement, the parties may also agree on other content based on the principle of autonomy of will. For example, regarding the arbitration procedure, the parties may negotiate and decide on several important matters. Regarding the method of hearing, the parties may choose between an oral hearing or a documentary hearing based on the specific circumstances of the case and their own needs. An oral hearing allows the parties to fully present their case, debate, and cross-examine evidence, facilitating the arbitral tribunal's comprehensive understanding of the case. A documentary hearing is more convenient and efficient, suitable for cases where the facts are clear, the evidence is sufficient, and the dispute is not significant. For instance, for a simple contract dispute where the parties have little disagreement on the facts but differ on the application of law, they may agree to choose a documentary hearing to save time and costs, with the arbitral tribunal rendering an award based on the documentary materials. Regarding the form of the hearing, the parties may agree on whether the arbitration should be conducted publicly or privately. Arbitration is private in principle, which helps protect the parties' commercial secrets and privacy, avoiding negative impacts that might arise from public hearings. However, if the parties believe that a public hearing would help enhance their corporate image or have demonstrative significance for the industry, they may also agree to choose a public hearing. Additionally, the parties may agree on procedural matters such as the time limit for arbitration, rules of evidence, and the method of constituting the arbitral tribunal. As long as such agreements do not violate mandatory legal provisions, the arbitral tribunal should respect the parties' wishes and proceed in accordance with their agreement.

2. **The Principle of Autonomy of Will and Other Principles**

The principle of autonomy of will in arbitration is closely related to and interacts with other arbitration principles. Compared with the principle of independence, the principle of autonomy of will is its premise and foundation. The principle of independence emphasizes that arbitration institutions and arbitral tribunals exercise their arbitration power independently according to law, free from interference by administrative organs, social organizations, and individuals. The principle of autonomy of will, on the other hand, grants the parties the right to autonomously choose the arbitration institution and arbitrators, making the power of the arbitration institution and arbitrators derive from the authorization of the parties, rather than external coercion. Through voluntarily concluding an arbitration agreement and selecting a trusted arbitration institution and arbitrators, the parties create the conditions for the arbitration institution and tribunal to exercise their arbitration power independently. At the same time, the principle of independence also provides a guarantee for the realization of the principle of autonomy of will, ensuring that arbitration can proceed according to law and the parties' wishes without interference, thereby safeguarding the legitimate rights and interests of the parties.

The principle of autonomy of will in arbitration and the principle of fairness and reasonableness complement each other. The principle of fairness and reasonableness requires the arbitral tribunal to resolve disputes fairly based on facts and law during the arbitration process, equally protecting the rights and interests of all parties. Under the principle of autonomy of will, the parties, through autonomously choosing the method of arbitration, the institution, and the arbitrators, expect a fair and reasonable award. When following the principle of fairness and reasonableness, the arbitral tribunal also needs to fully respect the voluntary choices of the parties and consider the matters and intentions agreed upon in the arbitration agreement. However, it is also necessary to note that taking full party autonomy one step further can lead to the abuse of party autonomy. Parties may agree on the arbitration procedure through the arbitration agreement, but the agreed procedure might ultimately fail to be properly executed, sacrificing the inherent attributes of dispute resolution that arbitration should possess. Moreover, coordinating the conflict between party autonomy and efficiency, and balancing the clash between party autonomy and fairness and legality, can sometimes be highly challenging. Furthermore, as an agreement, an arbitration agreement follows the principle of privity and does not bind third parties. This may lead to inconsistencies in the methods and outcomes of resolving related disputes, placing the parties in an awkward position. For example, if a dispute between a domestic buyer and a foreign trade company is resolved through litigation, while the dispute between the foreign trade company and the foreign seller is resolved through arbitration, the foreign trade company might find itself in a predicament where it bears liability from both sides. Similarly, if the main contract and the subcontract stipulate different dispute resolution methods, similar problems may arise. This also becomes a drawback of arbitration as a quasi-judicial procedure. Arbitration excludes third parties and usually cannot consolidate multiple parties, and thus, it cannot completely avoid conflicting awards.

The principle of autonomy of will in arbitration is also closely linked to the principle of finality of the award. The principle of finality means that an arbitral award becomes legally effective upon being rendered, and the parties may not apply for arbitration again or bring a lawsuit before a court regarding the same dispute. The principle of autonomy of will means that when choosing arbitration, the parties are already aware of and accept the outcome of finality. Based on their trust in arbitration and voluntary choice, the parties relinquish the right to resolve the dispute again through other means, such as litigation, in exchange for the efficiency of arbitration. Simultaneously, the principle of finality also prompts the parties to be more prudent when selecting the arbitration institution, arbitrators, and agreeing on the matters for arbitration, comprehensively considering their own interests and risks to ensure the smooth progress of the procedure and the effective enforcement of the award.

3. **Exceptions to the Principle of Autonomy of Will**

Although the principle of autonomy of will in arbitration grants the parties extensive autonomous choice, in practice, this right is not absolute and is subject to limitations from various aspects:

A. Limitations by Laws and Regulations. To safeguard social public interests, ensure fairness and justice, and maintain the stability of the legal order, laws and regulations set certain boundaries on the parties' autonomous choice in arbitration. On one hand, laws and regulations explicitly stipulate that certain disputes cannot be resolved through arbitration, such as disputes concerning marriage, adoption, guardianship, support, and succession, as well as administrative disputes that shall be handled by administrative organs according to law. These disputes involve special areas like personal status relationships, social public interests, and administrative management order, requiring handling through specialized legal procedures and institutions. Parties may not bring these matters within the scope of arbitration through an arbitration agreement, thus limiting their autonomous choice regarding arbitrable matters. On the other hand, during the arbitration proceedings, the parties' autonomous agreements must also comply with mandatory provisions of laws and regulations. For example, regarding the selection of arbitrators, although the parties have the right to autonomously choose arbitrators, the selected arbitrators must meet the statutory qualification requirements, such as possessing corresponding legal knowledge, professional experience, and professional ethics; otherwise, the selection may be invalid. Furthermore, the progression of the arbitration procedure must follow statutory procedural rules. Parties may not arbitrarily circumvent mandatory legal requirements through agreement, to ensure the legality and fairness of the arbitration activities.

B. Considerations of Public Interest. Arbitration not only involves the private interests of the parties but may also affect public interests. If the autonomous choices of the parties could harm public interests, such choices will be restricted. For instance, in disputes closely related to social public interests, such as those involving environmental pollution, food safety, and labor disputes, if the arbitration procedure agreed by the parties or the outcome of the award might lead to damage to public interests, the arbitration institution or the court may review and intervene in the relevant agreement. In some cross-border arbitration cases, if the enforcement of an arbitral award might affect national sovereignty, security, or public order, the relevant national court has the right to refuse recognition and enforcement of the award based on public interest. Such considerations based on public interest limit the parties' complete autonomous choice in arbitration, reflecting the role of law in balancing private interests and public interests.

C. Constraints of Arbitration Rules. To ensure the orderly conduct of the arbitration procedure and the fairness and authority of the award, arbitration institutions have established a series of arbitration rules. By choosing a particular arbitration institution, the parties must comply with that institution's arbitration rules. Although arbitration rules to some extent reflect party autonomy, allowing the parties to autonomously agree on certain aspects, they also regulate and constrain the parties' right to choose. For example, arbitration rules typically provide detailed provisions on the application for and acceptance of arbitration, the composition of the arbitral tribunal, the hearing procedure, rules of evidence, the rendering of awards, etc. Some of these provisions are mandatory, and the parties may not exclude them through agreement.

4. **Third Parties in Arbitration**

This Article stipulates that if there is no arbitration agreement, and one party applies for arbitration, the arbitration institution shall not accept the case. An arbitration agreement only binds the parties who signed it. However, in practice, the concept of a third party sometimes arises. Here, a third party refers to a person who has no original contractual or succession relationship with the parties to the arbitration agreement, or with whom an arbitration agreement exists in some other form—meaning a person with whom the parties to the arbitration agreement have no arbitration agreement of any form.[13] According to the principle of privity of contract, which states that a contract only binds its parties, an arbitration agreement does not have binding force on third parties. The involvement of third parties is inherently contrary to the consensual nature of arbitration.

In practice, in situations involving interconnected transactions or related parties, issues concerning third parties can arise either at the stage of initiating arbitration or during the arbitration proceedings, aiming for more convenient dispute resolution.

Take a contract for the benefit of a third party as an example. Under traditional principles, in a contract for the benefit of a third party, the third party can only initiate arbitration if they have, in some form, reached an arbitration agreement with one of the contractual parties. At that point, the former third party has effectively become a party to a new arbitration agreement, rather than being a third party with no arbitration agreement whatsoever with the other party.

A contract for the benefit of a third party, or a third-party beneficiary contract. According to traditional contract law theory, a relationship of privity exists between the contracting parties, and this privity is the prerequisite for the contract to bind the parties. For non-parties to the contract, the contract has no effect.[14] The principle of privity was a fundamental principle of contract law until the twentieth century, with numerous judicial precedents upholding it. However, since the twentieth century, the laws of many countries have introduced some exceptions to the principle of privity.[15] One such exception is the third-party beneficiary contract. A third-party beneficiary contract refers to a contract where one party does not set rights for themselves but sets them for a third party, and agrees that the other party will perform the obligation towards the third party, thereby granting the third party the right to directly request performance. In such contracts, the intention of the parties includes a component that benefits the third party, and the contractual rights involve the third party. The rights and interests enjoyed by this third party include: the benefit stipulated in the contract by the parties to be enjoyed by the third party; the right to request performance; the right to raise defenses, including defenses against the promisee.

Recognizing third-party beneficiary contracts constitutes a breakthrough in the principle of privity. This means that if A and B enter into a contract benefiting C, and B breaches the contract, C can also claim against B for the breach. C's right includes not only the right to claim damages but also a right of action. C's right of action does not arise from tort or other reasons but from the contractual obligation. This contract is the one concluded between A and B. C can sue based on the breach. If the contract does not contain an arbitration clause, undoubtedly, the dispute should be brought before a court. However, if this contract contains a valid arbitration clause and

---

[13] For a detailed discussion on arbitration and third parties, see Chap. 3.

[14] For instance, Article 1119 of the French Civil Code states that as a rule, one may, bind oneself and stipulate in his own name, only for oneself. Article 1165 states that agreements produce effect only between the contracting parties.

[15] See Section 328 of the German Civil Code; Section 2-318 of the US Uniform Commercial Code; Article 1121 of the French Civil Code; and Article 537 of the Japanese Civil Code.

designates an arbitration institution in China, can C invoke this arbitration clause to initiate arbitration? Two situations must be distinguished: 1. if C subsequently acknowledges the arbitration agreement in writing, then it is binding upon A, B and C; 2. if C does not provide written confirmation, then it is necessary to analyze whether a valid arbitration agreement has been reached between B and C. First, it should be acknowledged that the contract is a written contract, and the arbitration clause is also a written arbitration clause. Secondly, arbitration is the true intention of the parties. In the example above, A and B stipulated in the contract that any potential disputes would be resolved through arbitration. Simultaneously, the contract designates C as the beneficiary. The performance of this contract constitutes performance towards both C and A. Moreover, performance towards C is the main content of this third-party beneficiary contract and the primary obligation of B (the obligor). B's obligation towards A becomes a subsidiary obligation after the contract's formation. Generally, modifications or amendments to the contract do not affect the rights and interests of the third party and require prior consent from the third party who has an interest in the contract. In this contract, a potential dispute arises precisely from B's breach of the contractual promise made to A, i.e., failing to confer the stipulated benefit upon C. This dispute is essentially about B's non-performance and C's consequent failure to receive the benefit. Therefore, from B's perspective, the dispute with C is foreseeable and stipulated in its contract with A; it represents B's true intention. From C's perspective, once the third-party beneficiary contract is formed, the third party directly acquires the rights created by the contract. When C accepts[16] even a part of the performance, it indicates their acceptance of the rights created by the contract. C then enjoys the aforementioned rights; these rights include the right of action under the contract and, in the case of an existing arbitration clause, the right to request arbitration. C's acceptance constitutes acceptance of the entire contract. When a dispute arises between C and B, this contract is the basis for C's claim. C can claim for losses due to the breach of contract and can certainly use the dispute resolution clause stipulated in the contract as the means to resolve the dispute. An arbitration agreement formed in this manner should also fall under the "other written forms" stipulated in Article 16 of the New Arbitration Law. In essence, C is not inheriting the original arbitration agreement from the contract but is, through acceptance, forming a new arbitration agreement. The contractual arbitration clause remains binding on B and A.

Illustrative Cases

Case 1: *Sun and others v. Shengke Company*[17]

In April 2018, borrower Sunfei Company entered into a Loan Contract with lender Zeng through an online lending platform due to capital needs. Sun provided a mortgage guarantee for the loan with his own real estate and signed a Tripartite Mortgage

[16] C can accept through express or implied methods, directed towards the promisee or the promisor. C can also choose not to accept.

[17] (2022) Gui 71 Min Te No. 21; See also the 10 Typical Cases on Judicial Review of Arbitration published by the SPC in January 2024.

Contract. Both contracts stipulated that any disputes should be under the jurisdiction of the people's court where the collateral was located. Subsequently, the creditor's rights under the contract were transferred three times and were ultimately assigned to Shengke Company. Shengke Company filed an arbitration application with an arbitration commission, which issued an arbitral award in November 2019. Sunfei Company and Sun applied to the Nanning Railway Transport Intermediate Court for setting aside the aforementioned arbitral award, on the grounds that there was no arbitration agreement between them and Shengke Company.

The Nanning Railway Transport Intermediate Court held that the arbitration clause in the involved Loan Contract was stamped as a seal in a blank space within the contract terms, while the arbitration clause in the Tripartite Mortgage Contract was handwritten under Article 11 ("Other Agreed Matters"). Both the stamped and handwritten contents constituted amendments to the dispute resolution clause. Since Sun and Sunfei Company denied the validity of the arbitration clause, and such amendments lacked confirmation by Sunfei Company and Sun through signatures or other means, and Shengke Company also failed to provide evidence proving that the stamped and handwritten contents had been confirmed by Sunfei Company and Sun, it could not be determined that Zeng, Sunfei Company, and Sun had reached a valid agreement to change the dispute resolution method under the Loan Contract and the Tripartite Mortgage Contract to arbitration. Therefore, no valid and legally effective arbitration agreement existed in this case. The court ruled to set aside the involved arbitral award.

Case 2: *A Company v. B*[18]

On August 17, 2012, B opened an account with A Company, signing the Customer Account Application Form (Individual), Account Application Form (Individual), and Account Service Confirmation Form. Article 2 of the Customer Account Application Form (Individual) stated, "I have read the Important Notes and Instructions for Completing the Form on the reverse side of this form and clearly

[18] See the Typical Cases on Judicial Review of Arbitration published by the Zhejiang Province Hangzhou Intermediate Court in March 2024. When financial consumers participate in investment activities, their transactions with financial service providers are typically arranged through a series of documents such as application forms and confirmation forms. This series of related documents constitutes proof of the financial service contract relationship and reflects the rights and obligations of both parties. In practice, the standard texts of these relevant documents are generally provided by the financial service provider. The dispute resolution method of arbitration stipulated therein substantially affects the procedural rights and interests of the financial consumer, and it is appropriate for the financial service provider to provide special notice regarding the corresponding arbitration clause. Where there is evidence proving that the financial service provider gave special notice and the financial consumer signed and received the relevant documents containing the arbitration clause, if the financial consumer subsequently claims the arbitration agreement is invalid on the grounds that the financial service provider did not inform them of the content of the arbitration clause or that they were unaware of its content, the people's court will not support such a claim. The handling of this case, on one hand, provides normative guidance for financial service providers when formulating and specially notifying about arbitration clauses, and on the other hand, guides financial consumers to pay attention to reviewing arbitration clauses when signing relevant documents.

understand them, along with the accompanying Securities Investment Fund Investor Rights Guide and Service Confirmation and Risk Disclosure Statement for account opening, and voluntarily comply with the relevant regulations and assume the associated risks." Article 6 of the Notes and Instructions for Completing the Form on the reverse side stipulated, "The customer's submission of this application form indicates that the customer has agreed to and accepted all regulations of our company regarding open-end fund business." Article 2 in the upper part of the Account Application Form (Individual) stated, "I hereby confirm that I have read and clearly understood the Securities Investment Fund Investor Rights Guide and Service Confirmation and Risk Disclosure Statement attached to this account opening application and am willing to assume the relevant risks." On the Account Service Confirmation Form, checkmarks were placed before the listed documents, Securities Investment Fund Investor Rights Guide, Service Confirmation and Risk Disclosure Statement. B signed at the customer declaration section, which stated, "1. I have duly received the above documents. 2. The company's investment advisor has clearly explained the content of the documents. 3. I have carefully read and understood the content of the above documents and the risks that may be faced when participating in investments. 4. If I still have questions, I understand that I can seek independent professional advice." Among these, Article 6, Section (3) of the Securities Investment Fund Investor Rights Guide, stipulated, "Any dispute arising from or in connection with the Fund Contract, if cannot be resolved through negotiation or mediation, may be submitted by the fund investor to the China International Economic and Trade Arbitration Commission for arbitration in accordance with its arbitration rules in effect at the time. The place of arbitration shall be the place agreed in the Fund Contract. The arbitral award is final and binding upon all parties." It also stated below, "Before investing in the fund, investors should carefully read the Fund Contract, Prospectus, and other documents, and choose funds that match their own risk tolerance." On January 29, 2016, B, as the investor, signed the Fund Contract with the fund manager and the fund custodian.

On November 19, 2020, B initiated the first-instance lawsuit in the Jianggan Primary People's Court of Hangzhou, claiming that A Company had committed fraudulent acts and unreasonable recommendations, among other major faults, leading to the improper use of B's funds and resulting in losses. Therefore, B requested the court to order A Company to compensate for economic losses and corresponding interest losses. During the trial of this case, A Company raised a jurisdictional objection. The former Jianggan Primary People's Court of Hangzhou, after trial, issued a first-instance civil ruling dismissing A Company's jurisdictional objection.

The Zhejiang Province Hangzhou Intermediate Court held that, based on the statements in B's complaint and the preliminary evidence submitted, this lawsuit was initiated regarding whether A Company, as a fund distribution agency, had fulfilled its obligation. When B opened an account with A Company, a series of documents, including the Customer Account Application Form (Individual), Account Application Form (Individual), and Account Service Confirmation Form, were formed, constituting the contractual content between the two parties. When B applied to open the account and filled out the corresponding forms, he was informed that he should abide by the relevant agreements in the Securities Investment Fund Investor Rights Guide. B also signed the form, indicating that he had received and understood the content of the Securities Investment Fund Investor Rights Guide. Therefore, the relevant agreements in the Securities Investment Fund Investor Rights Guide were binding on both parties. The Securities Investment Fund Investor Rights Guide contained an arbitration clause. This arbitration clause contained an expression of intention to request arbitration, specified the arbitration matters, and designated a specific arbitration institution, complying with Article 16 of the Arbitration Law (2017). Furthermore, it did not fall under the invalid circumstances stipulated in Article 17 of the same law; thus, it should be deemed a valid arbitration clause. As B initiated this lawsuit based on A Company's violation of obligation, and the obligation is a pre-contractual obligation, and B's signing of the Fund Contract with the fund manager was related to A Company, A Company's obligation was closely connected with the conclusion of the involved Fund Contract. Therefore, this case should be considered a dispute related to the Fund Contract. Since the arbitration clause agreed in the Securities Investment Fund Investor Rights Guide existed between B and A Company, and the dispute in this case fell within the scope of disputes covered by the arbitration clause in the Securities Investment Fund Investor Rights Guide, this arbitration clause should apply, and the court lacked jurisdiction. The Court consequently revoked the first-instance civil ruling and dismissed B's claims.

Case 3: *Leidi Company v. Germany IBG Company*[19]
Leidi Company and Germany IBG Company entered into the IBG Agreement. Article 14.2 of this agreement stipulated that either party had the right to bring a lawsuit to the competent court regarding disputes arising from this agreement. Article 14.3 stipulated that disputes arising from or in connection with this agreement shall be submitted to the German Arbitration Institute for arbitration. Subsequently, a dispute arose between the parties regarding the performance of this agreement, and Leidi Company filed a lawsuit with the Jiangsu Province Nanjing Intermediate People's Court. Germany IBG Company raised an objection to jurisdiction, arguing that the parties had concluded an arbitration clause and that the people's court had no jurisdiction over the case. The Court held that the contract involved contained an arbitration clause, and the case should be submitted for

[19] (2021) Su 01 Min Chu No. 321, (2021) Su Min Zhong No. 606; See also the 10 Typical Cases on Judicial Review of Commercial Arbitration published by the Jiangsu High People's Court in July 2024. According to Article 18 of the Law of the Application of Law for Foreign-related Civil Relations, if the parties have not chosen the law applicable to the arbitration agreement, the law of the place where the arbitration institution is located or the law of the seat of arbitration shall apply. Therefore, if the chosen seat of arbitration or the location of the arbitration institution in a foreign-related arbitration agreement is in a foreign country, foreign law needs to be applied. This case ascertained the legal provisions of the German Code of Civil Procedure concerning the validity of arbitration agreements, referenced German court precedents on the validity of "arbitration or litigation" agreements, correctly interpreted German law, upheld the parties' right to choose arbitration, and provided guidance for handling similar cases.

arbitration. It accordingly ruled to dismiss Leidi Company's lawsuit. Leidi Company, dissatisfied with this ruling, appealed to the High People's Court of Jiangsu Province, arguing that the IBG Agreement provided for both litigation and arbitration options without specifying an order of precedence, constituting an "arbitration or litigation" clause which should be invalid.

The High People's Court of Jiangsu Province held that the arbitration institution designated in Article 14.3 of the IBG Agreement was the German Arbitration Institute, whose location was in Germany. The validity of this arbitration clause should be governed by German law. The High People's Court of Jiangsu Province ascertained that the German Code of Civil Procedure did not stipulate that "arbitration or litigation" clauses were invalid. German court precedents held that "arbitration or litigation" clauses were not contradictory, could be applied concurrently, and disputes should be submitted for arbitration; the agreement on court jurisdiction applied only if the parties did not invoke the arbitration agreement or waive arbitration. In this case, Germany IBG Company argued that an arbitration agreement existed between the parties and the dispute should be submitted for arbitration; therefore, the arbitration clause involved was valid. The High People's Court of Jiangsu Province dismissed the appeal and upheld the original ruling.

Case 4: *Fanhai Company v. Guo*[20]

In December 2019, Guo, the fund manager, MS Wealth Management Company, and the fund custodian, CMS Company, signed the Fund Contract, the Fund Supplementary Confirmation Letter, and the Confirmation of Subscription (Purchase). On the same day, Guo paid 4.3 million RMB as agreed into the designated fundraising account of MS Wealth Management Company. The Fund Contract stipulated that any dispute arising from or in connection with the contract, if not resolved through friendly negotiation, shall be submitted to a specified arbitration commission for arbitration. In October 2014, Fanhai Company issued a Letter of Commitment to MS Wealth Management Company, committing to provide credit enhancement support for the liquidity and asset security of asset management products initiated and actively managed by MS Wealth Management Company. In September 2021, Guo filed an application for arbitration with the agreed arbitration commission, naming MS Wealth Management Company, CMS Company, and Fanhai Company as respondents. In November 2021, Fanhai Company submitted an Arbitration Jurisdictional Objection Application to this arbitration commission, arguing that the commission had no jurisdiction over the dispute between Guo and

[20] (2022) Jing 74 Min Te No. 13; See also the 10 Typical Cases on Judicial Review of Arbitration published by the SPC in January 2024. This case is a typical example concerning the determination of the extended effect of an arbitration clause from a principal contract to an ancillary contract. Party autonomy is the cornerstone of arbitration agreements. The people's court fully respects the parties' intention to arbitrate. Based on the relationship between the principal and ancillary contracts, the particularity of arbitration, and the formal requirements of arbitration clauses, and in the absence of an arbitration clause in the ancillary contract, the court determined that the arbitration clause in the principal contract did not bind the ancillary contract. This case provides useful guidance for standardizing the extension of the effect of arbitration clauses.

itself. In January 2022, the Beijing Financial Court accepted the case filed by Fanhai Company, applying to confirm the validity of the arbitration agreement.

The Beijing Financial Court held that Fanhai Company did not directly sign the Fund Contract with Guo, and the Letter of Commitment was not issued by Fanhai Company to Guo. There was no clear expression of intention to resolve disputes through arbitration between Fanhai Company and Guo, and no arbitration agreement existed between them. Fanhai Company raised the objection before the first hearing of the arbitral tribunal, complying with relevant procedural rules. Upon inquiring with the specified arbitration commission, the Court found that the arbitration commission had not made a decision on the objection to the arbitration agreement's validity. The court ruled to confirm that no arbitration agreement existed between Fanhai Company and Guo.

Case 5: ***A Company and others, v. Luo***[21]

On May 20, 2013, A Company, B Company, and C Company signed the Authorized Cooperation Agreement, whereby A Company and B Company jointly agreed to authorize C Company to carry out the development and operation of the project involving the subject land parcel. On October 10, 2013, C Company and D Company signed the Cooperation Development Contract. This contract stipulated, "If any dispute or claim arises from or relates to this Contract, or concerning the interpretation, breach, termination, or validity thereof, it shall be resolved by the parties through friendly consultation. If consultation fails, the parties agree to submit the dispute to the Chengdu Arbitration Commission for arbitration." On December 15, 2015, A Company, B Company, and C Company (collectively as Party A) and D Company (as Party B) signed the Contract Termination Agreement. This Contract Termination Agreement did not contain any arbitration clause. On July 15, 2020, the assignor D Company and the assignee Luo signed the Claims Transfer Agreement, stipulating that D Company transferred all claims against A Company, B Company, and C Company under the Contract Termination Agreement to Luo. Subsequently, Luo applied for arbitration based on the arbitration clause in the Cooperation Development Contract, which was accepted by the Chengdu Arbitration Commission. A Company, B Company, and C Company filed a lawsuit with the Sichuan Province Chengdu Intermediate People's Court, requesting confirmation that no arbitration agreement existed between them and Luo.

The Sichuan Province Chengdu Intermediate People's Court held that in this case, A Company and B Company authorized C Company to handle matters related to the subject land parcel project, including approving all external commitments, agreements, contracts, meeting memoranda, etc., made by C Company during the project operation, and all debts and credits arising from the project, and jointly assumed joint and several liability. The Cooperation Development Contract signed between C Company and D Company clearly contained an arbitration clause. Therefore, the arbitration clause in the Cooperation Development Contract signed

[21] See the 9 Typical Cases on Judicial Review of Arbitration released by the Sichuan Province Chengdu Intermediate People's Court in May 2025.

by C Company and D Company was binding on A Company and B Company. Subsequently, the Contract Termination Agreement signed by A Company, B Company, C Company, and D Company confirmed the termination of the Cooperation Development Contract and addressed subsequent matters, but did not affect the validity of the arbitration clause in the Cooperation Development Contract. Disputes arising therefrom should be submitted to the Chengdu Arbitration Commission for arbitration by the parties as agreed. Luo, as the assignee of D Company's rights in this case, was entitled to initiate arbitration based on the arbitration clause in the Cooperation Development Contract. Accordingly, the Court ruled to dismiss the application of A Company, B Company, and C Company.

Case 6: ***Fan v. M Entertainment Company***[22]
Fan and M Entertainment Company (registered in the Cayman Islands) signed a Notice of Grant of Ordinary Share Options, which stipulated that Fan's signing of this notice would be deemed as an agreement to and signing of the Ordinary Share Option Grant Agreement. The dispute resolution clause in this agreement stipulated, "(a) Except for matters concerning the enforceability, arbitrability, etc., of this agreement, all other disputes shall be resolved through arbitration, without precluding Fan's right to apply to a court for interim measures, injunctions, etc.; (b) If Fan's place of employment is Hong Kong, Singapore, or the Chinese Mainland, etc., the dispute shall be submitted to the HKIAC for arbitration under its rules. ... (i) Simultaneously, the Company (but not Fan) has the right, at its sole discretion, if Fan's place of employment is China, to initiate arbitration with the CIETAC in Shanghai under its arbitration rules, to which Fan shall agree and may not choose another arbitral tribunal." Subsequently, M Entertainment Company applied to CIETAC for arbitration regarding disputes arising from the performance of the aforementioned contract. Fan applied to the court to confirm the arbitration agreement invalid, on the grounds that the clause provided for both litigation and arbitration as dispute resolution methods and referred to multiple arbitration institutions.

The Court held that, based on the express choice of the parties, the involved foreign-related arbitration clause was governed by Chinese law. The dispute resolution clause in question only granted both parties the right to apply to a court for interim measures and injunctions; it did not express an intention to submit substantive disputes to a court for resolution, and thus it could not be determined that court jurisdiction was agreed upon. On the other hand, Fan's location was the Chinese Mainland. According to the agreement, Fan could apply for arbitration with HKIAC, while M Entertainment Company could choose to apply for arbitration with either HKIAC or CIETAC. When M Entertainment Company chose arbitration with CIETAC, Fan was required to agree to this. As M Entertainment Company had

[22] See the 2nd batch of 10 Typical Cases on Judicial Review of Arbitration published by the High People's Court of Guangdong Province in August 2025. Where a specific arbitration institution can be determined through a unilateral optional arbitration clause, it does not constitute a situation where the arbitration institution is ambiguously agreed upon. This case reflects full respect for party autonomy and flexible choice in arbitration, and holds strong guiding significance for similar cases regarding the rules.

already applied to CIETAC for arbitration and the case had been accepted, the parties had formed a definite and exclusive arbitration agreement, selecting a specific arbitration institution. Therefore, the arbitration clause was legal and valid, and Fan's application should be dismissed.

Case 7: *X Communications Company v. Y Bank*[23]

X Communications Company and Y Bank entered into the Pledge Agreement on July 28, 2015. The clauses regarding governing law and dispute resolution in this agreement were primarily as follows: "22. GOVERNING LAW (This Agreement shall be governed by and construed in accordance with the laws of Country J.); 23. DISPUTE RESOLUTION 23.1 Unless the Pledgee elects otherwise, any dispute, controversy or claim arising out of or relating to this agreement, including questions regarding its existence, validity, interpretation, performance, shall be submitted to [X] Arbitration Commission for arbitration which shall be conducted in accordance with the arbitration rules of the arbitration commission in effect at the time of applying for arbitration. The seat of arbitration shall be Beijing. The arbitration shall be final. The language of the arbitration proceedings shall be English. 23.2 Notwithstanding Article 23.1, if the Pledgee so elects, the parties shall submit to the non-exclusive jurisdiction of the courts of Country J."

Y Bank submitted an application for arbitration to X Arbitration Commission on September 3, 2021, regarding disputes arising from the performance of this agreement, and X Arbitration Commission has formally accepted the case. X Communications Company argued that the arbitration clause in the Pledge Agreement was invalid and applied to the court to confirm the invalidity of the arbitration clause.

The Court held that the Pledge Agreement signed by X Communications Company and Y Bank contained an arbitration clause. The involved arbitration clause should legally be recognized as an arbitration agreement reached by the parties before the dispute arose. The content of this arbitration agreement contained a clear expression of intention to request arbitration and specified the arbitration matters, and it designated a specific arbitration commission to conduct the arbitration, thus meeting the elements required for a valid arbitration agreement under the aforementioned legal provisions. X Communications Company argued that this arbitration clause was a standard term and lacked sufficient notice and explanation. However, it did not provide evidence to prove that the text of the Pledge Agreement was pre-formulated by Y Bank for repeated use and lacked negotiation between the parties. Furthermore, even if the contract text adopted standard terms, the corresponding dispute resolution method applied equally to both parties, was not an exclusion of liability clause, and did not increase the responsibilities of X Communications Company. Therefore, this claim by X Communications Company lacked legal basis and was not accepted by the Court. X Communications Company also argued that Articles 23.1 and 23.2 of the Pledge Agreement constituted an

[23] See the 10 Typical Cases on Judicial Review of Financial Arbitration published by the Beijing Financial Court in October 2023.

"arbitration or litigation" clause. Regarding this, the Court held that Article 7 of the Arbitration Law Interpretation stipulated that if the parties agreed that disputes could be submitted to an arbitration institution for arbitration or to a people's court for litigation, the arbitration agreement was invalid. Therefore, the defining criterion for an "arbitration or litigation" agreement was that it provided for arbitration and litigation as parallel or alternative dispute resolution methods, leading to jurisdictional uncertainty. In this case, the involved dispute resolution clause was a unilateral optional dispute resolution clause, whose nature depended on Y Bank election. This agreement was the result of negotiation and consensus between the parties; there was no legal prohibition against such an arrangement, and the agreement did not constitute a clear unfairness in the rights and obligations of the parties.

Therefore, in this case, the parties' autonomy should be respected. The agreement's provision to submit disputes to the Arbitration Commission for arbitration did not violate Article 6 of the Arbitration Law (2017). Moreover, the selection of the arbitration institution by the parties through the agreement was specific and did not fall under the situation of an ambiguous designation of the arbitration institution referred to in Article 18 of the Arbitration Law (2017). Given that Y Bank had already applied for arbitration to X Arbitration Commission and explicitly waived its right to litigate in court, the involved dispute resolution clause had formed a definite and exclusive arbitration agreement.

Case 8: *Ningbo N Company v. Zhou*[24]

Ningbo N Company and X Construction Company signed the General Agreement, which stipulated that disputes should be submitted to Y Arbitration Institution. X Construction Company subsequently signed the Subcontracting Contract with Zhou, agreeing that disputes would be resolved by Z Arbitration Institution. Zhou then filed a lawsuit against Ningbo N Company as the defendant and X Construction Company as the third party, claiming payment for the project. Ningbo N Company raised a jurisdictional objection.

The Zhejiang Province Ningbo Intermediate People's Court held that Zhou was not a party to the General Agreement. Although the Subcontracting Contract signed by Zhou was explicitly based on the General Agreement, and he should have been aware of its arbitration clause, the Subcontracting Contract designated a different arbitration institution than the one stipulated in the General Agreement. This should be regarded as Zhou's refusal to accept the arbitration clause from the General Agreement. Furthermore, the legal relationship underlying the claims in this case was based on the Subcontracting Contract. Zhou's lawsuit against Ningbo N

[24] See the 10 Typical Cases on Judicial Review of Commercial Arbitration published by the Zhejiang Province Ningbo Intermediate People's Court in June 2024. In judicial practice, the right of action granted by law to the actual constructor against the developer/owner is sometimes abused. This case determined that the statutory remedy available to the actual constructor cannot override the parties' agreement to choose arbitration. It rejected the attempt to circumvent arbitration by adding a party not bound by the arbitration clause as a co-defendant. This case holds typical demonstrative significance for balancing the substantive and procedural rights of the parties and fostering a judicial environment that respects the intention to arbitrate.

Company and X Construction Company clearly violated the arbitration agreement between Zhou and X Construction Company. Therefore, the Court dismissed the claim.

Case 9: *Yu v. Li and others*[25]

Zimu Company provided a maximum amount guarantee for the loan debt of its shareholder Li to X Bank and signed the Guarantee Contract. Subsequently, Zimu Company was dissolved, and its shareholders, Yu and Li, as members of the liquidation team, signed the Liquidation Report. The Report stated that the company had no debts or credits and promised that the submitted liquidation materials were true and complete; they would bear all resulting responsibilities. Later, X Bank, on the grounds that Yu and Li had failed to liquidate according to law, causing damage to its claim, applied for arbitration to the Guangzhou Arbitration Commission based on the arbitration clause stipulated in the Guarantee Contract, demanding that Yu bear joint and several liability for Li's debt. After hearing the case, the Guangzhou Arbitration Commission issued an award stating that Yu shall bear joint and several liability for the loan debt, attorney fees, arbitration costs, and other debts owed by Li. Yu applied to the Court to set aside the aforementioned arbitral award, on the grounds that Yu was not a party to the Guarantee Contract and the involved arbitration agreement was not binding.

The Court held that although Yu was a member of Zimu Company's liquidation team, Yu was neither a party to the Guarantee Contract, nor a successor to the rights and obligations of Zimu Company, nor a transferee of the claims or debts. Furthermore, Yu had not expressed any intention to be bound by the arbitration clause in the contract. Therefore, the arbitration clause was not binding on Yu. The court accordingly ruled to set aside the part of the arbitral award that required Yu to bear joint and several liability.

Article 5

Where the parties have concluded an arbitration agreement and a party launches an action in a people's court, the people's court shall not accept the case, unless the arbitration agreement is null and void or otherwise provided by law.

Notes

This Article establishes the preclusive effect of an arbitration agreement regarding court jurisdiction, i.e., its anti-suit effect. Corresponding to Article 4, which stipulates that an arbitration institution shall not accept a case without an arbitration

---

[25] See the 2nd batch of the 10 Typical Cases on Judicial Review of Arbitration published by the Guangdong Province High People's Court in August 2025. The people's court, according to law, determined that when a company's liquidation team member is requested to bear liquidation liability towards the company's creditors, they are not bound by the arbitration clause previously concluded in the company's name. The case clarifies the scope of effect of arbitration agreements, legally restricts the extended effect of arbitration agreements, and fully respects the parties' true intention regarding the choice of dispute resolution method. It holds strong guiding significance for the adjudication rules of such cases.

agreement, this Article stipulates that a court shall not accept a case where a valid arbitration agreement exists. According to this Article, when a valid arbitration agreement exists between the parties, the court can promptly identify this fact and refer the case to arbitration, avoiding unnecessary waste of judicial resources while respecting the parties' autonomous choice. It also encourages parties to consider the terms of the arbitration agreement more carefully when concluding contracts, as entering into a valid arbitration agreement signifies the relinquishment of the right to institute court proceedings in favor of resolving disputes through arbitration. This Article draws a distinction between arbitration and litigation as dispute resolution methods, with the existence of an arbitration agreement serving as the demarcation line.

1. **Similarities and Differences Between Arbitration and Litigation**

From the perspective of being a method for resolving disputes, arbitration is not substantially different from litigation; both aim to settle the original dispute through a specific procedure. The similarities between arbitration and litigation are as follows:

Firstly, both arbitration and litigation involve the adjudication of a case by an impartial third party outside the dispute, based on law and facts. Arbitration is conducted by an arbitral tribunal, while litigation is conducted by a court. Both possess characteristics of independence and impartiality, perform similar functions to a certain extent, exercise comparable powers, and assume similar obligations and responsibilities. Furthermore, the adjudicating bodies in both systems feature specialization, and this trend towards specialization is becoming increasingly evident.

Secondly, similarities exist in procedural matters. Many procedures found in litigation are also present in arbitration, such as application (filing a claim) and defense, conservatory measures, hearings, cross-examination of evidence, and challenges (to arbitrators/judges). The often-mentioned "judicialization" of arbitration is also reflected in the convergence of procedural aspects between arbitration and litigation, potentially at the cost of the flexibility and voluntary nature that arbitration should possess.

Thirdly, the decisions rendered have legal effect. Generally, a valid arbitral award has the same legal effect as a court judgment, and both parties must conscientiously and fully comply with it. This is also stipulated by the statutory law of many countries. If one party fails to comply with an effective arbitral award, the prevailing party may, according to the applicable law or convention, apply to a court to enforce it through compulsory execution procedures.

Finally, generally speaking, the substantive legal norms applied by courts must also be applied by the arbitral tribunal when rendering an award. Furthermore, the arbitral tribunal applies the same conflict of laws rules as the court, rendering a decision on the merits of the dispute based on the substantive norms indicated by those rules.

Indeed, the differences between arbitration and litigation are also evident. Litigation procedures are a manifestation of the state exercising judicial power and constitute an important component of a country's judicial system. The right of individuals to seek dispute resolution is a constitutional right that cannot be derogated from save by the parties' express agreement. Arbitration is a quasi-judicial procedure and thus remains significantly different from litigation. For instance, arbitrators do not necessarily possess all the powers that judges have in litigation proceedings. Arbitration is conducted privately in principle, whereas litigation is conducted publicly in principle. The acceptance of a case in arbitration requires an arbitration agreement as its basis, whereas the establishment of court jurisdiction does not require an agreement between the parties to submit to court jurisdiction. If a valid arbitration agreement exists between the parties, it excludes the jurisdiction of the court. Regarding the scope of accepted cases, commercial arbitration only accepts commercial cases, whereas the scope of cases accepted by courts is not limited; courts exercise adjudicative power based on state coercive power. Any type of case can be submitted for resolution through litigation. In principle, parties to arbitration can freely agree on the applicable procedural rules, whereas court procedures cannot be modified by the free will of the parties. Arbitration follows the system of finality of the award, unlike litigation which typically follows a two-tier (or multi-tier) system of final appeal. This enables the expeditious resolution of parties' disputes, whereas litigation is subject to multi-tiered adjudication proceedings.

2. **Circumstances where a People's Court Accepts the Case**

As analyzed in the commentary on other provisions of this book, there are multiple scenarios in which an arbitration agreement may be deemed invalid. These include, but are not limited to:

A. ***The arbitration agreement violates legal provisions.*** For example, its form fails to comply with the written form explicitly required by the New Arbitration Law; or the matters agreed upon for arbitration fall outside the scope of what is legally arbitrable; or the agreement is ambiguous and cannot be supplemented by a subsequent agreement.

B. ***The arbitration agreement is concluded by a person without or with limited capacity for civil conduct.***

C. ***The expression of intent is not genuine.*** For instance, if one party induces the other party to sign the arbitration agreement by fraudulent means, in contravention of the latter's true will, the agreement is invalid. If one party coerces the other into signing the arbitration agreement, which violates the coerced party's true intention, the agreement shall be invalid. Where a material misunderstanding arises in respect of the content of the arbitration agreement, resulting in a discrepancy between the parties' true intent and the express content of the agreement, the agreement may be deemed invalid.

D. ***A Violation of public order and good morals***. For example, if the parties enter into an arbitration agreement for the purpose of concealing an illegal transaction by way of arbitration, the agreement shall be invalid for violating public order. Where the performance of the arbitration agreement would impair the lawful rights and interests of a third party, it may also be deemed invalid.

This Article also stipulates that, under circumstances otherwise provided by law, the court may accept a case even if an arbitration agreement exists. However, it does not provide a detailed list of the specific types of such circumstances. This Article reserves possibilities for special situations that may be stipulated in other laws. In judicial practice, there may be differing interpretations regarding which situations fall under "circumstances otherwise provided by law." For example, in certain complex cases involving intellectual property disputes or anti-monopoly disputes, various views exist concerning the relationship between arbitration agreements and court jurisdiction. Some argue that the specific nature of these fields dictates the priority application of special legal provisions in the relevant areas, potentially granting courts jurisdiction even if an arbitration agreement exists. Others contend that as long as the arbitration agreement is valid, the principle of arbitration priority should be followed, unless specific laws explicitly exclude arbitration.

In addition, certain laws exclusively prescribe litigation jurisdiction for specific circumstances. For example, Article 12 of the Anti-Foreign Sanctions Law of the People's Republic of China stipulates that where any organization or individual enforces or renders assistance in enforcing discriminatory restrictive measures imposed by a foreign state against citizens or organizations of the People's Republic of China, thereby infringing upon the lawful rights and interests of such citizens or organizations, the aggrieved citizens or organizations of the People's Republic of China may institute legal proceedings in a people's court in accordance with the law, claiming an order for cessation of the infringement and compensation for losses. If an underlying transaction containing an arbitration agreement involves sanctions, a situation may arise where a party elects to resolve the dispute through litigation rather than arbitration.

Generally, the following types of litigation require handling by the courts:

A. ***Disputes over the validity of the arbitration agreement***. Courts can accept cases concerning disputes over the validity of an arbitration agreement. For instance, if the parties disagree on whether the arbitration agreement is valid, and one party applies to the arbitration institution to confirm its validity while the other party initiates a lawsuit in court, the court has the authority to accept the case and issue a ruling.

B. ***Setting aside and enforcement of arbitral awards***. In proceedings for setting aside or enforcing an arbitral award, courts review and handle matters related to the arbitration. Even if an arbitration agreement exists, the court needs to intervene as required by law.

Furthermore, regarding bankruptcy disputes, Article 20 of the Enterprise Bankruptcy Law stipulates that after a people's court accepts a bankruptcy application, any pending civil lawsuits or arbitrations concerning the debtor shall be suspended; after the administrator takes over the debtor's property, such lawsuits or arbitrations shall proceed. Therefore, generally, bankruptcy does not affect the validity of the arbitration agreement. However, if the arbitration agreement is concluded after the acceptance of the bankruptcy application by the debtor and a creditor, since civil disputes concerning the debtor have already fallen within the exclusive jurisdiction of the bankruptcy proceedings, and the parties likely intend to evade this exclusive jurisdiction, such an arbitration clause will usually also be deemed invalid, and the parties may file a lawsuit in court.

When hearing whether to accept a case, courts need to pay attention to the issue of the independence of the arbitration agreement. The independence of the arbitration agreement is one of the important principles of the New Arbitration Law. The arbitration agreement is independent of the main contract. Even if the validity of the main contract changes, the validity of the arbitration agreement remains unaffected. In the event that the main contract is terminated due to one party's breach, the arbitration agreement remains valid, and the parties must still submit the dispute to arbitration in accordance with the arbitration agreement. Therefore, even if the main contract is invalid, the court can still refuse jurisdiction based on a valid arbitration agreement, ensuring that the parties' intention to resolve disputes through arbitration can be realized.

Additionally, it is important to acknowledge that courts in different regions may apply inconsistent standards when determining the validity of arbitration agreements. Given China's extensive jurisdiction, variations in judicial interpretation and application of the law across different levels of courts are noticeable, particularly in assessing arbitration agreements. Some courts adopt a stringent approach, rigorously evaluating both formal and substantive requirements. Minor imperfections, such as slight inaccuracies in naming the arbitration institution or imprecise descriptions of arbitrable matters, often lead these courts to invalidate the arbitration agreement. In contrast, other courts demonstrate a more flexible and arbitration-friendly stance. When faced with defects in an arbitration agreement, they consider a range of factors, including the parties' genuine intent, the overall purpose of the contract, and prevailing industry practices, striving to uphold the agreement's validity through interpretation and supplementation to direct disputes toward arbitration. This divergence in judicial standards results in similar or identical arbitration agreements potentially yielding different outcomes depending on the court. Such inconsistency underscores the need to enhance uniformity and fairness in the application of the law, as it introduces uncertainty for parties when selecting dispute resolution mechanisms.

Illustrative Case

X Capital Management Company v. Y Securities Company and others[26]

The involved bonds were listed on the Shanghai Stock Exchange on February 14, 2019, and traded to institutional investors among qualified investors. The issuance scale was RMB 1 billion, with an annual coupon rate of 6.5%, an issuance price of RMB 100 per bond, and a term of 3 years.

Section 5 of the Prospectus stipulated that if the issuer failed to perform or violated any commitments under the agreement, which would substantially affect its obligation to repay the principal and interest of the bonds, and such default persisted

[26] See the 10 typical Cases on Judicial Review of Financial Arbitration published by the Beijing Financial Court in October 2023.

for 30 working days without being fully remedied after written notice from the bond trustee or from bondholders holding no less than 20% of the outstanding principal amount of the bonds, it would constitute a default event under the bonds. The agreement was governed by and interpreted in accordance with Chinese law. Any disputes arising from or relating to the agreement were first to be resolved through negotiation between the parties. If the parties failed to resolve the dispute through consultation, it was to be submitted to Z Arbitration Commission for arbitration in accordance with its arbitration rules effective at the time of applying for arbitration. The place of arbitration was Beijing, and the arbitral award was final and binding on the parties to the agreement.

Section 10 of the Prospectus stipulated that any investor who legally acquired and held the bonds through subscription, transfer, gift, inheritance, or other lawful means was deemed to have accepted the terms and conditions of the Bond Trusteeship Agreement and authorized the bond trustee to perform its duties thereunder. The governing law and dispute resolution method in this section provided that any disputes arising from or relating to the agreement were first to be resolved through negotiation between the parties. If the parties failed to resolve the dispute through consultation, it was to be submitted to Z Arbitration Commission for arbitration in accordance with its arbitration rules effective at the time of applying for arbitration. The place of arbitration was Beijing, and the arbitral award was final and binding on the parties to the agreement.

X Capital Management Company filed a lawsuit with the Beijing Financial Court based on bond misrepresentation liabilities, claiming: (1) that Y Securities Company, the accounting firm, the law firm, and the appraisal company (collectively referred to the "Respondents") be ordered to jointly and severally compensate X Capital Management Company for losses of bond principal and interest; (2) that the Respondents be ordered to jointly and severally compensate for losses of overdue interest; (3) that the Respondents be ordered to jointly and severally compensate the X Capital Management Company for reasonable expenses incurred in enforcing the claims.

The Beijing Financial Court held that Article 119(4) of the Civil Procedure Law stipulated that a lawsuit must meet the following conditions: (4) the case falls within the scope of civil cases accepted by the courts and under the jurisdiction of the court where the lawsuit is filed. Article 124(2) provided that the court shall handle the following lawsuits respectively according to the specific circumstances: where the parties have reached a written arbitration agreement pursuant to the law and applied for arbitration, and therefore shall not file a lawsuit with the court, the plaintiff shall be informed to apply for arbitration with an arbitration institution. Article 216 of the Civil Procedure Law Interpretation provided that where the defendant raised an objection to the acceptance of the civil case on the grounds of having a written arbitration agreement before the first court hearing, the court shall conduct a review. If, upon review, any of the following circumstances was met, the court shall rule to dismiss the lawsuit: (1) the arbitration institution or the court had already confirmed the validity of the arbitration agreement; (2) the parties did not raise an objection to the validity of the arbitration agreement before the first arbitration hearing; (3) the arbitration agreement complied with Article 16 of the Arbitration Law and did not fall under the circumstances specified in Article 17 of the Arbitration Law.

In this case, based on the established facts, the Prospectus stated that any investor who legally acquired and held the bonds through subscription, transfer, gift, inheritance, or other lawful means was deemed to have accepted the provisions in the Prospectus regarding the rights and obligations of the issuer, bondholders, bond trustee, and other relevant parties, and to have agreed to the terms and conditions of the Bond Trusteeship Agreement. Any disputes arising from or relating to the agreement were first to be resolved through negotiation between the parties. If the parties failed to resolve the dispute through consultation, it was to be submitted to Z Arbitration Agreement for arbitration in accordance with its arbitration rules effective at the time of applying for arbitration.

According to the above provisions, by holding the bonds involved in the case, bond investors were deemed to have accepted the constraints imposed by the Prospectus on the issuer and the bond trustee, and the aforementioned arbitration clause thereby became legally binding on them. Therefore, the claims for compensation filed by X Capital Management Company should be resolved through arbitration proceedings. The Court therefore ruled to dismiss the action.

Article 6
The arbitration institution shall be selected by the parties through agreement.

There shall be no jurisdiction by level and no territorial jurisdiction in arbitration.

Notes

The principle of party autonomy is fundamental in the arbitration system, and this is particularly evident in the selection of an arbitration institution. According to the New Arbitration Law, parties are free to agree on the selection of an arbitration institution, granting them significant autonomy. In international commercial arbitration, based on considerations such as professional capability, reputation, and familiarity with the arbitration rules of different institutions, parties can autonomously decide which arbitration institution to submit their dispute to for resolution. For example, in a dispute arising from a cross-border sale of goods contract, the parties might jointly agree to submit the dispute to a specific arbitration institution because that institution has extensive experience and a professional panel of arbitrators in the field of international trade. This right to freely choose the arbitration institution fully embodies the principle of party autonomy, enabling the parties to construct an arbitration framework most suitable for resolving their dispute based on their actual needs and interests.

Under the framework of Chinese arbitration law, it is crucial to clearly specify the name of the arbitration institution in the arbitration agreement. A clear designation allows for the identification of the arbitration institution and the smooth initiation of arbitration proceedings. If the name of the arbitration institution is ambiguously stated in the arbitration agreement, it may become impossible to determine the specific institution, thereby affecting the validity of the arbitration agreement and giving rise to jurisdictional disputes.

When an arbitration agreement ambiguously refers to the arbitration institution, the parties may clarify the institution by reaching a supplementary agreement through negotiation. If the parties cannot reach a supplementary agreement on the choice of arbitration institution, according to the New Arbitration Law, the arbitration agreement will be deemed invalid, and the parties can only resort to other means, such as litigation, to resolve their dispute.

Furthermore, if an arbitration agreement only specifies the arbitration rules but does not clearly designate the arbitration institution, some arbitration rules themselves stipulate the corresponding institution.

In arbitration involving foreign elements, parties may choose foreign arbitration institutions. It is important to note that different countries and regions have varying requirements concerning the conduct of arbitration proceedings and the recognition and enforcement of arbitral awards. When choosing a foreign arbitration institution, parties must fully consider these factors, carefully assess the risks, and seek professional legal advice, where necessary, to ensure that the arbitral award can be effectively recognized and enforced when needed.

The second paragraph of this Article stipulates that arbitration does not follow hierarchical or territorial jurisdiction. In the traditional litigation model, parties are often strictly bound by territorial and hierarchical jurisdiction and must file lawsuits with courts in specific locations and at specific levels. For example, in a general contract dispute, according to the Civil Procedure Law, the lawsuit might need to be filed with the primary people's courts in the defendant's domicile or the place of contract performance. If the case involves a large amount in dispute, it might need to be filed with an intermediate people's court or a high court according to the rules on hierarchical jurisdiction. While these strict jurisdictional rules have their rationale in maintaining judicial order and facilitating case management, they somewhat restrict the parties' autonomous right to choose.

In arbitration, parties can completely bypass these restrictions. They may choose an arbitration institution based on their understanding of and trust in the institution, as well as the specific circumstances of the case. Regardless of the institution's location and its connection to the parties' domiciles, the place of contract performance, or the place where the dispute arose, as long as both parties agree, they can submit the dispute to that institution for arbitration. This cross-regional choice fully demonstrates the flexibility of arbitration regarding jurisdiction, allowing parties to break free from geographical and hierarchical constraints and select the arbitration institution most suitable for resolving their dispute according to their own needs, thereby meeting the diverse needs of different parties in dispute resolution. This approach allows arbitration to focus more time and energy on the substantive hearing of the case, thereby improving the efficiency of dispute resolution.

Furthermore, when selecting an arbitration institution, parties often consider the panel of arbitrators available at that institution. Since arbitration is not subject to hierarchical or territorial jurisdiction, parties can choose from a wider range of arbitration institutions, thereby gaining access to arbitrators from more specialized fields. Different arbitration institutions often have professional advantages in specific areas, possessing a panel of arbitrators with extensive experience and high professional competence in those fields. This optimized allocation of professional arbitrator resources enables parties to select the most suitable arbitrators to hear their case based on the nature and characteristics of the dispute. This ensures that the arbitral award fully considers the professional issues involved, enhances the quality and fairness of the award, and effectively safeguards the legitimate rights and interests of the parties.

It is also important to recognize that while the arbitration institution itself is a matter of choice, the court for enforcing the arbitral award must be determined according to law. Determining the competent court for enforcement in arbitral award execution can be complex. A party applying for enforcement of an arbitral award shall file the application with the intermediate people's court of the place where the person against whom the application is made is domiciled or where the property subject to enforcement is located. However, in practice, the domicile of the person against whom enforcement is sought and the location of the enforceable assets might be in different jurisdictions, or even involve multiple jurisdictions, which gives rise to difficulties in determining the competent enforcement court. Furthermore, if the person against whom enforcement is sought has property in multiple jurisdictions, and the claimant applies for enforcement to multiple courts with jurisdiction, issues of jurisdictional conflict may arise, requiring resolution based on relevant legal provisions and judicial interpretations to confirm the ultimately competent court for enforcement.

Illustrative Case

Party A v. Party B[27]

Both Party A and Party B were U.S. citizens. Party B entrusted Party A to hold the original shares of Company A (registered in the Cayman Islands) on its behalf. The two parties signed the Share Custody Agreement in Hangzhou, China, on February 20, 2012. Article 9 of the agreement stipulated, "Any disputes arising from the performance of this agreement shall be resolved through friendly negotiations between the parties; if mediation through consultation proves ineffective, both parties agree to submit the dispute to the Hangzhou Arbitration Commission for arbitration. The arbitration shall be final and binding on both parties to the agreement." On April 28, 2023, the Hangzhou Arbitration Commission accepted the contract dispute case between Party A and Party B. Before the first hearing of the arbitral tribunal, Party A applied to the Zhejiang Province Hangzhou Intermediate People's Court for confirmation that the arbitration agreement was invalid.

The Zhejiang Province Hangzhou Intermediate People's Court held that the arbitration agreement involved in the case constituted a "foreign-related arbitration

[27] See the Typical Cases on Judicial Review of Arbitration published by the Zhejiang Province Hangzhou Intermediate People's Court in March 2024. Parties to a foreign-related contract may conclude an arbitration agreement choosing to apply to a Chinese arbitration institution, which has no actual connection to the dispute.

agreement." As the parties did not choose the applicable law for determining the validity of this foreign-related arbitration agreement, the law of the place of the designated arbitration institution, i.e., the law of the People's Republic of China, should apply. The Hangzhou Arbitration Commission was an arbitration institution established after the implementation of the Arbitration Law (2017). According to Article 3 of the Notice of the General Office of the State Council on Several Issues Requiring Clarification for the Implementation of the Arbitration Law of the People's Republic of China, which stated that the primary duty of newly established arbitration commissions is to accept domestic arbitration cases; if parties to a foreign-related arbitration case voluntarily choose to submit their dispute to a newly established arbitration commission, the newly established arbitration commission may accept the case;… and Article 128 of the then-effective Contract Law, which provided that parties to a foreign-related contract may apply to a Chinese arbitration institution or another arbitration institution for arbitration in accordance with the arbitration agreement, the parties were permitted to agree in their arbitration clause to submit foreign-related disputes to a Chinese arbitration institution for arbitration. Pursuant to Article 6 of the Arbitration Law (2017), Party A's claim that the arbitration agreement was invalid on the grounds that the chosen arbitration institution was not located in a place having a factual connection to the dispute lacked legal basis. The Court ruled to dismiss the action.

Article 7
In arbitration, disputes shall be resolved on the basis of facts, in compliance with the law and in an equitable and reasonable manner.

Notes
Article 7 of the New Arbitration Law establishes the basis for the substantive award: facts, law, and fairness and reasonableness. The arbitration rules of major Chinese arbitration institutions generally adopt similar wording.

1. **On the basis of facts**

Resolved on the basis of facts is the premise for an arbitral award and the primary condition for achieving a fair and equitable resolution of the dispute. Its core implication is that the arbitral tribunal must base its decision on the objective facts of the case, restoring the true factual circumstances through the examination and evaluation of evidence, and must not engage in subjective presumptions or render awards without basis or substantiation. Objective facts directly related to the dispute, such as the time of contract conclusion, the content of performance, the occurrence of breach of contract, and the specific amounts of damages, form the basis for determining the rights and obligations of the parties and constitute the main subject-matter of the arbitral tribunal's hearing. When ascertaining facts, the arbitral tribunal primarily needs to adhere to the following requirements:

A. ***Objectivity Requirement***. The arbitral tribunal shall base its findings on objective evidence, unaffected by the parties' subjective statements or emotional factors, and shall comprehensively and truthfully restore the facts of the case. When examining

evidence, it shall strictly review the authenticity, legality, and relevance of the evidence, excluding false or illegal evidence.
B. ***Comprehensiveness Requirement***. The arbitral tribunal shall comprehensively collect evidence relevant to the facts of the case. It must not only examine the evidence provided by the parties but may also, upon the application of a party or on its own initiative, proactively investigate and collect evidence (such as obtaining documentary or physical evidence from relevant entities or individuals, questioning witnesses, etc.), ensuring that there are no omissions or deviations in the determination of the case facts.

C. ***Standard of High Probability***. In civil and commercial arbitration, since case facts often occurred in the past and evidence may be incomplete or contradictory, the arbitral tribunal typically adopts the standard of "high probability" for fact-finding. This means that when the evidence provided by one party can prove that the occurrence of a case fact is highly probable, the arbitral tribunal may determine that the fact is established, unless contrary evidence provided by the other party can overturn this determination.

2. **In compliance with the law**

In compliance with the law is the guarantee of the legality of the arbitral award and an important prerequisite for the arbitration system to receive judicial support. Its core connotation is that, based on the ascertained facts, the arbitral tribunal must render its award on the rights and obligations of the parties according to currently effective legal norms (including laws, administrative regulations, local regulations, rules, and judicial interpretations), and must not violate mandatory legal provisions or public order and good morals.

Regarding the approach of the arbitral tribunal in applying the law, arbitration statutes or arbitration rules generally provide for two main methods. One method stipulates that if the parties have agreed on a choice of law, the agreed-upon law shall apply; in the absence of such agreement, the law of the state with the closest connection shall apply; if a contract is involved, the tribunal shall also base its decision on the contract terms and take relevant practices into account; the legal system chosen by the parties shall be construed as referring to its substantive law. Furthermore, such provisions may also address the issue of amiable composition (*ex aequo et bono*). This approach employs the closest connection principle as the direct basis for determining the applicable law in the absence of party agreement, as seen in the arbitration laws of Germany[28] and Japan. According to the Japanese Arbitration Act (2003), the arbitral tribunal shall decide the dispute in accordance with the legal rules designated by the parties as applicable to the substance of the dispute. In such cases, unless otherwise indicated, any designation of the law or legal system of a specific state shall be construed as directly referring to the substantive law of that state, and not to its conflict-of-laws rules. The arbitral tribunal may decide *ex aequo*

[28] See Article 1051 of German Arbitration Law (1998).

et bono or as amiable compositeur only if the parties have expressly authorized it to do so. In the absence of express authorization or agreement, the arbitral tribunal shall apply the law of the state with the closest connection to the civil dispute involved in the arbitration proceedings. If a contract is involved in the civil dispute related to the arbitration proceedings, the arbitral tribunal shall make its decision based on the terms of that contract and shall take into account any applicable practices relevant to the civil dispute.[29]

The other method stipulates that the arbitral tribunal's discretion serves as the direct basis for determining the applicable law in the absence of party agreement, as seen in Section 46 of the UK Arbitration Act 1996. It is evident that the primary difference between the two lies in the extent of the arbitral tribunal's discretion in the absence of party agreement, while the provisions concerning amiable composition and the application of contract terms and trade practices are largely similar.

3. **In an equitable and reasonable manner**

"In an equitable and reasonable manner" is the value pursuit of an arbitral award. Its core connotation is that, based on the facts and in conformity with legal provisions, the arbitral tribunal should fully consider the actual circumstances of the parties, the specific background of the case, and the basic concept of fairness and justice, to render a just and reasonable award that balances the interests between the parties and avoids obviously unfair outcomes. Equity and reasonableness in arbitration are mainly reflected in the following three dimensions:

A. ***Equality of the Parties***. The arbitral tribunal shall ensure that both parties enjoy equal rights and status in the arbitration proceedings and must not favor either party. For example, during the hearing, it should give both parties sufficient opportunity to present their case, adduce evidence, cross-examine, and debate; when serving arbitration documents, it should ensure that both parties can obtain relevant information timely and equally; when rendering an award, it should base its determination of the parties' rights and obligations on the same facts and legal grounds.

B. ***Balance of Interests***. The arbitral tribunal should comprehensively consider the interest relationship between the parties. While protecting the legitimate rights and interests of one party, it should also take into account the reasonable demands of the other party, avoiding a situation where one party suffers excessive loss while the other gains excessive benefit. For instance, when handling a breach of contract dispute, the tribunal should not only determine the liability of the breaching party but also consider the reasons for the breach (such as force majeure, change of circumstances, etc.), the actual loss caused by the breach, and the non-breaching party's duty to mitigate losses, to reasonably determine the amount of liquidated damages or the scope of compensation, thereby achieving a balance of interests between the parties.

C. ***Reasonableness of the Outcome***. The result of the arbitral award should conform to the basic concept of fairness and justice and the general perception of the public,

[29] See Article 36 of the Japanese Arbitration Act (2003).

possessing reasonableness and acceptability. Even in cases where the legal provisions are clear, if strictly applying the law would lead to a manifestly unfair result, the arbitral tribunal may, without violating mandatory legal provisions, make appropriate adjustments to the award based on the principle of fairness and reasonableness.

The reference to "equitable and reasonable" in the New Arbitration Law does not refer to amiable compositeur. Amiable compositeur (or *ex aequo et bono*) is also a practice in commercial arbitration, generally referring to a dispute resolution method where the arbitrator renders an award based on standards that they consider fair and reasonable. Amiable compositeur usually requires two conditions: first, authorization by the parties; second, non-violation of the provisions of the law of the seat of arbitration. Arbitrators typically render awards as amiable compositeur only if the parties agree and the law of the seat of arbitration does not prohibit it. For example, Article 33(2) of the UNCITRAL Arbitration Rules states that the arbitral tribunal shall decide as amiable compositeur or *ex aequo et bono* only if the parties have expressly authorized it to do so and if the law applicable to the arbitration procedure permits such arbitration. Section 1051(3) of the German Arbitration Act stipulates that the arbitral tribunal shall decide as amiable compositeur or *ex aequo et bono* only if the parties have expressly authorized it to do so. The parties may authorize the arbitral tribunal up to the time of the making of its decision. Due to the abstract nature of principles like equity and good conscience, and fairness and justice, which form the basis of amiable compositeur, arbitrators in such proceedings possess significant discretionary power. Therefore, unless expressly authorized by the parties and not violating the mandatory provisions of the law applicable to the arbitration procedure, arbitration should not resolve the parties' dispute as amiable compositeur.

Chinese legislation does not provide for amiable compositeur. The principle of fairness and reasonableness is one basis for amiable compositeur. However, the New Arbitration Law adheres to this principle under the premise of complying with the law, treating it only as a supplement, without implying its independent application. In practice, there are instances where the principle of fairness and reasonableness is used as a supplement, but examples of awards based solely on this principle are rare. In recent practice, some institutional arbitration rules have begun to introduce amiable compositeur.

Article 8
Arbitration shall follow the principle of good faith.

Notes

The principle of good faith is the paramount principle in the field of civil and commercial law. Article 7 of the General Provisions of the Civil Code expressly stipulates that when engaging in civil activities, civil subjects should abide by the principle of good faith, uphold honesty, and abide by their commitments. In addition to Article 7, provisions such as Articles 142, 500, and 509 further elaborate on the principle of good faith. For instance, Article 142 states that the interpretation of an expression of intent manifested to a relative person shall be determined based on the words and sentences used, in conjunction with the relevant provisions, the nature and purpose of the act, custom, and the principle of good faith, to ascertain the meaning of the expression of intent. The interpretation of an expression of intent not manifested to a relative person shall not be completely bound by the words and sentences used, but shall be made in conjunction with the relevant provisions, the nature and purpose of the act, custom, and the principle of good faith, to determine the true intent of the actor. Particularly, this provision explicitly indicates that when interpreting an "expression of intent," the "principle of good faith" must also be considered to determine the true intent. Furthermore, Article 500 establishes a punitive mechanism for violations of the principle of good faith during contract formation. Specifically, if a party, in the course of concluding a contract, commits other acts violating the principle of good faith, thereby causing losses to the other party, it shall be liable for compensation.

Therefore, this principle of good faith requires civil activities to uphold honesty and abide by commitments, to balance the rights and interests of others and social public welfare while pursuing personal interests, and to maintain market moral order through balancing the interests of all parties. It represents the equilibrium between morality and law.

With increasingly complex economic interactions, many acts violating good faith have emerged in arbitration practice, such as false statements by parties, concealment of key evidence, malicious delay of arbitration proceedings, and evasion of arbitral award enforcement. These acts not only disrupt the order of arbitration and increase arbitration costs but also damage the authority of the arbitration system. The inclusion of this Article in the New Arbitration Law introduces the principle of good faith into arbitration legislation, establishing both moral and legal bottom lines for arbitration activities. It is of great significance for ensuring the fairness of arbitration procedures, protecting the legitimate rights and interests of the parties, and enhancing the credibility of arbitration. Although neither the Arbitration Law (1994) nor the Arbitration Law (2017) contains explicit provisions requiring arbitration activities to follow the principle of good faith, in practice, the main Chinese arbitration institutions have already incorporated this principle into their arbitration rules. Arbitration institutions such as CIETAC, BAC, and SCIA have all included provisions on "arbitration in good faith" in their formulated arbitration rules. For example, Article 9 of the CIETAC Arbitration Rules stipulates that the participants in the arbitration proceedings shall follow the principle of good faith in conducting the arbitration proceedings. Another example is Article 2(4) of the BAC Arbitration Rules, which states that the BAC, the Arbitral Tribunal, the parties and their representatives shall act in accordance with the principles of good faith, collaboration, and appropriate resolution of the dispute.

The principle of good faith in arbitration, also known as the principle of honesty and credit in arbitration, refers to the requirement that during arbitration activities, the parties, arbitrators, and arbitration institutions shall uphold honesty, abide by credit, exercise rights and perform obligations in good faith, and shall not abuse rights, evade obligations, or engage in acts contrary to good faith such as fraud or concealment.

The parties are the initiators and core participants of the arbitration procedure, and their good faith obligations run through the entire arbitration process. The regulation of the parties mainly lies in prohibiting the abuse of rights. For example, the principle of estoppel applies; a party shall not assert a claim or defense in the arbitration proceedings that contradicts their prior words or actions. Abusing procedural rights is prohibited; parties shall not exercise rights such as applying for a challenge or raising jurisdictional objections for illegal purposes, like delaying the procedure or increasing the other party's costs. At the stage of initiating the procedure, parties shall truthfully submit arbitration application materials and shall not fabricate facts or forge evidence; if an arbitration agreement exists, they must truthfully explain the conclusion and performance of the agreement and shall not conceal key information affecting the validity of the arbitration agreement. During the hearing stage, parties shall truthfully state the facts of the case and shall not make false or contradictory statements; they shall submit evidence related to the case in a timely and comprehensive manner and shall not conceal evidence unfavorable to themselves but crucial for the fair adjudication of the case; they shall comply with the procedural arrangements of the arbitral tribunal and shall not delay procedures such as evidence submission and hearings without justifiable reasons, such as intentionally submitting evidence after the deadline or absenting themselves from hearings without cause. At the stage of award enforcement, parties shall respect and proactively fulfill the effective arbitral award and shall not maliciously transfer property or evade performance obligations; if they have objections to the award result, they must assert their rights through legal channels (such as applying to set aside or not enforce the arbitral award) and shall not resort to illegal means such as violence or threats to resist enforcement.

Arbitrators are the makers of arbitral awards, and their level of good faith directly determines the fairness of arbitration. Upon accepting the appointment or selection as an arbitrator, they shall promptly disclose to the arbitration institution any relationships with the parties or their agents that may affect impartial adjudication, such as family relationships, economic dealings, or prior commercial cooperation. If grounds for challenge exist, they must proactively apply for withdrawal. During the hearing process, arbitrators shall hear the case neutrally and objectively and shall not show favor to any party; they shall diligently hear the statements and arguments of both parties, conduct comprehensive review of evidence, and shall not let personal bias, emotions, or external interference influence their judgment of the case; they shall strictly comply with the provisions of the arbitration procedure and shall not simplify or alter the procedure without authorization, ensuring the parties' procedural rights are fully protected. Arbitrators shall maintain confidentiality regarding the hearing process, case facts, evidentiary materials, and the content of the award, and shall not disclose case information to the outside world or comment on the case outside the arbitration proceedings, thereby safeguarding the confidentiality and authority of arbitration.

Arbitration institutions are the organizers and managers of the arbitration procedure. They shall handle matters such as the acceptance of arbitration cases, service, formation of the tribunal, and hearings in a timely and standardized manner according to the arbitration rules, and shall not intentionally delay the procedure or engage in irregular operations; they shall fully inform the parties of their procedural rights and obligations, fee standards, and other information, and shall not conceal or mislead. Simultaneously, arbitration institutions shall provide necessary arbitration service support for the parties and arbitrators, such as providing hearing venues and organizing case materials, to ensure the smooth progress of the arbitration procedure; they shall not use their position to seek improper benefits, such as demanding additional fees from parties or favoring specific parties.

It should be recognized that although the New Arbitration Law and some arbitration rules codify the principle of good faith, its application in practice sometimes encounters problems. Currently, in arbitration practice, there is a lack of unified and clear standards for defining "acts violating good faith." For example, how is the scope of "concealing evidence" defined? Does a party's failure to submit evidence with less relevance to the case constitute "concealment"? How is "false statement" distinguished from "inconsistent statements due to memory deviation"? The lack of clear provisions on these issues leads arbitral tribunals to rely on subjective judgment when making determinations, making different rulings in similar cases likely. For parties violating good faith, some tribunals only issue reprimands, while others rule that they bear additional arbitration costs, or even dismiss their arbitration claims. Furthermore, due to the confidentiality of arbitration and information asymmetry between parties, identifying and obtaining evidence of acts violating good faith faces many difficulties. For instance, acts such as false statements or concealment of evidence by parties are often covert. The arbitral tribunal primarily relies on the parties' statements and submitted evidence for judgment. If parties collude to provide false evidence (such as forging contracts or fabricating transactions), it is difficult for the tribunal to detect. If a party claims the other party has violated good faith (e.g., by concealing evidence), they need to provide evidence proving that the other party possesses such evidence and that it is crucial for the fair adjudication of the case. However, parties often struggle to obtain clues about the evidence held by the other party (such as internal documents or transaction records). Although the arbitral tribunal can investigate and collect evidence on its own initiative, it is limited by the principle of "respecting party autonomy," restricting the scope and intensity of investigation, making it difficult to effectively obtain key evidence.

Some arbitration institutions have further refined and adjusted the principle of good faith in their existing rules based on their own practice. Some arbitration institutions have already conducted relatively in-depth explorations in this area. For example, the SCIA Arbitration Rules (2025 Amendment), based on the principle of good faith, provide further details. In Article 7, it clearly states that (1) the parties and their representatives shall participate in the arbitration in accordance with the principles of good faith and cooperative goodwill; (2) if a party or its representative violates the provisions of these Rules, the agreement between the parties, or the order of the arbitral tribunal, resulting in procedural delay or increased costs, the arbitral tribunal has the power to decide that such party shall bear the corresponding consequences. (3) The parties and their representatives shall ensure the authenticity of their statements and submitted materials, otherwise the party shall bear the corresponding consequences. The rules clearly indicate the concerns regarding good faith cooperation and the consequences of violating it, thereby enhancing the enforceability of the principle. Similar provisions can also be found in Shanghai Arbitration Commission Arbitration Rules (2022).

Illustrative Cases

Case 1: *Henglong Company v. Yixiangyuan Company*[30]

Henglong Company applied to set aside an arbitral award rendered by the Zaozhuang Arbitration Commission, with one of the grounds for setting aside being that the evidence on which the award was based was forged.

Henglong Company claimed that the seal of Yixiangyuan Company on Exhibit 3, the Agreement, submitted by Yixiangyuan Company during the arbitration hearing, was forged and did not represent the true intent of Yixiangyuan Company; therefore, this Agreement was not valid. This very Agreement was the main evidence upon which the arbitral award relied. Furthermore, Yixiangyuan Company also forged the seal of the Z Engineering Construction Supervision Company and the signature of the chief supervising engineer on the Project Settlement Statement and the Drawing Review Record.

Yixiangyuan Company argued that the Agreement was not forged. This Agreement was formed by the parties on April 14, 2020, and Yixiangyuan Company affixed its seal at a later stage. This seal belonged to the company's official seal after its name change and was not forged. Henglong Company had also not objected to the authenticity of this evidence during the arbitration proceedings. The "Project Settlement Statement" was a settlement document submitted by Yixiangyuan Company to Henglong Company and the audit institution based on the Agreement. It was submitted to Henglong Company along with other construction documents on July 6, 2020, and Henglong Company forwarded it to the audit institution the next day. Furthermore, the preparation of this Project Settlement Statement had a factual and contractual basis. Additionally, the Drawing Review Record was not among the evidence adopted by the arbitral award and thus fell outside the scope of review in this case.

The Shandong Province Zaozhuang Intermediate People's Court held that the Shandong Hengyou Mansion Building 1# Project Handover Form, jointly signed and sealed by Henglong Company, Yixiangyuan Company, the supervision unit, and the audit unit, had already confirmed the specific completed quantity of work by the respondent. The completed quantity of work stated in the Project Settlement Statement was based on the quantity of work confirmed in the aforementioned handover form. Simultaneously, the Project Settlement Statement was submitted by the respondent to the claimant, who then forwarded it to the audit institution. Even if the Project Settlement Statement did not match the actual situation, the claimant,

[30] (2022) Lu 04 Min Te No. 9.

as the employer, upon receiving the Project Settlement Statement, was aware that the Agreement dated April 14, 2020, which both parties concluded, clearly stipulated the settlement method. However, the claimant neglected its duty of review and should bear the adverse legal consequences. Therefore, the court dismissed Henglong Company's claims. During the arbitration proceedings, the Agreement was submitted by Yixiangyuan Company, and Henglong Company recognized its authenticity during cross-examination. In its defense in this case, Yixiangyuan Company stated that the seal on the agreement was affixed at a later stage. Given Yixiangyuan Company's reasonable explanation and based on the principle of estoppel, the claimant's claim that the Agreement was forged could not be sustained.

Case 2: *Zhang Lan and others v. La Dolce Vita Fine Dining Group Holdings Limited*[31]

On December 13, 2013, the various parties, including Zhang Lan, Grand Lan Holdings Group (BVI) Limited ("Grand Lan Holdings"), La Dolce Vita Fine Dining Group Holdings Limited ("La Dolce Vita Group"), signed the Share Purchase Agreement, which contained an arbitration clause. After the arbitral award was rendered, Zhang Lan and Grand Lan Holdings sought to have the award set aside, arguing that the composition of the arbitral tribunal was inconsistent with the arbitration rules.

The court held that revisions, gap-filling, or interpretation and application of the arbitration rules fell within the autonomous scope of arbitration institutions and should not be interfered with through judicial review of arbitration. The court accordingly dismissed the application.

The SPC held that CIETAC afforded the parties sufficient time to present their opinions and diligently considered the views of all sides. After accepting the arbitration case, CIETAC issued four notices to the parties concerning the selection of arbitrators and other matters, soliciting their input. In these notices, CIETAC elaborated in detail on its position and the basis thereof to the respondents in the arbitration case. The method chosen by CIETAC for constituting the arbitral tribunal was well-founded and had been clearly explained to the arbitration respondent. At the request of the arbitration respondent, CIETAC repeatedly granted extensions for this party to appoint an arbitrator. The period from CIETAC's first notice informing the arbitration respondent of the need to determine an arbitrator to its fourth notice confirming the composition of the arbitral tribunal lasted 1 year and 4 months, which provided the arbitration respondent with ample time to carefully consider and appoint an arbitrator.

In this case, although there were two entities on the arbitration respondent's side, Zhang Lan was the sole shareholder and the only director of Grand Lan Holdings, and both were defined as the purchasers under the Agreement, constituting one party to the arbitration with aligned interests. The arbitration clause involved granted

[31] (2019) Zui Gao Fa Min Te No. 5.

this party the right to jointly appoint one arbitrator, and there were no practical obstacles preventing the implementation of this provision. The claimants for setting aside the award, on the grounds that they could not reach an agreement on the candidate for arbitrator, repeatedly refused to jointly appoint one arbitrator, which violated the principle of good faith. Such conduct should not be encouraged. Moreover, although the claimants declared that they reserved their right to raise objections, they ultimately jointly appointed Zhou as an arbitrator, meaning they did not fail to jointly appoint an arbitrator. The practice of parties conditionally reserving objections during the arbitration proceedings as leverage to apply for setting aside the arbitral award after an unfavorable outcome should not be encouraged. The court held that the arbitral award should not be set aside.

Article 9
Arbitration shall be carried out independently according to law, free from interference of administrative organs, social organizations or individuals.

Notes
This Article concerns the independence of arbitration. Prior to the implementation of the Arbitration Law (1994), the domestic arbitration system in China long carried strong administrative characteristics. Many arbitration institutions were directly established within administrative organs, and their operational models were difficult to clearly distinguish from administrative acts. In market economic activities, the outcomes of dispute resolution often concern local interests or the interests of specific industry sectors. Without the rigid constraint of the principle of independent arbitration, there was potential for administrative organs, social organizations, or even influential individuals to exert pressure on the arbitral tribunal, either explicitly or implicitly. The promulgation of the Arbitration Law (1994) aimed to promote the decoupling of arbitration from administration, facilitating the transition from traditional arbitration to modern commercial arbitration.

The independence of arbitration primarily includes two aspects:

A. ***Independence of arbitration institutions***. Arbitration institutions are not subordinate to any administrative organs. Their establishment, funding, and personnel management should follow market-oriented or privatized principles (e.g., most arbitration institutions are self-funded through arbitration fees rather than relying on fiscal allocations), severing dependencies on administrative organs. Although arbitration institutions are established uniformly by municipal people's governments organizing relevant departments and chambers of commerce, and are registered with the judicial administration departments of provinces, autonomous regions, and municipalities directly under the Central Government, they are independent of administrative organs and have no subordinate relationship with them. The New Arbitration Law safeguards the independence of arbitration institutions through a series of institutional designs. The primary source of funding for arbitration institutions is arbitration fees, not fiscal allocations, ensuring their economic independence. The members of arbitration institutions are composed of experts in law and economic trade, and persons with practical work experience. The chairman, vice-chairmen, and committee members must be experts in law and economic trade and persons with practical work experience, reducing the possibility of administrative interference. Regarding internal governance, arbitration institutions implement a committee system, stipulating their duties and rules of procedure through their articles of association, ensuring democratic and scientific decision-making. In practice, some local arbitration institutions still retain administrative characteristics, requiring further reform of arbitration institutions to promote the implementation of the principle of independence.

B. ***The independent adjudication of cases by arbitrators.*** The arbitration rules of various arbitration commissions clearly stipulate the principle of independent adjudication by the arbitral tribunal. For example, they stipulate that the arbitral tribunal has independent decision-making power and the autonomy to decide on hearing dates, evidence submission deadlines, and the scope of examination. Administrative organs or social organizations have no authority to issue orders regarding procedural details. On this point, it is particularly important to emphasize that the arbitral tribunal is also independent from the arbitration institution to which it belongs. The arbitral tribunal can decide on procedural matters (such as hearing dates, evidence admission) and substantive matters on its own, without needing to seek instructions from the arbitration institution. The arbitration institution must not provide guidance on the content of the award in individual cases or interfere with the outcome of the award.

Moreover, the independence of arbitration institutions is defined in relation to the courts. Precisely because arbitral tribunals render decisions independently and in accordance with the law, their awards are endowed with the same final and binding effect as legally effective court judgments. Although the courts possess supervisory authority over arbitration as prescribed by law (such as setting aside or refusing enforcement of arbitral awards), such supervision must adhere to statutorily defined grounds and procedures. In essence, it constitutes an *ex post facto* and limited judicial review, rather than intervention or direction during the arbitration proceedings.

Of course, the independence of arbitration is not absolute freedom, but rather independence within the legal framework. The independence of arbitration is relative; arbitration activities must comply with the New Arbitration Law and other relevant laws and regulations, and must not violate mandatory legal provisions or the public interest. Arbitration institutions and tribunals must conduct arbitration activities in accordance with their own arbitration rules. Courts have the authority to review the validity of arbitration agreements, the legality of arbitration procedures, and the enforcement of arbitral awards.

In practice, it is also necessary to distinguish between the relationship of arbitration independence and external supervision, clearly recognizing their essential differences to avoid misinterpreting "supervision" as "interference." Supervision is statutory and neutral in nature; its purpose is to ensure the legality of the arbitration procedure and the fairness of the outcome, not to alter the content of the award. For example, when a court reviews whether an award involves "forged evidence" or "violation of statutory procedures" pursuant to the New Arbitration Law, it constitutes statutory supervision and does not amount to interference with arbitration independence.

In contrast, external interference lacks a legal basis and aims to skew the arbitration outcome in favor of a specific party, thereby undermining the equal standing of the parties. For instance, if an administrative authority, for the benefit of a local enterprise, demands that the arbitral tribunal "prioritize local economic stability" by lowering compensation standards, this constitutes typical interference.

The key criterion lies in determining whether the action "affects the arbitral tribunal's autonomous judgment based on facts and law." If the external action merely ensures procedural compliance (such as urging the tribunal to adhere to the schedule) without intervening in the substantive decision, it does not constitute interference. If it directly or indirectly influences the outcome of the award, it crosses the boundary of independence.

Furthermore, it is essential to understand the differences between arbitration independence and judicial independence. Although both emphasize the independent exercise of authority, distinct differences exist. Firstly, the degree of independence differs. While court trials are independent, they must still adhere to the rules of territorial and hierarchical jurisdiction. Arbitration, however, is selected by the parties' agreement on the arbitration institution and remains free from interference by administrative organs, social organizations, or individuals. Secondly, the sources of authority differ. Specifically, judicial power derives from state authorization and is inherently mandatory, whereas arbitration authority stems from the parties' contractual agreement and is of a contractual nature. Thirdly, the supervision mechanisms differ. Courts operate under multiple supervision mechanisms, including internal supervision and oversight by the people's congresses. Arbitration primarily accepts judicial supervision, and the scope of such judicial supervision is limited.

The independence of arbitration is the keystone of the due process of arbitration procedures universally recognized by the international community. Whether a country's arbitration law can effectively guarantee independence is a primary factor considered by international commercial entities when choosing that place as the seat of arbitration. The development of the arbitration system ultimately relies on the general trust of the public, especially commercial entities. The principle of independence helps create a fair, transparent, and predictable business environment, reducing transaction costs. Simultaneously, the principle of independence safeguards the right of market entities to resolve disputes through arbitration, providing them with an efficient and fair dispute resolution channel. With the development of the market economy, the next step regarding the independence of arbitration requires improving the governance structure of arbitration institutions. Specifically, it is necessary to promote the establishment of sound modern governance structures within arbitration institutions, refine their constitutions and rules of procedure, and enhance the scientific and democratic nature of decision-making. Concurrently, industry self-regulation for arbitration institutions should be strengthened by establishing sound industry norms and standards, thereby enhancing their independence and professionalism. Furthermore, promoting the international development of arbitration institutions by drawing on internationally advanced practices will improve the international competitiveness of arbitration.

Illustrative Case

Company A v. Company B and others[32]

On November 30, 2016, Company A and Company B signed the Financial Lease Contract. On the same day, Company A, Company B, and Company C signed a Sale and Purchase Contract as an annex to the Financial Lease Contract. Both the Financial contracts stipulated that the method of dispute resolution was to submit the dispute to the Hangzhou Arbitration Commission for arbitration under its then-effective arbitration rules.

On March 26, 2018, Company A, as the arbitration claimant, filed an application for arbitration with the Hangzhou Arbitration Commission against Company B and Company C as respondents, citing a financial lease contract dispute as the cause of action. Company B filed a counterclaim against Company A with the Hangzhou Arbitration Commission. The Hangzhou Arbitration Commission formed an arbitral tribunal to hear the case. Subsequently, Company A applied to withdraw its main claim, and the counterclaim proceedings continued. On November 15, 2018, Company A applied to the Hangzhou Arbitration Commission to suspend the proceedings on the grounds that Company C was suspected of contract fraud, and this arbitration case involved suspected economic crime. The Hangzhou Arbitration Commission held that the current facts did not support that Company B was suspected of contract fraud and therefore found no necessity to suspend the proceedings. On January 14, 2019, and January 29, 2019, Company A again submitted applications to suspend the proceedings to the Hangzhou Arbitration Commission, along with a "Case Filing Decision" issued by X Public Security Bureau. On April 23, 2019, the Hangzhou Arbitration Commission issued a decision, stating that the outcome of the separate case does not constitute a prerequisite for handling Company B's arbitration claim in this arbitration case; the public security organ's case filing decision is insufficient for the arbitral tribunal to examine whether this

[32] See the Typical Cases on Judicial Review of Arbitration published by the Zhejiang Province Hangzhou Intermediate People's Court on 15 March 2024. In accordance with provisions and the fundamental principles of arbitration, the arbitration institution exercises its arbitration power independently according to law. Regarding how an arbitral tribunal should handle cases involving suspected economic crimes, there is currently no clear legal stipulation. The Hangzhou Arbitration Commission Arbitration Rules also stipulate that even if the civil dispute involved in an arbitration case may involve suspected economic crimes, the arbitral tribunal may decide whether it can continue the hearing based on the facts already ascertained. In other words, regarding whether to suspend the proceedings when an arbitration case involves a criminal filing, the arbitral tribunal enjoys discretionary power based on the specific circumstances of the case. Whether the financial lease contract dispute handled in the involved arbitration case constitutes a criminal offense has not been conclusively determined by an effective judgment. The mere filing decision document from the public security organ is insufficient to negate the characterization of the dispute as a civil one. The arbitral tribunal's decision not to suspend the proceedings was an exercise of its discretionary power based on the arbitration rules, and this discretionary power does not violate legal provisions.

arbitration case involves suspicion of economic crime and to decide whether to transfer the arbitration case to the public security organ. It therefore rejected Company A's application to suspend the proceedings, and the arbitration procedure continued. On November 16, 2020, the Hangzhou Arbitration Commission rendered an arbitral award. On May 14, 2021, Company A applied to the Hangzhou Intermediate Court to set aside this arbitral award.

The Zhejiang Province Hangzhou Intermediate People's Court held that Article 63 of the Hangzhou Arbitration Commission Arbitration Rules stipulated that if both parties jointly request or special circumstances arise during the arbitration process requiring suspension, the arbitration proceedings may be suspended. Article 64 stipulates that the involvement of a criminal case in an arbitration matter, even if formally filed by an investigative organ, does not necessarily lead to the suspension of the arbitration proceedings; the arbitral tribunal may make a decision based on the facts already ascertained. According to the aforementioned arbitration rules, the arbitral tribunal enjoyed the power to decide on its own authority whether the arbitration case needed to be suspended, including in situations where the case involved a criminal matter that had been formally filed with an investigation authority. This discretionary power did not violate legal provisions. Therefore, the failure to suspend the proceedings in the involved arbitration case did not constitute a violation of arbitration procedure. Moreover, the arbitral award addressed a dispute over civil rights and obligations arising from a financial lease contract between two equal subjects, Company A and Company B. The outcome of the arbitral award represented an adjustment and distribution of interests between specific civil subjects. There was no violation of the fundamental principles of Chinese law, no harm to national or public security, no contravention of social morality, and no endangerment of fundamental public interests. Consequently, this ground for setting aside the award put forward by Company A could not be sustained.

Article 10

Arbitration shall follow the system of finality of arbitral awards. Where a party applies for arbitration to an arbitration institution or brings an action in a people's court regarding the same dispute after an arbitral award has been made, the arbitration institution or the people's court shall not accept the case.

Where an arbitral award is set aside or its enforcement is denied by the people's court in accordance with the law, with respect to the same dispute, a party may apply for arbitration according to a new arbitration agreement concluded by the parties, or bring an action in the people's court.

Notes

Finality of the arbitral award is one of the fundamental characteristics of arbitration and a core operational rule. This Article establishes the system of finality of the arbitral award in modern commercial arbitration in China. In today's increasingly diversified landscape of commercial dispute resolution mechanisms, the principle of finality is a significant reason why arbitration has become a primary alternative to litigation. By endowing arbitral awards with immediate legal effect upon being rendered, it avoids the lengthy procedures such as appeals and retrials that may occur in litigation, thereby reducing the time cost and uncertainty of dispute resolution. This meets the inherent demand for efficiency in commercial activities and conserves valuable judicial and social resources.

This Article is divided into two paragraphs. The first paragraph establishes the core rule of finality of the arbitral award, clarifying the binding effect of the award on the parties, arbitration institutions, and courts after it becomes effective. Parties may not repeatedly seek remedies for the same dispute, and both arbitration institutions and courts must refuse to accept repeated applications, thereby procedurally terminating the contentious state of the dispute.

Once an award is rendered, it becomes binding on the parties and prohibits them from asserting claims repeatedly regarding the same dispute. What constitutes the same dispute? Generally, the same dispute must satisfy two core elements: identity of the subject matter and identity of the legal relationship. Identity of the subject matter requires that the subject matter of the dispute in the subsequent claim must be entirely identical to the previous one. For instance, regarding a payment dispute under the same contract, a party cannot split the claim for that payment or initiate repeated arbitration/litigation proceedings. Identity of the legal relationship means that the legal relationship underlying the dispute (such as a contractual relationship or a tort relationship) must be consistent with the one already adjudicated in the award. If a party asserts a claim based on new facts or new legal grounds (such as a newly discovered breach of contract after the award is rendered), it does not qualify as the "same dispute." In practice, common scenarios of "repeated claims" by parties include: applying to another arbitration institution for arbitration concerning a dispute already adjudicated by an award, initiating litigation in court regarding such a dispute, or raising claims in litigation that contradict the outcome of the arbitral award. According to the first paragraph of this article, any such application or lawsuit must be dismissed.

Once an award is rendered, it becomes binding on arbitration institutions, prohibiting them from accepting repeated applications. Regardless of whether a party applies to the original arbitration institution or another arbitration institution, the arbitration institution must refuse acceptance based on the first paragraph of Article 10. The core purpose of this Article is to avoid conflicting awards resulting from multiple arbitrations and to uphold the finality of arbitral awards.

Furthermore, once an award is rendered, it also becomes binding on the courts, which should not accept lawsuits for the same dispute. When a party initiates litigation in court over the same dispute that has already been subject to an effective arbitral award, the court should identify this during the case filing review stage and rule not to accept the case; if discovered after case acceptance, it must rule to dismiss the lawsuit. If the party does not disclose the arbitral award during the litigation and the court discovers through trial that the dispute has already been resolved by an arbitral award, it must terminate the proceedings and dismiss the claims, rather than rendering a judgment that conflicts with the arbitral award.

Of course, the principle of finality does not mean that an arbitral award is immune from any form of supervision. An exception to this principle allows for awards to be set aside or non-enforcement by a court on legally specified grounds. The finality of an award is superseded only in the extreme circumstances where a court, following judicial review, issues a ruling to set aside or non-enforcement. This framework both confers the authority of *res judicata* upon the arbitral award, thereby precluding the parties from re-litigating the same dispute, and delineates the strict boundaries within which state judicial power may intervene in arbitration, namely, only for the limited and statutorily prescribed reasons.

When an arbitral award contains fundamental defects as stipulated in Articles 71 and 76 of the New Arbitration Law, such as the absence of a valid arbitration agreement, a serious violation of due process, or the award being contrary to public policy, and the court, upon judicial review, confirms these defects and consequently rules to set aside or refuse enforcement, the final and binding effect of the original award is nullified. In such a scenario, the law does not mandate that the parties must resort to litigation or initiate a new arbitration. Instead, the choice of subsequent procedure is returned to the parties themselves. They may either enter into a new arbitration agreement to submit their dispute to arbitration once more, or either party may initiate litigation in a competent court. This provision signifies that if the parties maintain mutual trust and still wish to resolve their dispute through arbitration, they can arrive at a new agreement to do so; failing which, the matter will be resolved through judicial proceedings.

In commercial arbitration, an award becomes legally binding immediately upon its issuance, which fundamentally distinguishes it from the two-tiered trial system or even a three-tiered appellate review system in judicial proceedings. It should be clarified that while some commercial arbitration mechanisms incorporate internal appeal procedures within their rules, such features do not undermine the core framework of arbitration finality. The essential value of the finality principle lies in its simplification of the dispute resolution process, enabling prompt and definitive resolution of commercial disputes between parties, effectively reducing temporal and procedural costs, and aligning with the commercial sector's fundamental demand for efficiency.

However, like any institutional design, this finality carries inherent limitations for the arbitration mechanism. In practice, a significant concern that deters parties from choosing arbitration is the substantially elevated risk associated with the outcome. Unlike litigation, where multiple layers of review are available, arbitration generally offers no second opportunity for a substantive review of the case. If an award proves unjust or contains substantive errors in the application of law, parties typically lack recourse to correct these deficiencies through re-examination on the merits. For parties in specific cases, this irreversible finality may, in extreme situations, lead to irreparable harm to their legitimate rights and interests.

Consequently, when selecting a dispute resolution method, parties should carefully consider various factors, including the nature of the case, the value of the dispute, and their own risk tolerance. The ultimate choice must be grounded in the specific circumstances of each case.

Illustrative Cases

Case 1: *Funing X Bureau v. Yaxin Company*[33]

Funing X Bureau signed a contract for the Grant of Law Use with Yang. Subsequently, the parties agreed that Yaxin Company would succeed to Yang's rights and obligations under the Grant of Law Use. On November 4, 2019, Yaxin Company applied for arbitration with Y Arbitration Commission, requesting an award to rescind the Grant of Law Use, ordering the Funing X Bureau to return the land grant fee, and pay liquidated damages. Y Arbitration Commission rendered an arbitral award on June 18, 2020, ordering the rescission of the contract for the grant of the right to use state-owned construction land and the return of the land grant fee by the Funing X Bureau, but dismissed Yaxin Company's claim for payment of liquidated damages. Afterwards, Yaxin Company again applied for arbitration with the same Y Arbitration Commission, requesting an award ordering the Funing X Bureau to compensate for losses. Y Arbitration Commission rendered another arbitral award on January 19, 2021, ordering the Funing X Bureau to pay Yaxin Company interest related to the land grant fee. The Funing X Bureau contended that this arbitral award constituted re-arbitration and violated statutory procedures, and applied to the Jiangsu Province Yancheng Intermediate People's Court to set aside the award.

The Jiangsu Province Yancheng Intermediate People's Court held that when Yaxin Company applied for arbitration in the previous case, it requested the Funing X Bureau to pay liquidated damages, and in the subsequent case, it requested compensation for losses. This essentially negated the outcome of the previous arbitral award. After Y Arbitration Commission dismissed Yaxin Company's claim for payment of liquidated damages, it then rendered an award supporting Yaxin Company's claim for compensation for losses, which constituted re-arbitration, violated the principle of "finality of the arbitral award," and violated statutory procedures. The Court ruled to set aside the arbitral award.

Case 2: *SIPC v. UNI-TOP*[34]

---

[33] (2021) Su 09 Min Te No. 22; See the 10 Typical Cases on Judicial Review of Commercial Arbitration published by the High People's Court of Jiangsu Province in July 2024. "Finality of the arbitral award" is a fundamental principle of arbitration stipulated by the Arbitration Law. Re-arbitration violates the principle of "finality of the arbitral award" and is detrimental to maintaining the stability of the parties' rights and obligations. The handling of this case further clarifies the adjudication approach for "re-arbitration" and upholds the finality of arbitral awards.

[34] (2017) Jing 04 Min Te No. 39. This case represents the first instance in 2020 where an arbitral award rendered by CIETAC was set aside. Involving a foreign-related arbitral award, the Beijing Fourth Intermediate People's Court reported the case to the SPC for review. Upon approval, the subsequent award was vacated on grounds that it violated the principle of finality in arbitration, falling under the circumstance where "the matters decided in the award exceed the scope of the

On March 4, 2005, SIPC and UNI-TOP signed the Agency Agreement, stipulating that SIPC appointed UNI-TOP as its exclusive agent to assist SIPC in directly or indirectly acquiring shares of Petro Kazakhstan Inc. ("**PK Company**") through SIPC's affiliated companies according to relevant laws or regulations, and to assist SIPC in obtaining relevant government approvals. Subsequently, the PK Company acquisition project was changed to proceed through a public tender process. In 2005, the China National Petroleum Corporation (CNPC) successfully bid USD 4.18 billion to acquire 100% of PK Company's shares, which received approval from the Canadian government. In 2006, the CNPC group sold 33% of the total issued share capital of PK Company that it held to the Kazakh national oil company. SIPC and UNI-TOP signed three Extension Agreements on March 2, 2007, March 14, 2008, and June 13, 2008, respectively. Additionally, the two parties signed a Supplementary Agreement on June 13, 2008, adding a stipulation for UNI-TOP to carry out coordination work with the Kazakh government.

On August 30, 2012, UNI-TOP, based on the Agency Agreement and other agreements, applied for arbitration with the CIETAC, requesting SIPC to pay the agency remuneration and compensate for expected profit losses, etc. On December 30, 2013, the arbitral tribunal rendered the (2013) CIETAC Jing Award No. 0907 arbitral award ("Prior Award"), dismissing all of UNI-TOP's arbitration claims on the grounds that the conditions for payment of the remuneration stipulated in the Agency Agreement had not been fulfilled.

On September 30, 2015, UNI-TOP, based on SIPC's failure to actively pursue equity or other related rights in PK Company from the CNPC, again applied for arbitration with CIETAC, requesting confirmation that the conditions for payment of the remuneration under the Agency Agreement had been fulfilled, that SIPC should pay the agency remuneration and interest as agreed, and compensation for expected profit losses, etc. On June 30, 2017, the arbitral tribunal rendered the (2017) CIETAC Jing Award No. 0836 award ("**Subsequent Award**"), confirming that the conditions for payment of the remuneration under the Agency Agreement had been fulfilled and ordering SIPC to pay UNI-TOP the remuneration under the Agency Agreement and interest.

Subsequently, SIPC applied to the Beijing No.4 Intermediate People's Court to set aside the Subsequent Award. One of the grounds for setting aside was that CIETAC's acceptance of UNI-TOP's arbitration application for the same dispute, and the arbitral tribunal's re-adjudication of the same claims raised by UNI-TOP, violated the legal provision of "finality of the arbitral award" and the involved Arbitration Rules. In response, UNI-TOP argued that determining whether there was a violation of "finality of the arbitral award" fell within the scope of the arbitral tribunal's substantive review and was not within the scope of the court's review in setting aside an arbitral award case. Furthermore, new facts had arisen after the

arbitration agreement or the arbitration institution lacks jurisdiction to arbitrate." Notably, in its reply regarding this case, the SPC clarified that the provision concerning "new facts" under the Judicial Interpretation of the Civil Procedure Law applies solely to civil litigation procedures and does not extend to arbitration proceedings. This position diverges significantly from the practices adopted by some local courts in the judicial review of arbitration cases.

Prior Award was rendered, and UNI-TOP's arbitration claims in the subsequent case were based on these new facts, which did not violate the principle of "finality of the arbitral award."

The Beijing No.4 Intermediate People's Court held that first, regarding whether the two cases constituted the "same dispute" as stipulated in the Arbitration Law (2017), this could be determined through a procedural review based on the parties, the subject matter of the dispute, and the arbitration claims, and did not belong to the scope of substantive review of the case. Second, the parties, the subject matter of the dispute, and the arbitration claims were identical in both the Prior Award and Subsequent Award, constituting the "same dispute." The situation cited by UNI-TOP regarding SIPC's failure to pursue the relevant rights and interests did not constitute "new facts." Therefore, the Subsequent Award violated the principle of "finality of the arbitral award" stipulated in Article 9 of the Arbitration Law (2017) and fell under the circumstance for setting aside an arbitral award specified in Article 274(1)(4) of the Civil Procedure Law, namely "the matters awarded exceed the scope of the arbitration agreement or the authority of the arbitration institution."

Pursuant to the SPC's Provisions on the Reporting and Review System for Judicial Review of Arbitral awards, the Court referred the case to the Beijing High People's Court for review. The Beijing High People's Court, following the established procedure, subsequently referred the case to the SPC (the "SPC") for its review. Upon examination, the SPC issued an official reply stating that the two successive arbitral awards rendered by CIETAC involved identical parties, an identical subject matter, and identical claims for relief, thus constituting the same dispute, and thus CIETAC violated the statutory system of the final-and-binding nature of arbitral awards. Furthermore, the SPC clarified that the circumstance alleged by UNI-TOP, namely, that the other party had failed to diligently pursue certain rights and interests, did not constitute "new facts." It also emphasized that Article 248 of the Civil Procedure Law Interpretation applied specifically to civil litigation procedures and is not applicable to arbitration proceedings. Accordingly, the Court decided to set aside the Subsequent Award.

Article 11
Arbitration activities may be conducted online through information networks, unless the parties explicitly object thereto.

Arbitration activities conducted online through information networks have the same legal effect as offline arbitration activities.

Notes
The impact of the global COVID-19 pandemic has transformed online hearings and electronic service from temporary, alternative emergency measures into normalized, prioritized procedural options. Some arbitration institutions revised their arbitration rules during and after the pandemic to facilitate arbitration proceedings under special circumstances. Practice has demonstrated the immense value of online arbitration in ensuring uninterrupted proceedings and enhancing efficiency. Against this backdrop, the law must provide clear legal confirmation for this widely

established practice to eliminate doubts among participants and provide a stable legal expectation for the long-term development of online arbitration. Furthermore, with the rapid development of the digital economy, civil and commercial disputes exhibit new characteristics such as cross-regional scope, high frequency, and a demand for high efficiency. The limitations of the traditional offline arbitration model regarding time costs, spatial constraints, and procedural efficiency have become increasingly apparent. In this context, to meet the dispute resolution needs of the digital era, the New Arbitration Law newly establishes this Article, whose core purpose is to formally grant online arbitration equal legal status with offline arbitration.

Looking at the text of the provision itself, the first paragraph grants legitimacy to online arbitration but returns the final decision-making power to the parties. Parties may choose offline procedures for reasons such as exceptional case complexity, involvement of core confidential evidence, poor network conditions, or a simple preference for face-to-face communication. The law fully respects this. This can also prevent situations where technical failures or a party's lack of digital skills place them at a disadvantage in the proceedings, leading to substantive unfairness. Arbitration institutions may proactively use online methods to conduct arbitration activities in the absence of special circumstances, covering the entire arbitration process. This may specifically include:

A. ***Procedure Initiation Stage***. Parties can submit arbitration applications, upload evidence materials, and pay arbitration fees through the arbitration institution's online platform; the institution can serve notices of acceptance, arbitration rules, lists of arbitrators, and other documents via online means.

B. ***Hearing Stage***. Core procedures such as evidence exchange, cross-examination, and hearings can be conducted via video conferencing, online chat tools, electronic signatures, etc.; arbitrators can review evidence and organize debates online, and parties can submit supplementary materials in real-time online.

C. ***Award Rendering and Service Stage***. The arbitral tribunal can draft the award online and serve it to the parties via electronic service; parties can also confirm receipt of the award online, shortening the service period.

Regarding the parties' right to object, attention must be paid to the method and timing of raising an objection. The parties' expression of intent must be clear. Parties need to clearly express their unwillingness to proceed with online arbitration, either in writing (e.g., submitting a written objection letter to the arbitration institution, selecting the "disagree with online arbitration" option on the online platform) or orally (e.g., making a clear statement during a hearing, which must be recorded). Parties should raise objections at the initial stage of the arbitration proceedings; if an objection is raised after online procedures have partially commenced (e.g., online evidence exchange has been completed), the arbitration institution may consider factors such as the progress of the proceedings and cost savings when deciding whether to switch to offline procedures, preventing parties from abusing the right to object to delay the proceedings. Parties may object to conducting all arbitration activities online, or only object to specific stages being conducted online. The arbitration institution should respect the parties' choices regarding specific stages and adopt a hybrid "online + offline" model for conducting arbitration activities.

The second paragraph stipulates the equal legal effect of offline and online arbitration activities. This means: firstly, online arbitration must also comply with the procedural requirements stipulated in the New Arbitration Law (such as arbitrator challenges, protection of the parties' right to cross-examine evidence and debate). As long as the procedure is compliant, the awards rendered online possess the same procedural legitimacy as offline awards. Courts will not impose additional review standards specifically because the proceedings were conducted "online" when reviewing applications to set aside or refuse enforcement of arbitral awards. Secondly, electronic evidence submitted online (e.g., electronic contracts, chat records, transfer vouchers), upon review by the arbitral tribunal and meeting the requirements of authenticity, legality, and relevance, has the same effect as physical evidence submitted offline; evidence preserved by arbitration institutions through online preservation technologies (such as blockchain preservation) also has its probative force recognized. Thirdly, effective awards rendered through online arbitration, like offline awards, can serve as the basis for applying to the court for enforcement; when parties apply to the court for enforcement, the court does not need to conduct additional review of the "online arbitration" format itself, but only reviews the legality and enforceability of the award according to standard practices. Previously, due to the lack of a clear legal basis, some parties and arbitration institutions had concerns about the legal effect of online arbitration (e.g., worrying that online awards might be challenged during enforcement). This clause explicitly states that online arbitration has equal legal effect with offline arbitration, laying the legal foundation for the promotion and application of online arbitration and enhancing market entities' trust in it.

In practice, online arbitration plays an important role. Firstly, it enhances arbitration efficiency and reduces dispute resolution costs. Online arbitration breaks through time and space constraints; parties do not need to travel for offline meetings and can complete processes like application, evidence submission, and hearings via information networks, significantly shortening the arbitration cycle. Simultaneously, it saves costs such as transportation and accommodation, reducing expenses for both parties and arbitration institutions. Secondly, online arbitration helps expand the coverage of arbitration services and adapts to the needs of cross-regional disputes. Against the backdrop of economic globalization and domestic regional economic integration, cross-regional civil and commercial disputes are increasing. Online arbitration can break geographical restrictions, allowing parties from different regions to conveniently participate in arbitration, especially providing more accessible dispute resolution channels for market entities such as small and medium-sized enterprises and individual businesses.

Additionally, attention must be paid to the technical and legal dimensions of perfecting online arbitration. While online arbitration relies on information technology support, its technical safeguard mechanisms still require further development. For instance, regarding data security risks: data generated during arbitration proceedings, including party information, evidentiary materials, and hearing records, faces potential risks of data breaches or manipulation if encryption measures during storage and transmission are inadequate. A concrete example would be a platform suffering a cyberattack, leading to compromised evidence integrity. Furthermore, some small and medium-sized arbitration institutions have limited technical investments, resulting in weaker data security protection capabilities.

Regarding technical operational challenges, some parties may lack familiarity with online platforms, potentially hindering their ability to exercise procedural rights due to difficulties in uploading evidence or connecting to video hearings. If arbitration institutions fail to provide adequate technical guidance, such as user manuals or customer support, parties might be forced to abandon online arbitration due to technical obstacles.

Moreover, current online arbitration rules vary across different institutions. For example, institutions may adopt different methods of electronic service, such as email, SMS, or platform notifications, and apply different criteria for determining successful service, such as whether an email has been read or an SMS delivered. Some institutions have not established clear remedial measures for electronic service failures, such as procedures for handling situations where a party fails to receive the electronic award, which could adversely affect parties' access to rights protection mechanisms.

Currently, several Chinese arbitration institutions have incorporated provisions related to online arbitration into their arbitration rules. For instance, Article 6(5) of the SCIA Arbitration Rules stipulates that unless otherwise agreed by the parties, SCIA or the arbitral tribunal may decide that the parties shall directly send arbitration documents and evidence materials to other parties or to SCIA's online arbitration service platform and submit the service records to SCIA. The time of service shall be determined by SCIA or the arbitral tribunal based on the service records. Article 67 further provides that unless otherwise agreed by the parties, SCIA or the arbitral tribunal may decide that all or part of the arbitration proceedings be conducted by means of information technology, including but not limited to online case filing, service, hearing, and examination of evidence.

Similarly, Article 25 of the BAC Arbitration Rules, governing the manner of hearing, states that the arbitral tribunal shall hear the case by means of an oral hearing. Methods for oral hearings include on-site hearings and online hearings; an online hearing refers to a situation where one, multiple, or all parties to the arbitration participate in the oral hearing via telephone conference, video conference, or by using other communication technologies (or a combination thereof).

Furthermore, Article 8 of the CIETAC Arbitration Rules, addressing service and time periods, provides that any written correspondence, notices, and materials (hereinafter collectively referred to as "**Arbitration Documents**") related to the arbitration may be delivered through hand delivery, registered mail, express courier, fax, electronic means, or any other communication method that provides a record of delivery, or by any other method deemed appropriate by the CIETAC or the arbitral tribunal. Service by electronic means includes delivery of Arbitration Documents to an email address or other electronic communication address agreed upon or designated by a party, as well as delivery in electronic form via CIETAC's information storage system or any information system accessible without obstruction by the parties; and electronic means of service may be given priority in the service of Arbitration Documents.

Illustrative Cases

Case 1: *Hairun Company v. Song*[35]

Runhai Company filed an application seeking the revocation of the arbitral award rendered by the BAC, arguing that the arbitration proceedings had violated statutory procedures. The arbitral award stated in its first section that during the hearing, Song had presented original documents of Evidence 1 and Evidence 2, as well as the original storage medium of Evidence 3, and the arbitral tribunal had verified the consistency between the copies and the originals. However, the case was conducted through an online hearing, where Song's evidence was displayed via video conference. Runhai Company contended that it was impossible to confirm whether the materials presented online were original documents, thereby casting doubt on the authenticity of the claimant's evidence. Citing Articles 7, 43, and 45 of the Arbitration Law (2017), which respectively require arbitration to be based on facts and conducted in accordance with the law, obligate parties to provide evidence for their claims, and stipulate that evidence shall be presented at the hearing for cross-examination, Runhai Company argued that the online format prevented proper verification of evidence authenticity. This was particularly critical for the Investor Share Confirmation Letter and bank transaction records, which were central to proving Song's capital contribution. The company emphasized that if these documents were forged, and given the absence of the respondent Huawu Company at the hearing, there was no confirmation that the investment funds had actually been paid. In such a scenario, Song's claims would lack merit, and Runhai Company should not bear repayment liability. Runhai Company further asserted that the arbitral tribunal had determined the facts of the case arbitrarily without verifying the authenticity of the evidence, especially since none of the respondents had confirmed its validity. It invoked Article 58(3) of the Arbitration Law (2017), which allows for setting aside an award if the arbitration procedure violates statutory provisions. On these grounds, Runhai Company maintained that the arbitration proceedings had been unlawful and requested the court to revoke the award.

The Beijing Financial Court found that the arbitral award indicated Song had presented the original documents of Evidence 1 and Evidence 2, along with the original storage medium of Evidence 3, during the hearing. The arbitral tribunal had verified the consistency between the copies and the originals/original storage

[35] (2023) Jing 74 Min Te No. 37.

medium. The tribunal determined that the evidence submitted by Song was mutually corroborative. Given that neither Runhai Company nor Huawu Company had submitted any evidentiary materials, Huawu Company had not provided cross-examination opinions, and Runhai Company had not denied the authenticity of this evidence, the arbitral tribunal admitted the authenticity of the evidence submitted by Song. The tribunal further noted that the probative purposes and relevance of this evidence were respectively reflected in its subsequent analysis.

The Beijing Financial Court held that, regarding Runhai Company's claim that the arbitration procedure was unlawful because the original copies of evidence had not been physically verified during the hearing, the arbitral award indicated that Song had presented the original document and the original storage medium containing the bank transaction records during the online hearing. The arbitral tribunal had organized the parties to cross-examine the evidence in accordance with legal procedures, and Runhai Company had explicitly expressed its cross-examination opinions. The Court noted that if Runhai Company believed the online format prevented proper verification of the original evidence, it should have requested an offline verification from the arbitral tribunal. However, Runhai Company had not raised any objection to the online verification process, nor had it requested physical verification. The arbitral tribunal's conduct of the hearing online and its verification of the original evidence through digital means pursuant to the BAC Online Hearing Guidelines were deemed appropriate. Regarding the evidence, Runhai Company's cross-examination opinion was that the authenticity of the document could not be verified and that it was unrelated to Runhai Company. This implied that since the document was not issued by Runhai Company, its authenticity could not be confirmed by them, regardless of whether the original was examined. As for the bank transaction records, Runhai Company's cross-examination opinion was that their authenticity should be determined by the arbitral tribunal. Accordingly, the court determined that Runhai Company had waived its right to verify the original documents and cross-examine them, and had accepted the authenticity of the bank transaction records as determined by the arbitral tribunal. The arbitral tribunal's confirmation of the evidence's authenticity based on the original documents and storage media presented by Song during the hearing was considered proper. Therefore, the court dismissed Runhai Company's claims.

Case 2: *Shenzhen M Construction Company v. Zhuhai M Technology Company*[36]
Shenzhen M Construction Company applied for arbitration with the Zhuhai Court of International Arbitration against Zhuhai M Technology Company due to a construction project contract dispute, seeking payment of project funds and interest. During the arbitration process, Shenzhen M Construction Company submitted a property preservation application through the case management system of the Zhuhai Court of International Arbitration, requesting the preservation of properties

[36] See the 2nd batch of the Typical Cases on Judicial Review of Arbitration published by the High People's Court of Guangdong Province in 2025.

under the name of Zhuhai M Technology Company and provided a guarantee bond as security. After receiving the application, the Zhuhai Court of International Arbitration transmitted the property preservation application online to the Hengqin-Guangdong-Macao Deep Cooperation Zone People's Court via the adjudication-arbitration collaboration platform.

The Court simultaneously received the arbitration preservation application materials and electronically retrieved the arbitration case file through the adjudication-arbitration collaboration platform. The court accepted and reviewed the case on the same day, promptly issuing a civil ruling. The enforcement department utilized the online inquiry and control system to verify the property information under Zhuhai M Technology Company's name, successfully freezing the company's bank accounts and sealing its real estate properties. This entire process, conducted paper-free, efficiently completed the province's first online handling of an arbitration property preservation case.

Article 12
China supports arbitration institutions in strengthening exchanges and cooperation with overseas arbitration institutions and relevant international organizations, and in actively participating in the formulation of international arbitration rules.

Notes
With China's deep integration into the global economic system, the complexity and specialization of cross-border commercial disputes have increased significantly. Global arbitration centers are showing a trend towards multipolar development, with Beijing, Shanghai, and Shenzhen now ranking among the world's most popular arbitration seats. The need and necessity for participating in the formulation of international arbitration rules are also becoming increasingly prominent. Against this backdrop, legislating to clarify the state's supportive stance is a positive declaration.

Establishing a dispute resolution mechanism widely trusted by the international community is key to ensuring stable and long-term cooperation. By legislating to explicitly support arbitration institutions in conducting international exchanges and cooperation, the state aims to build a cadre of arbitrators and arbitration institutions capable of serving national strategies and possessing global reputations. This will provide efficient, neutral, and professional arbitration services for Chinese and foreign enterprises, thereby fostering a legalized and internationalized business environment.

Globally, traditional and emerging arbitration centers like Paris, London, Singapore, and Hong Kong are continuously optimizing their legal environments and actively attracting international arbitration cases. Within this landscape, if Chinese arbitration isolates itself, it will inevitably become marginalized. Article 12, in the form of national legislation, encourages and authorizes Chinese arbitration institutions to "go global," to compete on the same stage as their international counterparts, learn advanced experiences through exchange and mutual learning, and enhance their own international competitiveness. The aim is to establish China as an international arbitration hub with global influence.

Strengthening exchanges and cooperation with foreign arbitration institutions and relevant international organizations is a pathway to capacity building. This entails:

A. ***Personnel Exchange***. Supporting Chinese arbitrators and case managers for internships, employment, or observer roles at internationally renowned arbitration institutions to absorb advanced project management experience.

B. ***Business Cooperation***. Promoting joint arbitration, combined arbitration-mediation, procedural management services, and other forms of collaboration between Chinese and foreign arbitration institutions to jointly handle complex cross-border disputes.

C. ***Knowledge Sharing***. Hosting high-caliber international arbitration forums and introducing cutting-edge international arbitration theory and practical outcomes.

The declaration of actively participating in the formulation of international arbitration rules signifies that the Chinese arbitration community must engage more deeply in the discussions and revisions of arbitration model laws and rules within international organizations such as the UNCITRAL, proposing recommendations that align with the evolution of international commercial practice and reflect China's interests. Concurrently, it involves summarizing and refining the systems and practices proven effective in Chinese arbitration practice, promoting them to the world, and striving for their incorporation into internationally accepted "soft law" or rules. Furthermore, Chinese arbitration institutions, especially those dedicated to international business, should be encouraged to formulate more open, inclusive, and advanced arbitration rules, referencing international best practices, making them a procedural option preferred by international commercial entities. Additionally, the Chinese arbitration community should be encouraged to introduce and communicate information about Chinese arbitration to the international legal and business communities, increasing its recognition and acceptance.

Through "bringing in," advanced international concepts and practices will compel domestic arbitration institutions to deepen reforms and enhance service quality. Through "going global," successful international experiences will, in turn, feed back into and enrich domestic arbitration theory and practice, raising the overall standard of Chinese arbitration. The enhancement of domestic arbitration levels strengthens international competitiveness, while the expansion of international influence brings more opportunities and higher standards to domestic arbitration. This two-way development is the most beneficial kind of progress.

Chapter 2
Arbitration Institutions, Arbitrators and Arbitration Associations

Article 13
Arbitration institutions may be established in municipalities directly under the Central Government, in cities where the people's governments of provinces and autonomous regions are located, as well as in other cities divided into districts as needed. They shall not be established tier by tier, corresponding to the administrative divisions.

Arbitration institutions shall be established in a unified manner by the relevant departments and chambers of commerce organized by the people's governments of the cities referred to in the preceding paragraph, and it is a public welfare non-profit legal person.

Notes
Prior to the enactment of the Arbitration Law (1994), arbitration institutions handling economic contract disputes in China were predominantly established within administrative agencies, carrying strong administrative characteristics. The primary objective of enacting Article 13 of the Arbitration Law (1994) was to remove administrative attributes from the arbitration system, breaking away from the old model of establishing arbitration institutions based on administrative divisions and government departments, and preventing arbitration from becoming a "second court" or an extension of administrative power. This provision remains in the New Arbitration Law, and it has been refined based on practical circumstances. Since the implementation of the Arbitration Law (1994), the nature of arbitration institutions has been continuously debated within the industry, with no consensus reached on their nature. In practice, arbitration institutions of various natures have coexisted. During the process of this revision, there were strong calls from various sectors to further clarify the nature of arbitration institutions. The key addition in this revised Article is the stipulation that arbitration institutions are non-profit legal persons serving the public interest.

Y. Lin, *New Arbitration Law in China*, China Arbitration Yearbook,
https://doi.org/10.1007/978-981-92-0642-1_2

In past practice, numerous arbitration institutions in China lacked a uniformly defined legal status, leading to varied practices in institutional management, financial management, and tax treatment. Were they public institutions, social organizations, or other types of entities? This uncertainty significantly hindered the standardized management and long-term development of arbitration institutions. According to the provisions on legal persons in Chapter III of the Civil Code, legal persons are clearly categorized into three types: for-profit legal persons, non-profit legal persons, and special legal persons. The New Arbitration Law characterizes them as "non-profit legal persons serving the public interest," directly aligning with the Civil Code's classification of legal persons and endowing arbitration institutions with a clear and unambiguous legal personality. Article 87 of the Civil Code stipulates that a legal person established for public welfare or other non-profit purposes, which does not distribute profits to contributors, founders, or members, is a non-profit legal person. Non-profit legal persons include public institutions, social organizations, foundations, social service agencies, etc. Furthermore, Article 88 specifies that a public institution that meets the requirements for legal person status, is established to provide public services in line with economic and social development needs, and is registered in accordance with the law, acquires the status of a public institution legal person; where legal person registration is not required by law, it obtains the status of a public institution legal person from the date of establishment. Chinese arbitration institutions fall under this category of non-profit legal persons serving the public interest, and their legal status, rights, obligations, and asset disposal must comply with the provisions on non-profit legal persons in the Civil Code.

At the international level, the primary forms of arbitration institutions can be categorized into four types: corporate entities, incorporated associations, affiliates of chambers of commerce and other models. Common law jurisdictions generally adopt the form of a corporate entity, or a company limited by guarantee, while civil law jurisdictions typically adopt the form of an incorporated association. Both forms undergo independent registration. Furthermore, a significant number of arbitration institutions are established under chambers of commerce. This is closely related to the historical origins of arbitration, where merchants initially resolved commercial disputes among themselves privately by engaging trusted third parties. Arbitration institutions established by chambers of commerce represent one of the major models globally. Even for institutions not directly founded by chambers of commerce, chambers of commerce often participate as co-founders in many countries. Other industry associations with functions similar to chambers of commerce have also established a considerable number of arbitration institutions, such as the arbitration departments of the Federation of Oils, Seeds and Fats Association Limited (GAFTA) and the Grain and Feed Trade Association (FOSFA). As representatives of the business community or their respective industries, chambers of commerce and industry associations naturally play a crucial role in establishing arbitration institutions. Other models include entities like the Netherlands Arbitration Institute (NAI) and the Arbitration Foundation of Southern Africa (AFSA), which exist in the form of foundations.

Beyond arbitration institutions from these two major legal systems, several international organizations have also established their own arbitration bodies to provide services for the resolution of commercial disputes through arbitration. The ICC International Court of Arbitration, established in 1923, has developed into one of the world's most significant and renowned international commercial arbitration institutions. Affiliated with the ICC, the ICC International Court of Arbitration has the primary mandate of resolving international commercial disputes through arbitration in accordance with its rules, thereby facilitating the normal conduct of international business activities. Unlike other arbitration institutions that are affiliated with a particular country, the ICC International Court of Arbitration is independent of any state, while the parties involved in the cases it administers and the arbitrators who hear these cases may come from any country, making it a quintessentially international commercial arbitration institution. The ICSID is an independent institution within the World Bank Group. Established on October 14, 1966, pursuant to the Convention on the Settlement of Investment Disputes between States and Nationals of Other States (the 1965 Washington Convention) signed under the auspices of the World Bank in March 1965, it is a global permanent arbitration institution specializing in the resolution of international investment disputes. The ICSID is headquartered in Washington, D.C. Other examples include the Arbitration and Mediation Center of the World Intellectual Property Organization (WIPO Arbitration and Mediation Center) and the Commercial Arbitration and Mediation Center of the Americas (CAMCA), among others.

Differences in the forms of arbitration institutions reflect differing national conceptions of arbitration and the distinct legal contexts in which they operate. Yet a review of most arbitration institutions shows that, as permanent bodies, they largely possess four key characteristics regardless of their origin in common or civil law systems: public-interest orientation, non-profit status, independence, and a non-governmental nature.

The appropriate positioning of arbitration institutions in China is an issue deeply rooted in the country's specific conditions. The landscape of establishment models for arbitration institutions in China can be categorized into several types: firstly, the traditional model where the institution is established within a chamber of commerce; secondly, institutions created by the government based on cooperative relationships with chambers of commerce or other bodies; and thirdly, the model implemented after the Arbitration Law (1994), where relevant departments and chambers jointly establish an institution that is not situated within a chamber of commerce. Moreover, with economic development, innovative models like the statutory bodies may emerge.

From a legislative perspective, Article 24 of the New Arbitration Law explicitly stipulates: "Arbitration institutions shall be independent from administrative organs and shall not be subordinate to administrative organs." A literal interpretation of this Article unequivocally indicates that: firstly, arbitration institutions are not administrative organs; secondly, arbitration institutions shall not be subordinate to any administrative organ; and thirdly, arbitration institutions are independent from administrative organs. This provision in the New Arbitration Law reflects both the independence of arbitration institutions and their non-governmental (or private) character. Thus, the independence and non-governmental (or private) nature of arbitration institutions are clearly prescribed by law.

The explicit wording of this Article of public-interest orientation and non-profit status provides an accurate legal definition for the social function of arbitration institutions. As an integral component of the state-endorsed diversified dispute resolution framework, the fundamental value of arbitration resides in delivering impartial and efficient public services to society, rather than pursuing profit maximization. This article legally precludes arbitration institutions from prioritizing economic outcomes over social value, thereby ensuring their commitment to enhancing case handling quality, optimizing procedural services, and safeguarding arbitration integrity. The very establishment of arbitration institutions aims to provide fair and efficient arbitration services for resolving contractual disputes and other property-related conflicts between equal parties. Operational revenues, such as arbitration fees, are to be exclusively used for covering institutional costs, including arbitrator remuneration and administrative expenses, with no distribution of profits to funders or founding entities (such as governments or chambers of commerce). Any surplus funds must be reinvested to enhance arbitration service capabilities, such as through digital transformation initiatives and professional development programs.

Arbitration institutions share certain similarities with enterprises: both require a market to operate and provide services for a fee. However, they are fundamentally distinguished by their non-profit nature and the judicial enforceability of their awards on property rights disputes. The essential purpose of an arbitration institution is not profit-generation. Similarly, arbitration institutions are not the same as social organizations. Although both are classified as non-profit legal entities and function within specific professional domains, critical differences exist. Arbitration institutions maintain a panel of arbitrators, but this differs fundamentally from the membership structure of social organizations. While social organizations can pass resolutions binding only upon their members, the relationship between an arbitration institution and its arbitrators is not based on membership; it is fundamentally a relationship of mutual selection. Moreover, arbitration institutions possess the legal authority to adjudicate property disputes and render legally binding awards—a judicial power that social organizations lack. Social organizations may only exercise administrative authority over their own members, without the power to issue decisions enforceable by state coercion.

By prohibiting the establishment of arbitration institutions at each tier of the administrative hierarchy, the law severs their institutional connection to local jurisdictions. This liberates them from parochial local interests, allowing their development into regional or national dispute resolution hubs. The resulting freedom of parties to choose any arbitration institution across the country provides the structural basis for the principle of arbitration independence.

The requirement that a municipal government shall organize the relevant departments and chambers of commerce to uniformly establish an arbitration institution is designed to ensure that the institution possesses substantial credibility and wide representativeness from the very beginning. Government involvement provides essential authority and resources, while chamber of commerce participation infuses elements of commercial practice. This combination facilitates the creation of an institution that is both credible and market-oriented. Establishment, however, does not imply management or control. The government's role is that of an initiator and coordinator, responsible for integrating resources during the initial phase. Once legally established, the arbitration commission becomes an independent legal person. Article 24 of the New Arbitration Law explicitly stipulates the independence of arbitration institutions from administrative organs and from each other, legally securing their autonomous position in handling cases, free from interference by the municipal government or other entities involved in their formation.

This Article regarding the establishment of arbitration institutions exemplifies the unity of principle and flexibility. On the one hand, they guarantee that arbitration institutions are established in major central cities to satisfy basic requirements. On the other hand, they allow for establishment in other cities where genuine need exists, contingent upon local factors such as economic development level, the number of disputes, and their nature. This prevents a simplistic, one-size-fits-all approach to institutional setup and avoids resource misallocation, thereby fostering a properly scaled and strategically distributed network of arbitration services that corresponds with economic and social development needs.

Presently, more than 280 arbitration institutions have been established in China. The sector continues to grapple with the challenge of reconciling operational self-sufficiency and competitive positioning for talent with the non-profit mandate, all while propelling the development of arbitration law and practice. A critical point warranting emphasis is that the recent revisions *de facto* extend certain powers, traditionally associated with arbitration institutions, to include *ad hoc* tribunals and foreign-based arbitration bodies. While Chinese law imposes very strict requirements on arbitration institutions established domestically, the international landscape varies significantly, with some jurisdictions having minimal requirements or classifying such entities simply as commercial companies. This conceptual gap creates a risk that parties might establish arbitration institutions overseas, motivated purely by profit and leveraging the generalized powers conferred on arbitration institutions by the arbitration law to advance their private commercial interests. This potential loophole requires diligent follow-up research by the relevant administrative bodies and should be addressed through targeted regulatory measures.

Article 14
The arbitration institution established in accordance with Article 13 of this Law shall be registered with the administrative department of justice of the relevant province, autonomous region or municipality directly under the Central Government.

The arbitration institution established by the China Chamber of International Commerce with approval of the State Council shall be filed with the administrative department of justice of the State Council.

The specific measures for the registration and administration of arbitration institutions shall be formulated by the State Council.

Notes

This Article establishes specific provisions concerning the registration, filing requirements, and the authority to formulate administration measures for arbitration institutions, thereby constructing the fundamental framework for their market access and oversight in China. The legislative intent stems from the inherent need to build a unified, standardized, and transparent governance system for the arbitration industry. It aims to legally institute a dual-track system combining "registration" and "filing," thereby clarifying the legal status of arbitration institutions and assigning regulatory responsibilities at the institutional level.

The judicial administrative organ at the provincial level bears the responsibility for registering arbitration institutions established in accordance with Article 13. This registration is defined as an administrative licensing act, not a simple filing, mandating a substantive examination of factors including the institution's establishment criteria, articles of association, organizational and personnel structure, and its list of arbitrators. This process serves as a foundational guarantee that the institution possesses the capability to deliver professional arbitration services and adheres to its statutory status as a "non-profit legal person serving the public interest." This approach assists the judicial administrative department in the coordinated planning of arbitration resources within its jurisdiction, avoiding duplication and disordered competition. It also furnishes the legal basis for implementing continuous supervision, covering areas such as fee standardization, monitoring of information disclosure, and daily operational oversight. It is crucial to underscore that the supervision by the judicial administrative organ must operate within clearly delineated boundaries, limited to verifying the legality and regulatory compliance of the institution's establishment and operations, and should not intrude upon its internal governance or the substantive aspects of its arbitral awards.

Firstly, the decision to designate the judicial administrative departments of provinces, autonomous regions, and centrally-administered municipalities—rather than those at the prefectural level—as the registration authority underscores the legislative prudence regarding the establishment of arbitration institutions. Vesting this gatekeeping role in a higher administrative tier effectively prevents arbitrary establishment. An arbitration institution that fails to obtain provincial-level registration lacks legitimate legal status, and its awards may be set aside or denied enforcement due to the institution's invalid standing. Therefore, registration constitutes the fundamental prerequisite for an arbitration institution to practice lawfully.

To apply for establishment registration under the Provisional Measures for the Registration of Arbitration Commissions, the following documents must be submitted to the registration authority: (1) a written application to establish an arbitration commission; (2) the official document from the municipal people's government authorizing its formation; (3) the arbitration commission's articles of association; (4) verification of necessary operating funds; (5) certification of the arbitration commission's domicile; (6) copies of the appointment letters for the commission's constituent members; (7) the proposed panel of arbitrators to be appointed. The registration authority shall, within a period of ten days from receiving the documents required under Article 3(3) of these Measures, grant establishment registration and issue a registration certificate to an arbitration commission meeting all conditions. Where the conditions are met, but the submitted documents do not fully comply with Article 3(3), registration shall be granted after necessary supplements are made. Where the claimant fails to meet the conditions stipulated in Article 3(1), registration shall be denied.[1]

Secondly, a distinct filing procedure applies to arbitration institutions that are established by the China Chamber of International Commerce (CCOIC) upon obtaining State Council approval, requiring them to file with the State Council's judicial administrative department. These entities, exemplified by the China International Economic and Trade Arbitration Commission (CIETAC), are endowed from the outset with the specialized function of adjudicating international commercial disputes and serving the national policy of opening-up. Subjecting them to a filing mechanism instead of a formal registration regime is driven by a dual rationale: it safeguards their international stature and operational agility, while also ensuring their integration into the country's consolidated system of legal governance. This nuanced approach exemplifies a deliberate synthesis of regulatory principles and adaptive flexibility.

Thirdly, the State Council has been authorized to enact systematic administrative measures for the registration of arbitration institutions. This empowers it to issue comprehensive rules governing the conditions, procedures, and documentary requirements for registration and filing, alongside provisions for annual reporting, supervision, inspections, and legal consequences, thereby furnishing judicial administrative authorities with a definitive and practical basis for regulation. The Arbitration Law, serving as the superior law, deliberately sets forth only the basic principles and structural framework for managing arbitration institution registration, expressly delegating the specification of detailed implementation rules to the State Council via administrative regulations. In the over twenty-five years since the Arbitration Law took effect in 1995, the State Council has not yet issued dedicated nationwide administrative measures for the registration of arbitration institutions. Operational guidance currently derives largely from normative documents like the Provisional Measures for the Registration of Arbitration Commissions. These Provisional Measures, having been implemented for nearly three decades, now contain elements that are increasingly misaligned with the practical requirements for the development of arbitration institutions today. Ultimately, with the introduction of the relevant State Council measures and the refinement of supporting institutional frameworks, not only will the establishment and operation of arbitration institutions be further standardized, but China's arbitration service market is also expected to achieve orderly development, holistically enhancing the international competitiveness of China's arbitration sector.

[1] See Articles 3 & 4 of the Provisional Measures Provisional Measures for the Registration of Arbitration Commissions.

Against the backdrop of comprehensively advancing law-based government and optimizing the business environment, this provision not only specifies the statutory procedures for establishing arbitration institutions and clarifies the regulatory authority and responsibilities of judicial administrative departments at all levels, but also, by standardizing institutional access thresholds, safeguards the professionalism, impartiality, and authority of arbitration services. This establishes a solid institutional foundation for parties to access efficient and lawful dispute resolution mechanisms.

Article 15
An arbitration institution shall meet the following conditions:

(1) **Having its own name, domicile and charter;**
(2) **Having the necessary property;**
(3) **Having the personnel that meet the provisions of this Law; and**
(4) **Having appointed arbitrators.**

The charter of an arbitration institution shall be formulated in accordance with this Law.

Notes
Arbitration in China is predominantly conducted through institutional arbitration. The arbitration institution serves as the central pillar of this system, and the substantive rigor of its establishment conditions is crucial. It directly determines whether arbitration activities can be conducted justly and efficiently and affects the system's overall functional effectiveness. Consequently, some localities have historically emphasized creation over compliance during establishment, leading to institutions that are nominally present but devoid of a substantive operational basis. The independence and public trust in an arbitration institution cannot be assumed; they require a foundation of robust material support and professional expertise. This article institutionalizes this foundation by stipulating four mandatory conditions. Furthermore, it provides judicial administrative authorities with objective, consistent, and substantive benchmarks for registration review, thereby ensuring that every newly formed arbitration institution is, from the outset, a fully-structured and functionally capable entity, rather than an empty shell.

Paragraph 1 of Article 15 primarily stipulates the material and personnel foundations for an arbitration institution. Possessing a standardized name, a fixed domicile, and comprehensive articles of association constitute the fundamental prerequisites for its establishment. The name serves as the institution's identifier, requiring distinctiveness and recognizability to facilitate party identification and choice, while also embodying its brand image and social reputation. The domicile provides a permanent physical space for daily operations, necessary for conducting arbitration activities, receiving parties, and archiving records. The charter, acting as the institution's "constitution," defines its purpose, business scope, organizational structure, operational mechanisms, and internal management systems. This provides the fundamental governance framework for standardized and institutionalized operation, ensuring all activities proceed orderly under a unified set of rules.

Sufficient assets are the material foundation for sustaining the normal operation of an arbitration institution. The institution must cover various expenditures in its daily activities, including office premises, equipment acquisition and maintenance, personnel remuneration, and case administration costs. Ample financial resources facilitate a conducive working environment, the deployment of advanced facilities and technologies, and the ability to attract and retain highly qualified professionals, thereby enabling the delivery of high-quality and efficient arbitration services to the parties. Furthermore, necessary assets enhance the institution's independence and risk resilience, allowing it to maintain stable operations under complex circumstances and avoid excessive susceptibility to external influences.

Qualified constituent personnel form the core force enabling an arbitration institution to perform its functions. These personnel, including the director, deputy directors, and committee members, bear leadership, management, and decision-making responsibilities. They shall be primarily sourced from the fields of law and economic trade, possessing substantial practical experience. Profound professional competence and practical expertise enable them to accurately grasp legal principles and economic norms, leverage their specialized strengths in institutional governance and case-related decisions, and ensure the impartial and efficient progress of arbitration activities.

Arbitrators, as the primary actors in the arbitration process, directly influence the quality and credibility of arbitral awards through their caliber and competence. They must possess sound ethics, solid professional expertise, and substantial practical experience across diverse fields such as law, economics, finance, and engineering. This multidisciplinary composition enables them to handle complex disputes, conduct professional analyses from multiple perspectives, and integrate knowledge and experience to render impartial and reasoned awards, thereby meeting the diverse dispute resolution needs of the parties.

Paragraph 2 requires that the charter of an arbitration institution be established in accordance with this Law. Functioning as the basic code of conduct for the institution, the charter addresses various pivotal issues and plays a significant guiding role in the development of arbitration institutions. They elaborate on the functions of the arbitration commission, confirming its role in providing leadership, management, and decision-making within arbitration proceedings, thereby ensuring its operations comply with the law and promote procedural justice and efficiency. With respect to rules of procedure, the charter establishes strict formal requirements, specifying concrete procedures for calling and chairing meetings, voting, and other key stages to ensure that decision-making is both reasoned and inclusive. The remit of the executive body is also clearly set out in the articles, encompassing detailed functions and processes, including case administration, service of documents, and file management, thus ensuring it delivers effective and methodical support for the conduct of arbitration.

The charter plays an irreplaceable role in regulating organizational structure and conduct. They provide a clear basis for all operational activities, ensuring institutional functioning is rule-based, standardized, and orderly. Within arbitration proceedings, the charter guarantees procedural legality and impartiality, securing strict adherence to statutory rules in case handling and effectively safeguarding the lawful rights and interests of the parties. Simultaneously, the charter establishes the institutional framework for internal governance, promoting standardized and systematic development while enhancing administrative efficiency and service quality. Furthermore, the charter communicates the institution's mission, principles, and operational methods to the public, strengthening societal trust and recognition of arbitration.

Article 13 unequivocally defines arbitration institutions as non-profit legal persons serving the public interest. Regarding their public-interest nature, these institutions are not established primarily for profit but are dedicated to providing professional dispute resolution services to society, upholding fairness and justice, and maintaining stable economic order. This enables them to focus more intently on facts and law when handling cases, remaining detached from commercial interests, thereby enhancing the impartiality and authority of their awards. As for their non-profit character, their operations do not pursue profit; generated income is primarily used to ensure normal functioning and sustainable development, such as improving facilities, enhancing service quality, and strengthening staff training. This attribute effectively prevents the institution from deviating from its mission of justice due to profit-seeking, further solidifying party confidence in the arbitration mechanism. Under this legal identity, the establishment criteria set forth in Article 15, together with other relevant provisions in this Chapter of the New Arbitration Law, form an organic whole. They provide systematic safeguards for the effective operation and impartial adjudication of arbitration institutions across multiple critical dimensions, including organizational structure, material foundation, and personnel composition.

Article 16
If an arbitration institution changes its name, domicile, charter, legal representative, or members, it shall register such changes in accordance with the law.

Notes
Article 5 of the Provisional Measures for the Registration of Arbitration Commissions stipulated that an arbitration commission must file a record with the registration authority within 10 days after any change to its domicile or composition of personnel, submitting relevant documents related to the change. The newly added article in the New Arbitration Law now explicitly specifies five categories of matters for which an arbitration institution must undergo modification registration: its name, domicile, charter, legal representative, and composition of personnel. These elements constitute the fundamental attributes of an arbitration institution; a change in any of them directly affects its identity, operational capacity, and organizational credibility. For instance, a charter amendment may involve significant revisions to arbitration rules or adjustments to the institution's fundamental purpose, while changes to the legal representative or constituent personnel (e.g., council members) directly impact its decision-making orientation and governance standards. It is

particularly important to note that an arbitration institution's "domicile" holds profound legal significance, as it is often closely linked to the "Seat of Arbitration." This connection determines the procedural law governing the arbitration and the competent court exercising judicial supervision. Unregistered arbitrary changes to the domicile could obscure the seat, potentially triggering serious jurisdictional conflicts and legal application chaos. By mandating the registration of domicile changes, Article 16 fundamentally precludes this risk, providing robust protection for the stability of arbitration proceedings.

Article 16 establishes a systematic modification registration system, marking a significant enhancement in the standardized supervision of arbitration institutions. Compared to the simple filing mechanism for changes in domicile and personnel composition under the Provisional Measures for the Registration of Arbitration Commissions, the new law imposes stricter regulatory control over fundamental institutional attributes. The expansion of the scope of modification registration to include the name, charter, and legal representative reflects a legislative intent to conduct comprehensive oversight of an institution's core identity and operational framework. This mechanism ensures that any substantial changes to the institution undergo scrutiny by the registration authority, maintaining the accuracy and timeliness of registration information. More importantly, it effectively prevents potential irregularities arising from unreported alterations to key institutional elements, thereby safeguarding the interests of arbitration users and the orderly functioning of the arbitration service market. This provision substantially reinforces the ex-post regulatory capacity of judicial administrative departments, creating a closed-loop regulatory process that connects seamlessly with the ex-ante registration system for institutional establishment.

The modification registration system essentially operates as a mechanism for public transparency. Following the registration of significant changes to an arbitration institution's details, such information is generally disseminated via suitable platforms. This allows concerned parties and the broader public to access up-to-date information about the institution's status. By fostering such transparency, the system strengthens societal confidence in arbitration institutions and encourages parties to select arbitration as their preferred method for resolving disputes.

Article 17
When an arbitration institution terminates, it shall cancel its registration in accordance with the law.

Notes
The Arbitration Law (2017) contains explicit provisions regarding the establishment of arbitration institutions but remains silent on matters concerning their modification and termination. This Article, newly introduced in the New Arbitration Law, represents a proactive legal response to the dynamic nature of arbitration institutions as legal persons and addresses potential malpractices observed in practice, such as institutions persisting as "legally extant but operationally defunct." Furthermore, the article aligns with the general provision in Article 68 of the Civil

Code, which stipulates that the termination of a legal person shall be followed by deregistration in accordance with the law. As "non-profit legal persons serving the public interest," arbitration institutions are naturally bound by this universal rule upon their termination.

With the deepening of the de-administrative reform of arbitration institutions and the development of the arbitration services market, competition among institutions has become increasingly evident. In a market-oriented environment, it is inevitable that some institutions will struggle to sustain operations due to poor service quality, scarce caseloads, mismanagement, or regional restructuring, and will consequently need to exit the market. In the absence of a statutory exit mechanism, these institutions would remain in an awkward state of being "defunct yet not formally dissolved," unnecessarily consuming public resources and potentially causing subsequent legal disputes due to their ambiguous legal status. Article 17 provides a clear legal pathway for the stable and orderly exit of such institutions.

The deregistration of an arbitration institution is not merely a procedural formality but possesses a dual nature, combining elements of "administrative confirmation" and "termination of legal person status." Through reviewing the grounds for termination and the handling of remaining affairs, the judicial administrative organ (or other competent authority) confirms that the institution meets the criteria for deregistration, which is an act falling within the scope of administrative supervision. Upon completion of the deregistration, the legal personality of the arbitration institution is formally extinguished. It consequently loses its capacity for civil rights and civil conduct, and is permanently barred from conducting arbitration activities in its own name.

In accordance with Articles 6 and 7 of the Provisional Measures for the Registration of Arbitration Commissions, an arbitration commission applying for deregistration shall submit the following documents or certificates to the registration authority: (1) a written application for deregistration; (2) the document issued by the municipal people's government that established the arbitration commission, approving its deregistration; (3) a liquidation report confirmed by the relevant authority; (4) the arbitration commission's registration certificate. The registration authority shall, within ten days from receiving the documents and certificates specified in Paragraph 2, Article 6 of Provisional Measures for the Registration of Arbitration Commissions, deregister any arbitration commission that meets the termination conditions and retrieve its registration certificate.

Upon completion of the deregistration process, the following legal consequences shall arise: (1) extinguishment of legal personality: the arbitration institution ceases to possess legal personality and can no longer enter into contracts, participate in litigation, or conduct arbitration activities in its own name; (2) succession to rights and obligations: any outstanding claims and debts shall be handled by the liquidation panel (or a successor entity designated by the competent authority); (3) nullification of seals and certificates: the institution's official seal, panel of arbitrators, administrative licenses, and other relevant certificates must be surrendered to the competent authority for destruction or cancellation, with electronic certificates being deregistered simultaneously; (4) information disclosure obligation: the competent authority must publicize the deregistration of the arbitration institution through its official website, credit information platforms, and other channels, notifying the public that the institution has been terminated to prevent parties from mistakenly selecting it.

Article 18

The members of an arbitration institution shall be composed of one chairman, two to four vice chairmen and seven to eleven committee members.

The members of the arbitration institution are composed of experts in the field of law, economic and trade, and science and technology, as well as persons with practical working experience. Experts in the field of law, economic and trade, science and technology shall account for at least two-thirds of the people forming an arbitration institution.

The members of the arbitration institution serve a term of five years, and upon the expiration of their term, they shall be replaced in accordance with the law, with no less than one-third of the members to be replaced.

Notes

This Article addresses the makeup of the constituent personnel within an arbitration institution. In China's current practice, the top-tier decision-making body of an arbitration institution may be called a commission or a council. Operational history shows that the number of persons and the structure of these decision-making layers differed significantly among institutions. Some bodies were constituted with an excessive number of members, leading to poor deliberative efficiency, while others had too few members, failing to provide meaningful representativeness. The first paragraph of this Article now sets a consistent and moderate national standard for the size of this core body, specifically requiring two to four deputy directors and seven to eleven members. This standardized scale guarantees that decision-making benefits from necessary collective intelligence and a representative base, while effectively circumventing the risks of reduced accountability ("collective non-responsibility") and operational inefficiency associated with overly large memberships.

The decision-making of arbitration institutions, including the revision of arbitration rules, the appointment and disciplinary oversight of arbitrators, and the formulation of major procedural policies, is highly specialized. Should the decision-making body predominantly consist of individuals lacking relevant expertise, it would be difficult to render scientifically sound judgments on core operational matters. Paragraph 2 mandatorily requires that no less than two-thirds of the members must be experts in law, economics, trade, or science and technology. This legally enshrines the principle of "professional leadership by professionals." Legal experts ensure operations remain within the rule-of-law framework; economic and trade experts align with arbitration's primary function of serving commercial activities; and science and technology experts equip the institution to handle the growing number of disputes involving specialized technical knowledge. This diversified expert structure guarantees, at the source, the professional caliber of major institutional decisions and prevents arbitration institutions from deviating from their essential nature as providers of specialized services.

The absence of a regular and orderly succession mechanism can lead to rigid thinking, entrenched interests, and even "insider control" within the decision-making body. Paragraph 3 addresses this by establishing a fixed five-year term and a mandatory requirement to replace "no less than one-third" of the members, thereby striking a balance between governance continuity and the need for organizational renewal.

Article 19
Arbitration institutions shall establish and improve their internal governance structure in accordance with laws, regulations, and charters, specifying the responsibilities, powers, and procedures for decision-making, execution, and supervision.

Arbitration institutions shall establish and improve internal systems governing democratic deliberation, personnel management, fees and financial administration, document management, and complaint handling.

Arbitration institutions shall strengthen supervision over their members, staff, and arbitrators, and shall investigate and address any violations of laws or disciplinary rules committed during arbitration activities in a timely manner and in accordance with the law. Where legal liability should be pursued, the matter shall be promptly transferred to the relevant authorities for handling.

Notes
This Article, introduced into the New Arbitration Law, is grounded in a profound synthesis of decades of development experience with arbitration institutions in China. It aims to address common weaknesses and potential risks observed in their internal governance practices. Certain arbitration institutions have faced issues such as excessive concentration of power, irregular deliberation procedures, and a lack of internal oversight within their decision-making and execution processes. These shortcomings not only contravene fundamental principles of legal person governance but also create potential for power abuse and flawed decision-making. Paragraph 1 explicitly mandates the establishment of sound internal governance structures, legally compelling the adoption of a modern corporate governance model centered on checks and balances and procedural fairness. A robust legal person governance structure should typically comprise: (1) a decision-making body, such as the plenary session of the arbitration commission, a council, or board of directors, responsible for formulating development strategies, reviewing major issues, and amending the charter; (2) an executive body, such as the administrative office under the leadership of the Secretary-General, handling daily administration, case management, and personnel matters; (3) a supervisory body, such as a supervisory committee or disciplinary committee, operating independently from the executive body and overseeing the conduct of arbitrators and staff.

Furthermore, to prevent the internal management systems of arbitration institutions from becoming mere formalities or leaving regulatory gaps, Paragraph 2 specifically emphasizes the establishment of systems for democratic decision-making, personnel management, and financial administration. Deficiencies in these specific systems can lead to operation without stable and predictable rules, resulting in arbitrary management that undermines both the professionalism and stability of services. For instance, chaos in fee collection and financial management directly conflicts with their mandated "public-interest and non-profit" nature.

The fairness of arbitration is ultimately reflected in the conduct of its constituent personnel, staff, and arbitrators. In practice, the rare but serious cases involving ethical breaches by arbitrators or procedural violations by secretarial personnel have significantly tarnished the overall reputation of arbitration. Paragraph 3 explicitly assigns the supervisory responsibility to the arbitration institution and mandates the establishment of a comprehensive handling chain, from internal investigation to external referral. The subjects of supervision encompass all relevant parties, from the decision-making level to the executive level, and from administrative staff to core case-handling personnel. Illegal acts refer to violations of national laws such as the Arbitration Law, the Criminal Law, and the Civil Code, including arbitrator bribery or rendering an award contrary to law. Disciplinary breaches refer to violations of the institution's internal regulations, such as the arbitrator code of conduct or staff behavior guidelines, including breaches of confidentiality, unjustified procedural delays, or improper contact with parties. The institution possesses the primary authority to investigate and impose disciplinary sanctions, such as warnings, reprimands, temporary suspension from appointment, or even removal from the panel. Should any conduct be suspected as criminal or warrant administrative penalty, the institution is obligated to refer the matter to relevant authorities, prohibiting internal resolution and reflecting a "zero-tolerance" stance towards serious misconduct.

The three paragraphs of this Article are interlinked and establish mandatory legal obligations, not merely aspirational norms. Arbitration institutions failing to implement corresponding structures will face compliance risks. For the institutions, this raises the threshold for establishment and operation, prompting a shift in focus from merely pursuing case volume to enhancing the quality of internal governance. For arbitrators, it introduces stricter professional disciplinary constraints while, through institutional safeguards, reduces pressures arising from improper interference. Such provisions also help bolster the parties' trust in and predictability of the arbitration process.

Article 20
Arbitration institutions shall establish an information disclosure system to promptly make public their charters, registration records, arbitration rules, panel of arbitrators, service processes, fee standards, annual business reports, and financial reports; and shall proactively accept social supervision.

Notes

The mandatory provisions on information disclosure by arbitration institutions under this Article represent a significant step towards modernization, transparency, and enhanced credibility for China's arbitration system. The eight categories of information specified cover fundamental aspects of institutional governance (charters, registration, and filing documents), the basis for procedural operations (arbitration rules, panel of arbitrators), key user experience elements (service procedures, fee schedules), and operational status (annual business and financial reports). This Article is logically interconnected with Article 19. While Article 19 focuses internally, requiring the establishment of sound internal structures and systems, this Article primarily addresses external transparency, mandating the public disclosure of internal governance outcomes and key operational information for public scrutiny.

Publishing the charter demonstrates the legality of its governance structure. Publishing the arbitration rules allows parties to clearly anticipate the entire procedural flow before choosing arbitration, safeguarding their right to procedural information. Making a detailed and regularly updated panel of arbitrators publicly available is fundamental to protecting the parties' right of selection and constitutes the foundation of procedural justice under the "panel system" model. Transparent service procedures and publicly available fee schedules effectively manage party expectations and reduce misunderstandings arising from information asymmetry. The annual business report serves as a "report card" of the institution's professional capability and operational efficiency. Disclosure of the annual financial report is crucial for ensuring the institution's financial independence and non-profit nature. Subjecting the sources and uses of funds to public scrutiny effectively prevents asset misappropriation, ensuring resources are dedicated to the cause of arbitration. The registration and filing information constitute the basic data proving the institution's lawful establishment and legal personality.

This Article imposes a positive duty on arbitration institutions to accept supervision from society. The supervisory body includes not only the parties involved but also lawyers, academics, media, other arbitration institutions, and the general public, forming a comprehensive, multi-faceted oversight network. Operating the institution's organizational structure, fee schedules, and annual operational and financial status under public scrutiny serves the deeper purpose of reinforcing its public-interest orientation and social responsibility. Issues identified through societal oversight can be fed back into the "complaint handling system" described in Article 19 or reported directly to the supervisory authorities, thereby forming a complete governance loop: from internal governance to information disclosure, then to societal feedback, and finally back to internal rectification and external accountability.

A critical consideration in applying this Article is maintaining a clear boundary between an institution's duty to disclose information and its obligation to maintain case confidentiality. The disclosure requirement pertains exclusively to general, institutional data rather than any particulars concerning individual arbitration proceedings. Operational clarity must be achieved through supplementary regulations and specific guidance to avoid potential confusion during enforcement.

As progress is made in modernizing the national governance system and governance capacity, the operation of arbitration must evolve beyond a closed or semi-closed model, given its role as a key part of the diversified dispute resolution system. This article stipulates the compulsory publication of information encompassing the institution's charter, arbitration rules, list of arbitrators, and service procedures. This allows potential parties to adequately assess the unique profiles, rule distinctions, and professional backgrounds of arbitrators across different institutions before initiating proceedings. Thereby, the principle of party autonomy is effectively advanced and substantiated at the pre-application phase, supporting a rational choice aligned with specific requirements.

Article 21
The arbitrators appointed by the arbitration institution should be fair and impartial, possess good professional qualities, be diligent and responsible, maintain integrity and honesty, and adhere to professional ethics.

Notes
As adjudicators of arbitration cases, the capacity of arbitrators directly determines the impartiality, professionalism, and credibility of arbitral awards. This Article establishes the core criteria for the appointment of arbitrators, forming a crucial institutional foundation for safeguarding the quality of arbitration. Together with Article 22, it constitutes the essential considerations for arbitrator appointment. The Article defines five core qualification requirements for arbitrators from multiple dimensions, including "moral integrity," "professional competence," and "sense of responsibility." These requirements, while relatively independent, are mutually reinforcing and collectively establish the professional threshold for arbitrators.

"Fairness and impartiality" constitutes the primary ethical requirement for arbitrators, emphasizing that they must maintain neutrality, remain uninfluenced by factors such as the parties' identity, interests, or social connections, and handle disputes with a fair and just attitude. In legal terms, this requirement permeates the entire arbitration process: at the case acceptance stage, arbitrators should proactively disclose any interests that may affect their neutrality; during the proceedings, they must equally safeguard both parties' rights to present evidence and debate; and at the award-rendering stage, they should base their decisions objectively on facts and law, avoiding "biased awards." In practice, "fairness and impartiality" is often assessed through specific behaviors, such as whether there was any private contact with one party, whether a party's right to debate was suppressed during hearings, and whether the reasoning in the award is logical and free from apparent bias.

"Good professional qualities" constitute the core capability requirement for arbitrators to perform their duties. Its connotation extends beyond legal expertise to encompass a composite knowledge structure suited to the specific type of case. This specifically includes three aspects: first, legal professional ability, requiring familiarity with relevant laws and regulations such as the arbitration law and the Civil Code, and the capacity to accurately apply legal provisions; second, industry-specific expertise, necessitating command of specialized knowledge in fields like finance, construction, or intellectual property when handling such cases, for instance, understanding cost standards in construction or rules for determining IP infringement; third, procedural operational skills, requiring familiarity with arbitration procedural rules and the ability to organize hearings, identify key issues in dispute, and draft arbitral awards.

"Diligence and responsibility" requires arbitrators to execute their functions with conscientiousness and responsibility, eschewing perfunctory execution and procedural delays. In practice, this entails: first, temporal diligence by adhering to prescribed timelines for case proceedings, such as promptly convening hearings and rendering awards; second, substantive diligence through meticulous review of evidentiary materials and a comprehensive understanding of case facts to prevent erroneous awards; third, procedural diligence by timely informing parties of case progress and their relevant rights and obligations.

"Integrity and honesty" represents the fundamental ethical baseline that arbitrators must uphold, requiring them to refrain from exploiting their position for personal gain and from accepting bribes, gifts, or any other improper benefits from the parties. This requirement complements "Integrity and Impartiality": while the latter emphasizes neutrality in subjective attitude, the former focuses on integrity in objective conduct, together establishing a protective barrier for arbitration justice.

"Adherence to professional ethics" synthesizes and extends the preceding four requirements, representing the comprehensive code of conduct for arbitrators in their professional practice. This encompasses professional ethics, confidentiality obligations, and the maintenance of professional standing, among other aspects. For instance, arbitrators must uphold confidentiality by refraining from disclosing case information, hearing details, or award contents (unless otherwise required by law or agreed by the parties); they shall safeguard the profession's reputation by avoiding public statements that could undermine the credibility of arbitration institutions; and they must diligently honor their duty of disclosure and withdrawal, proactively recusing themselves from cases where circumstances exist that may compromise their neutrality.

Regarding the appointment and assessment of arbitrators, major Chinese arbitration institutions have generally established corresponding standards. For reference, please consult the relevant provisions on arbitrators issued by institutions such as the China International Economic and Trade Arbitration Commission (CIETAC), the Shenzhen Court of International Arbitration (SCIA), and the Beijing Arbitration Commission (BAC).

From the perspective of its institutional value, the importance of this Article is mainly reflected in three key areas: first, it ensures the impartial nature of arbitral awards, guaranteeing that decisions are founded on facts and law and safeguarding the parties' legal rights and interests. Second, it improves the professional quality of arbitration services, securing through various dimensions that arbitrators can address complicated disputes with efficiency and precision. Third, it preserves the credibility of the arbitration system, reinforcing users' confidence in opting for arbitration, thus facilitating its expanded role in the diversified mechanism for dispute resolution.

Article 22
An arbitrator shall meet one of the following conditions:

(1) **Having passed the national uniform legal profession qualification examination and obtained legal professional qualifications, and having engaged in arbitration work for at least eight years;**
(2) **Having practiced as a lawyer for at least eight years;**
(3) **Having served as a judge or prosecutor for at least eight years;**
(4) **Having been engaged in legal research or legal education, possessing a senior professional title; or**
(5) **Having acquired knowledge of law, engaged in professional work in the field of law, economic and trade, maritime affairs, science and technology, etc., possessing a senior professional title or having an equivalent professional level.**

Where laws such as the Supervisory Officers Law of the People's Republic of China, the Judges Law of the People's Republic of China, and the Prosecutors Law of the People's Republic of China provide that certain public officials shall not serve concurrently as arbitrators, such provisions shall prevail; with respect to other public officials serving concurrently as arbitrators, relevant regulations shall be observed.

An arbitration institution may appoint arbitrators from among foreigners with special knowledge in the fields of law, economic and trade, maritime affairs, science and technology, etc.

Notes
Arbitration institutions in China employ a panel-based system, under which they engage qualified arbitrators and include them in an official panel for the parties to choose from. Excellent arbitrators are the key element in securing the fair and timely settlement of controversies. The domains covered by modern commercial arbitration have far exceeded traditional sales of goods, having widely extended to highly specialized sectors including investment and financing, intellectual property, maritime and commercial shipping, construction engineering, and the digital economy. The equitable resolution of these disputes relies on the chosen arbitrators being well-versed not just in law but also having deep industry-specific knowledge.

Paragraph 1 establishes a diversified access system through five parallel criteria. This structural design aims to prevent excessive homogeneity in arbitrators' backgrounds. Criteria one through four all center on substantial legal education or long-term legal practice. Whether passing the national unified legal professional qualification examination with eight years of arbitration experience, practicing as a lawyer, former judge, or prosecutor for eight years, or serving as a law professor engaged in teaching and research, all such candidates have undergone prolonged, systematic legal training and practical experience. This ensures arbitration activities remain within the rule-of-law framework and that awards withstand legal scrutiny. The fifth criterion reflects the strategy for diversifying expertise. Appointing industry experts with "senior professional title or having an equivalent professional level" as arbitrators ensures the tribunal can accurately grasp the technical core of disputes and render decisions consistent with industry logic and commercial realities.

In practice, the concurrent service of public officials (particularly judges and prosecutors) as arbitrators may raise concerns over role conflict and potential undue influence, potentially compromising the impartiality of their primary duties. The newly added Paragraph 2, by referencing laws such as the Judges Law, Prosecutors Law, and Supervisory Officers Law, explicitly prohibits specific public officials from serving and imposes a "compliance with relevant regulations" prerequisite for other public officials. This legally clarifies the boundary between arbitration activities and the exercise of public authority, serving as a crucial measure to uphold arbitration independence and prevent improper power interference.

In disputes involving foreign investment and cross-border transactions, parties often expect the arbitral tribunal to possess an international perspective and cross-cultural understanding. Paragraph 3 expressly permits the inclusion of outstanding foreign arbitrators. In practice, when appointing foreign arbitrators, institutions emphasize their professional background, practical experience, and international reputation. Typically selected from internationally renowned law firms, academic institutions, research organizations, and international bodies, these foreign arbitrators possess substantial experience in international arbitration. They are generally well-versed in international commercial arbitration rules (such as the UNCITRAL Arbitration Rules) and various legal systems, enabling them to effectively address legal conflicts and procedural issues in foreign-related cases. The appointment of foreign arbitrators helps alleviate foreign parties' concerns about "local arbitration favoritism," thereby attracting more international cases to Chinese arbitration institutions. Concurrently, these arbitrators introduce advanced international arbitration concepts, procedural rules, and professional knowledge, providing diverse perspectives for handling foreign-related cases and promoting the alignment of China's arbitration system with international standards.

Regarding the qualification requirements for arbitrators, major Chinese arbitration institutions generally establish corresponding standards based on statutory provisions, with some instituting more stringent criteria. For instance, pursuant to Article 2 of the CIETAC Provisions on the Accreditation of Arbitrators, "a Chinese arbitrator shall satisfy the following conditions: 1. Be dedicated to the cause of arbitration, impartial and upright, with high moral character, and adhere to the principle of independent and impartial case handling; 2. Have passed the national unified legal professional qualification examination and obtained the legal professional qualification, and have been engaged in arbitration work for eight years; or have been engaged in practice as a lawyer for eight years; or have served as a judge for eight years; or have been engaged in legal research or teaching and hold a senior professional title; or possess legal knowledge and have been engaged in professional work in economic, trade, or other fields and hold a senior professional title or possess an equivalent professional level; 3. Endorse the Commission's Charter and be willing to abide by the Commission's Arbitration Rules, Code of Conduct for Arbitrators, and other relevant provisions; 4. Command a foreign language to the extent that it can serve as a working language, with appropriate flexibility for a minority of renowned individuals; 5. Be able to commit time to arbitration cases; 6. Fulfill other conditions stipulated by the Commission. A foreign arbitrator shall satisfy the following conditions: 1. Be dedicated to the cause of arbitration, impartial and upright, with high moral character, and adhere to the principle of independent and impartial case handling; 2. Possess professional knowledge and practical experience in law, economic trade, or other fields; 3. Endorse the Commission's Charter and be willing to abide by the Commission's Arbitration Rules, Code of Conduct for Arbitrators, and other relevant provisions; 4. Have a basic command of Chinese, with appropriate flexibility for a minority of renowned individuals; 5. Fulfill other conditions stipulated by the Arbitration Commission. The accreditation of arbitrators from Hong Kong, Macao, and Taiwan shall be implemented with reference to the conditions for foreign arbitrators." Similar stipulations are found in Article 2 of the Beijing Arbitration Commission Arbitrator Appointment and Management Measures.

Article 23
Arbitration institutions shall establish panels of arbitrators classified by professional field.

Where an arbitrator has been dismissed from public office, has their lawyer's practice certificate revoked, or has their senior professional title canceled, thus no longer meeting the qualifications to serve as an arbitrator, the arbitration institution shall remove such person from the panel of arbitrators.

Notes

1. **Panel System**

Paragraph 1 of this Article pertains to the system of a panel of arbitrators in China. In most countries, the arbitration system permits the coexistence of different types of arbitration, such as *ad hoc* arbitration and institutional arbitration operating in parallel. However, some countries implement only institutional arbitration, which can result in institutions establishing a panel to select qualified arbitrators. There are various practices regarding the panel system: the first is a mandatory panel; the second is a recommended panel; the third involves operation without a panel. China has traditionally relied predominantly on institutional arbitration, and the use of a panel has been the consistent method in practice.

Under a mandatory panel framework, arbitration institutions stipulate that only arbitrators listed on their official panel may hear cases. China's historical practice has been fundamentally rooted in this mandatory panel model. Such institutions generally curate one or more specialized panels, requiring that arbitrator selection for any dispute category be confined to the relevant list. Consequently, in these jurisdictions or institutional settings, prospective arbitrators must achieve listing on the panel and secure formal accreditation before becoming eligible for appointment by either the disputing parties or the institution itself. Nevertheless, reflections on potential administrative challenges within institutions and the inherent subjectivity of appointment standards suggest that a rigid mandatory system can inadvertently hinder the free flow of skilled arbitrators and potentially stifle sectoral growth. In response, certain Chinese arbitration bodies are now exploring hybrid models, integrating features of a recommended panel alongside mechanisms from non- panel systems that prioritize the principle of party autonomy, thereby augmenting the traditional mandatory approach.

The recommended panel system, also known as a non-compulsory panel of arbitrators, describes a practice wherein an arbitration institution establishes a panel that is not mandatory but acts primarily in a recommendatory capacity. Within this framework, the parties retain the freedom to select their arbitrators either from the names on the panel or, if they so agree, from individuals not listed on it. Provisions for this system might be included in the arbitration rules, or they might not be directly specified. A recommended panel serves to gather a body of specialized experts within the field, yet it does not confine the possible choice of arbitrators solely to this group, thereby offering litigants other potential avenues for selection. Typically, the arbitration institution upholds relatively high standards when evaluating applications for inclusion in this type of panel.

Another approach is to operate without a panel. Institutions employing this method do not maintain a panel of arbitrators, allowing parties to freely appoint any qualified individual as an arbitrator. Examples include the ICC International Court of Arbitration, the London Court of International Arbitration (LCIA), and the Arbitration Institute of the Stockholm Chamber of Commerce (SCC Arbitration Institute). However, even institutions without a formal panel may maintain an internal, non-public list to facilitate arbitrator appointments when necessary. The institution's role in appointing arbitrators makes this practice entirely feasible. For instance, based on accumulated experience, an institution might compile a list of arbitrators it may appoint in the future (a positive list) and a list of those it will not reappoint (a negative or grey list). Such lists are strictly for the institution's internal reference and carry no external effect.

Modern commercial disputes are becoming increasingly specialized in areas such as intellectual property, financial derivatives, maritime affairs, construction engineering, international investment, and the digital economy, demanding highly specialized knowledge from arbitrators. A single, undifferentiated panel forces parties to search for a needle in a haystack when selecting arbitrators, making it difficult to quickly identify genuine experts in the specific field of dispute. The mandate in Paragraph 1 for institutions to have a panel of arbitrators in different specializations aims to promote the scientific classification of an institution's talent pool. By rendering arbitrators' specific competencies visible and easily identifiable, it serves to provide the parties with a precise directory for attaining adjudication by experts.

2. **Removal**

The second paragraph governs the removal of arbitrators from the panel. A sound mechanism for removal is a necessary tool to weed out unqualified arbitrators and cleanse the arbitration ranks. Situations warranting removal can be classified as "circumstances of statutory disqualification" and "other circumstances of no longer meeting the conditions," which specifically comprise:

A. having been discharged from public employment: this applies to public office holders (for instance, former judges, prosecutors, or government workers) who were dismissed for violations of law or discipline, implying serious deficiencies in their professional ethics or behavioral compliance, conflicting with the basic requirement for arbitrators to be "impartial and upright," and thus disqualifying them.

B. having one's lawyer's practicing certificate revoked: this certificate is the statutory credential for a lawyer to practice law. Its revocation normally occurs due to serious unlawful or disciplinary acts by the lawyer (such as fabricating evidence, bribing a judge, or harming a client's interests). Such conduct directly contradicts the professional ethics and practice discipline expected of an arbitrator and constitutes a statutory ground for removal.

C. having a senior professional title revoked: A senior professional title (e.g., professor, senior engineer, senior economist) is a core qualification for certain arbitrators. Its revocation might be due to academic misconduct, insufficient professional capability, or obtaining the title improperly, indicating that their professional level no longer satisfies the requirements for an arbitrator and necessitates removal.

D. other circumstances of no longer meeting the conditions: Beyond the aforementioned statutory scenarios, practice also includes cases such as the arbitrator's death, loss of capacity for civil conduct (e.g., due to illness rendering them unable to perform duties), being investigated for criminal liability (for crimes like fraud or intentional injury), failing to participate in the hearing of arbitration cases for consecutive years without legitimate reason, or engaging in behavior that seriously violates arbitrator ethics (like privately contacting a party or leaking case secrets).

Article 24
Arbitration institutions shall be independent from administrative organs and shall not be subordinate to administrative organs.

There shall be no subordinate relationships between arbitration institutions.

Notes
Arbitration, serving as an alternative dispute resolution method outside court litigation, derives its primary strengths from three fundamental attributes: independence, adaptability and specialized expertise. Crucially, the autonomy of arbitration institutions themselves forms the essential foundation underpinning the system's integrity and equitable functioning. This Article provides a statutory basis for this institutional autonomy. It achieves this by clearly defining the independent legal standing of arbitration institutions. Moreover, it clarifies the relationship boundaries, stating that arbitration institutions are independent from administrative organs and that the various arbitration institutions exist on a footing of equality with one another.

Arbitration institutions have no subordinate relationship with administrative organs, which is specifically reflected in their independence in four aspects: organizational structure, personnel management, financial affairs and professional business operations.

First, organizational independence: although established uniformly by municipal people's governments in conjunction with relevant departments and chambers of commerce pursuant to the New Arbitration Law, an arbitration institution becomes an independent legal person upon its establishment, with no subordinate relationship to its establishing authorities. Its organizational structure and the selection of its responsible persons are autonomously determined according to its charter, free from direct administration or control by administrative organs.

Second, personnel independence: matters of personnel management, including the selection, assessment, and dismissal of the institution's staff and arbitrators, are conducted independently by the arbitration institution pursuant to its internal rules, without interference from administrative organs. Administrative organs have no authority to directly appoint the institution's responsible persons nor to designate arbitrators for specific cases.

Third, financial independence: the funding of arbitration institutions derives primarily from case acceptance and handling fees. They practice independent accounting and self-management, are not incorporated into the fiscal budgets of administrative organs, and are not subject to their financial supervision. Administrative organs may not appropriate or divert their funds, nor require them to bear administrative expenses.

Fourth, operational independence: in all professional activities, including case acceptance, arbitrator appointment, procedural arrangements, and the rendering of awards, arbitration institutions operate autonomously in accordance with the Arbitration Law and relevant arbitration rules, free from any directive or interference by administrative organs. Administrative organs may not offer predisposed opinions on individual cases, nor intervene in the adjudication process or its outcome.

No subordinate relationship exists between arbitration institutions themselves. This principle fundamentally establishes their equal legal status, transcends geographical or hierarchical constraints, safeguards the parties' freedom to choose an arbitration institution, and fosters healthy competition among institutions. Regardless of their location, scale, or founding date, all arbitration institutions enjoy equal legal status. There are no "superior-subordinate" or "leadership-followership" relationships between them. Jurisdictional scope is determined solely by the parties' arbitration agreement, free from administrative divisions or hierarchical structures. Parties may autonomously select any arbitration institution nationwide based on case characteristics and their own needs. Each institution independently formulates arbitration rules, manages arbitrators, and handles cases, with no mutual relationship of guidance, supervision, or subordination in their operations. The legislative intent behind this design is to fully respect party autonomy and stimulate arbitration institutions to enhance their professional standards and service quality through constructive competition.

With the growing independence of arbitration institutions and the broadening range of choices for parties, China's arbitration industry has developed a landscape of flourishing diversity and competition. Major institutions leverage their comprehensive strengths to build advantages in areas such as foreign-related arbitration, financial arbitration, and investment arbitration, while local institutions cultivate specialized brands by leveraging local industrial characteristics. Although institutions remain independent of each other, they still engage in exchange and cooperation through various channels, like industry associations and professional seminars to promote the overall development of the sector.

A well-defined independent status and equal relationships provide arbitration institutions with a stable institutional environment, enabling them to focus on enhancing the quality of arbitration services, free from administrative interference or hierarchical pressure. This institutional arrangement has promoted the standardization and market-oriented development of China's arbitration industry, accelerated its alignment with international arbitration systems, and strengthened the overall competitiveness of arbitration in China. Independent arbitration institutions are more likely to gain the trust of parties, particularly in foreign-related arbitration, where foreign parties generally prefer institutions independent of administrative organs. This helps elevate international recognition and supports China's goal of establishing itself as an international arbitration hub.

Article 25

China Arbitration Association is a social organization with the status of a legal person. Arbitration institutions are members of China Arbitration Association. The charter of China Arbitration Association shall be formulated by its national congress of members.

China Arbitration Association is a self-disciplined organization of arbitration institutions. It shall supervise the behavior of arbitration institutions and their members, personnel and arbitrators in arbitration activities in accordance with its charter.

China Arbitration Association shall formulate model arbitration rules in accordance with this Law and the relevant provisions of the Civil Procedure Law of the People's Republic of China.

Notes

This Article concerns the China Arbitration Association. At the international level, self-regulatory organizations for arbitration institutions mandated by law, such as the China Arbitration Association, are relatively uncommon.[2] The establishment of the China Arbitration Association was originally provided for in the Arbitration Law (1994). In 1994, the General Office of the State Council issued a notice stating that the reorganization of arbitration institutions should be undertaken first, and on that basis, the China Arbitration Association could then be prepared. Preparatory work for the association could begin earlier. However, for various reasons, the China Arbitration Association has never been formally established.

[2] Although bearing the designation "association," arbitration associations in other countries, such as the American Arbitration Association (AAA) and the Swiss Arbitration Association (ASA), are not identical in concept to the China Arbitration Association.

According to paragraph 1 of this Article, the legal nature of the Arbitration Association is that of a social organization as a legal person. This signifies that the China Arbitration Association is not an administrative organ, but rather a non-profit social organization voluntarily formed by arbitration institutions and established through legal registration. It enjoys independent property rights as a legal person and may conduct civil activities in its own name, such as formulating rules, implementing supervision, and participating in professional exchanges. This nature dictates that its operations must adhere to the principles of "voluntary participation, self-governance, and self-regulation," distinguishing it from the "management and subordination" relationship characteristic of administrative organs and making it more aligned with the values of arbitration and the specific characteristics of the arbitration profession.

The organizational structure is built upon a membership model and is governed primarily by its charter. Specifying that "arbitration institutions are members of China Arbitration Association" ensures the association represents their collective interests. Stipulating that the "charter of China Arbitration Association shall be formulated by its national congress of members" means core rules, such as members' rights and obligations, procedural rules, and supervisory processes, require collective determination by all members, embodying the principle of "member autonomy" and preventing the association's decisions from diverging from the industry's actual needs.

Paragraph 2 clarifies the "self-regulatory supervision" function of the Arbitration Association. Its supervision scope is comprehensive, covering both "arbitration institutions" (such as domestic and foreign-related arbitration institutions) and their "constituent personnel" (e.g., council members, responsible persons), "staff" (e.g., case managers, administrative personnel), as well as "arbitrators". Supervision must be conducted "in accordance with the charter," requiring that the standards, procedures, and disciplinary measures for supervision are explicitly defined within the charter to prevent arbitrariness. The focus of supervision is on "conduct during arbitration activities," ensuring that such oversight does not interfere with the substantive adjudication of arbitration cases (such as refraining from reviewing factual findings or legal application in awards).

Paragraph 3 empowers the Arbitration Association to formulate model arbitration rules. These model rules must comply with mandatory provisions of the New Arbitration Law and the Civil Procedure Law, avoiding any content that conflicts with the law. The model rules are positioned as reference templates, not as a "mandatory standard." Individual arbitration institutions may develop customized rules (e.g., for intellectual property or financial arbitration) based on these model rules, taking into account their specific characteristics, such as specialized fields or case types.

Furthermore, the relationship between the Arbitration Association and individual arbitration institutions must be clearly understood. As the Association is merely an organization composed of members, no relationship of operational guidance exists between them. The Association cannot interfere with an institution's case development or individual case management. Arbitration institutions remain solely responsible for the procedural management of their cases. While the Association may organize arbitrator training, it cannot entirely replace the training conducted by the institutions themselves.

Article 26
The administrative department of justice of the State Council legally guides and supervises national arbitration work, improves relevant work systems, and coordinates the planning of arbitration development.

The administrative department of justice of the people's governments of provinces, autonomous regions, and municipalities directly under the central government shall guide and supervise arbitration work within their respective administrative areas in accordance with the law.

Notes
In past practice, regulatory responsibilities over arbitration institutions may have overlapped or existed in gray areas, leading to either regulatory duplication or regulatory gaps. By clearly vesting the judicial administrative department of the State Council with the responsibility to "guide and supervise" the work of arbitration institutions nationwide, this provision fundamentally addresses the core issue of "who regulates," achieving unification and legalization of the regulatory authority. This Article works in tandem with the industry self-regulation function of the arbitration association established under Article 25 of this New Arbitration Law, together forming a governance system that combines "administrative supervision" with "industry self-regulation." The supervision by the judicial administrative departments focuses on macro-level policies, institutional approval, development planning, and compliance oversight; whereas the association's supervision emphasizes professional ethics, disciplinary rules, and operational standards.

This Article establishes a "graded responsibility system, creating a two-tier supervision framework involving the "judicial administrative department of the State Council" and the "judicial administrative departments of the people's governments of provinces, autonomous regions, and municipalities directly under the central government." This structure conforms to China's general administrative principles. It ensures the uniformity of national policies while leveraging the advantages of local governments, such as proximity to actual conditions and administrative convenience, thereby enhancing the targeted nature and efficiency of supervision. Guidance and supervision constitute external oversight conducted in accordance with the law, focusing on ensuring that arbitration institutions and their activities comply with the provisions of the New Arbitration Law and other relevant laws and regulations.

It improves the relevant work systems, including authorizing the department to take the lead in formulating or promoting the improvement of supporting regulations and systems aligned with the New Arbitration Law, such as measures for the administration of arbitration institution registration, measures for the administration of arbitration fee collection, and basic guidelines for arbitrator professional ethics.

This aims to provide a unified and standardized institutional foundation for arbitration work nationwide.

Coordinating and planning the development of the arbitration sector means that the judicial administrative departments need to formulate medium- to long-term plans for the development of China's arbitration industry from the perspective of national governance and opening-up. This involves defining development goals, key tasks, and regional layouts, and guiding resource allocation, for instance, prioritizing support for the establishment of international arbitration centers and promoting the development of arbitration in specific, specialized fields.

Amidst these powers of guidance and supervision, how to preserve the independence of arbitration institutions becomes a question the arbitration industry must seriously consider. Guidance and supervision must be strictly confined within the bounds of "in accordance with the law," focusing on regulating institutional operations and procedural fairness, rather than intervening in individual case determinations. It is imperative to strictly guard against the erosion of arbitration independence by administrative management.

Judicial administrative departments at all levels need to be staffed with personnel possessing professional arbitration knowledge and management capabilities; otherwise, guidance and supervision may become merely formalistic or deviate from their intended purpose.

For the judicial administrative departments, corresponding implementation rules and lists of powers should be issued promptly to clarify the specific content, methods, and procedures of guidance and supervision at each level, ensuring that power is exercised lawfully, normatively, and transparently.

For arbitration institutions, they should proactively adapt to development within the new regulatory environment, actively cooperate with the lawful supervision and guidance of judicial administrative departments, and view it as an opportunity to standardize themselves and enhance their brand. Furthermore, this provision reserves space for the establishment and functional positioning of the China Arbitration Association. In the future, judicial administrative departments can gradually transfer some self-regulatory and administrative functions to the industry association, forming a governance model where "administrative supervision" and "industry self-regulation" are more coordinated.

Chapter 3
Arbitration Agreements

Article 27
An arbitration agreement shall include arbitration clauses stipulated in a contract and agreements of submission to arbitration that are concluded in other written forms before or after disputes arise.

An arbitration agreement shall contain the following particulars:

(1) **The expression of intention to apply for arbitration;**
(2) **The matters for arbitration; and**
(3) **The designated arbitration institution.**

If one party claims that there is an arbitration agreement when applying for arbitration, and the other party does not deny this before the first hearing, it will be considered that there is an arbitration agreement between the parties, as prompted and recorded by the arbitral tribunal.

Notes

1. **Definition and Classification of Arbitration Agreements**

It is generally accepted that an arbitration agreement refers to an agreement by the parties to submit to arbitration disputes which have arisen or which may arise between them. Article 7(1) of the UNCITRAL Model Law defines an "arbitration agreement" as an agreement by the parties to submit to arbitration all or certain disputes which have arisen or which may arise between them in respect of a defined legal relationship, whether contractual or not. Various jurisdictions typically define it directly or indirectly in their arbitration legislation.

For example, Section 6 of the UK Arbitration Act 1996 states that an "arbitration agreement" means an agreement to submit to arbitration present or future disputes (whether they are contractual or not), and the reference in an agreement to a written form of arbitration clause or to a document containing an arbitration clause constitutes an arbitration agreement if the reference is such as to make that clause part of

Y. Lin, *New Arbitration Law in China*, China Arbitration Yearbook,
https://doi.org/10.1007/978-981-92-0642-1_3

the agreement. Section 1029 of the German Code of Civil Procedure (1998) states that "Arbitration agreement" is an agreement by the parties to submit to arbitration all or certain disputes which have arisen or which may arise between them in respect of a defined legal relationship, whether contractual or not, and an arbitration agreement may be in the form of a separate agreement ("separate arbitration agreement") or in the form of a clause in a contract ("arbitration clause").

In the context of the arbitration law framework, arbitration agreements may be divided into two categories based on the timing of the parties' agreement: those reached before the dispute arises and those reached after the dispute arises. As parties often reach a deadlock due to conflicting interests after a dispute arises, making it difficult to reach a new consensus on the dispute resolution method, pre-agreed arbitration agreements are the most common form in practice, effectively avoiding subsequent disagreements on the dispute resolution process. An agreement where parties specifically agree to "submit to arbitration" for the resolution of a specific dispute only after it has actually occurred (e.g., after a breach of contract or the occurrence of a tort) relies on the parties' consensus through negotiation after the dispute erupts. However, limited by the adversarial nature post-dispute, the probability of reaching such an agreement is low, and it is only occasionally used when the parties wish to resolve the dispute quickly and flexibly (e.g., to avoid lengthy litigation proceedings).

From a formal perspective, arbitration agreements may be primarily categorized into three types, each corresponding to different conclusion scenarios and legal effects:

A. ***Arbitration Clauses in Contracts***. These are specific clauses embedded within a main contract (such as a sales or service contract). They represent the typical form of an arbitration agreement concluded before any dispute arises. While closely connected to the main contract, an arbitration clause possesses relative independence. Consequently, even if the main contract is held invalid, the arbitration clause typically remains effective, ensuring that disputes can still be resolved through arbitration as agreed.

B. ***Separately Concluded Arbitration Agreements***. These are agreements reached by the parties in a written form separate from the main contract (such as a standalone agreement or exchange of correspondence). Such agreements may be made either before a dispute arises, concerning potential future disputes, or after a dispute has arisen, specifically to address that existing dispute.

C. ***Arbitration Agreements by Incorporation and Other Forms***. These are agreements where the parties indirectly establish their consent to arbitrate by "incorporating" a pre-existing arbitration clause or set of arbitration rules. For example, a contract may state that "matters not covered in this contract shall be governed by the terms of [XX Contract], including its arbitration clause," or it may directly incorporate a rule from an arbitration institution's rules stating that "acceptance of these rules constitutes agreement to arbitrate."

D. ***Furthermore, in specialized areas such as investment treaty arbitration, the form of a* "Standing Offer" *exists*.** A State party, by concluding an international investment treaty, makes a standing offer to investors from other State parties, agreeing that "future investment disputes may be submitted to arbitration." An investor can then accept this offer by initiating arbitration proceedings, thereby forming a valid arbitration agreement.

From the perspective of comparative legislative practice, legal restrictions historically existed regarding the validity of arbitration agreements concerning future disputes. Early legislation in some countries held that agreements to submit such disputes to arbitration were invalid, as the content of potential future disputes was inherently uncertain. However, with the evolution of arbitration systems and the demands of commercial practice, this limitation has been abandoned by most jurisdictions. Contemporary national legislation generally recognizes the validity of arbitration agreements relating to future disputes. This is reinforced by Article II (1) of the New York Convention, which explicitly extends the application of arbitration agreements to all or any differences which have arisen or which may arise, thereby confirming the legitimacy of future dispute arbitration agreements at the international convention level and establishing a uniform foundational rule for cross-border arbitration.

2. **Three Core Elements**

The content of an arbitration agreement is highly flexible and may be tailored to include diverse elements according to the parties' needs, covering matters for arbitration, arbitration procedure, appointment of arbitrators, effect of the award, language of arbitration, seat of arbitration, and applicable law, among others. From the perspective of validity determination, these contents can be divided into essential elements (whose absence may affect the validity of the agreement) and discretionary agreements (which parties may choose to include or not). Together, they constitute the complete content system of an arbitration agreement.

According to the New Arbitration Law, an arbitration agreement under institutional arbitration typically requires three core elements: an expression of intention to request arbitration, the matters for arbitration, and a designated arbitration institution.

A. "***The expression of intention to apply for arbitration***" is the primary prerequisite for the validity of an arbitration agreement. If the parties lack a genuine and mutual intention to resolve disputes through arbitration, even if the agreement is labeled "arbitration," it cannot be recognized as a valid arbitration agreement. In practice, ambiguous expressions may lead to the invalidity of an arbitration agreement, thereby precluding the initiation of arbitration proceedings. For instance, parties may stipulate an "arbitration or litigation" clause, whereby they agree to either submit disputes to arbitration or to litigation in the event of a dispute. Generally, such a clause shall be deemed invalid. Nonetheless, such a clause is not entirely void; if the parties have designated the competent court, the validity of such designation shall be determined in accordance with the applicable laws and judicial interpretations.[1]

B. "***The matters for arbitration***" are the basis for the arbitration institution's exercise of jurisdiction and an essential element of the arbitration agreement. The matters for arbitration are an important basis for defining the jurisdiction of the arbitration institution and must clearly point to the scope of "commercial disputes." For the determination of "commercial nature," reference can be made to the broad interpretation of "commercial" in the UNCITRAL Model Law and the definition of "contractual and non-contractual commercial legal relationships" in the Notice on the Implementation of the New York Convention, covering disputes arising from various commercial interactions such as trade, investment, and services. Article 2 of the Arbitration Law Interpretation further specifies that if the parties generally agree that the matters for arbitration are "contract disputes", disputes arising from the formation, validity, modification, transfer, performance, liability for breach, interpretation, rescission, and other matters, of the contract shall be deemed as matters for arbitration. This interpretation clarifies the legal effect of "general agreements," avoiding jurisdictional disputes caused by vague descriptions of the matters for arbitration.

C. "***The designated arbitration institution***" refers to China's implementation of a system of institutional arbitration. If an arbitration agreement does not designate a specific arbitration institution, this may easily give rise to jurisdictional disputes, thereby affecting arbitration efficiency. Therefore, "selecting a clear arbitration institution' is one of the substantive requirements for a valid arbitration agreement under Chinese law.

When selecting an arbitration institution, parties shall choose an appropriate institution based on the nature of the dispute and the institution's expertise, while ensuring the designation is clear to avoid disputes over validity. Different arbitration institutions have advantages in specific fields (e.g., the WIPO Arbitration and Mediation Center is proficient in intellectual property disputes, the China Maritime Arbitration Commission specializes in maritime disputes). Parties should select a specialized institution according to the type of dispute.

It is important to note that if the parties agree to adopt *ad hoc* arbitration (non-institutional arbitration), there is no need to designate an arbitration institution. However, the New Arbitration Law only provides for *ad hoc* arbitration in specific fields and regions. Notably, in jurisdictions where *ad hoc* arbitration is recognized, an arbitration institution does not necessarily need to be designated in the arbitration agreement. In ***Svensk Company v. Changli Company***,[2] the dispute involved the interpretation of the following dispute resolution clause: "in case of disputes governed by Swedish law, and that disputes should be settled by Expedited Arbitration in Sweden." Based on the parties' expressions regarding the Chinese meaning of

---

[1] Official Reply of the SPC on Several Issues Concerning the Application of Law in the Jurisdiction over Certain Civil Cases, Fa shi (2025) No. 15.

[2] (2018) Su 01 Xie Wai Ren No. 8.

this clause, both parties had no objection to resolving disputes through expedited arbitration in Sweden, but disagreed on whether such expedited arbitration could be conducted through *ad hoc* proceedings. The court determined that while the parties had agreed to resolve their disputes through expedited arbitration, this agreement did not exclude the possibility of *ad hoc* arbitration. Furthermore, the parties had not raised any objections to the *ad hoc* arbitration during the arbitration hearings. Under these circumstances, the rendering of an award by an *ad hoc* arbitral tribunal was consistent with the parties' mutual agreement. Therefore, it was concluded that the handling of the dispute by an *ad hoc* arbitral tribunal did not constitute any inconsistency with the arbitration agreement.

3. **Other Contents**

In addition to the above three elements, other contents can be agreed upon in the arbitration agreement, such as the following:

A. ***Arbitration Procedure***. Parties may autonomously determine the arbitration procedure through agreement. They may either directly select existing arbitration rules or formulate special procedures themselves, provided that such agreement does not violate the mandatory provisions of the law of the seat of arbitration. In institutional arbitration, most arbitration institutions have established standard arbitration rules. Parties may expressly provide in the agreement that "this dispute shall be submitted to the XX Arbitration Institution for adjudication in accordance with its currently effective arbitration rules." Some laws and arbitration rules directly stipulate that "the parties' choice of an arbitration institution shall be deemed as consent to apply the rules of that institution," rendering an additional clause on the application of rules unnecessary.

Parties may agree on special procedures according to the characteristics of the dispute (e.g., deadlines for evidence exchange, methods of hearing), which is particularly crucial in ad hoc arbitration, where procedural agreements are key to ensuring the smooth progress of arbitration. Even when institutional rules are selected, most rules allow parties to deviate from non-mandatory provisions through agreement.

B. ***Arbitrators.*** The appointment of arbitrators directly affects the fairness and professionalism of the arbitral award. Parties may agree on the number, qualifications, and appointment methods of arbitrators while also complying with the mandatory requirements of the law and arbitration rules. The New Arbitration Law clearly stipulates the number of arbitrators in a tribunal as "one or three,' and parties must agree within this range. Most jurisdictions (e.g., Article 10 of the UNCITRAL Model Law) do not impose limits on the number of arbitrators, allowing parties to agree freely; only when the parties have not agreed is the default number three arbitrators. Parties can agree on the professional qualifications required for arbitrators (e.g., "having more than 10 years of practical experience in international trade law"), but the terms of such agreement must not violate mandatory legal provisions (e.g., some countries prohibit persons without capacity for civil conduct from serving as arbitrators). The significance of such agreements is that when parties cannot appoint arbitrators themselves, the arbitration institution or court can appoint them based on the agreed qualifications.

China implements a "panel system" for arbitrators. Even if parties agree on arbitrator qualifications, the ultimately appointed arbitrator must still be on the arbitration institution's panel of arbitrators. Only in specific cases (e.g., foreign-related cases, cases involving pilot free trade zones) do some arbitration institutions allow the appointment of arbitrators outside the panel, subject to the confirmation by the institution.

Parties may agree that arbitrators be appointed by a specific institution (e.g., an industry association, a third-party organization), or agree on specific procedures such as "each party selects one arbitrator, and then both jointly select the presiding arbitrator." If the appointment method is not agreed upon, it shall be determined according to the law of the seat of arbitration or the arbitration rules (e.g., in institutional arbitration, arbitrators are appointed by the arbitration institution).

C. ***Language of Arbitration***. The agreement on the language of arbitration relates to the parties' right to participate in the proceedings and the protection of their rights and interests. Parties may choose autonomously; it does not need to be consistent with the language of the contract. Parties may agree to use one or more languages for all aspects of the arbitration procedure (e.g., hearings, rendering of the award) or for specific aspects (e.g., submission of evidentiary materials, such as "the arbitration procedure shall be conducted primarily in Chinese, English exhibits must be accompanied by a Chinese translation"). When agreeing, consideration should be given to the actual circumstances of the case (e.g., nationality of the parties, language of evidence) to avoid affecting the parties' rights due to language barriers (e.g., if foreign parties agree to use only Chinese, ensure they have Chinese communication skills or can obtain translation support). Some Chinese arbitration institutions default to "if the language of arbitration is not agreed upon, Chinese shall be the formal language," a rule adapted to the high proportion of domestic cases. However, for institutions handling a significant number of foreign-related cases, the language of arbitration is usually determined by the arbitral tribunal or the institution based on the circumstances of the case (e.g., nationality of the parties, place connected to the dispute).

D. ***Seat of Arbitration, i.e., the Legal Nexus of the Arbitration Procedure***. The seat of arbitration is a key connecting point for the validity of the arbitration agreement, the procedural rules, and the judicial review of the award. Its designation directly affects the legality and enforceability of arbitration. When agreeing on the seat of arbitration, parties need to comprehensively assess the following points: (a) arbitrability and enforceability of the agreement. Confirm that the dispute is arbitrable under the law of the seat of arbitration and that the arbitration agreement complies with local formal and substantive requirements; (b) judicial practice. Preference should be given to countries or regions that adopt a "pro-arbitration" stance, whose courts typically intervene less in arbitration procedures and can provide necessary assistance (e.g., property preservation, evidence collection); (c) convenience. Consider practical conditions such as transportation, accommodation, and translation services at the seat of arbitration to facilitate the participation of the parties and arbitrators in the proceedings.

4. **Participation in Proceedings Deemed as Consent to Arbitrate**

Article 3 is a newly added clause in the New Arbitration Law. The foundation of arbitration is party autonomy. Both the UNCITRAL Model Law and the arbitration laws of most developed jurisdictions adopt a relatively liberal approach towards the form and content of arbitration agreements, emphasizing the ascertainment of the parties' genuine intent. Through years of judicial interpretations and case-specific replies, the SPC has progressively developed a judicial policy of "supporting arbitration" and "endeavoring to uphold the validity of arbitration agreements." While retaining the core elements of an arbitration agreement, the revised version shifts the focus of review from "whether the agreement is formally perfect" to "whether the parties possess a genuine mutual intent to resolve disputes through arbitration" by introducing a default presumption rule of "deemed existence."

The Arbitration Law (2017) provided that arbitration agreements to be concluded in writing, but did not explicitly address the effect of agreements reached by participating in arbitration proceedings. However, the provisions in Article 13(1) and Article 27(1) of the Arbitration Law Interpretation reflected the judicial practice approach of "failure to raise an objection during arbitration proceedings being deemed as acquiescence to the validity of the arbitration agreement." The New Arbitration Law incorporates these judicial interpretations, affirming that parties may conclude an arbitration agreement by implied conduct, thereby broadening the methods for determining an arbitration agreement and significantly enhancing procedural certainty.

It establishes a clear temporal threshold, i.e., "before the first hearing." It stipulates that if a party fails to raise an objection to the arbitration agreement within this period, they will be estopped from denying it subsequently. This grants parties a sufficient period to object while preventing them from exploiting procedural loopholes for "ambush" tactics or malicious delay. The arbitral tribunal, after providing a "prompt and recording" of the situation, may proceed with the proceedings, effectively avoiding interruptions caused by jurisdictional challenges. Simultaneously, this clause substantively strengthens the arbitral tribunal's authority to handle challenges to its own jurisdiction. When a party does not deny jurisdiction within the statutory period, the arbitral tribunal is empowered by this legal provision to directly "deem" the jurisdictional basis as established and proceed to hear the case.

Illustrative Cases

Case 1: *X Communications Company v. Y Bank*[3]

X Communications Company and Y Bank entered into a Pledge Agreement on July 28, 2015. The clauses concerning the governing law and dispute resolution in the agreement were primarily as follows: GOVERNING LAW (The agreement was to

[3] See the 10 Typical Cases on Judicial Review of Financial Arbitration published by the Beijing Financial Court in October 2023. This case involves a unilateral optional arbitration clause.

be governed by and construed in accordance with the laws of Country J.). 22 DISPUTE RESOLUTION: Unless the Pledgee elected otherwise, all disputes, controversies, or claims arising out of or relating to this agreement, including issues concerning its existence, validity, interpretation, or performance, were to be submitted to Z Arbitration Commission for arbitration. The arbitration was to be conducted in accordance with the arbitration rules effective at the time of applying for arbitration, with the seat of arbitration in Beijing. The arbitration was to be final, and the proceedings were to be conducted in English. 23.2 Notwithstanding Article 23.1, if the Pledgee so elected, both parties were to submit to the non-exclusive jurisdiction of the courts of Country J.

Y Bank submitted an application for arbitration to the Z Arbitration Commission on September 3, 2021, concerning disputes arising from the performance of the agreement, and the arbitration commission formally accepted the case. The claimant, X Communications Company, contended that the arbitration clause in the Pledge Agreement was invalid and applied to the court for a ruling to confirm the invalidity of the arbitration clause.

In this case, the Pledge Agreement executed between X Communications Company and Y Bank contained an arbitration clause. This arbitration clause was determined to be an arbitration agreement reached by the parties before the dispute arose. The content of this arbitration agreement included a clear expression of intent to submit to arbitration, specified the matters subject to arbitration, and designated a specific arbitration commission, thus satisfying the elements required for a valid arbitration agreement under the relevant legal provisions. X Communications Company argued that the arbitration clause constituted a standard form term which had not been highlighted or explained. However, it failed to provide evidence to the court proving that the text of the agreement in question was pre-drafted by Y Bank for repeated use and lacked negotiation between the parties. Furthermore, even if the contract text contained standard terms, the corresponding dispute resolution method applied equally to both parties, did not constitute an exemption clause, and did not increase X Communications Company's liabilities. Therefore, this claim by X Communications Company lacked legal basis and was not supported by the Court.

X Communications Company also argued that Articles 23.1 and 23.2 of the agreement constituted an invalid "arbitrate-or-litigate" scenario. Regarding this, the Court held that Article 7 of the Arbitration Law Interpretation stipulated that if the parties agreed that disputes could either be submitted to an arbitration institution for arbitration or brought before the court, the arbitration agreement would be invalid. Consequently, the defining criterion for an "arbitrate-or-litigate" agreement was the parallel or alternative stipulation of both arbitration and litigation as dispute resolution methods, leading to jurisdictional conflicts. In this case, the disputed arbitration clause was a unilateral optional dispute resolution clause, the nature of which depended on the choice of Y Bank. This stipulation was the result of mutual agreement between the parties; there was no legal prohibition against such a stipulation, and it was not sufficient to constitute a clear unfairness in the rights and obligations of the parties. Therefore, the Court respected the principle of party autonomy in this case. The agreement's stipulation to submit disputes to an arbitration commission for arbitration did not violate Article 6 of the Arbitration Law. Furthermore, the parties' selection of the arbitration institution through the agreement was exclusive and did not fall under the circumstance of an unclear designation of the arbitration institution referred to in Article 18 of the Arbitration Law. Under the circumstances where Y Bank had already applied for arbitration to Z Arbitration Commission and explicitly waived its right to initiate legal proceedings in court, the disputed clause formed a definite and exclusive arbitration consensus. It did not constitute the type of invalid "arbitrate-or-litigate" clause identified by the Arbitration Law Interpretation. Instead, it complied with the requirements for a valid arbitration clause under the Arbitration Law and was therefore deemed legally valid.

Case 2: *M Securities Company v. N Company*[4]

In March 2017, N Company issued the 01 Prospectus, offering the first series of medium-term notes for 2017 with an issuance amount of RMB 2 billion. In October 2017, N Company issued the 04 Prospectus, offering the fourth series of medium-term notes for 2017 with an issuance amount of RMB 1.2 billion. Both Prospectuses stipulated that the issuer's issuance of the debt financing instruments, the lead underwriter's underwriting of the instruments, and the holders' subscription or purchase of the instruments were deemed to constitute agreement and acceptance of the provisions under the Prospectuses, which contained arbitration agreements. M Securities Company sought to confirm the existence of an arbitration agreement between itself and N Company.

In this case, N Company issued the two Prospectuses. From a legal perspective, the 01 Prospectus and the 04 Prospectus should be regarded as an invitation to offer under Article 473 of the Civil Code. However, these prospectuses explicitly stipulated that "the issuer's issuance of the debt financing instruments, the lead underwriter's underwriting of the instruments, and the holders' subscription or purchase of the instruments were deemed to constitute agreement and acceptance of the aforementioned provisions, and these provisions were recognized as legally binding contractual obligations." Moreover, there was no evidence showing that M Securities Company and N Company had reached any other agreements when M Securities Company purchased the medium-term notes. Therefore, the contents set out in the 01 Prospectus and the 04 Prospectus could be regarded as the agreed text between the two parties and were legally binding on the investors and the issuer.

The Court held that the arbitration clause at the end of the 01 Prospectus and the 04 Prospectus stipulated that the issuance of the debt financing instruments by the issuer, the underwriting of the instruments by the lead underwriter, and the subscription or purchase of the instruments by the holders were all deemed to constitute agreement and acceptance of the aforementioned provisions. These provisions were recognized as legally binding contractual obligations. It further stated that if the issuer violated these provisions, investors had the right to submit the dispute to X Arbitration Commission for arbitration. The convening of holders' meetings shall

[4] See the 10 Typical Cases on Judicial Review of Financial Arbitration published by the Beijing Financial Court in October 2023.

not violate the Prospectuses. In terms of content, the wording of this arbitration clause consistently referred to "this series of medium-term notes." Therefore, the phrase "the aforementioned provisions" in the arbitration clause referred to all content in the 01 Prospectus and the 04 Prospectus related to the issuance of this series of medium-term notes. Although different dispute resolution methods were stipulated sequentially under the "Investor Protection Mechanism" in both the 01 Prospectus and the 04 Prospectus, there was no provision allowing investors to choose between litigation and arbitration. Consequently, regarding the choice of dispute resolution method for investor protection issues, the last clear expression of intention between the parties should prevail. The involved arbitration clause met the formal requirements stipulated in Article 16 of the Arbitration Law (2017) and constituted a valid arbitration clause.

Case 3: ***A Company and others, v. Luo***[5]

On May 20, 2013, A Company, B Company, and C Company signed the Authorized Cooperation Agreement, whereby A Company and B Company jointly authorized C Company to carry out the development and operation of the project involving the subject land parcel. On October 10, 2013, C Company and D Company signed the Cooperation Development Contract. This contract stipulated, "If any dispute or claim arises from or relates to this Contract, or concerning the interpretation, breach, termination, or validity thereof, it shall be resolved by the parties through friendly consultation. If consultation fails, the parties agree to submit the dispute to the Chengdu Arbitration Commission for arbitration." On December 15, 2015, A Company, B Company, and C Company (collectively referred to as Party A) and D Company (as Party B) signed the Contract Termination Agreement. This Contract Termination Agreement did not contain any arbitration clause. On July 15, 2020, the assignor D Company and the assignee Luo signed the Claims Transfer Agreement, stipulating that D Company transferred all claims against A Company, B Company, and C Company under the Contract Termination Agreement to Luo. Subsequently, Luo applied for arbitration based on the arbitration clause in the Cooperation Development Contract, which was accepted by the Chengdu Arbitration Commission. A Company, B Company, and C Company filed a lawsuit with the Sichuan Province Chengdu Intermediate People's Court, requesting confirmation that no arbitration agreement existed between them and Luo.

The Sichuan Province Chengdu Intermediate People's Court held that in this case, A Company and B Company authorized C Company to handle matters related to the subject land parcel project, including approving all external commitments, agreements, contracts, minutes of meeting, etc., made by C Company during the project operation, and all debts and credits arising from the project, and assumed joint and several liability. The Cooperation Development Contract signed between C Company and D Company clearly contained an arbitration clause. Therefore, the arbitration clause in the Cooperation Development Contract signed by C Company

---

[5] See the 9 Typical Cases on Judicial Review of Arbitration released by the Sichuan Province Chengdu Intermediate People's Court in May 2025.

and D Company was binding on A Company and B Company. Subsequently, the Contract Termination Agreement signed by A Company, B Company, C Company, and D Company confirmed the termination of the Cooperation Development Contract and addressed subsequent matters, but such termination did not affect the validity of the arbitration clause in the Cooperation Development Contract. Disputes arising therefrom should be submitted to the Chengdu Arbitration Commission for arbitration by the parties as agreed. Luo, as the assignee of D Company's rights in this case, was entitled to initiate arbitration based on the arbitration clause in the Cooperation Development Contract. Accordingly, the Court ruled to dismiss the application of A Company, B Company, and C Company.

Case 4: ***Wu v. A Fund Sales Company***[6]
Based on the recommendation of A Fund Sales Company, Wu purchased a fund product issued and managed by B Asset Management Company. Wu agreed with A Fund Sales Company that disputes would be submitted to the X Arbitration Institution, and with B Asset Management Company that disputes would be submitted to Y Arbitration Institution. Wu filed the present lawsuit against A Fund Sales Company and B Asset Management Company, alleging gross fraud and joint tort. B Asset Management Company and A Fund Sales Company raised objections to the court's jurisdiction.

The Zhejiang Province Cixi Intermediate People's Court held that the three parties had neither reached a new arbitration agreement regarding the dispute in question nor selected a single arbitration institution. As Wu claimed that the two companies should bear joint and several liability, which constituted a necessary joint action, the court should accept the case. The Court further concluded that the valid arbitration clauses between Wu and the two companies stipulated different arbitration institutions, and Wu shall commence separate arbitration proceedings before the respective arbitration institutions as agreed. Accordingly, the Court dismissed the claims.

Case 5: ***W Company v. Ningde M Company and others***[7]

[6] See the 10 Typical Cases on Judicial Review of Commercial Arbitration published by the Zhejiang Province Ningbo Intermediate People's Court in June 2024. This case holds positive reference significance for determining the jurisdiction between courts and arbitration institutions when investors have agreed to arbitration clauses with different arbitration institutions in their agreements with the fund issuer and the fund seller respectively.

[7] (2018) Min 07 Ren Gang No. 1. This case is among the six typical cases released by the SPC in September 2024 that demonstrate support for arbitration in Hong Kong. The core issue in this case is whether a valid arbitration agreement exists between the parties. In accordance with the provisions of Article 7(1)(1) of the Arrangement, which states that "the arbitration agreement is invalid under the law to which the parties have subjected it or, failing any indication thereon, under the law of the place where the arbitral award was made," the case first accurately determines that the governing law of the arbitration agreement is Hong Kong law. It then identifies and applies the provisions concerning the "written form" of arbitration agreements under Sections 19(1) and 19(2) of the Hong Kong Arbitration Ordinance. Finally, based on the specific facts of the case, it provides a detailed analysis of whether the arbitration agreement in question satisfies the constitutive requirements of the "written form."

W Company and Ningde M Company signed a Supply Agreement on October 20, 2008. Article 16 of this agreement stipulated that, "any dispute arising from the performance of this agreement shall be arbitrated at HKIAC." During the performance, these two companies and N Carbon Industry Company signed the Amendment Agreement. This Amendment Agreement was confirmed by the three parties: the new clauses added in the Amendment Agreement should be added as new terms to the Supply Agreement; the amended clauses should be governed by the Amendment Agreement; except for Articles 6, 7, and 10 to 13, the remaining unamended terms should be resolved according to the provisions of the Supply Agreement. Subsequently, because both Ningde M Company and N Carbon Industry Company violated the Amendment Agreement, W Company applied for arbitration to HKIAC. HKIAC issued multiple arbitral awards between March 23 and December 28, 2016. W Company applied to the Fujian Province Nanping Intermediate People's Court for recognition and enforcement of the involved arbitral awards. N Carbon Industry Company argued that the Amendment Agreement did not contain an arbitration clause, and no arbitration agreement existed between N Carbon Industry Company and W Company. According to Article VII(1)(a) of the Arrangements Concerning Mutual Enforcement of Awards, the involved arbitral awards should not be recognized or enforced.

The Court held that the Amendment Agreement explicitly referenced the Supply Agreement and stipulated that the amendments made by the Amendment Agreement to the Supply Agreement formed part of the Supply Agreement. This indicated that N Carbon Industry Company had the intention to resolve disputes according to the arbitration clause in the Supply Agreement. The Hong Kong Arbitration Ordinance allowed the incorporation of an arbitration clause from another document by reference to satisfy the requirement for a written arbitration agreement, without requiring the parties to sign the referenced document. Therefore, a valid arbitration agreement regarding dispute matters was reached between N Carbon Industry Company and W Company. Accordingly, the Court ruled to recognize and enforce the involved arbitral awards.

Article 28
An arbitration agreement shall be null and void under one of the following circumstances:

(1) **The agreed matters for arbitration exceed the scope of arbitrable matters as specified by law;**
(2) **A party was under incapacity or limited capacity for civil conduct when the arbitration agreement was concluded; or**
(3) **A party coerced the other party into concluding the arbitration agreement.**

Notes
The circumstances rendering an arbitration agreement invalid are diverse. This Article, through enumeration, clarifies three statutory scenarios of invalidity, serving as an important basis for determining the validity of arbitration agreements in judicial practice. It centered on three core aspects, namely, "arbitrability of disputes," "capacity of the contracting parties," and "authenticity of the declaration of intent". This Article 28 excludes the validity of arbitration agreements lacking

legality and legitimacy, while also reserving space for the legal interpretation and application of other grounds for invalidity (such as lack of formal requirements, ambiguous designation of the arbitration institution, etc.).

1. **Arbitrability**

This Article delineates the boundary between the exercise of arbitration power and judicial power. As a private dispute resolution mechanism, the jurisdictional scope of arbitration must be clearly prescribed by law. Disputes falling outside this scope are matters under the exclusive jurisdiction of the courts (e.g., disputes concerning personal status relationships, administrative disputes, etc.). If such disputes are agreed to be submitted to arbitration, the arbitration agreement is void ab initio. According to Article 2 of the New Arbitration Law, the statutory scope of arbitration in China is "contractual disputes and other disputes over property rights and interests between equal subjects—citizens, legal persons, and other organizations." Article 3 of the Arbitration Law further specifies two categories of non-arbitrable matters: Firstly, disputes concerning marriage, adoption, guardianship, support, and succession (these involve personal relationships, concern the confirmation of status rights, and relate to national public order and good morals, and should be exclusively adjudicated by courts); Secondly, administrative disputes that shall be handled by administrative organs according to law (e.g., disputes arising from administrative licensing or administrative penalties, which fall within the purview of administrative power and are beyond the jurisdiction of arbitration institutions).

Furthermore, contractual disputes arising from the transfer or licensing of intellectual property rights are disputes over property rights and interests and can be agreed to be arbitrated. However, some intellectual property disputes involving aspects of administrative confirmation of rights are not arbitrable. Although the term "arbitration" is used for labor disputes, its nature is administrative arbitration and requires a mandatory prior labor arbitration procedure; it does not fall under the "commercial arbitration" defined by the Arbitration Law. Therefore, parties cannot agree to submit labor disputes to a commercial arbitration institution under the Arbitration Law.

2. **Capacity of the Contracting Parties**

An arbitration agreement is essentially a special type of civil contract, and its formation must comply with the provisions of the Civil Code regarding capacity for civil conduct. A person without capacity for civil conduct cannot independently perform juristic acts. A person with limited capacity for civil conduct can only perform juristic acts appropriate to their age, intelligence, and mental health status. Since an arbitration agreement involves the disposition of the right to resolve disputes, it is a relatively complex civil act and must be concluded independently by a person with full capacity for civil conduct; otherwise, it will be void due to defects in the subject's capacity.

In practice, attention must be paid to the timing for determining capacity and the burden of proof. The general benchmark is the capacity status "at the time of concluding the arbitration agreement," not "when the dispute arises" or "when applying for arbitration." For example, if a party had full capacity when concluding the agreement but later lost capacity, this does not affect the validity of the agreement. Conversely, if a party had limited capacity when concluding the agreement, even if they later obtained full capacity, the arbitration agreement may still be deemed invalid.

According to the Civil Code, the juristic acts of persons without capacity or with limited capacity for civil conduct shall be performed by their statutory agents on their behalf. If a statutory agent (e.g., parents of a minor, guardian of a person with mental disorder) concludes an arbitration agreement in the name of the person represented, the following conditions must be met for it to be deemed valid: The agency act must be in the interest of the person represented (e.g., agreeing to arbitration to resolve their property dispute); The agency act must not exceed the scope of statutory agency authority (a statutory agent may not dispose of the core rights of the person represented, such as waiving the right to arbitrate, except within necessary limits).

3. **Authenticity of the Declaration of Intent**

The cornerstone of the arbitration system is party autonomy. The conclusion of an arbitration agreement must be based on the genuine and voluntary mutual assent of both parties. Coercive conduct deprives a party of its autonomous right to choose and violates the fundamental principles of arbitration; therefore, such arbitration agreements are invalid by law. The party concerned may directly apply to the court to confirm the invalidity of the arbitration agreement or raise a jurisdictional objection during the arbitration proceedings.

In practice, some parties may claim the arbitration agreement is invalid on grounds of coercion during the arbitration proceedings or at the judicial review stage. Establishing "coercion" requires the simultaneous fulfillment of the following elements: One party engaged in coercive conduct, i.e., made a threat to harm the lawful rights and interests of the other party (e.g., threatening "to sign the agreement or else trade secrets will be disclosed," or "failure to cooperate will result in stopping supplies causing losses," etc.); This conduct caused the other party to fall into a state of fear and make the declaration of intent to conclude the arbitration agreement based on that fear (i.e., a direct causal relationship exists between the coercive act and the conclusion of the agreement). In practice, it is important to distinguish between "coercion" and "normal commercial pressure."

4. **Other Circumstances**

Although Article 28 of the New Arbitration Law only enumerates three scenarios of invalidity, the circumstances rendering an arbitration agreement invalid in practice are diverse and require comprehensive judgment by combining other provisions of the New Arbitration Law and relevant judicial interpretations. For example:

A. ***Defects in Formal Requirements***. An arbitration agreement must be in writing, including arbitration clauses in contracts, separately concluded arbitration agreements, and agreements reached through correspondence, data messages, etc. If the arbitration agreement is oral (except in jurisdictions that recognize oral arbitration agreements), or if the written form has major defects (e.g., merely a unilateral statement not confirmed by the other party), it is invalid due to failure to meet formal requirements.

B. *Ambiguous Designation of the Arbitration Institution Without Possibility of Correction.* According to the New Arbitration Law, an arbitration agreement should designate an arbitration institution. If the designation of the arbitration institution is ambiguous and the parties cannot clarify it through a supplementary agreement, the arbitration agreement is invalid. In practice, courts have adopted a more lenient approach towards determining "ambiguous designation": if the arbitration institution can be uniquely identified from the context of the agreement, or if there is a minor clerical error in the institution's name but it corresponds to a unique entity, the agreement is usually found valid.

C. *Content of the Arbitration Agreement Violates Mandatory Legal Provisions.* Apart from the scenarios listed in this Article, if the content of the arbitration agreement violates other mandatory legal provisions, it is also invalid. For example, stipulating that "no application may be made to the court to set aside or refuse enforcement of the arbitral award after it is rendered" is invalid because such a stipulation excludes the parties' statutory right to seek remedies and violates the mandatory provisions of the Arbitration Law concerning judicial review of awards.

By clarifying the circumstances rendering an arbitration agreement invalid, this Article provides clear adjudication guidance for judicial practice. Considering practical needs, parties should pay attention to the following key points when concluding an arbitration agreement: ensure the matters for arbitration fall within disputes over property rights and interests, avoiding involvement in personal status relationships or administrative disputes; ensure the contracting parties have full capacity for civil conduct, and if a statutory agent acts on behalf of a party, the agent's authority should be clear; the agreement should be based on equal negotiation, avoiding coercing or defrauding the other party into acceptance.

Illustrative Cases

Case 1: *Lianping A Company v. Huang*[8]

Lianping A Company sought to: confirm that the arbitration clause reached in the Annual Economic Responsibility Document signed by Lianping A Company and

[8] (2023) Yue 01 Min Te No. 185. An agreement signed between an employer and an employee may contain both labor contract elements and provisions regarding rights and obligations in civil and commercial activities between equal subjects. If the parties agree to resolve disputes through arbitration, one cannot simply argue that all disputes arising from the agreement are non-arbitrable solely because the agreement contains labor contract elements. When judicially reviewing the validity of an arbitration clause, the type of dispute should be distinguished. For other civil and commercial disputes between the parties that do not constitute labor disputes, the parties' intention to arbitrate should be respected, and the part of the arbitration clause concerning other civil and commercial disputes should be deemed valid.

the respondent Huang was legal and valid; and that the application fee was to be borne by the respondent Huang.

Huang argued that a labor relationship was formed between Huang and Lianping A Company during the performance of the Economic Responsibility Document and the disputes arising therefrom were labor disputes. The involved arbitration clause was invalid because the agreed-upon matters for arbitration exceeded the scope of arbitration permitted by law.

The Guangdong Province Guangzhou Intermediate People's Court held that: it confirmed that the content within the arbitration clause of the Economic Responsibility Document regarding disputes arising from losses caused to Lianping A Company by Huang's acts within his scope of employment, which could be submitted to the Guangzhou Arbitration Commission for arbitration, was valid. This case was an application to confirm the validity of an arbitration agreement, and should be reviewed according to Articles 16 and 17 of the Arbitration Law (2017). The involved Economic Responsibility Document stipulated, "All disputes arising from the performance of this Responsibility Document shall be resolved by both parties through friendly consultation. If consultation fails, either party may apply to the Guangzhou Arbitration Commission for arbitration." This stipulation on dispute resolution contained an expression of intent to request arbitration, clearly specified the matters and scope for arbitration, and designated the Guangzhou Arbitration Commission as the arbitration institution, thus satisfying the content required by law for a valid arbitration agreement.

The agreed matter for arbitration was "all disputes arising from the performance of this Responsibility Document." Huang was a professional manager of Lianping A Company. The Economic Responsibility Document stipulated Huang's job responsibilities, 2017 annual operation targets, remuneration, as well as assessment management and restraint mechanisms. Consequently, disputes arising from the performance of the Economic Responsibility Document included both labor disputes arising from remuneration and disputes arising from losses caused to the company by Huang in the course of performing his duties as a professional manager. Labor disputes did not fall within the scope of commercial arbitration. However, disputes between the parties that did not constitute labor disputes could be submitted to a commercial arbitration institution. Therefore, the content within the arbitration clause of the Economic Responsibility Document regarding disputes arising from losses caused to Lianping A Company by Huang's acts within his scope of employment, which could be submitted to the Guangzhou Arbitration Commission for arbitration, did not fall under the invalid circumstances stipulated in Article 17 of the Arbitration Law and should be deemed valid according to law.

Case 2: *Li v. A Culture Company*[9]

On November 27, 2019, A Culture Company and Li signed a Client Subscription Contract. The contract stipulated that, "any disputes arising during the performance

[9] See the 10 Typical Cases on Judicial Review of Domestic Arbitration published by the Beijing No. 4 Intermediate People's Court in 2022.

of this agreement shall be resolved through friendly consultation between Party A and Party B. If consultation fails, both parties agree to be under the jurisdiction of the Beijing Arbitration Commission." On the same day, Li paid the investment sum, and A Culture Company issued a receipt to Li.

In November 2021, Li Jia, the guardian of Li, applied to the Court for confirmation that the arbitration clause agreed in the Client Subscription Contract signed between Li and A Culture Company was invalid.

Upon review, it was found that Li obtained a disability certificate in October 2009, which indicated Li was a person with a mental disability, classified as Grade 1. The Dongcheng Primary People's Court of Beijing issued a civil judgment on July 8, 2021, which determined, based on judicial appraisal, that Li suffered from severe cognitive dysfunction and was assessed as having no capacity for civil conduct. Accordingly, Li was adjudicated as a person with no capacity for civil conduct, and Li Jia was appointed as Li's guardian. Therefore, the Court confirmed that the arbitration clause stipulated in the Client Subscription Contract was invalid.

Case 3: *Wang v. Huya Company*[10]

Wang claimed that due to physical illness and other reasons, she was recuperating at home and attempted to engage in live streaming. Lacking understanding of this new field, she was allegedly entrapped by Huya Company personnel during her trial broadcasts, who took partial payment from her. She was threatened that if she did not participate in Huya Company's live streaming management, she would face legal liability. Besides being forced to refund the full amount of over 200,000 RMB, she was also falsely accused of potentially committing crimes such as money laundering. Furthermore, she was threatened with the public release of an indecent video from her previous broadcasts. Consequently, Wang claimed she had no choice but to accept all of Huya Company's terms and was coerced into signing the Huya Anchor Exclusive Cooperation Agreement. Regarding the content of the agreement, Wang stated she never read it at the time, did not know its specific terms, and was unaware of the default clauses or the arbitration clause. All contract documents were sent back to the claimant's address as requested by Huya Company. She argued the agreement did not represent her genuine intent and was signed under duress from the respondent. Additionally, during her broadcasts, Huya Company allegedly restricted and controlled her through various means, and its staff demanded she engage in unethical and illegal activities. As Huya Company was now seeking to hold her liable for breaching the contract, she applied to the court to confirm the agreement was invalid.

Huya Company argued that the Huya Anchor Exclusive Cooperation Agreement and its arbitration clause represented the genuine intent of both parties. Their reasons were as follows: First, Huya Company never coerced Wang into signing the agreement or its arbitration clause. The agreement was voluntarily signed after negotiations and reflected the true will of both parties. Wang provided no evidence to prove Huya Company coerced her. Second, Wang was aware of and accepted the

[10] (2020) Chuan 13 Min Te No. 34.

terms of the agreement. By signing and fingerprinting the agreement, Wang demonstrated her acceptance of its contents, including the default clauses and the arbitration clause. Furthermore, on November 19, 2019, Wang sent an email to Huya Company staff, admitting that her live streaming on Douyin constituted a breach of contract and expressing her desire to return to Huya for streaming, which also indicated her knowledge and acceptance of the agreement's terms. Additionally, Wang herself stated in her application that Huya Company had mailed the agreement to her, giving her ample time and opportunity to read the terms and raise objections. Even if Wang did not read the terms before signing, her unawareness of the specific content was due to her own negligence and would not render the agreement or its arbitration clause invalid. Third, Both parties had performed the agreement for nearly two years. After enjoying the rights and benefits under the agreement, Wang failed to perform her main obligations and now refused to resolve disputes or bear liability for breach by claiming the agreement and its arbitration clause were invalid, which violated the basic principle of the consistency of rights and obligations. In summary, the arbitration clause contained a clear expression of intent to arbitrate, specified the matters for arbitration, and designated an arbitration commission, complying with Article 16 of the Arbitration Law (2017) and lacking any invalid circumstances stipulated in Articles 17 or 18 of the Arbitration Law (2017). Therefore, it should be deemed valid.

The Court opined that this case involved an application to confirm the validity of an arbitration agreement. The provisions of Articles 16, 17, and 18 of the Arbitration Law (2017) constituted statutory grounds for the people's court to confirm the invalidity of an arbitration agreement. In this case, Wang sought to confirm that the involved arbitration agreement was invalid, arguing that Huya Company used duress to force her to sign the entire Huya Anchor Exclusive Cooperation Agreement, including the arbitration clause. Therefore, the focus of the dispute was whether Huya Company used duress to force Wang to sign the involved arbitration agreement. Huya Company sent the agreement text to Wang, who signed and fingerprinted it before returning it to Huya Company for sealing. Wang claimed that before signing the agreement, she had received partial payment from Huya Company, and during the signing, she was threatened that failure to participate in Huya's live stream management would lead to legal liability, requiring full refund and facing exaggerated accusations of crimes like money laundering, along with threats to release her previous indecent live video. Huya Company denied these allegations. Wang failed to provide evidence to substantiate her claims, so the Court did not uphold them. As for whether Huya Company provided Wang with the final signed and sealed agreement, and whether Wang read the agreement's content, these factors did not demonstrate that Huya Company used duress to compel her to sign the agreement. Furthermore, the liability for breach of contract involved in the agreement, such as Wang bearing a large sum of liquidated damages if she breached, could not lead to the inference that Huya Company used duress. Regarding the chat records submitted by Wang, Huya Company argued that the person Wang chatted with was not its employee. The Court held that even if the chatter was a Huya Company employee, this evidence merely reflected negotiations about potentially signing a new contract and could not be used to infer the circumstances surrounding the signing of the original involved agreement, nor could it prove Huya Company used duress to sign the involved agreement. Regarding the media reports submitted by Wang, regardless of their truthfulness, they could not prove that Wang was coerced into signing the involved agreement.

The Court further held that, in summary, the arbitration clause in the involved agreement contained a clear expression of intent to arbitrate, designated an arbitration institution, and specified the matters for arbitration, thus meeting the formal requirements for a valid arbitration clause. There was no evidence proving otherwise. Therefore, the Court dismissed the claims.

Case 4: *Qu v. Zhai*[11]

Qu was judicially determined to be a person with limited capacity for civil conduct. The legal representative of Qu sought to invalidate the arbitration clauses in the loan contract and mortgage contract entered into between Qu and Zhai. The court held that Zhai had not engaged in adequate communication with Qu regarding the arbitration clauses at the time of contract execution, and therefore, it could not be concluded that the arbitration clauses represented the mutual intention of both parties. Given the short timeframe between the execution of the contracts in question and the judicial determination of Qu as a person with limited capacity for civil conduct, coupled with the persistent nature of the illness that led to Qu's classification as such, the court ruled to invalidate the arbitration clauses involved in the case.

Case 5: *Fang v. B Education Company*[12]

In August 2022, after communicating with the staff of B Education Company about purchasing training courses, Fang reached a purchase intention, and the two parties formally signed the Course Contract. This contract was drafted by B Education Company and then provided to Fang for signing. Article 10 stipulated that disputes arising from the signing or performance of the contract should be resolved by arbitration through the Beijing Arbitration Commission. Fang subsequently filed a lawsuit with the court, claiming that she had not noticed the involved arbitration clause when signing the contract. She argued that the Course Contract provided by B Education Company was a standard form contract, and the dispute resolution method designed in the agreement intentionally excluded litigation and adopted the high-cost method of arbitration, which violated the principle of fairness and should

---

[11] See the Annual Report on Judicial Review of Commercial Arbitration published by the SPC in December 2025.

[12] See the 10 Typical Cases on Judicial Review of Domestic Arbitration Judicial Review published by Beijing No. 4 Intermediate People's Court's in July 2022. The key focus of review in this case was whether the contract setup was grossly unfair. Both arbitration and litigation are methods of dispute resolution; choosing arbitration does not inherently violate the principle of fairness. Parties engaging in civil activities should reasonably be aware of and guard against relevant risks. If there are objections to the content of the contract, including the dispute resolution clause, they should communicate and negotiate with the counterparty to strive for a dispute resolution method that they accept.

be deemed invalid according to law. Upon review, the Court ruled to dismiss Fang's application.

Article 29
Where an arbitration agreement contains no or unclear provisions concerning the matters for arbitration or the arbitration institution, the parties may reach a supplementary agreement. Where no such supplementary agreement may be reached, the arbitration agreement shall be void.

Notes
According to the New Arbitration Law, one of the required elements of an arbitration agreement is the clear designation of the matters for arbitration and the arbitration institution. This Article further stipulates that even if the parties have the intention to arbitrate, if the matters for arbitration or the arbitration institution are not agreed upon and no supplementary agreement can be reached, the arbitration clause is invalid. But what constitutes a clear designation? It must be clarified that if, based on various circumstances, the matters for arbitration or the arbitration institution can be inferred as clear, then it is considered a clear designation, and the arbitration agreement is not invalid for this reason. If the governing law of the arbitration agreement is the New Arbitration Law, then whether the agreement regarding the matters for arbitration or the arbitration institution complies with the New Arbitration Law and whether it is clear directly affects the arbitration procedure and the validity of the arbitral award.

1. **Matters for Arbitration**

Matters for arbitration refer to the scope of disputes agreed to be submitted to arbitration, i.e., which disputes can be arbitrated. In general arbitration clauses, the agreement on matters for arbitration can adopt an all-inclusive approach, a specific approach, or a hybrid approach. The all-inclusive approach means the arbitration agreement stipulates that all disputes arising from or related to the contract shall be submitted to arbitration. The specific approach means only one or several specific types of disputes are submitted to arbitration. The hybrid approach means all issues related to a certain aspect of the contract are submitted to arbitration. In the latter two cases, situations exceeding the scope of the arbitration agreement are prone to occur. For example, issues submitted to arbitration and decided by the arbitral tribunal might not be the specific types of disputes designated in the arbitration agreement, or might not fall within the designated aspect of the contract covered by the arbitration agreement. For matters not within the scope of the arbitration agreement, the parties have no right to submit them, and the arbitral tribunal has no power to rule on them. Not being within the scope of arbitration means the parties have not authorized the arbitral tribunal to decide such matters, and the tribunal naturally cannot contravene the parties' intent and rule on them of its own accord.

Among the three elements of an arbitration agreement stipulated by the New Arbitration Law, the ones frequently disputed are mainly whether the expression of intent to arbitrate is genuine and exists, and whether the designated arbitration institution is clear. Relatively speaking, potential disputes among parties regarding the matters for arbitration mainly focus on arbitrability. If the disputes agreed upon cannot be resolved through arbitration according to the applicable law, then such matters are not arbitrable, and the arbitral tribunal cannot make a ruling on them. For instance, in certain contracts that have both administrative contract functions and commercial functions, because administrative contracts are not arbitrable under the New Arbitration Law, awards can only be made on matters within the scope of arbitration that can be resolved through commercial arbitration.

Arbitrability, or the scope of application of arbitration, simply put, refers to which disputes can be resolved through arbitration and which cannot. It is a restriction on the autonomous will of the parties (primarily embodied in the arbitration agreement), involves the validity of the award, and determines whether the award can be recognized and enforced by the court. From this perspective, although arbitrability is not included among the three elements, the subject matter of the dispute being arbitrable is a prerequisite for the validity of the arbitration agreement. If the law of a country stipulates that certain disputes cannot be resolved through arbitration, then agreements regarding such disputes cannot be resolved through arbitration by signing an arbitration agreement.

When determining the matters for arbitration, the explicit expression of the parties in the arbitration agreement should be the primary basis. If the parties intend to submit all related disputes to arbitration, it is advisable to use general, all-inclusive expressions, avoiding specific or restrictive language, to prevent further disputes later about whether a matter falls within the scope of arbitration. During the hearing of a case, the arbitral tribunal should carefully identify the consistency between the arbitration claims and the matters agreed upon in the arbitration agreement. Specifically, the scope of the arbitral tribunal's hearing should be limited to the matters agreed upon in the arbitration agreement, and it should respond to the parties' arbitration requests within this scope. In practice, parties might raise claims in their arbitration application that exceed the scope of the arbitration agreement; in such cases, the arbitral tribunal should proactively review and limit them. The validity of the award may be affected if any of the following situations occur: the matters decided in the award, although not exceeding the scope of the arbitration agreement, were not claimed by the parties; the matters decided in the award exceed the scope of the arbitration agreement; or the matters decided in the award exceed the scope of the parties' arbitration claims. In these situations, the parties may apply to the court to set aside the award or refuse enforcement according to law. If it involves a foreign arbitral award, the court may refuse enforcement based on the New York Convention.

2. **Arbitration Institution**

In the practice of judicial review, a considerable number of cases involve one party challenging the validity of the arbitration agreement on the grounds of the agreement regarding the arbitration institution. Several scenarios are listed below.

A. Inaccurate Designation of the Arbitration Institution's Name

For various reasons, when signing the contract, the parties might not accurately describe the name of the arbitration institution, resulting in additional., omitting or incorrect characters. Article 3 of the Arbitration Law Interpretation states that if the name of the arbitration institution agreed upon in the arbitration agreement is inaccurate, but the specific arbitration institution can be determined, it shall be deemed that the arbitration institution has been selected.

In fact, this is a basic principle of determination when challenges to the arbitration agreement involve issues with the arbitration institution. Previously, in a reply regarding a case where the name of the chosen arbitration institution in the arbitration clause was missing a character but did not affect the validity of the arbitration clause,[13] the SPC pointed out that although the parties' arbitration clause omitted the word "Economic" in the name of the China International Economic and Trade Arbitration Commission, it did not affect the validity of the arbitration clause. Therefore, CIETAC had jurisdiction over all disputes arising from the performance of the joint venture contract or related to it among the aforementioned three parties. This approach has been consistently followed in prior judicial practice.

B. Designated Arbitration Rules Without Naming the Arbitration Institution
Some arbitration clauses only stipulate the applicable arbitration rules without directly designating the arbitration institution administering the arbitration. In fact, many arbitration institutions can apply other institutions' arbitration rules to conduct arbitration proceedings. It cannot be assumed that agreeing to a certain institution's rules necessarily means agreeing to arbitrate at that institution, unless the rules themselves stipulate that choosing those rules is deemed as the parties' agreement for arbitration to be administered by that institution. Article 4 of the Arbitration Law Interpretation stipulates that if the arbitration agreement only specifies the arbitration rules applicable to the disputes, the parties shall be deemed not to have agreed upon on an arbitration institution, unless the parties have reached a supplementary agreement or the arbitration institution can be determined according to the agreed arbitration rules. Therefore, if it is agreed that arbitration shall be conducted according to the arbitration rules of a certain Chinese institution, and those rules stipulate that choosing the rules is deemed as agreement to submit to that institution, it should be recognized as agreement to submit to that institution. If the agreed arbitration rules cannot determine the arbitration institution and the parties cannot reach a supplementary agreement, then agreeing to a certain institution's arbitration rules is, under the New Arbitration Law, deemed as not having agreed upon an arbitration institution.

C. Designating a Non-Existent Arbitration Institution
Parties might designate a non-existent institution due to a lack of knowledge about the setup of arbitration institutions. The validity of such agreements needs to be determined based on different legal jurisdictions. In *Baoyuan Trading Company v.*

[13] See Fa Jing (1998) No. 159.

Yu,[14] the case involved a sales contract signed on May 27, 2006. The contract stipulated in Article 8 that disputes be submitted to the "Fujian Jinjiang Arbitration Commission" for arbitration. The SPC, in its reply on the request for instructions regarding the arbitration clause in the sales contract between Baoyuan Trading Company and Yu held that since the "Fujian Jinjiang Arbitration Commission" did not exist, there were no other arbitration institutions in Jinjiang City, and the parties could not reach a supplementary agreement on this matter, according to Article 18 of the Arbitration Law (1994), the arbitration clause involved in this case should be confirmed as invalid.

D. Designating Two Arbitration Institutions

Some arbitration clauses may designate two or more arbitration institutions. According to Article 5 of the Arbitration Law Interpretation, if an arbitration agreement designates two or more arbitration institutions, the parties may agree to choose one of them to apply for arbitration; if the parties cannot reach an agreement on the choice of arbitration institution, the arbitration agreement is invalid. Many countries have more than one commercial arbitration institution. China now has over 270 arbitration institutions. In such cases, parties drafting an arbitration clause might select two or more arbitration institutions. In previous arbitration practice, courts at all levels, including the SPC, adopted a lenient aproach towards arbitration clauses designating two arbitration institutions.[15] However, according to Article 5 of the Arbitration Law Interpretation, if the arbitration agreement designates two or more arbitration institutions and the parties fail to agree on choosing one to apply for arbitration, the arbitration agreement is invalid.

The foregoing briefly discusses several scenarios regarding matters for arbitration and arbitration institutions. Furthermore, from a practical perspective, the application of this Article involves three levels: firstly, identifying the defect, meaning the arbitration agreement lacks clarity or is missing regarding the two core elements of "matters for arbitration" or "arbitration institution"; secondly, initiating the remedial procedure, where the law grants the parties the right "may" to reach a supplementary

[14] (2007) Min Si Ta Zi No. 38.

[15] The SPC previously issued an official reply in 1996 concerning the validity of an arbitration clause selecting two arbitration institutions simultaneously. This is documented in the Official Reply of the SPC on the Validity of an Arbitration Clause Selecting Two Arbitration Institutions (Fa Han [1996] No. 176, dated December 12, 1996). The arbitration clause in the contract between the parties involved in the referenced case stipulated that "disputes arising from the contract shall be submitted to the Foreign Economic and Trade Arbitration Commission of the China Council for the Promotion of International Trade, or to the Arbitration Institute of the Stockholm Chamber of Commerce for arbitration." The SPC held that the designation of the arbitration institution in this arbitration clause was clear and capable of being performed. The parties could proceed to arbitration by selecting one of the agreed-upon institutions. With reference to this Reply, in a situation where arbitration is agreed to be conducted by either Institution A or Institution B, the agreement on the arbitration institution is clear and enforceable, as the parties may arbitrate by choosing either designated institution. Therefore, the arbitration clause in this case is valid.

agreement through negotiation. Here, the word "may" indicates this is an authorizing norm rather than an obligatory norm, giving the parties the option of whether to attempt remediation; finally, determining the legal consequence. If the parties successfully reach a supplementary agreement, the defect is cured, and the arbitration agreement is complete *ab initio*; if, after reasonable efforts, no agreement can be reached, the arbitration agreement is definitively void. In practice, when applying this Article, arbitration institutions and courts should adopt a pro-arbitration stance, investigate and guide whether there is a possibility for the parties to reach a supplementary agreement, and should not preclude arbitration prematurely in the early stages of the procedure merely because the agreement contains defects.

Illustrative Cases

Case 1: *Rongcheng Company v. Li and others*[16]

In June 2017, Rongcheng Company signed the Property Management Service Agreement with homeowners Li and Lin. Article 9 of the agreement stipulated, "If a dispute arises between the homeowner and the property management enterprise regarding this agreement and consultation fails, it shall be referred to the property management authority for mediation or submitted to the Shengzhou Arbitration Commission for a ruling according to law." In July 2021, Rongcheng Company submitted an arbitration application to the Shaoxing Arbitration Commission, requesting that Li and Lin pay the outstanding property service fees and corresponding late payment penalties. In August 2021, Li and Lin submitted a written objection to the arbitration jurisdiction to the arbitration commission, arguing that the arbitration institution agreed upon in the agreement did not exist, the arbitration agreement was invalid, and therefore the Shaoxing Arbitration Commission had no jurisdiction over their dispute. In October 2021, the Zhejiang Province Shaoxing Intermediate People's Court accepted the case filed by Rongcheng Company applying for confirmation of the validity of the arbitration agreement.

The Zhejiang Province Shaoxing Intermediate People's Court held that the arbitration clause in the Property Management Service Agreement stipulated that disputes should be arbitrated by the "Shengzhou Arbitration Commission." Although the arbitration institution named in the clause did not exist, Shengzhou City was under the administrative jurisdiction of Shaoxing City, and there was only one arbitration institution in Shaoxing City, namely the Shaoxing Arbitration Commission.

[16] (2021) Zhe 06 Min Te No. 47; See the 10 Typical Cases on Judicial Review of Commercial Arbitration published by the High People's Court of Zhejiang Province. This case is a typical example of how to determine the validity of an arbitration agreement when the agreed-upon arbitration institution does not exist or is unclear. When reviewing the validity of such arbitration agreements, the principle of striving to uphold the validity of the arbitration agreement should be adopted, fully respecting the parties' intention to arbitrate. The arbitration agreement should be interpreted in good faith using textual, contextual, and purposive interpretation methods. If a specific arbitration institution chosen by the parties can be determined, the arbitration agreement should be recognized as valid according to law.

Furthermore, the parties involved in the case had a clear intention to submit disputes to arbitration and to resolve them in Shengzhou City, Shaoxing. According to Article 6 of the Arbitration Law Interpretation, which states that if an arbitration agreement provides for arbitration by an arbitration institution at a certain location and there is only one arbitration institution at that location, that arbitration institution shall be deemed to be the arbitration institution stipulated in the agreement, the Shaoxing Arbitration Commission could be deemed as the arbitration institution agreed upon by the parties. Accordingly, the Court ruled to confirm that the arbitration agreement signed by the parties was valid.

Case 2: *Chen v. Hong Company*[17]
Chen and Hong Company signed the Project Contract Agreement, which stipulated that disputes arising from the contract shall be submitted to arbitration before the Guangzhou Arbitration Commission. Due to an increase in the project scope, the parties subsequently signed the Project Responsibility Contract, under which Article 11 stipulated that contract disputes shall be submitted to the local arbitration commission. Later, a dispute arose from the performance of the contract, and Chen filed a lawsuit with the Dongguan No. 1 People's Court, requesting Hong Company to pay the project payment. Chen acknowledged that the Project Responsibility Contract was the one actually performed, but argued that the arbitration clause therein did not designate a specific arbitration institution and should therefore be invalid. The Dongguan No. 1 People's Court dismissed Chen's claims on the grounds that the contract contained an arbitration clause. Chen appealed.

The Dongguan Intermediate People's Court held that Chen acknowledged the Project Responsibility Contract was the one actually performed, and its arbitration clause stipulated arbitration by the "local arbitration commission." Although the contract did not specify the exact location of "local," the contract was a construction project contract, and both the location of the contract's subject matter and the place of performance were fixed. The agreement between Chen and Hong Company to arbitrate by the "local arbitration commission" should be construed as referring to the arbitration commission in Dongguan, the location of the contract's subject matter and place of performance. At the time the contract was signed, there was only one arbitration institution in Dongguan, i.e., the Dongguan Branch of the Guangzhou Arbitration Commission. In accordance with Article 6

[17] See the 1st batch of Typical Cases on Judicial Review of Arbitration published by the High People's Court of Guangdong Province in February 2024. The parties' agreement in a contract to refer disputes to the "local arbitration institution" for arbitration is one of the common expressions found in arbitration agreements. If the specific arbitration institution can be determined by considering the nature of the contract, as well as factors such as the domicile of the parties, the place of contract conclusion, the place of contract performance, and the location of the subject matter of the contract, the parties' intention to arbitrate should be respected, and the determination should be made in accordance with the principle favoring the validity of the arbitration agreement.

of the Arbitration Law Interpretation, the disputes arising from the said contract between Chen and Hong Company shall be submitted to the Dongguan Branch of the Guangzhou Arbitration Commission. Consequently, the Court ruled to dismiss the appeal.

Case 3: *A Logistics Company v. B Shipping Company*[18]

A Logistics Company and B Shipping Company signed the Contract of Affreightment, which stipulated that all disputes arising from this contract shall be submitted to the Shanghai Headquarters of the China Maritime Arbitration Commission for arbitration. However, an appendix to the contract, the General Logistics Terms, stipulated that any dispute arising from these General Logistics Terms shall be submitted to the Shanghai Sub-Commission of the CIETAC for arbitration in accordance with that commission's arbitration rules. Later, cargo damage occurred during this shipment. A Logistics Company filed the present lawsuit with the Court but did not submit the involved Contract of Affreightment and its appendix, the General Logistics Terms. After the court accepted the case, B Shipping Company raised an objection to the court's jurisdiction and stated that A Logistics Company could choose either one of the two agreed-upon arbitration institutions, and B Shipping Company would accept either choice. The Court ultimately dismissed the lawsuit filed by A Logistics Company.

The Court held that the Contract of Affreightment and its appendix, the General Logistics Terms, each designated one arbitration institution. According to Article 5 of the Arbitration Law Interpretation, if an arbitration agreement designates two or more arbitration institutions, the parties have the obligation to negotiate and select one of them for arbitration. A Logistics Company did not provide evidence proving that it had fulfilled the corresponding obligation to negotiate. B Shipping Company, on the other hand, agreed to let A Logistics Company "choose either one" of the stipulated arbitration institutions. Therefore, it should be determined that the parties could reach an agreement on selecting one of the arbitration institutions, and the involved arbitration clause could not be deemed invalid. Accordingly, the dispute concerning the cargo damage fell within the scope of arbitration and did not fall under the accepted case types of the People's Court.

Case 4: *Shan Company v. Niu Company*[19]

---

[18] See the Typical Cases on Judicial Review of Arbitration from 2020–2024 published by the Shanghai High People's Court. This case is a typical case concerning the confirmation of the validity of an arbitration clause designating two arbitration institutions. In practice, after a dispute arises, it is often difficult for the parties to calmly renegotiate the choice of an arbitration institution. The adjudication in this case provides a reference path for resolving such impasses: if one party clearly indicates its willingness to accept any of the selectable arbitration institutions, and the arbitration agreement is free from other grounds for invalidity, the arbitration agreement should be deemed valid. The other party's refusal to choose does not affect the valid determination of the arbitration agreement. This rule aligns with the principle of "favoring the validity of the arbitration agreement" in determining effectiveness.

[19] See the 2nd batch of the 10 Typical Cases on Judicial Review of Arbitration published by the High People's Court of Guangdong Province in August 2025. The people's court accurately ascertained and applied Australian arbitration law, adhered to the principles of good faith interpretation and supporting arbitration, prudently reviewed the enforceability and validity of the foreign-related

Shan Company and Niu Company entered into the Purchase Contract, which stipulated that relevant disputes shall be "submitted to the New South Wales International Economic and Trade Arbitration Commission for arbitration in accordance with its arbitration rules, with the seat of arbitration in Sydney. The arbitral award shall be final and binding upon both parties." The agreement did not stipulate the procedure for appointing arbitrators. Later, a dispute arose between the parties. Niu Company argued that the "New South Wales International Economic and Trade Arbitration Commission" stipulated in the Purchase Contract did not actually exist. According to Australian law, this arbitration agreement should be invalid. Consequently, Niu Company filed a lawsuit with the court based on the dispute resolution clause and submitted a legal opinion provided by a legal expert it had commissioned. During the first-instance trial, the court also commissioned a legal ascertainment institution, which issued an ascertainment report concluding that the involved arbitration agreement should be valid under Australian law. The court of the first instance therefore ruled to dismiss Niu Company's claims. Niu Company appealed.

The Court of the second instance held that the parties did not agree on the applicable law for determining the validity of the arbitration agreement, but they did agree that the seat of arbitration was Sydney. According to Article 16 of the Arbitration Law Interpretation, the validity of the arbitration clause in this case shall be reviewed under the law of the seat of arbitration, namely, Australian law. Niu Company and the court of the first instance commissioned legal experts and a legal ascertainment institution, respectively, to provide legal opinions, which reached different conclusions. However, the legal opinion commissioned by the court of the first instance was more persuasive in terms of formal completeness and relevance of the ascertained law; therefore, that ascertainment report was adopted. According to the ascertained Australian law, the court's interpretation of the validity of the arbitration agreement should apply a liberal principle favoring arbitration. The term "New South Wales International Economic and Trade Arbitration Commission" was not a defined term in the contract, and it could be inferred that the parties' true intention was to "submit disputes to an arbitration institution in Sydney, New South Wales." The Australian Centre for International Commercial Arbitration (ACICA) was the only default appointing authority in Sydney capable of performing the function of appointing arbitrators under the International Arbitration Act. Therefore, the parties' true intention should be presumed to be submission to the ACICA for arbitration. The court of the second instance held that this arbitration clause was valid and enforceable. Consequently, it dismissed the appeal and upheld the original ruling.

Case 5: *Tianjin A Hotel Management Company v. Hong Kong B Company*[20]
Tianjin A Hotel Management Company and Hong Kong B Company signed the Management Contract on January 25, 2013. The contract stipulated that it was to be

arbitration agreement with a defective institutional name, and fully respected the parties' expression of intent to submit disputes to arbitration.

[20] (2021) Jin 01 Min Te No. 1; See the 6 Typical Cases Supporting Hong Kong Arbitration published by the SPC in September 2024. This case involves the principle for determining the governing law of the validity of an arbitration clause. The parties in this case only agreed on the law

construed in accordance with the law of the Chinese Mainland, while the arbitration clause stipulated that disputes arising from the contract were to be "resolved by arbitration by the International Chamber of Commerce in accordance with the ICC Arbitration Rules effective on the date the request for arbitration is received (or any similar subsequent rules). The appointing authority shall be the International Chamber of Commerce. The place of arbitration shall be Hong Kong." Tianjin A Hotel Management Company argued that the "International Chamber of Commerce" mentioned in the clause did not possess arbitration functions and that no arbitration institution named "International Chamber of Commerce" existed. It therefore applied to the court for confirmation that the arbitration clause was invalid.

The Tianjin No. 1 Intermediate People's Court held that the Management Contract signed between Tianjin A Hotel Management Company and Hong Kong B Company only specified the law governing the contract itself. This could not be used as the law applicable to determining the validity of the arbitration clause within the contract. Instead, the law of the agreed seat of arbitration, namely, Hong Kong law, should be applied to determine the validity of the arbitration clause. According to the provisions of the Hong Kong Arbitration Ordinance, the validity of an arbitration clause depends on the parties' expression of intent to submit disputes to arbitration. In this case, the arbitration clause signed by Tianjin A Hotel Management Company and Hong Kong B Company contained the parties' expression of intent to refer disputes to arbitration. It should therefore be recognized as a valid arbitration clause. Consequently, the court ruled to dismiss Tianjin A Hotel Management Company's application to confirm the arbitration agreement as invalid.

Case 6: *Liu v. Long*[21]

---

governing the contract (the proper law of the contract), but did not specify the governing law of the arbitration agreement. Therefore, referring to Article 18 of the Choice of Law Interpretation, the law of the seat of arbitration, namely Hong Kong law, should be applied to determine the validity of the arbitration agreement. According to the Hong Kong Arbitration Ordinance, an arbitration agreement is an agreement by the parties to submit to arbitration all or certain disputes which have arisen or which may arise between them in respect of a defined legal relationship, whether contractual or not. An arbitration agreement may be in the form of an arbitration clause in a contract or in the form of a separate agreement. Thus, Hong Kong law does not require the clear and specific designation of an arbitration institution as an essential element for determining the validity of an arbitration agreement. In this case, the parties had a clear written expression of intent to submit disputes to arbitration, which satisfied the requirements for the validity of an arbitration clause under Hong Kong law. Therefore, the arbitration clause in question should be recognized as valid.

[21] (2022) Yue 03 Min Chu No. 7444; See the 10 Typical Cases on Judicial Review of Arbitration for 2024 published by the Guangdong Province Shenzhen Intermediate People's Court in July 2025; See also the 6 Typical Cases Supporting Hong Kong Arbitration published by the SPC in September 2024. Whether an inaccurately named arbitration institution in a party's agreement (a defective arbitration agreement) affects the validity of the arbitration agreement and the subsequent arbitration proceedings is a common issue in the judicial review practice of arbitration. In this case, the respondent submitted a legal opinion from a Hong Kong barrister, arguing that the inaccuracy in the arbitration institution's name meant the subsequent proceedings should be conducted as ad hoc arbitration. Based on the Hong Kong law ascertained through a commissioned legal ascertainment institution, and identifying the key characteristic "International Economic and Trade Arbitration Commission" contained within the name "Hong Kong International Economic and Trade

Liu and Long signed three Loan Agreements, which stipulated the loan amount, term, interest, and other details. The agreements also stipulated that "any disputes and controversies under this agreement, if unable to be resolved through friendly consultation, shall be submitted to the Hong Kong International Economic and Trade Arbitration Commission for arbitration in accordance with the prevailing procedural rules of the Hong Kong International Economic and Trade Arbitration Commission." As Long failed to repay the principal and interest on time, Liu applied for arbitration to the China International Economic and Trade Arbitration Commission Hong Kong Arbitration Center (hereinafter referred to as the CIETAC Hong Kong Arbitration Center). After the CIETAC Hong Kong Arbitration Center rendered an arbitral award, Liu applied to the Guangdong Province Shenzhen Intermediate People's Court for recognition and enforcement. Long argued that the involved award should not be recognized and enforced, primarily on the grounds that the "Hong Kong International Economic and Trade Arbitration Commission" stipulated in the arbitration clause could not designate a specified arbitration institution, and therefore, the arbitration clause was invalid. Long also submitted a legal opinion commissioned from a Hong Kong barrister, arguing that the arbitration institution agreed upon was unclear, and accordingly, under Section 10 of the Hong Kong Arbitration Ordinance and Chapter 609C, the Hong Kong International Arbitration Centre should issue specific directions regarding the service of documents, the appointment of arbitrators, and the number of arbitrators. The Guangdong Province Shenzhen Intermediate People's Court commissioned a Legal Ascertainment and Commercial Mediation Centre to ascertain Hong Kong law, which obtained a legal opinion from a Hong Kong barrister stating that Hong Kong court precedents indicated defective arbitration agreements were not uncommon, and the Court should consider and give effect to the true intention of the contracting parties, directing them to the most suitable arbitral tribunal that best reflected their mutual intention.

The Guangdong Province Shenzhen Intermediate People's Court held that since the involved award was made in Hong Kong, Hong Kong law should be applied to review the validity of the arbitration clause. Although the name of the arbitration institution in the involved arbitration clause was inaccurately written, the parties' intention to arbitrate was clear, and under Hong Kong law, this arbitration clause was valid. The court analyzed the discrepancies between the two Hong Kong legal opinions and ultimately adopted the legal opinion provided by the X legal ascertainment and commercial mediation centre, namely that the court should choose the interpretation that best conformed to the intention expressed by the parties through the contract language, which was more reasonable and more effective. The Court held that, based on the stipulations in the involved arbitration clause, although the name of the arbitration institution was inaccurate, the parties clearly favored institutional arbitration. Furthermore, among the eight existing

---

Arbitration Commission," the court determined that the CIETAC Hong Kong Arbitration Center was the arbitration institution agreed upon by the parties. This finding aligned with the Hong Kong courts' rules for interpreting arbitration clauses and effectively promoted and realized the parties' intention for institutional arbitration.

arbitration institutions in Hong Kong, only the "China International Economic and Trade Arbitration Commission Hong Kong Arbitration Center" used "International Economic and Trade Arbitration Commission" as part of its proper name, which was the closest match to the name stipulated in the arbitration clause. Therefore, the Court determined that the parties had chosen the CIETAC Hong Kong Arbitration Center as the arbitration institution. Accordingly, the court ruled to recognize and enforce the award.

Article 30
An arbitration agreement shall exist independently. The formation, amendment, ineffectiveness, termination, revocation or invalidity of a contract shall not affect the validity of the arbitration agreement that has been reached.

The arbitral tribunal shall have the power to affirm the validity of a contract.

Notes
The independence of an arbitration agreement, also known as "separability" or "autonomy," is one of the core concepts of the arbitration system. Its essential meaning is that the arbitration agreement exists independently from the underlying contract and other contract clauses at the legal level. As a keystone of the arbitration system, this principle aims to ensure the stability and predictability of the dispute resolution mechanism, preventing changes in the validity of the underlying contract from affecting the progress of arbitration proceedings. According to the principle of independence, the validity of the arbitration agreement previously reached by the parties remains unaffected regardless of whether the underlying contract is formed, modified, non-effective, terminated, rescinded or invalidated. This principle has gained broad consensus in both international and domestic arbitration legal systems. For example, Article 16 of the UNCITRAL Model Law explicitly states that the arbitration clause which forms part of a contract shall be treated as an agreement independent of the other terms of the contract. The New Arbitration Law has also incorporated relevant rules, but in practice, the specific circumstances under which an arbitration agreement is deemed independently effective shall be determined on a case-by-case basis and require reasonable analysis based on the facts.

1. **Theoretical Basis for Arbitration Agreement Independence**

The jurisprudential support for arbitration agreement independence primarily stems from the following four aspects, which together form the foundation of its institutional legitimacy:

A. Core Embodiment of the Principle of Autonomy of Will. The parties' agreement to resolve disputes through arbitration is a direct reflection of their true intention. Unless there is evidence to the contrary proving the absence of mutual consent, the law should prioritize respecting the parties' agreement to submit disputes to arbitration. This is an inherent requirement of the "party autonomy" essence of the arbitration system.

B. Extension of the Principle of Contract Severability. Contract clauses are not entirely inseparable; some clauses can exist independently based on specific functions and purposes. The arbitration agreement, as a "collateral agreement" for dispute resolution, serves the function of providing a path for resolving disputes arising during contract performance, possessing specificity and independence distinct from the rights and obligations clauses of the main contract.

C. Practical Necessity for Diversion of Litigation Case Load. With the surge in the number and increasing complexity of civil and commercial disputes, the pressure on court caseloads continues to intensify. Supporting the independence of arbitration agreements helps facilitate the diversion of more dispute to arbitration, thereby achieving a rational allocation of dispute resolution resources and alleviating the burden on the judicial system.

D. International Trend of Pro-Arbitration. From the global adoption of the New York Convention to the revision and improvement of modern arbitration laws in various countries, "pro-arbitration" has become the mainstream direction in international commercial dispute resolution. The principle of arbitration agreement independence is precisely the key institutional mechanism that ensures the efficient progress of arbitration proceedings and maintains the authority of the arbitration system.

2. **Controversies: Relative Theory vs. Absolute Theory**

Regarding whether there are boundaries to the application of arbitration agreement independence, that is, whether the arbitration agreement can be independent of the underlying contract under specific circumstances, there are two opposing views in theory and practice:

Relative Theory. Advocates distinguish the types of defects in the validity of the underlying contract. If the underlying contract is void *ab initio* or fundamentally non-existent, the arbitration agreement should also be void accordingly. The core rationale is that a contract being void *ab initio* or non-existent means the parties never reached a consensus on the underlying contract, and since the arbitration agreement is part of the contract, it naturally lacks a basis for consensus. In such cases, disputes should not be resolved through arbitration.

Absolute Theory. The supporters hold that there is no need to distinguish the specific circumstances of defects in the validity of the underlying contract; the independence of the arbitration agreement should apply throughout. If the substantive issues have not been heard, the arbitral tribunal cannot pre-judge whether the claim that the arbitration agreement does not exist or is invalid is true. At this point, regardless of adopting the relative or absolute theory, if different bodies accept the case first, it may fall into the dilemma of "which comes first, determining the contract's validity or confirming the arbitration agreement's validity?" Therefore, the specific handling depends on the legal provisions of each country and the approach of the judicial authorities towards arbitration.

3. **Impacts of the New Arbitration Law**

Article 19 of the Arbitration Law (2017), while establishing the principle of the independence of arbitration agreement, only lists four situations: "modification, rescission, termination, or invalidity of the contract." It did not cover key defective states such as "non-establishment of the contract" or "non-effectiveness of the contract," leading to legislative gaps and practical disputes. For instance, when the main contract is not established *ab initio* due to lack of signature or seal by one party, or is not effective due to unfulfilled conditions like approval or registration, does the included arbitration agreement fail as well, based on the principle "when the skin (main contract) is gone, the hair (arbitration clause) cannot adhere"?

In fact, even before the 2025 revision, China's judicial practice had clearly shown a trend supporting the "Absolute Theory":

The SPC, through judicial case practice and the release of several guiding cases,[22] explicitly stated that the determination of the existence and establishment of an arbitration agreement should be independent of the review of the main contract's validity. This essentially extended the scope of application of the independence principle to the preliminary issue of "whether the contract is established." Article 10 of the Arbitration Law Interpretation clearly stipulates that if the parties have reached an arbitration agreement on disputes when concluding the contract, the fact that the contract is not established does not affect the validity of the arbitration agreement.

The New Arbitration Law adjusted the original Article 19 to Article 30. The core change is the incorporation into the legislative text of the consensus formed in judicial practice that "non-establishment or non-effectiveness of the contract does not affect the validity of the arbitration agreement," thoroughly implementing the principle of "priority to the parties' arbitration agreement." The jurisprudential basis for this revision is that the true intention of the parties to resolve disputes through arbitration, with the core being "resolving disputes through arbitration rather than litigation when disputes arise, should not necessarily be negated simply because the main contract has defects in its formation or effectiveness. The introduction of the new provision ensures that the initial agreement of the parties to resolve disputes receives legal recognition and is given continuing effect.

4. The Connection between the Principles of Independence and *Kompetenz-Kompetenz*

It is important to clarify that the independence of the arbitration agreement refers to "the standards and procedures for determining the validity of the arbitration agreement are separate from those for determining the validity of the main contract," not that "the arbitration agreement is necessarily valid." Whether the arbitration agreement is valid still needs to be examined and confirmed through statutory procedures, and the arbitral tribunal has the power to review this. If the arbitral tribunal determines that the arbitration agreement is invalid, it should terminate the proceedings and may not continue to exercise jurisdiction.

[22] For example, *Yunyu Company v. Zhongyuan Company* (Guiding Case No. 196).

Based on the severability of the arbitration clause, claims or findings regarding the validity of the main contract do not affect the review of the arbitration clause's validity. The arbitral tribunal should still accept the case based on the arbitration clause, but must first make a decision on its own jurisdiction. This involves the "*Kompetenz-Kompetenz*" principle in the arbitration system, meaning that regardless of adopting the relative or absolute theory, the arbitral tribunal first enjoys the "competence to rule on its own jurisdiction" and has the power to examine and decide whether it has jurisdiction over the case.

Regarding the connotation of the "*Kompetenz-Kompetenz*" principle, there are two major understandings:

A. ***Principle in the Strict Sense***. Advocates of this understanding maintain that the arbitral tribunals shall have the ultimate authority to determine their own jurisdiction, and this decision is not subject to judicial power. However, this model grants excessive power to the arbitral tribunal and has gradually been abandoned by few jurisdictions. For example, Germany, the country of origin of this principle, abolished the provision that "parties may authorize the arbitral tribunal to make a final decision on jurisdiction" when revising the German Arbitration Act 1998. The original version allowed parties to agree that jurisdiction issues fall under the exclusive jurisdiction of the arbitral tribunal, excluding court intervention. After the revision, it clearly stated that in any case, the issue of the arbitral tribunal's jurisdiction shall be ultimately decided by the court.

B. ***Principle in the Broad Sense***. Advocates of this understanding hold that the arbitral tribunal shall have the power to examine and decide on its own jurisdiction, but this decision is not final and remains subject to judicial supervision. This is the mainstream model in international commercial arbitration today. Most countries, while establishing the severability of the arbitration agreement in their legislation, adopt this kind of "*Kompetenz-Kompetenz*" principle, both ensuring the procedural authority of the arbitral tribunal and protecting the legitimate rights and interests of the parties through judicial supervision, achieving a balance between arbitration efficiency and judicial fairness.

In judicial practice, Chinese courts, based on a pro-arbitration stance, apply the principle of independence of arbitration agreements to determine the validity of arbitration agreements. In ***Ningbo A Biotechnology Company et al. v. Shanghai A Technology Company***, based on the concept of supporting arbitration and fully respecting the legislative intent and party autonomy, the court interpreted the independence of the arbitration agreement in good faith, clarifying that the establishment of an arbitration clause can be independent of the underlying contractual relationship. It interpreted this in conjunction with the contract negotiation process and transaction background such as announcements released by the listed company, determining that an agreement had been reached regarding the offer and acceptance of the arbitration clause, thereby confirming the validity of the arbitration agreement. This interpretive approach serves as a reference for similar cases.

Illustrative Cases

Case 1: *Ningbo X Biotechnology Company and others v. Shanghai Y Technology Company*[23]

The respondent, Shanghai Y Technology Company, intended to acquire the equity of the claimant, Ningbo X Biotechnology Company. In March 2022, the respondent sent the Equity Acquisition Agreement, which had been negotiated and finalized by both parties, to the claimant, requesting that the claimant sign first. The "Dispute Resolution" clause therein stipulated that any disputes should be settled by arbitration by the Shanghai International Arbitration Center. After the agreement was signed by the claimant and other transferors, it was delivered to the respondent for its signature and seal. As a listed company, the respondent subsequently issued announcements regarding the involved transaction, disclosing all key elements of the Equity Acquisition Agreement and directly quoting the aforementioned arbitration clause. In July 2022, the respondent returned all originals of the Equity Acquisition Agreement, which it had not signed, to the claimant and refused to execute the agreement. The claimant argued that although the respondent had not signed the Equity Acquisition Agreement, both parties had reached an agreement on the arbitration clause, and therefore requested the court to confirm that the arbitration clause in the Equity Acquisition Agreement was effective for all parties. The Court ultimately ruled to confirm the validity of the arbitration clause in the Equity Acquisition Agreement.

The Court held that an arbitration clause was independent, and its formation and validity should be examined independently from the other clauses of the contract. Based on the negotiation process of the Equity Acquisition Agreement in this case, the parties had exchanged the agreement containing the arbitration clause during negotiations with the intent to conclude a contract. The final version of the contract was sent by the respondent, and the claimant had delivered the signed original agreement to the respondent. The respondent, through its listed company announcements, admitted that the Equity Acquisition Agreement had been signed and disclosed the involved arbitration clause in the "Dispute Resolution" section. There was no evidence proving that the respondent had raised any objection to the arbitration clause. Although the respondent did not sign or seal the Equity Acquisition

[23] See the 10 Typical Cases on Judicial Review of Arbitration from 2020–2024 published by the Shanghai High People's Court in July 2025. Generally, an insurance contract consists of the insurance application form, the insurance policy, and the insurance terms and conditions. When there is an inconsistency between the application form and the policy regarding the agreed method of dispute resolution, determining which document governs often becomes the core issue in applications filed by the parties to confirm the validity of an arbitration agreement. The insurance application form is signed and sealed by the policyholder, and its contents represent the genuine intent of the policyholder. The insurer should issue the insurance policy based on the dispute resolution method stipulated in the application form (with litigation being the default if none is specified). If the dispute resolution clause contained in the issued policy differs from the one agreed upon in the application form, the insurer must specifically draw this discrepancy to the policyholder's attention, provide an explanation, and obtain the policyholder's consent. Otherwise, the arbitration clause contained in the policy will not be effective against the policyholder, as it lacks the policyholder's expression of intent to submit disputes to arbitration.

Agreement, based on the principle of the independence of the arbitration agreement, the parties had reached a consensus on the arbitration clause contained within the Equity Acquisition Agreement. Therefore, the involved arbitration clause was valid.

Case 2: *J Company v. P Insurance Company*[24]
In August 2020, J Company applied for insurance from P Insurance Company for its construction project and affixed its seal to the Application Form. The "Dispute Resolution" section of the Application Form provided options for "Litigation" and "Arbitration," and specified the Shanghai Arbitration Commission as the arbitration institution, but J Company did not select any option. In September 2020, P Insurance Company issued the Insurance Policy, which stipulated arbitration as the dispute resolution method and designated the S Arbitration Commission as the institution; the attached Insurance Clauses also stipulated that disputes shall be submitted to the arbitration institution specified in the Insurance Policy. In August 2023, P Insurance Company applied for arbitration to the arbitration institution based on the arbitration clause in the Insurance Policy. After the arbitration institution accepted the case, J Company applied to the court, requesting confirmation that no valid arbitration agreement existed between the parties.

The Shanghai Financial Court held that Article 14 of the Insurance Law Interpretation stated that where the contents recorded in an insurance contract are inconsistent, they shall be determined according to the following rules: "If the contents recorded in an insurance contract are inconsistent, they shall be determined according to the following rules: (1) Where the insurance application form is inconsistent with the insurance policy or other insurance certificate, the insurance application form shall prevail, unless such inconsistency arises from the insurer's explanation and the policyholder's consent, in which case the contents recorded in the insurance policy or other insurance certificate signed and received by the policyholder shall prevail; (2) Where non-standard terms are inconsistent with standard terms, the non-standard terms shall prevail." In the present case, first, although J Company had affixed its seal to the Application Form when completing it, it did not clearly select either litigation or arbitration in the "Dispute Resolution" section. Therefore, it was difficult to establish that J Company had the intention to submit disputes related to the insurance contract to arbitration at the time of application. Second, the Insurance Policy was a standard form issued by P Insurance Company. Although it contained a clause submitting disputes to arbitration, there was no evidence proving that P Insurance Company had prompted, explained, and obtained J Company's consent regarding the dispute resolution clause in the Insurance Policy. Given that J Company explicitly denied agreeing to the dispute resolution method in the Insurance Policy, this clause was not effective against J Company. Furthermore, according to Article 1 of the Insurance Clauses attached to the Insurance Policy, the insurance contract consisted of the Application Form, the Insurance Policy or other insurance certificates, and the attached clauses, etc. There was a clear inconsistency

[24] See the Typical Cases on Judicial Review of Financial Arbitration published by the Shanghai Financial Court in November 2024.

in the dispute resolution methods stipulated between the Application Form and the Insurance Policy within the involved insurance contract, and the insurer had not clearly explained such inconsistency to the claimant and obtained its consent. Finally, the Insurance Policy issued by the insurer in this case made a substantive change to the dispute resolution method content in the Application Form filled out by the claimant. The content regarding the dispute resolution method in the Insurance Policy constituted a new offer. The dispute resolution clause is of an independent nature in the contract and is of significant interest to the parties. The insurer's new offer regarding the dispute resolution method required the claimant's explicit acceptance. The act of paying the insurance premium shall not be deemed as the claimant's implied acceptance of the insurer's new offer. Consequently, no valid arbitration agreement existed between J Company and P Insurance Company.

Case 3: *H Securities Company v. L Bank*[25]

H Securities Company was the manager of a certain trust beneficiary rights asset-backed special plan. L Bank entered into a Subscription Agreement with H Securities Company to subscribe to asset-backed securities. Article 5 of the Subscription Agreement stipulated that the Plan Description and the Standard Terms, together with the Subscription Agreement, constituted the asset management contract executed between the claimant and the respondent. The template texts of the Plan Description, the Standard Terms, and the Subscription Agreement were uniformly drafted by H Securities Company and uploaded by it to the Shanghai Stock Exchange's Bond Filing and Review System before September 2017. Among these documents, the arbitration clause stipulated in the Plan Description was that disputes be submitted to C Arbitration Commission for arbitration in Shenzhen in accordance with its then-effective arbitration rules. The arbitration clause stipulated in the Standard Terms was that disputes be submitted to C Arbitration Commission for arbitration in Shanghai in accordance with its then-effective arbitration rules. The arbitration clause in the Subscription Agreement stipulated that disputes be submitted to S Arbitration Commission for arbitration in Shanghai in accordance with its rules. In February 2024, S Arbitration Commission rendered an arbitral award. H Securities Company applied to the Shanghai Financial Court to set aside the arbitral award on the grounds that S Arbitration Commission lacked jurisdiction.

The Shanghai Financial Court held that the arbitration clause in a contract text existed independently, and its formation and validity were separate and severable from the other clauses of the contract. Therefore, the different arbitration clauses in the three documents in this case should be considered separately from the other

[25] See the 10 Typical Cases on Judicial Review of Financial Arbitration published by the Shanghai Financial Court in October 2024. The three bond issuance documents involved in this case stipulated three different arbitration clauses. Based on the principle of independence, the incorporation of other contract clauses and the incorporation of arbitration clauses should be considered separately. In this case, the court confirmed the formation and effectiveness of the arbitration clause stipulated in the "Subscription Agreement" by considering both the form of the arbitration clause texts and the intention of the parties.

contract clauses regarding their formation and effectiveness. The incorporation of other contract clauses did not imply the incorporation of the arbitration clauses.

First, regarding the form of the parties' expression of intent towards the three arbitration clauses, only the text of the Subscription Agreement bore the signatures and seals of both H Securities Company and L Bank. The Plan Description and Standard Terms did not bear L Bank's signature or seal. Although the signing or sealing of the Plan Description and Standard Terms did not affect the fact that their other clauses formed part of the transaction documents, the arbitration clauses contained within the Plan Description and Standard Terms lacked a separate expression of intent from L Bank in the form of signature or seal.

Second, regarding the substance of the parties' expression of intent towards the three arbitration clauses, the Subscription Agreement was signed after negotiation between the parties. The filling in of corresponding content and changes to clauses reflected, from a different perspective, that the parties had reached a consensus on the content agreed in this text through the exchange of intentions. Furthermore, both H Securities Company and L Bank acknowledged in this case that the Plan Description and Standard Terms constituted invitations to treat, only becoming part of the overall contract after the Subscription Agreement was signed. Therefore, although the standard texts of the three documents were uniformly created, the negotiation and finalization of the Subscription Agreement text occurred afterward. Thus, it should be considered that the parties reached a final, separate agreement on the arbitration clause stated in the Subscription Agreement. The arbitration clauses stipulated in the Plan Descriptions and Standard Terms were not formed due to the lack of a mutual expression of intent by the parties. Accordingly, the Court ruled to dismiss H Securities Company's claims.

Article 31

Where a party challenges the validity of an arbitration agreement, they may request the arbitration institution or arbitral tribunal to make a decision or apply to the people's court for a ruling. Where one party requests the arbitration institution or arbitral tribunal to make a decision and the other party applies to the people's court for a ruling, the people's court shall render a ruling.

A party's challenge of the validity of the arbitration agreement shall be raised prior to the arbitral tribunal's first hearing.

Notes

Raising a jurisdictional challenge before the arbitration institution or filing an application with the court to confirm the validity of an arbitration agreement is one of the most common procedural tactics in arbitration, also most easily used as a delay strategy. Without clear rules, parties might submit the same challenge separately to both the arbitration institution and the court, leading to conflicts of "parallel proceedings," resulting in wasted resources and uncertainty regarding the award's validity. Furthermore, the respondent might deliberately raise a challenge at a late stage of the arbitration proceedings, or even after the award is rendered, severely undermining procedural efficiency and the legitimate rights and interests of the other party. The existence of this clause aims precisely to close these procedural loopholes. It respects the power of the arbitration institution or the arbitral tribunal to decide on its jurisdiction, while also establishing the court's ultimate decision-making authority when the parties' choices conflict, reflecting the principle of coexistence of judicial support and supervision over arbitration.

In China's arbitration practice, both arbitration institutions and courts have the authority to determine the validity of an arbitration agreement. If a party raises an objection to the validity of an arbitration agreement and one party applies to an arbitration institution for confirmation while the other party requests a people's court to declare the agreement invalid, the people's court shall not accept the case if the arbitration institution accepted the application and rendered a decision prior to the court. If the arbitration institution has accepted the application but has not yet rendered a decision, the people's court shall accept the case and simultaneously notify the arbitration institution to suspend the arbitration proceedings.

Traditionally, in arbitration proceedings administered by Chinese arbitration institutions, the arbitral tribunal does not directly accept parties' requests to decide on challenges to the validity of the arbitration agreement. The Arbitration Law (2017) vested this decision-making power in the "arbitration commission". Although in recent arbitration practice, arbitration institution typically authorize the arbitral tribunal to make such decisions, this discrepancy in the legislative text remains a distinctive feature of Chinese arbitration law. After the 2025 revision, a party challenging the validity of the arbitration agreement may request a decision from either the arbitration institution or the arbitral tribunal. Literally, this could be a tribunal under the administration of an arbitration institution, or an *ad ho*c tribunal. Thus, the concept of *Kompetenz-Kompetenz* has been formally codified in the Chinese arbitration legislation.

The principle of *Kompetenz-Kompetenz* is one of the fundamental principles of modern commercial arbitration law. Its core connotation is that the arbitral tribunal has the power to rule on its own jurisdiction, including the power to decide on the existence, validity, and scope of the arbitration agreement. In short, it means the arbitral tribunal has the authority to decide on its own jurisdiction. This principle aims to vest the power to determine jurisdiction primarily in the arbitral tribunal itself, rather than the courts, thereby safeguarding the efficiency and independence of the arbitration proceedings.

Modern arbitration law generally tends to support and encourage dispute resolution through arbitration. *Kompetenz-Kompetenz* is a specific manifestation of this policy inclination, empowering the arbitral tribunal to initiate proceedings and exclude improper interference. If any jurisdictional challenge had to be first submitted to a court for adjudication, it would repeatedly interrupt the arbitration proceedings, causing serious delays and waste of resources. *Kompetenz-Kompetenz* ensures that the arbitration proceedings can "commence first," preventing parties from employing delay tactics by abusively raising jurisdictional challenges.

However, *Kompetenz-Kompetenz* is not an absolute or unlimited principle. The arbitral tribunal's power to decide on its jurisdiction does not exclude the ultimate supervision of the courts but rather forms a coordinated mechanism of "parallel and staged" review. The typical model is that the arbitral tribunal decides first, subject to subsequent court supervision. When a party raises a jurisdictional challenge, the mainstream approach is to encourage the arbitral tribunal to first exercise its *Kompetenz-Kompetenz*, make a preliminary or final decision, and continue advancing the arbitration proceedings. During this period, the courts generally do not intervene. Courts generally exercise subsequent supervision over the arbitral tribunal's decision, primarily at two stages:

Stage One: Setting aside proceedings regarding the jurisdiction decision. After the arbitral tribunal rules that it has jurisdiction and subsequently renders a substantive award, the other party may request judicial review by the court in proceedings to set aside the arbitral award, citing the lack of jurisdiction of the arbitral tribunal.
Stage Two: Review at the stage of setting aside or enforcing the award. When applying to set aside or enforce an arbitral award, a party may request the court to set aside or refuse enforcement of the award on the grounds that the arbitral tribunal lacked jurisdiction.

It is also important to note that this Article stipulates parties may raise challenges either with the arbitration institution or with the court, but when there is a conflict, the court has the superseding authority to decide. This, to some extent, weakens the effect of *Kompetenz-Kompetenz*, as a party can interrupt the arbitration at an early stage by filing a lawsuit with the court.

The second paragraph stipulates that the challenge must be raised before the first hearing of the arbitral tribunal, preventing malicious delay of the arbitration proceedings. If the parties have already invested significant resources in substantive defense and hearings, only to have the preliminary proceedings nullified due to a challenge that could have been raised earlier, it would cause enormous waste of resources. Failure to raise the challenge within the time limit is deemed in law to constitute a waiver by the party of its right to object and implicitly accepting the jurisdiction of the arbitral tribunal.

Illustrative Cases

Case 1: *Hui A Company and others v. Hua B Bank*[26]

[26] See the 10 Typical Cases on Judicial Review of Arbitration published by the High People's Court of Guangdong Province in February 2024. Challenging the validity of an arbitration agreement is a right conferred upon the parties by law. In situations where neither of the parties has raised an objection to the validity of the arbitration agreement, the fact that an arbitration institution proceeds to examine and make a determination on its own initiative does not affect the parties' right to apply to a people's court for confirmation of the arbitration agreement's validity in accordance with the law. As long as the application submitted by the parties meets the time limit requirements stipulated in the Arbitration Law (2017), the people's court shall conduct a review to safeguard the parties' right to raise objections regarding the validity of the arbitration agreement before a judicial authority.

Hua A Bank (the lender) and Zhou (the borrower) signed a Personal Micro-loan Contract, which stipulated that disputes arising from the contract shall be submitted to X Arbitration Institution for arbitration. Hui A Company and Yang separately signed Maximum Amount Guarantee Contracts with Hua A Bank, agreeing to provide guarantee liability for Zhou's loan, and stipulating that contract disputes shall be resolved according to the method agreed in the main loan contract. Hua A Bank applied for arbitration to X Arbitration Institution based on the involved arbitration clause. After accepting the case, X Arbitration Institution promptly issued a Decision, affirming that the involved arbitration clause was legal and valid and that the case fell within its jurisdiction. It then served the arbitration application, arbitration rules, and the aforementioned Decision to both Hui A Company and Yang. Subsequently, Hui A Company and Yang applied to the Guangdong Province Guangzhou Intermediate People's Court to confirm the invalidity of the involved arbitration clause. Hui A Company, Yang, and Hua A Bank all confirmed that no party had filed an application for objection to jurisdiction with X Arbitration Institution.

The Guangdong Province Guangzhou Intermediate People's Court held that although X Arbitration Institution had already issued a Decision affirming the legality and validity of the involved arbitration clause and its jurisdiction over the dispute, this Decision was not made in response to any party's challenge as to the validity of the arbitration agreement. Now, Hui A Company and Yang applied to the Court to confirm the invalidity of the involved arbitration clause. Pursuant to Article 20(2) of the Arbitration Law (2017), the Court determined that the involved arbitration clause was legal and valid. Consequently, the Court ruled to dismiss the claims of Hui A Company and Yang.

Case 2: *Lin v. X Education Technology Company*[27]

Lin and X Education Technology Company entered into the Intellectual Property Agreement, which stipulated that any dispute arising from or related to the contract shall be submitted to the SCIA for arbitration. Neither party had applied for arbitration by an arbitration institution nor filed a lawsuit regarding the performance of the contract. Lin applied to the people's court to confirm the invalidity of the arbitration agreement. The court of first instance, after review, held that Article 20 of the Arbitration Law (2017) stipulated that if a party challenged the validity of the arbitration agreement, the challenge must be raised prior to the arbitral tribunal's first hearing. According to this article, parties could only seek the people's court to rule on a dispute concerning the validity of an arbitration agreement after arbitration proceedings had commenced. As the parties in this case had not applied for

[27] See the 2nd batch of the 10 Typical Cases on Judicial Review of Arbitration published by the High People's Court of Guangdong Province in August 2025. This case clarifies that parties have the right to directly confirm the validity of an arbitration agreement through judicial proceedings before a dispute arises, and clarifies the application of relevant legal rules.

arbitration to an arbitration institution, the application did not meet the prerequisite. Consequently, the court ruled to dismiss Lin's claim. Lin appealed.

The court of the second instance held that according to Article 20 of the Arbitration Law (2017), which provided that if a party challenged the validity of an arbitration agreement, they could request the arbitration commission to make a decision or apply to the people's court for a ruling. Where one party requested the arbitration commission to make a decision while the other party applied to the people's court for a ruling, the people's court would have the authority to rule. Any challenge to the validity of an arbitration agreement had to be raised before the first hearing of the arbitral tribunal. This meant that the existing law did not require the existence of an actual dispute or the initiation of arbitration proceedings as a precondition for a party to apply to the people's court to determine the validity of an arbitration agreement. Where a party applied for confirmation of the validity of an arbitration agreement even before any dispute had arisen, the people's court should accept the case. Accordingly, the court set aside the first instance ruling and instructed the court of the first instance to hear the case. that according to Article 20 of the Arbitration Law (2017), which provided that if a party challenged the validity of an arbitration agreement, they could request the arbitration commission to make a decision or apply to the people's court for a ruling. Where one party requested the arbitration commission to make a decision while the other party applied to the people's court for a ruling, the people's court would have the authority to rule. Any challenge to the validity of an arbitration agreement had to be raised before the first hearing of the arbitral tribunal. This meant that the existing law did not require the existence of an actual dispute or the initiation of arbitration proceedings as a precondition for a party to apply to the people's court to determine the validity of an arbitration agreement. Where a party applied for confirmation of the validity of an arbitration agreement even before any dispute had arisen, the people's court should accept the case. Accordingly, the court set aside the first instance ruling and instructed the court of the first instance to hear the case.

Chapter 4
Arbitration Proceedings

Section 1 Application and Acceptance

Article 32
A party's application for arbitration shall meet the following requirements:

(1) **There is an arbitration agreement;**
(2) **There are specific arbitration claims, relevant facts and reasons; and**
(3) **The application is within the scope of the arbitration institution's jurisdiction.**

Notes
This Article stipulates the conditions that must be met for a party to apply for arbitration. Applying for arbitration refers to the act whereby natural persons, legal persons, and other organizations of equal status, regarding contractual disputes and other disputes over property rights and interests that have arisen between them, submit the dispute to the relevant arbitration institution for arbitration based on an arbitration agreement concluded either beforehand or afterwards. After a dispute arises, either party to the dispute may, in accordance with an arbitration agreement concluded between the parties before or after the dispute arose, submit an application for arbitration to the chosen arbitration institution according to law. The arbitration process is initiated by a party's application for arbitration. The arbitration process truly begins only after the arbitration application is accepted upon review. A party's submission of an arbitration application does not guarantee its acceptance. To prevent parties from abusing their rights and wasting arbitration resources, and to ensure the arbitration process proceeds on a legal, standardized, and effective track from the outset, a party's application for arbitration must meet the basic conditions stipulated by law.

The principle of party autonomy is the cornerstone of the arbitration system. Unlike the judicial power of courts, which derives from state authority, the jurisdiction of arbitration derives entirely from the expression of intent of the parties. This

Y. Lin, *New Arbitration Law in China*, China Arbitration Yearbook,
https://doi.org/10.1007/978-981-92-0642-1_4

requires that the initiation of arbitration proceedings must be based on an arbitration agreement between the parties. In the absence of an arbitration agreement, initiating arbitration based solely on a unilateral application by one party would infringe upon the other party's statutory right to resolve disputes through litigation, and could also lead to the subsequent award being set aside or denied enforcement by the court due to lack of jurisdictional basis. The jurisdiction of the arbitral tribunal should be confined to the specific arbitration claims, facts, and reasons presented by the parties. This reflects respect for party autonomy on the one hand, and helps safeguard the expertise and efficiency of arbitration on the other. Furthermore, the jurisdiction of the arbitral tribunal should be limited to the types of disputes permitted by law for arbitration and to the arbitration institution selected by the parties in the arbitration agreement, to avoid potential jurisdictional conflicts.

The New Arbitration Law clarifies the minimum formal requirements for initiating arbitration proceedings by enumerating specific conditions, designating the arbitration agreement as the primary condition for accepting a case, and defining the boundaries and basic requirements for the scope of cases that an arbitration institution can accept.

1. **The Requirement of an Arbitration Agreement**

The existence of a valid arbitration agreement between the parties is a mandatory condition. Typically, without an arbitration agreement, parties cannot demand resolution of their dispute through arbitration, and the arbitration institution will not accept the arbitration application submitted by the claimant. In exceptional circumstances, even if no arbitration agreement exists between the parties at the time of application, if one party insists on submitting the dispute to arbitration, the arbitration institution may, after explaining the legal provisions to that party, attempt to accept the case and notify the respondent. If the respondent clearly indicates that it does not object to submitting the dispute to arbitration, the parties may subsequently sign an arbitration agreement, and the arbitration proceedings shall continue.

2. **The Requirement of Specificity**

Arbitration claims refer to the assertions of rights made by the claimant against the respondent. That is, they clarify what issue the party seeks to resolve through arbitration, what obligation the respondent should be required to perform, and thereby what legitimate rights and interests of the claimant should be protected. Arbitration claims shall be clear, specific, and enforceable; they cannot be vague or abstract. Arbitration claims must also be supported by certain facts and reasons, and preliminary evidence should be provided. Facts refer to the objective circumstances, primarily the course of events leading to the dispute. Based on this, the parties shall state the specific reasons, explaining the rationale and legality behind their arbitration claims. Reasons refer to subjective understandings, primarily the party's interpretation of the relationship between the facts, the relevant laws and regulations, and the claims raised.

3. **The Requirement of the Scope of Jurisdiction**

This item actually encompasses two requirements: First, the arbitration institution accepting the party's application for arbitration shall be the institution selected by the parties in their arbitration agreement, or an institution that can be determined based on the arbitration agreement (see detailed provisions in Article 6 of the New Arbitration Law). Second, the matters for which the party applies for arbitration must fall within the scope stipulated in Article 3 of the New Arbitration Law and must not be matters that are legally excluded from arbitration. Specifically, the disputes submitted for arbitration by the parties shall be contractual disputes and other disputes over property rights and interests that arise between citizens, legal persons, and other organizations of equal status. They cannot be disputes concerning marriage, adoption, guardianship, support, or succession, nor disputes that shall by law be handled by administrative organs. If an arbitration institution accepts a dispute that clearly exceeds its authority, the award may be set aside by the court pursuant to the provisions of Chapter V of the New Arbitration Law.

Article 33
Where a party applies for arbitration, they shall submit the arbitration agreement and a written application for arbitration together with copies thereof to the arbitration institution.

Notes
Article 33 supplements Article 32, further clarifying the essential documents that parties must submit when applying for arbitration. From a comparative law perspective, legislation in various jurisdictions and the rules of different arbitration institutions generally require parties to submit documents in a written form. By explicitly listing the three basic items, i.e., "arbitration agreement and a written application for arbitration together with copies thereof to the arbitration institution", this Article helps standardize the initiation of arbitration proceedings, enhances the efficiency of case acceptance, and can reduce procedural delays or jurisdictional disputes caused by incomplete documentation.

The arbitration agreement is a prerequisite for the parties to submit their dispute to arbitration, the legal basis for the arbitral tribunal to hear the parties' dispute, and a crucial precondition for the enforcement of the arbitral award. By submitting the arbitration agreement, the parties demonstrate to the arbitration institution the existence of their mutual consent of arbitration, while also proving that the institution is the forum selected by the parties in their agreement, thereby establishing a legitimate jurisdictional basis for the dispute submitted for arbitration. Current international arbitration legislation generally emphasizes the written form of the arbitration agreement and the genuineness of the expression of intent.

The application for arbitration typically states the specific claims made by the party and the facts and reasons relied upon for applying for arbitration. It is a key condition for initiating arbitration proceedings, serves as an important basis for the arbitration institution to accept the case, decide on the applicable procedures, and collect advance arbitration fees. For the arbitration institution, a written application facilitates a preliminary assessment of whether the dispute falls within its scope of acceptance and aids in notifying the respondent, enabling the respondent to prepare a targeted defense and safeguarding its procedural rights. Furthermore, under the arbitration rules of some institutions, the date the application is submitted is considered the official commencement date of the arbitration proceedings. For instance, Article 11 of the CIETAC Arbitration Rules states that the arbitration proceedings commence on the date the arbitration institution receives the Request for Arbitration. If the claimant submits the application in writing and/or applies through the online case filing system, the proceedings commence on the date of the earliest receipt. Similarly, Article 11(4) of the SCIA Arbitration Rules stipulates that the arbitration proceedings commence on the date the SCIA receives the Notice of Arbitration.

Article 34
A written application for arbitration shall specify the following particulars:

(1) **The name, gender, age, occupation, work unit, domicile, and contact information, or the name and domicile of legal persons or non-legal person organizations and the names, positions and contact information of their legal representatives or chief responsible persons;**
(2) **The arbitration claims and facts and reasons on which it is based; and**
(3) **The evidence, the source of the evidence and the names and domiciles of witnesses.**

Notes
The standardization of the application for arbitration is crucial for ensuring due process and the efficiency of arbitration proceedings. In practice, procedural disputes arising from incomplete content or unstructured formatting of the arbitration application occur from time to time. Examples include: missing party information, such as failure to list the legal representative or contact details, leading to difficulties in serving arbitration documents; ambiguous claims, where arbitration requests lack factual or legal basis, requiring repeated clarification by the arbitral tribunal; and unstructured evidence submission, where the source of evidence or witness information is not specified, hindering the efficiency of fact-finding.

Therefore, Article 34 standardizes the documents submitted by the parties when applying for arbitration by enumerating the essential elements of an application for arbitration. This aims to avoid procedural delays and repetition, safeguard the legitimacy and traceability of arbitration proceedings, and enhance the efficiency of such proceedings. Specifically, the party initiating an arbitration proceeding shall clearly state the following matters:

1. Basic Information of the Parties. This includes the name, gender, age, profession, work unit, domicile, and contact information of the claimant and the respondent. If a party is a legal person or other organization, its name, domicile, and the name, position, and contact information of its legal representative or responsible person shall be stated. If a party has authorized an agent, the basic information of the agent shall be stated after that of the claimant, accompanied by a power of attorney. The claimant shall ensure the information provided is accurate and sufficient.

This facilitates the arbitration institution's review and confirmation of the parties' identities when accepting the case and enables the institution to contact the parties promptly based on this information.

It is advisable for the claimant, when applying for arbitration, to carefully verify the respondent's name and domicile, and to provide the arbitration institution, to the extent possible, with the respondent's last-known contact address and methods, such as postal address, post code, telephone, telex, fax, and email. If the information provided by a party contains errors or omissions, it may lead to defects in service, procedural delays, repetition, or even invalidity. There have been instances in judicial practice where arbitral awards were set aside or enforcement was refused due to defects in service in the arbitration proceedings.

2. Claims, Facts, and Reasons. This constitutes the core content of the application for arbitration. The claimant shall explicitly state the arbitration claims, which should be specific and clear, avoiding vague or overly broad statements. For instance, for monetary claims, the claimed amount or a clear calculation method, including the calculation period and formula, should be listed. For non-monetary claims, the specific action requested or the intended effect of the requested action should be listed. The arbitral tribunal ultimately renders an award based on the claims made by the parties. Therefore, the parties' claims directly determine the focus of the tribunal's examination and findings, consequently affecting the enforceability of the parties' claims.

The claimant shall also provide a detailed description of the disputed facts related to the arbitration claims and accurately elaborate on the basis of the claim, i.e., the legal provisions and contractual agreements; the reasoning should be sufficient and logically clear. Where multiple claims are involved, their internal logic should be reasonable, avoiding contradictions.

3. Evidence and the Source of Evidence. Article 55 of the New Arbitration Law stipulates that the parties shall provide evidence in support of their assertions. Therefore, when submitting an application for arbitration, the claimant shall simultaneously provide necessary evidence, indicate the sources of evidence, and provide the names and domiciles of witnesses. This Article, on one hand, encourages the claimant to present the true circumstances of the case and prevents abuse of rights; on the other hand, it facilitates verification of relevant facts by the arbitral tribunal and, if necessary, allows for appropriate investigation, thereby enabling timely resolution of the case. Evidence must possess authenticity, legality, and relevance. For witness evidence, the witness's name, domicile, and contact information should be listed, and identity verification documents should be submitted if necessary; for electronic evidence, it is advisable to prepare the original storage media or notarized documents in advance.

Additionally, the application for arbitration shall state the name of the arbitration institution and the date of submission. The claimant shall also sign or affix its seal. In practice, arbitration institutions typically specify the detailed contents required in the application for arbitration within their arbitration rules, or provide templates for the claimant's reference.

Illustrative Case

Singapore M Company v. Ningbo N Company[1]

Singapore M Company (seller) and Ningbo N Company (buyer) entered into a contract for the sale of oil, with payment by irrevocable letter of credit. The contract stipulated that the method for resolving disputes was to apply for arbitration at SIAC. Subsequently, the parties proceeded to arbitration in Singapore concerning a dispute under the underlying contract. After the Zhejiang Province Ningbo Intermediate People's Court accepted the case concerning an alleged letter of credit fraud filed by the buyer, the seller subsequently applied to the Court to confirm the validity of the arbitration agreement. This application included a request to confirm that the following disputes constituted the agreed matters for arbitration and fell within the scope of the valid arbitration agreement: a) the place of shipment of the goods; b) the country of origin of the goods; c) the probative value of the Certificate of Origin, bill of lading, and related documents regarding the performance of the contract; etc.

The Zhejiang Province Ningbo Intermediate People's Court held that the arbitration agreement stipulated in the contract involved in the case was valid, and disputes related to the contract, including those arising from its formation, validity, modification, or termination, should all fall within the matters for arbitration. However, the scope of arbitration was confined to disputes related to the underlying contract. The legal relationship under the letter of credit was independent of the underlying contractual relationship, and no grounds under the underlying contract could affect the letter of credit legal relationship. The aforementioned findings of fact regarding the place of shipment and origin were not themselves claims in litigation or applications for arbitration, that is, they did not constitute so-called "disputes" under the arbitration agreement. Therefore, such a request did not fall within the scope of judicial review of the arbitration agreement by the Court. Singapore M Company sought to preclude the Court's authority to determine relevant facts through this case, thereby challenging the Court's jurisdiction over the letter of credit dispute. This view was inconsistent with legal provisions and was not accepted. The Court accordingly dismissed the relevant application filed by the Singapore company.

Article 35

Where an arbitration institution receives a written application for arbitration and considers that the application complies with the conditions for acceptance, it shall accept the application and notify the claimant within five days from the date of receipt. Where the arbitration institution considers that the application does not comply with the conditions for acceptance, it shall inform the claimant in writing of its rejection of the application and explain the reasons for rejection.

[1] See the 10 Typical Cases on Judicial Review of Arbitration published by the Zhejiang Province Ningbo Intermediate People's Court in June 2024. This case delineates the jurisdictional boundaries and establishes principles between litigation concerning domestic letter of credit disputes and arbitration concerning the underlying international trade dispute. In international judicial practice, courts and arbitral tribunals are permitted to hold differing opinions regarding the determination of the same objective factual situation and the legal significance attributed to those facts in litigation or arbitration arising from the same legal facts. One party cannot seek to negate the court's jurisdiction over a letter of credit dispute by attempting to exclude the court's power to determine relevant facts.

Notes

While the preceding two Articles address the conditions and required materials for parties submitting an arbitration application, this Article primarily governs the arbitration institution, specifying the time limit for its review of applications for acceptance and its obligation to notify the parties of the outcome of such reivew.

In institutional arbitration, after parties submit the documents required for applying for arbitration, as stipulated by law and arbitration rules, the arbitration institution conducts a preliminary review of the application. The arbitration institution has the authority to decide whether to accept the case. Acceptance is a crucial milestone in the arbitration process; under the rules of some arbitration institutions, acceptance marks the official commencement of the arbitration proceedings.

If the arbitration institution delays in processing the arbitration application, it will leave the parties' procedural rights in a state of prolonged uncertainty, potentially affecting the protection of their substantive rights and interests. If the arbitration institution, after review, decides not to accept the arbitration application, it has an obligation to ensure procedural transparency and fairness, to inform the party of the reasons for its decision, so that the party can decide whether or how to seek other remedies. Efficiency and speed are significant advantages of arbitration, which impose higher demands for the expeditious progress of every stage of the arbitration process. Therefore, the law specifies the time limit for the arbitration institution to review and decide on accepting a party's arbitration application and stipulates the arbitration institution's obligation to provide written notice when it decides not to accept the application. This aims to uphold the efficiency, fairness, transparency, and predictability of arbitration, safeguarding the parties' procedural and substantive rights.

Acceptance refers to the act whereby the arbitration institution, after receiving a party's arbitration application and upon review finding that it meets the statutory conditions for applying for arbitration, decides to accept it and begins organizing and conducting the arbitration activities. The conditions for acceptance here refer to the three conditions for applying for arbitration stipulated in Article 32 of the New Arbitration Law. In practice, arbitration institutions review the submitted arbitration application regarding the following aspects: the existence of a written arbitration agreement; whether the arbitration institution has jurisdiction, including reviewing whether the matters for arbitration exceed the scope prescribed by law and whether the parties have selected that institution as the adjudicating body; whether the parties to the arbitration are appropriate; and whether the application for arbitration sets put specific claims, facts, and reasons, and is accompanied by corresponding evidentiary materials, etc. Regarding the review of arbitration applications, arbitration institutions generally adopt a liberal approach, meaning they will typically register the case as long as they find a clear expression of intent to arbitration by the parties, clear claims, and corresponding evidence. Any ambiguities in the interpretation of the arbitration agreement that might arise are often left to be resolved at the stage of deciding on jurisdiction, aiming to hear both parties' views for a fair determination.

The law requires the arbitration institution to decide whether to accept the case within five days from the date of receiving the application for arbitration and to notify the claimant. If the decision is to accept the case, the claimant may be notified orally or in writing; if the decision is not to accept the case, the claimant must be notified in writing, and the reasons for non-acceptance should be provided. This ensures the party understands why the application was not accepted, allowing them to pursue other avenues for dispute resolution and rights protection. The five-day period stipulated in this Article is calculated from the day following the arbitration institution's receipt of the application for arbitration, excluding the day of receipt itself. If the application materials lack non-essential content (such as missing copies of evidence), the arbitration institution may request supplementation; the period taken for such supplementation shall not be included in the five-day time limit.

Article 36
After an arbitration institution accepts an application for arbitration, it shall, within the time limit specified in the arbitration rules, deliver a copy of the arbitration rules and the panel of arbitrators to the claimant, and serve one copy of the application for arbitration together with the arbitration rules and the panel of arbitrators on the respondent.

After receiving the copy of the application for arbitration, the respondent shall submit a written defense to the arbitration institution within the time limit specified in the arbitration rules. After receiving the written defense, the arbitration institution shall serve a copy thereof on the claimant within the time limit specified in the arbitration rules. The respondent's failure to submit a written defense shall not affect the progress of the arbitration proceedings.

Notes
The right to defense is a fundamental right of the respondent. Through the defense, the respondent responds to the claimant's application and presents their own position. This facilitates the clarification of the facts of the case and resolving the dispute between the parties. If the respondent fails to defend for reasons not attributable to itself, it may affect the efficiency of the arbitration and the enforcement of the award. If the respondent fails to defend or fails to defend adequately due to its own reasons, it will affect its own rights and interests. The respondent should submit a Statement of Defense within the time limit specified in the arbitration institution's rules; however, failure by the respondent to submit it within this period does not affect the continuation of the arbitration proceedings. After receiving the copy of the application for arbitration, the respondent shall submit a statement of defense within the time limit prescribed by the arbitration rules. The arbitration institution shall, upon receiving the statement of defense, serve a copy thereof to the claimant within the time limit prescribed by the arbitration rules. Failure of the respondent to submit a statement of defense does not affect the continuation of the arbitration proceedings.

This Article stipulates the arbitration institution's obligation to serve documents after accepting an arbitration application and the procedure for the respondent's defense. It is a crucial step after the initiation of arbitration proceedings to safeguard the parties' right to know, right to participate, and right to debate. Paragraph 1 requires the arbitration institution to serve the applicable arbitration rules and the panel of arbitrators on the claimant, and to serve a copy of the application for arbitration submitted by the claimant, the arbitration rules, and the panel of arbitrators on the respondent, all within the time limit specified in the arbitration rules. This Article aims to ensure that both parties are promptly informed of the procedural rules and the range of available arbitrators, laying the groundwork for subsequent procedures (such as arbitrator selection and defense preparation).

Service must be conducted in a lawful and effective manner. In arbitration practice, the most common methods include personal service, service by mail, and service by leaving the documents at the recipient's address. Where the parties have agreed upon a method of service, that agreed method shall prevail. Service by public announcement is not applicable in arbitration. However, arbitration rules typically stipulate circumstances under which service is deemed to have been effectuated. For example, Article 6(3) of the SCIA Arbitration Rules stipulates that arbitration documents, notices, or materials sent by the Court to a party or its representative(s) shall be deemed to have been served under any of the following circumstances: (1) When delivered to any one of the following addresses of the recipient: place of business, registered address, domicile, registered residence address, address on identity card, any address confirmed orally or in writing to the institute; any effective address used publicly, the address specified in the parties' agreement, or any other contact address that the institution deems appropriate; (2) When, after reasonable inquiry, none of the addresses specified above can be found, and the documents are sent by mail or by any other means capable of providing a delivery record to the last known contact address of the recipient; (3) When, after the party or its representative(s) has received arbitration documents, notices, or materials served by the Court and subsequently changes its address without notifying the Court, the Court sends subsequent arbitration documents, notices, or materials to the original address where service was effected.

Paragraph 2 of this Article concerns the defense. An arbitration defense refers to the act of the respondent in an arbitration case replying and arguing against the arbitration claims and the facts and reasons relied upon and put forward by the claimant in the Application for Arbitration, in order to protect their own rights and interests. This paragraph contains three aspects. First, after receiving the aforementioned documents served by the arbitration institution, the respondent shall submit a statement of defense to the arbitration institution within the time limit prescribed by the arbitration rules. In practice, the defense periods stipulated in different arbitration rules vary slightly. Second, the arbitration institution shall promptly serve the statement of defense and other materials submitted by the respondent to the claimant. During the arbitration process, in principle, all case-related materials submitted by any party should be promptly transmitted by the arbitration institution to the other parties. Failure to do so may constitute a procedural defect, potentially challenging the final award. Third, if the respondent fails to submit its defense on time, it means the respondent voluntarily waives its right to defend, and this does not affect the continuation of the arbitration proceedings. The arbitral tribunal has the power to hear the case based on existing materials. This provision primarily aims to prevent respondents from delaying proceedings through passive defense, reflecting the efficiency advantage of arbitration.

The defense should address each of the claimant's claims and the basis thereof point by point. If a claim is justified, it may be admitted or not disputed; if a claim is unjustified, it should be rebutted; if a claim is partially justified, it may be partially admitted and partially rebutted. When making rebuttals, facts should be presented and evidence provided, based on law or practice, respecting legally established contracts, and reasons should be clearly explained. Furthermore, the language used in the defense should be moderate, maintaining reason and restraint, and avoiding using provocative or even insulting language, lest it exacerbate existing conflicts.

In practice, some respondents, while not substantively abandoning their defense, intentionally exceed the time limit to conduct a "surprise" or "ambush" defense during the hearing. Although the arbitral tribunal, for the purpose of clarifying the facts, may ultimately not refuse or reject the overdue defense, such surprise tactics are highly inadvisable. This behavior still carries the risk of the claimant arguing that the respondent has waived the right to defend. Secondly, it delays the arbitration process, significantly reduces the efficiency of the hearing, and is not conducive to the timely resolution of the dispute, which is detrimental to all parties involved. If the respondent genuinely faces objective difficulties in submitting the defense on time, arbitration rules usually allow the respondent to apply for an extension of the defense period. The respondent should submit a written application explaining the reasons in advance.

A special circumstance is when the respondent, after receiving the arbitration documents served by the arbitration institution, raises an objection to the jurisdiction. It may, within the defense period stipulated by the rules, submit a "jurisdiction challenge" instead of a statement of defense.

If the respondent fails to appear or participate until the conclusion of the arbitration proceedings, the arbitral tribunal will render a default award. For cases heard and decided by default, both the arbitration institution and the arbitral tribunal must pay special attention to safeguarding all procedural rights of the respondent and should ensure that the relevant arbitration materials have indeed been effectively served.

In summary, the procedures stipulated in this Article reflect the following principles of the arbitration system:

1. Procedural Fairness and Transparency. By mandating that the arbitration institution serve the arbitration rules, the panel of arbitrators, and a copy of the application for arbitration within statutory time limits, it ensures that both parties participate in the arbitration proceedings on the basis of equal access to information.

2. Efficiency. Requiring the respondent to submit the Statement of Defense within the specified time limit and explicitly stating that "failure to submit a Statement of

Defense does not affect the continuation of the arbitration proceedings" prevents delays caused by the respondent's passive response.

3. Party Autonomy and Procedural Certainty. The specific time limits prescribed arbitration rules are determined by each arbitration institution, which respects institutional autonomy while ensuring procedural standardization and predictability through the legal framework.

Article 37

Where the parties have concluded an arbitration agreement and one party has brought an action in a people's court without declaring the existence of the arbitration agreement and, after the people's court has accepted the case, the other party submits the arbitration agreement prior to the first hearing, the people's court shall dismiss the case unless the arbitration agreement is void or otherwise provided by law. If, prior to the first hearing, the other party has not raised an objection to the people's court's acceptance of the case, they shall be deemed to have renounced the arbitration agreement and the people's court shall continue to try the case.

Notes

This Article focuses on the rules for coordinating conflicts between arbitration agreements and court jurisdiction, embodying the core balance between the "principle of party autonomy" and the "principle of judicial supervision" in the arbitration system. This Article follows the framework of the original Article 26 of the Arbitration Law (2017) but strengthens the preclusive effect of the arbitration agreement on litigation proceedings by refining procedural steps and clarifying legal consequences. The core intent of the revision primarily points to three principles: ***(1) Principle of Party Autonomy in Arbitration Agreements.*** When a valid arbitration agreement exists, the court should respect the parties' expressed intention to choose arbitration, avoiding improper judicial intervention. ***(2) Preventing Abuse of Procedure.*** Setting a final deadline for raising objections, using before the first hearing as the cut-off point for exercising the right to object, prevents parties from abusing procedural rights to delay dispute resolution. ***(3) Waiver of the Right to Object.*** Additionally, we note that this revision specifically adds exceptional reasons for the People's Court not to dismiss the lawsuit.

1. **Excluding Court Jurisdiction**

The application of the new Article 37 presupposes that the arbitration agreement is valid. If the arbitration agreement is invalid, the court need not dismiss the lawsuit. The validity of an arbitration agreement requires the three elements stipulated in Article 16 of the New Arbitration Law: an expression of intent to apply for arbitration, matters for arbitration, and a designated arbitration institution. When reviewing the validity of an arbitration agreement, the court adopts a formal review standard, requiring only a preliminary assessment on whether the agreement possesses the basic elements, without delving into substantive disputes. Generally, if the validity of the arbitration agreement is very obvious, the court will directly require the parties to proceed to arbitration. If the arbitration agreement is invalid, the court need not dismiss the lawsuit. However, if the parties dispute the validity of the arbitration agreement, the court must also determine the validity of the arbitration agreement within that procedure.

By signing an arbitration agreement, the parties agree on the method of dispute resolution, choosing arbitration and excluding the court. A valid arbitration agreement has the effect of excluding court jurisdiction. This effect is prescribed by law. For example, section 1032(1) of the German Arbitration Act 1998 stipulates that a court before which an action is brought in a matter which is the subject of an arbitration agreement shall, if the respondent raises an objection before the beginning of the oral hearing on the substance of the dispute, reject the action as inadmissible unless the court finds that the arbitration agreement is null and void, inoperative or incapable of being performed.

The New Arbitration Law contains similar provisions. There are considerable cases in this regard. Courts will, based on the arbitration clause in the contract, find that they lack jurisdiction and dismiss the plaintiff's lawsuit. Of course, excluding the court's jurisdiction to hear the merits of the case does not mean excluding other procedural jurisdictions of the court. For instance, parties may request the court to take interim measures, appoint arbitrators, or administer oaths; such procedural matters still fall within the purview of the competent court. The court's jurisdiction in these instances does not conflict with the arbitration agreement.

In ***Hydraulic Company v. Technology Company***,[2] contracts stipulated that "any disputes arising from the performance of this contract shall be resolved through friendly negotiation between the parties. If an agreement cannot be reached through negotiation, the dispute shall be submitted to arbitration. The arbitration shall be conducted in Wuhan, the location where the contract was signed, and administered by the Wuhan Arbitration Institution." The court held that this stipulation constituted an arbitration clause agreed upon by both parties in the contract. In accordance with Article 5 of the Arbitration Law (2017) and Article 6 of the Arbitration Law Interpretation, the court lacked jurisdiction over the dispute. Accordingly, the court dismissed the action filed by Hydraulic Company.

In ***Technology Company v. Catering Management Company***,[3] the court held that Technology Company and Catering Management Company had included an arbitration clause in the transfer agreement. Therefore, any disputes arising from the transfer agreement should be resolved through arbitration, and the court lacked jurisdiction over the case. Accordingly, the court dismissed the action filed by the plaintiff, Technology Company.

In ***Huang v. G Company***,[4] the court held that the dispute in this case was a contractual dispute between Huang and G Company. Huang filed the lawsuit based on the Cooperation Agreement dated May 1, 2007. This Cooperation Agreement

[2] (2009) Da Min Chu Zi No. 3868.

[3] (2009) Feng Min Chu Zi No. 04471.

[4] (2009) Hai Min Chu Zi No. 10243.

clearly stipulated that any dispute related to the contract, either party has the right to apply to the BAC for arbitration to resolve the dispute through arbitration. The arbitration agreement. Accordingly, the jurisdictional challenge raised by G Company was well-founded, and thus the court dismissed the action filed by the plaintiff, Huang.

Similarly, numerous other cases can be cited, for example: ***Lin v. F Company***,[5] ***Linying G Company v. Pingdingshan H Company***,[6] ***LH Transport Company v. J Property Insurance Company***,[7] ***Wang v. K Property Insurance Company***,[8] ***Guangxi L Company v. Beijing M Company***,[9] ***Beijing N Company v. O Bank***,[10] ***Yang v. P Insurance Company***,[11] ***Q Bank v. Cheng et al.***,[12] ***Henan R Company v. Huangchuan S Company***.[13] In these and other cases, the courts all held that the court lacked jurisdiction by reason of the existence of an arbitration clause.

In all the cases mentioned above, the parties raised objections to the court's jurisdiction based on the existence of an arbitration agreement. The courts also correctly applied the relevant laws and judicial interpretations, thereby realizing the true intention of the parties at the time of contract signing to resolve disputes through arbitration. Of course, if the arbitration agreement is defective, leading the court to find the agreement invalid, the court will rule not to stay the litigation proceedings or will find the arbitration agreement invalid. This can be seen in other cases discussed later.

2. **Procedure for Raising an Objection with the Court: Time Limits and Handling Methods**

Jurisdictional objections must be raised before the first hearing. Therefore, objections raised during the hearing itself shall not be deemed valid jurisdictional challenges. Failure to raise an objection before the court's first hearing shall deemed a waiver of the arbitration agreement. Similarly, if the case is submitted to an arbitration institution for arbitration, failure to raise an objection before the first hearing and continuing with the arbitration proceedings shall constitute a waiver of the jurisdictional challenge.

In ***H Company v. B***,[14] H Company sought to set aside the arbitral award on the grounds that the arbitral tribunal lacked jurisdiction over the case. The SPC held that pursuant to Article 20(2) of the Arbitration Law (2017), if a party challenged the

---

[5] (2009) Yuan Min Yi Chu Zi No. 52.

[6] (2009) Ping Min Chu Zi No. 82.

[7] (2009) Yuan Min San Chu Zi No. 42.

[8] (2009) Tai Min Chu Zi No. 1348.

[9] (2009) Da Min Chu Zi No. 8125.

[10] (2009) Xi Min Chu Zi No. 4851.

[11] (2009) Xuan Min Chu Zi No. 8327.

[12] (2009) Da Min Chu Zi No. 10645.

[13] (2009) Xing Min Er Chu Zi No. 461.

[14] [2009] Min Si Ta Zi No. 1.

validity of the arbitration agreement, the challenge should be raised before the first hearing of the arbitral tribunal. H Company did not raise a jurisdictional objection during the arbitration hearing but instead presented a substantive defense. According to Article 8 of the CIETAC Arbitration Rules, it should be deemed that the party waived its right to raise an objection, and the arbitral tribunal had jurisdiction over the case.

The phrase "prior to the first hearing" refers to a preclusive period for a party to raise an objection, which is determined based on the commencement of the court's formal hearing, such as the court investigation or debate stages. In practice, attention should be paid to the flexible nature of the "reasonable period". If a party fails to raise an objection in time due to legitimate reasons (such as not having received the response materials), the court may extend the period at its discretion, subject to strict scrutiny of the authenticity of the reasons provided. An objection may be manifested through a written application, an oral statement made in court, or even implied conduct (such as filing a defense on the merits). However, it must clearly express the intent to contest the court's jurisdiction.

The New Arbitration Law clarifies that after accepting a lawsuit, the court shall conduct an active examination of the existence of an arbitration agreement, but it need not dismiss the lawsuit *sua sponte*; instead, it waits for a party to raise an objection. This adjustment reduces the court's review burden but may create risks of information asymmetry: If the defendant intentionally fails to respond, the court might proceed with the hearing unaware of the arbitration agreement, easily leading to disputes at the subsequent enforcement stage. Furthermore, the lack of a stipulation regarding the court's duty to inform may cause uninformed parties to lose their right to object. To understand the procedure stipulated in this Article, the following three key points are essential:

A. No Declaration of Arbitration Agreement upon Filing. When one party files a lawsuit with a people's court without declaring the existence of a valid arbitration agreement, the court accepts the case in accordance with the law.

B. Time Limit for Raising an Objection. If the other party does not agree to waive the arbitration agreement and revert to litigation, it must submit the arbitration agreement and raise an objection before the first hearing (referring to the formal hearing after the expiration of the defense period, and excluding preparatory procedures such as pre-trial conferences). If the defendant is absent or fails to enter an appearance and defend the case, this shall not be deemed a waiver of the arbitration agreement.

C. Court's Disposition. If the objection raised by the other party is upheld, meaning the court finds the arbitration agreement valid, it shall issue a ruling to dismiss the lawsuit. If the objection is not raised before the first hearing, the party is deemed to have waived the arbitration agreement, and the court shall continue to hear the case.

In its application, this Article also presents certain limitations. First, while the purpose of this Article is to give effect to the arbitration agreement, a question arises: should the court review the validity of the arbitration agreement *ex officio* (on its own initiative) or only passively upon a party's defense? The wording of this

Article suggests the court's review is primarily passive. In practice, however, during case filing review or trial proceedings, the court may sometimes discover the existence of an arbitration agreement on its own (e.g., an arbitration clause within the disputed contract), or a party may be absent. In such scenarios, the court should not remain entirely passive, merely waiting for a party to declare the existence of an arbitration agreement or to submit it before the first hearing. A more proactive approach would better reflect a judicial policy supportive of arbitration. Second, the stipulation of "prior the first hearing" may be exploited by parties to delay proceedings. To enhance the efficiency of arbitration procedures, it might be preferable for the law to set an absolute deadline to prevent excessive delays. This deadline would ideally align with the period stipulated for the first substantive defense in the arbitration rules applicable to the case. Under exceptional circumstances, such as force majeure or the loss of original evidence, the court may exercise its discretion to accept an objection raised after the deadline.

3. **Waiver of the Right to Object**

However, it should also be noted that even if a valid arbitration agreement exists, the parties may subsequently mutually agree to terminate it. Furthermore, if one party files a lawsuit and the other party fails to duly raise an objection and instead proceeds with the litigation, this constitutes a waiver of the right to arbitrate. If a party fails to raise an objection within the specified time limit, it will result in the termination of the arbitration agreement's effect, and the court will exercise exclusive jurisdiction. The irreversibility of the waiver is reflected in the principle of estoppel; the party cannot subsequently reassert the validity of the arbitration agreement in arbitration or enforcement proceedings. Only in cases involving fraud, duress, or violation of public policy may a party apply to set aside the court's judgment, but the standards for recognition in practice are extremely high. Arbitration laws in other countries (such as the UK and Germany) have similar provisions.

In some cases, the waiver of the arbitration agreement is express, with both parties jointly expressing the intention to waive. For example, in ***N Bank v. Wen and others***,[15] although the parties agreed to submit to the Shaoyang Arbitration Commission, N Bank did not inform the court about the existence of the arbitration agreement when filing the lawsuit. During the court's first hearing, neither defendant raised an objection. Upon inquiry by the judge, both defendants stated they did not want arbitration. Therefore, the people's court could continue the trial.

In other cases, even after clearly expressing a waiver of the arbitration agreement, the losing party may still seek to overturn the adverse judgment by citing the existence of the arbitration agreement. For instance, in ***Henan X Bureau v. Y Company***,[16] Y Company claimed that the Construction Project Contract contained a clear agreement that disputes should be submitted to the Nanyang Arbitration Commission. After the court of the first instance accepted the case, Y Company

[15] (2009) Dong Min Chu Zi No. 794.

[16] (2009) Yu Fa Min Yi Zhong Zi No. 5.

raised an objection, but the court of the first instance continued the trial. The court of second instance found that the arbitration was valid. During the trial held by the court of first instance on January 16, 2008, Henan X Bureau agreed to waive the arbitration clause. Regarding the legality of the first-instance procedure, the court, based on Article 26 of the Arbitration Law (1994), held that after the Henan X Bureau expressed its waiver of the arbitration clause during the first-instance trial, it was not improper for the court of first instance to continue hearing the case. Therefore, the court of the second instance dismissed the action.

Similar situations arose in cases like ***W School v. Huang,***[17] ***Deng v. X Insurance Company***,[18] and ***Liu v. Y Property Insurance Company***.[19] Of course, this is a procedural right of the parties, but it will only be supported by the court if there is sufficient evidence.

An arbitration agreement may be effectively waived not only through an express declaration but also by implication. If a party fails to raise a jurisdictional objection before the first hearing, it is deemed to have waived the arbitration agreement. In ***Dai v. Z Property Insurance Company***,[20] the defendant argued that the Insurance Contract contained an arbitration agreement, the court should not have jurisdiction, and the plaintiff should apply to the arbitration commission. The defendant further argued during the trial that the plaintiff should apply to the arbitration commission for arbitration. On this issue, the court held that the Insurance Policy in this case stated that the method for resolving disputes under the Insurance Contract was submission to the Zhengzhou Arbitration Commission, and this agreement should constitute a valid arbitration agreement. However, according to Article 26 of the Arbitration Law (1994), the defendant did not raise an objection to the court's acceptance of the case before the first hearing, so the court should continue the trial, and the defendant's defense opinion should not be adopted. The defendant subsequently appealed.[21] The court of the second instance found that Z Property Insurance Company and Dai signed the Insurance Policy, which stipulated the insured coverage and the method for resolving disputes under the Insurance Contract. The court of the first instance found the contract legally valid and found that the appellant had not objected to the court of first instance before the first hearing. According to the Insurance Contract, the court of first instance lawfully rendered a judgment based on the liability limits stated in the Insurance Policy for the traffic accident involving the insured vehicle, which complied with legal provisions. The appellant argued on appeal that it had orally raised an objection to the court of first instance before the formal opening of the court session on the hearing day, claiming the first-instance judgment deprived it of the right to choose the dispute resolution method. As the appellant provided no relevant evidence to support its grounds for appeal, the court

---

[17] (2009) Min Yi Zhong Zi No. 359.

[18] (2009) Bei Min Yi Chu Zi No. 836.

[19] (2009) Zhan Min Chu Zi No. 669.

[20] (2009) Nei Min Chu Zi No. 248.

[21] (2009) An Min San Zhong Zi No. 239.

of the second instance found the appellant's grounds insufficient and did not accept them. The first-instance judgment was clear in its findings of facts and correct in its application of law and should be affirmed.

The above cases illustrate that any objection shall be raised in writing before the first hearing; if raised orally, corresponding evidence must be adduced to prove the same; otherwise, it will be difficult for the court to recognize that the objection was effectively raised.

4. **Exceptional Grounds for the People's Court Not to Dismiss the Action**

According to the original Article 26 of the Arbitration Law (2017), where a valid arbitration agreement exists between the parties and one party files a lawsuit with a people's court without disclosing the existence of such an agreement, the court, having accepted the case, shall dismiss the lawsuit if the other party submits the arbitration agreement before the first hearing, unless the arbitration agreement is invalid. Compared with the Arbitration Law (2017), the New Arbitration Law introduces a key addition to the exception under which the people's court may dismiss the lawsuit. In addition to the circumstance where the arbitration agreement is invalid, the new law includes the phrase "otherwise provided by law." This means that in such cases, even if one party submits the arbitration agreement before the first hearing, the people's court is not necessarily required to dismiss the lawsuit.

If the arbitration agreement is invalid, then the people's court has jurisdiction over the lawsuit. However, the specific situations encompassed by the phrase 'otherwise provided by law" require particular attention in subsequent arbitration and judicial practice.

Illustrative Cases

Case 1: *GY Company v. S Transportation Bureau*[22]

GY Company claimed that SCIA had rendered a decision on February 20, 2020, to issue a new award regarding its dispute with the S Transportation Bureau. The case had not yet been reconstituted by the tribunal and was still at the stage before the first hearing. The two case proceedings were independent of each other. Therefore, the present application to confirm the validity of the arbitration agreement should be considered as being made "before the first hearing." The first-instance ruling's application of Article 13 of the Arbitration Law Interpretation constituted an error in the application of the law.

S Transportation Bureau argued that the involved arbitration case had its first hearing on August 18, 2017. During the hearing, GY Company confirmed in court that it had no objection to the procedures already conducted by the arbitral tribunal. GY Company had already accepted the jurisdiction of the SCIA over the involved arbitration case and could not regain rights it had previously waived simply because the case entered re-arbitration proceedings. The first-instance ruling correctly applied the law.

[22] SPC Guiding Case No. 197.

The Court found that SIAC accepted the involved arbitration case in 2016. On August 18, 2017, the arbitral tribunal conducted a hearing. Before the arbitration claimant stated and finalized the facts and reasons supporting its arbitration claims, the arbitral tribunal inquired whether "the parties have any objections to the procedures already conducted in this case." The claimant in this case [i.e., GY Company in the judicial review proceeding] replied, "No objections." At the conclusion of the hearing, the claimant in this case stated that it had "no objections to the arbitration procedures conducted up to now." On March 29, 2018, SCIA rendered an arbitral award. After the award was made, GY Company applied to the Guangdong Province Shenzhen Intermediate People's Court to non-enforcement of the arbitral award. The court, upon review, held that the case could be remitted to the arbitral tribunal for re-arbitration. As the arbitral tribunal had agreed to re-arbitrate within the time limit specified by the court, the procedure for reviewing the refusal of enforcement of the arbitral award should be terminated. On February 26, 2020, the court ruled to terminate the review procedure of that case. The Guangdong Province Shenzhen Intermediate People's Court dismissed the action filed by GY Company. GY Company subsequently appealed to the High People's Court of Guangdong Province. The High People's Court of Guangdong Province dismissed the action and upheld the lower court's decision.

The High People's Court of Guangdong Province held that Article 20(2) of the Arbitration Law (2017) stipulated that any challenge to the validity of an arbitration agreement must be raised before the first hearing of the arbitral tribunal. If a party failed to raise an objection to the validity of the arbitration agreement before the first hearing of the arbitral tribunal, it would be deemed that the party had accepted the tribunal's jurisdiction over the case. Although this case had entered a re-arbitration procedure, it still concerned the same dispute. GY Company had not raised any objection to the validity of the arbitration agreement during the arbitration process and had confirmed that it had no objection to the arbitration proceedings. Its conduct remained effective during the re-arbitration process. In accordance with Article 13 of the Arbitration Law Interpretation, which stated that if a party did not raise an objection to the validity of the arbitration agreement before the first hearing of the arbitral tribunal in accordance with Article 20(2) of the Arbitration Law (2017), but subsequently applied to the people's court to confirm the invalidity of the arbitration agreement, the people's court shall not accept the application, the court of first instance should not have accepted GY Company's application to confirm the validity of the arbitration agreement. After accepting the case, the court of first instance, pursuant to Article 8(1) of the Arbitration Judicial Review Provisions, dismissed the action and upheld the first instance decision.

Case 2: ***A Holding Company and others v. C Company and others***[23]
A Holding Company and B Management Company (collectively referred to as the "**plaintiffs**") filed a lawsuit against C Company, D Insurance Company, and E Property Management Company (collectively referred to as the "**defendants**") in

[23] (2018) Zui Gao Fa Min Xia Zhong No. 453.

the High People's Court of Beijing. The plaintiffs requested that the defendants deliver the houses to the plaintiffs and compensate the plaintiffs for economic losses caused by tortious acts.

Before the first hearing, the defendants raised objections to the court's jurisdiction over the case. Specifically, they argued that the case did not constitute a tort liability dispute and should not be governed by tort legal relationships. The rights allegedly infringed upon and claimed by the plaintiff should be classified as creditors' rights, which lacked absoluteness and publicity and therefore did not fall within the scope of protection under the Tort Liability Law. The rights and interests asserted by the plaintiff were contractual obligations enjoyed by specific parties under the contract and thus did not constitute a situation where liability for breach of contract and tort liability concurred as defined by law. Even if the court considered the case to be a tort liability dispute, the exception to the arbitration clause jurisdiction established by the SPC for certain joint tort cases should not apply, and the arbitration clause should continue to bind the parties to the arbitration agreement. The attempt by the defendants to evade the jurisdiction of the arbitration clause should not be upheld. D Insurance Company raised objections. It argued that matters related to the property involved were governed by a clear arbitration clause and should be submitted to arbitration for resolution. A Holding Company had no connection to the case, and the court should dismiss its claims. D Insurance Company was not involved in the disputes concerning the property and was not a proper defendant in the case. Instead, it was included as a litigation connection point by the plaintiff to circumvent the arbitration clause. Therefore, the court lacked jurisdiction over the case. Since a clear arbitration clause existed regarding matters related to the property involved, any tort claims arising from such matters should be submitted to arbitration for jurisdiction. E Property Management Company raised objections. It contended that the disputes involved should be submitted to CIETAC.

The Beijing High People's Court rendered a civil ruling, dismissing the complaint filed by the plaintiffs. A Holding Company and B Management Company appealed to SPC. The Court issued a civil ruling, dismissing the appeal and upholding the original ruling.

With regard to one of the main contested issues in this case, i.e., whether the tort dispute between the parties was subject to the arbitration clause, the SPC held the following: Article 29 of the House Lease Contract explicitly stipulated an arbitration clause, which was legally valid. Disputes between the parties arising from the House Lease Contract, whether raised as contract disputes or as tort disputes, should be submitted for arbitration in accordance with the parties' agreement, and the people's court did not have jurisdiction. Although B Management Company filed corresponding claims against the C Company, D Insurance Company, and E Property Management Company in this case on tort grounds, such disputes still fell within the scope of the arbitration clause in the House Lease Contract. The court did not support the attempt to circumvent the contractual arbitration clause by initiating a tort lawsuit. In other words, even though B Management Company raised claims on tort grounds in this case, these claims still fell within the effective scope of the arbitration clause in their House Lease Contract, thereby excluding the jurisdiction of the people's court. The SPC upheld the lower court's decision.

Article 38

The claimant may renounce or amend its arbitration claim. The respondent may accept or refute an arbitration claim and shall have the right to make a counter-claim.

Notes

This Article establishes the fundamental principles for parties to exercise their procedural and substantive rights in arbitration proceedings, embodying the core of the principle of party autonomy within the arbitration process. It clarifies the respective rights of the claimant and the respondent concerning arbitration claims, forming the foundation for the progression and adversarial nature of arbitration proceedings.

The power of arbitration stems from the parties' mutual consent. Since choosing arbitration is an exercise of the parties' procedural rights, the disposition of substantive rights during arbitration should naturally also be a right enjoyed by the parties. During the arbitration process, the claimant may waive or amend its arbitration claims, and the respondent may admit or challenge the arbitration claims and has the right to raise a counterclaim. By granting both parties a series of procedural rights, the fairness, efficiency, and adversarial nature of the arbitration process are ensured, enabling the arbitral tribunal to ascertain the facts and clarify liabilities within a fully debated environment, thereby rendering a just award. The legal status of both parties in an arbitration case is equal, and the matters submitted for arbitration are those which the parties are entitled to dispose of. These actions precisely represent the parties' exercise or disposition of their rights and are therefore appropriate. When a respondent raises a counterclaim, it must also comply with the requirements of the arbitration scope and the arbitration agreement. Simultaneously, due to the equal status of the parties in arbitration, once the respondent raises a counterclaim, the claimant also has the right to defend against it.

The claimant's renouncement of arbitration claims primarily refers to the claimant explicitly informing the arbitral tribunal in writing that it no longer insists on all or part of its previously raised arbitration claims. This is the claimant's disposition of its substantive rights, equivalent to a "withdrawal of the action" in litigation.

Amending arbitration claims refers to the claimant modifying, supplementing, or adjusting the already raised arbitration claims during the course of the arbitration proceedings. This includes increasing or decreasing the claimed amount, changing the subject matter of the claims, etc. It can be a quantitative amendment, altering the amount claimed, or a qualitative amendment, changing the legal nature or content of the claim.

The respondent's admission of the claimant's arbitration claims means that the respondent acknowledges and accepts the claims raised by the claimant, equivalent to a self-admission of the facts and rights asserted by the claimant.

The respondents' refusal to the claimant's arbitration claims involves contesting or negating the claims raised by the claimant, and the reasons relied upon, primarily from the aspects of facts, evidence, and application of law. This can be done through submitting a statement of defense, providing contrary evidence, cross-examining evidence, participating in hearing debates, etc. It is more of a defensive right, aimed at rendering the claimant's claims unfounded either wholly or in part.

The respondent's raising of a counterclaim is an independent claim made by the respondent against the claimant (who becomes the respondent to the counterclaim) before the same arbitral tribunal, which is factually or legally connected to the claims in the original arbitration. This is an important right for the respondent to switch from defense to offense, aiming to offset, absorb, or negate the claimant's arbitration claims, or to render them meaningless. Sometimes it even involves asserting independent rights against the claimant to protect its own legitimate rights and interests. The respondent should comprehensively assess the case circumstances and choose the most advantageous strategy—whether to simply challenge the claims or to proactively raise a counterclaim—requires careful consideration based on facts and law. Another significant purpose of allowing counterclaims is to simplify the arbitration process and improve efficiency. Since the counterclaim is raised in response to the original claim and both claims are based on the same dispute, they can be consolidated in the arbitration, enabling a thorough and early resolution of the parties' dispute and saving costs.

A counterclaim is both related to and relatively independent from the original claim. The connection is mainly reflected in: the counterclaim must be raised against the claimant of the original arbitration claim; the subject matter of the counterclaim must be based on the same facts or legal relationship as the subject matter of the arbitration claim, or there must be other direct connections between them; the counterclaim must fall within the scope of the arbitration agreement and be under the jurisdiction of the same arbitral tribunal. The independence of the counterclaim is mainly shown in: the counterclaim is an independent claim—if the respondent does not raise it in the already commenced arbitration proceedings, it may apply for arbitration separately; if the respondent raises a counterclaim before the arbitral award is rendered and the claimant withdraws its arbitration application, the arbitration proceedings do not cease or conclude as a result, and the arbitral tribunal shall render an award on the counterclaim. If the claimant does not withdraw the original claim, and the arbitral tribunal consolidates the hearing of the original claim and the counterclaim, it should separately address the original claim and the counterclaim in the award.

It is important to note that parties must strictly adhere to the time limits prescribed by the arbitration rules when exercising rights such as waiver, amendment, or counterclaim. Exercising these rights after the deadline may not be accepted by the arbitral tribunal. The exercise of the aforementioned rights must be submitted to the arbitration commission in writing and transmitted by the arbitral tribunal to the other party. The parties' right of disposition is not absolute. The arbitral tribunal has the power to review whether the waiver, amendment, or counterclaim is lawful, falls within the scope of the arbitration agreement, or would unduly delay the proceedings, and shall ultimately decide whether to permit it.

Article 39
A party may apply for property preservation, request to compel the other party to take certain actions or prohibit them from taking certain actions if it may become difficult for the party to enforce the award or cause other damages to the party due to acts of the other party or other causes. Where a party applies for property preservation, the arbitration institution shall submit the party's application to the people's court in accordance with the relevant provisions of the Civil Procedure Law of the People's Republic of China, the people's court should handle cases in a timely manner according to the law.

Due to the emergency situation, the parties to the arbitration agreement may apply to the people's court for property preservation in accordance with the relevant provisions of the Civil Procedure Law of the People's Republic of China before applying for arbitration, and request the court to order the other party to take certain actions or to prohibit them from taking certain actions. When a party applies for preservation, the people's court shall handle it in a timely manner in accordance with the law.

Where an application for property preservation has been wrongfully made, the claimant shall compensate the party against whom the application has been made for any loss incurred from property preservation.

Notes
While arbitration offers advantages such as efficiency and flexibility, arbitration institutions and tribunals lack coercive enforcement power. If a party maliciously transfers assets or engages in acts that may prejudice the enforcement of an award, the arbitral award may be rendered unenforceable. The coercive power of the courts serves as a supplement to the authority of arbitration institutions and tribunals, integrating judicial support with the arbitration process to better safeguard the legitimate rights and interests of the parties to the arbitration.

In the context of Chinese law, preservation measures generally include property preservation, evidence preservation, and conduct preservation. Compared to the provisions of the Arbitration Law (1994), the New Arbitration Law adds provisions concerning conduct preservation alongside the original property preservation. Furthermore, in addition to the arbitration proceedings, the New Arbitration Law also grants parties the right to apply for preservation measures before applying for arbitration. Thus, the provisions on preservation measures in the New Arbitration Law have become more aligned with the Civil Procedure Law.

In the field of international arbitration, preservation measures constitute a type of interim measure. With reference to the provisions on interim measures in the UNCITRAL Model Law, an interim measure is any temporary measure, whether in the form of an award or in another form, by which an arbitral tribunal orders a party, at any time prior to the issuance of the award that finally decides the dispute, to: (a) maintain or restore the status quo pending determination of the dispute; (b) take action that would prevent, or refrain from taking action that is likely to cause, current or imminent harm or prejudice to the arbitration process itself; (c) provide a means of preserving assets out of which a subsequent award may be satisfied; or (d) preserve evidence that may be relevant and material to the resolution of the dispute. According to the Model Law, the arbitral tribunal is the body authorized to decide on interim measures.

Unlike the Model Law, the New Arbitration Law does not grant arbitral tribunals the power to order interim measures. Instead, the arbitration institution forwards the party's application to the court, which then makes the decision. This collaborative mechanism between the judiciary and the arbitration process strengthens the authority and enforceability of arbitral awards. The revisions in this article reflect both the internal demands of China's market economy development and the external impetus to align with international commercial arbitration rules. In its application, cooperation among arbitration institutions/tribunals, courts, and parties is required, pursuing efficiency while adhering to the bottom line of procedural justice and substantive fairness. This clause not only lays a solid foundation for the improvement of China's arbitration system but also provides a strong guarantee for fostering an internationalized, rule-of-law-based business environment.

This Article is divided into three paragraphs, stipulating preservative measures during arbitration, preservative measures before arbitration, and liability for compensation in case of erroneous preservation, respectively. Its core lies in using the coercive power of the courts to compensate for the limitation of arbitration institutions lacking enforcement power, thereby ensuring the effectiveness of the arbitration process and the enforceability of awards.

Paragraph 1 concerns preservation measures during arbitration, including both property preservation and conduct preservation. If one party believes that the acts of another party or other reasons may render the award difficult to enforce or cause other harm, it may apply to the arbitration institution for property preservation or conduct preservation. The term "other harm" here is an open-textured concept, encompassing not only economic losses but also non-pecuniary damages such as harm to business reputation or loss of competitive advantage. Property preservation aims to provide the party with post-hoc relief by ensuring the respondent possesses sufficient assets to compensate the claimant after harm has occurred. Applications for property preservation are generally suitable for cases involving monetary claims or claims convertible into monetary claims. The main methods of preservation include sealing up, distraining, or freezing assets. Conduct preservation focuses on pre-hoc relief, prohibiting the respondent from engaging in acts that could harm the claimant's interests before the harm occurs. It is mainly applicable to cases requiring a party to perform or refrain from performing specific acts, commonly seen in areas such as intellectual property infringement, equity disputes, and non-competition agreements.

Upon receiving a party's application for preservation measures, the arbitration institution does not conduct a substantive review of the application but submits it to the competent court. The court reviews the application and issues a ruling in accordance with the relevant provisions of the Civil Procedure Law, reflecting the dual attributes of judicial support for and supervision over arbitration.

Paragraph 2 regulates preservation measures before arbitration, applicable under the precondition of an "emergency." Emergencies mean that if one waits until the formal arbitration proceedings are initiated to apply for preservation, or if the party does not apply for preservation immediately, the purpose of the preservation will be unattainable or the party's legitimate rights and interests will suffer irreparable harm. For example, the respondent is about to transfer the disputed assets overseas or is rapidly destroying electronic evidence. In such cases, the party may apply directly to the court for preservation but must promptly initiate arbitration thereafter.

Paragraph 3 stipulates liability for compensation in case of erroneous preservation, which constitutes a tort liability. It requires the claimant to have acted with intent or gross negligence, the application to lack a proper basis, the preservation measures to be inconsistent with the actual needs, and the respondent to have suffered actual losses. This clause protects the legitimate rights and interests of the respondent while also restraining the claimant from abusing its rights, embodying the principle of fairness.

It is important to note that the preservation measures provided for in this Article are initiated upon the application of a party; arbitration institutions and courts cannot order preservation on their own initiative, which differs from the litigation procedure.

Overall, Article 39 of the New Arbitration Law, through the cooperative mechanism between arbitration institutions and courts, strengthens the authority and enforceability of arbitral awards. This aligns with the development trends of international commercial arbitration and serves the practical need for China to optimize the business environment. In practice, courts must conduct substantive reviews of preservation applications based on the provisions of the Civil Procedure Law, ensuring their necessity and reasonableness, thereby achieving a unity of procedural efficiency and substantive justice.

In fact, even before this, there have been some successful practical cases. For instance, in October 2024, the Beijing Arbitration Commission accepted an international technology development and service dispute. The claimant applied to the arbitral tribunal for interim measures. The tribunal promptly made procedural arrangements based on the application, held a pre-hearing conference for the interim measures, heard the parties' statements and arguments, conducted necessary investigations, and issued a decision on interim measures after the conference. This decision was ultimately enforced by the Beijing No. 4 Intermediate People's Court.

Illustrative Cases

Case 1: ***A Resources Company v. B Industrial Company***[24]

The case concerning the enforcement of a foreign-related arbitral award between A Resources Company and B Industrial Company was the first foreign-related arbitration enforcement case in Beijing after the jurisdictional adjustments for foreign-related cases in 2024. The focal point of the dispute was whether certain parts of the arbitral award had substantive enforceable content. Item 1 of the arbitral award stated that "The Respondent shall acquire the 20% equity interest in a certain

[24] See the 10 Typical Cases on Judicial Review of Arbitration published by the Beijing No. 4 Intermediate People's Court in November 2024.

company held by the Claimant for 76 million RMB," and Item 4 stated that "The 5 million RMB equity transfer payment already actually paid by the Respondent to the Claimant shall be deducted from the total equity transfer price (i.e., 76 million RMB)." Regarding whether the aforementioned award items had enforceable content, the Court sent a letter to the arbitration institution requesting confirmation. The arbitration institution indicated that the arbitral award was a confirmation made by the arbitral tribunal regarding the amount of the equity transfer price based on the parties' arbitration claims.

The Beijing No. 4 Intermediate People's Court determined that the content of the aforementioned arbitral award constituted confirmation of the equity transfer price amount between the parties; it did not contain a payment obligation, nor did it fall within the category of enforcement involving the delivery of property or the performance of specific acts. Therefore, the enforcement application filed by the A Resources Company should be dismissed by ruling. However, considering the litigation burden and economic costs for the parties, the Court did not simply issue a dismissal ruling but instead strived for a substantive resolution of the dispute. The Court channeled the case into mediation through the Beijing Court's One-Stop Diversified International Commercial Dispute Resolution Platform via "enforcement-source referral." During the mediation process, the judge actively communicated and coordinated with multiple departments, including tax authorities, banks, and the State Administration of Foreign Exchange, to find solutions for obstacles present in the foreign-related case, such as foreign exchange payment barriers, tax payment difficulties, the drafting and signing of the equity transfer agreement, and trust restoration. Through the efficient linkage of "enforcement-mediation," the parties were successfully facilitated to reach a settlement and complete performance. This case fully demonstrates the effectiveness of the Court's construction of a diversified dispute resolution mechanism that organically connects mediation, arbitration, and the judiciary, working together to build a first-class preferred destination for international commercial dispute resolution.

Case 2: *Shenzhen A Company v. Zhuhai B Company*[25]

Shenzhen A Company applied to the Zhuhai International Arbitration Court for arbitration due to a construction project contract dispute with Zhuhai B Company, requesting Zhuhai B Company to pay the project payment, interest, and other sums. During the arbitration process, Shenzhen A Company submitted an application for property preservation through the case handling system of the Zhuhai International Arbitration Court, seeking to preserve the property under the name of Zhuhai B Company and providing a guarantee letter as security. Upon receiving the application, the Zhuhai International Arbitration Court, relying on the arbitration-judicial collaboration platform, transmitted the property preservation application online to the People's Court of the Guangdong-Macao In-Depth Cooperation Zone in Hengqin.

[25] See the 10 Typical Cases on Judicial Review of Arbitration Published by the High People's Court of Guangdong Province in August 2025.

The Court simultaneously received the application materials for arbitration preservation and, through the arbitration-judicial collaboration platform, retrieved the electronic arbitration case file with one click. It registered the case for review on the same day and promptly issued a civil ruling. The enforcement department verified the property clues under the name of Zhuhai B Company using the online inquiry and control system, successfully freezing and sealing the bank accounts and real estate under the name of Zhuhai B Company. The entire process was fully paperless, efficiently completing the province's first online handling of an arbitration property preservation case.

Case 3: ***UK M Company v. Hong Kong N Company and others***[26]
The claimant, UK M Company, initiated arbitration at the HKIAC against twenty-seven parties, including the respondents Hong Kong N Company, A, B, C, D, E, F, and G, concerning a share repurchase dispute arising from the Restated Shareholders Agreement signed on October 27, 2017, and the Share Purchase Agreement signed on September 5, 2017. The arbitration was accepted by HKIAC. During the arbitration proceedings, UK M Company, to prevent the respondents, including Hong Kong N Company from hiding, transferring assets, or encumbering property, and to ensure the practical enforcement of the future arbitral award, applied to the Zhejiang Province Hangzhou Intermediate People's Court for property preservation. It requested the freezing of bank deposits amounting to RMB 503,720,313.5 belonging to the respondents. For this purpose, UK M Company submitted materials, including a liability insurance policy for litigation property preservation as security to the Zhejiang Province Hangzhou Intermediate People's Court.

The Zhejiang Province Hangzhou Intermediate People's Court held that this case involved an application for court-ordered assistance in preservation within proceedings already accepted by the HKIAC. This arbitration case constituted a "Hong Kong arbitration proceeding" as defined in Article 2 of the Arrangement Concerning Mutual Enforcement of Awards. Article 3 of the Arrangement Concerning Mutual Enforcement of Awards provided that a party to Hong Kong arbitration proceedings might, before the rendering of an arbitral award, apply to a Mainland Intermediate People's Court in the place of the domicile of the respondent, or the place where the property or evidence is located, for interim measures. In this case, five respondents had their domicile and property located within Hangzhou; therefore, the Zhejiang Province Hangzhou Intermediate People's Court had the authority to accept this application for arbitration preservation. According to the Work Guidance on Further Regulating the Handling of Property Preservation Cases (Pilot) by the High People's Court of Zhejiang Province, when conducting property preservation work, the people's court should prudently adopt preservation measures, equally protect the legitimate rights and interests of all parties, and review whether the respondent's circumstances involve a situation where the enforcement of the effective legal

[26] See the 10 Typical Cases on Judicial Review of Arbitration published by the Zhejiang Province Hangzhou Intermediate People's Court in March 2024.

document may become difficult and the necessity of preservation. Upon review, the arbitration claims of the claimant in this case showed no indication of being "clearly unfounded." There were clear leads regarding the property, and suitable security was provided, and the claimant also submitted explanatory materials indicating that the respondents' business conditions were deteriorating and they might lose their ability to perform their obligations. Thus, preservation was necessary in this case. The preservation application by UK M Company complied with legal provisions and should be granted according to the law. Consequently, the court ruled to freeze bank deposits of RMB 503,720,313.5 belonging to the respondents, including Hong Kong N Company, or to seal, distrain, or seize other property of equivalent value. In the same month, the Hangzhou Intermediate Court froze the 60.91% equity in O Company held by Hong Kong N Company.

Article 40

A party or statutory agent may appoint a lawyer or other agent to carry out arbitration activities. Where a lawyer or other agent is appointed to carry out arbitration activities, a power of attorney shall be submitted to the arbitration institution.

Notes

An arbitration agent refers to a person who, upon authorization by a party, their legal representative, or the legal representative of a legal person, and within the scope of such authorization, participates in arbitration activities in the name of the principal. Parties not only have the right to choose arbitration as the method for resolving disputes but also have the autonomy to select agents they trust to participate in this process, a right fully respected and guaranteed by law. Given that arbitration procedures possess both legal professionalism and technicality, allowing parties to be represented by professionals (especially lawyers) ensures their claims are fully and effectively presented and safeguarded, preventing potential disadvantages arising from unfamiliarity with procedures or the law. Simultaneously, to prevent unauthorized agency or ultra vires acts by agents that could infringe upon the parties' rights and interests, and to ensure the seriousness and standardization of arbitration activities, if a party or their legal representative appoints an agent to conduct arbitration activities, a written power of attorney should be signed. This also facilitates the standardized management of arbitration cases by the arbitration institution.

According to this Article, individuals eligible to serve as arbitration agents are primarily divided into two categories: first, lawyers, i.e., practicing personnel who have lawfully obtained a lawyer's practice certificate and provide legal services to clients upon engagement; second, other individuals who meet the stipulated requirements. In practice, these typically include close relatives of the party, personnel recommended by the party's employing unit, or other citizens permitted by the arbitration commission. When appointing an arbitration agent to participate in arbitration activities, the written power of attorney must be submitted. The power of attorney usually specifies information such as the principal, the agent, and the scope of authority. The power of attorney must be personally signed by the principal or bear the principal's official seal. In foreign-related cases, arbitration institutions generally also require that powers of attorney formed outside the Chinese Mainland be notarized by a local notary public and authenticated by the relevant Chinese embassy or consulate. Whether this is a mandatory requirement is determined specifically by the arbitration institution or the arbitral tribunal.

Based on the scope of authorized powers, the entrusted arbitration agency can be divided into a general agency and a special agency. An agent with general agency authority can only perform routine arbitration acts such as submitting applications, participating in hearings, and presenting opinions; whereas an agent with special agency authority, in addition to exercising the powers of general agency, can also, based on special authorization, perform acts such as admitting, waiving, or amending arbitration claims, participating in settlement, and accepting mediation.

In practice, the arbitration rules of some arbitration institutions may contain more specific provisions regarding the identity of the arbitration agent, the number of agents, and the addition or change of agents. For example, Article 24 of the SCIA Arbitration Rules stipulates that a party may be represented by persons it appoints, including legal practitioners from the Chinese Mainland, the Hong Kong Special Administrative Region, the Macao Special Administrative Region, the Taiwan region and foreign lawyers. Where a party appoints a representative to participate in arbitration, a Power of Attorney specifying the authorized matters and scope of authority shall be submitted to SCIA.

Article 22 of the CIETAC Arbitration Rules stipulates that a party may authorize Chinese and/or foreign arbitration representatives to handle matters relating to the arbitration. The party or its arbitration representatives shall submit a Power of Attorney to the CIETAC, and the CIETAC shall forward the Power of Attorney to the relevant parties and the arbitral tribunal. If a party changes or adds its arbitration representatives after the formation of the arbitral tribunal, the chairperson of the CIETAC may, taking into consideration the opinions expressed by the parties on the challenge of arbitrators within a reasonable time and the progress of the arbitration proceedings, take necessary measures to avoid conflicts of interest arising from such change or addition, including excluding the new arbitration representatives from participating in the arbitration proceedings.

Illustrative Case

Singapore A Company v. Ningbo B Company[27]

Singapore A Company applied for recognition and enforcement of an arbitral award rendered by the SIAC on the grounds that Ningbo B Company had failed to fulfill the award. Ningbo B Company argued that it had not authorized Lawyer W to

[27] See the 10 Typical Cases on Judicial Review of Arbitration published by the Zhejiang Province Ningbo Intermediate People's Court in June 2024. In arbitration, whether the representative acts of a practicing lawyer can be effective against a party should be examined in light of the specific process of the arbitration and in accordance with the arbitration rules of the relevant arbitration institution. Where there is evidence proving that a practicing lawyer represented a party in the

participate in the aforementioned arbitration and that there was no effective service by the arbitral tribunal, resulting in it not receiving proper notice of the arbitration and thus being unable to participate and present its case.

The Zhejiang Province Ningbo Intermediate People's Court held that since both China and Singapore are member states of the New York Convention, and the involved arbitration did not violate the commercial reservation declaration made by China upon its accession to the New York Convention, this case should be reviewed under the New York Convention. Although Ningbo B Company did not submit a written power of attorney authorizing Lawyer W to the SIAC, the arbitration process showed that Lawyer W clearly stated his representation of Ningbo B Company in the arbitration, provided the arbitral tribunal with relevant information about Ningbo B Company, and replied to the arbitral tribunal after it sent notifications to Ningbo B Company's email address. These circumstances indicated that Lawyer W possessed the outward appearance of authority to represent Ningbo B Company. The SIAC's determination, based on this, that Lawyer W represented Ningbo B Company in the arbitration did not violate the relevant provisions of the SIAC Arbitration Rules. Furthermore, the SIAC's dispatch of arbitration notices via email complied with the SIAC Arbitration Rules and constituted valid service. The emails sent by the SIAC to Lawyer W should be deemed as proper notice to Ningbo B Company, and the effect of Lawyer W's participation in the arbitration proceedings and full presentation of arguments should also extend to the company. That is to say, this case did not involve the circumstance stipulated in Article V(1)(b) of the New York Convention, which would result in the refusal of recognition and enforcement. Therefore, the Court ruled to recognize and enforce the arbitral award.

Article 41

The arbitration documents shall be served in a reasonable manner agreed upon by the parties; if the parties have not agreed or the agreement is unclear, they shall be served according to the methods prescribed by the arbitration rules.

Notes

Service of process is the fundamental guarantee of a party's right to know and participate in the proceedings. The legitimacy and efficiency of arbitration proceedings largely depend on whether arbitration documents can be effectively served upon all parties. Only through lawful and effective service can parties become aware of the initiation, progress, and key stages of the proceedings, thereby having the opportunity to exercise a series of core rights such as defending, presenting evidence, cross-examining evidence, selecting arbitrators, and participating in hearings. Without service, there can be no talk of a party's participation in the proceedings.

---

arbitration, it is not appropriate to simply find the existence of circumstances stipulated in Article V(1)(b) of the New York Convention merely because the party did not submit written authorization materials. This case is the first case since the establishment of the Ningbo International Commercial Court to rule on the recognition and enforcement of a foreign arbitral award by applying the New York Convention.

Both domestic and international arbitration legislation and practice recognize "failure to receive proper notice" as a statutory ground for setting aside or refusing the enforcement of an arbitral award. If improper service results in a party being unable to attend the hearing or present its case, the legal validity of that award faces significant challenges. In practice, the rigor of the service procedure and whether all reasonable efforts have been exhausted often become the primary point of attack for the unsuccessful party to challenge the award's validity. An award that is substantively impeccable may nonetheless be entirely undermined by a minor procedural flaw in service.

For a long time, the system for serving arbitration documents was primarily stipulated in the arbitration rules of various arbitration institutions, without being clearly defined in laws and regulations. In practice, situations where effective service is impossible due to reasons such as changes to a party's registered address or invalid contact methods occur frequently. Even though some arbitration rules allow service to be completed and deemed effective through "the last known method of service for the party," this often leads to delays in the arbitration process because the specific circumstances of this "last known" method need to be determined. Furthermore, it is not uncommon for parties to intentionally evade service and subsequently apply to set aside or refuse enforcement of the award on the grounds of defects in the service procedure after the award is rendered.

This Article, for the first time at the level of arbitration legislation, marks the first time at the level of arbitration legislation to clarify the system for serving arbitration documents, establishing a service system centered on party autonomy and supplemented by arbitration rules. This provides a clear legal basis and institutional guarantee for determining service issues in future arbitration practice.

First, if the parties have agreed upon a method of service, arbitration documents shall be served by a reasonable method as agreed upon by the parties. This is a typical manifestation and extension of the principle of party autonomy in arbitration, specifically applied to procedural matters. Parties may clearly stipulate service provisions as part of the dispute resolution clause when entering into the main contract, or they may agree on service matters through a supplementary agreement after a dispute arises but before or during the initiation of arbitration proceedings. The advantage of such a prior arrangement lies in its ability to provide a high degree of certainty and predictability for any subsequent procedures, effectively avoiding secondary disputes arising from service issues and thereby enhancing arbitration efficiency. The qualifier "reasonable method" in this clause establishes a necessary boundary for party autonomy. It requires that the parties' agreement cannot be arbitrary or impractical; it must consider the verifiability and accessibility of the chosen method. Parties may refer to commercial practices or international customs when making such agreements. If, during the arbitration proceedings, a clearly established and reasonable agreement between the parties is disregarded, and another method of service is used arbitrarily, this may constitute a significant procedural defect. Subsequently, the unsuccessful party may fully rely on this ground to apply for setting aside or refusal of enforcement of the award after it is rendered. Therefore, in arbitration practice, verifying whether an effective service agreement exists between the parties is a crucial preliminary task, both for the parties themselves and for the arbitration institution at the outset of the proceedings.

Second, where the parties have not agreed or the agreement is unclear, the law authorizes the arbitration rules to fill this gap. To ensure smooth proceedings, various arbitration institutions have detailed and operational provisions on service in their rules. Taking the service provisions in the CIETAC Arbitration Rules, SCIA Arbitration Rules, and BAC Arbitration Rules as examples. Regarding the enumeration of service methods, these rules stipulate traditional methods such as personal delivery, mail, courier, fax, etc., and also include electronic methods like email and other electronic means of service. Further, to address the difficulty of service encountered in practice, especially situations where the respondent maliciously avoids service or fails to notify of an address change, the arbitration rules stipulate the criteria for deeming service effective. This is a key design balancing procedural efficiency and procedural fairness. Its core logic is that if the arbitration institution sends the documents to an address provided by the party or the last known address determined through reasonable inquiry, as required by the rules, and the documents are not actually received due to the party's own reasons, service is legally deemed effective. For instance, the CIETAC Arbitration Rules stipulate that any arbitration documents sent to a party or its representative(s) are deemed to have been served if delivered in person to the addressee or sent to the addressee's business address, registration address, domicile, habitual residence, or mailing address, or, if none of these addresses can be found after reasonable inquiry by the other party, sent by the CIETAC to the addressee's last-known business address, registration address, domicile, habitual residence, or mailing address by registered or express mail, or by any other means that can provide a record of delivery, including notarized service, entrusted service, and service by detention. Furthermore, some arbitration rules are experimenting with more efficient service models. For example, the SCIA Arbitration Rules stipulate that, unless otherwise agreed by the parties, the SCIA or the arbitral tribunal may decide that the parties shall directly send arbitration documents and supporting evidence to the other parties or to the SCIA's online arbitration service platform when submitting them, and submit the service record to the SCIA. The time of service is determined by the SCIA or the arbitral tribunal based on the service record.

Based on the above provisions, to minimize legal risks arising from service issues, it is recommended that parties consider clearly specifying the service address, service method, obligation to notify changes of address, and consequences of failing to fulfill the notification obligation at the contract drafting stage. During arbitration proceedings, the claimant should adhere to the principle of good faith and proactively and fully disclose all possible contact methods of the respondent known to it to the arbitration institution. For the arbitration institution and the arbitral tribunal, their core responsibility is to fulfill the obligation of diligent service. When the parties have an agreement, they must strictly comply with it; when there is no agreement, they must adhere to the arbitration rules, upholding the principles of reasonableness and diligence.

Illustrative Cases

Case 1: *Wu v. X Investment Company*[28]

X Investment Company and Wu signed a lease contract stipulating that disputes would be arbitrated by the M Arbitration Institution. Due to Wu's failure to pay rent on time, X Investment Company applied for arbitration. The M Arbitration Institution issued an award, among other things, rescinding the lease contract. Wu applied to set aside the arbitral award on the grounds of procedural violations in the service of process.

The Zhejiang Province Ningbo Intermediate People's Court held that Wu's rented residence was in the same building as X Investment Company, and X Investment Company's payment demand letters had been successfully delivered to and signed for at the address of Wu's rented factory premises. However, the arbitration institution used only Wu's registered domicile address for service. Without confirming that the first mailing was signed for by Wu, it continued multiple deliveries to his registered domicile address, all of which went unsigned for. This service did not comply with the arbitration rules, meaning the subsequent service attempts could not be deemed to have been effectively served. Consequently, the Court ruled to set aside the arbitral award due to procedural violations.

Case 2: *B Trading Company v. C Import & Export Company*[29]

In this case, the question presented was whether the arbitration institution violated statutory procedures by using a non-existent address provided by C Import & Export Company as the service address for B Trading Company without verifying its authenticity.

The Beijing No. 4 Intermediate People's Court, upon review, held that service in arbitration is a crucial part of the arbitration process, impacting its smooth progression and the authority of the award. Lawful and effective service is not only an inherent requirement of due process, safeguarding the parties' right to know and participate equally in arbitration, but also a necessary foundation for substantive justice in arbitration and a strong guarantee for enhancing the credibility of arbitration. Based on respect and support for arbitration, when reviewing whether service in arbitration violates statutory procedures, the people's court should strictly adhere to the arbitration rules, examining both whether the specific method of service complies with the rules and whether the service address for the opposing party provided by one party is genuine. Although the arbitration institution attempted service by mail and notarized service to B Trading Company, the service address provided by C Import & Export Company did not exist. This resulted in B Trading Company failing to receive the relevant arbitration documents and materials, being absent from the arbitration hearing, and being unable to exercise rights such as presenting its case. In summary, the Court found that the arbitration institution's service

---

[28] See the 10 Typical Cases on Judicial Review of Commercial Arbitration published by the Zhejiang Province Ningbo Intermediate People's Court in June 2024.

[29] See the 10 Typical Cases on Judicial Review of Domestic Arbitration published by the Beijing No. 4 Intermediate People's Court in July 2024.

violated statutory procedures. It then notified the arbitration institution to conduct re-arbitration. After the arbitration institution agreed, the court terminated the setting-aside procedure. This case, by notifying re-arbitration, corrected the procedural issue while maximizing the preservation of the parties' arbitration agreement, reducing the parties' cost of safeguarding their rights, and providing a useful reference for standardizing and improving arbitration service procedures.

Case 3: *TH Company v. JZ Company*[30]
JZ Company applied to an arbitration commission for arbitration, requesting TH Company to pay project funds and compensate for losses due to delayed payment. JZ Company's application stated TH Company's address as a location in the Economic Development Zone, Tongshan District, Xuzhou City, which was the project site, while TH Company's registered domicile was a different address on Taishan Road, Xuzhou City. After accepting the case, the arbitration commission served the application, tribunal formation notice, hearing notice, and other arbitration documents to TH Company at the address stated in JZ Company's application. The arbitral tribunal, citing TH Company's failure to appear after lawful summons, conducted the hearing in absentia and rendered an award. The arbitration commission subsequently served the arbitral award to TH Company at the same address provided by JZ Company. TH Company applied to the Xuzhou Intermediate People's Court to set aside the arbitral award, arguing that the arbitration commission's failure to serve arbitration documents according to its rules constituted a violation of statutory procedures.

The Jiangsu Province Xuzhou Intermediate People's Court held that failure to notify a party of the hearing in an appropriate manner constitutes a violation of statutory procedures. According to the arbitration commission's Arbitration Rules, arbitration documents, notices, and materials are deemed served if personally delivered to the recipient or mailed to the recipient's business address, habitual residence, or contact address. In this case, the arbitration commission served documents to TH Company based on the address provided by JZ Company. This address was merely the project site, and there was no evidence proving it was TH Company's business address, habitual residence, or contact address. The arbitration commission's service did not comply with its Arbitration Rules, resulting in TH Company's non-participation in the arbitration, which could affect the fairness of the award. The court therefore ruled to set aside the arbitral award.

Case 4: *SVM Company v. Wansheng Company*[31]
In March 2017, SVM Company and Wansheng Company signed a sales contract stipulating that disputes related to the contract shall be submitted to the International

---

[30] (2021) Su 03 Min Te No. 51-2.

[31] (2019) Su 05 Xie Wai Ren No. 6; See the 10 Typical Cases on Judicial Review of Commercial Arbitration published by the High People's Court of Jiangsu Province in July 2024. This case determined that minor defects in the service procedure of a foreign arbitral tribunal, which did not affect the party's receipt of arbitration notice, do not constitute the circumstance of "was not given proper notice" under Article V(1)(b) of the New York Convention. The court ruled to recognize and enforce the Ukrainian arbitral award.

Commercial Arbitration Court at the Ukrainian Chamber of Commerce and Industry (the ICAC) for arbitration. The contract listed Wansheng Company's address as "BAIZIGANG ROAD". In September 2017, after SVM Company applied for arbitration, the ICAC sent arbitration materials to Wansheng Company by express mail to the address "BAIRIGANG ROAD". This mail was signed by "LISA". Subsequently, the arbitral tribunal sent the hearing notice, tribunal formation notice, etc., by express mail to the address stated in the contract, "BAIZIGANG ROAD". This mail was signed by Shen, who was then the General Manager of Wansheng Company. Wansheng Company did not participate in the hearing. The ICAC rendered an arbitral award ordering Wansheng Company to refund the advance payment. SVM Company applied to the Jiangsu Province Suzhou Intermediate People's Court for recognition and enforcement of this arbitral award. Wansheng Company argued that the arbitral tribunal had not served the arbitration documents upon it, and thus the award should not be recognized and enforced.

The Jiangsu Province Suzhou Intermediate People's Court held that since both China and Ukraine are contracting states to the New York Convention, this case should be reviewed under the relevant provisions of the Convention. According to the Ukrainian law on international commercial arbitration and the ICAC Arbitration Rules, notices in arbitration proceedings could be served by mail. In September 2017, the arbitral tribunal sent arbitration materials to Wansheng Company by express mail. Although there was a slight discrepancy between the mailing address and the address in the contract, the city, building, and company name were all correct. Therefore, the express mailing address could be determined as Wansheng Company's address, and the mail had been signed for. In November 2017, the arbitral tribunal sent the hearing notice and tribunal formation notice to the address stated in the contract for Wansheng Company, which was signed by Wansheng Company's General Manager. Consequently, there was no situation in the involved arbitral award where Wansheng Company was not properly notified, leading to its inability to participate in the arbitration proceedings. The court thus ruled to recognize and enforce the foreign arbitral award.

Case 5: *WRE Company v. APM Company*[32]

On July 26, 2018, an arbitration commission sent the arbitration notice, arbitration rules, and panel of arbitrators to WRE Company by express mail based on the address provided by APM Company in the arbitration application. The mail was returned due to "incorrect name/address". On August 6, 2018, APM Company submitted the Reply Regarding Case Service Issues, confirming WRE Company's effective service address as a center on Binhu Road, Binhu District, Wuxi City, and agreed to serve arbitration documents by notarized service. The arbitration commission again sent the arbitration notice, arbitration rules, panel of arbitrators, arbitration application, and attachments to WRE Company. On September 25, 2018, it sent the tribunal formation notice, hearing notice, and their attachments to WRE Company. All documents were successfully delivered. WRE Company did not participate in the

[32] (2019) Su 02 Zhi Yi No. 49.

arbitration hearing, and the arbitral tribunal rendered a default award. WRE Company applied to the Jiangsu Province Wuxi Intermediate People's Court to refuse enforcement of the involved arbitral award, citing the arbitration commission's failure to effectively serve the arbitration materials as a violation of statutory procedures.

The Jiangsu Province Wuxi Intermediate People's Court held that Article 8 of the arbitration commission's arbitration rules stipulated that arbitration documents sent to a party or its arbitration agent are deemed effectively served if personally delivered or sent to the recipient's business place, registered address, domicile, habitual residence, or contact address, or if, after reasonable inquiry by the other party, none of these addresses can be found, sent by the arbitration commission by registered mail, express mail, or any other means providing a record of delivery (including notarized service, entrusted service, and service by detention) to the recipient's last-known business place, registered address, domicile, habitual residence, or contact address. Both WRE Company and APM Company acknowledged that APM Company had visited WRE Company in April 2018 to discuss contract termination matters. APM Company claimed this was the last address it knew from WRE Company. Although WRE Company claimed it had orally informed APM Company of its impending relocation, APM Company denied this and WRE Company failed to provide evidence. Therefore, it could be determined that this address was the last address known to APM Company for WRE Company. The arbitration commission's service by mail to this address according to its Arbitration Rules should be deemed effective service. The Court thus ruled to dismiss WRE Company's action.

Case 6: *Indian D Company v. Shanghai E Company*[33]
Indian D Company and Shanghai E Company signed an agreement stipulating that disputes would be submitted to the SIAC for administration and arbitrated according to the SIAC Rules in effect. The SIAC initiated arbitration based on this clause. The arbitral tribunal held hearings in Singapore and rendered a final award, ordering Shanghai E Company to pay Indian D Company compensation for breach of contract, legal costs, arbitration costs, and interest on these items. As Shanghai E Company failed to fulfill the award, Indian D Company requested the Chinese court to recognize and enforce the final award. Shanghai E Company argued that it never received a written arbitration hearing notice, and all applications and evidentiary materials from Indian D Company were sent by the arbitration center via email, not mailed, preventing timely verification of the evidence's authenticity.

The Court held that the SIAC Arbitration Rules permitted service by email. The SIAC had sent multiple arbitration notices to Shanghai E Company via email. Subsequently, Liu, representing Shanghai E Company, emailed the arbitration center inquiring about the case, indicating that the email address used by the center for

---

[33] See the Typical Cases on Judicial Review of Arbitration published by the Shanghai High People's Court in July 2025. Service is a critical link in arbitration proceedings. Compared to court service in litigation, service by an arbitral tribunal has its particularities and must comply with the arbitration rules. In this case, according to the SIAC Rules, email is one permissible method of service. The arbitral tribunal's service of the hearing notice and evidence via email, and the related service and hearing procedures, complied with the arbitration rules.

Shanghai E Company was correct. After Liu, on behalf of Shanghai E Company, applied for a postponement of the hearing, the arbitral tribunal decided to adjourn the hearing date, to which Shanghai E Company raised no objection and confirmed receipt of the opposing party's evidence. Although Shanghai E Company claimed it could not attend the hearing due to Liu's departure, this was an internal management issue. Liu, representing Shanghai E Company, had confirmed the new hearing date. Therefore, the arbitration hearing notice and the opposing party's evidence were served to Shanghai E Company via email, and this service method complied with the arbitration rules. Consequently, the arbitral award involved should be recognized and enforced according to the provisions of the New York Convention.

Case 7: *A Company v. B Company*[34]
A Company's industrial and commercial registration address was Address X, and its legal representative was Jia. The parties had agreed in the contract that the "notification method" for A Company was Jia's contact information (another address for A Company, contact phone number, and email address). After the Hangzhou Arbitration Commission accepted the lease dispute case between B Company and A Company, it mailed the arbitration documents six times to A Company's registration address, addressed to Jia. Except for the first mail being returned due to "addressee refused," the remaining mails were returned due to "no such person at original address." The arbitral tribunal then proceeded with an absentia hearing and rendered an award. A Company applied to the Zhejiang Province Hangzhou Intermediate People's Court to set aside the arbitral award, arguing that the Hangzhou Arbitration Commission's failure to serve notices to the address agreed in the contract resulted in it not receiving arbitration notices, effectively depriving it of the rights to defend, present evidence, and debate.

The Zhejiang Province Hangzhou Intermediate People's Court held that the parties had clearly agreed on another contact address for A Company in the contract. When service to A Company's registration address was not normally received, the Hangzhou Arbitration Commission, without attempting service to the other contact address agreed upon in the contract, deemed service effective and proceeded with an absentia hearing and award. This service in fact violated the relevant provisions on service in the arbitration rules and resulted in the deprivation of A Company's relevant rights, such as defense, presentation of evidence, and debate. This constituted the circumstance stipulated in Article 58 of the Arbitration Law (2017) that the composition of the arbitral tribunal or the arbitration procedure violated the

[34] See the Typical Cases on Judicial Review of Arbitration published by the Zhejiang Province Hangzhou Intermediate People's Court in March 2024. "Deemed service" constitutes a special circumstance beyond "personal service" or "service by leaving documents." It applies in situations where the recipient in an arbitration case subjectively refuses to accept the arbitration documents or where the arbitration institution is objectively unable to effect service upon the recipient. Once the conditions stipulated in the arbitration rules are met, the documents are deemed to have been lawfully served even if the recipient did not actually receive them, and the recipient bears the legal consequences of "having been served." The arbitration institution must make reasonable inquiries and accurately determine the service address before it can serve documents to that address in accordance with the arbitration rules and apply the concept of "deemed service."

statutory procedure. Upon reporting level-by-level and obtaining approval from the SPC, the Court ruled to set aside the arbitral award.

Section 2 Composition of Arbitral Tribunal

Article 42

An arbitral tribunal may be composed of either three arbitrators or one arbitrator. An arbitral tribunal composed of three arbitrators shall have a presiding arbitrator.

Notes

The parties' selection, or the appointment by an authorized body acting under party authorization, law, or arbitration rules, forms the arbitral tribunal. This tribunal hears the disputed matters submitted to arbitration, advances the arbitration proceedings, and ultimately renders a final and substantive award on the merits.

In the vast majority of cases, the arbitral tribunal is composed of an odd number of arbitrators. The most common tribunal compositions are a sole-arbitrator tribunal (one arbitrator) and a collegiate tribunal (three arbitrators). In international commercial arbitration legislation and practice, the number of arbitrators composing the tribunal is determined by party agreement or by the arbitration rules agreed upon by the parties. If the parties have not clearly agreed, the arbitration institution has the authority to determine the number of arbitrators for the case's tribunal according to its rules. For example, Article 10 of the UNCITRAL Model Law stipulates that if the parties have not agreed on the number of arbitrators, and the respondent, upon receiving the notice of arbitration, fails to agree on a sole arbitrator within a specified period, the default is three arbitrators, to be selected by the parties and the relevant appointing authority. Differing from the Model Law approach, the AAA Commercial Arbitration Rules state that if the arbitration agreement does not specify the number of arbitrators or is ambiguous, and the parties do not otherwise agree, the dispute will be heard and determined by one arbitrator, unless the AAA, in its discretion, directs that three arbitrators be appointed. A party may request three arbitrators in its claim or defense, and the AAA will exercise its discretion regarding the number of arbitrators based on that request.

To ensure the proper exercise of parties' rights, many countries impose corresponding legal restrictions on the parties' choice regarding the tribunal's composition. As stipulated in this Article, the arbitral tribunal shall be composed of either three arbitrators or one arbitrator. A tribunal composed of three arbitrators is commonly referred to as a collegiate tribunal or a three-member tribunal, while a tribunal composed of one arbitrator is commonly referred to as a sole-arbitrator tribunal or a one-member tribunal.

This Article clarifies the two basic forms of arbitral tribunal composition: first, a tribunal composed of one arbitrator, and second, a tribunal composed of three arbitrators. In practice, the composition of the tribunal is often applied flexibly based on factors such as the nature of the case, the amount in dispute, and the parties' intentions, to ensure the suitability and efficiency of the arbitration.

A tribunal composed of one arbitrator is commonly referred to in practice as a sole-arbitrator tribunal. Under this form, the single arbitrator is solely responsible for hearing and deciding the disputed case submitted by the parties for arbitration. The sole arbitrator is usually jointly selected by the parties or appointed by the arbitration institution. The advantage of a sole-arbitrator tribunal lies in its simplicity and cost-effectiveness. Since only one arbitrator needs to be appointed, the formation process is relatively straightforward, allowing for a quick start to the arbitration proceedings and avoiding delays caused by multi-party coordination. For instance, in cases involving smaller amounts in dispute and clear facts, a sole-arbitrator tribunal can significantly reduce the parties' arbitration costs, including time and financial costs. However, since the outcome of the award relies entirely on the judgment of a single arbitrator, any shortcomings in the arbitrator's professional competence, experience, or impartiality could lead to erroneous or biased awards. Furthermore, the sole-arbitrator tribunal lacks a system of checks and balances; if the arbitrator makes procedural or substantive errors, the cost of correction is relatively high. Therefore, a sole-arbitrator tribunal is more suitable for relatively straightforward disputes where the parties have a high degree of trust.

A tribunal composed of three arbitrators is commonly referred to in practice as a collegiate tribunal or a three-member tribunal. The claimant and the respondent each appoint one arbitrator, and the third arbitrator, the presiding arbitrator, is jointly selected by the parties or appointed by the arbitration institution. Within the collegiate tribunal, the presiding arbitrator plays a very central role. Regarding the progress of the arbitration proceedings, the presiding arbitrator acts as the chairperson, requiring thorough familiarity with arbitration procedure. Should any procedural inefficiencies arise, they should promptly study the matter with the other tribunal members to control the process. Regarding decisions on substantive issues, while expressing their independent opinion, the presiding arbitrator should synthesize the opinions of the other arbitrators to formulate the award document. In situations where a majority opinion of the tribunal cannot be formed, the opinion of the presiding arbitrator becomes decisive. The advantage of a collegiate tribunal lies in its collective decision-making mechanism. Three arbitrators can examine the case from different perspectives, discuss and complement each other, contributing to a more comprehensive grasp of the issues and reducing potential biases from individual judgment, thereby making the award more prudent and sound. Simultaneously, the parties' right to appoint arbitrators enhances their sense of participation and trust in the arbitration process. However, compared to a sole-arbitrator tribunal, the formation process for a collegiate tribunal is somewhat longer, and the costs are naturally higher.

Illustrative Cases

Case 1: ***A International Logistics Company v. Singapore B Shipping Company***[35]

A International Logistics Company and Singapore B Shipping Company entered into the Charter Party Agreement stipulating that disputes would be arbitrated in London under English law and the LMAA Terms. After a dispute arose, A International Logistics Company sent a Notice of Arbitration to Singapore B Shipping Company, stating that arbitration had been commenced pursuant to the arbitration clause and that an arbitrator had been appointed. It requested Singapore B Shipping Company to appoint its arbitrator within 14 days. Subsequently, A International Logistics Company sent another email to Singapore B Shipping Company, noting the lack of response regarding the arbitrator appointment and stating that, according to the 2021 LMAA Terms, the arbitrator it appointed would serve as the sole arbitrator. During the arbitration, Singapore B Shipping Company submitted a Defense and Counterclaim and a Reply to Defense. After the arbitral award was rendered and Singapore B Shipping Company failed to comply, A International Logistics Company applied to a Chinese court for recognition and enforcement. Singapore B Shipping Company argued that it had not participated in the appointment of the arbitrator, and that the sole arbitrator was not a full member of the LMAA, thus not complying with the LMAA Terms. The court ultimately ruled to recognize and enforce the arbitral award.

The court held that the involved award was an English maritime arbitral award. As both China and the UK are contracting states to the New York Convention, the award should be reviewed under the Convention. Regarding the composition of the arbitral tribunal, the LMAA Terms contained no requirement for a sole arbitrator to be a full member, nor was there any such agreement between the parties. The Notice of Arbitration sent by A International Logistics Company clearly stated its appointment of an arbitrator and requested Singapore B Shipping Company to appoint its arbitrator within 14 days. This Notice alerted Singapore B Shipping Company to the potential consequences and gave it a choice. Singapore B Shipping Company did not respond and instead participated in the entire arbitration proceeding by submitting defenses and a counterclaim on the merits, constituting an implied waiver of its right to object. This should be deemed as the parties having agreed to appoint the arbitrator designated by A International Logistics Company as the sole arbitrator. Therefore, the composition of the arbitral tribunal in this case complied with the LMAA Terms.

[35] See the Typical Cases from 202-2024 on Judicial Review of Arbitration published by the Shanghai High People's Court in July 2025. The composition of the arbitral tribunal or the arbitration procedure not being in accordance with the agreement of the parties or the arbitration rules constitutes a ground for refusing recognition and enforcement of an arbitral award under the New York Convention. In this case, the court examined the parties' agreement, including the arbitration clause and arbitration rules, the parties' conduct during the arbitration, and the law of the seat of arbitration, determining that the composition of the arbitral tribunal was not inconsistent with the parties' agreement or the arbitration rules. Furthermore, applying the law of the seat, English law, it pointed out that the respondent had participated in the entire arbitration proceeding and failed to raise an objection promptly as required by English law, constituting a waiver.

Case 2: ***C Finance Company v. D Salt Company***[36]

On December 11, 2007, C Finance Company and D Salt Company signed the Loan Contract stipulating that any dispute shall be finally settled by arbitration under the UNCITRAL Arbitration Rules. The place of arbitration shall be Hong Kong. The appointing authority shall be the HKIAC. The arbitral tribunal shall consist of three arbitrators. As D Salt Company failed to repay the loan as agreed, C Finance Company applied for arbitration to the HKIAC. The HKIAC rendered an arbitral award on August 12, 2019. C Finance Company applied to the Sichuan Province Zigong Intermediate People's Court for recognition and enforcement of the award on August 17, 2020. D Salt Company argued that the Loan Contract stipulated a tribunal of three arbitrators, but HKIAC appointed a sole arbitrator. Therefore, the award should not be enforced. Investigation revealed that the award stated that the parties had written to HKIAC requesting the appointment of an arbitrator. After Bao was appointed as the sole arbitrator for the dispute, the parties confirmed this appointment through a jointly signed letter.

The Sichuan Province Zigong Intermediate People's Court held that although the composition of the arbitral tribunal changed the original agreement in the Loan Contract for a three-member tribunal, this change to a sole arbitrator was based on a consensus reached with both parties' consent. Furthermore, D Salt Company did not raise an objection to the appointment of the sole arbitrator during the arbitration in accordance with the relevant provisions of the UNCITRAL Arbitration Rules. The Court accordingly ruled to enforce the involved arbitral award.

Case 3: ***German SE Company and others v. J Company***[37]

German SE Company, German SA Company, E Company, and J Company had business dealings since 2013. After J Company and German SE Company confirmed orders via email exchange, J Company signed two procurement agreements

[36] (2020) Chuan 03 Ren Gang No. 1; See the 6 Typical Cases Supporting Hong Kong Arbitration published by the SPC in September 2024. The core of international commercial arbitration lies in fully respecting party autonomy. International commercial arbitration allows parties to select, initiate, modify, and advance the entire arbitration process through their autonomous will. Although the agreement in this case stipulated a tribunal of three arbitrators, the change during the arbitration proceedings to appoint a sole arbitrator, confirmed by a jointly signed written letter, did not constitute the ground for refusal of enforcement under Article 7(1)(4) of the Arrangement Concerning Mutual Enforcement of Awards which concerns the composition of the arbitral tribunal not being in accordance with the agreement of the parties.

[37] See the 6 Typical Cases Supporting Hong Kong Arbitration published by the SPC in September 2024. Once chosen by the parties, the arbitration rules become the procedural norms to be followed by the arbitration institution, the arbitral tribunal, and the parties during the arbitration process. They also serve as the primary basis for the People's Court to determine the legality of the arbitral tribunal's composition and the arbitration procedure at the recognition and enforcement stage. When a party violates a procedural order, the arbitral tribunal has the power, within the framework of the arbitration rules, to make determinations and decide how to proceed. This case also elaborated on issues such as awards rendered by the ICC International Court of Arbitration in Hong Kong being Hong Kong awards, and that the award did not violate the social public interest of the Chinese Mainland, finally ruling to recognize and enforce the involved award based on the Arrangement Concerning Mutual Enforcement of Awards.

with German SA Company and E Company, respectively. Both agreements stipulated that disputes should be submitted to the ICC International Court of Arbitration for arbitration under the ICC Arbitration Rules, with the seat of arbitration in Hong Kong. German SE Company, German SA Company, and E Company applied to the ICC International Court of Arbitration for arbitration, alleging breach of contract by J Company. The ICC International Court of Arbitration rendered a final award on September 4, 2020, ordering J Company to pay E Company €4,962,980 for the goods, plus lost profits, damages, default interest, etc. German SE Company et al. applied to the Beijing Fourth Intermediate People's Court for recognition and enforcement of the award on January 4, 2021. J Company argued that the award should not be recognized and enforced, primarily on the grounds that: E Company submitted its Procedural Timetable later than the deadline set by the tribunal's Procedural Order No. 1, and this Procedural Order represented the parties' procedural agreement; the appointment of the presiding arbitrator violated Article 12(5) of the ICC Arbitration Rules, thus constituting a situation where the arbitration procedure was not in accordance with the parties' agreement; the subject matter involved excessively high electromagnetic radiation, endangering public safety, and enforcement would violate the social public interest of the Mainland, etc.

The Beijing No. 4 Intermediate People's Court held that the arbitral award rendered by the ICC International Court of Arbitration in Hong Kong should be recognized as a Hong Kong arbitral award. Regarding whether the composition of the arbitral tribunal and the arbitration procedure were inconsistent with the parties' agreement, since J Company failed to provide evidence proving that the parties had agreed on another procedure for appointing the third arbitrator, according to Articles 12(5) and 13(2) of the ICC Arbitration Rules, the third arbitrator, who serves as the presiding arbitrator, shall be appointed by the Court, and the Secretary General may confirm a candidate nominated jointly by the co-arbitrators as the presiding arbitrator. In this case, the presiding arbitrator was jointly nominated by the co-arbitrators and confirmed by the Secretary General of the Court. This appointment procedure did not violate the aforementioned provisions of the ICC Arbitration Rules. Article 22(2) of the ICC Arbitration Rules states: "To ensure effective case management, the arbitral tribunal, after consulting the parties, may adopt such procedural measures as it considers appropriate, provided that they are not contrary to any agreement of the parties." For a party's failure to submit documents according to the procedural timetable set by the tribunal, the tribunal has the discretion to decide whether to accept them. The tribunal's acceptance of E Company's belated Procedural Timetable did not violate the ICC Arbitration Rules or the parties' agreement. Furthermore, the dispute involved a contractual dispute between equal civil subjects, and its outcome only affected the contracting parties, not involving social public safety. Whether the products met the inspection standards agreed in the contract was also not a basis for determining that the award harmed social and public safety. In summary, the award involved did not contain any circumstances listed in Article 7 of the Arrangement Concerning Mutual Enforcement of Awards, and the Court ruled to recognize and enforce it.

Article 43
Where the parties agree that the arbitral tribunal shall be composed of three arbitrators, they shall each appoint or entrust the chairman of the arbitration institution to appoint one arbitrator according to the procedure stipulated in the arbitration rules. The third arbitrator shall be jointly appointed by the parties, or may be appointed by the chairman of the arbitration institution upon joint authorization by the parties in accordance with the procedure stipulated in the arbitration rules. Where the parties have agreed that the third arbitrator shall be jointly selected by their respective appointed arbitrators, such agreement shall prevail. The third arbitrator shall serve as the presiding arbitrator.
Where the parties agree that the arbitral tribunal shall be composed of one arbitrator, they shall jointly appoint or jointly entrust the chairman of the arbitration institution to appoint the arbitrator according to the procedure stipulated in the arbitration rules.

Notes
The appointment of arbitrators for a specific case, forming the arbitral tribunal, may occur through different methods. The primary method is appointment by agreement of the parties. In institutional arbitration, different institutions may impose certain review processes or require confirmation for the appointment of arbitrators. The main methods for appointing arbitrators include selection by the parties themselves, selection by the parties themselves followed by confirmation by the appointing authority, appointment by a designated appointing authority, court appointment of an arbitrator, appointment of an arbitrator by the administering institution, and appointment of the presiding arbitrator by the already-appointed arbitrators. Most arbitration laws or rules contain provisions, whether detailed or brief, regarding the appointment of arbitrators.

As a reflection of the consensual nature of arbitration, the parties' right to select arbitrators is an important right and the primary method agreed upon by the parties for arbitrator appointment. A party's failure to receive notice regarding the appointment of an arbitrator may render the award unenforceable. Parties can select arbitrators according to their own will. Arbitrators selected in this manner are the customary approach in the majority of arbitration cases. Parties, besides agreeing to select arbitrators themselves, may also agree on other methods of appointment, such as designating a third party to appoint the arbitrator. Parties can agree on the arbitrator(s) in the arbitration clause, agree on them in an arbitration agreement after a dispute arises, or select an arbitrator after the commencement of arbitration proceedings, upon notice from the arbitral tribunal or the other party.

The principle of party autonomy in arbitration dictates that, in addition to selecting their respective arbitrators, parties can negotiate to determine the candidate for the presiding arbitrator or the sole arbitrator. Parties can also agree on the qualifications and other conditions for arbitrators or agree on the method for selecting arbitrators. They can directly nominate a specific individual to serve as the presiding arbitrator or sole arbitrator. For instance, the parties may separately or jointly nominate A as the presiding arbitrator or sole arbitrator. This method best reflects party autonomy. The practical difficulty with this method is that, as it occurs after the dispute has arisen, any proposal from one party may be met with distrust by the other, making the likelihood of jointly selecting a specific arbitrator very small. Failing joint selection, the parties may resort to jointly entrusting an institution or an individual to appoint the presiding arbitrator/sole arbitrator.

In situations where the parties fail to jointly select or jointly entrust the appointment of an arbitrator, the common practice in China is for the chairman of the arbitration commission to make the appointment on their behalf. This approach has the same effect as joint entrustment for appointment, as the chairman exercises the power to appoint the presiding arbitrator.

Regarding the number of arbitrators, this Article primarily stipulates two forms of tribunal composition: the three-member collegiate tribunal and the sole-arbitrator tribunal. If the parties agree on a tribunal composed of three arbitrators, including two co-arbitrators and one presiding arbitrator, the selection of arbitrators must go through the following stages: First, each party shall select or entrust the chairman of the arbitration commission to appoint one arbitrator. The general rule is that a party is deemed to have completed the selection by designating a qualified arbitrator from the panel of arbitrators provided by the arbitration institution. In cases involving complex transactional arrangements, the arbitration clause may involve multiple parties. In such instances, the multiple parties on the same side shall jointly appoint one arbitrator. Second, the third arbitrator, the presiding arbitrator, shall be jointly selected by the parties or jointly entrusted to the chairman of the arbitration commission for appointment. The presiding arbitrator is generated primarily through three methods: firstly, the parties jointly select one arbitrator as the presiding arbitrator; secondly, the parties jointly entrust the arbitration institution, which then appoints the presiding arbitrator according to the procedures stipulated in the arbitration rules; thirdly, the parties may agree that the two already-appointed arbitrators shall jointly select the third, presiding arbitrator.

In practice, it is often difficult for the parties to effectively negotiate the choice of the presiding arbitrator. Many arbitration rules establish specific mechanisms for the appointment of the presiding arbitrator. Currently, the mechanisms adopted by major domestic arbitration institutions in China can be summarized into the following three categories: The first is the recommendation system, which requires each party to recommend several candidates for the presiding arbitrator. If there is an identical candidate on both parties' recommendation lists, that person is typically appointed as the presiding arbitrator. If there is more than one identical candidate, the chairman of the arbitration commission usually appoints one from among them. If there is no overlap in the lists, the chairman of the arbitration commission decides and appoints a presiding arbitrator from outside the recommendation lists. Although this method provides some possibility for the parties to jointly select the presiding arbitrator, it faces two main issues in practice: firstly, due to the adversarial nature of arbitration itself, parties often lack the initiative to proactively recommend candidates and may even directly waive their right to recommend; secondly, given the large number of arbitrators on the panel, it is extremely difficult for parties acting 'back-to-back' to recommend the same person, often resulting in the recommended candidates being directly excluded from subsequent appointment. Of course, in some cases, parties might also use the recommendation system as a procedural tactic to exclude undesired candidates from becoming the presiding arbitrator. The second is the list system, where, upon party agreement or joint application, the arbitration institution provides a list containing several candidates. The parties can make positive selections or negative exclusions from the list and give feedback on the results to the institution. If a candidate remains on both parties' final lists, that person is appointed as the presiding arbitrator. If multiple candidates remain, the chairman of the arbitration commission makes the appointment. If no candidates overlap, the chairman appoints from outside the list. The third is selection by the co-arbitrators. This Article specifically mentions this method but emphasizes that it applies when the parties have agreed that the two co-arbitrators will jointly select the presiding arbitrator. This raises a question: can this method be used if the parties have not agreed upon it? This can be understood in conjunction with the provisions of Article 44 below, which states that if the parties have not agreed on the method for forming the tribunal or selecting arbitrators, the chairman of the arbitration commission shall appoint the arbitrators according to the procedure determined by the arbitration rules. Based on this provision, we return to the third category of presiding arbitrator appointment mechanisms summarized earlier. As the phrase "if the parties have agreed that the third arbitrator is to be jointly selected by the arbitrators they have respectively selected, such agreement shall prevail" is newly added content in this revision, the specific issues that may arise in practice require further observation.

Illustrative Case

***A Company v. J*[38]**

In 2018, A Company and J entered into the House Commission Lease Contract, which stipulated, "disputes arising from or in connection with this Agreement shall be settled through friendly negotiations between the parties. If a dispute is not resolved within thirty (30) days after one party issues written notice to the other party, either party shall have the right to submit the dispute to the Hangzhou Arbitration Commission for arbitration in Hangzhou in accordance with its arbitration rules effective at that time. For the purpose of arbitration, a tribunal of three arbitrators shall be constituted. Each party to the dispute shall select one arbitrator,

[38] See the Typical Cases on Judicial Review of Arbitration published by the Zhejiang Province Hangzhou Intermediate Court in March 2024. This case involves the issue of how to determine the legitimacy and legality of arbitration procedures when a special stipulation in the arbitration clause conflicts with the arbitration rules of the arbitration institution. The arbitration clause in this case stipulated the composition of the arbitral tribunal, which effectively precluded the application of the summary procedure under the arbitration rules. This can be understood as a specially agreed arbitration procedure by the parties. Unless subject to a "special reminder" by the arbitrator, this special agreement is not overridden by the parties' acceptance of the arbitration institution's rules, and an arbitrator's non-specific inquiry directed at the parties does not constitute a "special reminder".

and the third arbitrator shall be jointly appointed by the parties to the dispute. The two arbitrators appointed in this manner shall jointly appoint the third arbitrator. If either party fails to appoint an arbitrator within fifteen (15) working days from receipt of the notice of arbitration, or if the two arbitrators appointed by the parties fail to agree on the third arbitrator within fifteen (15) working days from the appointment of the second arbitrator, then any arbitrator not appointed as provided above shall be appointed by the Hangzhou Arbitration Commission in accordance with its arbitration rules effective at that time." In 2019, J applied for arbitration to the Hangzhou Arbitration Commission. On October 30, 2019, the Hangzhou Arbitration Commission sent the Notice of Response to Arbitration (Summary Procedure) to A Company. On November 15, the Hangzhou Arbitration Commission appointed a sole arbitrator to form the arbitral tribunal. On November 18, the Hangzhou Arbitration Commission sent the Notice of Tribunal Composition to A Company, informing it that "If you wish to challenge any of the above members of the arbitral tribunal, please submit a written application stating the reasons before the hearing." The sole arbitrator heard the case using the summary procedure and inquired in court whether A Company had any objections to the prior arbitration procedures, but did not specifically remind the parties that the composition of the tribunal was inconsistent with their agreement. A Company stated it did not apply for a challenge and had no objections to the prior procedures. After the Hangzhou Arbitration Commission rendered an arbitral award, A Company applied to the Zhejiang Province Hangzhou Intermediate People's Court to set it aside.

The Zhejiang Province Hangzhou Intermediate People's Court held that, according to the wording of the arbitration clause signed by A Company and J, the parties agreed to arbitrate according to the Hangzhou Arbitration Commission's rules, but simultaneously made a specific agreement regarding the composition of a three-member tribunal and the appointment of arbitrators. This constituted a special agreement on the composition of the arbitral tribunal, which clearly precluded the application of the summary procedure contained in the Hangzhou Arbitration Commission Arbitration Rules. Without obtaining A Company's consent, the Hangzhou Arbitration Commission directly sent the Notice of Response to Arbitration (Summary Procedure), requiring A Company and J to jointly select or jointly entrust the Chairman of the Arbitration Commission to appoint a sole arbitrator and to apply the summary procedure. This violated the parties' special agreement on the arbitration procedure. The resulting arbitral award violated statutory procedures, falling under the circumstances for setting aside an arbitral award stipulated in Article 14 of the Arbitral Award Enforcement Provisions. During the hearing of the arbitration case, the sole arbitrator did inquire in court whether the parties had objections to the prior procedures, and A Company did not raise an objection to the composition of the tribunal. However, the sole arbitrator's inquiry was not a specific reminder directed at the parties regarding their choice of a sole arbitrator and the application of the summary procedure for the case. It did not meet the requirement of a "special reminder" stipulated in Article 14 of the aforementioned judicial interpretation. Therefore, it could not alter the determination that the arbitration violated statutory procedures. Consequently, upon reporting level-by-level and obtaining approval from the SPC, the Zhejiang Province Hangzhou Intermediate People's Court ruled to set aside the arbitral award.

Article 44
Where the parties fail to agree on the method of composition of the arbitral tribunal or to appoint the arbitrators within the time limit specified in the arbitration rules, the arbitrators shall be determined or appointed by the chairman of the arbitration institution following the procedures stipulated in the arbitration rules.

Notes
In arbitration practice, due to the substantive conflict of interest between the parties, it may be difficult or even impossible for them to reach an agreement on the composition of the arbitral tribunal through negotiation. If the arbitration agreement also fails to clearly stipulate the form of tribunal composition, the arbitration proceedings may reach a deadlock due to party inaction or disagreement. The core function of this article is to ensure that the arbitration proceedings do not stall due to the passive conduct or disagreements of the parties. By empowering the chairman of the arbitration institution to appoint arbitrators for the parties according to the procedures determined by the applicable arbitration provisions, this clause provides an institutional guarantee for the smooth progress of the arbitration.

When applying Article 44, it is important to note that the chairman's power of appointment is conditional upon the parties' failure to agree on the composition of the arbitral tribunal or to select arbitrators within the specified time limit, and must follow the procedures prescribed by the applicable arbitration rules. In other words, if the parties fail to reach an agreement on the composition of the arbitral tribunal within a certain period, and also fail to select or jointly select arbitrators within that period, then the chairman of the arbitration institution, according to law, has the power to appoint arbitrators on behalf of the parties. However, the appointment of arbitrators must be conducted in accordance with the procedures stipulated in the arbitration rules.

The forms of tribunal composition typically include a sole-arbitrator tribunal and a three-member tribunal. Parties may agree on the composition of the tribunal, such as the number of arbitrators and how each arbitrator is to be appointed. The parties' agreement takes precedence. If the parties have not agreed, the chairman of the arbitration institution will determine the number of arbitrators and the method of their appointment according to the arbitration rules.

Currently, the arbitration rules of most domestic arbitration institutions distinguish between the ordinary procedure, which applies to three-member tribunals, and the fast-track procedure (or summary procedure, etc.), which applies to sole-arbitrator tribunals. For example, Article 29(2) of the SCIA Arbitration Rules stipulates that unless otherwise agreed by the parties or provided by these Rules, the arbitral tribunal shall be composed of three arbitrators. Article 56 stipulates: (1) the fast-track procedure shall apply where the amount in dispute does not exceed RMB 10 million, or where the amount in dispute exceeds RMB 10 million but the parties have agreed in writing, or where the parties have agreed to apply the fast-track or summary procedure; (2) where the amount in dispute is not clear, the SCIA Court shall decide whether to apply the fast-track procedure based on a comprehensive consideration of the complexity of the case, the interests involved, and other relevant factors. Article 20(1) of the BAC Arbitration Rules stipulates that unless otherwise agreed by the parties or provided by these Rules, the arbitral tribunal shall be composed of three arbitrators. Articles 54 and 55 stipulate that, unless otherwise agreed by the parties, the summary procedure shall apply where the amount of the claim does not exceed RMB 5 million. Cases applying the summary procedure shall be heard by a sole arbitrator.

For cases applying a three-member tribunal, the parties shall, within the specified time limit, each select one arbitrator and jointly select a presiding arbitrator. For cases applying a sole-arbitrator tribunal, the parties shall, within the specified time limit, jointly select one sole arbitrator. In practice, most arbitration rules stipulate that the aforementioned time limit is usually 15 days from the date the party receives the Notice of Arbitration. If the parties fail to select arbitrators within the time limit, the chairman of the arbitration institution shall appoint the arbitrators according to the procedure determined by the arbitration rules. Generally, factors such as expertise, reputation, arbitration experience, efficiency, availability, qualifications, working language, domicile, nationality, age, education level, and personality traits may all be considered by the arbitration institution when determining the arbitrator for a specific case. The final determination of the specific candidate requires a comprehensive consideration of various factors. Some arbitration rules have provisions on this matter. For example, Article 30 of the CIETAC Arbitration Rules stipulates that when appointing an arbitrator, the Chairman of the Arbitration Commission shall consider the applicable law of the dispute, the place of arbitration, the language of arbitration, the nationalities of the parties, the type of dispute, and any other factors the Chairman considers relevant.

The appointing entity "chairman of the arbitration institution" stipulated in this Article can be understood as a functional role within the arbitration institution, rather than a specific individual. Therefore, the act of the chairman appointing arbitrators for the parties is not an arbitrary subjective decision but must strictly follow the procedures prescribed by the arbitration rules, ensuring that the procedure for appointing arbitrators is legal and compliant, and that the appointed arbitrator is suitable for the specific case.

Article 45
If an arbitrator falls under any circumstance that may cause the parties to reasonably doubt his or her independence or impartiality, the arbitrator should promptly disclose in writing to the arbitration institution.

The arbitration institution shall notify the parties in writing of the arbitrators' disclosures and the composition of the arbitral tribunal.

Notes
The ability of arbitrators to exercise their power impartially and independently is the fundamental guarantee for the proper resolution of commercial disputes through

the arbitration mechanism. Impartiality requires arbitrators to maintain an unbiased stance towards both parties and in rendering awards; independence emphasizes that arbitrators should make objective judgments based on the facts and the law, free from interference by any party or external factors. Impartiality and independence permeate all stages, including the qualification and selection of arbitrators and the conduct of hearings, and are also reflected in specific institutional arrangements such as the boundaries of the parties' right to challenge an arbitrator and the scope of the arbitrator's duty of disclosure.

Although the New Arbitration Law provides a withdrawal system for arbitrators, its function cannot replace the disclosure system. For a long time, the arbitrator's duty of disclosure has been primarily stipulated by various arbitration institutions in their arbitration rules or codes of conduct for arbitrators. The lack of provisions at the legislative level has led to issues in judicial review practice concerning the arbitrator's duty of disclosure, including unclear standards for the duty of disclosure, divergences in the application of law, and inconsistent rulings in similar cases.

The disclosure system and the withdrawal system are essentially two sides of the same coin: the former emphasizes the arbitrator's proactive notification of circumstances that may affect impartiality, reflecting self-discipline and ex-ante prevention; the latter relies on the parties raising objections, belonging to ex-post remedy and passive response. The two systems are complementary in function, each with its own focus, and cannot replace each other.

The New Arbitration Law explicitly codifies the arbitrator's duty of disclosure, forming an effective connection and closed-loop management between the disclosure and challenge systems, filling the previous legislative gap. The system helps to more comprehensively safeguard the independence and impartiality of arbitrators and enhance the credibility of arbitration outcomes. Simultaneously, it provides a clear basis for judicial review, helps unify the standards for applying the law, reduces inconsistent rulings in similar cases due to vague rules, and improves the predictability and consistency of judicial practice.

Article 45(1) stipulates the arbitrator's active duty of disclosure. If an arbitrator believes circumstances exist that could give rise to justifiable doubts regarding their independence or impartiality, the arbitrator shall promptly disclose these circumstances to the arbitration institution in writing.

Under what circumstances must an arbitrator make a disclosure? This involves determining the specific standard for the arbitrator's duty of disclosure. Judging from the content of the provision, whenever an arbitrator believes that facts objectively exist which could give rise to justifiable doubts about their independence or impartiality, they must fulfill the duty of disclosure. As the subject of the disclosure obligation, the arbitrator should determine whether to disclose and which facts to disclose from the perspective of a reasonable third party. Common situations include, but are not limited to: the arbitrator having an economic interest or business dealings with a party; having close social relationships such as familial, collegial, or comrade-in-arms ties with a party or its representative; having previously provided advisory opinions or expressed biased views on the matters in dispute; and other circumstances that may affect independent judgment. In practice, the principle of "when in doubt, disclose" is usually followed.

Besides the matters for disclosure, it should also be noted that: firstly, disclosure is not limited to before accepting the appointment but is an ongoing obligation. If matters requiring disclosure arise during the course of the proceedings, they should also be promptly disclosed. Secondly, disclosure does not constitute a denial of the arbitrator's impartiality and independence. The purpose of disclosure is to provide information for the parties to decide whether to challenge the arbitrator, and it does not necessarily lead to the arbitrator's challenge.

Article 45 (2) stipulates the arbitration institution's duty to notify, meaning the arbitration institution shall promptly, accurately, and comprehensively inform the parties of the content disclosed by the arbitrator and the composition of the arbitral tribunal in writing. In practice, many arbitration institutions require that when an arbitrator is appointed by a party or the chairman of the arbitration institution, they must sign a written declaration guaranteeing independent and impartial arbitration. If facts exist that could give rise to justifiable doubts about their impartiality and independence, they should proactively disclose them in this declaration. When the arbitration institution notifies the parties of the tribunal's composition in writing, it attaches the declaration signed by the arbitrator(s). For example, Article 32 of the SCIA Arbitration Rules stipulates that after being appointed, an arbitrator shall sign a declaration of impartiality and independence. The arbitrator shall disclose in the declaration any circumstances likely to give rise to justifiable doubts as to his/her impartiality or independence of which he/she is aware. Should any circumstances requiring disclosure arise during the arbitration proceedings after the declaration is signed, the arbitrator shall promptly disclose them in writing.

Illustrative Cases

Case 1: *A Engineering Company v. TB Company*[39]

In March 2017, TB Company filed an arbitration application with an arbitration commission against A Engineering Company due to a construction project contract dispute. A Engineering Company raised a counterclaim. After hearing the case, the arbitral tribunal, considering the complexity of the case and the large amount in dispute, consulted the expert advisory committee of that arbitration commission on the disputed issues in April 2018. In July 2018, the arbitral tribunal rendered an award. A Engineering Company applied to the Wenzhou Intermediate People's Court of Zhejiang Province to set aside the aforementioned arbitral award on the grounds that the composition of the arbitral tribunal violated procedures, among other reasons.

[39] (2018) Zhe 03 Min Te No. 63; See the 10 Typical Cases on Judicial Review of Arbitration published by the SPC in January 2024.In this case, the arbitrator failed to fully fulfill the disclosure obligation in accordance with the arbitration rules, which, to a certain extent, affected the party's exercise of the right to challenge. This constituted a circumstance that might affect the fairness of the award. Therefore, the people's court set aside the arbitral award on the grounds that "the composition of the arbitral tribunal or the arbitration procedure was not in accordance with the statutory procedure".

The Zhejiang Province Wenzhou Intermediate People's Court held that Yang, the agent for TB Company in the arbitration case, had previously worked at the same law firm as the arbitrator Chen. During Yang's tenure as the director of the expert advisory committee of the arbitration commission, both Chen and the presiding arbitrator in the arbitration case were expert members of that committee. However, the arbitrator profile for Yang on the arbitration commission's official webpage did not indicate his position as director of the expert advisory committee, and his status as director was not disclosed during the arbitration proceedings. According to Article 56(1)(3) of that arbitration commission's arbitration rules, an arbitrator who has other relationships with a party or its agent in a case that may affect the impartiality of the award shall voluntarily disclose this to the arbitration commission and request a withdrawal, and the parties also have the right to apply for withdrawal. During the arbitration proceedings of the involved case, Chen and others failed to disclose their relationship with TB Company's agent in accordance with the arbitration rules, which, to a certain extent, affected the parties' exercise of their right to challenge and constituted a circumstance that might affect the fairness of the award. Although the expert advisory committee of the arbitration commission stated that the members for the expert advisory meeting held in April 2018 were determined by lot drawing by the commission, because it refused to provide the meeting minutes of this meeting to the people's court, and as there were currently no relevant records concerning the lot drawing in the arbitration case file materials, reasonable suspicion that Yang, as the director of the expert advisory committee, exerted improper influence on this discussion could not be ruled out. Accordingly, the court ruled to set aside the aforementioned award rendered by the arbitration commission.

Case 2: *Wang v. B Bank*[40]

Fang, the deputy branch manager of the Tianjin Branch of B Bank (this branch was not involved in the business related to the arbitration case), met with the presiding arbitrator Hong, under the pretext of being a student, and attempted to discuss legal application issues related to the arbitration case. Arbitrator Hong, suspecting it might be related to an arbitration case he was handling, refused to comment and left. Subsequently, the arbitrator did not disclose this incident. After the arbitral award was rendered, the respondent Wang applied to the Court to set aside the arbitral award made by the SCIA, on the grounds that presiding arbitrator Hong violated the provisions on arbitrator withdrawal under Article 34(3) of the Arbitration Law (2017).

---

[40] See the Typical Cases on Judicial Review of Arbitration published by the Guangdong Province Shenzhen Intermediate People's Court in July 2025. Determining whether an arbitrator should withdraw due to private meetings with a party requires considering whether the meeting process is sufficient to raise justifiable doubts about the arbitrator's impartiality, rather than requiring withdrawal merely because a meeting occurred. In this case, although the meeting participant Fang was an employee of Bank B, the branch where he worked was not involved in the business related to the case, and the arbitrator was unaware of his professional identity. The arbitrator left immediately upon learning the purpose of the meeting. The facts of the arbitration case were not discussed. Such circumstances would not raise justifiable doubts about the arbitrator's impartiality and therefore did not constitute grounds for the arbitrator's withdrawal.

The Guangdong Province Shenzhen Intermediate People's Court held that Wang was aware of the meeting between Fang and the arbitrator before the first hearing of the arbitral tribunal, but did not apply for the arbitrator's withdrawal on this ground. According to Article 14(3) of the Arbitral Award Enforcement Provisions, Wang's application to set aside the involved arbitral award on the grounds that the presiding arbitrator violated Article 32(2) of the SCIA Arbitration Rules could not be established and should not be supported. Fang, as the deputy branch manager of B Bank's Tianjin Branch, had no connection between the business involved in the arbitration case and B Bank's Tianjin Branch. Fang did not disclose his employer or other identity information before contacting the arbitrator, and the arbitrator was unaware of Fang's professional identity. Fang met the arbitrator in his personal capacity, not as a party to the arbitration case. Furthermore, the arbitrator left immediately upon learning that Fang was an employee of B Bank, and the facts of the arbitration case were not discussed. Such circumstances did not affect the fair handling of the arbitration case. Therefore, the arbitrator did not violate Articles 34(3) or (4) of the Arbitration Law (2017). Wang's application to set aside the involved arbitral award on this ground was unfounded, and his claim was not supported. The Court accordingly ruled to dismiss Wang's action.

Article 46

Under any one of the following circumstances, the arbitrator must withdraw, and the parties shall also have the right to challenge the arbitrator for a withdrawal:

(1) **The arbitrator is a party, an agent in the case or a close relative of a party or of an agent in the case;**
(2) **The arbitrator has a personal interest in the case;**
(3) **The arbitrator has other relationship with a party or their agent in the case which may affect the impartiality of arbitration; or**
(4) **The arbitrator has privately met with a party or agent or accepted an invitation to entertainment or a gift from a party or agent.**

Notes

Ensuring the fairness and credibility of arbitration proceedings hinges on safeguarding the independence and impartiality of arbitrators. The essence of arbitration lies in the adjudication by a third party chosen by the parties. Its authority stems not only from legal mandate but is also rooted in the trust of the parties. The foundation of this trust is the arbitrator's ability to make unbiased judgments based on facts and law, free from any external interference.

However, in the complex landscape of commercial and social practice, various explicit or implicit interest connections may exist between an arbitrator and the parties, their representatives, or other related entities. These connections could arise from commercial cooperation, financial dealings, familial relationships, teacher-student bonds, or prior professional associations. Failure to regulate such situations, even if the arbitrator subjectively believes they can remain impartial, makes it difficult to fully dispel any reasonable doubts from the parties and the public regarding the arbitrator's neutrality, thereby fundamentally undermining the just foundation of the arbitration system. The arbitrator's duty of disclosure stipulated in Article 45 requires arbitrators to proactively and promptly inform the arbitration institution of any circumstances likely to give rise to justifiable doubts as to their impartiality or independence. What to disclose and whether to disclose in practice relies on the arbitrator's professional ethics, expert judgment, and the subsequent review by the arbitration institution.

The system for challenging arbitrators is a crucial measure to ensure the fairness and independence of arbitration, constituting a mandatory procedural norm with severe consequences. Once a circumstance for challenge expressly provided by law exists, the arbitrator no longer has discretion and must withdraw from the case. Their continued participation directly risks the arbitral award being set aside or enforcement being refused. For instance, after an award is rendered, a party may invoke grounds such as "the composition of the arbitral tribunal or the arbitration procedure was not in accordance with the statutory procedure" or "the composition of the arbitral tribunal or the arbitration procedure was not in accordance with the arbitration rules" to argue that the arbitrator violated disclosure or challenge obligations and apply to set aside the arbitral award.

It can be considered that the circumstances for challenge explicitly listed by law constitute the minimum, yet most core, requirements for an arbitrator's duty of disclosure. These are legally defined red lines that undoubtedly may affect impartial arbitration. Arbitrators not only bear the responsibility to proactively disclose these circumstances but also, upon disclosure or upon a party's request, bear the mandatory obligation to withdraw according to law.

The provisions on the duty of disclosure in Article 45 provide a crucial pre-discovery and filtering mechanism for the effective implementation of the challenge system in this Article. Together, they form indispensable procedural pillars for safeguarding arbitration fairness. Their ultimate purpose is to maintain the purity and authority of the arbitration process by eliminating, to the greatest extent possible, any factors that could affect neutrality.

This Article clearly stipulates the statutory circumstances under which an arbitrator must withdraw. If an arbitrator falls under any of the four categories listed in this Article, they shall voluntarily withdraw themselves from the case and must not continue to participate in the arbitration proceedings. Simultaneously, parties have the right, upon discovering that an arbitrator falls under the aforementioned circumstances, to raise an objection with the arbitration institution and request the withdrawal of that arbitrator. This right is a vital component of the parties' procedural rights.

Specifically, the circumstances for withdrawal stipulated in this Article include the following four categories:

(1) Where there is an identity overlap between the arbitrator and the case, for instance, if the arbitrator is a party to the case, an agent, or a close relative of a party or agent. This category constitutes the most obvious and fundamental

conflict of interest, as it involves a direct identity connection between the arbitrator and the subject of the case.

(2) Where the arbitrator has an interest in the case. The term "interest" typically refers to a situation where the arbitrator personally, or specific related persons (such as family members, parties with actual beneficial links), have a direct or indirect economic, reputational, or other legal stake in the outcome of the case, such that it may affect the neutrality and objectivity of their adjudication.

(3) Where there exists another relationship between the arbitrator and a party or its agent in a case that may affect the impartiality of the arbitration. This category covers a broad range of relationships, which may include special social connections such as teacher-student, colleague, business partner, or debtor-creditor relationships. The core of the determination lies in whether the relationship would, in the view of a reasonable person, be sufficient to cause actual or potential influence on the arbitrator's independent judgment.

(4) Where the arbitrator has engaged in conduct that violates professional ethics, such as privately meeting with a party or its agent, or accepting entertainment or gifts from them. Such conduct not only directly contravenes the arbitrator's integrity and duty of confidentiality but also seriously undermines the propriety and credibility of the arbitration process.

Among these four categories, the first and fourth are relatively easier to identify and determine in practice due to their strong objectivity and obvious impropriety. In contrast, the second category and the third category are often more concealed and subject to interpretation, requiring comprehensive judgment based on the specific case facts, societal norms, and arbitration practice.

In practice, arbitrators should, based on the principle of good faith, proactively disclose any potential conflicts of interest. Parties also have the right to file a challenge application based on justifiable doubts. However, the final decision on whether the arbitrator should withdraw must be reviewed and determined by the arbitration institution according to statutory procedures, ensuring procedural propriety and the validity of the decision.

Illustrative Cases

Case 1: *A Office v. B Company*[41]

[41] See the 9 Typical Cases on Judicial Review of Arbitration published by the Sichuan Province Chengdu Intermediate People's Court in May 2025. The issue of arbitrators' conflicts of interest and the recusal system are receiving increasing attention in the field of domestic arbitration. On one hand, due to the temporary and non-full-time nature of the arbitrator profession, and particularly as the legal profession has become a significant source of arbitrators, the different roles of being both a lawyer and an arbitrator inevitably involve various professional conflicts of interest. On the other hand, although the Arbitration Law stipulates a catch-all recusal clause for "other relationships with the parties or their agents that may affect impartial arbitration," specific guidance is lacking. In practice, the approach of detailing recusal circumstances through arbitration rules is not yet widespread. This case establishes a clear rule: where the law firm of an arbitrator has ongoing business dealings with one party, and the arbitrator neither recuses themselves nor

B Company, due to a dispute with A Office arising from the performance of a contract, applied for arbitration to an arbitration commission in accordance with the arbitration clause. The arbitration commission subsequently rendered an arbitral award in the case. Later, A Office applied to the Sichuan Province Chengdu Intermediate People's Court, stating that the presiding arbitrator Luo of the arbitral tribunal was the head and legal representative of Law Firm Z. However, Law Firm Z had cooperated with B Company for many years and maintained a close relationship. The presiding arbitrator, Luo, had an interest in the case and should have withdrawn himself according to the law, but did not do so. Therefore, A Office sought to set aside the arbitral award on the grounds that the composition of the arbitral tribunal violated statutory procedures.

The Sichuan Province Chengdu Intermediate People's Court held that relevant documents showed that in recent years, several lawyers from Law Firm Z had served as entrusted litigation agents for B Company in multiple cases. The presiding arbitrator, Luo, was appointed by the arbitration commission. Although Arbitrator Luo did not serve as an entrusted litigation agent in the aforementioned cases, the affiliated Law Firm Z indeed had ongoing business dealings with B Company. Furthermore, the presiding arbitrator, Luo, was also the head of Law Firm Z. Therefore, a specific relationship existed between Luo and B Company that could affect impartial arbitration. The presiding arbitrator, Luo, neither voluntarily withdrew nor disclosed the business dealings between the law firm and B Company, leading to reasonable doubts about the impartiality of the award rendered by the arbitral tribunal. Consequently, the Court supported A Office's argument that the composition of the arbitral tribunal violated statutory procedures, but determined that the matter could be handled by reconstituting the arbitral tribunal for a renewed arbitration. The Court then notified the arbitration commission to conduct a renewed arbitration.

Case 2: *M Company v. N Company*[42]

M Company and N Company entered into the Construction Contract, agreeing to submit disputes related to the contract to X Arbitration Commission for arbitration. M Company applied for arbitration to the selected arbitration commission. M Company selected Shen as an arbitrator, N Company selected Tao as an arbitrator, and the director of X Arbitration Commission designated Zhou as the presiding arbitrator. The arbitral tribunal rendered an arbitral award, dismissing all of M Company's arbitration claims. M Company applied to the Jiangsu Province Nantong Intermediate People's Court to set aside this arbitral award, arguing that Arbitrator

discloses this, it shall be recognized as an "other relationship" under Item 3, Article 34 of the Arbitration Law of the People's Republic of China that "may affect impartial arbitration."

[42] (2023) Su 06 Min Te No. 34; See the 10 Typical Cases on Judicial Review of Commercial Arbitration in July 2024 published by the High People's Court of Jiangsu Province in July 2024. To elaborate on the provision of Article 34 of the Arbitration Law regarding "other relationships with the parties or their agents that may affect impartial arbitration," arbitration institutions have specified concrete circumstances concerning "other relationships" in their rules. People's Courts may invoke these arbitration rules when making determinations in judicial review of arbitration.

Tao and Sha, the agent of N Company, had a teacher-student relationship, had previously worked at the same law firm, and held positions in the Intellectual Property Committee of the Y City Lawyers Association, which might affect impartial arbitration. M Company contended that Tao should have withdrawn himself, but did not, thus the composition of the tribunal violated statutory procedures.

The Jiangsu Province Nantong Intermediate People's Court held that the circumstances of this case did not fall within those specified in the Arbitrator Code of Conduct of X Arbitration Commission, where an arbitrator must withdraw themselves. During Sha's period of study at the school, Tao did not have a direct teacher-student instructional relationship with him. Although Sha and arbitrator Tao had previously worked at the same law firm, Tao had left that law firm in 2008. By the time of the arbitration in 2020, this far exceeded the circumstances stipulated in the Arbitrator Code of Conduct of X Arbitration Commission regarding "having worked in the same unit and left their posts less than two years ago." M Company did not submit evidence proving that Tao and Sha held positions in the Intellectual Property Committee of the Y City Lawyers Association. Therefore, it could not be determined that a relationship existed between the two that might affect the arbitrator's independence or impartiality. Consequently, the court ruled to dismiss M Company's application to set aside the arbitral award.

Article 47

Where a party challenges an arbitrator, they shall state the reasons for the challenge prior to the first hearing. Where the causes giving rise to the challenge became known after the first hearing, the challenge may be made before the conclusion of the final hearing of the case.

Notes

The parties involved in the application have the right to challenge an arbitrator who raises reasonable doubts in their minds. This is a procedural right of the parties. Rights may be abused. In practice, the challenge system is inevitably exploited by some parties who, based on so-called arbitration strategy or other considerations, challenge arbitrators to achieve improper purposes such as delaying the arbitration proceedings.

One major advantage of arbitration over litigation is its efficiency and speed. If parties could raise challenge applications at any time, even before or after the award is rendered, it would lead to prolonged uncertainty in the arbitration proceedings and could easily be maliciously used as a tactical tool to delay the process and exhaust the opposing party. Stipulating a general principle of a time limit for challenge applications aims to urge the parties to exercise due diligence, to discover and raise issues as early as possible, and to resolve potential qualification disputes before the substantive hearing, thereby ensuring that the arbitration proceedings can proceed smoothly and uninterrupted, which aligns with the intrinsic value of efficiency in arbitration.

A party may challenge an arbitrator at the following two junctures:

A. ***Before the first hearing.*** After the arbitral tribunal is constituted, the arbitration commission shall notify the parties in writing of the tribunal's composition. At the commencement of the hearing, the sole arbitrator or the presiding arbitrator must inform the parties of their right to apply for the arbitrator's challenge and inquire whether they wish to do so.

B. ***Before the conclusion of the final hearing.*** For various reasons, a party may not be fully aware of whether an arbitrator is subject to statutory grounds for challenge prior to the first hearing. It may only discover or learn of such grounds during the course of the proceedings. To safeguard the parties' right to fully exercise their rights and ensure the fairness of the arbitration, the law permits a party to submit a challenge application before the conclusion of the final hearing. However, if the oral hearings have concluded and the tribunal has entered the deliberation phase or has already rendered an award, a challenge can no longer be filed. In such a case, the party may only seek a remedy by applying to a people's court to set aside the arbitral award in accordance with legal provisions.

In practice, arbitration institutions typically stipulate more specific provisions and requirements regarding challenges in their arbitration rules. For example, Article 23(2) of the BAC Arbitration Rules stipulates that a party shall submit a challenge application in writing, state the reasons, and provide corresponding evidence. Paragraph (3) stipulates that for cases not involving further hearings or conducted through written procedure, the challenge shall be submitted within 10 days of the date the party becomes aware of the grounds for challenge. Paragraph (7) stipulates that if an agent appointed by a party after becoming aware of the composition of the arbitral tribunal has a relationship with an arbitrator that constitutes grounds for challenge, that party shall be deemed to have waived its right to challenge the arbitrator based on such grounds. Article 33(1) of the SCIA Arbitration Rules stipulates that if a party challenges an arbitrator based on information disclosed by the arbitrator, it shall submit the challenge in writing within 10 days of receiving the arbitrator's written disclosure. If no challenge is filed within this period, the party may not subsequently challenge the arbitrator based on the disclosed matters. Paragraph (6) stipulates that if a party, after receiving the notice of the constitution of the arbitral tribunal, appoints an agent whose relationship with an arbitrator constitutes grounds for challenge, that party loses the right to challenge the arbitrator on such grounds, but the other party's right to challenge remains unaffected. If this causes a delay in the arbitration proceedings, the party responsible for the circumstance giving rise to the challenge shall bear the corresponding consequences, including but not limited to the costs incurred thereby.

Illustrative Case

Li v. A Fund and others[43]

[43] See the Typical Cases from 2020–2024 on Judicial Review of Arbitration published by the Shanghai High People's Court in July 2025. On the one hand, arbitrators shall proactively disclose any matters that may affect their neutrality, including potential conflicts of interest such as past relationships with the parties or their representatives, professional background, or commercial

A dispute arbitration case was formed with a tribunal composed of three arbitrators. Among them, A Fund selected Cheng as an arbitrator. Arbitrator Cheng issued a disclosure letter. It stated that although there were no circumstances requiring mandatory withdrawal, to avoid reasonable doubts by the parties, he disclosed that he and the agent lawyer of A Fund had previously worked at the same law firm, but they belonged to different practice teams and had no business cooperation or other interactions. The parties in the arbitration case had all received the disclosure letter during the arbitration proceedings. During the arbitration hearing, upon inquiry by the arbitral tribunal, all parties expressed no objection to the composition of the arbitral tribunal and did not apply for withdrawal. After the arbitral tribunal rendered an award in the aforementioned arbitration case, Li applied to the court to set aside the arbitral award on the grounds that a special relationship existed between Arbitrator Cheng and the agent of A Fund, which would inevitably affect impartial arbitration. Li argued that even though he did not apply for withdrawal, the arbitrator should have voluntarily withdrawn himself, and otherwise, the composition of the arbitral tribunal violated statutory procedures. The court ultimately ruled to dismiss Li's application to set aside the award.

The court held that Arbitrator Cheng had voluntarily disclosed the situation between himself and Liu, the agent of A Fund, that might cause reasonable doubt among the parties. After receiving the disclosure letter, Li did not raise a challenge application within the time limit stipulated by the arbitration rules. In subsequent court hearings, when questioned again by the arbitral tribunal, Li repeatedly replied that he was aware of the content of the disclosure letter, had no objection to the composition of the arbitral tribunal, and did not apply for the arbitrator's withdrawal. These facts could be regarded as Li's self-admission that the content involved in the disclosure letter was insufficient to affect the impartial adjudication of the case, and that he voluntarily waived his right to object to the composition of the arbitral tribunal and to request the arbitrator's withdrawal. Now, after the award was rendered, Li again uses the disclosure letter as a basis to claim that the arbitrator should have withdrawn himself but did not, which is inconsistent with the provisions of the arbitration rules. Therefore, the court dismissed Li's action.

Article 48

The chairman of the arbitration institution shall decide whether the arbitrator should withdraw or not. The arbitration institution shall make the decision collectively if the arbitrator is the chairman of the arbitration institution.

---

associations. This transparency helps reduce reasonable doubts regarding the arbitrator's impartiality and provides parties with an opportunity to promptly submit a challenge. On the other hand, parties shall exercise their right to challenge in a timely manner. If a party, without justifiable reason, fails to submit a challenge within the prescribed period after becoming aware of the disclosed matter, it shall be deemed to have waived such right. Thereafter, if the party seeks to set aside the arbitral award on the basis of the disclosed matter, such request may be considered contrary to the principle of good faith and is unlikely to be upheld by the court.

Notes

The approval procedures for withdrawal differ depending on the subject of the withdrawal. According to this Article, whether an arbitrator withdraws themselves is decided by the director of the arbitration institution. If the arbitrator is the director of the arbitration institution, whether to withdraw is decided collectively by the arbitration institution. In practice, the director of the arbitration institution may make the decision on withdrawal without stating reasons.

It should be noted that whether the withdrawal provisions apply to recording personnel, interpreters, and appraisal personnel is not explicitly stipulated in the New Arbitration Law, but in practice, it is generally considered that the withdrawal provisions similarly apply to them. The withdrawal decision should be made based on a review of the party's application reasons in accordance with the law. After review, if it meets the statutory conditions, a withdrawal decision should be made. After the decision is made, the arbitrator should withdraw from the arbitration of the case; if it does not meet the statutory conditions, the party should be persuaded to withdraw the application, or the application should be directly dismissed, making a decision not to allow withdrawal. It should be noted here that whether it is a decision to allow withdrawal or not to allow withdrawal, it should be made in writing, and not orally.

In practice, there is a situation where after a party applies for an arbitrator's withdrawal, the other party agrees to the withdrawal application, or the challenged arbitrator voluntarily proposes to no longer serve as the arbitrator for the case. In such a case, no decision by the chairman of the arbitration institution is needed, and that arbitrator no longer serves as the arbitrator for the case. However, this situation does not mean that the reasons for the challenge raised by the party are valid. Some arbitration institutions have explicitly stipulated this in their arbitration rules. For example, Article 32(5) of the CIETAC Arbitration Rules stipulates that if one party challenges an arbitrator, the other party agrees to the challenge, or the challenged arbitrator voluntarily withdraws from serving as the arbitrator for the case, then the arbitrator shall no longer serve as the arbitrator for the case. The above situations do not indicate that the reasons for the challenge raised by the party are valid.

To ensure the continuity of the arbitration proceedings, generally, before a decision on whether to withdraw is made, the arbitrator should continue to perform their duties. That is to say, after a party raises a challenge application, the arbitration proceedings will not be suspended as a result. In practice, the director of the arbitration institution or the arbitration institution usually reviews the party's challenge application promptly after receiving it and makes a decision as soon as possible.

Once a withdrawal decision is made, it will inevitably produce corresponding legal consequences in the arbitration proceedings, typically including: possible postponement of the hearing; reselection or appointment of arbitrators, reconstitution of the arbitral tribunal; and possibly the restart of the arbitration proceedings.

Article 49
Where an arbitrator cannot perform his or her duties due to their withdrawal or for other reasons, a substitute arbitrator shall be selected or appointed in accordance with this Law.

After a substitute arbitrator has been selected or appointed on account of an arbitrator's withdrawal, a party may request that the arbitration proceedings already carried out should be carried out anew, and the arbitral tribunal shall decide whether to approve it or not. The arbitral tribunal may also take its own initiative to decide whether the arbitration proceedings already carried out should be carried out again.

Notes
If an arbitrator is unable to continue performing their duties due to illness, death, resignation, or the acceptance of a party's challenge against the arbitrator, it involves the issue of arbitrator replacement or reconstitution of the arbitral tribunal. The reconstitution of the arbitral tribunal typically involves discussion on two issues: firstly, the method of reconstituting the tribunal, and secondly, the impact after the tribunal is reconstituted. Generally, the method for reappointing or selecting an arbitrator and reconstituting the arbitral tribunal is substantially the same as the method used for the original appointment or selection of the arbitrator and constitution of the tribunal.

The UNCITRAL Arbitration Rules stipulate that the procedure for appointing or selecting a substitute arbitrator shall be the same as the procedure used for appointing or selecting the original arbitrator. The ICSID Arbitration Rules stipulate that any vacancy resulting from the disqualification, death, incapacity, or resignation of an arbitrator shall be filled promptly by the same method pursuant to which the original appointment was made. To prevent parties from abusing the power of appointment to delay the arbitration process, this provision applies with an exception: in the case of a vacancy arising from the resignation of an arbitrator appointed by a party, the substitute shall not be appointed by that party but shall be appointed by the Chairman of the Administrative Council, unless the remaining members of the Tribunal have agreed otherwise. The CIETAC Arbitration Rules have also adopted this practice.

In *ad hoc* arbitration, if the parties have not agreed on the method for filling a vacancy in the position of arbitrator, and a vacancy occurs, if the parties still cannot reach an agreement, the court shall decide on the method for selecting or choosing a replacement arbitrator. At this point, since an arbitral tribunal already exists and the seat of arbitration is mostly already determined, there is generally no issue regarding which court should handle the filling of the arbitrator vacancy. The application for replacing the arbitrator can be made directly to the court at the seat of arbitration. In view of this, it is very important to ensure that the relevant court has the power to appoint a substitute arbitrator. Most countries with well-developed arbitration legislation have granted this power of appointment to the courts.

If an arbitrator withdraws themselves, voluntarily withdraws, or is unable to perform their duties as an arbitrator for other reasons, according to the provisions of Article 49(1), a new arbitrator shall be selected or appointed, and the selection or appointment shall be conducted in accordance with the preceding provisions of this Law. Other reasons generally may include situations such as the arbitrator being unable to continue participating in the arbitration proceedings due to health problems; the death or imprisonment of the arbitrator; the arbitrator becoming a person without or with limited capacity for civil conduct; or the arbitrator becoming a judge, etc., which factually or legally prevents the arbitrator from continuing to perform their duties. Some arbitration rules also empower the arbitration institution or its chairman to proactively decide to replace an arbitrator, applicable in situations where it is determined that the arbitrator has not performed their duties in accordance with the requirements of the rules.

After a new arbitrator is selected or appointed, how should the previously conducted arbitration proceedings be handled? Article 49(2) stipulates that, firstly, a party may request that the proceedings already conducted be repeated, but whether to repeat them is to be decided by the newly constituted arbitral tribunal. Secondly, even if the parties do not express an opinion on this matter, the arbitral tribunal may, on its own initiative, decide whether or not the proceedings already conducted shall be repeated.

In practice, after a tribunal member is replaced, the newly appointed arbitrator does not participate in the prior hearings, which might affect their understanding of the entire arbitration process, the case, and the performance of their duties as an arbitrator. Therefore, in practice, the arbitration rules of some institutions also contain provisions regarding the proceedings after arbitrator replacement, consistent with the spirit of the second paragraph of this Article, vesting the power to decide how the proceedings continue and whether they should be repeated in the arbitral tribunal. For example, Article 4 of the SCIA Arbitration Rules stipulates that, unless otherwise agreed by the parties, after the replacement of an arbitrator, the arbitral tribunal shall decide whether and to what extent the proceedings conducted previously shall be repeated. If the arbitral tribunal decides to repeat the proceedings in their entirety, the time limit for rendering an award stipulated in Article 50 of these Rules shall be calculated from the date of the arbitral tribunal's decision to repeat the proceedings.

Furthermore, it is important to note that, generally, although the reconstituted tribunal has the power to decide whether the proceedings should be repeated, any effective decisions made by the original tribunal shall remain effective, unless explicitly set aside or modified by the reconstituted tribunal.

Illustrative Cases

Case 1: *Chongqing A Company v. HT Company*[44]

Chongqing A Company applied for non-enforcement of an arbitral award rendered by the SCIA. One of its main reasons was that the selection and replacement of the

[44] (2024) Yu 03 Zhi Yi No. 2.

presiding arbitrator in this case seriously violated the basic principles of the Civil Code and the Arbitration Law (2017), and accordingly, the rendered award was erroneous. This case involved four presiding arbitrators. Two of them were replaced after Chongqing A Company raised challenge applications due to their direct interest relationship with HT Company. The presiding arbitrator, Yang, who had an interest relationship with HT Company, participated in the hearing. The replacement arbitrator, Lan did not reconvene a hearing, did not conduct cross-examination of supplementary evidence, did not ascertain the facts, and did not respond to or investigate Chongqing A Company's applications for adding a third party or for investigating and collecting evidence. The award, rendered in favor of HT Company based on the hearing opinions of presiding arbitrator Yang, who had an interest relationship with HT Company, was erroneous and severely lacked credibility.

The court held that, firstly, regarding the replacement of arbitrators in the arbitration proceedings of this case, although the construction company had applied for the recusal of the presiding arbitrators Yang and Lu on two separate occasions, and the Shenzhen Court of International Arbitration had issued Notices of Arbitrator Replacement to replace them accordingly, there was no evidence to prove that there existed any statutory grounds requiring their recusal upon the parties' application or that warranted the arbitrators' voluntary recusal during the replacement procedures for Yang and Lu. Moreover, in the Notices of Arbitrator Replacement issued, the SCIA had informed the parties that if they had any grounds for recusal against the arbitrator, they should submit such requests in accordance with Article 33 of the SCIA Arbitration Rules within the prescribed time to ensure the smooth progress of the arbitration proceedings. During the hearing conducted by the tribunal composed of presiding arbitrator Yang and the two arbitrators respectively appointed by the parties, the tribunal inquired whether the claimant and the respondents had any recusal requests, and both parties indicated that they did not. Additionally, both presiding arbitrators, Yang and Lu, were jointly appointed by the arbitrators respectively designated by the parties in accordance with Article 30(3) of the SCIA Arbitration Rules, which complied with statutory procedures.

Secondly, regarding whether a new hearing should have been conducted after the replacement of arbitrators, Article 37 of the Arbitration Law (2017) stipulated that if an arbitrator was unable to perform his or her duties due to recusal or other reasons, a new arbitrator should be selected or appointed in accordance with the provisions of this Law. After a new arbitrator was selected or appointed due to recusal, the parties could request that the arbitration proceedings already conducted continue, subject to the tribunal's decision on whether to permit it; the tribunal could also decide on its own whether the arbitration proceedings already conducted should be repeated. Furthermore, Article 34(4) (Replacement of Arbitrators) of the SCIA Arbitration Rules provided that unless otherwise agreed by the parties, after the replacement of an arbitrator, the tribunal would decide whether all or part of the hearings already conducted needed to be repeated. Therefore, after the presiding arbitrator was replaced three times in the arbitration proceedings of this case, whether the hearings already conducted needed to be repeated was to be determined by the tribunal composed of the presiding arbitrator Lan Muhong, who was appointed in the last replacement, and arbitrators Liu and Li. In summary, the claimant's ground for opposing the enforcement of the arbitral award lacked evidentiary support and was unfounded.

Case 2: *Shandong B Company v. Jinan C Company*[45]
Claimant Shandong B Company applied to set aside an award rendered by the Jinan Arbitration Commission. One of the reasons was that after the arbitrator was replaced, no new hearing was conducted. The claimant received a new Notice of Composition of the Arbitral tribunal from the Jinan Arbitration Commission on December 13, 2022, stating that arbitrator Guo had passed away due to illness, and the respondent had newly selected Yu as the arbitrator. However, after the arbitral tribunal was reconstituted, no hearing was conducted in this case, and an award was rendered directly.

The court held as follows: according to Article 37 of the Arbitration Law (2017), if an arbitrator was unable to perform his or her duties due to withdrawal or other reasons, a new arbitrator should be selected or appointed. After a new arbitrator is selected or appointed due to withdrawal, the parties were allowed to request that the procedures already carried out be repeated; whether to approve this should be decided by the arbitral tribunal. The arbitral tribunal could also decide on its own initiative whether the procedures already carried out shall be repeated. Furthermore, according to Article 14 of the Arbitral Award Enforcement Provisions, the Court dismissed the claim made by the claimant.

Article 50
Where an arbitrator is involved in the circumstances described in item (4) of Article 46 of this Law and the circumstances are serious or involve the circumstances described in item (6) of Article 71 of this Law, they shall assume legal liability according to law and the arbitration institution shall remove their name from the register of arbitrators.

Notes
The arbitrator is the master of the arbitration proceedings. A very important corresponding issue is the liability of arbitrators. Arbitrator liability refers to the price an arbitrator should pay for violating contractual or legal obligations, primarily referring to the arbitrator's legal liability, including civil and criminal liability, but also encompassing moral and professional responsibility.

From the perspective of comparative legal studies, due to differing arbitration philosophies and other reasons, countries have different provisions regarding arbitrator liability. According to the English Arbitration Act 2025, an arbitrator is liable only for acts done in bad faith and enjoys immunity from suit for acts or omissions in the discharge of their functions. The US Uniform Arbitration Act states that an arbitrator or arbitration organization is immune from civil liability to the same extent as a judge of a court of this state acting in a judicial capacity. The Japanese

---

[45] (2023) Lu 01 Min Te No. 154.

Arbitration Act primarily stipulates criminal liability for bribery. An arbitrator who accepts, demands, or agrees to accept a bribe in connection with their duties shall be punishable by imprisonment with work for not more than five years. In this case, if the arbitrator agrees to act in response to a request, they shall be liable to penal servitude for not more than seven years. If a person to be appointed as an arbitrator, regarding the duties they are to perform, accepts, demands, or agrees to accept a bribe, agreeing to act in response to a request, they shall, if appointed, be punishable by imprisonment with work for not more than five years.

Regarding arbitrator liability, the main issues to be addressed can be divided into two aspects: first, whether liability needs to be borne, and second, what form of liability is to be borne. Surveying the legislative examples of various countries, it can be generally seen that the literal expressions concerning arbitrator liability mainly include the following: (1) no liability for negligence, but liability for fraud or intentional acts, such as provisions in the arbitration laws of Australia and Sri Lanka; (2) no liability for negligence, but liability for misconduct in the arbitration case itself, such as in Singapore; (3) no liability, such as in the Netherlands and under the ICC Rules; (4)no liability, except for breaches of good faith, such as in the UK; (5) liability, such as in China and Japan.

From the legislative provisions of various countries, it can be seen that arbitrator liability involves the following types of arbitrator behavior: (1) negligence. Most countries stipulate that arbitrators are not liable for negligence in performing their duties. However, in countries that fully support the contractual relationship between arbitrators and parties, arbitrators may still be liable for contractual negligence, such as compensating parties for losses or being unable to receive remuneration. The arbitration laws of Israel and Argentina are of this type; (2) intentional misconduct or improper conduct; (3) fraud; (4) accepting bribes. Japan is a typical country where criminal liability is stipulated in its arbitration law.

Article 50 stipulates the liability of arbitrators, specifying only two types of conduct for which arbitrators shall bear legal liability: the circumstances set forth in Article 46(4), namely, meeting privately with a party or its representative or accepting an invitation to entertainment or gifts from a party or its representative under serious circumstances; and the circumstances set forth in Article 71(1)(6), namely, soliciting or accepting bribes, engaging in malpractices for personal gain, or perverting the law in rendering an arbitral award. However, the specific forms of liability are not detailed. In 2006, a new criminal offense was formally added to Chinese criminal law: the Crime of Perverting the Law in Rendering an Arbitral award. The Amendment (VI) to the Criminal Law stipulates that one article is added after Article 399 as Article 399 bis: "Any person bearing arbitration duties according to law who, in arbitration activities, intentionally perverts the law by rendering an award contrary to facts and law, if the circumstances are serious, shall be sentenced to fixed-term imprisonment of not more than three years or criminal detention; if the circumstances are especially serious, shall be sentenced to fixed-term imprisonment of not less than three years but not more than seven years."

This Article adopts an enumerative approach to specify the circumstances under which an arbitrator needs to bear legal liability. According to this Article, if an arbitrator engages in either of the following two types of conduct, they shall both be subject to removal from the panel of arbitrators by the arbitration institution and bear corresponding legal liability. First, if the arbitrator meets with a party or their agent in private or accepts entertainment or gifts from them, and the circumstances are serious. This provision requires that the arbitrator's aforementioned conduct meet the standard of "serious circumstances." Serious circumstances generally refer to repeatedly or multiple times of dining, accepting gifts, meeting with parties, or causing a negative impact. Second, if the arbitrator, in arbitrating a case, demands or accepts bribes, engages in malpractices for personal gain, or perverts the law.

It should be noted that the provisions of Article 50 on arbitrator liability are not complete or clear. In practice, examples of arbitrators bearing liability seem to be rare. However, once an arbitrator's misconduct (including acts requiring other liability and acts not requiring other liability) is disclosed, the arbitrator is inevitably placed on the moral judgment platform. Not only will their public image and reputation be damaged, but their career development in the arbitration industry and even the legal profession will be significantly affected. Furthermore, many domestic arbitration institutions have currently formulated codes of conduct for arbitrators, specifying clear and specific requirements for arbitrators' performance of their duties. Some arbitration institutions also stipulate the liability of arbitration-related personnel, including arbitrators, in their arbitration rules.

Section 3 Hearing and Award

Article 51

Arbitration shall be conducted in the form of oral hearings. Where the parties agree to arbitrate without oral hearings, the arbitral tribunal may render an arbitral award on the basis of the written application for arbitration, the written defense and other materials.

Notes

This Article continues the core content of the original Article 39 of the Arbitration Law (2017). It establishes the basic procedural framework of "hearings as the principle, and written proceedings as the exception." With the development of commercial arbitration practice, particularly the impact of the global pandemic on in-person proceedings, the value of the written procedure model in resolving disputes efficiently has become increasingly prominent. This provision emphasizes the balance between party autonomy and the arbitral tribunal's discretion, which holds particular significance in the era of the digital economy, as it accommodates the demand for dispute resolution mechanisms that are "streamlined, low-cost, and highly adaptable."

Furthermore, this Article also clarifies the arbitral tribunal's authority over the procedure. The use of the word "may" in this Article grants discretionary power to the arbitral tribunal, not an obligation. Even if the parties agree to dispense with a hearing, the arbitral tribunal has the right to request supplementary evidence or initiate an oral hearing if it considers the written materials insufficient to fully reflect the facts of the case. The arbitral tribunal needs to assess whether the written materials are sufficient to determine the facts of the case; if the evidence is complex or there are major disputes, the arbitral tribunal may still decide to hold a hearing to prevent the simplification of the procedure from compromising substantive justice. This design avoids the abuse of procedural choice by the parties and strengthens the arbitral tribunal's responsibility for controlling the quality of the procedure.

In arbitration, there are two forms of case hearing: oral hearings and written proceedings. In some cases, a combination of oral hearings and written proceedings can be adopted according to the actual situation. Both oral hearings and written proceedings have their pros and cons. Oral hearings facilitate the parties' presentation of evidence, cross-examination, and oral arguments in court, which is conducive to the arbitral tribunal accurately clarifying the case facts, but it may delay the rendering of the award and increase the parties' expenses. Although written proceedings are conducive to rendering an arbitral award promptly and help the parties save costs, as the parties do not have the opportunity for face-to-face oral statements, and the arbitral tribunal relies solely on the written materials submitted by the parties, it may not fully understand the actual case situation, and the accuracy of the award rendered might be compromised.

Article 51 clearly states that "the parties agree to arbitrate without oral hearings" can serve as a prerequisite for written proceedings, giving priority of procedural choice to the parties. This design reflects the core concept distinguishing arbitration from litigation, i.e., the parties' mutual agreement is the basis for procedural advancement, and the arbitral tribunal's authority derives from the parties' authorization rather than state coercion. Hearing procedures usually involve costs such as venue, time, and travel; for cases with small amounts in dispute or clear facts, written proceedings can significantly reduce resource consumption. This Article allows the arbitral tribunal to render an award based on written materials with the parties' agreement, avoiding unnecessary procedural delays, which aligns with commercial entities' expectations for "rapid dispute resolution," and is particularly suitable for high-frequency, low-value disputes such as cross-border trade and e-commerce. At the same time, this Article does not completely abandon the safeguarding function of oral hearings, but uses "hearings as the principle" as a guarantee of procedural justice.

Although the New Arbitration Law stipulates that arbitration cases shall be heard orally as a principle, it also allows the arbitral tribunal to conduct written proceedings under certain circumstances. So-called written proceedings refer to the situation where the arbitral tribunal, based on the agreement of the parties, only conducts the case and renders an arbitral award based on the written materials provided by the parties. The written materials mentioned here mainly refer to the application for arbitration, the statement of defense, the contract between the parties, correspondence, and other relevant written materials.

During written proceedings, the arbitral tribunal does not hold hearings, and the arbitrators cannot listen to the statements and arguments of the parties and their agents face-to-face; they only make judgments on the case based on written materials. To ensure the fairness and accuracy of the arbitral tribunal's hearing, written proceedings are only conducted when two conditions are met simultaneously: the parties' agreement and the arbitral tribunal's approval.

First, written proceedings must be based on the parties' agreement. Since the parties have the right to dispose of the matters under arbitration, and arbitration itself exists based on the parties' will, determining whether to conduct an oral hearing or written proceedings should, of course, respect the parties' will. If the parties agree to dispense with a hearing, the arbitral tribunal may render an award based on the application for arbitration, the statement of defense, and other materials.

Secondly, cases subject to written proceedings should generally be those involving small amounts in dispute, simple case details, and clear facts. Otherwise, for cases involving large amounts, complex case details, or unclear facts, during written proceedings, the arbitral tribunal may find it difficult to ascertain the facts, thus being unable to render a correct award, which is not conducive to protecting the legitimate rights and interests of the parties.

Written proceedings do not require hearings, saving many statutory procedures with specified time limits of oral hearings, which is conducive to the arbitral tribunal rendering an award promptly. At the same time, written proceedings can significantly reduce the time and expenses spent on travel for the parties and their agents, arbitrators, and other arbitration participants, making it convenient for the parties. However, to effectively ensure the quality of written proceedings and avoid situations where the arbitral award may be set aside or enforcement refused due to procedural reasons, the following issues should be noted during written proceedings:

(1) Ensuring the comprehensiveness and effectiveness of service. The arbitration institution shall promptly deliver the written materials provided by one party to the other party. Besides delivering the copy of the application for arbitration and the copy of the statement of defense to the other party as required, the arbitration institution should also deliver all evidential materials and statements provided by the parties to the arbitral tribunal within a reasonable period to the other party. Furthermore, written documents such as witness statements, expert conclusions, and inspection records collected by the arbitral tribunal on its own initiative should also be delivered to all parties. This is also a common practice in modern commercial arbitration. For example, Article 24(3) of the UNCITRAL Model Law states that all statements, documents, or other information supplied to the arbitral tribunal by one party shall be communicated to the other party, and any expert report or evidentiary document on which the arbitral tribunal may rely in making its decision shall be communicated to the parties. When the arbitration institution delivers the aforementioned written materials, it should simultaneously require or remind the recipient to promptly comment on or respond to the received materials.

(2) Setting a necessary time limit for the parties to provide materials. To facilitate the smooth progress of written proceedings, the arbitral tribunal shall set a necessary time limit for the parties to submit materials. In other words, all parties must provide materials within the specified time limit; otherwise, they will be deemed to have waived the right to submit materials. If a party provides materials after the time limit, the arbitral tribunal may refuse to accept them.

(3) Ensuring proper notification. Written proceedings do not absolutely preclude the arbitral tribunal from notifying one party to come to the place of hearing (generally the location of the arbitration commission) to inquire about certain issues in the case. However, the arbitral tribunal must promptly inform the other party of all the circumstances of the inquiry to ensure fairness. This situation is a necessary exception to written proceedings and a manifestation of the flexibility of arbitration.

Illustrative Case

Chen v. Y Trust Company and others[46]

In 2017, Y Trust Company, as the trustee, signed the Trust Contract with Chen (the subordinated beneficiary) and P Bank (the senior beneficiary) respectively, stipulating that Chen and P Bank would join the H Collective Fund Trust Plan and agreeing that contract disputes would be submitted to C Arbitration Commission for arbitration in Shanghai. Simultaneously, Chen and P Bank separately signed the Cooperation Agreement, stipulating that Party A P Bank was the senior beneficiary of the H Collective Fund Trust Plan, and Party B Chen was the subordinated

[46] See the 10 Typical Cases on Judicial Review of Financial Arbitration published by the Shanghai Financial Court in October 2024.Regarding whether an arbitration claimant or an arbitration institution can include disputes involving a "chain of contracts" within the same arbitration proceeding for resolution, many arbitration rules have made clear provisions. For example, Article 10 of the ICC Arbitration Rules (2021) stipulates: The Court may, at the request of a party, consolidate two or more arbitrations pending under the Rules into a single arbitration, provided certain conditions are met, such as: a) the parties have agreed to consolidation; or b) all the claims in the arbitrations are made under the same arbitration agreement; or c) the claims are made under more than one arbitration agreement, the arbitrations are between the same parties, the disputes arise in connection with the same legal relationship, and the Court finds the arbitration agreements compatible. Another example is found in Schedule 2 of the Hong Kong Special Administrative Region's Arbitration Ordinance (2022), which stipulates that the Court of First Instance may, on the application of a party, order the consolidation of two or more arbitration proceedings if it is satisfied that common questions of law or fact arise in both or all of them, or that the rights to relief claimed arise out of the same transaction or series of transactions, etc., on such terms as it thinks just. In this case, by interpreting the transaction structure of the related contracts and the content of the arbitration clauses, allowing the arbitration parties to bring specific related transactions into a single arbitration proceeding for resolution is conducive to improving the efficiency of the arbitration procedure.

beneficiary. Disputes related to this Cooperation Agreement concerning arbitration were to be submitted to C Arbitration Commission for arbitration in Shanghai. In 2020, Chen filed an application for arbitration with C Arbitration Commission, naming Y Trust Company and P Bank as joint respondents.

Later, P Bank applied to the Shanghai Financial Court, arguing that it was not a party to the Trust Contract signed between Chen and Y Trust Company, and therefore, the arbitration agreement between Chen and Y Trust Company was not binding on P Bank.

The Shanghai Financial Court held that the arbitration clauses agreed upon in the Trust Contract and the Cooperation Agreement were lawful and valid. The privity of mutual consent in concluding an arbitration agreement should be determined comprehensively based on the contract texts and the legal relationships involved. In this case, Chen, as the subordinated beneficiary, and P Bank, as the senior beneficiary, respectively signed the Trust Contract with Y Trust Company concerning the same trust asset, and these contracts contained arbitration clauses. Furthermore, Chen and P Bank, based on the same trust asset, made clear arrangements regarding the rights and obligations between the subordinated beneficiary and the senior beneficiary, and signed the Cooperation Agreement for this purpose, which also contained an arbitration clause. Moreover, the arbitration institution designated in both the Trust Contract and the Cooperation Agreement was the same. Based on this, P Bank, Chen, and Y Trust Company, concerning the trust legal relationship in which they jointly participated, entered into contracts pairwise and selected the same arbitration institution. This could be considered as the three parties having formed a common intention to agree to arbitration. The Court accordingly ruled to dismiss P Bank's action.

Article 52

Arbitration shall be conducted in private. Where the parties agree to a public hearing, the arbitration may be conducted in public unless state secrets, trade secrets of other parties, or personal privacy are involved.

Notes

Confidentiality or non-public nature is one of the characteristics of arbitration. Many arbitration rules, such as those of the ICC International Court of Arbitration and the UNCITRAL Arbitration Rules, stipulate that hearings shall be held in private.[47] The non-public nature of the arbitration proceedings, including the award, helps prevent the disclosure of certain commercial secrets between the parties, protects their commercial reputation, makes it emotionally easier for the parties to accept the outcome, and facilitates future business dealings. Of course, confidentiality often also means that societal resources can only be partially and limitedly utilized and further developed. Unless in procedures requiring disclosure, a potentially highly impactful and valuable arbitration case may, due to the confidentiality of arbitration, only benefit the parties involved. Perspectives and practices regarding

[47] See Article 21 and Article 25 respectively.

confidentiality may differ across countries. For example, in the United States, neither the Federal Arbitration Act nor the Uniform Arbitration Act includes provisions requiring parties or arbitrators to maintain confidentiality concerning the arbitration proceedings they are involved in. France adheres to a strict principle of confidentiality, while Sweden seems to disregard arbitration confidentiality.

Article 52 of the New Arbitration Law essentially retains the provision of the original Article 40, establishing non-public arbitration as the principle, and stipulates exceptions and exceptions to those exceptions. Confidentiality is one of the core attractions for parties choosing arbitration over litigation. However, there is growing global reflection on "excessive confidentiality" in arbitration, particularly in cases involving public interest, investment arbitration, or industry standards, where calls for increased transparency are rising. Simultaneously, as the internationalization of Chinese arbitration practice continues to deepen, legislators need to seek a careful balance between international trends and local practice, and between the private interests of the parties and the public interest.

In principle, in arbitration, whether the case is heard orally or through documentary procedures, it should not be conducted publicly. The principle of non-public hearing is generally understood as the principle of confidentiality. Arbitration should be conducted confidentially. During oral hearings, non-participants should not be allowed to attend, and journalists should not be permitted to interview or report. Arbitrators must strictly maintain arbitration secrecy and must not disclose any substantive or procedural information about the arbitration case to the outside world, including the case details, the hearing process, and the opinions of the collegial panel, etc. Secretariat staff of arbitration institutions also bear a duty of confidentiality. When conducting academic discussions or exchanging arbitration experiences, appropriate confidentiality measures should be taken regarding the cases involved. The "Arbitration Law" does not stipulate whether other arbitration participants bear a duty of confidentiality, but considering the nature of arbitration, they should maintain confidentiality for the arbitration.

This provision is opposite to the corresponding provisions in the Civil Procedure Law, Criminal Procedure Law, and Administrative Procedure Law. Litigation implements the principle of public trial, except when involving party privacy and state secrets. Because judicial adjudication is an exercise of state power, stipulating the principle of publicity is necessary to reflect the fairness of the judicial organs exercising state adjudicative power and is conducive to accepting societal supervision. Arbitration, however, is different. The power of arbitration is granted by the parties. In essence, arbitration is a private adjudicative act, and there is no need to make this private act public. What parties submit to arbitration are contractual disputes and other disputes over property rights and interests. When adjudicating these disputes, to some extent, they will involve technical information and business information that is not known to the public, can bring economic benefits to the parties, has practical utility, and for which the parties have adopted confidentiality measures—that is, the trade secrets of the parties[48] and other confidential business information. If arbitration implemented a system of public hearings, allowing outsiders to attend, or even permitting journalists to conduct interviews and reports, it would not be conducive to the parties maintaining their trade or confidential commercial information secrets. Of course, if all parties believe that there are no commercial secrets or business secrets involved in their dispute, they can, based on mutual agreement, allow the arbitration to be conducted publicly, except where state secrets are involved.

Confidentiality is one of the distinctive features that sets arbitration apart from the public trial system of litigation and is also a key factor attracting commercial entities. Sensitive commercial information, financial data, or technical secrets disclosed during arbitration proceedings may cause irreversible harm to the parties if made public. This clause, while establishing the principle of non-public proceedings, provides for the circumstance where "the parties agree to a public hearing" as an exception to the principle of non-publicity. However, immediately following, the clause further creates an exception to this exception through a proviso, stating that even if the parties agree to make it public, it shall not be public if state secrets, the commercial secrets of others, or personal privacy are involved. It delineates the boundaries of party autonomy and establishes the absolute priority of public interest and the rights and interests of third parties. This mandatory provision reflects the legislator's protection of higher-level legal interests and ensures that arbitration activities operate within the legal framework, avoiding legal prohibitions due to procedural choices.

Another important issue is the balance between confidentiality and the public interest principle. Can the principle of confidentiality be breached where legitimate public interest requires it? An increasing number of cases involve such situations, for instance, those requiring public disclosure according to relevant securities regulatory laws and regulations, or where disclosure is necessary in other court proceedings.

Illustrative Case

A Airlines v. B Aircraft Leasing Company[49]

The case where A Airlines and others applied to set aside an arbitral award against B Aircraft Leasing Company is the first judicial review case nationwide involving an application to set aside an arbitral award concerning third-party funding. The focus of the dispute was whether the participation of a third-party funder in the arbitration should be disclosed and whether such participation violated the principle of confidentiality.

---

[48] See the Anti-Unfair Competition Law of the People's Republic of China.

[49] See the 10 Typical Cases on Judicial Review of Arbitration published by the Beijing No. 4 Intermediate People's Court in November 2024. The case established the necessity and scope of disclosure obligations for third-party funding in arbitration, as well as the proportionality standard for assessing confidentiality principles. This approach not only respected the principle of party autonomy but also set a reasonable and feasible standard for the judicial review of international commercial arbitration within the framework of Chinese law.

The Beijing No. 4 Intermediate People's Court held that existing laws did not contain prohibitive provisions regarding third-party funding institutions supporting and funding parties in arbitration. The conduct of civil entities in choosing arbitration and opting for third-party funding during arbitration should be evaluated based on legality and the principle of party autonomy. The key to the confidentiality of arbitration lies in keeping the details of the case undisclosed to the public to protect the parties' commercial secrets and social reputation. While arbitration rules prohibited the disclosure of information to the "outside world," they did not restrict relevant personnel from accessing such information. In the absence of existing arbitration rules prohibiting third-party funding institutions from supporting parties in arbitration, the establishment of a funding relationship between a third-party funding institution and a party did not violate arbitration confidentiality rules. In summary, the arguments raised by A Airlines, such as the alleged violation of arbitration confidentiality principles by the third-party funding institution, were unfounded. The Court accordingly dismissed their application.

Article 53

The arbitration institution shall notify the parties of the date of the hearing within the time limit specified in the arbitration rules. A party with justified reasons may, within the time limit specified in the arbitration rules, request a postponement of the hearing. The arbitral tribunal shall decide whether or not to postpone the hearing.

Notes

With the continuous increase in the number of arbitration cases in China and the growing complexity of case types, the standardization, predictability, and efficiency of procedural management have become important benchmarks for measuring the quality of arbitration. The standards for judicial review of arbitration are largely consistent regarding procedural issues. In practice, procedural disputes arising from improper notification of hearing dates or mishandling of hearing postponements occur from time to time and have even become grounds for parties to subsequently apply to set aside or not enforce arbitral awards. The legislation regarding the notification of hearing dates establishes a framework that balances principle with flexibility. Timely and formal notice of a hearing ensures that both parties have reasonable and sufficient time to prepare before the hearing, including organizing evidence, engaging agents, and preparing written statements and defense points. It is fundamental for safeguarding the parties' equal participation in the procedure and the effective exercise of the right to defend, preventing harm to substantive justice due to "surprise hearings." While emphasizing procedural stability, the law also includes an exception stating that "a party with justified reasons may, within the time limit specified in the arbitration rules, request a postponement of the hearing," reflecting the legislator's necessary consideration for procedural flexibility. Commercial activities are complex and variable; parties may be unable to proceed with the hearing as scheduled due to justified reasons such as force majeure, sudden illness, or the unavailability of key witnesses. Allowing applications for postponement ensures that while efficiency is pursued, substantive justice in individual case adjudication is not sacrificed by rigidly adhering to deadlines.

This Article continues the original Article 41 of the Arbitration Law (20170) and pertains to the provisions regarding notice of hearings and postponement of hearings in arbitration proceedings. Various arbitration institutions must establish clear and reasonable time standards in their respective rules. If the procedural rules are complied with, any future objection raised by the losing party on this ground will not be supported. Once the arbitral tribunal is constituted, the secretariat of the arbitration commission shall promptly transfer the case files to the arbitral tribunal. The arbitral tribunal hall determine an appropriate hearing date based on factors such as the handling of evidence, documents, and procedural matters—for instance, whether evidence that should be submitted by the parties has been submitted, whether specialized issues requiring appraisal have been appraised, whether sites and items requiring inspection have been inspected, whether evidence and property requiring preservation have been preserved, whether documents that the parties need to supplement have been fully supplemented, and whether relevant personnel for whom grounds for challenge have been discovered have been challenged—while also coordinating the work schedules of the arbitrators. After the hearing date is determined, the arbitration commission shall, through its functional office (the secretariat), notify the parties of the hearing date within the time limit specified in the arbitration rules.

Generally, once the hearing date is set, for the convenience of the arbitration commission, the arbitral tribunal, and the parties in making necessary preparations for the hearing, arbitrators and parties should not arbitrarily request changes to the hearing date. Under special circumstances, if a party requests a postponement, it should submit an application to the arbitral tribunal a reasonable time before the hearing. If justified reasons exist, the arbitral tribunal may agree to postpone the hearing. The arbitrators of the tribunal should contact the arbitration commission to promptly readjust the hearing schedule and determine a new hearing date. If an arbitrator needs to postpone the hearing due to special circumstances, they should also notify the arbitration commission in advance, and the latter will notify the parties. The new hearing time should be determined and communicated to the parties as soon as possible.

Furthermore, regarding the place of hearing, the New Arbitration Law does not provide explicit stipulations. It is generally understood that in domestic arbitration, the location of the arbitration commission chosen by the parties in the arbitration agreement is the place of hearing. If the parties have agreed on another venue for the hearing, their agreement may be followed, depending on the circumstances.

According to this Article, the legislator grants the ultimate decision-making power regarding postponement to the arbitral tribunal, rather than to the parties or the arbitration institution, with the aim of: first, preventing parties from abusing the right to postpone to delay the proceedings; and second, ensuring that the decision is based on a professional assessment of the overall circumstances of the case. As the master of the procedure, the arbitral tribunal is best positioned to balance the reasonableness of the postponement request, the opinions of the other party, the impact on the overall progress of the procedure, and the needs of the fair adjudication of the case.

Illustrative Case
Du v. SH Company[50]
Du applied for non-enforcement of a certain award rendered by the BAC. One of the reasons was that the arbitration procedure violated statutory procedures. On the eve of the rehearing after the arbitration commission had newly appointed an arbitrator, Du was unable to attend the hearing due to illness and applied for a postponement. However, the arbitration commission did not agree to the postponement and requested that the agent attend the hearing. The agent was not in Beijing, and Du was also unable to participate in the hearing, resulting in a failure to apply for the repetition of the proceedings that had already been conducted.

The court held that, according to Article 41 of the Arbitration Law (2017), the arbitration commission shall notify the parties of the date of the hearing within the time limit specified in the arbitration rules. A party may request a postponement of the hearing within the time limit specified in the arbitration rules if it has justified reasons. Whether to postpone the hearing shall be determined by the arbitral tribunal. Thus, whether to grant a postponement is decided by the arbitration commission. In this case, the arbitration commission's decision not to grant Du's application for postponement was an exercise of its discretionary power. In other words, before receiving notice of approval, Du should have been prepared to appear in court on time. As for Du's claim that his failure to appear in court led to his inability to apply for the repetition of the proceedings already conducted, this court holds that there is no necessary connection between applying for the repetition of proceedings already conducted and appearing in court. According to the provisions of the Arbitration Rules, Du could have made the request after the arbitration commission reconstituted the tribunal; it did not need to be raised during the hearing. His failure to make the request after the tribunal was reconstituted constitutes negligence in exercising his rights, and he shall bear the legal consequences himself. His current claim during the non-enforcement review stage that the arbitration procedure violated statutory procedures on this ground lacks factual and legal basis, and hence the court dismissed the action.

Article 54
Where the claimant fails to attend the hearing without justified reasons after having been notified in writing or leaves the hearing prior to its conclusion without the permission of the arbitral tribunal, they may be deemed to have withdrawn their application for arbitration.

Where the respondent fails to attend the hearing without justified reasons after having been notified in writing or leaves the hearing prior to its conclusion without the permission of the arbitral tribunal, a default award may be made.

---

[50] (2020) Su 11 Zhi Yi No. 21.

Notes

Article 54 of the New Arbitration Law fully inherits the provisions of the original Article 42, aiming to address situations where parties passively participate or even maliciously delay proceedings, thereby preventing the arbitration process from reaching a deadlock due to one party's non-cooperation. Although the wording of the article remains unchanged in this revision, its context carries new characteristics of the times: on one hand, commercial entities have enhanced awareness of protecting their rights, but some parties may also abuse procedural rights; on the other hand, the internationalization of arbitration is deepening, requiring Chinese arbitration procedures to possess a high degree of certainty and predictability to align with internationally accepted rules. It is particularly important to note that in today's environment of increasingly complex cases, business models, and commercial atmospheres, accurately handling procedural and substantive aspects in cases of default awards has become a significant issue that arbitral tribunals need to actively address and contemplate.

At every stage of the arbitration process, close cooperation from the parties is essential. Hearings are a crucial phase in arbitration proceedings, playing an important role in clarifying the facts of the case, making the parties' cooperation even more vital. Parties should appear in court on time and participate in the hearing activities under the direction of the arbitral tribunal. Participating in the hearing is both a right and an obligation of the parties. As a right, the parties can, of course, waive it; but as an obligation, if a party fails to fulfill it, it may affect the progress of the arbitration and thereby cause prejudice to the other party. Therefore, certain legal consequences must be imposed on parties who fail to fulfill their obligation to attend the hearing.

The main purpose of this Article is to ensure the efficient progress of the procedure and prevent malicious delays. In commercial arbitration, "time is money." One party (especially a respondent with a high expectation of losing the case) may intentionally delay the proceedings by failing to appear or withdrawing during the hearing, consuming the other party's time and financial resources. Addressing improper conduct by the claimant, the provision stipulates that it "shall be deemed to have withdrawn its application for arbitration," making it bear the consequence of termination of the proceedings. Addressing improper conduct by the respondent, the provision stipulates that the tribunal "may proceed with the arbitration and make a default award," allowing the procedure to continue in its absence. This effectively deprives the malicious delayer of the right to obstruct the procedure and ensures the efficiency of dispute resolution.

It is important to note that this Article grants the arbitral tribunal necessary procedural discretion. The use of the word "may" in both instances within the clause means that even if a party fails to appear or withdraws from the hearing without justified reasons, the arbitral tribunal is not obligated to make a decision of "deemed withdrawal" or "default award," but rather has the power to exercise discretion based on the circumstances of the case. For example, if some joint claimants or joint respondents are present, the arbitral tribunal may decide to continue the hearing for those who are present.

When making a default award, the arbitral tribunal should be especially cautious and must render an award based on the law, respecting the evidence, ascertaining the facts, and distinguishing right from wrong. If the claimant's claim is unfounded or insufficient, a favorable award for the claimant cannot be made simply because the respondent is absent; if the respondent is in the right, an adverse award cannot be made against them merely because they failed to appear or withdrew from the hearing without reason. This is an inevitable requirement of arbitration fairness. Certainly, if a party fails to appear or withdraws during the hearing, it will inevitably affect their ability to present evidence or state their case. If this consequently hinders the arbitral tribunal's ability to distinguish right from wrong, the party shall bear the consequences themselves.

Regarding similar situations, Article 129 of Civil Procedure Law stipulates that if the plaintiff, having been served with a summons, refuses to appear in court without justified reasons, or withdraws from the court session without the permission of the court, the case may be considered as withdrawn by the plaintiff; if the defendant has filed a counterclaim, a judgment by default may be rendered. However, in the New Arbitration Law, when the claimant is deemed to have withdrawn its arbitration claim, there is no explicit provision on how to handle a counterclaim raised by the respondent. This does not negatively impact arbitration practice because all provisions concerning the claimant's arbitration claim also apply to counterclaims raised by the respondent. If the respondent raises a counterclaim, the arbitration proceedings do not terminate merely because the claimant is deemed to have withdrawn its claim. On the contrary, the arbitral tribunal simply ceases to hear the claimant's arbitration claim but must continue to hear and render an award on the respondent's counterclaim.

Illustrative Case

Sun v. Lu[51]

Sun authorized her husband, Lu, to attend the arbitration hearing at the SCIA with their identity card. However, Sun and Lu did not submit any power of attorney or authorization procedures to the SCIA. Furthermore, Lu arrived at the SCIA nearly 40 minutes later than the time specified in the hearing notice. After the hearing concluded, Lu contacted the arbitration secretary, who informed him that he could apply for another hearing. However, neither Sun nor Lu applied for a rehearing. Subsequently, Sun applied to the Intermediate Court to set aside the arbitral award

[51] See the 10 Typical Cases for 2024 on Judicial Review of Arbitration published by the Guangdong Province Shenzhen Intermediate People's Court in July 2025. Parties shall strictly comply with the provisions of the Arbitration Law of the People's Republic of China and the relevant arbitration rules, actively fulfill their procedural obligations to ensure they fully enjoy their corresponding rights. A party's failure to participate in the arbitration proceedings due to its own reasons does not constitute a violation of statutory procedures by the arbitration proceedings. Consequently, the court will not set aside the arbitral award rendered by the arbitral tribunal in accordance with the arbitration rules. This case fully demonstrates the seriousness of the rules and order inherent in arbitration as a quasi-judicial process. It also reflects judicial support for the authority of arbitral tribunals in handling cases according to law and rules, as well as for their public credibility.

on the grounds that the SCIA rendered the award in her absence, thereby violating legal procedures.

The Guangdong Province Shenzhen Intermediate People's Court held that Sun and Lu did not submit any power of attorney or authorization procedures to the SCIA. The SCIA's handling of the matter complied with Article 24 of the SCIA Arbitration Rules. Lu arrived at the SCIA nearly 40 minutes later than the scheduled hearing time, and the arbitral tribunal proceeded with the hearing in his absence, which was in accordance with Article 39 of the SCIA Arbitration Rules. Therefore, there was no circumstance in this case where the arbitration procedure violated statutory procedures. Accordingly, the Court ruled to dismiss Sun's action.

Article 55
The parties shall provide the evidence in support of their own arguments.

The arbitral tribunal may, as it considers necessary, collect the evidence on its own. If necessary, assistance may be requested from the relevant parties in accordance with the law.

Notes
This Article corresponds to the original Article 43 of the Arbitration Law (2017) and is a core provision regarding the arbitration evidence system. As arbitration becomes one of the mainstream methods for resolving commercial disputes, the cases involved are increasingly specialized and complex, and new forms and types of evidence are also emerging. A purely "adversarial" model of evidence presentation may, in some circumstances, lead to difficulties in ascertaining facts, especially when crucial evidence is held by third parties outside the case or involves public interest. On the other hand, overemphasizing the arbitral tribunal's investigative power could contradict the principles of confidentiality, efficiency, and party autonomy in arbitration. Therefore, this revision helps to further clarify and balance the parties' primary responsibility in presenting evidence with the arbitral tribunal's auxiliary function of investigating and collecting evidence to ascertain the facts, thereby adapting to the needs of modern commercial dispute resolution.

The parties bear the responsibility to prove their claims, which reflects the principle of "he who asserts must prove" from civil procedural law in the field of arbitration. Its primary purpose is to clarify the parties' central role and primary responsibility in the arbitration proceedings. Arbitration originates from the parties' agreement, and the resources required for dispute resolution should primarily be borne by the parties. This provision encourages parties to prudently assert their claims and actively search for and submit evidence in support of their case, reflecting the adversarial nature of arbitration. Almost all major international arbitration rules contain similar provisions. For example, Article 24(1) of the UNCITRAL Arbitration Rules on evidence and hearings stipulates that each party shall have the burden of proving the facts relied on to support its claim or defense.

Paragraph 2 grants the arbitral tribunal the power to "collect evidence on its own initiative." The fundamental purpose is to compensate for shortcomings in the parties' ability to present evidence and prevent unjust outcomes due to obstacles in evidence production. In specific circumstances, such as when evidence involves state archives, bank records, professional data held by third parties, etc., the parties may be unable to obtain it themselves. In such cases, collection by a neutral and authoritative arbitral tribunal helps reveal the objective facts of the case, ensuring the award is based on as complete an evidentiary foundation as possible, thereby achieving substantive justice.

The newly added provision stating that "when necessary, assistance may be requested from the relevant parties in accordance with the law," while acknowledging that arbitration is a private dispute resolution mechanism, in fact grants the arbitral tribunal greater power to investigate and collect evidence than before. When necessary to ascertain the facts, the arbitral tribunal can request cooperation from judicial organs, administrative agencies, or other societal entities. This both safeguards the independence of arbitration and provides it with a necessary channel for public support, helping to enhance the social credibility of the arbitration system in resolving complex disputes.

In certain situations, the arbitral tribunal may also collect evidence on its own initiative, but evidence obtained by the tribunal in this manner must be disclosed to the parties. Typically, it is only necessary for the arbitral tribunal to exercise this discretionary power when the parties are unable to obtain the evidence themselves. The arbitral tribunal enjoys broad discretion in deciding whether to actively collect evidence and whether to request assistance. This power is not an obligation; the arbitral tribunal does not need to respond to every investigation request from the parties. Its decision should be based on a judgment of "necessity," i.e., whether it is crucial for determining key facts of the case and the parties genuinely face difficulties in obtaining it themselves. This prevents parties from shifting the burden of proof onto the arbitral tribunal and avoids excessive intervention by the tribunal that could harm the adversarial nature and efficiency of the proceedings.

Illustrative Cases

Case 1: *Hong Kong A Company v. B Company and others*[52]

In September 2024, the SHIAC accepted an arbitration case concerning a cross-border data service contract dispute between the claimant, Hong Kong A Company, and the respondents, B Company and C Company. The core of the dispute involved determining whether the contract was formed between the parties by identifying the identities of the transaction representatives for each party. As the transaction representative information consisted only of WeChat IDs, and the parties were unable to verify the subject details themselves, they applied to the arbitral tribunal for investigation and evidence collection. The arbitration institution issued an assistance inquiry letter to a third party, but it was refused. Subsequently, in April 2025, the arbitral tribunal issued an interim measure decision, granting the claimant's request for investigation and evidence collection. The arbitration institution, through the

[52] See the Typical Cases from 2020–2024 on Judicial Review of Arbitration published by the Shanghai High People's Court in July 2025.

"Shanghai Court International Commercial One-Stop Dispute Resolution Platform," applied to the People's Court for the issuance of a court investigation order to assist in the arbitration's evidence collection. Upon review, the court granted permission and issued an investigation order to assist the arbitration in accordance with the law.

The court held that first, the evidence for which the arbitration institution sought assistance was relevant to the arbitration case and constituted necessary evidence for the dispute under arbitration. Second, both the parties and the arbitral tribunal, despite efforts and attempts, were unable to collect this evidence themselves. Third, the interim measure decision made by the arbitral tribunal in accordance with the arbitration rules and common practices in international commercial arbitration complied with due process, and the tribunal's opinion on whether to adopt interim measures, based on its review of the arbitration case, could serve as an important reference for the people's court in reviewing the issuance of the investigation order. Therefore, the court agreed to issue the investigation order in accordance with the law.

Case 2: *A v. B*[53]

The Zhuhai International Arbitration Court accepted a Macao-related loan contract case. The parties involved reached a settlement agreement on their own regarding the loan contract dispute and jointly applied to the arbitration court for an award with enforceability. Upon review, the arbitral tribunal decided to obtain the parties' bank transaction records to verify facts related to the loan. As banking institutions typically do not open such item inquiries to institutions or individuals other than judicial organs, citing customer privacy protection, the arbitral tribunal faced difficulties in collecting the evidence itself. It therefore submitted an application to the Guangdong Province Zhuhai Intermediate People's Court for the issuance of an investigation order.

The Guangdong Province Zhuhai Intermediate People's Court held that the arbitration case involved Macao-related elements, and both the location of the arbitration institution and the evidence was in Zhuhai City. According to Article 3, the High People's Court of Guangdong Measures on Issuing Investigation Orders to Assist Commercial Arbitration Institutions in Evidence Collection (Pilot), the Court had jurisdiction over the application. Although the arbitration parties had reached a settlement agreement on the loan dispute, the arbitration institution still needed to review the authenticity of the loan relationship. The relevant bank transaction details requested by the arbitration institution constituted evidence related to the facts to be proven, necessary for collection, and which the arbitration institution could not

[53] See the 2nd batch of the 10 Typical Cases on Judicial Review of Arbitration published by the High People's Court of Guangdong Province in August 2025. This case involves the province's first investigation order to assist arbitration issued after the implementation of the "Guangdong High People's Court Measures on Issuing Investigation Orders to Assist Commercial Arbitration Institutions in Evidence Collection (For Trial Implementation)," and is also the nation's first investigation order involving a Macao-related commercial arbitration case. The court's assistance in issuing the investigation order effectively resolved the difficulty faced by the arbitration institution in evidence collection.

collect on its own. Consequently, the Court issued an investigation order to the arbitration institution.

Article 56
The parties may apply to the arbitral tribunal for an appraisal on specialized issues of fact. Where the arbitral tribunal based on the application of the parties or its own discretion, considers that a special issue requires appraisal, it may refer the issue for appraisal to an appraiser agreed on by the parties or to an appraiser designated by the arbitral tribunal.

If requested by a party or required by the arbitral tribunal, the appraiser shall attend the hearing upon notice from the arbitral tribunal. Subject to the permission of the arbitral tribunal, the parties may question the appraiser.

Notes
This Article corresponds to the original Article 44 under the Arbitration Law (2017) and pertains to the expert appraisal mechanism within arbitration proceedings. With technological advancements and the exponential growth in the complexity of commercial disputes, factual determinations involving specialized knowledge have become a common challenge for arbitral tribunals. The original appraisal provision was relatively broad in practice. This revision focuses specifically on appraisals for specialized issues concerning facts, ensuring that when faced with highly specialized disputes, the arbitral tribunal can both leverage expert wisdom and maintain control over the fact-finding process.

This Article first clarifies the parties' rights regarding the appraisal procedure. Simultaneously, it clearly grants the arbitral tribunal the power to decide whether to initiate an appraisal, aiming to prevent crucial facts from remaining unascertained due to strategic inaction by a party. This dual-track initiation mechanism ensures that if either party is unwilling to apply for an appraisal due to cost or strategic reasons, but the issue is decisive for the award, the arbitral tribunal may proactively initiate the procedure to safeguard substantive justice.

This Article encourages the parties to reach a consensus on the appraisal institution early in the proceedings, which helps enhance their trust in the appraisal process and their acceptance of the appraisal results. The arbitral tribunal exercises its appointment power only when the parties fail to agree. This respects the contractual nature of arbitration and ensures the procedure does not stall due to a deadlock in selection. This approach is also commonly adopted in arbitration practice, i.e., the parties first negotiate to determine the appraisal institution, and if no agreement is reached, the arbitral tribunal decides.

Paragraph 2 stipulates that "the appraiser shall attend the hearing upon notice from the arbitral tribunal" and, with permission, accept questions. Through courtroom cross-examination, the parties can directly question the expert appraiser on specialized aspects such as the basis, methodology, samples, and reasoning process of the appraisal, thereby exposing potential flaws, biases, or limitations in the expert opinion. This effectively avoids the scenario of a written expert opinion being the sole, unchallenged word, compels the expert appraiser to assume professional responsibility for their conclusions, and provides a foundation for the arbitral tribunal to decide whether to admit, partially admit, or exclude this evidence.

Prior to this revision, the arbitration rules of most arbitration institutions contained specific provisions regarding appraisal within arbitration proceedings. For instance:

Article 35 of the BAC Arbitration Rules stipulates that if a party applies for an appraisal and the arbitral tribunal agrees, or if the arbitral tribunal deems an appraisal necessary even without a party application, the tribunal may notify the parties to jointly select an appraiser within a specified period or may appoint one itself. The parties shall pre-pay the appraisal fees according to the agreed ratio or the ratio determined by the arbitral tribunal. Failure to pre-pay grants the arbitral tribunal the right to decide against proceeding with the relevant appraisal. The arbitral tribunal has the right to require, and the parties have the obligation to provide or present to the appraiser, any documents, data, property, or other items necessary for the appraisal. Any dispute between a party and the appraiser regarding whether provided items are case-related shall be decided by the arbitral tribunal. The appraiser shall submit a written expert opinion, copies of which shall be delivered to the parties, who have the right to comment thereon. If the arbitral tribunal deems it necessary or, upon a party's request, it may notify the appraiser to participate in the hearing. With the arbitral tribunal's permission, the parties may question the appraiser on matters related to the expert opinion. The appraisal period is not included in the time limit for rendering the award. Article 38 states that the arbitral tribunal shall decide whether to adopt the expert opinion.

Article 44 of the CIETAC Arbitration Rules stipulates that the arbitral tribunal may consult experts or appoint appraisers regarding specialized issues in the case. Experts and appraisers can be institutions or individuals, domestic or foreign. The arbitral tribunal has the power to require the parties, who are obligated, to provide or disclose to the expert or appraiser any relevant materials, documents, property, or objects for review, inspection, or appraisal. Copies of expert reports and appraisal reports shall be forwarded to the parties, giving them an opportunity to comment. If a party applies or the arbitral tribunal requires the expert or appraiser to participate in the hearing, they shall do so and, if the arbitral tribunal deems necessary, explain their report.

Article 45 of the SCIA Arbitration Rules stipulates that if the arbitral tribunal deems it necessary, or upon a party's request approved by the arbitral tribunal, the tribunal may decide to engage an expert to conduct an appraisal, audit, valuation, testing, or consultation and provide an expert report. The arbitral tribunal may notify the parties to jointly select an expert within a specified period; if the parties cannot agree, the arbitral tribunal shall make the appointment.

Illustrative Case

***X Fire Protection Company v. Y Engineering Company*[54]**

[54] See the Typical Cases for 2024 on Judicial Review of Arbitration published by the Guangdong Province Shenzhen Intermediate People's Court in July 2025. During the hearing of an arbitration

Y Engineering Company (subcontractor) and X Fire Protection Company (contractor) entered into the Fire Protection Engineering Labor Subcontract, agreeing on a contract price of 430,000 RMB. Y Engineering Company, believing it had fulfilled its contractual obligations, filed for arbitration with the SCIA, requesting X Fire Protection Company to pay 246,957 RMB in project payments and interest, among other claims. During the arbitration proceedings, X Fire Protection Company, contending that there was a significant dispute between the parties regarding the actual construction volume, applied to the arbitral tribunal for a project cost appraisal. The arbitral tribunal did not grant the appraisal application, reasoning that the contract stipulated a fixed lump sum for the project, the main components of the disputed payment had low relevance to the quantities specified within the contract, the disputed amount related to the contractually agreed quantities was small, and the issues could be ascertained through methods such as the parties presenting and cross-examining evidence, making an entrusted appraisal unnecessary. The arbitral tribunal rendered an award, ordering X Fire Protection Company to pay Y Engineering Company 181,483 RMB in project labor fees and interest losses, etc. X Fire Protection Company applied to the Guangdong Province Shenzhen Intermediate People's Court to set aside the arbitral award, arguing that its application for a project cost appraisal during the arbitration stage was denied, and the tribunal proceeded to rule directly without an appraisal, constituting a procedural violation. Thus, the award should be set aside according to the law.

The Guangdong Province Shenzhen Intermediate People's Court held that issues such as assessment and appraisal applications raised by the parties during arbitration proceedings essentially pertained to the allocation of the burden of proof and the ascertainment of facts. The arbitral tribunal had the authority to handle such matters based on the specific circumstances of the case. In this case, X Fire Protection Company had applied for a construction cost appraisal during the arbitration. The arbitral tribunal, considering the circumstances of the case hearing, determined that the relevant facts could be ascertained without such an appraisal. Such determination fell within the arbitral tribunal's authority and should not be considered a violation of procedural rules. X Fire Protection Company's application did not fall within the statutory grounds for setting aside an arbitral award as stipulated in Article 58 of the Arbitration Law (2017). Therefore, its application should not be supported. Accordingly, the Court dismissed X Fire Protection Company's action.

---

case, the decision on whether to initiate an appraisal to ascertain the facts of the case falls within the authority of the arbitral tribunal. It involves the tribunal's comprehensive assessment of factors such as the allocation of the burden of proof between the parties, the probative value of existing evidence, whether a party has applied for an appraisal, and the feasibility of an appraisal. An arbitral tribunal's decision not to proceed with an appraisal based on the circumstances of the case, against which a party raises an objection and applies to set aside the arbitral award, essentially reflects the party's dissatisfaction with the tribunal's review of evidence and findings of fact. The tribunal's decision does not constitute a violation of statutory procedures.

Article 57
The evidence shall be presented during the hearings and may be examined by the parties.

Notes
This Article continues the provisions of the original Arbitration Law (2017), stipulating one of the rules of evidence in practice: the presentation and cross-examination of evidence during the hearing. This Article embodies the principle of "due process" in arbitration proceedings. With the increasing complexity of arbitration cases and the widespread use of electronic evidence, the procedural fairness of the evidence presentation and cross-examination phase has an increasingly prominent and decisive impact on the entire arbitration outcome. In commercial arbitration practice, a party's failure to obtain a reasonable opportunity to present its case and evidence, including the inability to effectively cross-examine evidence, is one of the significant grounds for setting aside or refusing enforcement of an arbitral award.

Hearings facilitate the parties' presentation of evidence, cross-examination, and oral arguments, which is conducive to the arbitral tribunal accurately clarifying the facts of the case. Of course, it may also delay the rendering of the award and increase the parties' expenses.

The requirement for evidence to be presented and cross-examined during the hearing is beneficial for the arbitral tribunal to observe the reactions of the parties and witnesses to the evidence in real-time and on-site throughout the evidence examination process, thereby forming its inner conviction. The arbitral tribunal can obtain a richer and more intuitive basis for its conviction than by reviewing written materials. This procedural requirement prevents the arbitral tribunal from relying on evidence formed outside the hearing that has not been cross-examined as the basis for its award. The right to cross-examine is a crucial part of the parties' procedural rights. By challenging the authenticity, legality, and relevance of the opposing party's evidence and debating the probative value of the evidence, the parties can effectively participate in the fact-finding process.

In arbitration, hearings are relatively common. For cases with more complex facts and significant disputes, holding a hearing allows both parties to cross-examine the presented evidence and state their respective viewpoints and arguments, thereby gradually clarifying the case details and the various legal relationships involved.

Generally, during the court investigation, the claimant states the case first, followed by the respondent's defense. Arbitrators may ask the parties questions about the case, and with the permission of the arbitral tribunal, the parties may also ask questions of the opposing party. Parties may present new evidence during the hearing and may cross-examine evidence presented at the hearing. However, this provision seems to lack flexibility and risks excluding written proceedings. Article 51 stipulates that if the parties agree to dispense with a hearing, the arbitral tribunal shall conduct a written review. But whether the arbitral tribunal can actively decide to conduct a written review of a case is not explicitly stipulated. Furthermore, since the New Arbitration Law does not provide for pre-hearing exchange of evidence, this provision seems to imply that whenever there is new evidence, a hearing must be held to allow for its "presentation at the hearing," unless the parties agree to dispense with a hearing, or, interpreting from the perspective of arbitration autonomy, the parties agree to adopt alternative methods.

Illustrative Case
Yantai A Company v. Shandong B Company[55]
Yantai A Company and Shandong B Company signed the Cooperation Agreement. During the performance of the agreement, a dispute arose between the parties. Shandong B Company applied for arbitration to the Qingdao Arbitration Commission in accordance with the cooperation agreement. After hearing the case, the Qingdao Arbitration Commission rendered an award, finding that Yantai A Company had breached the contract and should bear liability for breach. Subsequently, Yantai A Company applied to the Shandong Province Qingdao Intermediate People's Court to set aside the arbitral award on the grounds of procedural violations in the arbitration.

The Shandong Province Qingdao Intermediate People's Court found that the "Calculation Details" relied upon by the arbitral tribunal in its award were created after the arbitration hearing. Furthermore, the "Calculation Details" represented the unilateral statement of Shandong B Company, and their content was cited multiple times in the arbitral award, depriving Yantai A Company of its right to defend and violating the arbitration procedure. In accordance with Article 61 of the Arbitration Law (2017), the Court notified the arbitral tribunal to conduct a renewed arbitration. After the arbitral tribunal agreed to renew the arbitration, the setting-aside procedure for this case was concluded.

Article 58
Under circumstances where the evidence may be destroyed, lost or difficult to obtain at a later time, a party may apply for preservation of the evidence. Where a party applies for preservation of the evidence, the arbitration institution shall submit the application to the primary people's court in the place where the evidence is located, and the people's court shall handle it in a timely manner according to the law.

In an emergency, the parties to the arbitration agreement may apply to the people's court for evidence preservation in accordance with the relevant provisions of the Civil Procedure Law of the People's Republic of China before applying for arbitration. When a party applies for evidence preservation, the people's court shall handle it in a timely manner according to the law.

---

[55] See the Typical Cases on Judicial Review of Commercial Arbitration published by the Shandong Province Qingdao Intermediate People's Court in 2018–2021. Evidence relied upon by the arbitral tribunal in determining the facts of the case shall be presented at the hearing. Violation of this arbitration procedure constitutes the circumstance "the arbitration procedure violates the statutory procedure" as stipulated in Article 58(1) of the Arbitration Law (2017). In this case, the "Calculation Details" relied upon by the arbitral tribunal in ascertaining the facts were not cross-examined by the parties. The rendering of the arbitral award violated statutory procedures, and the court notified the arbitral tribunal to conduct a renewed arbitration in accordance with the law.

Notes

This Article corresponds to the original Article 46 under the Arbitration Law (2017) and is a core provision regarding the system of evidence preservation in arbitration proceedings. In commercial arbitration practice, the timely fixation and preservation of evidence often directly affect the ascertainment of case facts and the fairness of the final award. With arbitration cases involving increasingly complex technical fields, a growing proportion of electronic evidence, and the dispersal of evidence due to frequent cross-border commercial activities, the practical risks of evidence being destroyed or becoming difficult to obtain have increased significantly. Simultaneously, the international trend of judicial support for arbitration demands the establishment of a more robust system for preservation in arbitration, enhancing China's attractiveness as a seat of arbitration. Furthermore, while retaining the basic framework connecting arbitration and the judiciary, the revised clause further clarifies the independent status of pre-arbitration evidence preservation.

Evidence preservation in arbitration refers to compulsory protective and fixation measures taken by the people's court at the location of the evidence during the arbitration process, upon a party's application submitted via the arbitration commission, regarding evidence that may be destroyed or become difficult to obtain later.

The purpose of establishing the evidence preservation system in the Arbitration Law (2025) is to prevent evidence from being destroyed or becoming difficult to obtain later, thereby ensuring the correct and timely adjudication of cases and resolution of disputes. Thus, evidence preservation is a measure taken by the People's Court to protect the legitimate rights and interests of parties in arbitration, reflecting judicial support for arbitration. There are two situations requiring evidence preservation measures: First, evidence risks being destroyed. For example, a key witness in the case is currently seriously ill or even at risk of death; if their testimony is not promptly obtained through preservation measures, this potentially obtainable evidence will be lost if the witness unfortunately dies. Another example is an item that could serve as evidence being perishable or prone to decay; if preservation measures are not taken promptly, and the item deteriorates, deforms, due to natural or human factors, losing its original state, it loses its probative value, and as potential evidence, it is destroyed. Second, evidence will be difficult to obtain later. For example, a citizen who can serve as a witness is going abroad for several years of study or to settle overseas; obtaining testimony from this witness later would be comparatively difficult, so preservation measures should be taken promptly to extract their testimony.

At one time, in practice, if arbitration proceedings had not yet commenced, an interested party could not apply for evidence preservation. If an emergency situation requiring preservation arose at that time, the interested party could apply for notarization to preserve the probative effect of the relevant evidence through notarization. The newly added Paragraph 2 explicitly states that an application for evidence preservation may be filed "before applying for arbitration," which is a significant advancement in this revision, establishing the pre-arbitration evidence preservation system clearly through legislation. This provision recognizes the independent value of evidence preservation, elevating it from an ancillary status within arbitration proceedings to an independent remedy, ensuring that parties can act swiftly when facing emergencies, preventing the loss of preservation opportunities due to procedural limitations.

If a party applies for evidence preservation, it should submit a written application for evidence preservation to the arbitration commission. The application shall specify the following: the content of the evidence requiring preservation; the location of the evidence and witnesses; the relevance of the evidence requiring preservation to the case; and the reasons for taking evidence preservation measures. Upon receiving the application, the arbitration commission shall promptly submit it to the primary people's court at the location of the evidence. The court, upon receiving the application, shall review it promptly. If it deems preservation necessary, it shall promptly issue a ruling on evidence preservation, take preservation measures promptly, and notify the party and the arbitration commission. If it finds preservation unnecessary, it shall notify the party and the arbitration commission. Furthermore, other matters related to evidence preservation shall be handled by reference to the relevant provisions of the Civil Procedure Law.

Illustrative Cases

Case 1: *HC Company v. JL Company*[56]

HC Company asked the court to set aside a certain arbitral award rendered by CIETAC according to the law. One of the reasons was that the arbitration procedure violated statutory procedures. The arbitral tribunal's refusal to grant the application for evidence preservation violated the provisions of Article 46 of the Arbitration Law (2017). HC Company's arbitration claim was to demand JL Company compensate for its loss of working time during the suspension of work, including machinery losses and labor losses. The labor loss consisted of two parts: first, the wages paid by HC Company to the workers during the suspension period; second, the Labor Bureau of M County, directly deducted 2.4 million RMB from the project payment payable by JL Company to HC Company to disburse wages, including those for the suspension period, to the migrant workers on behalf of HC Company. To obtain evidential support, HC Company applied to CIETAC to go to the Labor Bureau of M County to obtain the payroll roster and list, because the Labor Bureau only cooperated with case-handling units such as public security, procuratorates, and courts, making it impossible for HC Company to obtain this evidence itself. This evidence involved over a million RMB in losses for HC Company and was crucial to HC Company's arbitration claim. On May 7, 2022, HC Company submitted an Application for Obtaining Evidence to CIETAC, requesting to obtain relevant evidence from the Labor Bureau of M County regarding the disbursement of wages to migrant workers on its behalf. After receiving the application, CIETAC served it to JL Company to solicit its opinion. JL Company replied in writing that it disagreed with the application. CIETAC then served a notice to HC Company and decided not to approve HC Company's application for obtaining evidence. After receiving this

[56] (2023) Jing 04 Min Te No. 298.

letter, HC Company raised an objection, arguing that a party's application to obtain evidence did not require the consent of the other party, and therefore applied again, submitting Opinions on the Letter Regarding the Construction Contract Dispute Case No. DP20220537 and a Re-application for Obtaining Evidence. After receiving the application, CIETAC served a notice to HC Company and again decided not to approve HC Company's application. In response to CIETAC's two decisions disapproving its request to obtain evidence, HC Company, in accordance with Article 46 of the Arbitration Law (2017), submitted an Application for Evidence Preservation to CIETAC. CIETAC decided not to approve HC Company's application for evidence preservation, which constituted a serious violation of statutory procedures. According to Article 46 of the Arbitration Law (2017), CIETAC violated this mandatory legal provision, made its own decision, and arbitrarily decided not to approve HC Company's evidence preservation application, thereby depriving HC Company of its right to apply for evidence preservation.

The court held that Article 46 of the Arbitration Law (2017) provides that where evidence might be lost or difficult to obtain later, a party may apply for evidence preservation; when a party applies for evidence preservation, the arbitration commission shall submit the party's application to the basic-level people's court at the place where the evidence is located. In this case, during the arbitration process, the arbitral tribunal, having considered HC Company's application to collect evidence as set out in its "Application for Evidence Preservation" and the actual circumstances of the case, decided not to grant HC Company's application. In this regard, the court held that the arbitral tribunal had the authority to review whether a party's application for evidence preservation complied with the provisions of Article 46 of the Arbitration Law (2017) and also had the authority to decide whether to grant such an application. During the arbitration, the arbitral tribunal, taking into account the actual circumstances of the case, decided not to grant the application submitted by HC Company, which did not violate the provisions of the Arbitration Rules.

Case 2: *Lin v. Zhuang*[57]

The claimant, Lin, sought to set aside an arbitral award rendered by the Shenzhen Arbitration Commission on the ground that the arbitration violated statutory procedures. Lin submitted an "Application for Evidence Preservation" to the arbitral tribunal on May 4, 2017, and a Request to Issue a Certificate to Obtain Huang's Identity Information on May 8. Since Huang's ID card and bank card had been cancelled, and the specific account number could no longer be provided, evidence could only be obtained through investigation and evidence collection. However, the arbitral tribunal also refused preservation on the grounds that it was irrelevant to the case and did not inform Lin of the relevant progress. The arbitral tribunal's refusal to preserve the evidence clearly violated legal provisions and significantly harmed Lin's legitimate rights and interests.

The court held that Article 46 of the Arbitration Law (2017) provided that where evidence might be lost or difficult to obtain later, a party could apply for evidence

[57] (2017) Yue 03 Min Te No. 465.

preservation. When a party applied for evidence preservation, the arbitration commission was required to submit the party's application to the basic-level people's court at the place where the evidence was located. The court stated that the subject of an evidence preservation application should be relevant to the adjudication of the case, and the evidence should be at risk of being lost or becoming difficult to obtain later. The arbitration commission (or arbitral tribunal), being responsible for hearing the case, was best positioned to understand the relevance of the evidence to the case and the necessity of its preservation. Therefore, it could conduct a preliminary review of a party's evidence preservation application. If the application met the statutory conditions for preservation and the preservation (or lack thereof) could affect the correct adjudication of the case, the commission (or tribunal) should submit the application to the basic-level people's court at the location of the evidence. Conversely, if the application did not meet the legal requirements or the preservation would not affect the correct adjudication of the case, then the arbitration commission's (or tribunal's) failure to submit the application to the court did not constitute a violation of statutory procedures. In this case, the subject of Lin's evidence preservation application was the detailed account information of a non-party, Huang, at the Industrial and Commercial Bank of China Shenzhen Xinian Sub-branch and China Merchants Bank Shenzhen Branch Tairan Sub-branch, from November 2012 to November 2014. The purpose was to prove that Huang had repaid part of the loan on Lin's behalf. However, Huang was neither a party to the arbitration nor a witness. There was no evidence demonstrating Huang's connection to the arbitration case, and Huang's account details alone were insufficient to prove that the transfers were made to repay the loan in dispute on Lin's behalf. Lin failed to demonstrate that the subject of the preservation application was relevant to the case adjudication. Consequently, the arbitration commission's decision not to support the evidence preservation application and not to submit it to the basic-level people's court did not affect the correct adjudication of the case and did not violate statutory procedures.

Article 59
The parties shall have the right to debate in the course of arbitration. At the end of the debate, the presiding arbitrator or sole arbitrator shall solicit final opinions from the parties.

Notes
This Article pertains to the principle of debate and final statements within arbitration proceedings. This revision continues the wording of the original Arbitration Law (2017). As arbitration cases involve increasingly complex technical facts and legal issues, the need for parties to clarify the points of dispute through full debate becomes more pronounced. Protecting the parties' right to debate is a core element of due process and directly relates to the validity and enforcement of the award. Under the principle of debate, parties can present their factual bases and legal arguments to the arbitral tribunal through direct oral confrontation. This process can effectively expose contradictions in evidence, clarify legal disputes, and aid the arbitral tribunal in making accurate determinations. It is important to note that in

practice, debate and final statements can sometimes become mere formalities, with the debate segment lacking effective guidance and final statements being a simple procedural step. Arbitration institutions or experienced arbitral tribunals need to provide appropriate guidance for these procedures to ensure the fairness and efficiency of the hearing and to protect the parties' rights.

During the hearing, the parties and their agents, under the direction of the arbitral tribunal, may at any time state their respective positions regarding the facts of the case and the application of law, refuting and arguing against each other to protect their own legitimate rights and interests. Debate is a right of the parties, but when exercising this right, the parties should not stray from the scope of the case or discuss issues unrelated to the case, and must not insult or slander the other party or its agents. While informing the parties of their full opportunity to state their case and debate, the arbitral tribunal should remind the parties to comply with the order of the hearing. The respondent should not interrupt and refute while the claimant is stating its case, and the claimant should not arbitrarily interrupt while the respondent is presenting its defense.

For the arbitral tribunal, a full debate between the parties can lay a solid foundation for ascertaining the facts, clarifying rights and wrongs, correctly applying the law, and rendering an award. At the conclusion of the debate, the arbitral tribunal shall solicit the final opinions of the parties. Before adjourning the hearing, the arbitral tribunal may, depending on the circumstances, require the parties to submit supplementary materials and statements; it may make arrangements or notify the parties later regarding whether it needs to collect evidence on its own initiative, whether to conduct an appraisal on certain issues of the case, or whether another hearing is necessary.

In practice, some arbitration rules stipulate that the arbitral tribunal may require the parties to submit written arguments based on the progress of the hearing. Similarly, the parties' final opinions may be presented orally during the hearing or submitted in writing within the time limit specified by the arbitral tribunal. For example, refer to Articles 39 and 40 of the BAC Arbitration Rules. Article 35 of the CIETAC Arbitration Rules, on the manner of hearing, stipulates that unless otherwise agreed by the parties, the arbitral tribunal may conduct the hearing in an inquisitorial or an adversarial manner, depending on the specific circumstances of the case.

Illustrative Cases

Case 1: ***Hua Company v. Guang Company***[58]

[58] See the 1st batch of the Typical Cases on Judicial Review of Arbitration published by the High People's Court of Guangdong Province in February 2024. The cross-examination of evidence is a fundamental arbitration right of the parties and an important means to ensure the fairness of the arbitral award's outcome. If an arbitration institution fails to organize the parties to cross-examine supplementary evidence used to determine the facts of the case, it may affect the correct adjudication of the case. Under such circumstances, the people's court may notify the arbitral tribunal to renew the arbitration, giving the tribunal an opportunity to remedy the procedural defect.

A dispute arose between Hua Company and Guang Company over project payments, leading Hua Company to apply for arbitration with X Arbitration Commission. During the arbitration, X Arbitration Commission initiated an appraisal procedure. The appraisal institution issued an appraisal opinion and subsequently provided a supplementary explanation, issuing a "Reply." X Arbitration Commission rendered an arbitral award requiring Guang Company to pay the outstanding project sum and interest to Hua Company. Hua Company argued that the arbitral tribunal did not treat the "Reply" issued by the appraisal institution as evidence by organizing the parties to cross-examine it, nor did it review or affirm it in the award. Therefore, Hua Company applied to set aside the arbitral award on the grounds that the arbitration violated statutory procedures.

The Guangdong Province Zhuhai Intermediate People's Court held that, according to the arbitration rules of X Arbitration Commission, if the parties submit supplementary evidential materials before the conclusion of the hearing, and the arbitral tribunal decides to accept them but not to hold another hearing, it may require the parties to submit written cross-examination opinions within a specified period. The "Reply" issued by the appraisal institution constituted a supplementary explanation to the appraisal opinion and was an integral part of it. The content of the "Reply" could affect the review and determination of the probative value of the appraisal opinion. The arbitral tribunal's failure to treat the "Reply" as evidence and organize the parties to cross-examine it deprived the parties of their right to debate, violated the arbitration rules, and potentially affected the correct adjudication of the case. Considering the need to remedy the procedural defect in the arbitration and resolve the parties' dispute promptly, the Court notified the arbitral tribunal to renew the arbitration within a specified period and simultaneously ruled to suspend the setting-aside procedure. Subsequently, X Arbitration Commission renewed the arbitration, and the Court ruled to conclude the setting-aside procedure.

Case 2: *ZT Company v. JG Company*[59]

In November 2018, the Hangzhou Arbitration Commission accepted the case concerning a construction contract dispute between ZT Company and JG Company, among others. Before rendering a partial award, the arbitral tribunal in this case held four hearing sessions, but only conducted procedures such as statements, defenses, presentation, and cross-examination of evidence, handling of appraisal matters, and

---

[59] (2022) Zhe 01 Min Te No. 226; See the 10 Typical Cases on Judicial Review of Commercial Arbitration published by the High People's Court of Zhejiang Province. The principle for arbitration hearing procedures is that hearings "shall be conducted," with "agreement to dispense with hearings" as the exception. An arbitral tribunal rendering a partial award should also adhere to this procedural principle. In this case, the arbitral tribunal did not complete a full hearing process over four separate hearing sessions. Before the conclusion of the final hearing, the arbitration claimant applied to amend its arbitration claims. Since the scope of the prior hearings did not cover the amended claims, and one party explicitly requested another hearing regarding the amended claims, it was improper for the arbitral tribunal to render a partial award without holding a hearing, based solely on materials submitted by the parties after the hearings. Where defects exist in the arbitration procedure, the People's Court may notify the arbitral tribunal to remedy them by renewing the arbitration within the existing arbitration case.

factual inquiries, never completing a full hearing process. During the final hearing session, JG Company added and amended its arbitration claims and applied for a partial award. Upon inquiry by the arbitral tribunal, ZT Company explicitly replied that another hearing should be held. After the hearing, the parties submitted applications and corresponding statements of defense to the arbitral tribunal. The arbitral tribunal rendered a partial award without holding any further hearings. Subsequently, ZT Company applied to the Zhejiang Province Hangzhou Intermediate People's Court to set aside the arbitral award on the grounds of procedural violations in the arbitration.

The Zhejiang Province Hangzhou Intermediate People's Court held that after a party added and amended its relevant arbitration claims, and the opposing party requested an oral hearing, the arbitral tribunal, without conducting an oral hearing and relying solely on materials submitted after the hearings, rendered a partial award on that dispute. This failed to safeguard the parties' rights to debate and present final opinions, violated statutory procedures, and constituted a statutory ground for setting aside the award. As this case involved a partial award and there were still unresolved matters pending in the arbitration case, it was not appropriate to set aside this partial award, which could lead to jurisdictional disputes and hearing obstacles. Furthermore, this ground for setting aside could still be remedied by renewing the arbitration within the existing arbitration case, allowing the arbitral tribunal to do so. Based on this, the Court notified the arbitral tribunal to renew the arbitration within the existing arbitration case. After the arbitral tribunal indicated its agreement, the Court ruled to conclude the judicial review procedure for the arbitration.

Case 3: *Zhang v. HX Company*[60]

The X Arbitration Commission accepted a case concerning a contract dispute between HX Company and Zhang arising from the Agency Agreement and rendered an arbitral award in April 2022. Zhang asserted that he had no relationship with HX Company, that the main evidence, the Agency Agreement, relied upon by the arbitration commission for its award was not signed by him, and that although the name of the bank account holder in the agreement matched his name, the ID number of the account holder did not match his ID number. The contact phone number provided by HX Company to the arbitral tribunal was also not Zhang's mobile number, resulting in Zhang not receiving the hearing notice and arbitration documents, being unable to participate in the arbitration hearing, and losing the opportunity to debate. Zhang requested the setting aside of the arbitral award on the grounds that the evidence on which the award was based was forged.

The Fujian Province Xiamen Intermediate People's Court held that the evidence provided by Zhang indicated that his identity information might have been misused to sign the contract in question with HX Company. Determining whether the

[60] (2022) Min 02 Min Te No. 273; See the 10 Typical Cases on Judicial Review of Arbitration published by the SPC in January 2024. Where the identity of an arbitration party may be incorrect or defects exist in the arbitration procedure, the People's Court may notify the arbitration institution to renew the arbitration, giving the arbitral tribunal an opportunity to remedy the procedural defects.

signature and fingerprint on the contract were made by Zhang himself would require an appraisal. Considering the need to correct the procedural defect in the arbitration and resolve the dispute between the parties promptly, the Court notified the arbitral tribunal to renew the arbitration within a specified period and simultaneously ruled to suspend the setting-aside procedure. Subsequently, the arbitration commission renewed the arbitration, and the Court then ruled to conclude the setting-aside procedure. During the renewed arbitration process, the claimant, HX Company, withdrew its arbitration application.

Article 60

An arbitral tribunal shall make records of the hearings in writing. The parties and other participants in the arbitration shall have the right to apply for supplementation or correction of the record of their own statements if they consider that such record contains omissions or errors. If the application for supplementation or corrections is rejected, the application shall be recorded.

The record shall be signed or sealed by the arbitrators, the recordist, the parties and other participants in the arbitration.

Notes

This Article concerns the recording and confirmation of arbitration proceedings. The New Arbitration Law retains the wording of the original provision. Against the backdrop of increasingly standardized and internationalized arbitration practice, the legal status and normative requirements of hearing transcripts have become more prominent in importance. With the proliferation of new hearing methods such as electronic arbitration and online hearings, the form and confirmation mechanisms of hearing records face new challenges. In practice, the hearing transcript serves not only as an important basis for the arbitral tribunal's award but also aids in subsequent judicial review proceedings to determine the legality and compliance of the arbitration.

The hearing transcript is a record of the hearing activities. It is one of the important documents in arbitration, serving as a basis for case deliberation and even for summarizing arbitration work experience. Making a proper hearing transcript is a key responsibility of the recording personnel. The primary purpose of the transcript is to establish an official record of the arbitration procedure. Crucial procedural nodes and content from the hearing, such as the presentation of evidence, cross-examination, debate, admissions, waivers, and amendments to arbitration claims, are fixed in the form of the transcript. This Article can serve as an accurate basis for the arbitral tribunal's deliberations and award, and also preserves first-hand materials for potential judicial review, ensuring the entire arbitration process is traceable and enhancing the transparency and credibility of the procedure.

This Article also safeguards the parties' right to object to the procedural record. If a party believes the record of its statements has omissions or errors, it has the right to apply for correction or supplementation. This ensures the record can truthfully and completely reflect the intentions expressed by all parties during the hearing, preventing deviations in the basis of the award due to inaccuracies in the record.

Even if the arbitral tribunal finds the application for correction unfounded, it must record the application itself in the transcript, forming a complete procedural record. This ensures the parties' procedural rights are fully reflected and provides a basis for subsequent review of whether the arbitration procedure was proper, preventing the validity of the award from being affected by procedural oversights.

It is common practice for arbitrators, recording personnel, parties, and other arbitration participants to sign or affix their seals to the transcript. The act of signing or sealing signifies confirmation of the recorded content by the respective parties. However, in international commercial arbitration practice, signing the transcript, or even the transcript itself, may not be a mandatory requirement.

In arbitration practice, arbitration institutions generally stipulate corresponding provisions for hearing records in their arbitration rules. For example:

Article 41 of the BAC Arbitration Rules stipulates that the arbitral tribunal shall record the hearing circumstances in the transcript, except for mediation circumstances; the arbitral tribunal may audio or video record the hearing; parties and other arbitration participants have the right to apply for correction if they believe the record of their statements has omissions or errors; if the arbitral tribunal does not allow the correction, it shall record the application; the transcript shall be signed or sealed by the arbitrators, recording personnel, parties, and other arbitration participants. For online hearings, confirmation of the transcript shall be conducted in the manner determined by the arbitral tribunal; upon application by all parties, or application by one party and approval by the Commission, the parties may engage stenographers to record the hearing circumstances, the costs of which shall be advanced by the parties.

Article 41(1) of the SCIA Arbitration Rules stipulates that, upon a party's application, the hearing transcript may be provided to the parties; Paragraph (3) stipulates that upon joint application by the parties, or upon application by one party and consent of the arbitral tribunal, or at the arbitral tribunal's own discretion, the SCIA may engage professional stenographers or use other methods to prepare the hearing transcript for the arbitral tribunal.

Article 61

If the arbitral tribunal finds that a party unilaterally fabricates fundamental facts to apply for arbitration, or that the parties are colluding maliciously with the intention of harming national interests, social public interests, or the legitimate rights and interests of others through arbitration, it shall reject their arbitration request.

Notes

This Article is a new addition in this revision, legislatively regulating the abuse of process for false arbitration. The formulation of this clause stems from the increasingly prominent issues of false arbitration and malicious arbitration in recent arbitration practice. As arbitration's status in the social dispute resolution system has risen, its advantages of efficiency, confidentiality, and finality have been abused by a minority of parties. Instances have emerged where parties unilaterally fabricate facts or engage in malicious collusion to obtain illegal awards through arbitration procedures, thereby harming the legitimate rights and interests of the state, society, and third parties. Such actions severely undermine the credibility of the arbitration system and also pose a challenge to the social integrity system. Under the framework of the Arbitration Law (2017), arbitral tribunals faced with obviously false or malicious arbitration lacked clear authorization for proactive intervention, relying mainly on post-hoc correction through court procedures for setting aside or refusing enforcement. This not only wasted judicial resources but also struggled to effectively curb such behaviors. The addition of this Article fills this legal gap in the Arbitration Law (2017), granting arbitral tribunals clear power to detect and sanction dishonest arbitration conduct during the proceedings, thereby safeguarding the integrity of the arbitration order at its source.

As arbitration becomes a mainstream channel for resolving commercial disputes, its advantages, such as confidentiality and efficiency, may be abused by malicious parties. In areas such as financial lending, real estate transactions, and corporate equity, cases are heard where arbitral awards are obtained by fabricating creditor-debtor relationships or forging guarantee contracts, to subsequently participate in asset distribution, evade enforcement, or harm third-party interests. Under the previous legal framework, the regulation of false arbitration and malicious collusion primarily relied on setting-aside and non-enforcement procedures. This model, focusing on post-hoc relief, could lead to drawbacks such as damage already occurring, the need to initiate complex litigation separately, and high costs.

This Article also embodies the concrete application of the principle of good faith in arbitration proceedings. One of the vital forces of the arbitration system lies not only in fairness and efficiency but also in the good faith of all parties. Unilateral fabrication of basic facts by a party or malicious collusion between parties constitutes a fundamental undermining of the arbitration system. By authorizing arbitral tribunals to directly dismiss such claims, it effectively removes toxins from the arbitration process, defending the fairness and authority of arbitration as a quasi-judicial mechanism.

This Article distinguishes dishonest arbitration conduct into two types: a party unilaterally fabricates basic facts and malicious collusion between the parties, corresponding to different constituent elements and standards of proof. The former focuses on the requirement for the authenticity of objective facts, while the latter emphasizes the conspiratorial nature of subjective intent. This distinction covers the main types of dishonest conduct in practice and provides clear guidance for the typological review by arbitral tribunals. In terms of balancing interests, the clause constructs protection for "infringement of national interests, public social interests, or the lawful rights and interests of others," establishing the bottom line of public order in arbitration proceedings.

Furthermore, regarding the allocation of power, on one hand, it clearly grants arbitral tribunals the power to actively review and dismiss dishonest claims; on the other hand, it imposes reasonable constraints on the arbitral tribunal's discretion through the mandatory wording "shall reject," preventing abuse of power.

In practice, the application of this Article generally adopts a progressive review method. In the initial stages of the procedure, the arbitral tribunal conducts preliminary screening by reviewing materials such as the application for arbitration and the statement of defense. During the evidence exchange stage, the focus is on key evidence regarding its formation time, source, and interrelationships. During the hearing process, in-depth investigation and cross-examination are conducted on doubtful issues. When applying this Article, the arbitral tribunal should fully protect the parties' procedural rights, including informing them of the suspected grounds, providing opportunities for defense, and allowing supplementary evidence. Determining false arbitration relies on the arbitral tribunal's comprehensive hearing of the case. The assessment of involved subjective and objective elements requires the arbitral tribunal to use professional knowledge, logical reasoning, and everyday experience to form its inner conviction.

One point to note is that the boundary determination when reviewing for false arbitration requires careful consideration. Modern commercial transactions are increasingly complex, with innovative transaction models and structures, some of which may not be widely familiar. The arbitral tribunal should avoid two extremes: first, excessive review, mischaracterizing normal commercial risks or performance disputes as dishonest conduct; second, insufficient review, adopting a laissez-faire attitude towards obvious false arbitration.

When parties maliciously collude to obtain legal documents legitimizing false legal relationships through arbitration procedures to achieve their illegal purposes, it not only wastes judicial resources and undermines judicial credibility but also harms the legitimate rights and interests of relevant entities. Apart from the arbitral tribunal's adjudication within the arbitration proceedings, courts may also need to address false arbitration during the judicial review stage. By meticulously examining to uncover the truth and severely cracking down on false arbitration, the correct implementation of the law and judicial fairness can be effectively maintained, safeguarding the legitimate rights and interests of relevant entities from unlawful infringement.

Illustrative Cases

Case 1: ***A Asset Management Company v. B Industrial Development Company***[61]

In the case concerning the arbitral award for the construction project contract dispute between C Construction Company and B Industrial Development Company, the Chengdu Arbitration Commission rendered Award No. 882 (2021) on October 19, 2022 (hereinafter referred to as Arbitral award No. 882), ordering: B Industrial Development Company to pay C Construction Company 182,917,334.88 RMB in outstanding project payments and interest; C Construction Company enjoys a priority right to compensation within the scope of 74,773,257.84 RMB from the auction or discounted price of the unsold properties in Building #1 and the villa area of a

[61] See the 9 Typical Cases on Judicial Review of Arbitration published by the Sichuan Province Chengdu Intermediate People's Court May 2025.

certain real estate project located in Longquanyi District, Chengdu, owned by B Industrial Development Company.

On March 7, 2023, the Sichuan Province Chengdu Intermediate People's Court accepted the construction company's application for enforcement, with the enforcement case number (2023) Chuan 01 Zhi No. 844. A non-party, A Asset Management Company, claimed that Zhong and Zhang were the actual constructors of the involved Phase II villa project mentioned above. By concealing this significant fact and collaborating with the parties in this case to submit a false "Situation Statement" to the arbitration commission, it led the arbitral tribunal to determine that C Construction Company was the performing entity of the construction contract for the involved Phase II villa project and to award C Construction Company the corresponding project payment claim and priority right, thereby harming its legitimate interests as a creditor in another case. It requested not to enforce Award Document No. 882 according to law.

After review, the Sichuan Province Chengdu Intermediate People's Court held that the involved Phase II villa project was actually completed by Zhong and Zhang, not undertaken by C Construction Company. The arbitration parties' confirmation that C Construction Company undertook the Phase II villa project constituted fabrication of case facts. Zhong and Zhang, as individuals, do not legally enjoy the priority right to project payments. C Construction Company did not undertake the project and thus should not enjoy the priority right to the project payment for the involved Phase II villa project. Because the second item of Arbitral award No. 882 regarding the priority right to project payments affected the order of debt repayment, leading to the setting aside of A Asset Management Company's in-kind debt repayment ruling, it severely harmed the legitimate rights and interests of that company. Therefore, the court ruled not to enforce the second item of Arbitral award No. 882, namely, "C Construction Company enjoys a priority right to compensation within the scope of 74,773,257.84 RMB from the auction or discounted price of the unsold properties in Building #1 and the villa area of a certain real estate project located in Longquanyi District, Chengdu, owned by B Industrial Development Company."

C Construction Company disagreed and applied to the High People's Court of Sichuan Province for reconsideration. After review, the Sichuan High Court ruled to dismiss the application for reconsideration and upheld the original enforcement ruling.

Case 2: ***HS Company v. HD Company and other***[62]

In 2011, HJ Company entered into a maximum amount guarantee contract with the Ningbo Branch of SPD Bank, agreeing that HJ Company would provide a joint and several liability guarantee for the debts of a non-party, Wanxin Company, up to 88 million RMB. In 2013, HS Company and HJ Company entered into a transfer contract, whereby HJ Company transferred its movable and immovable properties,

---

[62] (2020) Su 09 Zhi Yi No. 11; (2021) Su Zhi Fu No. 83; See also the 10 Typical Cases on Judicial Review of Commercial Arbitration published by the High People's Court of Jiangsu Province in July 2024.

including sea area use rights, to HS Company, and agreed to submit disputes arising from this contract to a certain arbitration commission for arbitration. Between May and June 2014, HS Company remitted a total of over 38.99 million RMB to HJ Company via bank transfers. In June 2014, the Ningbo Branch of SPD Bank filed a lawsuit, which later resulted in a civil mediation statement stating that HJ Company would bear joint and several liability for Wanxin Company's debts within the scope of 88 million RMB. In April 2015, the Ningbo Branch of SPD Bank filed another lawsuit, requesting the court to rescind the transfer contract between HJ Company and HS Company. The effective judgment of the people's court supported the above claim by the Ningbo Branch of SPD Bank. In 2017, HS Company applied for arbitration with a certain arbitration commission, claiming that the transfer contract had been rescinded by a court judgment and requesting an order for HJ Company to return the transfer payment. The arbitration commission rendered an arbitral award ordering HJ Company to return the transfer payment. Ningbo Branch of SPD Bank transferred the involved claim to HD Company. HD Company applied to the Jiangsu Province Yancheng Intermediate People's Court for non-enforcement of this arbitral award, asserting that a false arbitration existed between HJ Company and HS Company. During the proceedings, the Jiangsu Province Yancheng Intermediate People's Court ascertained that there were familial relationships between the shareholders of HJ Company and HS Company. Furthermore, the obtained bank transfer records proved that the transfer payments made by HS Company to HJ Company originated from the accounts of HS Company's shareholders, and HJ Company remitted the funds back to the accounts of HS Company's shareholders within a short period. The Jiangsu Province Yancheng Intermediate People's Court held that false arbitration existed between HS Company and HJ Company and ruled not to enforce the arbitral award. HS Company disagreed with this ruling and applied to the High People's Court of Jiangsu Province for reconsideration.

The High People's Court of Jiangsu Province held that HD Company retained a legal and genuine claim against HJ Company. Familial relationships existed between the shareholders of HS Company and HJ Company. The funds remitted by HS Company to HJ Company originated from HS Company's shareholders, and HJ Company remitted the funds back to HS Company's shareholders' accounts within a very short time. The parties could not provide a reasonable explanation for the remittance of large sums. It could be determined that HS Company and HJ Company had fabricated the legal relationship and facts of the case. The arbitral award ordering HJ Company to return the transfer payment to HS Company was erroneous. Based on this arbitral award, HS Company could participate in the distribution of proceeds from the court auction, affecting the realization of HD Company's claim and harming HD Company's legitimate rights and interests. The High People's Court of Jiangsu Province ruled to dismiss HS Company's application for reconsideration.

Article 62

After an application for arbitration has been made, the parties may settle their dispute on their own. Where the parties have reached a settlement agreement,

they may request the arbitral tribunal to make an arbitral award in accordance with the settlement agreement; alternatively, they may withdraw their application for arbitration.

Notes

This Article pertains to the system of settlement by the parties within arbitration proceedings. With the continuous increase in the number of arbitration cases and the diversification of dispute types, encouraging parties to resolve disputes through mutual agreement not only aligns with the efficiency value of arbitration but also reflects the full respect for party autonomy in modern dispute resolution mechanisms. In practice, settlement within arbitration proceedings possesses unique institutional advantages: on one hand, it allows parties, under the professional guidance of the arbitral tribunal and considering commercial interests and long-term cooperation, to creatively reach solutions that may extend beyond the strict confines of legal adjudication; on the other hand, the issue of enforceability of settlement agreements has always been a bottleneck restricting their full effectiveness. Transforming a settlement into an arbitral award combines these two different mechanisms, constructing a more flexible and efficient path for dispute resolution.

After applying for arbitration, a party has the right to settle with the other party at any time. So-called settlement refers to the act whereby the parties, through negotiation, reach their own solution for the dispute already submitted to arbitration. Since the parties have complete dispositive power over the matters submitted to arbitration, settlement is an embodiment of the parties disposing of their own civil rights. Settlement can occur either during a hearing or outside of hearings, but in all cases, it is reached by the parties themselves without the arbitral tribunal's direct involvement. The power of arbitration originates from the parties' consensual authorization, and the parties similarly have the right to terminate or alter the course of the arbitration proceedings through mutual agreement. This provision confirms that the parties retain ultimate control over the method of dispute resolution throughout the arbitration process. Even after arbitration proceedings have commenced, they can still choose to conclude the dispute through settlement based on changing circumstances and commercial considerations.

Typically, settlements arise for three main reasons: first, the claimant withdraws its arbitration claim (the same applies to counterclaims, similarly hereinafter); second, the respondent admits the claimant's arbitration claim; third, the parties find a solution to their dispute through negotiation. Regardless of the cause, a settlement will lead to the following outcomes: First, if the settlement results from the claimant withdrawing its claim, the claimant may withdraw the arbitration application, or the arbitration commission may decide to close the case based on the circumstances. Both methods will result in concluding the case. Second, if the settlement results from the respondent admitting the claim or the parties finding a solution through negotiation, it will lead to the parties reaching a settlement agreement. The parties may then request the arbitral tribunal to render an arbitral award based on the settlement agreement, or they may apply to close the case based on the agreement, or they may agree to conclude the case by other means not prohibited by the arbitration rules.

In practice, a mere settlement agreement only possesses contractual effect and lacks enforceability. By converting it into an arbitral award, the parties can obtain the same legal effect as an ordinary arbitral award, allowing them to directly apply to the court for compulsory enforcement if one party fails to perform. This significantly enhances the incentive for parties to choose settlement, making it a truly effective method of dispute resolution. However, it must be pointed out that when an arbitral tribunal renders an award based on a settlement agreement, it should conduct a necessary review. If the content of the settlement agreement violates mandatory legal provisions, it cannot be confirmed or supported.

This Article focuses on promoting the substantive resolution of disputes. Compared to awards rendered by the arbitral tribunal, settlement agreements voluntarily reached by the parties are often more aligned with their respective commercial interests, leading to a stronger willingness to perform and achieving the effect of truly resolving the case. This both reduces the burden of adjudication on the arbitral tribunal and helps preserve the commercial relationship between the parties, achieving a unity of legal and social effect.

Article 63
Where a party repudiates the settlement agreement after the application for arbitration has been withdrawn, they may apply for arbitration again in accordance with the arbitration agreement.

Notes
In arbitration practice, after parties withdraw an arbitration application based on a settlement agreement, situations may arise where a party reneges for various reasons, such as one party failing to perform the settlement agreement, the settlement agreement being based on a significant misunderstanding or gross unfairness, or the emergence of new circumstances. Some parties worry that once the arbitration application is withdrawn, they will lose the right to resolve the dispute through arbitration; other parties may maliciously use the settlement procedure to delay, refusing to perform the agreement after withdrawing the application and then reapplying for arbitration, resulting in procedural inefficiency and resource waste. This Article provides parties with clear behavioral expectations and procedural safeguards.

This Article, together with Article 62, forms the basic framework of the arbitration settlement system. Article 61 regulates the conclusion of a settlement and its procedural handling, while this Article stipulates the remedies available after the failure of a settlement. A settlement agreement is essentially a civil contract and may be void, voidable, or impossible to perform. If the right to arbitration relief were permanently lost simply because a settlement was reached and the application withdrawn, it would lead to substantive injustice. This Article confirms that the validity of the original arbitration agreement is not extinguished by the procedural withdrawal, ensuring that parties can return to the arbitration process when the basis for the settlement ceases to exist. This Article legislatively affirms the specific application of the separability of the arbitration agreement in the context of settlement, providing a clear legal basis for parties to resume arbitration proceedings.

Regarding whether parties can apply for arbitration again based on the original arbitration agreement after reaching a settlement agreement, withdrawing the arbitration application, and then reneging, there were historically two different views: one held that they could apply for arbitration again, and the other held that they could not. The New Arbitration Law adopts the first view, stipulating that in such circumstances, the parties have the right to apply for arbitration based on the arbitration agreement. It is important to note that the precondition for the parties' right to apply for arbitration under this Article is that the parties have breached the settlement agreement. Theoretically, the primary basis for determining whether parties can apply for arbitration is the existence of a valid arbitration agreement. When parties withdraw an arbitration application due to reaching a settlement, the arbitration proceedings have not yet concluded, and the original arbitration agreement remains valid. Therefore, the parties can still apply for arbitration based on this valid arbitration agreement.

Illustrative Case

CM Company v. Chen[63]

CM Company filed a lawsuit with the court, requesting modification of the Settlement Agreement signed by the parties when determining the rights and obligations of the loan. CM Company argued that the Settlement Agreement disposed of the loan relationship between the parties, was signed hastily by CM Company in order to lift a seizure without carefully checking the original vouchers, that the amount stated differed so greatly from the actual amount that it did not represent CM Company's true intent, and that there was obviously a significant misunderstanding. Performing according to it would also violate the principle of fairness. Since the aforementioned Settlement Agreement was a document independent of the Repayment Agreement (whose authenticity and legality were disputed by the parties and would be resolved separately), the parties did not agree on a dispute resolution clause applicable to the Settlement Agreement itself. It only stipulated that if CM Company breached by failing to pay, Chen could apply for arbitration at the Shanghai Arbitration Commission based on the loan contract. However, in fact, there was no loan contract between the parties, and after the Settlement Agreement was signed, there was no situation where CM Company failed to pay when due. Therefore, the arbitration method was not suitable for resolving disputes related to the aforementioned Settlement Agreement. Since, in the current loan dispute, Chen was the one who should pay the money, and CM Company was the recipient,

[63] (2018) Jin 02 Min Chu No. 1050.

according to relevant legal provisions, the court at CM Company's domicile had jurisdiction over this case.

The court held that the parties involved had entered into a repayment agreement that contained an arbitration clause. Chen had initially filed for arbitration with the Shanghai Arbitration Commission. Subsequently, the parties reached an out-of-court settlement during the arbitration proceedings, and Chen withdrew the arbitration application. CM Company's lawsuit essentially constituted a repudiation of both the settlement agreement and the repayment agreement, and therefore remained subject to the arbitration clause in the repayment agreement. Furthermore, in accordance with Article 50 of the Arbitration Law (2017), if a party regretted after reaching a settlement agreement and withdrawing the arbitration application, it could apply for arbitration based on the arbitration agreement. Consequently, the court determined that it lacked jurisdiction over the case and ruled that CM Company should submit the dispute to the Shanghai Arbitration Commission for arbitration.

Article 64
Prior to issuing an arbitral award, an arbitral tribunal may carry out conciliation. Where both parties voluntarily seek conciliation, the arbitral tribunal shall conduct conciliation. Where conciliation is unsuccessful, an arbitral award shall be made promptly.

Where conciliation leads to a settlement agreement, the arbitral tribunal shall make a written conciliation statement or make an arbitral award in accordance with the result of the settlement agreement. A written conciliation statement and an arbitral award shall have equal legal effect.

Notes
Conciliation is often regarded as a primary form of ADR. ADR is the abbreviation for Alternative Dispute Resolution,[64] commonly translated as alternative dispute resolution or optional dispute resolution. Compared to arbitration, ADR methods like conciliation have different characteristics: the popularity of ADR methods reflects, to some extent, the parties' desire to further reduce dispute resolution costs; the outcome of ADR procedures is not intended to produce a binding decision on the parties' rights or obligations, but merely requires the parties to jointly attempt to reach a settlement to resolve the dispute; it is often conducted alongside litigation or arbitration proceedings; it is not an independent procedure for resolving disputes—if the parties fail to reach a settlement, resolving the dispute still requires litigation or arbitration. The differences between arbitration and ADR are mainly manifested in:

A. Enforceability of the outcome. An arbitral award is final, and the parties can apply to the court for compulsory enforcement. The outcome of ADR generally

[64] Some institutions or countries view ADR as an abbreviation for other concepts, such as Amicable Dispute Resolution or Administrative Dispute Resolution.

lacks enforceability or only has contractual enforceability; parties may not comply, necessitating further court or arbitration proceedings to obtain a final decision.

B. Limitations on party autonomy. Once parties decide to proceed with arbitration, the arbitration agreement cannot be terminated unless both parties unanimously agree not to arbitrate. Currently, however, using ADR methods does not have this restriction; for example, in conciliation proceedings, any party can decide to stop participating in the conciliation at any time.

C. The functions of adjudicators. Arbitrators act as adjudicators, while neutrals in ADR typically only facilitate, assisting the parties in reaching a settlement.

Since adopting ADR methods often requires consideration of the specific circumstances of the dispute, ADR methods can be diverse. Moreover, with societal development, various alternative resolution methods also evolve; their forms are not fixed, and their procedures are flexible and variable. It is generally believed that the most common forms of ADR include binding arbitration, conciliation, mediation, expert evaluation, non-binding arbitration, private judging, mini-trials, court-annexed ADR, etc. Beyond these, as an open concept, ADR methods keep pace with the times, continuously generating new methods, such as ODR (Online Dispute Resolution), which is also becoming popular. These procedures can be conducted separately or in combination. The principle behind establishing these procedures is flexibility, aiming to resolve disputes, and they possess several characteristics mentioned earlier.

The mechanism combining arbitration and conciliation has long been regarded as an important embodiment of Eastern experience, but it also faces new challenges and opportunities in its practical development. With the in-depth development of diversified dispute resolution mechanisms, parties have raised higher demands for control over the dispute resolution process and the acceptability of the outcome. The importance attached to conciliation in international arbitration practice is also increasing. In the context of judicial reform, arbitration needs to fully leverage its advantages of flexibility and efficiency, and conciliation is an important path to achieving this goal. This Article, from a legislative level, affirms the legal status of combining arbitration and conciliation, distinguishing China's arbitration system from arbitration models in other jurisdictions. This institutional design both inherits China's traditional culture of discouraging litigation and aligns with the development trends of modern ADR, reflecting the unique value of China's arbitration system.

Conciliation in arbitration refers to a method, agreed upon by all parties and conducted under the auspices of the arbitral tribunal, where the parties reach a consensus based on voluntary negotiation and mutual understanding and accommodation to resolve their dispute. From the perspective of Chinese arbitration practice, there are three methods of conciliation: First, the arbitral tribunal conducts joint consultations with all parties. Second, the parties conduct their own consultations and, upon reaching an agreement, inform the arbitral tribunal of this agreement. Third, the arbitral tribunal conducts separate consultations with each party. This situation is equivalent to "good offices." This form is suitable for the early stages of conciliation where the differences between the parties are significant. Through "good offices," the arbitral tribunal avoids the embarrassment parties might feel from compromising or admitting mistakes face-to-face, potentially helping the parties eliminate differences and seek common ground. However, this situation should not be considered as arbitrators meeting privately or unilaterally with one party or its agent, as prior consent from the parties has been obtained.

After a settlement is reached through conciliation, the arbitral tribunal shall prepare a conciliation statement or render an award based on the outcome of the conciliation agreement. The parties may also agree on other ways to conclude the case. By stipulating that the conciliation statement has the same legal effect as an arbitral award, the issue of the enforceability of conciliation outcomes is fundamentally resolved. Granting the conciliation statement the same compulsory enforceability as an arbitral award eliminates parties' concerns about the outcomes of conciliation and enhances the practical value and attractiveness of conciliation as a dispute resolution method. This provision allows successful conciliation to maintain the atmosphere of an amicable dispute resolution while also obtaining the guarantee of state coercive power.

In fact, conciliation can be conducted during the arbitration proceedings or after the arbitration proceedings have concluded. A general principle, from the perspective of dispute resolution, is to maintain an open and flexible attitude towards the dispute resolution method itself.

Some arbitration institutions have corresponding provisions regarding conciliation in their rules. Article 48 of the SCIA Arbitration Rules stipulates that if a party applies for a non-party to participate in conciliation, and all parties and that non-party agree in writing, the arbitral tribunal may notify the non-party to participate in the conciliation. If the conciliation is unsuccessful, no party may invoke any statement, opinion, view, suggestion, or proposition made by any party or arbitrator during the conciliation process in subsequent arbitration proceedings, judicial proceedings, or any other proceedings as support for its claim, defense, or counterclaim. Articles 54 and 55 of the SIAC Arbitration Rules respectively stipulate "Conciliation by a Conciliator" and "Conciliation by the Arbitral tribunal," specifying matters requiring attention during the conciliation process at different stages. Article 57 stipulates that if conciliation is unsuccessful, no party may invoke the opinions, views, statements, suggestions, or propositions expressed, raised, made, assented to, or denied by the other party, the conciliator, or the arbitral tribunal during the conciliation process in subsequent arbitration proceedings, judicial proceedings, or any other proceedings as a basis for its claim, defense, or counterclaim.

Illustrative Cases

Case 1: *EL Company v. KH Travel Agency*[65]

---

[65] See the 10 Typical Cases on Judicial Review of People's Courts Serving and Guaranteeing the Construction of Pilot Free Trade Zones published by the SPC in February 2022.

EL Company provided international tourism services. Starting from 2017, EL Company was entrusted by KH Travel Agency to be responsible for the reception services for tourist groups organized by the travel agency to Russia. The reception service fees were advanced by EL Company, and KH Travel Agency was to pay EL Company according to the tour schedule. Due to KH Travel Agency's delayed payments, EL Company filed a lawsuit, demanding that KH Travel Agency pay the reception service fees and interest for overdue payment.

After the Chongqing Pilot Free Trade Zone People's Court accepted the case, and fully respecting the parties' intentions, the Court relied on the "one-stop" dispute resolution mechanism for foreign-related commercial litigation, arbitration, and conciliation spearheaded by the Court. Both parties unanimously agreed to refer the case to the CIETAC Southwest Sub-Commission for arbitration. EL Company submitted an application to the Court to withdraw the lawsuit, simultaneously filed an arbitration application with CIETAC Southwest Sub-Commission, and the Court approved the withdrawal and transferred the case materials to CIETAC Southwest Sub-Commission. CIETAC Southwest Sub-Commission organized a conciliation between the parties, ultimately resolving the dispute through an arbitration conciliation statement.

Case 2: ***A Bank v. B Fund Company***[66]

An asset management plan product managed by B Fund Company faced a credit rating downgrade due to a bond issuer's default, leading to a trading halt of the held bonds and a lowered bond pledge ratio. The value of the original collateral became insufficient, requiring the asset management plan product to promptly provide additional collateral or repay part of the financing. As the fund company, the manager of the asset management plan, failed to provide additional collateral in time, the custodian bank, A Bank, actually paid the liquidation advance pursuant to the relevant agreement. Subsequently, the custodian bank, A Bank, applied for arbitration with an arbitration commission regarding the advance payment, demanding that B Fund Company pay the advanced funds. An arbitration commission legally awarded that the fund company shall compensate the bank for the liquidation advance and bear corresponding interest, preservation fees, arbitration fees, etc., totaling 1.176 billion RMB. After the case entered the enforcement procedure, it attracted significant social attention. The fund company faced enormous redemption pressure, with investors redeeming an average of nearly 5 billion RMB monthly, directly affecting the vital interests of 2.3 million investors holding positions in the company.

Through the Beijing Financial Court's active coordination, third-party investment was introduced, and the parties reached a settlement agreement during enforcement. This not only avoided compliance risks for the fund company's operations but also quickly stabilized the morale of the over 300-person investment team and restored the confidence of 2.3 million position-holding investors in the fund company.

---

[66] See the 10 Typical Cases on Judicial Review of Financial Arbitration published by the Beijing Financial Court in October 2023.

Article 65
A written conciliation statement shall specify the arbitration claim and the results of the settlement agreed by the parties. The written conciliation statement shall be signed by the arbitrators, sealed by the arbitration institution, and then served on both parties.

The written conciliation statement shall become legally effective immediately after both parties have signed for it.

Where a party repudiates the written conciliation statement before they signs for it, the arbitral tribunal shall promptly make an arbitral award.

Notes
Against the backdrop of increasingly well-established practice in arbitration conciliation, conciliation statements also require corresponding standardization. Issues such as non-standard preparation of conciliation statements, unclear effective time points, and parties reneging directly affect the stability and enforceability of conciliation outcomes. Unifying the preparation standards for conciliation statements is an inevitable requirement for improving the quality of arbitration documents; clarifying the effective time point of a conciliation statement is an institutional guarantee for stabilizing legal relationships; finally, promptly addressing situations where parties renege before signing the conciliation statement is also conducive to maintaining procedural seriousness and avoiding procedural delays. Article 65 of the New Arbitration Law concerns the provisions on arbitration conciliation statements, clarifying important content such as the content of the conciliation statement, formal requirements, the effective mechanism, and how to handle parties reneging. This is of significant importance for standardizing the arbitration conciliation procedure and protecting the legitimate rights and interests of the parties.

The conciliation statement shall specify the arbitration claims and the result of the parties' agreement. The arbitration claims refer to the specific demands raised by the parties in the arbitration proceedings; the result of the parties' agreement refers to the settlement content reached by the parties through conciliation. This provision ensures the clarity and verifiability of the conciliation content, enables the parties to clearly know their rights and obligations, and also provides a clear basis for subsequent possible enforcement procedures, avoiding future disputes arising from unclear conciliation content.

The formal requirements for an effective conciliation statement include the arbitrator's signature, the seal of the arbitration institution, service, and acknowledgment of receipt. The conciliation statement is signed by the arbitrator(s), reflecting the arbitral tribunal's recognition of the conciliation agreement and signifying the arbitral tribunal's responsibility for the conciliation process and outcome. Affixing the seal of the arbitration institution is to confirm the formality and authority of the conciliation statement. The seal of the arbitration institution is the official identifier of the arbitration institution; its presence gives the conciliation statement higher credibility, allowing the parties and the public to trust that the conciliation statement was produced and issued by a legitimate arbitration institution.

The conciliation statement needs to be served on both parties and acknowledged by them to ensure that the parties are aware of the conciliation content. Only when the parties actually receive the conciliation statement can they truly understand the outcome of the conciliation and decide their next steps based on its content. The conciliation statement becomes legally effective after being acknowledged by both parties. Once effective, it possesses the same legal effect as an arbitral award, and the parties can directly apply to the court for compulsory enforcement based on the conciliation statement.

This Article also stipulates provisions regarding reneging. According to this Article, parties are only effective in reneging before acknowledgment; reneging after acknowledgment is not permitted and is considered acceptance of the conciliation outcome. If a party reneges before acknowledgment, the arbitral tribunal must promptly render an award. This is to avoid procedural delays and ensure the efficiency of dispute resolution. The arbitral tribunal should resume the arbitration proceedings as soon as possible after a party reneges, hear the matters in dispute, and render an award, so that the parties' rights and obligations can be determined promptly.

Illustrative Cases

Case 1: *Guangzhou A Investment Company and others v. Liu*[67]

In 2016, Liu applied to the people's court for compulsory enforcement based on an arbitration conciliation statement rendered by the Guangzhou Arbitration Commission. During the enforcement process, the judgment debtors, Guangzhou A Investment Company, Guangzhou B Hotel, and Fang, applied for non-enforcement of part of the claims confirmed in the arbitration conciliation statement, citing reasons such as forged evidence, illegal arbitration procedures, and false arbitration. These judgment debtors had previously applied to the people's court in 2017 to set aside this arbitration conciliation statement, but their application was dismissed by a ruling according to law; they again applied for arbitration concerning this portion of the claim dispute in 2023, which was dismissed by the Guangzhou Arbitration Commission.

The effective judgment held that the judgment debtors, Guangzhou A Investment Company, Guangzhou B Hotel, and Fang delayed enforcement by applying to set aside the arbitration conciliation statement and filing a separate arbitration application. Having failed to gain support through these means, they then raised the current application for non-enforcement based on grounds such as forged evidence, illegal arbitration procedures, and false arbitration. According to Article 17 of the Arbitral Award Enforcement Provisions, non-enforcement of an arbitration conciliation statement is limited solely to circumstances involving a "violation of public interests." This case involved an ordinary private lending dispute, and there was no

[67] See the 2nd batch of the 10 Typical Cases on Judicial Review of Arbitration published by the High People's Court of Guangdong Province in August 2025. According to Article 17 of the Arbitral Award Enforcement Provisions, violation of public interests is the sole statutory ground for non-enforcement of an arbitration conciliation statement.

evidence indicating that the arbitration conciliation statement violated public interests. Therefore, the court ruled to dismiss the application for non-enforcement.

Case 2: *Zhao vs. Chongqing A College*[68]
On January 22, 2020, the Chongqing Arbitration Commission accepted the case concerning a contract dispute between the parties based on the arbitration clause in the Cooperation Agreement signed by Zhao and Chongqing A College. On April 17, 2020, the Chongqing Arbitration Commission rendered Conciliation Statement No. 149 (2020). The Conciliation Statement confirmed that the Cooperation Agreement signed by the parties was valid, that both parties would continue performance, and that the arbitration fees and attorney fees would be borne by Chongqing A College. On August 17, 2020, Chongqing A College applied to the Chongqing No. 1 Intermediate People's Court to set aside the aforementioned arbitration conciliation statement, citing reasons including that the evidence on which the conciliation statement was based was forged.

The Chongqing No. 1 Intermediate People's Court ascertained that during the arbitration proceedings, the entrusted agent Zhang for Chongqing A College was a former employee of the college. Zhang participated in the arbitration initiated by Zhao against Chongqing A College with the Chongqing Arbitration Commission without obtaining authorization from Chongqing A College, and reached a conciliation agreement with Zhao, fully agreeing to Zhao's arbitration claims. The seal used by Zhang in the arbitration proceedings was one that Chongqing A College had reported lost in a newspaper announcement and filed with the public security organ before the Chongqing Arbitration Commission accepted the case. Furthermore, the relevant arbitration documents were all wrongfully taken by Zhang and were not acturally served upon Chongqing A College, resulting in Chongqing A College not substantially participating in the arbitration activities.

The Chongqing No. 1 Intermediate People's Court held that, according to Article 51 and Article 58 of the Arbitration Law (2017), an arbitration conciliation statement should have the same legal effect as an arbitral award; therefore, arbitration conciliation statements should also fall within the scope of judicial review. Judicial review of an arbitration conciliation statement did not constitute interference with the party autonomy exercised during the arbitration proceedings, but was a necessary safeguard for the "voluntary" and "fair" principles of arbitration. This case involved a false arbitration initiated by Zhao in collusion with Zhang. The arbitration conciliation statement rendered by the Chongqing Arbitration Commission did

[68] See the 10 Typical Cases for 2016–2020 on Judicial Review of Commercial Arbitration published by the High People's Court of Chongqing. Whether an arbitration conciliation statement can be applied for setting aside was theoretically controversial due to unclear legal provisions, and judicial practice also involved different approaches. For those arbitration conciliation statements resulting from false arbitration that violate the "voluntary" principle of conciliation, if parties whose rights and interests are harmed are not allowed to seek relief through judicial review, their legitimate rights and interests would inevitably be impaired, and the credibility of the arbitration system and arbitration institutions would be further damaged. Therefore, bringing arbitration conciliation statements within the scope of judicial review of arbitration is reasonable and necessary.

not represent the true intent of the party (Chongqing A College) and harmed the legitimate rights and interests of Chongqing A College, which did not participate in the arbitration. Consequently, the Court ruled to set aside the involved arbitration conciliation statement.

Article 66

The arbitral award shall be made in accordance with the opinion of the majority of the arbitrators, and the opinion of the minority of the arbitrators may be entered in the record. If the arbitral tribunal is unable to form a majority opinion, the arbitral award shall be made in accordance with the opinion of the presiding arbitrator.

Notes

This Article concerns the deliberative and decision-making mechanism of the arbitral tribunal, also known as the voting mechanism. Three-member arbitral tribunals are commonly used in complex commercial arbitrations, and the question of how to effectively resolve reasonable differences among arbitrators on professional issues through legal procedures is a problem frequently encountered in practice.

In practice, in the majority of arbitration cases, the tribunal can reach a unanimous opinion. However, it is also not uncommon for decisions to be made based on a majority opinion or the presiding arbitrator's opinion, especially in cases involving new business models, cutting-edge technical issues, or significant interest balancing. It is normal for arbitrators to have differences based on diverse professional backgrounds and adjudicative philosophies. Legislation needs to ensure the democratic and scientific nature of the tribunal's decision-making. One of the original intentions behind the design of a three-member tribunal is to ensure the quality of the award through collective wisdom and prevent autocratic decision-making by an individual. The principle of majority decision-making can effectively integrate different professional perspectives and adjudicative experiences, ensuring the final award is based on full discussion and rational deliberation, thereby maximizing the accuracy of factual findings and the appropriateness of legal application.

The majority decision and presiding arbitrator decision mechanisms stipulated in this Article protect each arbitrator's right to express their opinion independently while ensuring the tribunal can produce an effective award promptly through clear decision-making rules, preventing the collegial system from falling into the dilemma of "deliberation without decision." Generally, it is a common practice in arbitration systems worldwide that the award shall be made according to the opinion of the majority of the arbitrators. The Arbitration Law (2025) stipulates that an arbitral tribunal may be composed of either three arbitrators or one sole arbitrator. When a sole arbitrator conducts the arbitration alone, there is no issue of differing opinions. When the tribunal is composed of three arbitrators, if any two arbitrators share the same opinion and the other (regardless of whether they are the presiding arbitrator) holds a different opinion, the award shall be made according to the majority opinion, and the dissenting opinion of the minority arbitrator can be recorded in the transcript. If each of the three arbitrators holds a different opinion, the award shall be made according to the opinion of the presiding arbitrator. It is worth noting that, to enhance the transparency and fairness of arbitration, whether dissenting opinions of arbitrators not adopted as the basis for the award should be attached to the award and served on the parties is a question worthy of study.

Arbitration laws worldwide consistently require that awards or other decisions should be made according to the opinion of the majority of the arbitrators. However, they differ in their methods for handling situations where a majority opinion cannot be formed. These may be summarized into four scenarios: First, for any decision, a majority vote must be achieved through consultation, concession, or compromise. For example, Article 591 of the 1983 Austrian Code of Civil Procedure stipulates that if the required majority for a decision cannot be reached, or if two arbitrators cannot reach a unanimous opinion, unless otherwise agreed, the parties may request the competent court to declare the arbitration agreement invalid. Similar provisions exist in Article 1057 of the 1986 Dutch Arbitration Act, Article 11 of the 1973 Korean Arbitration Act, etc. Second, for procedural matters, the presiding arbitrator may decide alone. Examples include Article 31 of the 1976 UNCITRAL Arbitration Rules, Article 29 of the 1985 Model Law, and Section 1052 of the 1998 German Code of Civil Procedure. Third, the tribunal makes decisions in the manner stipulated by the arbitration agreement. This content is found in Article 1701 of the 1998 Belgian Judicial Code and the arbitration laws of many countries. Fourth, the method adopted by the New Arbitration Law is also followed by many other countries. Examples include Article 189 of the 1987 Swiss Federal Act on Private International Law, Section 30 of the Swedish Arbitration Act 1999, and so forth. Of course, these methods are not mutually exclusive; in practice, many countries and arbitration institutions allow several methods for making decisions simultaneously.

When the arbitral tribunal cannot form a majority opinion, the award shall be made according to the opinion of the presiding arbitrator. The purpose of this arrangement is to establish an effective mechanism for breaking decision-making deadlocks. When three arbitrators each hold different views and cannot form a majority, having the presiding arbitrator, who typically has relatively more experience and overall responsibility for the procedure, make the final decision can effectively prevent prolonged procedures due to arbitrator divergence and uphold the efficiency value of the arbitral award being "final and binding."

Illustrative Case

TH Company v. XD Company[69]

TH Company asked the court to set aside an arbitral award rendered by the Luoyang Arbitration Commission according to law. One of the reasons was that the presiding arbitrator refused to render the award according to the majority opinion of the arbitrators during the decision-making process. Instead, the award was issued based on the presiding arbitrator's own minority opinion, and both of the other arbitrators refused to sign the award, constituting a serious violation of the law.

[69] (2023) Yu 03 Min Te No. 60.

The Court held that regarding TH Company's contention that the arbitral award in this case was not rendered in accordance with the majority opinion of the arbitral tribunal, Article 53 of the Arbitration Law (2017) stipulated that an award shall be made in accordance with the majority opinion of the arbitrators, and the differing opinion of the minority arbitrator may be recorded in the transcript. If a majority opinion cannot be formed by the arbitral tribunal, the award shall be made in accordance with the opinion of the presiding arbitrator. The fundamental principle embodied in the above provisions was the democratic centralism principle, which in the deliberation rules of the arbitral tribunal, primarily manifested as the principle that the minority should submit to the majority during case deliberations. Upon reviewing the arbitration case file, the involved arbitration had been deliberated by the arbitral tribunal, and two arbitrators had reached a consensus on the majority of issues. The presiding arbitrator considered the opinions of the two arbitrators to be unclear and insufficiently specific, but neither requested further clarification from them nor adopted the majority opinion. Instead, he proceeded to render the arbitral award based solely on his individual minority opinion. Furthermore, neither of the two other arbitrators signed the arbitral award. This process failed to reflect the principle of the minority submitting to the majority within the collegial system, thereby violating statutory procedures. Consequently, the arbitral award was to be set aside.

Article 67

An arbitral award shall specify arbitration claims, facts of the dispute, reasons for the decision, results of the award, allocation of arbitration fees and the date of the award. Where the parties agree that they do not wish the facts of the dispute and the reasons for the decision to be specified in the arbitral award, these parts may be omitted. The arbitral award shall be signed by the arbitrators and sealed by the arbitration institution. An arbitrator with dissenting opinions to the arbitral award may choose to sign or not to sign the award.

Notes

This Article pertains to the formatting standards for arbitral awards. Against the backdrop of increasing internationalization and specialization in arbitration practice, the arbitral award, as the final output of the arbitration proceedings, must not only meet internationally accepted reasoning standards but also accommodate the specific needs of commercial arbitration. In practice, the need for the level of detail in an arbitral award varies significantly between cases: on one hand, cases involving significant public interest or complex legal disputes require thorough reasoning to enhance the award's credibility and enforceability; on the other hand, parties in some commercial disputes are more concerned with the efficiency of the award and wish to avoid lengthy reasoning processes. Furthermore, uniform standards are also needed regarding the signing of the award by arbitrators holding dissenting opinions.

The content of an arbitral award refers to the written statement of decisions made on procedural and substantive matters in the arbitration case. This Article explicitly lists the six essential elements that an arbitral award shall contain (the arbitration claims, the facts of the dispute, the reasons for the award, the result of the award, the allocation of arbitration costs, and the date of the award). Its primary purpose is to ensure the completeness and standardization of the award's content. This provision provides clear guidance for the arbitral tribunal in drafting the award, preventing issues affecting the award's validity or enforcement due to missing elements.

The proviso stating that where the parties agree that they do not wish the facts of the dispute and the reasons for the decision to be specified in the arbitral award, these parts may be omitted acknowledges the special needs of parties, such as pursuing procedural efficiency or protecting trade secrets, allowing them to waive certain procedural safeguards on an informed basis. Allowing an arbitrator with a dissenting opinion to choose not to sign respects their right to independent judgment and also enhances the seriousness of the deliberation process through a mechanism of procedural transparency. Simultaneously, the rule that a failure to sign does not affect the validity of the award ensures the finality of the tribunal's collective decision. In arbitration practice, the main arbitration institution's rules often contain further provisions regarding awards with minority opinions. For example, Article 49(3) of the BAC Arbitration Rules stipulates that an arbitrator who does not sign shall provide a separate opinion. The arbitration institution shall deliver this separate opinion to the parties along with the award, but the opinion does not form part of the award. Furthermore, some arbitration institution rules specifically clarify that an arbitrator's electronic signature has the same effect as a handwritten signature; the award delivered to the parties shall be a paper copy. If both parties agree, or the arbitration commission deems it necessary, the award may be delivered electronically. For instance, see Article 52(7) and (10) of the CIETAC Arbitration Rules.

This Article only lists the main contents of an arbitral award. As a complete arbitral award, it should also state the name and address of the arbitration institution, the serial number of the award, the basic information of the parties, information about their representatives, the composition of the arbitral tribunal, the names of the arbitrators, the hearing process and the place where the award was made, the time limit for performance of the award, etc. If any of the following situations occurred during the arbitration proceedings, they should also be stated: any decision made by the arbitration commission on its jurisdiction; any conservatory measures taken; any partial award or interim award rendered; the cross-examination of important evidence, especially evidence collected by the arbitral tribunal on its own initiative; the appointment of an appraiser, etc. Additionally, the award should indicate whether it is a final award, an interim award, or a partial award.

If the award is made based on a settlement agreement or the outcome of conciliation, it is called a consent award or an agreed award. Its content can be relatively simple. Unless the parties have agreed otherwise, it suffices to base it on the settlement agreement or conciliation outcome; it is not necessary to include the reasons.

Article 68

In arbitration proceedings, where a part of the facts involved has already become clear, the arbitral tribunal may make an award in respect of such part of the facts first.

Notes

In the context of increasingly complex commercial arbitration practice, the number of multi-dimensional and multi-issue complex disputes has increased significantly. The model where the arbitral tribunal renders a single award after the conclusion of the entire procedure may not always be conducive to the effective resolution of the case or the protection of a party's legitimate rights and interests. With the growth of arbitration cases in specialized fields such as construction engineering, financial derivatives, and intellectual property rights, the issues in dispute exhibit a clear characteristic of severability: some facts may become clear early due to sufficient evidence, while others require further adjudication. Parties may suffer unnecessary commercial losses due to the unresolved status of a key issue, or the progress of the entire procedure may be hindered by a localized dispute. Permitting the arbitral tribunal to issue a preliminary award on parts of the facts that have already been ascertained is an appropriate solution in such circumstances.

The preliminary award referred to in the New Arbitration Law is also referred to as a partial award. It is an award made by the arbitral tribunal during the process of hearing the case, concerning issues or facts that have already been ascertained, in order to facilitate the continued adjudication of other issues and to promptly protect the legitimate rights and interests of the parties. In arbitration theory, there are also concepts of interim awards or provisional awards, but China's Arbitration Law does not stipulate interim or provisional awards. However, interim awards do exist in Chinese arbitration practice and are similar to partial awards.

According to the New Arbitration Law and arbitration practice, a partial award may be rendered under the following circumstances: first, the matters in dispute in the arbitration are inherently separable or conducted in stages, and the parties have accordingly raised several arbitration claims. For instance, if a party purchased goods in several batches, has different opinions on the quality of these batches, and has raised different claims, and if the arbitral tribunal needs more time to fully clarify the entire case, but rendering an award on the already clarified part does not affect the subsequent hearing; second, an emergency arises during the arbitration process where failure to issue a preliminary award would cause loss to a party, such as preserving or selling perishable, deteriorating, or depreciating goods to prevent further losses. Third, procedural matters requiring the cooperation and action of the parties to enable the arbitral tribunal to carry out its work smoothly, such as assisting the tribunal in appointing experts to debug equipment or audit accounts.

By determining partial rights and obligations through a preliminary award, parties can obtain a basis for interim enforcement, effectively controlling the time and opportunity costs of dispute resolution. This phased processing mechanism can significantly shorten the time for parties to obtain effective relief, while simultaneously reducing the adjudicative pressure on the arbitral tribunal in complex cases, thereby optimizing the allocation of judicial resources. Furthermore, this Article grants the arbitral tribunal discretionary power based on the specific circumstances of the case. The tribunal needs to comprehensively consider the necessity and feasibility of a partial award and its impact on the overall procedure, rather than applying it mechanically. This flexible authorization respects the arbitral tribunal's functions in procedure and also requires arbitrators to possess higher capabilities in procedural management and case comprehension.

Article 69

Where there are literal or calculation errors in the arbitral award, or where the matters that have been decided by the arbitral tribunal are omitted in the arbitral award, the arbitral tribunal shall make due corrections or supplementation. The parties may, within 30 days from the date of receipt of the award, request the arbitral tribunal to make such corrections or supplementation.

Notes

This Article addresses the corrections and supplemental awards commonly encountered in practice. The former refers to formal or clerical issues in the award, such as wording or calculation errors, while the latter involves substantive matters and conclusions of the case. This revision retains the wording of the corresponding provision in the original Arbitration Law. With the increasing complexity of arbitration cases and the growing length of awards, the probability of technical errors like wording, numerical calculations, etc., has correspondingly increased, and omissions of certain adjudicated items also occur from time to time. In practice, the application of this Article might face issues such as an unclear definition of the scope for correction or supplementation, non-standardized procedures, and potentially unreasonable time limit settings.

Once an arbitral award becomes effective, neither party may seek to alter its content. However, countries typically allow the arbitral tribunal, either on its own initiative or upon a party's request within a specified period, to make a written correction to errors in the award, such as wording, typographical errors, calculation errors, or errors of a similar nature, or to address matters which were adjudicated by the tribunal but omitted from the award. According to this Article, corrections to the award are limited to three types, and parties must request them within 30 days of receiving the award: first, errors in wording; second, calculation errors; third, matters that have been adjudicated but were omitted from the award. The arbitral tribunal has no power to correct other errors, including errors in the award itself. This provision might seem somewhat unreasonable but it embodies the principle of finality of the award; overall, the benefits outweigh the drawbacks. As a document with legal enforceability, the precision of the wording, the accuracy of calculations, and the completeness of the adjudicated items in an award directly impact the vital interests of the parties and the reputation of arbitration. Establishing a correction mechanism allows for the timely rectification of technical errors, preventing formal defects from affecting the substantive validity of the award.

In practice, the rules of major arbitration institutions contain corresponding provisions. For example, Article 56 "Correction of the Award" of the CIETAC Arbitration Rules states that the arbitral tribunal may, on its own initiative, make a written correction of any clerical, typographical, or calculation error, or any error of a similar nature, or any omission in the award within a reasonable time after the award is issued. Any party may, within 30 days from its receipt of the award, request in writing that the arbitral tribunal correct any such error or omission in the award; if an error indeed exists, the arbitral tribunal shall make a written correction within 30 days of receiving the written request. Such a written correction forms part of the award and shall be subject to Article 52 "Making of Award". Article 57 "Additional Award" states that if any claim or counterclaim was adjudicated but omitted from the award, the arbitral tribunal may, on its own initiative, make an additional award within a reasonable time after the award is issued. Any party may, within 30 days from its receipt of the award, request in writing that the arbitral tribunal make an additional award on the omitted claim or counterclaim; if an omission indeed exists, the arbitral tribunal shall make an additional award within 30 days of receiving the written request. This additional award forms part of the award and shall be subject to paragraphs (4) to (10) of Article 52 "Making of Award".

It is important to note that while parties can request the arbitral tribunal to correct wording or calculation errors in the award, or address omitted matters which were adjudicated, they must follow relatively strict procedural requirements. If an explanation issued by the arbitration commission regarding the adjudicated items is clearly inconsistent in meaning with the dispositive part of the award, the enforcement court should investigate, by means such as notifying the arbitral tribunal to provide an explanation or consulting the arbitration case file from the arbitration commission, whether the explanation was made according to statutory procedures and has legal effect. Otherwise, the court cannot directly use this explanation as the basis for enforcement.

Related to the correction of awards is the issue of the arbitral tribunal's interpretation of its own award. For various reasons, an arbitral award might be unclear, or a court in enforcement or setting aside proceedings might have difficulty understanding a certain part of the award, or other circumstances might necessitate an authoritative interpretation by the original tribunal to facilitate the parties' smooth performance of the award or the court's proper handling of objections raised against the award. Therefore, it is necessary to empower the arbitral tribunal to interpret its award. The arbitration legislation of many countries and some arbitration rules provide the arbitral tribunal with the supplementary power to interpret the award. However, the New Arbitration Law contains no such provision.

Illustrative Cases

Case 1: ***Chen v. Kuang and others***[70]

Chen applied to the Guangdong Province Shenzhen Intermediate People's Court for non-enforcement of an arbitral award and a correction award rendered by the Shenzhen Arbitration Commission. One of the reasons was that since the involved arbitral award took legal effect, it had been applied for compulsory enforcement multiple times. During enforcement, serious errors in the original arbitral award led to significant enforcement issues. The erroneous results arising from the enforcement application based on the arbitral award should be corrected. The Court should rule not to enforce the arbitral award and the correction award according to law,

[70] (2021) Zui Gao Fa Min Ta No. 404.

immediately stopping the enforcement procedure for the second item of the original award, which was still in the process of resumed execution. Furthermore, the Shenzhen Arbitration Commission's issuance of the correction award violated the relevant provisions of the Arbitration Law (2017) and the Shenzhen Arbitration Commission Arbitration Rules. This case lacked the objective basis warranting a correction and far exceeded the 30-day correction time limit stipulated by law from the date of receiving the award.

The collegial panel of the Guangdong Province Shenzhen Intermediate People's Court, after deliberation, formed a unanimous opinion that, according to Article 8 of the Arbitral Award Enforcement Provisions, the application period is limited to 15 days. Although the involved Award No. 837 was rendered on October 22, 2013, the arbitral tribunal issued Correction Award No. 837-1 on July 27, 2020, stating that the correction formed part of the original award. Furthermore, the related enforcement case was still ongoing at the Court. Therefore, the application time limit should be recalculated from after the correction award was made. Chen's application to the Court on August 5, 2020, for non-enforcement of Award No. 837 and Correction Award No. 837-1 did not exceed the statutory time limit. Although Chen had applied to the Court to set aside the arbitral award in 2013 and was rejected, the grounds for that application were different from the grounds in this application for non-enforcement. This application was based on new facts arising from the arbitral tribunal's issuance of the correction award. Therefore, he had the right to apply for non-enforcement of the arbitral award.

Regarding whether the correction award rendered by the Shenzhen Arbitration Commission fell within the scope of permissible corrections and whether it violated the Arbitration Law (2017) and the Shenzhen Arbitration Commission Arbitration Rules, the Court's panel unanimously held the following: first, Article 20 of the Arbitration Law Interpretation stated that "violation of statutory procedures" as referred to in Article 58 of the Arbitration Law (2017) meant violation of the arbitration procedures stipulated in the Arbitration Law or the arbitration rules chosen by the parties, which could affect the correct adjudication of the case. Article 56 of the Arbitration Law (2017) limited the scope of corrections by the arbitral tribunal solely to "errors in wording, calculation in the award, or matters which have been adjudicated by the arbitral tribunal but were omitted from the award." Article 68 of the Shenzhen Arbitration Commission Arbitration Rules stipulated that if there were any errors in wording, calculation, or omissions in the award, the arbitral tribunal shall make corrections on its own initiative; a party may, within 30 days from the date of receiving the award, request the arbitral tribunal to make corrections, and the arbitral tribunal should make the corrections. The correction award shall form part of the original award." Regarding the time limit for corrections, the Arbitration Law (2017) and the Shenzhen Arbitration Commission Arbitration Rules only stipulated a 30-day limit for parties to apply for corrections from the date of receiving the award; they did not stipulate a time limit for the arbitral tribunal to make corrections on its own initiative. Second, there were no errors in wording or calculation, nor any omitted matters that had been adjudicated in the award. The arbitral tribunal, on its own initiative, seven years later, issued Correction Award No. 837-1, changing the original Item 2 to "and return all houses on the involved land to the Claimant." This constituted a substantive alteration of the parties' rights and obligations, exceeding the scope of correcting "errors in wording, calculation, or omitted matters." Third, the correction award only corrected the second item of the dispositive part of the award but did not correct the content of the preceding "Arbitral tribunal's Opinion" section. This resulted in an internal contradiction: the preceding "Arbitral tribunal's Opinion" still stated that Chen should return all houses on the involved land belonging to the Claimant to Kuang and Du, while the corrected dispositive item stated that "all houses on the involved land." Finally, the Court had already ascertained that after Kuang and Du leased the land, they built some sheet-metal houses on it. After Chen signed the contract and supplementary agreement with Kuang and Du, he invested in building fixed factory buildings, office buildings, and dormitories totaling over 7,500 square meters on the land. The arbitral tribunal, without ascertaining the relevant facts, directly corrected the award to order Chen to return all houses on the involved land to Kuang and Du. This was clearly lacking a basis, conflicted with the court judgment, and deprived the relevant parties of their right to defend themselves on this issue before the arbitral tribunal. Therefore, the act of the arbitral tribunal rendering the correction award violated the relevant provisions of the Arbitration Law (2017) and the Shenzhen Arbitration Commission Arbitration Rules. Therefore, the award should not be enforced.

The High People's Court of Guangdong Province held that according to the provisions regarding the scope of corrections to arbitral awards in Article 56 of the Arbitration Law (2017) and Article 68 of the Shenzhen Arbitration Commission Arbitration Rules, the corrections made by the arbitral tribunal's correction award are limited to errors in wording, calculation, or omitted matters in the original award. The Shenzhen Arbitration Commission, on its own initiative, seven years after rendering Award No. 837, issued Correction Award No. 837-1, changing the original second item to "and return all houses on the involved land to the Claimant." This was a substantive change to the parties' rights and obligations, did not constitute an error in wording, calculation, or an omitted matter, and contradicted the finding in the "Arbitral tribunal's Opinion" section of the original award, which stated that Chen should return all houses belonging to the arbitration claimant on the involved land to Kuang and Du. By using a correction award to alter the substantive rights and obligations confirmed in the original award, the arbitral tribunal deprived the parties of their right to defend themselves on this issue. This constituted the circumstance "the arbitration procedure violates the statutory procedure" as stipulated in Article 237 of the Civil Procedure Law. This case presented a situation where a partial non-enforcement of the arbitral award could be ruled. The High People's Court of Guangdong Province ruled not to enforce Correction Award No. 837-1.

Case 2: *Electric Power Company v. Construction Company*[71]

---

[71] (2023) Gan 01 Min Te No. 44; See the 5 Typical Cases on Judicial Review of Arbitration published by the High People's Court of Jiangxi Province. In this case, the people's court determined that the act of the arbitration commission substantially altering the original award result through a correction award without conducting arbitration proceedings might affect the correct adjudication

A dispute arose between Electric Power Company and Construction Company, which was submitted to the Nanchang Arbitration Commission for arbitration. On November 4, 2022, the Nanchang Arbitration Commission ruled that Electric Power Company must pay Construction Company project payments and interest for overdue payment. On December 9, 2022, the Nanchang Arbitration Commission issued a correction award, changing the start and end dates for calculating the interest specified in the second item of the dispositive part of the original award. On February 14, 2023, the Nanchang Arbitration Commission issued another correction award, deleting the reasoning regarding the "deduction of 6.76% management fee" from the project payment calculation section and correcting the corresponding project payment amount and overdue interest amount in the dispositive part.

The Jiangxi Province Nanchang Intermediate People's Court ruled to set aside the Nanchang Arbitration Commission's Arbitral Award No. 0634 (2020), Correction Award No. 0634 (2020), and Correction Award No. 0634-1 (2020).

The Jiangxi Province Nanchang Intermediate People's Court held that the arbitral tribunal must comply with the Arbitration Law (2017) and the arbitration rules when issuing a correction award. Making a substantial alteration to the original award in the form of a correction award without conducting arbitration proceedings might affect the correct adjudication of the case. This constituted a violation of statutory procedures, met the conditions for revoking the arbitral award, and the award should be set aside.

Article 70
The arbitral award shall be legally effective as of the date on which it is made.

Notes
This Article corresponds to the original Article 57 and concerns the effective date of an arbitral award. Before the Arbitration Law (1994) took effect, practices varied. Specifically, some awards became effective on the date they were made, while others became effective upon service. The Arbitration Law (1994) unified the practice, stipulating that the arbitral award becomes legally effective on the date it is made. In long-standing practice, an arbitral award becomes legally binding at the moment it is made, without requiring an appeal process or a specific confirmation procedure. From the moment the award is made, parties can arrange subsequent actions based on its content, including voluntary performance, applying for enforcement, or making relevant commercial decisions. Although the award becomes effective on the date it is made, parties still retain statutory remedies, such as applying to set aside the award or requesting corrections. In cases where arbitration rules stipulate various methods of service (including electronic service) as valid, discrepancies may arise between the date the award is made and the date it is served.

The primary purpose of this Article is to clarify the point in time when the arbitral award attains legal effect. This enables the parties to know clearly when the

---

of the case. Consequently, it ruled that this act by the arbitral tribunal violated statutory procedures, and the involved award met the statutory conditions for revocation and should be set aside.

award becomes binding upon them, allowing them to better exercise their rights and fulfill their obligations. Clarifying the effective time of the award can reduce disputes and delays between parties regarding the award's validity. Once the arbitral award becomes legally effective, the parties may not apply for arbitration again for the same dispute, nor may they bring a lawsuit in a People's Court. If one party fails to perform the obligations specified in the award, the other party may apply to the People's Court for enforcement in accordance with relevant regulations. Upon receiving the enforcement application, the People's Court will, according to the law, take appropriate compulsory enforcement measures against the party refusing to perform, to ensure the content of the award is realized.

The date of rendering, the date of service, and the date of performance are distinct concepts. The "date of rendering" typically refers to the date on which the arbitral tribunal, after hearing the case and conducting deliberations, forms its final award opinion. This date is generally clearly recorded in the award. In practice, it is important to note that the rendering of the award is not equivalent to its service; there exists a separate date of service. The arbitral award becomes legally effective from the date it is rendered. Regardless of whether the parties have received the award, they are obligated to comply with its contents. Different methods of service result in variations in the date of service. For instance, for service by mail, the date of service is the date the party actually signs for receipt; for service by electronic means, the date of service is the date the electronic document reaches the electronic address designated by the recipient. Even if service is delayed due to reasons attributable to a party itself (such as providing an incorrect address for service), this does not affect the legal consequence that the award becomes effective from the date it was rendered.

The date of performance usually refers to the date explicitly stipulated in the arbitral award by which the parties must perform their obligations under the award. It is the specific point in time when the parties must actually fulfill their legal responsibilities. In arbitration practice, the date of performance is generally explicitly agreed upon in the award or determined according to law. In most cases, the arbitral tribunal will directly specify the performance period within the award, for example: "The Respondent shall pay the Claimant compensation in the amount of XX within 15 days from the date this award is rendered." If a party fails to perform its obligations within this period, it constitutes delayed performance and requires bearing corresponding liabilities for the delay (such as paying default interest, penalties for breach of contract, etc.). If the arbitral award does not explicitly stipulate a performance period, the parties should perform their obligations within a reasonable period after receiving the award. The determination of a "reasonable period" requires a comprehensive assessment considering the specific circumstances of the case (such as the nature of the obligation, the amount involved, the difficulty of performance, etc.), generally guided by the principle of safeguarding the legitimate rights and interests of the obligee while also taking into account the obligor's capacity to perform.

Chapter 5
Application for Setting Aside an Arbitral Award

Article 71
A party may apply to the intermediate people's court in the place where the arbitration institution is located for setting aside an arbitral award if they can provide evidence that proves the arbitral award involves one of the following circumstances:

(1) **There is no arbitration agreement;**
(2) **The matters decided in the award exceed the scope of the arbitration agreement or go beyond the authority of the arbitration institution;**
(3) **The composition of the arbitral tribunal or the arbitration procedure was not in accordance with the statutory procedure;**
(4) **The evidence on which the award is based was forged;**
(5) **The other party has withheld evidence which is sufficient to affect the impartiality of arbitration; or.**
(6) **An arbitrator has solicitated or accepted bribes, done malpractices for personal benefits or perverted the law in the arbitration of the case.**

The people's court shall rule to set aside the arbitral award if, upon examination by a collegial panel, the award is verified to involve any of the circumstances specified in the preceding paragraph.

Where the people's court determines that the arbitral award violates the public interest, it shall rule to set aside the award.

Notes
This Article embodies the principle of limited judicial intervention in arbitration. It provides parties with a channel for the relief of rights and prevents the abuse of arbitration power, while simultaneously safeguarding the independence and efficiency of arbitration through strict setting-aside conditions and review procedures. In practice, it is generally understood that setting aside an award is confined to procedural irregularities. However, a purely "procedural review" model may be

Y. Lin, *New Arbitration Law in China*, China Arbitration Yearbook,
https://doi.org/10.1007/978-981-92-0642-1_5

insufficient in addressing extreme injustice. For instance, situations where a party wins an award based on forged evidence, or loses due to the other party's malicious concealment of crucial evidence, might be difficult to remedy under a purely procedural review. Including "the evidence on which the award is based is forged" (item 4) and "the other party has withheld the evidence which is sufficient to affect the impartiality of the arbitration" (item 5) as grounds for setting aside precisely aims to plug this legal loophole, providing a final judicial remedy for parties whose rights are harmed by the other party's dishonest conduct. This approach prevents excessive judicial intervention in arbitration while offering a judicial recourse for awards with significant procedural or substantive flaws. After an award is set aside, the dispute is not finally resolved. The parties may choose the following paths: reach a new arbitration agreement and apply for arbitration again, or initiate litigation in the people's court to resolve the dispute through judicial proceedings.

According to this Article, "parties" specifically refers to the claimant and respondent in the arbitration proceedings, and does not include non-parties who did not participate in the arbitration. Arbitration possesses a contractual nature, and its effects are limited to the parties who signed the arbitration agreement. If a non-party believes an award infringes upon their rights and interests, they should seek relief through other legal procedures.

The competent court for applying to set aside an award is the intermediate people's court at the place where the arbitration institution is located. Jurisdiction is based on the "location of the arbitration institution," not the parties' domicile or the place of contract performance. For example, if the arbitration institution is the BAC, even if both parties are in Shanghai, the application for setting aside must be filed with the competent intermediate people's court in Beijing. However, the New Arbitration Law provides for limited ad hoc arbitration, and its provisions regarding jurisdiction for setting aside such awards are not explicitly stated, requiring reference to subsequent judicial interpretations or other legal documents. Competent courts shall include the relevant intermediate people's courts within Pilot Free Trade Zones, the Hainan Free Trade Port, other areas specified by the state, or the intermediate people's court at the seat of arbitration.

This Article explicitly lists six circumstances under which an award may be set aside. The claimant must provide evidence proving the existence of at least one of these circumstances. These circumstances all involve major flaws in the arbitration procedure affecting the award's impartiality, which are difficult to remedy through correction procedures. Among them, the first to third circumstances relate to procedural flaws; the fourth and fifth relate to evidence flaws; and the sixth relates to arbitrator illegality. To a certain extent, although all are related to procedural matters, the fourth and fifth also touch upon substantive content. If a party presents evidence proving the existence of one of the aforementioned circumstances, and the people's court, after forming a collegiate panel to review and verify it, confirms it, the court shall rule to set aside the award. Additionally, if the award "violates the public interest," the court may set it aside on its own initiative, without requiring an application from a party.

1. **No Arbitration Agreement**

According to the New Arbitration Law and judicial practice, "no arbitration agreement" refers not only to the "physical absence of a relevant document" but mainly includes two types: first, where an arbitration agreement never existed from the beginning; and second, where an arbitration agreement was signed but is legally void or ineffective. The legal consequences of both are the same, both resulting in the arbitration institution lacking a jurisdictional basis, and awards made accordingly can be set aside.

A. ***No Arbitration Agreement from the Outset***

The parties never reached an agreement on "resolving disputes through arbitration," either before or after the dispute arose, and did not form any arbitration agreement meeting statutory requirements. The arbitration institution's jurisdiction lacks the parties' voluntary authorization.

(i) ***Before the dispute arises (e.g., during contract signing)***. The contract only stipulates rights and obligations clauses without any dispute resolution clause, or explicitly stipulates "disputes shall be under the jurisdiction of the People's Court," without mentioning arbitration.
(ii) ***After the dispute arises.*** One party proposes "resolution through arbitration," but the other party explicitly refuses; or although the parties negotiate arbitration matters, they fail to reach an agreement on core content, such as the arbitration institution or arbitration matters, and ultimately do not sign a written arbitration agreement. Special attention is needed: a unilateral expression of intent does not constitute an agreement. Merely one party expressing willingness to "accept arbitration" through letters, statements, etc., without obtaining the other party's acceptance, cannot form a valid arbitration agreement.

B. ***The arbitration agreement is deemed void***

Even if the parties have formally executed an arbitration agreement (such as an arbitration clause within a contract or a separate submission agreement), it may be deemed void *ab initio* if it fails to meet the statutory requirements for validity. The legal effect is equivalent to "no arbitration agreement." Common scenarios rendering an agreement invalid in practice include:

(i) ***The subject matter of arbitration exceeds the legal scope of arbitrability***. Disputes explicitly excluded from arbitration jurisdiction by law cannot be submitted to arbitration. If the parties agree to arbitrate such disputes, the agreement is void. For example, disputes concerning personal status relationships such as marriage, adoption, guardianship, support, and succession, as well as administrative disputes that shall be handled by administrative organs according to law (e.g., disputes over land ownership), all fall outside the scope of matters acceptable for arbitration. Related arbitration agreements concerning these matters are void.

(ii) ***Failure to designate the arbitration institution clearly and the inability to rectify.*** An arbitration agreement must designate a "specific and specified arbitration commission." If the designation is ambiguous (e.g., "arbitration by the arbitration institution at Party A's location," "arbitration by the arbitration commission at the place of contract performance") and the parties are unable to determine a specified institution through a supplementary agreement, the arbitration agreement is void. For instance, if the parties agree that "disputes shall be arbitrated by an arbitration institution in Beijing," but there are multiple institutions in Beijing such as the "Beijing Arbitration Commission" and the "China International Economic and Trade Arbitration Commission," and the parties subsequently fail to reach a clear agreement specifying one, the arbitration agreement is void due to the inability to identify the specific institution.

(iii) ***The signing party lacks civil capacity.*** An arbitration agreement is a type of civil contract. The parties concluding it must possess the corresponding capacity for civil conduct (typically meaning full capacity for civil conduct). Arbitration agreements signed by persons with no capacity for civil conduct (e.g., minors, persons with mental disorders) or with limited capacity for civil conduct are void due to the lack of a genuine and valid expression of intent.

(iv) ***The arbitration agreement was concluded under duress.*** Arbitration is fundamentally based on the principle of "party autonomy." If one party uses duress, such as violence, threats, or intimidation, to compel the other party to sign the arbitration agreement, this constitutes a situation where the "expression of intent is not genuine," and the agreement is void. For example, if A threatens to "publicly disclose B's personal private life" to force B to sign a contract containing an arbitration clause, the arbitration agreement is void due to the presence of duress.

(v) ***The form does not conform to statutory requirements.*** The New Arbitration Law explicitly requires that an arbitration agreement must be made in "written form" (including arbitration clauses in contracts, separate arbitration agreements, letters, data messages, etc.). A mere oral agreement, or a written agreement not genuinely signed or sealed by both parties (e.g., containing a forged signature, or signed by only one party), is void due to formal defects. For instance, if A forges B's signature to create an "Arbitration Agreement" and subsequently applies for arbitration based on it, the agreement is void because it lacks B's genuine intent and the signature is forged.

2. **The Matters Decided in the Award Exceed the Scope of the Arbitration Agreement or Go Beyond the Authority of the Arbitration Institution**

The scope of arbitration is limited to matters agreed upon by the parties; any part exceeding this scope may be set aside. Matters prohibited from arbitration by law (such as disputes concerning personal status relationships) cannot be arbitrated.

The scope of arbitration is confined to matters stipulated in the parties' arbitration agreement or permitted by law. An arbitral award that exceeds this scope may be set aside. The core purpose of this provision is to uphold the "contractual nature" of arbitration and its "statutory jurisdictional boundaries." The power of arbitration derives from the voluntary authorization of the parties and must not exceed the jurisdictional limits prescribed by law. If an arbitral tribunal adjudicates matters beyond its authority and renders an award, the award loses its legal foundation and should be corrected through judicial procedures. The specific implications, practical standards for determination, and legal consequences of the following two scenarios are analyzed below:

A. ***Ultra petita* or excess of authority**

"*Ultra petita*" is one of the most common grounds for setting aside an award in arbitration practice. It refers to the situation where the dispute matters adjudicated and decided by the arbitral tribunal exceed the scope for dispute resolution explicitly agreed upon by the parties in their arbitration agreement. The essence of arbitration power is "authorization by agreement"; the parties define the boundaries of the tribunal's adjudication through the arbitration agreement, and the tribunal has no authority to rule on matters outside the agreement. Based on judicial practice, "ultra petita" primarily includes three typical scenarios:

(i) Exceeding the agreed scope of arbitrable matters. The arbitration agreement explicitly limits the types of disputes, but the tribunal rules on matters not covered by the agreement. For example, the parties' arbitration agreement only stipulates that "disputes arising from contract payment shall be resolved by arbitration," but the tribunal also rules on a claim for "compensation for tortious injury related to goods quality." The tort compensation dispute falls outside the agreed scope of arbitration.
(ii) Exceeding the scope of the parties' claims. The content of the tribunal's award goes beyond the specific claims raised by the claimant in the arbitration proceedings. For example, the claimant only sought "payment of overdue goods payment of 1 million RMB by the respondent," but the tribunal awarded "payment of 1 million RMB for the goods plus 200,000 RMB in penalty interest." The penalty interest portion constitutes an ultra petita award.
(iii) Involving non-parties to the arbitration agreement. The arbitral award imposes obligations or confers rights on a third party who is not a signatory to the arbitration agreement. For example, A and B agreed to resolve their contract dispute through arbitration, but the tribunal ruled that "third party C shall bear joint and several liability for B's debt." Since C was not a party to the arbitration agreement, this part of the award constitutes ultra petita.

It is important to note that if the ultra petita portion can be clearly separated from the valid part of the award, the court may set aside only the ultra petita portion, leaving the remainder of the award effective. For instance, if an arbitral award contains both "payment for goods" and "tort compensation," and the tort compensation part constitutes ultra petita, the court may set aside only the tort compensation part of the award, preserving the validity of the payment for goods portion.

B. ***The arbitration institution lacks jurisdiction***

"Lack of jurisdiction" refers to a situation where the arbitration institution renders an award on a dispute that is explicitly prohibited from arbitration by law or falls outside its jurisdictional purview. The core issue is that the arbitration power has exceeded statutory boundaries. In such cases, regardless of any agreement between the parties, the arbitration institution lacks jurisdiction, and any award rendered on this basis should be set aside. According to the New Arbitration Law and related regulations, "lack of jurisdiction" primarily refers to disputes explicitly excluded from arbitration by law, which the arbitration institution has no authority to accept. These specifically include:

(i) Disputes Concerning Personal Status: Such as marriage, adoption, guardianship, support, and succession;
(ii) Administrative Disputes: Disputes that, according to law, should be handled by administrative organs, such as administrative confirmation of rights or administrative penalties;
(iii) Other Statutorily Excluded Circumstances: For example, labor disputes must undergo specialized labor arbitration procedures, and disputes over agricultural contract management within agricultural collective economic organizations are also not subject to ordinary arbitration procedures.

If, upon examination and verification, the court finds that the award involves "ultra petita" or deals with a matter over which the arbitration institution "lacks jurisdiction," it shall rule to set aside the entire award or the ultra petita portion. After an award is set aside, the parties may reach a new arbitration agreement and apply for arbitration again, or directly file a lawsuit in court. When applying to set aside the award, the parties must provide sufficient evidence to prove "ultra petita" or "lack of jurisdiction," such as the arbitration agreement, the application for arbitration, the award itself, etc., and clearly point out the specific content that exceeds authority or the legal basis for the lack of jurisdiction.

3. **The Formation of the Arbitral Tribunal or the Arbitration Procedure Was Not in Accordance with the Statutory Procedure**

In cases applying to set aside arbitral awards, procedural irregularities are frequently cited as a core defense. Whether the arbitration procedure complies with the parties' agreement, the arbitration rules, or legal provisions directly affects the fairness and enforceability of the award. The following two types of procedural flaws are particularly common.

A. ***Violation of statutory procedures in the composition of the arbitral tribunal***

The composition of the arbitral tribunal is the foundation for the legitimacy of the arbitration procedure and must strictly adhere to the express provisions of the New Arbitration Law and the rules of the arbitration institution. Any improper conduct occurring during the formation of the tribunal may constitute a statutory ground for setting aside the award. Specific manifestations include:

If the arbitration institution fails to effectively serve key documents such as the notice of acceptance and the panel of arbitrators during the tribunal formation process, or fails to clearly inform the parties' right to select arbitrators according to law, it constitutes a major procedural defect. Particularly, if a party has neither actively selected an arbitrator nor explicitly authorized the arbitration institution to make the appointment, and the institution nonetheless proceeds to appoint an arbitrator on its own initiative, it substantially deprives the party of its procedural autonomy, constituting a typical violation of the legal procedures for tribunal formation.

According to Article 46 of the New Arbitration Law, if an arbitrator falls under statutory circumstances for withdrawal—such as being a close relative of a party or their agent, having an interest in the case, or being involved in other situations that might affect the impartiality of the award—they must withdraw from the proceedings, either on their own initiative or upon request. If an arbitrator who should have withdrawn fails to do so, and this conduct could potentially affect the substantive fairness of the award, it constitutes a fundamental flaw in the tribunal's composition.

Parties have the right to make special agreements regarding the composition of the arbitral tribunal according to the law. For instance, if the parties explicitly agree that the case shall be heard by a three-arbitrator tribunal, but the arbitration institution arbitrarily applies a summary procedure and appoints a sole arbitrator, or otherwise violates the parties' explicit agreement, it constitutes a serious departure from the parties' procedural consensus and amounts to a violation of the legal procedures for tribunal formation.

B. ***Violation of statutory procedures in the conduct of the arbitration proceedings***

The conduct of the arbitration proceedings must also strictly comply with legal and rule requirements, especially concerning procedural steps that involve the fundamental rights of the parties. Otherwise, the award may be set aside due to serious procedural violations. For example:

If the arbitration institution fails to effectively serve key legal documents such as the notice of arbitration, notice of tribunal formation, or hearing summons to the parties in the manner prescribed by the New Arbitration Law or the applicable arbitration rules (e.g., personal service, service by mail, service by public announcement), resulting in a party being unable to exercise procedural rights such as the right to defend, present evidence, or appear at the hearing due to lack of notice, it constitutes a fundamental violation of the principles of due process.

Furthermore, the arbitration process must ensure that the parties enjoy and may in practice exercise basic procedural rights, such as applying for the withdrawal of an arbitrator, cross-examining evidence, engaging in debate, submitting evidence, and making final statements. If the arbitral tribunal fails to grant the parties a reasonable period for submitting their defense, or admits key evidence as the basis for its decision without allowing the parties to cross-examine it, these actions constitute a substantive impairment of procedural fairness.

4. **The Other Party Has Withheld Evidence Which Is Sufficient to Affect the Impartiality of the Arbitration**

In applications to set aside arbitral awards, "withholding evidence" is a claim frequently raised by claimants and a common ground upon which courts set aside awards. If the other party withheld evidence sufficient to affect the impartiality of the award, it will lead to the award being set aside. The rationale for this ground is that by withholding crucial evidence, one party causes the arbitral tribunal to deviate in its finding of the case's basic facts, consequently rendering an unjust award. With reference to the Arbitral Award Enforcement Provision and judicial practice, the determination of "withholding evidence" must satisfy strict requirements. Not all acts of withholding evidence constitute a statutory ground for setting aside.

According to Article 16(1) of the Arbitral Award Enforcement Provisions, the following conditions must be cumulatively satisfied to establish that a party has concealed evidence from the arbitration institution that was sufficient to affect the impartiality of the award: (i) The evidence constitutes crucial evidence for determining the basic facts of the case; (ii) The evidence was solely in the possession of the other party and was not submitted to the arbitral tribunal; (iii) The applying party knew of the existence of this evidence during the arbitration proceedings and requested the other party to produce it or asked the arbitral tribunal to order its production, but the other party failed to produce or submit it without a justifiable reason. It is evident that the Arbitral Award Enforcement Provisions set a relatively high threshold for establishing "withholding evidence," requiring the simultaneous fulfillment of all three conditions. This serves both to prevent parties from undermining fairness by concealing evidence and to avoid frivolous challenges to the validity of arbitral awards based on allegations of evidence concealment.

Firstly, the evidence must be material crucial for the tribunal's determination of the core facts of the case, not secondary or ancillary material. The absence of this evidence would undermine the foundation of the tribunal's findings on basic facts (such as whether a contract was performed, whether a breach occurred, how the amount of loss is determined, etc.) and could lead to a fundamental change in the outcome of the award. For example, in an arbitration concerning payment for goods, a delivery receipt proving "the buyer actually received the goods" or an inspection report proving "the seller's goods had quality defects" would typically constitute crucial evidence for determining basic facts. In contrast, communication records unrelated to the dispute or non-core transaction documents may not necessarily meet this requirement.

Secondly, the evidence must have been "solely in the possession of the other party and not submitted to the arbitral tribunal." This means the evidence was actually possessed or controlled by the other party, and the applying party was unable to obtain it themselves for objective reasons (e.g., internal ledgers kept by the other party, related contracts between the other party and a third party, proprietary technical data held by the other party). If the applying party could have obtained the evidence themselves (e.g., publicly available documents, materials jointly held by both parties), it does not meet the requirement of being "solely possessed by the other party."

Thirdly, the applying party must have "known of the existence of the evidence during the arbitration proceedings and have actively sought its production." The applying party cannot remain passive during the arbitration and only raise the claim of "withholding evidence" after the award is rendered. If a party made no request whatsoever, it is difficult to constitute statutory "concealment," even if the other party did withhold evidence.

Judging from judicial precedents, courts strictly adhere to the principle of "simultaneous satisfaction of the three requirements" when determining "withholding evidence." If only one or two requirements are met, the claim of "withholding evidence" is usually dismissed. For instance, in ***JQ Company and others v. JK Company and others***,[1] the court held that although S Exchange and JQ Company alleged that the other party "withheld" evidence related to the filing of documents with the competent authority during the arbitration, the filing work itself was a joint obligation of both parties. During the arbitration, S Exchange and JQ Company were fully capable of verifying the specific status of the document filing. Therefore, pursuant to the aforementioned judicial interpretation, the claim of 'withholding evidence' cannot be established." Similarly, in ***TZ Company v. WX Company***,[2] the court also held that evidence referred to in "withholding evidence sufficient to affect the impartiality of the award" should be evidence that is crucial for determining the basic facts of the case, was solely possessed by the other party but not submitted to the arbitral tribunal, and whose existence was known to a party during the arbitration proceedings, who then requested the other party to produce it or asked the tribunal to order its production, but the other party failed to produce or submit it without justifiable reason.

In practice, for a party applying to set aside an award and alleging "withholding evidence," the burden is on them to prove the importance of the evidence, that it was solely in the possession of the other party and they could not obtain it themselves, and that they requested its production during the proceedings. If they cannot simultaneously prove all three points, the claim of "withholding evidence" is unlikely to receive court support.

5. **The Evidence on Which the Award is Based was Forged**

The submission of forged evidence is also one of the circumstances stipulated by law upon which an application to set aside an arbitral award can be based. In arbitration proceedings, if one party forges crucial evidence used to determine the basic facts of the case, leading the arbitral tribunal to render an unjust award, this constitutes the circumstance of "forged evidence" which can negate the award. According to Article 15 of the Arbitral Award Enforcement Provisions, the people's court shall

[1] (2018) Jing 04 Min Te No. 23.

[2] (2019) Wan 06 Min Te No. 12.

recognize a circumstance as involving forged evidence where the following conditions are cumulatively satisfied:

(i) The evidence was already admitted and relied upon by the arbitral award;
(ii) The evidence constitutes crucial evidence for determining the basic facts of the case;
(iii) Upon investigation, the evidence is confirmed to have been created or obtained through illegal means such as fabrication, alteration, or provision of false certificates, violating the requirements of objectivity, relevance, and legality of evidence.

To establish that forged evidence has occurred, all three conditions stipulated in Article 15 of the Arbitral Award Enforcement Provisions must be met simultaneously. This is similar to the requirement for simultaneously satisfying three conditions when determining the withholding of evidence. For example, in ***Jiang v. JD Company***,[3] the Commercial Housing Sales Contract involved in the case was crucial evidence relied upon by the arbitral tribunal to determine the basic facts of the case. The court, based on a subsequent judicial expert opinion, determined that this Commercial Housing Sales Contract was forged. Consequently, the court ultimately held that the evidence on which the Huaihua Arbitration Commission's award was based was forged and set aside the arbitral award in this case. It can be seen that in this case, the court primarily relied on Article 15 of the "Enforcement Provisions" to determine that the Commercial Housing Sales Contract involved constituted forged evidence, thereby supporting the claimant's claim and setting aside the arbitral award.

6. **Arbitrator Misconduct or Violation of Law**

That an arbitrator solicited or accepted bribes, engaged in malpractices for personal gain, or perverted the law in rendering an arbitral award constitutes one of the statutory grounds for setting aside the award. Such conduct tramples upon the professional ethics and fundamental integrity expected of arbitrators, directly contravening the core principles of "independence and impartiality" in arbitration. In practice, these situations are relatively rare. The following analysis elaborates on the specific connotations, standards for determination, and key points of judicial practice concerning these three types of conduct:

Although an arbitrator's soliciting or accepting bribes, engaging in malpractice for personal gain, and perverting the law in rendering an award all fall under the category of "unlawful or negligent conduct," their manifestations and the basis for their determination differ. A specific distinction must be made based on the nature of the act and the objective evidence.

Soliciting or accepting bribes refers to an act where an arbitrator, by taking advantage of the authority and position afforded by adjudicating a case, directly or indirectly demands or accepts money, property, or other improper benefits from a

[3] (2019) Xiang 12 Min Te No. 1.

party. The core of such conduct lies in the "illegal exchange of official authority for personal gain." Soliciting bribes involves proactively demanding money or property from a party or its representative, with the party passively providing benefits in order to obtain a favorable award. Accepting bribes involves receiving money, property-related benefits (such as cash, real estate, equity, travel arrangements, luxury consumption, etc.), or non-property benefits (such as arranging employment for relatives or friends, providing official favors, etc.) that are proactively offered by a party or its representative, where such benefits are directly linked to the outcome of the case.

Engaging in malpractices for personal gain refers to an arbitrator intentionally deviating from an impartial stance due to personal relationships, interest connections, or other improper motives, and favoring one party over the other through acts such as concealing key facts or manipulating procedures. Its core elements are a "subjective intent to show favoritism" coupled with "objective acts of misconduct."

Perverting the law in rendering an arbitral award refers to a situation where an arbitrator, in the course of hearing a case, deliberately issues an award contrary to facts or law despite knowing that the fundamental facts are incorrectly determined or the law is erroneously applied. Its core element is "knowingly and deliberately acting in error," which distinguishes it from "deficiencies in an award resulting from a lack of competence." Particular attention must be paid to the fact that "perverting the law in rendering an arbitral award" requires the element of "subjective intent." If an arbitrator renders an inappropriate award due to a reasonable dispute over fact-finding or a misinterpretation of legal provisions—such as differing assessments of the probative value of evidence or scholarly disagreements on the application of law—it falls under "issues of adjudicative competence" and does not constitute perverting the law. Only conduct that involves "knowingly disregarding the correct facts and law, and deliberately rendering an erroneous award" meets the statutory requirement.

In applications to set aside arbitral awards heard by the courts, challenges raised on this ground are not uncommon, but the majority are dismissed. When reviewing whether an arbitrator has engaged in the aforementioned conduct, the courts apply a high threshold and stringent requirements. As such circumstances directly negate the arbitrator's professional integrity and the legality of the award, clear and sufficient evidence is required to prevent parties from making baseless accusations against arbitrators merely due to an unfavorable outcome. Article 18 of the Arbitration Judicial Review Provisions stipulates that an arbitrator's conduct of soliciting or accepting bribes, engaging in malpractices for personal gain, or perverting the law in rendering an arbitral award refers to conduct that has already been confirmed by an effective criminal legal document or a disciplinary decision. Furthermore, Article 399 of the Criminal Law provides that any person bearing arbitration duties according to law who, in arbitration activities, intentionally perverts the law by rendering an award contrary to facts and law, if the circumstances are serious, shall be sentenced to fixed-term imprisonment of not more than 3 years or criminal detention; if the circumstances are especially serious, shall be sentenced to fixed-term imprisonment of not less than 3 years but not more than 7 years.

Accordingly, an arbitrator alleged to have engaged in such conduct must have been convicted by a judgment of a judicial authority or subjected to a disciplinary decision by an arbitration commission or a disciplinary inspection commission. The party must produce documentary evidence, such as an effective criminal legal document or a disciplinary decision, that adjudicates or confirms the arbitrator's engagement in the aforementioned conduct. Only upon such a basis may the court set aside the arbitral award on these grounds.

7. **Violation of Public Interest**

Violation of public interest is one of the statutory grounds for parties to apply for setting aside or non-enforcement of an arbitral award, and it is also a circumstance under which courts may actively exercise judicial review of arbitral awards ex officio. As the last line of defense for public power to supervise arbitration, a private dispute resolution mechanism (private process), this provision reflects the necessary constraint of judicial authority on arbitration autonomy.

Similar to most countries, the New Arbitration Law does not specifically define the connotation and extension of "public interest." The original Arbitration Law (2017) used the term "social public interest, " while the New Arbitration Law adopts the term "public interest". Relevant expressions can also be found in the Civil Code, such as Article 117, which states that "where it is necessary for the public interest... fair and reasonable compensation shall be provided." Simultaneously, the Civil Code employs the concept of "public order and good morals," stipulating that civil subjects must not violate public order and good morals; otherwise, the relevant legal act shall be invalid.

Arbitral awards generally only bind the parties to the arbitration (following the principle of privity). However, if their content extends beyond the private domain and harms the interests of an unspecified majority, the fundamental order of the state, or the core values of society, it may constitute a violation of public interest. In practice, regardless of whether the terms "public interest, " "social public interest, " "public order and good morals, " or "public policy" are used, courts tend to interpret them consistently in judicial review of arbitration: they are generally considered to refer to the most fundamental legal and moral interests of society, concerning the common well-being of all members of society, specifically including two aspects: public order and public morality. The former refers to the basic order of social operation and life, while the latter refers to the moral standards universally recognized and followed by society.

From the perspective of the development of the arbitration system, the provision that "violation of public interest may lead to setting aside an award" has irreplaceable institutional value. Arbitration is essentially the institutionalized embodiment of private remedy. However, if party autonomy is entirely unrestricted, it may lead to malicious arbitration (such as using arbitration procedures to transfer illegal funds or evade mandatory legal provisions), thereby harming the overall interests of the state and society. This provision provides a clear basis for judicial intervention, preventing arbitration from becoming a tool for unlawful conduct. At the same time, it also defines the boundaries of party autonomy, clarifying that arbitration procedures and content must not breach the bottom line of law and public interest, thereby achieving a reasonable balance between party autonomy and state coercion.

For courts, when applying this provision, they should prudently determine public interest and avoid inappropriately interfering with the independence of arbitration on broad grounds. For parties, they should recognize that arbitration is not beyond the law, and any attempt to achieve illegal purposes through arbitration may be declared invalid due to violation of public interest. For arbitration institutions, during the adjudication process, they should proactively pay attention to whether the content of the award complies with national laws and public policies, thereby preventing such risks at the source and enhancing the credibility and overall quality of arbitration.

Illustrative Cases

Case 1: *C Company v. D Company*[4]

In October 2014, C Company issued a Letter of Commitment to D Company. The letter stated that C Company commits to providing credit enhancement support for the liquidity and asset security of the asset management products initiated and for which D Company undertakes active management responsibilities. It is clarified that the asset management products initiated and actively managed by D Company include: private funds and asset management plans where D Company acts as the asset manager, or which are co-developed by D Company and other financial institutions, and where D Company serves as the final investment decision-maker for the asset management product through roles such as investment advisor. On December 27, 2019, Guo, D Company, and X Securities Company signed a Fund Contract. In this Fund Contract, D Company acted as the fund manager. Article 25 of the contract stipulated, "all parties agree that any dispute arising from or related to this contract shall be resolved through consultation and mediation. If the dispute cannot be resolved through friendly consultation, it shall be submitted to Y Arbitration Commission for arbitration, with the seat of arbitration in Beijing, in accordance with the arbitration rules of that commission effective at that time." In September 2021, Guo applied for arbitration to Y Arbitration Commission, naming D Company, X Securities Company, and C Company as respondents. Y Arbitration Commission accepted the case. C Company raised objections to the arbitration jurisdiction twice. After review, the arbitral tribunal dismissed the objections and set February 22, 2022, as the date for the arbitration hearing. On January 19, 2022, C Company applied to the Beijing Financial Court to confirm the invalidity of the arbitration agreement. The Beijing Financial Court accepted the case on January 21, 2022. The claimant, C Company, requested the Court to confirm that no arbitration agreement existed between C Company and Guo.

---

[4] See the 10 Typical Cases on Judicial Review of Financial Arbitration published by the Beijing Financial Court in October 2023.

The Beijing Financial Court held that arbitration was based on the existence of a genuine and valid arbitration agreement between the parties. An arbitral tribunal could only obtain the authority to resolve disputes upon the explicit authorization of the parties. The expansion of arbitration's effect had specific boundaries and should not be subject to arbitrary broad interpretation. Currently, there were no explicit legal provisions stipulating whether an arbitration clause in a master contract may apply to an ancillary contract. Given the special nature of arbitration clauses and in the absence of clear legal grounds, the scope of an arbitration clause should not be arbitrarily expanded through interpretation. Instead, the parties' intention to resolve disputes through arbitration should be strictly ascertained.

In this case, C Company did not directly enter into the Fund Contract with Guo. The Letter of Commitment was not issued by C Company to Guo, and there was no clear expression of intent between the two parties to resolve disputes through arbitration. Consequently, no arbitration agreement existed between C Company and Guo. C Company raised an objection before the first hearing of the arbitral tribunal, which complied with the relevant procedural rules. Accordingly, the Court ruled to confirm that no arbitration agreement existed between C Company and Guo.

Case 2: *F Company v. G Management Committee*[5]
This case involved an application by F Company and G Management Committee to set aside an arbitral award. The legal issue presented was whether the matters decided in the arbitral award exceeded the scope of G Management Committee's arbitration claims. Specifically, the question was whether F Company's request to "confirm that the act of terminating (rescinding) the Land Use Contract in the 'Letter on Terminating the Land Grant Contract' issued by G Management Committee on December 27, 2006, had become legally effective" was consistent with the arbitral award which "confirmed that the act of terminating the Land Use Contract in the three separate 'Land Use Contract' termination notices issued by G Management Committee became legally effective on the date the award was rendered."

The Beijing No. 4 Intermediate People's Court held that the wording of the arbitration claims and the award's dispositive part were not entirely identical. However, the essence of both could be distilled to "confirming the legal effectiveness of the act of terminating the contract." Determining the scope of the claims required a comprehensive assessment based on factors such as the parties' purpose in arbitration, the facts and grounds asserted, and the arguments presented during the hearings. Although the three notices were issued at different times, were based on varying legal provisions and factual backgrounds, and were phrased differently, their core objective was consistent: G Management Committee (and its predecessor organization) intended to terminate the contract with F Company. The Court confirmed that the object of the management committee's request for arbitration was not the notice documents themselves, but rather the underlying request to terminate

[5] (2024) Jing 04 Min Te No. 287; See the 10 Typical Cases on Judicial Review of Arbitration published by the Beijing No. 4 Intermediate People's Court in November 2024.

the contract expressed within those notices. As for whether the contract could be terminated and the specific time of termination, the arbitral tribunal had the authority to make an independent determination based on the facts ascertained and the application of the law. In summary, the award did not exceed the scope of the management committee's arbitration claims. Consequently, the court ruled to dismiss F Company's application. This case established the rule that the court should look beyond the superficial wording to ascertain the parties' true intent when determining whether an arbitral award exceeds the scope of the arbitration claims. It reflected the principles of statutory review and limited supervision in judicial review of arbitration.

Case 3: *H Company v. I Company*[6]
H Company and I Company entered into the Cooperation Development Agreement. In 2010, I Company filed for arbitration with an arbitration commission against H Company as the respondent, based on the arbitration clause in the aforementioned contract. During the arbitration, I Company raised multiple claims, one of which was requesting H Company to pay the property rental income of over 82 million RMB stipulated in the contract, plus interest. Subsequently, the arbitral tribunal issued an award. Regarding the rental income claimed by I Company, the tribunal ruled that H Company should pay a total of over 87 million, comprising rent, taxes, and default penalties. After the award was rendered, H Company applied to the Beijing No.4 Intermediate People's Court to set aside the involved arbitral award on the grounds that "the matters decided in the award fell outside the scope of the arbitration agreement or the arbitration commission lacked jurisdiction to arbitrate," among other reasons.

The Beijing No.4 Intermediate People's Court found that the amount of rent payable awarded by the arbitral tribunal exceeded the amount claimed by I Company. The awarded sum included components such as taxes, which I Company had not requested. This part of the award exceeded the scope of the party's arbitration claims and constituted an excess of authority (*ultra petita*). Therefore, the Court ruled to set aside the relevant part of the award that constituted an excess of authority and dismissed the other applications.

Case 4: *Sun v. Lyu*[7]
Sun authorized her husband, Lyu, to attend the arbitration hearing at the SCIA with their identification cards. However, Sun and Lyu did not submit any power of attorney or authorization documents to the arbitration institution. Furthermore, Lyu arrived at the SCIA nearly 40 minutes later than the time specified in the hearing

---

[6] See the 10 Typical Cases on Judicial Review of Domestic Arbitration published by the Beijing No.4 Intermediate People's Court in July 2023.

[7] See the 10 Typical Cases on Judicial Review of Arbitration published by the Guangdong Province Shenzhen Intermediate People's Court in July 2025. Parties shall strictly comply with the provisions of the Arbitration Law (2017) and the arbitration rules, actively fulfill procedural obligations to ensure they fully enjoy relevant rights. A party's failure to participate in the arbitration proceedings due to its own reasons does not constitute a situation where the arbitration procedure violates

notice. After the hearing concluded, Lyu contacted the arbitration secretary, who informed him that he might apply for another hearing. Nevertheless, neither Sun nor Lyu applied for a further hearing. Subsequently, Sun applied to the Guangdong Province Shenzhen Intermediate People's Court to set aside the arbitral award, arguing that the award was rendered in her absence and that the arbitration procedure violated legal provisions.

The Guangdong Province Shenzhen Intermediate People's Court held that since Sun and Lyu failed to submit any power of attorney to the arbitration institution, SCIA's handling of the matter was in compliance with the arbitration rules. Regarding Lyu's late arrival nearly 40 minutes after the scheduled hearing time, the arbitral tribunal's decision to conduct the proceedings in his absence was in line with Article 39(2) of the Arbitration Rules. Therefore, the circumstances did not constitute a violation of statutory procedures in the arbitration process. Accordingly, the Court ruled to dismiss Sun's application.

Case 5: *J Company v. Fu and others*[8]

Fu and others were shareholders of a mining company, which held the exploration rights for a certain mine. In 2012, Fu and others signed the Equity Transfer Contract with J Company, stipulating that J Company would acquire partial equity in the mining company from Fu and others and take over full management of the mining company. In 2014, Fu and others, based on the arbitration clause in the Equity Transfer Contract, filed an arbitration application, claiming that after taking over the mining company, J Company failed to handle the renewal registration for the exploration rights, which led to the expiration and invalidation of two exploration rights owned by the mining company, thereby causing a severe devaluation of the mining company's equity. They requested the arbitral tribunal to order J Company to compensate for their losses totaling 140 million RMB. During the arbitration proceedings, J Company repeatedly applied to the arbitral tribunal for a suspension of the proceedings on the grounds that the administrative reconsideration concerning the invalidation of the involved exploration rights was still pending and no decision had been made. However, the arbitral tribunal decided not to suspend the arbitration proceedings and rendered an award. The award ruled in favor of Fu and others, supporting their claim on the grounds that J Company's failure to perform its contractual obligations resulted in the loss of the exploration rights.

---

statutory procedures. For arbitral awards rendered by the arbitration institution in accordance with the arbitration rules, the court shall not set them aside according to law. This case fully demonstrates the seriousness inherent in the rules and order of arbitration as a quasi-judicial process. It also exemplifies judicial support for the authority of arbitral tribunals in handling cases in accordance with the law and established rules, thereby reinforcing their social credibility.

[8] See the 10 Typical Cases for 2022 on Judicial Review of Domestic Arbitration published by the Beijing No. 4 Intermediate People's Court in July 2023. The Court respects the discretionary power of the arbitral tribunal, but the exercise of such power by the arbitration institution shall be limited by "not affecting the correct adjudication of the case." For arbitral awards that breach the "boundary of correct adjudication" and infringe upon the substantive rights of the parties, the court will provide relief to the lawful rights and interests of the parties by setting aside the award.

After the award was issued, J Company applied to the Beijing No.4 Intermediate People's Court to set aside the award, citing reasons including the arbitral tribunal's failure to suspend the proceedings, which constituted a violation of statutory procedures. During the court's proceedings, J Company submitted a reconsideration decision from the Ministry of Natural Resources, which revoked the invalidation of the involved exploration rights previously issued by the Provincial Department of Natural Resources, and the mining company's mineral resources exploration license was subsequently renewed. Upon reporting to and obtaining approval from the SPC, the Court ruled to set aside the involved arbitral award.

Case 6: *K Company v. Jiang*[9]

The M Arbitration Commission accepted the arbitration application on July 6, 2018, based on the application submitted by K Company, the arbitration clause in the Financial Lease Contract signed between K Company and the respondent Jiang on April 19, 2017, and the arbitration clause in the Joint Liability Guarantee Contract signed between K Company, Jiang, and Yan on April 19, 2017.

On November 22, 2018, the M Arbitration Commission rendered an award, which included the following rulings: (1) Jiang was to pay K Company the remaining rent of 188,341.2 RMB; (2) Jiang was to pay K Company a penalty of 5493.4 RMB calculated from October 21, 2017, to June 27, 2018, and a further penalty calculated from June 28, 2018, until the date of actual payment, based on the amount of 188,341.2 RMB at a daily rate of 0.05%; (3) Jiang was to pay K Company's attorney fees; (4) The arbitration fees for this case were to be borne by Jiang; (5) Yan was to assume joint and several liability for the payments Jiang was required to make to K Company under items (1) to (4) above; (6) K Company was entitled to priority in receiving compensation from the proceeds of the auction or sale of the tractor provided by Jiang as collateral, within the scope of items (1) to (4) of the award. Yan applied to the court to set aside item (5) of the award issued by the M Arbitration Commission, which required Yan to assume joint and several liability for the payments Jiang was required to make to the claimant under items (1) to (4) above.

The Beijing Financial Court held that the M Arbitration Commission's finding that Yan should bear joint and several guarantee liability to K Company was based on the Joint Liability Guarantee Contract. Although this contract contained an arbitration clause, a judicial appraisal conducted by a forensic appraisal center determined that the signature of "Yan" on the Joint Liability Guarantee Contract was not signed by Yan himself, and the fingerprint in the signature space for "Yan" was not impressed by him. Therefore, this case fell under the circumstances specified in Article 58(4) of the Arbitration Law (2017), where the evidence on which the award was based was forged. Consequently, as the signature and fingerprint of "Yan" on the Joint Liability Guarantee Contract were not his own, the contract was not binding on Yan. Accordingly, the Court set aside item (5) of the award issued by the M

[9] See the 10 Typical Cases on Judicial Review of Financial Arbitration published by the Beijing Financial Court in October 2023.

Arbitration Commission, namely the part requiring Yan to assume joint and several liability for the payments Jiang was required to make to K Company under items (1) to (4) above.

Case 7: *Zhang v. Nanchang L Culture Company*[10]

Zhang stated that around the end of July 2022, he received an enforcement notice from the Shanghai No.1 Intermediate People's Court, requiring him to pay Nanchang L Culture Company RMB 286,007.06. The basis for enforcement was the Award No. 20220259 rendered by the Xiamen Arbitration Commission on April 29, 2022. However, Zhang claimed he had no relationship whatsoever with Nanchang L Culture Company and had never had any prior contact or connection with them. The key evidence underlying the Xiamen Arbitration Commission's award, namely the Exclusive Anchor Cooperation Agency Agreement, was not signed by Zhang, nor had he received any so-called signing fee from Nanchang L Culture Company. Although the name of the payee's bank account in the agreement matched Zhang's name, the account number did not belong to him. The owner of that bank account was named Zhang, but their ID number was 422,823,197,410,232,366, which was completely different from Zhang's ID number. The contact phone number 13582612657 provided by Nanchang L Culture Company to the Xiamen Arbitration Commission was not Zhang's mobile number, which resulted in Zhang not receiving the hearing notice and arbitration documents, preventing him from participating in the hearing and losing the opportunity to defend himself. Therefore, Zhang argued that the evidence on which the arbitral award was based was forged. He requested the court to set aside the Award No. 20220259 rendered by the Xiamen Arbitration Commission. Nanchang L Culture Company stated that it was unclear about the situation described by Zhang. If the circumstances were true, then the case

[10] See the 10 Typical Cases on Judicial Review of Arbitration published by the Fujian Province Xiamen International Commercial Court in November 2023. This case is a judicial review case concerning an arbitral award, arising from a party's application to set aside the award. When hearing such cases, the court must prioritize the principle of efficiency in judicial review and carefully balance the conflict between the parties' procedural rights and judicial efficiency. In this case, Zhang claimed that the evidence on which the award was based was forged, on the grounds that he had never signed the involved contract. Unlike the substantive dispute over whether Zhang should bear contractual liability, the issue for review in this case was confined to whether the Agreement was signed by Zhang. The focus and standard of the court's review differed from those of the arbitral tribunal's review of the parties' substantive dispute. The former leaned towards a formal examination, while the latter should have conducted a substantive examination. Specifically, this case fully demonstrates the judicial value of both supporting and supervising arbitration in parallel. According to Article 104 of the Minutes on Foreign-Related Commercial and Maritime Trial Work, if an claimant applies to set aside an arbitral award and the court, upon review, finds circumstances warranting setting aside that could be remedied through a renewed arbitration, the court may notify the arbitral tribunal to conduct a renewed arbitration. In this case, the court issued a notice for renewed arbitration, providing the arbitral tribunal with a means to remedy procedural defects and preserve the award's validity. By allowing the arbitration institution to examine and determine the authenticity of the evidence based on substantive review standards, the court demonstrated that, in exercising its judicial supervisory power, it emphasizes both fairness and efficiency, safeguards the parties' lawful rights and interests, minimizes errors, and upholds the finality of arbitral awards.

might involve contract fraud, which should ultimately be adjudicated by the court according to law.

The Court found that the Xiamen Arbitration Commission accepted the contract dispute case between Nanchang L Culture Company and Zhang arising from the Exclusive Anchor Cooperation Agency Agreement and rendered an arbitral award in April 2022. The award ruled that Zhang should return the signing fee to Nanchang L Culture Company, pay a penalty, and bear the attorney fees and arbitration costs. Although the name of Party B's bank account in the involved agreement matched Zhang's name, a bank inquiry revealed that the citizen identity number of the account holder was inconsistent with Zhang's. Furthermore, the contact number for Zhang provided by Nanchang L Culture Company to the arbitral tribunal was not his personal mobile number. Zhang only learned of the arbitral award after receiving the court's enforcement notice.

The Court held that the evidence provided by Zhang indicated that his personal identity information might have been used by someone else to sign the involved contract with the respondent. Determining whether the signature and fingerprint on the contract were made by Zhang himself required an appraisal. To rectify the procedural issues in the arbitration, and considering the goals of saving litigation costs for the parties and resolving their dispute promptly, the court notified the arbitral tribunal to resume arbitration within a specified period and simultaneously suspended the setting-aside procedure. Subsequently, the arbitration commission resumed the arbitration proceedings, and the court therefore ruled to terminate the setting-aside procedure for this case.

Case 8: *LY Hotel v. JH Administration*[11]

In September 2020, LY Hotel and JH Administration entered into the House Lease Contract, under which LY Hotel leased premises from JH Administration for the period July 2020 to July 2025. A dispute later arose over rent, and the JH Administration filed an arbitration application with the Jinhua Arbitration Commission. The Commission ruled that the House Lease Contract had been terminated in August 2022 and ordered LY Hotel to pay the JH Administration outstanding rent, late fees, occupancy charges and unpaid utility bills. LY Hotel subsequently applied to the Zhejiang Province Jinhua Intermediate People's Court to set aside the award, alleging that the JH Administration had concealed evidence capable of affecting the impartiality of the award.

[11] (2023) Zhe 07 Min Te No. 58; See the 10 Typical Cases on Judicial Review of Commercial Arbitration published by the High People's Court of Zhejiang Province in November 2024. During the judicial review of arbitration, regarding the substantive handling of the arbitral award, the people's court should adhere to the principles of moderate and limited review. An arbitral award may only be set aside by ruling if the circumstances explicitly stipulated by law are met. In this case, the parties had signed an agreement regarding rent reduction, which was solely in the possession of the lessor who failed to voluntarily submit it to the arbitral tribunal. This constituted concealment of evidence sufficient to affect the impartiality of the award, meeting the circumstances for setting aside the arbitral award. The setting aside of the arbitral award in question not only upholds procedural justice but also safeguards the parties' lawful rights and interests in accordance with the law, thereby providing guidance for the review of similar cases.

The Zhejiang Province Jinhua Intermediate People's Court found that, during performance of the contract, the parties had signed an agreement providing for a six-month rent waiver for LY Hotel in respect of the 2022 COVID-19 period. JH Administration, however, neither referred to this fact nor produced the rent-waiver agreement during the arbitration.

The Court held that, since the dispute concerned the calculation of rent, both the rent-reduction policy and the rent-waiver agreement constituted key evidence going to the basic facts of the case and were exclusively within JH Administration's possession. By failing to produce that evidence, JH Administration had concealed evidence sufficient to affect the impartiality of the award. Accordingly, the ground for setting aside the award under Article 58(1)(v) of the Arbitration Law (2017) was established, and the Court ruled to set aside the arbitral award.

Case 9: *Li v. Wang*[12]
In January 2022, Li filed an arbitration application with an arbitration commission, relying on the Loan Contract signed with Wang, and claimed repayment of RMB one million. In August 2022, the arbitration commission rendered an award ordering Wang to repay the principal and interest to Li. Wang contended that the tribunal had overlooked the fact that the loan was used to finance gambling, had characterized the dispute as an ordinary civil loan, and had thereby violated public order and good morals. He applied to the Guizhou Province Guiyang Intermediate People's Court to set aside the award.

The Guizhou Province Guiyang Intermediate People's Court held that, as shown by the flow of funds, Li's younger sister, Li A, first transferred the money to Li, who then transferred it to Wang, who in turn transferred it back to Li A for the purchase of gambling chips. The evidence indicated that Li knew or should have known that his sister earned a living in Macao by lending money for gambling and taking a share of the profits. Accordingly, the Court found that the RMB one million was, in fact, gambling capital provided by Li A to Wang. The alleged loan from Li to Wang was inconsistent with common sense and with the parties' previous transaction practices; the underlying legally valid loan did not exist. Because all parties were aware that the money would be used for gambling, and gambling violated the public order and good morals of the mainland, the funds were not entitled to legal protection. The Court therefore ruled to set aside the arbitral award rendered by the arbitration commission.

Case 10: *A Company v. B Company and others*[13]
In July 2022, the Chengdu Arbitration Commission accepted a dispute over equity transfers among B Company, C Company, and other parties and rendered an award. After the award was issued, A Company, which held 40% of B Company's shares, applied in its own name to the court to set aside the arbitral award.

---

[12] (2023) Qian 01 Min Te No. 54; See the 10 Typical Cases on Judicial Review of Arbitration published by the SPC in January 2024.

[13] See the 9 Typical Cases on Judicial Review of Arbitration published by the Sichuan Province Chengdu Intermediate People's Court in May 2025. This case involves the issue of whether, in

The Sichuan Province Chengdu Intermediate People's Court held that, on the one hand, according to the provisions of Article 58 of the Arbitration Law (2017), the claimant for setting aside an arbitral award must be a party to the arbitration case. In this case, A Company was not a party to the arbitration case; it filed the application on behalf of B Company in its capacity as a shareholder of B Company, which did not comply with the aforementioned legal provisions. On the other hand, there was a clear distinction between civil and commercial litigation and judicial review. The shareholder derivative action system was not applicable to cases involving judicial review of arbitration. In terms of the subject of review, cases for setting aside arbitral awards differed from ordinary civil litigation procedures. They did not involve substantive examination of acts infringing upon the company's rights and interests or the identification of liable parties, but only reviewed whether the arbitral award fell under the statutory grounds for revocation. Regarding the underlying purpose of the systems, the shareholder derivative action system aimed to pursue claims against parties responsible for infringing upon the company's rights and interests, while the judicial review system for arbitration aimed to exercise judicial supervisory power, ensuring the procedural legality and fairness of the arbitral award and that it did not violate public interests. In summary, A Company lacked standing to apply for setting aside the arbitral award. Accordingly, the Court dismissed Company A's application.

Case 11: ***Lai v. O Real Estate Company***[14]

In 2016, O Real Estate Company and P Culture Company entered into the Lease Agreement. During the performance of the contract, a dispute arose between the two parties. P Culture Company filed for arbitration against O Real Estate Company as the respondent before an arbitration commission. After the arbitral award was rendered, Lai, a non-party to the case, applied to the people's court to set aside the aforementioned arbitral award, claiming to be a de facto shareholder of O Real Estate Company. Upon review, the court held that since Lai was not a party to the arbitration case, he lacked the standing to apply for setting aside the arbitral award. Consequently, the court dismissed Lai's action.

---

judicial review cases concerning arbitration, and claimant can reference the provisions on shareholder derivative lawsuits to apply for setting aside an arbitral award made against the company in the shareholder's own name. This case, analyzing from the perspectives of the scope of review and institutional purposes of the judicial review system for arbitration and the shareholder derivative lawsuit system, as well as the relationship between them, ultimately determined that if a shareholder files an application to set aside an arbitral award in their own name, the people's court shall dismiss it.

[14] See the 10 Typical Cases on Judicial Review of Domestic Arbitration published by the Beijing No. 4 Intermediate People's Court in July 2023. The party entitled to apply to the people's court for setting aside an arbitral award is limited to the parties to the arbitration; a non-party lacks the standing to apply for setting aside an arbitral award.

Case 12: ***AC Company v. BC Company***[15]
In March 2023, BC Company initiated arbitration proceedings before the CIETAC Sichuan Sub-branch, relying on the arbitration clause contained in the Integrated Logistics Services Agreement concluded between BC Company and AC Company. In December 2023, CIETAC Sichuan Sub-branch issued an arbitral award in the name of CIETAC. Subsequently, AC Company applied to the Sichuan Province Chengdu Intermediate People's Court to set aside the award, alleging that the circumstances specified in Article 58(1)(iii) of the Arbitration Law (2017) had been met.

The Sichuan Province Chengdu Intermediate People's Court held that Article 58(1) of the Arbitration Law (2017) stipulated that a party could apply to the intermediate people's court where the arbitration commission was located to set aside an award. Article 2(3) of the CIETAC Arbitration Rules provided that the CIETAC was based in Beijing, and its branch offices or arbitration centers were its branch offices, which, under the authorization of the CIETAC, accepted arbitration applications and administered arbitration cases. In this case, the CIETAC Sichuan Sub-Commission was a branch office of CIETAC. It could not render an award in its own name and did not possess the status of an independent arbitration entity. The involved arbitral award was issued in the name of CIETAC. Therefore, AC Company should have applied to set aside the award at the intermediate people's court where CIETAC was located. The Sichuan Province Chengdu Intermediate People's Court lacked jurisdiction over the case. Accordingly, the Court ruled to dismiss AC Company's action.

Case 13: ***R Technology Company v. S Electronics Company***[16]
In 2015, S Electronics Company and T Company entered into the Electronic Products Service Contract. Later, T Company underwent a transfer, and on January 5, 2018, its corporate name was changed to R Technology Company. Its legal representative was changed from Ye to Lin, and its registered address was also updated. All of these changes were registered and publicly disclosed with the company registration authority. In October 2018, S Electronics Company, relying on the arbitration clause in the Electronic Products Service Contract signed with T Company,

[15] See the 9 Typical Cases on Judicial Review of Arbitration published by the Sichuan Province Chengdu Intermediate People's Court in May 2025.

[16] See the 10 Typical Cases for 2022 on Judicial Review of Domestic Arbitration published by the Beijing No.4 Intermediate People's Court in July 2023. Rendering an award without proper service substantially deprives the respondent in the arbitration of the opportunity to present its case to the arbitral tribunal, infringes upon the procedural rights of the arbitration parties, may affect the correct adjudication of the case, and infringes upon the substantive rights and interests of the parties. The arbitration rules of various arbitration institutions typically include "the addressee's last known address" as a fallback provision for confirming the service address. However, given that China's legal system adopts the principle of service by the institution, where the arbitration institution, not the parties, is the subject responsible for effecting service, the arbitration institution bears the obligation to conduct necessary examination and verification of service information to protect the procedural rights of the party being served. Otherwise, it constitutes a violation of the arbitration procedure.

filed an arbitration application with the arbitration commission, naming T Company as the respondent. The arbitration commission sent arbitration-related documents by express mail to the address provided by S Electronics Company, which was T Company's former registered address. The documents were returned by the postal service with the note "no such person at this address, phone unreachable." Thereafter, S Electronics Company confirmed that this address was the last known business address, registered address, domicile, and correspondence address of T Company, and requested notarized service. All subsequent arbitration documents were then served by notarized delivery to the former address of T Company.

In 2019, the arbitral tribunal issued an award in favor of S Electronics Company's claims. Following the issuance of the award, S Electronics Company applied to the people's court for enforcement. In 2021, R Technology Company learned of the arbitration proceedings and applied to the court to set aside the arbitral award. Upon review, the People's Court determined that the service procedure in the arbitration had violated the arbitration rules and ruled to set aside the arbitral award.

Article 72
A party seeking to apply for setting aside an arbitral award shall submit such application within three months from the date of receipt of the award.

Notes

In the procedure for setting aside an arbitral award, the parties' right to apply for setting aside the award is strictly limited by a statutory time limit. According to the original Article 59 of the Arbitration Law (2017), the time limit for a party to apply for setting aside an arbitral award was 6 months; whereas the New Arbitration Law has shortened this time limit to 3 months. This provision applies to all applications for setting aside an arbitral award based on the New Arbitration Law and is a fundamental prerequisite for initiating the procedure.

This three-month period is legally characterized as a fixed period, to which the rules regarding suspension, interruption, or extension of the limitation of action do not apply. The party must submit the application for setting aside within 3 months from the day following the receipt of the award. If the application is filed after the expiration of this period, the people's court shall rule to dismiss the application and will not conduct a substantive review of the grounds for setting aside.

This period aligns with the core value of "efficiency and expediency" in the arbitration system. Arbitration follows the principle of finality, and the legal effect of an award should be determined promptly after it becomes effective, to prevent parties from abusing the setting aside procedure to delay the performance of obligations. The three-month period reserves reasonable time for parties to collect information and prepare the application, while also effectively preventing instability in the effectiveness of the award due to the untimely exercise of rights.

Regarding the commencement of the time limit, it should be calculated from the date the party actually receives the award, not the date the award is made or the date the arbitration institution dispatches it. If a party collects the award directly from the arbitration institution, the date of collection is deemed the date of receipt; if the arbitration institution serves the award by mail, the date the party signs for the mail is deemed the date of receipt (regardless of whether it is actually opened, signing is considered service); if the party refuses to accept it and the arbitration institution serves it by public announcement in accordance with the law, the date the announcement period expires is deemed the date of receipt. After receiving the award, if a party believes there are statutory grounds for setting aside, it should promptly prepare relevant evidence and file the application within the statutory time limit to avoid losing the right to relief due to delay.

Illustrative Case

Li and others v. Ma and others[17]

In this case, the Court held that the claimants, Li and Zhou, applied to set aside a non-foreign-related arbitral award rendered by a domestic arbitration institution in mainland China. Arbitration is an independent legal pathway for dispute resolution, whose fundamental value orientation is to respect party autonomy and resolve disputes promptly and efficiently. Judicial review of arbitration should and must fully respect the authority and efficiency of arbitration. Therefore, Article 59 of the Arbitration Law (2017) stipulated that a party applying to set aside an arbitral award must file the application within 6 months from the date of receiving the award. Article 8 of the Arbitration Judicial Review Provisions stipulated that if a people's court discovered after case-filing that the application did not meet the acceptance conditions, it shall dismiss the application. According to the aforementioned provisions, a party's application to set aside an arbitral award must be filed within the statutory period. If the application was filed after the expiry of the statutory period, the court should not accept the case; if the court discovered after case-filing that the acceptance conditions were not met, it should rule to dismiss the application.

The court held that in this case, after the Beijing Arbitration Commission rendered the award, it served the award on Li and Zhou on February 13, 2020, via notarized delivery (ordinary mail delivery). The delivery addresses were both in Heilongjiang Province, which were consistent with the addresses stated in the application for setting aside the arbitral award submitted by Li and Zhou, a married couple. This address was also the registered domicile address stated on Li′s valid identity card. Although Li and Zhou denied receiving the said award, the delivery procedure of the arbitral award complied with the arbitration rules and should be deemed as a valid service. An application to the court to set aside an arbitral award should be filed within 6 months of receiving the arbitral award. An application filed after this period did not meet the acceptance conditions of the people's court, and this statutory time limit was not subject to suspension or interruption. As the time when Li and Zhou filed the application to set aside the award had significantly exceeded the six-month statutory period, their application was dismissed.

[17] (2025) Jing 74 Min Te No. 104.

Article 73

The people's court shall, within two months from the date of accepting an application for setting aside an arbitral award, rule to set aside the award or to dismiss the application.

Notes

This Article establishes a mandatory provision regarding the time limit for the court's review of applications to set aside arbitral awards. It aims to prevent prolonged court reviews that leave arbitral awards in a state of uncertain validity for extended periods, while also reserving sufficient time for the court to conduct a substantive review, thereby ensuring the quality of judicial supervision.

The two-month time limit commences from the date the people's court formally accepts the application to set aside the award, not from the date the party submits the application. In practice, the court must first conduct a "formal review" of the application materials (such as whether the claimant is a party to the arbitration, whether the application was filed within three months, whether the court has proper jurisdiction, and whether the materials are complete). Only if the application meets the acceptance conditions will the court issue a "Case Acceptance Notice," and the time limit starts from the "acceptance date" indicated in this notice.

After conducting its review, the court must issue a ruling within two months: If the court finds the party's application unfounded, it will issue a ruling dismissing the application. The original arbitral award maintains its legal effect, and the parties must enforce it. If the court finds the party's grounds for the application valid, it will issue a ruling to set aside the award. The original arbitral award thereby loses its legal effect. The parties may then apply for arbitration based on a renewed arbitration agreement between them, or directly file a lawsuit with the People's Court.

However, attention must be paid to the re-arbitration procedure stipulated in Article 74 of the New Arbitration Law. During the court's review of the application to set aside the award, if the court considers it possible for the arbitral tribunal to conduct a re-arbitration, it shall notify the arbitral tribunal to conduct a re-arbitration within a specified time limit. In this scenario, the court shall rule to suspend the setting-aside procedure. If the arbitral tribunal commences re-arbitration, the court shall subsequently issue a separate ruling to terminate the setting-aside procedure. If the arbitral tribunal refuses to conduct re-arbitration, the court shall rule to resume the setting-aside procedure and, based on the circumstances of the case, decide whether to set aside the award.

Illustrative Case

YH Company v. ZH Company and others[18]

In December 2021, the M Arbitration Commission rendered an arbitral award ordering Chongqing A Hospital to pay ZH Company compensation for suspension losses,

[18] (2022) Yu 01 Min Te No. 104; See the 10 Typical Cases on Judicial Review of Arbitration published by the SPC in January 2024. The entity entitled to apply to the Intermediate People's Court of the place where the arbitration commission is located to set aside an arbitral award is limited to "parties." This case strictly adhered to the aforementioned provision of the Arbitration Law, clarifying that a non-party lacks the standing to apply for setting aside an arbitral award.

among other claims. In that arbitration case, the claimant was ZH Company and the respondent was Chongqing A Hospital. In March 2022, YH Company, as a non-party to the case, applied to the Chongqing First Intermediate People's Court to set aside the aforementioned arbitral award, citing the following grounds: first, the matters decided in the award exceeded the scope of the arbitration agreement; second, ZH Company and Chongqing A Hospital had colluded maliciously, leading to an erroneous arbitral award that infringed upon the legitimate rights and interests of YH Company.

The Chongqing No.1 Intermediate People's Court held that this was a case concerning an application to set aside a domestic arbitral award, and the examination of whether the claimant in this case was a proper party should be conducted pursuant to Article 58 of the Arbitration Law (2017). According to this article, only the parties to the arbitration case could apply to set aside an arbitral award. The term "parties" here referred to the claimant or the respondent in the arbitration case. The claimant in this case, YH Company, was neither the claimant nor the respondent in the relevant arbitration case. As a non-party, it lacked the standing to apply to set aside the arbitral award, and its application to set aside the arbitral award should therefore be dismissed. If YH Company believed that the arbitral award in question was erroneous and had harmed its legitimate rights and interests, it could, in accordance with the Arbitral Award Enforcement Provisions, apply to the people's court for a ruling not to enforce the said arbitral award. Accordingly, the Court ruled to dismiss YH Company's application.

Article 74

Where, after accepting an application for setting aside an arbitral award, the people's court considers that the case may be re-arbitrated by the arbitral tribunal, it shall notify the tribunal of re-arbitrating the case within a certain time limit and shall rule to stay the setting-aside procedure. If the arbitral tribunal begins to re-arbitrate, the people's court shall rule to terminate the setting-aside procedure. If the arbitral tribunal refuses to re-arbitrate the case, the people's court shall rule to resume the setting-aside procedure.

Notes

Resumption of arbitration is a special relief mechanism within the arbitration system. From the perspective of international practice, resumption of arbitration is primarily divided into two types: first, resumption of arbitration conducted after an arbitral award has been set aside; second, resumption of arbitration conducted by the arbitral tribunal upon notification by the court during the procedure for setting aside the award. The former involves the continuation of proceedings after an award is set aside, while the latter belongs to an intermediate relief arrangement within the process of judicial supervision. This Article pertains to the latter.

The resumption of the arbitration procedure stipulated in this Article is a special procedure within the setting-aside procedure. It refers to the situation where, after the people's court accepts an application to set aside an award, if it considers that the case can be referred back to the arbitral tribunal for resumption of arbitration, it notifies the arbitral tribunal to resume arbitration within a specified time limit and rules to suspend the setting-aside procedure. Since the provisions of the New Arbitration Law on resumption of arbitration are relatively principle-based and lack specific operational details, this has led to divergences in judicial practice and theoretical understanding. To address this, some courts have issued guiding opinions, such as the Provisions on Issues Concerning the People's Court's Notification of Resumption of Arbitration published by the High People's Court of Shanghai, which clarifies specific circumstances under which arbitration may be resumed: violation of statutory procedures in the arbitration proceedings; the evidence on which the award is based is forged (limited to domestic arbitration); the opposing party conceals evidence sufficient to affect the impartiality of the award (limited to domestic arbitration); the arbitral award involves "ultra petita" or "omitted adjudication."

The circumstances for resumption of arbitration stipulated in the Arbitration Law Interpretation include forgery of evidence and withholding of evidence, but these circumstances are not an exhaustive list; resumption of arbitration may also occur under other circumstances. Under certain conditions, the court may consider that the setting-aside procedure is an extremely severe negative procedure in terms of both degree and consequence. Where the arbitration procedure and award can be remedied in some way, the arbitral tribunal can be given the opportunity to rectify the procedural defects, thereby achieving a better balance between arbitration procedural defects and the finality of the arbitral award. Consequently, the court may choose to remand the case to the arbitral tribunal for resumption of arbitration, allowing it to re-examine the relevant procedural and substantive issues. From this perspective, resumption of arbitration is similar to remand for a new trial in litigation. However, resumption of arbitration is not equivalent to remand for a new trial in the litigation system, because the arbitral tribunal has its own judgment on whether to resume arbitration and may disagree with resuming it, a discretion which does not exist in the context of a remand for a new trial in litigation. If the arbitral tribunal commences the resumed arbitration within the time limit designated by the people's court, the people's court shall rule to terminate the setting-aside procedure; if it does not commence the resumed arbitration, the people's court shall rule to resume the setting-aside procedure.

Regarding procedural operation, the court's issuance of a notice for resumption of arbitration directly leads to the suspension of the setting-aside procedure. According to the judicial interpretation, the decision-making power on whether to resume arbitration lies with the arbitral tribunal: the arbitral tribunal can either accept the court's suggestion and initiate resumed arbitration or refuse to resume arbitration. If the arbitral tribunal refuses, the people's court shall rule to resume the setting-aside procedure and continue the judicial review of the award. If the arbitral tribunal commences the resumed arbitration, the people's court shall rule to terminate the setting-aside procedure. This is also the new wording added to this Article in the New Arbitration Law.

If a party is dissatisfied with the award rendered upon resumption of arbitration, it may, according to the provisions of Article 23 of the Arbitration Law Interpretation, apply to the people's court for setting aside within the prescribed time limit from the date of service of the resumption of the arbitral award. This reflects the judiciary's continuous supervision over the resumption of the arbitration procedure, ensuring a balance between arbitration fairness and the protection of parties' rights.

Overall, the system of resumption of arbitration serves as a bridge between safeguarding the efficiency of arbitration and maintaining procedural fairness. The consequence of setting aside an award is that the award's validity is void *ab initio*, and all previously conducted arbitration proceedings are rendered futile. If the defects in the award are only partial and remediable (for instance, certain non-core procedural defects or the inadvertent failure to adjudicate a minor claim), then completely setting aside the entire award undoubtedly constitutes a significant waste of procedural resources. The resumption of the arbitration system allows the arbitral tribunal to rectify the issues based on the original proceedings, rather than starting over from scratch, which greatly conserves judicial and arbitration resources and aligns with the principle of procedural economy. Furthermore, modern arbitration philosophy emphasizes that judicial supervision of arbitration should be supportive rather than interventionist. When defects arise in an award, the entity most familiar with the case details and most professionally capable of correcting them is the very arbitral tribunal that rendered the award. The court's power to remand the case for resumption of arbitration under specific circumstances is an embodiment of this philosophy. It acknowledges the arbitral tribunal as the preferred expert for dispute resolution, with the judiciary providing remedial channels only when necessary, thus avoiding the invalidation of the entire dispute resolution outcome due to minor defects and actively upholding the efficiency of the arbitration system.

Illustrative Case

BJ Company v. Zhou and others[19]

On July 25, 2022, the N Arbitration Commission rendered an arbitral award. BJ Company applied to the Jiangsu Province Nanjing Intermediate People's Court to set aside the arbitral award, arguing that the opposing parties, Zhou and Lu, had concealed bank transfer records dated before September 2017. This concealment allegedly prevented the arbitral tribunal from ascertaining the fact that the two individuals had obtained loans from financial institutions and subsequently engaged in relending the obtained funds, which was sufficient to affect the fairness of the ruling.

The Jiangsu Province Nanjing Intermediate People's Court obtained bank transfer vouchers of Zhou and others, and discovered that Zhou had indeed obtained bank funds and engaged in relending. The evidence concealed by Zhou was sufficient to affect a fair ruling. The Court held that the case could be reconsidered by the arbitral tribunal. Accordingly, it suspended the setting-aside proceedings and notified the N Arbitration Commission to resume the arbitration. Subsequently, the arbitration commission notified the parties to resume the arbitration and informed the Court in writing of the hearing notice. The Court then ruled to terminate the setting-aside proceedings. The parties involved reached a mediation agreement during the resumed arbitration process.

---

[19] (2022) Su 01 Min Te No. 212; See the 10 Typical Cases on Judicial Review of Commercial Arbitration published by the High People's Court of Jiangsu Province in July 2024.

Chapter 6
Enforcement

Article 75
The parties shall perform the arbitral award. Where a party fails to perform the arbitral award, the other party may apply to the people's court for enforcement in accordance with the relevant provisions of the Civil Procedure Law of the People's Republic of China. The people's court where the enforcement is sought shall enforce the award.

Notes
The ultimate purpose for parties in choosing arbitration is not merely to obtain a document, but to realize their lawful rights and interests through it. Compliance with an arbitral award is, first and foremost, a statutory obligation. When the obligated party refuses to perform voluntarily, the prevailing party may apply to a people's court for compulsory enforcement. Through a series of enforcement measures available to the court, including sealing up, seizure, freezing, and transfer of assets, imposition of consumption restrictions, and inclusion on the list of dishonest persons subject to enforcement, the court can effectively compel or even substitute for the judgment debtor in fulfilling the obligations. This ensures that the substantive outcome of an award, rendered by the arbitral tribunal following a fair procedure, can be genuinely realized.

Internationally, courts generally can confer compulsory enforceability upon awards and enforce them through three primary methods: first, by enforcing them in the same manner as a court judgment; second, by rendering a judgment based on the arbitral award and then enforcing it[1]; or third, by declaring the award enforceable and then enforcing it.[2] Courts enforce effective arbitral awards in accordance with the execution procedures prescribed by the civil procedure law. If a party is unable

[1] For example, Sections 66(1) and (2) of the UK Arbitration Act 1996.
[2] For example, Section 1060(1) of the German Arbitration Act 1998.

Y. Lin, *New Arbitration Law in China*, China Arbitration Yearbook,
https://doi.org/10.1007/978-981-92-0642-1_6

to have the arbitral award set aside through the setting-aside procedure, the arbitral award can be enforced within the country.

On March 1, 2018, the SPC issued the Arbitral Award Enforcement Provisions for cases where parties apply to people's courts for the enforcement of arbitral awards or arbitration mediation statements made by arbitration institutions in accordance with the Arbitration Law (2017). Only the main content partially relevant to this Article is excerpted here; other relevant content will be discussed together in Article 76 of the New Arbitration Law.

1. **Competent Courts**

In principle, applications for the enforcement of arbitral awards or arbitration mediation statements made by arbitration institutions shall fall under the jurisdiction of the intermediate people's court of the place where the person subject to enforcement has their domicile or where the property subject to enforcement is located. Under the following conditions and upon approval by a higher-level people's court, the intermediate people's court may designate a basic people's court to exercise jurisdiction: first, the amount of the subject matter of enforcement conforms to the level-based jurisdiction acceptance scope of the basic people's court for first-instance civil and commercial cases; second, the domicile of the person subject to enforcement or the location of the property subject to enforcement is within the jurisdiction of the designated basic people's court.

If the person subject to enforcement or a non-party applies for non-enforcement of the arbitral award in an enforcement case, the intermediate people's court responsible for enforcement shall separately file the case for review and handling; if the enforcement case has been assigned to a basic people's court for jurisdiction, it shall, within three days of receiving the application for non-enforcement, transfer the case to the original enforcement court for separate filing and review.

2. **Grounds for Dismissing the Action**

If the content of an arbitral award or arbitration mediation statement falls under any of the following circumstances, rendering enforcement impossible, the people's court may rule to dismiss the enforcement application; if it renders partial enforcement impossible, the court may rule to dismiss that part of the enforcement application; if it renders partial enforcement impossible and that part is indivisible from the rest, the court may rule to dismiss the enforcement application:

A. The subject of rights and obligations is unclear;
B. The specific amount of monetary payment is unclear, or the calculation method is unclear, making it impossible to determine the specific amount;
C. The specific property to be delivered is unclear or cannot be determined;
D. The standard, object, or scope of performance of an act is unclear.

If an arbitral award or arbitration mediation statement only determines the continued performance of a contract but does not specify the specific content of the rights and obligations to be performed, as well as the method and time limit for performance, etc., resulting in the impossibility of enforcement, it shall be handled in accordance with the preceding paragraph.

3. **Correction or Clarification of the Award**

If there are clerical or calculation errors in the main text of the arbitral award or the arbitration mediation statement, or if there are matters already determined by the arbitral tribunal but omitted from the main text of the award, which can be corrected or clarified, the people's court shall notify the arbitral tribunal in writing to make the correction or clarification, or shall consult the arbitration case file from the arbitration institution to ascertain the relevant facts. If the arbitral tribunal neither makes corrections nor provides clarification, and the enforceable content remains unclear and specific after the people's court has consulted the arbitration case file, making enforcement impossible, the court may rule to dismiss the enforcement application.

4. **Suspension of Enforcement**

If the person subject to enforcement applies to set aside the arbitral award and the application has been accepted by a people's court, or if the person subject to enforcement or a non-party applies for non-enforcement of the arbitral award in the enforcement case and provides appropriate security, the enforcement court shall rule to suspend enforcement. During the period of suspension of enforcement, the people's court shall cease dispositive measures, unless the enforcement claimant provides full and effective security and requests continued enforcement; before the sealing, distraint, or freezing period for the subject matter of enforcement expires, the people's court may, based on a party's application or on its own authority, handle procedures for continuing the sealing, distraint, or freezing.

5. **Property Preservation Measures**

During the judicial review period of cases involving applications to set aside an arbitral award or for non-enforcement of an arbitral award, if a party or a non-party applies for preservation measures against property other than that which is already sealed, distrained, or frozen, the people's court responsible for the review shall handle the matter with reference to Article 100 of the Civil Procedure Law. If enforcement still needs to continue after the judicial review, the preservation measures shall automatically convert into sealing, distraint, or freezing measures in the enforcement; if the people's court that imposed the preservation measures is different from the enforcement court, the preservation formalities shall be transferred to the enforcement court, and the preservation ruling shall be deemed as a ruling made by the enforcement court.

If a people's court rules to set aside an arbitral award or rules not to enforce an arbitral award based on the application of the person subject to enforcement, and the original person subject to enforcement applies for execution restitution or for the lifting of compulsory enforcement measures, the people's court shall support the application. If the original enforcement claimant applies for preservation of the money or property that has already been performed or compulsorily enforced by the people's court, the people's court shall permit it in accordance with the law; if the original enforcement claimant, within 30 days from the date the people's court adopted the preservation measures, fails to apply for arbitration anew based on a written arbitration agreement reached by both parties or to file a lawsuit with the people's court, the people's court shall rule to lift the preservation.

6. **Time Limit for Non-Enforcement Applications**

If a person subject to enforcement applies to the people's court for non-enforcement of an arbitral award, a written application shall be submitted within 15 days from the date of service of the enforcement notice; if there are circumstances specified in Article 237 of the Civil Procedure Law and the enforcement procedure has not yet concluded, the written application shall be submitted within 15 days from the date the party knew or should have known of the relevant facts or case.

If, before the expiry of the time limit specified in the preceding paragraph of this Article, the person subject to enforcement has applied to a competent people's court to set aside the arbitral award and the application has been accepted, the time limit shall be recalculated from the effective date of the court document rejecting the application to set aside the arbitral award.

If the person subject to enforcement or a non-party applies for non-enforcement of the arbitral award in the enforcement case after the expiry of the time limit, the people's court shall rule not to accept the application; if the application has already been accepted, the court shall rule to dismiss the application for non-enforcement.

7. **Non-Party Application for Non-Enforcement**

A non-party applying to the people's court for non-enforcement of an arbitral award or an arbitration mediation statement shall submit an application and evidence materials proving the validity of their claim, and shall meet the following conditions:

A. There is evidence proving that the parties in the arbitration case maliciously applied for arbitration or engaged in false arbitration, harming the legitimate rights and interests of the non-party.
B. The subject matter of enforcement involving the legitimate rights and interests claimed by the non-party has not yet reached the conclusion of enforcement;
C. The application is submitted within 30 days from the date the non-party knew or should have known that the people's court had taken enforcement measures against the subject matter.

8. **Court Hearing Procedure**

The people's court hearing a case concerning non-enforcement of an arbitral award shall form a collegial panel to review the grounds raised by the person subject to enforcement and the application of the non-party; grounds not raised by the person subject to enforcement shall not be reviewed, except where the arbitral award may violate public interest.

When the person subject to enforcement or a non-party applies for non-enforcement of the arbitral award in the enforcement case, the people's court shall conduct an inquiry; if the person subject to enforcement raises other grounds for non-enforcement before the conclusion of the inquiry, these shall be reviewed together. During the review, if the people's court deems it necessary, it may request the arbitral tribunal to provide an explanation or consult the arbitration case file from the arbitration institution.

The people's court's review of a case concerning non-enforcement of an arbitral award shall be completed and a ruling made within 2 months from the date of case filing; under special circumstances requiring an extension, the period may be extended by 1 month upon approval by the president of the court.

Article 76

Where the party against whom the enforcement is sought presents evidence which proves that the arbitral award involves one of the circumstances set forth in paragraph 1 of Article 71 of this Law, the people's court shall, after examination and verification by a collegial panel formed by the people's court, rule not to enforce the award.

Where the people's court finds that the enforcement of an award violates the public interest, it shall rule not to enforce it.

Notes

This Article concerns the non-enforcement of an arbitral award. For an award, non-enforcement and setting aside produce similar effects, namely, a negative assessment of the award. There have historically been differing views on the necessity of maintaining this dual-track system. One perspective argues that since the effects and the grounds for raising objections are the same, only one system should be retained. However, another viewpoint supports the coexistence of both systems, contending that the non-enforcement system provides a necessary remedy for respondents who did not participate in the setting-aside procedure. Applying to set aside an award is subject to a strict three-month time limit (Article 72 of the New Arbitration Law), and the initiative lies with the parties. The respondent may fail to apply for setting aside within the statutory time limit for various reasons (such as not becoming aware of their rights promptly, strategic considerations, or objective obstacles). When the prevailing party applies for compulsory enforcement after the expiry of the setting-aside period, the non-enforcement system offers the respondent another crucial opportunity for judicial review, ensuring they do not lose the right to challenge fundamental defects merely due to the passage of procedural time limits.

It should be recognized that, from a practical standpoint, the two procedures indeed possess distinct procedural values. The setting-aside procedure is an independent legal action, whereas the non-enforcement review is embedded within the enforcement proceedings. Their procedural nature, urgency, and focus differ. Non-enforcement review directly concerns whether state coercive power should be employed; its examination is more targeted, focusing on whether the award is "enforceable." For certain defects that only become apparent when the respondent raises a defense, the non-enforcement system provides a more contextually appropriate opportunity for rebuttal within the enforcement framework.

This Article explicitly lists six circumstances under which enforcement may be refused. If a party presents evidence proving the existence of any of the aforementioned circumstances, and the people's court, after forming a collegial bench to review and verify the evidence, confirms its validity, the court shall issue a ruling refusing enforcement of the award. Additionally, consistent with the court's considerations when setting aside an award, if the award "violates public policy," the court may, on its own initiative, set aside the award without requiring a party's application. For a discussion of the various circumstances, refer to Article 71.

1. **The Award Deals with Matters Not Falling within the Scope of the Arbitration Agreement or Matters which the Arbitration Institution Has no Power to Arbitrate**

If, upon examination by the people's court, any of the following circumstances is verified to be true, it shall be determined as "the award deals with matters not falling within the scope of the arbitration agreement or matters which the arbitration institution has no power to arbitrate" under Article 237(2)(2) of the Civil Procedure Law:

(1) The matters dealt with by the award exceed the scope of the arbitration agreement;
(2) The matters dealt with by the award are non-arbitrable matters as provided by law or the arbitration rules chosen by the parties;
(3) The content of the award exceeds the scope of the parties' arbitration claims;
(4) The arbitration institution that rendered the award is not the one agreed upon in the arbitration agreement.

2. **The Composition of the Arbitral Tribunal or the Arbitration Procedure Violates Statutory Procedures**

If the arbitration procedure violates the provisions of the New Arbitration Law, the arbitration rules chosen by the parties, or the special agreement of the parties on the arbitration procedure, and such violation may affect the fair rendering of the award, and upon examination by the people's court, the circumstance is verified to be true, it shall be determined as "the composition of the arbitral tribunal or the arbitration procedure violates statutory procedures" under item (3) of paragraph 2 of Article 237 of the Civil Procedure Law.

If a party claims that it was unable to participate in the arbitration due to failure to serve legal documents in the manner prescribed by the New Arbitration Law or the arbitration rules, or that an arbitrator should have recused themselves according to the New Arbitration Law or the arbitration rules but did not, and such circumstance may affect the fair rendering of the award, and upon examination, the claim is verified to be true, the people's court shall uphold the claim. If the arbitral tribunal served arbitration legal documents in accordance with the New Arbitration Law, the arbitration rules, or the method agreed upon by the parties, and the party claims that such service does not comply with the relevant provisions on service in the Civil Procedure Law, the people's court shall not uphold the claim.

If the applicable arbitration procedure or arbitration rules were specifically highlighted, and the party knew or should have known that the statutory arbitration procedure or the chosen arbitration rules were not complied with, but still participated or continued to participate in the arbitration proceedings without raising an objection, and then applies for non-enforcement of the arbitral award on the ground of violation of statutory procedures after the arbitral award is rendered, the people's court shall not uphold the claim.

3. **The Evidence on which the Award Is Based Is Forged**

The people's court shall determine a circumstance as "the evidence on which the award is based is forged" under item (4) of paragraph 2 of Article 237 of the Civil Procedure Law, if all the following conditions are met:

A. The evidence has been admitted by the arbitral award;
B. The evidence is a major piece of evidence for determining the basic facts of the case;
C. Upon investigation, the evidence is indeed formed or obtained through illegal means such as fabrication, alteration, or provision of false testimony, violating the requirements of objectivity, relevance, and legality of evidence.

4. **Concealment of Evidence Sufficient to Affect the Impartiality of the Award**

The people's court shall determine a circumstance as "the opposing party concealed evidence from the arbitration institution sufficient to affect the impartiality of the award" under item (5) of paragraph 2 of Article 237 of the Civil Procedure Law, if all the following conditions are met:

A. The evidence is a major piece of evidence for determining the basic facts of the case;
B. The evidence was solely in the possession of the opposing party but was not submitted to the arbitral tribunal;
C. During the arbitration proceedings, the party became aware of the existence of this evidence and requested the opposing party to produce it or petitioned the arbitral tribunal to order its submission, but the opposing party, without justifiable reason, failed to produce or submit it.

If a party conceals evidence in its own possession during the arbitration proceedings, and after the arbitral award is rendered, applies for non-enforcement of the arbitral award on the grounds that the evidence it concealed was sufficient to affect the impartiality of the award, the people's court shall not uphold the claim.

5. **Public Policy**

If a person against whom enforcement is sought applies for non-enforcement of an arbitration mediation statement or an arbitral award made based on a settlement agreement or mediation agreement between the parties, the people's court shall not uphold the application, except where such arbitration mediation statement or arbitral award violates public policy.

6. **Multiple Grounds**

If a person against whom enforcement is sought applies for non-enforcement of an arbitral award, they must assert all multiple grounds for non-enforcement of the same arbitral award simultaneously. If an application for non-enforcement of an arbitral award is rejected by a ruling, and a subsequent application is filed, the people's court shall not review it, except where there is new evidence proving the existence of circumstances specified in items (4) or (6) of paragraph 2 of Article 237 of the Civil Procedure Law.

7. **Application for Non-Enforcement by a Non-Party**

If a non-party or outsider applies for non-enforcement of an arbitral award or an arbitration mediation statement, and the following conditions are met, the people's court shall uphold the application:

A. The outsider is the holder of the right or interest;
B. The right or interest asserted by the outsider is legal and genuine;
C. There existed a fabrication of legal relationships or falsification of case facts between the parties to the arbitration case;
D. The dispositive part of the arbitral award or the outcome of the arbitration mediation statement regarding the civil rights and obligations of the parties is partially or entirely incorrect, infringing upon the legitimate rights and interests of the outsider.

Illustrative Cases

Case 1: *WS Company v. YSG Company*[3]

On July 26, 2018, the M Arbitration Commission sent the arbitration notice, arbitration rules, and the panel of arbitrators to WS Company by express mail to the address provided by YSG Company in the arbitration application, but the documents were returned due to "incorrect name/address." On August 6, 2018, YSG Company submitted the "Reply Regarding Service of Process in the Case," confirming the effective service address for WS Company as a specific center on Binhu Road, Binhu District, Wuxi City, and agreed to serve the arbitration documents by notarized delivery. The M Arbitration Commission again sent the arbitration notice, arbitration rules, panel of arbitrators, arbitration application, and attachments to WS Company. On September 25, 2018, it also sent the notice of tribunal formation, hearing notice, and their attachments to WS Company. All documents were successfully delivered. WS Company did not participate in the arbitration hearing, and the arbitral tribunal rendered a default award.

[3] (2019) Su 02 Zhi Yi 49; See the 10 Typical Cases on Judicial Review of Commercial Arbitration published by the High People's Court of Jiangsu Province in July 2024.

WS Company applied to the Jiangsu Province Wuxi Intermediate People's Court for non-enforcement of the involved arbitral award, arguing that the M Arbitration Commission had not effectively served the arbitration materials, thereby violating statutory procedures.

The Jiangsu Province Wuxi Intermediate People's Court held that Article 8 of the M Arbitration Commission Arbitration Rules stipulated that any arbitration documents dispatched to a party or its arbitration agent were deemed effectively served if they were either handed over to the recipient in person, sent to the recipient's place of business, registered address, domicile, habitual residence, or mailing address, or if, after reasonable inquiry by the other party, none of these addresses could be found, and the M Arbitration Commission sent the documents by registered mail, express delivery, or any other means capable of providing a delivery record (including notarized service, entrusted service, and service by leaving the documents) to the recipient's last known placce of business, registered address, domicile, habitual residence, or mailing address. Both WS Company and YSG Company acknowledged that YSG Company had visited WS Company's premises at the "specific center on Binhu Road, Binhu District, Wuxi City" in April 2018 to discuss matters such as contract termination. YSG Company claimed that this was the last address it knew for WS Company. Although WS Company asserted that it had orally informed YSG Company about its impending relocation, YSG Company did not acknowledge this, and WS Company failed to provide evidence to prove it. Therefore, the aforementioned address could be determined as WS Company's last known address by YSG Company. The M Arbitration Commission's mailing of the documents to this address in accordance with the Arbitration Rules was deemed to constitute effective service. Consequently, the Court ruled to dismiss WS Company's application for non-enforcement of the arbitral award.

Case 2*: Zhang v. C Company*[4]

In March 2018, Zhang, as the borrower, entered into the Loan Agreement with C Company through an online platform. The agreement stipulated that the parties would confirm their rights and obligations through a simplified procedure by submitting an arbitration mediation agreement to the N Arbitration Commission. On the same day, both parties entered into the Mediation Agreement, in which the borrower agreed that in the event of default, he would not raise any counterclaim

[4] See the Typical Cases on Judicial Review of Commercial Arbitration published by Guangdong Province Shenzhen Intermediate People's Court in 2024.

The SPC's Reply on the Application of Law to the Case Filing and Enforcement of 'Pre-dispute Arbitration' Awards or Mediation Statements by Arbitration Institutions stipulates that arbitral awards or mediation statements made by arbitration institutions before disputes arise between the parties concerning online loan contracts shall not serve as the basis for enforcement. Although the arbitral award in this case was rendered after the dispute arose, the court, during its review, strictly implemented the spirit of the Reply, determining that the arbitration institution, without ascertaining the specific performance of the contract and without safeguarding the basic procedural rights of the respondent in the arbitration, directly rendered an award based on the pre-set "Mediation Agreement" content before the dispute occurred, which constituted a violation of statutory procedures, and the award was likewise unenforceable.

against the lender's arbitration claim for repayment of the principal and interest, would not raise any objection to the amounts of the principal, interest, and related costs, would not challenge the relevant evidence materials submitted by the lender in the arbitration, and would waive his right to defense and other rights granted under the arbitration rules.

As Zhang failed to fully repay the loan principal and interest as agreed, C Company submitted an arbitration application to the N Arbitration Commission in May 2020. The arbitration commission sent arbitration documents, including the arbitration notice, tribunal formation notice, and hearing notice, to Zhang via the email address specified in the Mediation Agreement. Zhang did not submit any defense or participate in the arbitration hearing. In July 2020, the arbitration commission rendered an arbitral award based on the evidence submitted by C Company, including the Loan Agreement and the Mediation Agreement, upholding C Company's arbitration claims. Zhang applied to the court for non-enforcement of the arbitral award, arguing that the arbitration procedure was unlawful and that a "pre-emptive arbitration" could not be applied for compulsory enforcement.

The Court held that the arbitral tribunal's service of procedural documents, such as the arbitration notice, tribunal formation notice, and hearing notice, via email, did not comply with the N Arbitration Commission's Arbitration Rules, which stipulated that "documents deliverable via email shall be limited to awards, mediation agreements, decisions, and similar documents." This constituted a violation of the statutory procedure. Furthermore, Zhang and C Company signed the Mediation Agreement before any dispute arose, in which Zhang pre-emptively agreed not to raise any objections to the principal, interest, and related costs claimed by C Company in any future arbitration, and restricted Zhang's arbitration rights, including the right to defend, submit evidence, and apply to set aside the arbitral award. The arbitral tribunal directly adopted this Mediation Agreement as the basis for the award, failing to safeguard Zhang's fundamental procedural rights in the arbitration. This fell under the circumstance specified in the Civil Procedure Law where "the composition of the arbitral tribunal or the arbitration procedure violated the statutory procedure." Consequently, the court ruled not to enforce the arbitral award.

Case 3*: TH Company and others v. ZH Company*[5]

In 2015, the listed company TY Electromechanical conducted a private placement of shares, which ZH Company purchased through an "asset management plan." TH Company and Zhao, as shareholders of TY Electromechanical, issued a Letter of Commitment guaranteeing that the annualized return of the "asset management plan" would not be less than 10%, with TH Company covering any shortfall. Zhao provided a joint and several liability guarantee for TH Company's obligations. ZH Company applied for arbitration before an arbitration commission, requesting that TH Company and Zhao pay the shortfall compensation in accordance with the Letter of Commitment. The arbitral tribunal held that the Letter of Commitment did

[5] (2021) Su 05 Zhi Yi 150; See the 10 Typical Cases on Judicial Review of Commercial Arbitration by the High People's Court of Jiangsu Province in July 2024.

not violate mandatory provisions of laws or administrative regulations, nor did it contravene public order and good customs. It therefore deemed the commitment valid and rendered an arbitral award ordering TH Company and Zhao to pay the shortfall compensation. In 2021, TH Company and Zhao applied to the Jiangsu Province Suzhou Intermediate People's Court for non-enforcement of the arbitral award.

The Jiangsu Province Suzhou Intermediate People's Court held that investors participating in the stock market investments of a listed company should bear the risks associated with stock price fluctuations themselves. The Letter of Commitment in question was an agreement characterized as a "guaranteed return for a private placement." Providing a guaranteed return commitment to potential investors participating in the private placement by the listed company, its actual controllers, or other interested parties violated the legal principle of "equal rights for shares" and the fundamental rule of "caveat emptor" in the stock market. It distorted the pricing mechanism of the stock issuance market and disrupted the financial regulatory order. Consequently, the arbitral award, which recognized the validity of an agreement guaranteeing returns for a listed company's private placement, contravened public interest. Accordingly, the Court ruled not to enforce the arbitral award.

Case 4: *D Bank v. Wang*[6]

The Guizhou Province Liupanshui Intermediate People's Court accepted this case for enforcement based on the effective arbitral award rendered by the Guangzhou Arbitration Commission. After review, the Guizhou Province Liupanshui Intermediate People's Court held that during the arbitration proceedings, the arbitral tribunal failed to effectively protect the party's fundamental procedural rights. In accordance with Article 2 of the Reply of the SPC on the Application of Law to Issues Concerning the Case Filing and Enforcement of "Pre-emptive Arbitration" Awards or Mediation Statements by Arbitration Institutions and Article 157 of the Civil Procedure Law, the Guizhou Province Liupanshui Intermediate People's Court rendered a decision dismissing the enforcement application made by the D Bank.

D Bank refused to accept the enforcement ruling of the Guizhou Province Liupanshui Intermediate People's Court and applied to the High People's Court of Guizhou Province for reconsideration, requesting that the said enforcement ruling be set aside and that the Guizhou Province Liupanshui Intermediate People's Court be directed to accept the case for enforcement.

The claimant argued the following: first, the Guangzhou Arbitration Commission fully respected the intentions of both the enforcement claimant and the party against whom enforcement was sought during the arbitration process, strictly adhered to its arbitration rules, and utilized not only electronic service but also service by mail. Page 2 of the award (2020) Sui Zhong An Zi No. 27626 by the Guangzhou Arbitration Commission stated, "this Commission served the arbitration notice... to the electronic service address, mailing address, and domicile of the party against

[6] (2023) Zui Gao Fa Zhi Jian 427.

whom enforcement was sought." Furthermore, the Certificate of Service and Effectiveness issued by the Guangzhou Arbitration Commission also indicated that "service was also effected on the party against whom enforcement was sought by mail on March 18, 2021." Second, the arbitration in this case did not constitute "pre-emptive arbitration." The evidence submitted during the arbitration showed that the loan in dispute between D Bank and Wang had been in default since July 8, 2020. D Bank did not apply for arbitration until November 18, 2020, and the procedures followed by the Guangzhou Arbitration Commission during the arbitration complied with its arbitration rules and legal provisions. The core circumstance regulated as "pre-emptive arbitration" in the SPC on the Application of Law to Issues Concerning the Case Filing and Enforcement of "Pre-emptive Arbitration" Awards or Mediation Statements by Arbitration Institutions is "where parties to an online loan contract apply for enforcement of an arbitral award or mediation statement rendered by an arbitration institution before the occurrence of the dispute." In this case, D Bank initiated arbitration only after the contractual dispute had arisen. During the arbitration, the Guangzhou Arbitration Commission effected service in accordance with the law and conducted the arbitration based on the online arbitration rules agreed upon by both parties in the contract. Wang failed to provide effective contact information and could not be reached even after the Guangzhou Arbitration Commission attempted service at his domicile. Therefore, it was not improper for the Guangzhou Arbitration Commission to conduct the arbitration in his absence pursuant to its arbitration rules.

The High People's Court of Guizhou Province held that, pursuant to Article 25(1) of the Arbitration Law (2017), an arbitration institution must, during the arbitration process, protect the parties' fundamental procedural rights, such as the right to apply for the withdrawal of an arbitrator, the right to present evidence, and the right to defend. In this case, there was no evidence proving that Wang had received copies of arbitration documents such as the arbitration application, the arbitration rules, the notice of tribunal composition, or the hearing notice. As a party to the arbitration, he failed to appear and participate in the arbitration activities. The Guangzhou Arbitration Commission rendered the arbitral award in Wang's absence without protecting his fundamental procedural rights as stipulated by the Arbitration Law (2017). The Guizhou Province Liupanshui Intermediate People's Court's ruling to dismiss D Bank's enforcement application was not improper. However, the Guizhou Province Liupanshui Intermediate People's Court wrongly applied the Reply of the SPC on the Application of Law to Issues Concerning the Case Filing and Enforcement of "Pre-emptive Arbitration" Awards or Mediation Statements by Arbitration Institutions. Accordingly, the High People's Court of Guizhou Province rendered a decision, dismissing D Bank's application for reconsideration.

D Bank refused to accept the enforcement ruling of the High People's Court of Guizhou Province and petitioned for a retrial, requesting to set aside the said enforcement ruling of the High People's Court of Guizhou Province; to set aside the decision of the Guizhou Province Liupanshui Intermediate People's Court; and to instruct the Guizhou Province Liupanshui Intermediate People's Court to accept and enforce the arbitral award made by the Guangzhou Arbitration Commission.

The SPC opined that Article 3 and Article 4 of the Arbitral Award Enforcement Provisions stipulated the circumstances under which an enforcement application should be dismissed due to the unclear content of an arbitral award. Article 244 of the Civil Procedure Law prescribed the grounds for refusing enforcement of an arbitral award. According to the aforementioned legal provisions, during the enforcement proceeding of an arbitral award, a people's court could, in accordance with the law, examine whether the arbitral award could be accepted for enforcement and whether grounds for refusing enforcement existed.

Regarding the requirements for accepting enforcement cases concerning arbitral awards, Article 461(1) of the Civil Procedure Law Interpretation provided that the effective legal document for which a party applies to the people's court for enforcement shall meet the following conditions: (1) the subjects of rights and obligations are clear; (2) the content of performance is clear. According to Article 3 of the Arbitral award Enforcement Provisions, if the enforcement content of an arbitral award or arbitration mediation document falls under any of the following circumstances, making enforcement impossible, the people's court may rule to dismiss the enforcement application; if it makes partial enforcement impossible, the court may rule to dismiss that part of the enforcement application; if it makes partial enforcement impossible and that part is inseparable from the rest, the court may rule to dismiss the enforcement application: (1) the subjects of rights and obligations are unclear; (2) the specific amount of monetary payment is unclear or the calculation method is unclear, making it impossible to determine a specific amount; (3) the specific object to be delivered is unclear or cannot be determined; (4) the standard, object, or scope of conduct to be performed is unclear.

In this case, the primary reason the Guizhou Province Liupanshui Intermediate People's Court ruled to dismiss the enforcement application of D Bank was that the Guangzhou Arbitration Commission had failed to safeguard Wang's fundamental procedural rights in the arbitration. This reason fell within the grounds for refusing enforcement of an arbitral award stipulated in Article 244 of the Civil Procedure Law. It essentially pertained to a judicial review by the people's court regarding the legality of the arbitral award, rather than an examination of whether the award could be accepted for enforcement. The Guizhou Province Liupanshui Intermediate People's Court and the High People's Court of Guizhou Province had not examined whether the case met the statutory conditions for accepting an enforcement case concerning an arbitral award, and thus failed to clarify the facts. The Guizhou Province Liupanshui Intermediate People's Court and the High People's Court of Guizhou Province should have examined whether to accept the enforcement application from the D Bank in accordance with the relevant legal provisions governing the acceptance of enforcement cases for arbitral awards.

Case5: *YM Company v. XMD Company*[7]

On July 4, 2007, YM Company (Party A), XMD Company (Party B), and others jointly signed the Operation Contract. Article 12 of the contract, concerning dispute resolution and applicable law, stipulated that any dispute arising from the performance of this Contract between the parties shall be settled through friendly consultations if possible; If no agreement could be reached through consultation, any party shall have the right to submit the dispute to the Xiamen Arbitration Commission for arbitration.

On November 21, 2005, XMD Company, based on the aforementioned contract, filed an arbitration application against YM Company as the respondent with the Xiamen Arbitration Commission. XMD Company sought the arbitration commission to rule that YM Company continue to fully perform the Operation Contract; second, YM Company should pay compensation for relevant losses of RMB two million; and third, YM Company should bear the arbitration costs. After hearing the case, the Xiamen Arbitration Commission rendered the award Xia Arbitration Zi [2006] No. 0353, ruling that YM Company should continue to perform the aforementioned contract signed on July 4, 2003, and pay XMD Company a penalty of RMB 1.075 million. Subsequently, XMD Company applied to the court for enforcement of the said arbitral award.

After review, the court rendered the Civil Ruling (2007) Xia Zhi Zi No. 108-4. In this ruling, the court held that "the main focus of dispute in this case was whether there was insufficient evidence to determine that the Contract was an innominate contract involving a complex arrangement of rights and obligations related to real estate development, and whether the applicable law was indeed incorrect," and further held that "according to the provisions of the SPC's Interpretation on Issues Concerning the Application of Law in the Trial of Cases Involving Disputes over Contracts for the Right to Use State-Owned Land, the arbitral award's finding that the Contract was an innominate contract involving a complex arrangement of rights and obligations related to real estate development was based on insufficient evidence, which consequently determined that the law applied was indeed incorrect." Accordingly, the court ruled not to enforce the award Xia Arbitration Zi [2006] No. 0353 rendered by the Xiamen Arbitration Commission. On June 29, 2023, XMD Company, based on the aforementioned contract, applied to the Xiamen Arbitration Commission for arbitration, requesting the termination of the contract signed by both parties, and demanding that YM Company return the deposit in full, bear the penalty for overdue payments, compensate for losses, and return the funds already collected.

This case concerned the confirmation of the validity of an arbitration agreement. The main issue in dispute was whether the arbitration clause stipulated in Article 12 of the Contract for the Contracted Operation of the Commercial Housing Project of the Commercial Bank Center Guest Building was valid. YM Company argued that

[7] See the 10 Typical Cases on Judicial Review of Arbitration published by the Xiamen International Commercial Tribunal in 2023.

XMD Company's renewed application for arbitration based on the involved contract constituted repeated arbitration, and that the award Xia Arbitration Zi [2006] No. 0353 rendered by the Xiamen Arbitration Commission for disputes arising from this contract had been ruled unenforceable by the people's court, thereby rendering the arbitration clause in Article 12 of the involved contract invalid. The court did not support this argument for the following reasons:

First, Article 12 of the aforementioned contract stated, "1. Any dispute arising from the performance of this Contract between the parties shall be settled through friendly consultations if possible. If no agreement can be reached through consultation, any party shall have the right to submit the dispute to the Xiamen Arbitration Commission for arbitration. The arbitration rules shall be those in effect at the said Commission at the time the dispute arises." This clause contained a clear expression of intent to submit to arbitration and defined the matters for arbitration, clearly designated the Xiamen Arbitration Commission as the arbitration institution, and there were no corresponding circumstances constituting statutory invalidity. Therefore, it should be recognized as a valid and effective arbitration clause.

Second, YM Company argued that the original arbitration agreement was invalidated after the people's court ruled not to enforce the award Xia Arbitration Zi [2006] No. 0353. The court held that determining the validity of the original arbitration clause after an arbitral award has been ruled unenforceable by a people's court should be based on a careful consideration of the parties' arbitration claims, the grounds for non-enforcement, and the parties' arbitration agreement, among other factors. In this case, the arbitration claims raised by XMD Company in the arbitration case Xia Arbitration Zi [2006] No. 0353 were requests for YM Company to continue performing the contract and to compensate for losses due to delayed performance. Although this arbitral award was later ruled unenforceable by the court, the grounds for non-enforcement were not circumstances that negated the validity of the arbitration agreement, such as the absence of an arbitration agreement between the parties or the arbitral tribunal exceeding its authority. Therefore, based on the existing evidence on record, YM Company did not submit evidence proving that the arbitration clause in the involved contract signed by the parties had been altered or was invalid for other reasons. XMD Company had the right to request termination of the contract and claim civil compensation from the Xiamen Arbitration Commission based on the arbitration clause stipulated in the involved contract.

Finally, regarding YM Company's claim that XMD Company's renewed application for arbitration based on the involved contract constituted repeated arbitration and violated the principle of *ne bis in idem*, this, according to the law, did not fall within the scope of review for confirming the validity of an arbitration agreement, and the court did not review it here.

In summary, YM Company's application to confirm the invalidity of the arbitration clause in Article 12 of the Operation Contract was unfounded and was not supported. According to Article 20 of the Arbitration Law (2017), the court ruled to dismiss the action.

Article 77
Where one party applies for the enforcement of the arbitral award and the other party applies for setting aside the arbitral award, the people's court shall rule to suspend the procedure of enforcement.

Where the people's court rules to set aside the arbitral award, it shall rule to terminate the enforcement procedure. Where the people's court rules to dismiss the application for setting aside the arbitral award, it shall rule to resume the enforcement procedure.

Notes
This Article addresses the coordination between the enforcement procedure and the setting-aside procedure. When an application for enforcement by one party and an application to set aside the award by the other party occur simultaneously, the court shall rule to suspend enforcement, rather than proceeding with enforcement or directly dismissing the setting-aside application. The core rationale is that although the arbitral award has become effective, the filing of a setting-aside application indicates the potential existence of legal defects in the award (such as illegal arbitration procedures, forged evidence, etc.). If enforcement continues and the award is subsequently set aside, it will lead to the complex consequence of "restitution of enforcement," which not only wastes judicial resources but may also cause irreversible losses to the person against whom enforcement is sought. For example, if the person against whom enforcement is sought claims the arbitral award "exceeded the scope of the arbitration agreement" and applies to set it aside, but the court nonetheless forcibly freezes and transfers their assets, and the award is later set aside, restitution of the assets would be required through the restitution of enforcement procedure. This not only increases procedural costs but may also result in irreparable harm to the rights of the person against whom enforcement is sought if the assets have already been disposed of by the claimant. Suspending enforcement precisely serves to temporarily halt enforcement actions, allowing time for the review of the award's legality and avoiding the irreversible risk of erroneous enforcement.

If the court, after review, rules to set aside the award, it must then issue a ruling to terminate enforcement. Once an arbitral award is set aside, its legal effect is extinguished, and it loses its premise as a basis for enforcement. The enforcement procedure consequently loses its foundation to continue. In this case, terminating enforcement is not a result of inability to enforce, but rather a legal consequence of the invalidation of the basis for enforcement, and it is final. It is important to note that terminating enforcement is different from dismissing an application for enforcement: the former results from the invalidation of the basis for enforcement, leading to the termination of the procedure, while the latter results from the unenforceability due to unclear enforcement content. Their legal consequences and subsequent remedial paths are fundamentally different.

If the court rules to dismiss the application to set aside the award, it must then rule to resume enforcement and continue advancing the original enforcement procedure. In practice, some persons against whom enforcement is sought, even without legitimate grounds, may still file setting-aside applications based on fabricated reasons in an attempt to delay the procedure, transfer assets, or evade obligations. By clearly stipulating the legal conditions for resuming enforcement, this provision prevents the enforcement procedure from being indefinitely stalled by unjustified setting-aside applications, thereby safeguarding the timely realization of the legitimate rights and interests of the claimant for enforcement.

In addition to the provisions herein, according to the Arbitral Award Enforcement Provisions, effective March 1, 2018, if a party's application to a people's court to set aside an arbitral award has been dismissed, and the party subsequently raises the same grounds for opposing enforcement in the enforcement procedure, the people's court shall not support it; if a party's application to a people's court for non-enforcement has been dismissed, and the party subsequently applies to set aside the arbitral award on the same grounds, the people's court shall not support it. During the review period of a case concerning non-enforcement of an arbitral award, if a party files an application to set aside the arbitral award with a competent people's court and it is accepted, the people's court shall rule to suspend the review of the non-enforcement application; if the arbitral award is set aside or a decision is made to re-arbitrate, the people's court shall rule to terminate enforcement and conclude the review of the non-enforcement application; if the application to set aside the arbitral award is dismissed or the claimant for enforcement withdraws the application to set aside the arbitral award, the people's court shall resume the review of the non-enforcement application; if the person against whom enforcement is sought withdraws the application to set aside the arbitral award, the people's court shall rule to conclude the review of the non-enforcement application, unless the non-enforcement application was filed by an outsider.

In practice, specific details need to be considered. For example, while this provision states that enforcement shall be resumed after the setting-aside application is dismissed, it does not specify the exact timeframe for resumption—should the court resume enforcement immediately upon the dismissal ruling taking effect, or must the claimant reapply for resumption? Typically, it should be understood that after the ruling dismissing the setting-aside application takes effect, the enforcement court should proactively resume enforcement without requiring the claimant to reapply. The rationale for this approach is that if reapplication were required, the claimant's potential failure to apply promptly could lead to a stall in the enforcement procedure, giving the person against whom enforcement is sought an opportunity to transfer assets. The enforcement court proactively resuming enforcement ensures procedural continuity and promptly protects the claimant's rights. However, in practice, factors such as inefficiencies in case processing or delays in information synchronization in some courts may cause delays in resuming enforcement, requiring the parties to promptly notify the court or follow up.

Furthermore, for instance, if the claimant has already applied for property preservation (such as freezing the bank account of the person against whom enforcement is sought) during the arbitration proceedings, and the enforcement procedure is initiated but then suspended due to the person against whom enforcement is sought applying to set aside the award, can the person against whom enforcement is sought then apply to lift the preservation? Article 77 does not directly stipulate this, but in practice, two conditions usually need to be met: first, the person against whom enforcement is sought provides sufficient and effective security to ensure that the claimant's rights and interests can be protected if enforcement is later resumed; second, lifting the preservation would not harm the public interest or the lawful rights and interests of others.

Illustrative Case

ZG Shipbuilding Company v. YY Shipping Company[8]

On November 11, 2014, the claimant ZG Shipbuilding Company and the respondent YY Shipping Company signed a Ship Sale and Purchase Contract. It was agreed that YY Shipping Company (which did not possess a water transport license for bulk chemical carriers) would sell the bulk chemical carrier M/V "Offshore Oil 881" to ZG Shipbuilding Company for RMB 47 million. The contract stipulated that any disputes arising from the contract should be submitted to the CMAC Shanghai Sub-Commission for arbitration. On November 27, the vessel was delivered, and ZG Shipbuilding Company subsequently entrusted Haijiao Company with the repair of the vessel. (After delivery, the vessel was renamed M/V "Zhonggang Yongshun"). On April 10, 2015, YY Shipping Company applied to the CMAC Shanghai Sub-Commission for arbitration due to the contract dispute, requesting termination of the contract, return of the vessel, forfeiture of the earnest money, and compensation for related costs, among other claims.

On May 14, 2015, ZG Shipbuilding Company applied to the Xiamen Maritime Court for pre-litigation property preservation, requesting measures to restrict the disposal, transfer, mortgage, and bareboat charter of the M/V "Offshore Oil 881" belonging to YY Shipping Company. ZG Shipbuilding Company claimed that YY Shipping Company had breached the contract by failing to handle the ownership change and cancellation of the operation certificate, resulting in its inability to put the vessel into operation and causing economic losses exceeding RMB ten million. YY Shipping Company argued that it had performed the contract according to the agreement and had actually delivered the vessel. It claimed that ZG Shipbuilding Company's preservation action harmed its interests, including losses of RMB 7.614 million due to funds being tied up because of the unpaid balance of RMB 42.3 million, and potential losses exceeding RMB 23 million if the vessel's transfer was restricted, as the company intended to sell the vessel to other buyers to mitigate losses. As ZG Shipbuilding Company failed to provide valid security within the time limit, the Xiamen Maritime Court rendered the Civil Ruling (2015) Xia Hai Fa Bao No. 38 on June 17, 2015, dismissing ZG Shipbuilding Company's application for property preservation.

On May 28, 2015, ZG Shipbuilding Company filed a counterclaim in the arbitration, requesting that YY Shipping Company be ordered to pay ship repair costs, crew wages, costs for the bunker fuel on board, and return double the earnest money. It also applied to the CMAC Shanghai Sub-Commission for property preservation to restrict the rights of disposal, transfer, mortgage, and bareboat charter of the M/V

[8] (2016) Min 72 Min Chu No. 565.

"Zhonggang Yongshun" belonging to YY Shipping Company. The CMAC Shanghai Sub-Commission submitted this property preservation application to the Xiamen Maritime Court on July 2, 2015. During the period ordered for providing security, the claimant ZG Shipbuilding Company provided real estate with a total value exceeding RMB three million as security. On July 7, 2015, the Xiamen Maritime Court rendered the Civil Ruling (2015) Xia Hai Fa Bao No. 42, granting the property preservation application, freezing the rights of disposal, transfer, mortgage, and bareboat charter of the M/V "Offshore Oil 881" belonging to YY Shipping Company, and freezing the security properties.

On March 31, 2016, the CMAC Shanghai Sub-Commission rendered the arbitral award (2016) Hai Zhong Hu Cai No. 005, dismissing ZG Shipbuilding Company's counterclaim. On April 12, 2016, YY Shipping Company applied to lift the property preservation. ZG Shipbuilding Company argued that the arbitral award contained errors in both substance and procedure, that it intended to initiate an action to set aside the arbitral award, and thus disagreed with lifting the property preservation. On April 19, the Xiamen Maritime Court ruled to lift the preservation measures against the vessel involved in the case.

On June 24, 2016, YY Shipping Company filed a lawsuit with the Xiamen Maritime Court, claiming that since the arbitral award had dismissed ZG Shipbuilding Company's counterclaim, ZG Shipbuilding Company's erroneous preservation had caused its economic losses amounting to RMB 19.776 million.

Additionally, Haijiao Company sent a letter to ZG Shipbuilding Company on June 2, 2015, stating that the repair work on the M/V "Zhonggang Yongshun" had been completed. As it had not received the repair fees, berthage fees, and other related costs for the vessel, it would exercise a lien on the vessel until these fees and costs were settled in full, and would not allow the vessel to leave the berth or sail. The vessel remained under the company's lien. Separately, YY Shipping Company applied to the Ningbo Maritime Court for a mandatory order on July 2, 2015, demanding that ZG Shipbuilding Company immediately return the M/V "Zhonggang Yongshun". As the application fee was not paid, the Ningbo Maritime Court ruled on July 14, 2015, that the case would be treated as a withdrawal of the application for the mandatory order.

After hearing the case, the Xiamen Maritime Court held that ZG Shipbuilding Company had applied for property preservation to secure its claims, but these claims were ultimately all dismissed by the arbitral award. Therefore, its preservation application was deemed erroneous. However, before the preservation ruling was issued, the vessel had already been placed under lien by Haijiao Company, and the consequence of being unable to operate had already occurred. This state was maintained and continued even after the preservation was lifted. Under these circumstances, implementing the preservation to freeze the bareboat charter rights did not create additional or cause new damages; that is, there was no causal link between the preservation and the alleged damages. YY Shipping Company also failed to provide sufficient evidence regarding the losses from the vessel's inability to operate. On November 10, 2016, the court rendered the Civil Judgment (2016) Min 72 Min Chu No. 565, dismissing YY Shipping Company's claims.

On October 21, 2016, ZG Shipbuilding Company applied to the Shanghai Maritime Court to set aside the arbitral award (2016) Hai Zhong Hu Cai No. 005. After hearing the case, the Shanghai Maritime Court held that there were no statutory grounds for setting aside the award. On December 14, 2016, it rendered the Civil Ruling (2016) Hu 72 Min Te No. 277, dismissing ZG Shipbuilding Company's application to set aside the arbitral award (2016) Hai Zhong Hu Cai No. 005 rendered by the CMAC Shanghai Sub-Commission.

In January 2017, ZG Shipbuilding Company applied to lift the preservation measures on the security properties it had provided, on the grounds that the preservation action had not caused any damage to the respondent and the preservation case had concluded. On January 16, 2017, the Xiamen Maritime Court ruled to lift the preservation of the secured real estate.

Chapter 7
Special Provisions for Arbitration Involving Foreign Elements

Article 78
The provisions of this Chapter shall apply to the arbitration of disputes arising from economic, trade, transportation, maritime affairs and other disputes involving a foreign element. For matters not covered in this Chapter, the other relevant provisions of this Law shall apply.

Notes
With China's deep integration into the global economy, foreign-related commercial disputes have become increasingly complex and diverse. These disputes not only involve traditional areas such as foreign-related economic trade, transport, and maritime matters but may also extend to other civil and commercial disputes with foreign elements. Due to the potential involvement of parties, subject matter, or legal facts from different jurisdictions in foreign-related arbitration, it exhibits significant differences from purely domestic arbitration in aspects such as the composition of the arbitral tribunal, arbitration procedures, rules of evidence, applicable law, and the recognition and enforcement of awards. Arbitration procedural rules designed for domestic commercial arbitration may struggle to fully meet the specific expectations for international commercial arbitration practices in such disputes. Parties often anticipate a procedure that is more internationally inclusive, flexible, and aligned with international commercial practices. Applying the same set of rules indistinguishably to both foreign-related and domestic arbitration could not only weaken the attractiveness of Chinese arbitration in the international market but also, in practice, compromise the effectiveness and credibility of arbitration due to a lack of procedural flexibility. Differentiating between international (foreign-related) arbitration and domestic arbitration in legislation, by dedicating a separate chapter to foreign-related arbitration and granting it priority application, helps provide a more lenient procedural environment and broader party autonomy for international arbitration.

Y. Lin, *New Arbitration Law in China*, China Arbitration Yearbook,
https://doi.org/10.1007/978-981-92-0642-1_7

Furthermore, this Article addresses the issue of which legal basis should be primarily consulted when handling foreign-related arbitration. It first directs parties and arbitration institutions to apply the "special provisions" (this Chapter) designed for the characteristics of foreign-related cases. Only when gaps exist in these special provisions does it refer back to the "general provisions" (other parts of this Law). This provides certainty and predictability for the initiation and progression of arbitration procedures. This means that in foreign-related arbitration, matters such as the appointment of arbitrators (particularly the selection of foreign arbitrators), language of arbitration, methods of service, rules of evidence, interim measures, and even the standards for setting aside and enforcing awards will primarily follow the special arrangements in Chapter 7. These arrangements are typically more flexible, better reflect party autonomy, and are more conducive to alignment with international treaties such as the New York Convention, thereby creating the most suitable procedural environment for the fair and efficient resolution of foreign-related disputes. When the special provisions of Chapter 7 cannot cover every detail of the arbitration procedure—for instance, if procedural issues not addressed by the special provisions arise, such as the basic requirements for the validity of an arbitration agreement, the arbitral tribunal's competence-competence, or basic procedures for challenges—this Article serves as a fallback provision, providing the legal basis for such procedural issues.

From the perspective of whether to enact a separate international commercial arbitration law, the legislative approach to commercial arbitration mainly takes two forms. One is to include provisions related to international commercial arbitration within separate chapters of the arbitration law. The other is to enact separate domestic arbitration laws and international arbitration laws. China currently adopts the former approach, which has been the legislative model since the promulgation of the Arbitration Law (1994). In fact, Civil Procedure Law also adopts this model, containing special provisions for foreign-related litigation only in its Fourth Part.

Some countries internationally adopt a dualistic legislative model, such as Singapore. Singapore enacted its first arbitration law in 1953 and had only a unified arbitration law before 1994. In 1994, Singapore enacted the International Arbitration Act of Singapore, thereby establishing a dual-track arbitration legal system. The main reason for establishing this legislative model was the Singaporean legislature's recognition that a higher degree of freedom in international arbitration was necessary, while simultaneously believing that the lower level of judicial intervention characteristic of international arbitration was not suitable for domestic arbitration.

During the process of revising the New Arbitration Law, some viewpoints suggested enacting separate international commercial arbitration legislation. The rationale was that China's domestic commercial arbitration legislation contains certain aspects, such as the extent of court intervention and the functions of arbitration institutions, that differ from current international commercial arbitration systems or practices. Enacting separate legislation, it was argued, would be more conducive to the development of a country's international commercial arbitration. However, the model ultimately adopted in the revision remains the unified one. Nevertheless, the New Arbitration Law incorporates additional elements, such as a conditional ad hoc arbitration system, the seat of arbitration doctrine, arbitration cost systems, and an open attitude towards foreign arbitration institutions, aiming to promote further alignment with international commercial arbitration practices.

In the context of the new law's promulgation, it remains necessary to uphold the distinctive Chinese domestic commercial arbitration system that has proven effective in practice. Simultaneously, in line with the characteristics of foreign-related or international commercial arbitration, and embracing a spirit of innovation and development, we should continue to explore and advance the establishment of systems in specific rule application or institutional design that align with modern commercial arbitration practices.

Given that different provisions apply to foreign-related and purely domestic cases, the concept most likely to cause controversy in practice related to this Chapter is: what constitutes a foreign-related dispute? Referring to Article 522 of the Choice of Law Interpretation, a civil case can be identified as foreign-related under any of the following circumstances:

(1) One or both parties are foreigners, stateless persons, foreign enterprises, or foreign organizations;
(2) The habitual residence of one or both parties is outside the territory of the People's Republic of China;
(3) The subject matter is located outside the territory of the People's Republic of China;
(4) The legal facts that establish, alter, or extinguish the civil relationship occurred outside the territory of the People's Republic of China;
(5) Other circumstances that can be determined as a foreign-related civil case.

In practice, whether a dispute is foreign-related can usually be determined based on three elements: firstly, the subjects of the civil legal relationship involved in the case; secondly, the object of the civil legal relationship involved in the case; and thirdly, the content of the civil legal relationship, namely the legal facts that establish, alter, or extinguish the civil legal relationship. If any one of these elements is present, the dispute can be identified as foreign-related, thus allowing the application of this Chapter's provisions. Generally, whether a case is foreign-related can be easily determined. However, sometimes the foreign element may be concealed, requiring careful analysis to identify the foreign element, adopting a stance supportive of arbitration.

In judicial review practice, the presence of foreign elements affects the applicable law of the arbitration procedure. Therefore, improper application may be deemed a procedural defect. If there is an objection regarding whether the domestic arbitration procedure or the foreign-related arbitration procedure applies to the arbitration proceedings, it should be raised promptly; otherwise, it may constitute a waiver of the right to object. This is because arbitration embodies the principle of party autonomy. The parties can agree on specific arbitration procedures or accept different procedural agreements. Once accepted, or if no objection is raised, subsequently applying to set aside or not enforce the arbitral award on the grounds that the arbitration procedure did not conform to the arbitration rules during judicial review of the award would violate the fundamental principle of estoppel.

Illustrative Cases

Case 1*: Wang v. SZA Investment Company*[1]

One of the grounds upon which Wang applied to set aside the CIETAC arbitral award was that the case involved foreign-related elements, yet the arbitral tribunal, after review, applied the domestic arbitration procedure on the grounds that the case lacked such elements. Wang argued that this constituted an error in the arbitration procedure, falling under the circumstances for setting aside the award as stipulated in Article 58(3) of the Arbitration Law (2017). In fact, the relevant project was an overseas project, and the payment of the disputed funds also occurred overseas, indicating the presence of foreign-related elements. Wang claimed that after review, the arbitral tribunal had ascertained that the dispute involved foreign-related elements, yet still determined that no such elements existed and applied the domestic arbitration procedure, which constituted an error in the arbitration procedure.

SZA Company argued that the arbitration did not meet the staturoy criteria for foreign-related arbitration, and the application of the domestic arbitration procedure was correct. From the provisions of the CIETAC Arbitration Rules, particularly Chapter V "Special Provisions for Domestic Arbitration," it was evident that the differences between domestic and foreign-related procedures concerned only aspects such as costs, time limits for rendering the award, and service of documents. The substantive rights of the parties and the final outcome of the award were no different under either procedure. The claimant had participated in the arbitration proceedings from December 4, 2019, actively engaging in procedures such as selecting arbitrators, submitting defenses, and presenting evidence, thus fully exercising his procedural and substantive rights, and had never raised any objection to the application of the domestic procedure by the Arbitration Commission. The application of the domestic rules to the arbitration case neither violated the relevant provisions of the Arbitration Rules nor affected the correctness of the award.

Regarding the issue of whether the application of the domestic arbitration procedure to the case violated the arbitration procedure, the court held that according to Article 10 of the CIETAC Arbitration Rules, if a party, knowing or should have known that any provision of, or requirement under, these Rules or the arbitration agreement had not been complied with, nevertheless participated in or continued to participate in the arbitration proceedings without promptly and explicitly objecting in writing to such non-compliance, it was deemed to have waived its right to object. No evidence showed that Wang had raised any objection during the arbitration proceedings regarding the application of the "Special Provisions for Domestic Arbitration" to the arbitration procedure. He was thus deemed to have waived his right to object to the application of the domestic arbitration procedure. Consequently, the court did not accept this ground of the claimant's request to set aside the award.

---

[1] (2021) Jing 04 Min Te 667.

Case 2*: HR V Company. ZX Company*[2]

In 2017, HR Company and ZX Company entered into the License Agreement concerning the development and licensing of software related to computer vision technology. In July 2020, HR Company filed a lawsuit with the Zhejiang Province Hangzhou Intermediate People's Court, alleging that ZX Company had defaulted on payments and committed a malicious breach of contract. HR Company requested the Court to order ZX Company to continue performing its contractual obligations and to pay the outstanding amount under the agreement, along with interest, losses, and various other expenses incurred due to ZX Company's breach.

ZX Company defended itself by raising an objection to the Court's jurisdiction, arguing that disputes between the parties based on the contract should be submitted to the SIAC for arbitration in Singapore. Specifically, ZX Company argued as follows: first, according to the International Arbitration Act of Singapore and the Model Law, the parties had a genuine and valid arbitration agreement regarding the disputes in question. Second, the agreement involved was a foreign-related contract, and parties could legally agree to overseas arbitration. Both parties to the agreement were Sino-foreign joint ventures, and ZX Company was registered and established in a Pilot Free Trade Zone. At the time of signing the contract, HR Company was a wholly foreign-owned enterprise by the Bermuda-based X Company, indicating foreign-related elements. The subject matter of the contract largely involved intellectual property rights owned by HR Company overseas. Even if the contract lacked foreign-related elements, considering the facts that both parties were registered in the Pilot Free Trade Zone and were Sino-foreign joint ventures, it should be recognized that the parties had the right to agree to to submit the dispute to another arbitration institution.

The Zhejiang Province Hangzhou Intermediate People's Court held that although the parties clearly expressed their intention to submit the disputes to an overseas arbitration institution, the parties to the agreement, the subject matter of the contract, and the legal facts establishing, altering, or terminating the legal relationship all lacked foreign-related elements. The agreement did not constitute a foreign--related civil relationship. Regarding the parties to the contract: Whether Sino--foreign joint ventures or wholly foreign-owned enterprises, they were all enterprise legal persons registered within China and did not fall under the "foreign enterprises or organizations" as defined in Article 522 of the Civil Procedure Law. They also did not meet the conditions for applying foreign-related civil relations specified in Article 9 of the SPC's Opinions on Providing Judicial Services and Safeguards for the Construction of Pilot Free Trade Zones" (Fa Fa [2016] No. 34). The relevant content of the SPC's Notice on Clarifying the Jurisdiction Threshold Standards for First-Instance Foreign-Related Civil and Commercial Cases and Issues Concerning Centralized Handling" was only for adjusting the division of personnel among internal tribunals within the court and could not be used as a basis for determining that the parties in this case had foreign-related elements. Therefore, both parties to the

[2] (2021) Zui Gao Fa Zhi Min Xia Zhong 90.

dispute were Chinese legal persons. Regarding the subject matter of the contract: the main content of the agreement was that HR Company licensed ZX Company to use computer software owned by HR Company, and ZX Company paid licensing fees for this use. The involved computer software was developed by HR Company within China, and the intellectual property rights were owned by a domestic entity. Therefore, the subject matter of the contract between HR Company and ZX Company was not foreign-related. Even if it were true, as ZX Company claimed, that the mobile phone products using the involved software produced by ZX Company from 2018 to 2019 were mainly sold overseas, such sales activities did not alter the fundamental legal relationship between the parties and were insufficient to establish that the dispute had foreign-related elements. Therefore, the Zhejiang Province Hangzhou Intermediate People's Court ruled to dismiss the action. Subsequently, ZX Company's Appeal on the following grounds to the SPC, requesting the revocation of the ruling.

The SPC opined that the arbitration clause in the involved agreement was an overseas arbitration clause agreed upon by domestic parties for a dispute lacking foreign-related elements, and thus was an invalid arbitration clause. ZX Company was registered and established in the China (Shanghai) Pilot Free Trade Zone and was a limited liability company jointly funded by Chinese parties. HR Company was registered in Zhejiang Province and was a Sino-foreign joint venture listed company. Although the arbitration clause in the involved agreement clearly expressed the intention to submit disputes to an overseas arbitration institution and the designated arbitration institution was specific and clear, according to Article 271 of the Civil Procedure Law and Article 65 of the Arbitration Law (2017), Chinese law did not permit domestic parties to submit disputes lacking foreign-related elements to foreign arbitration. Referring to Article 522 of the Choice of Law Interpretation, the parties in this case were all Chinese legal persons, the conclusion of the involved agreement and its subject matter were both within Chinese territory, and the legal facts giving rise to, altering, or extinguishing the legal relationship between the parties also lacked foreign-related elements. Therefore, the SPC ruled to dismiss the appeal.

Article 79

Where a party to a foreign-related arbitration applies for evidence preservation, the arbitration institution shall submit the application to the intermediate people's court in the place where the evidence is located, and the people's court shall handle matters in a timely manner according to the law.

Notes

This Article, whose basic formulation remains the same as Article 68 of the Arbitration Law (2017), primarily concerns the competent court for evidence preservation in foreign-related arbitration. Evidence preservation in arbitration refers to compulsory protective or fixing measures taken by the people's court at the location of the evidence during the arbitration process, upon application by a party, regarding evidence that might be destroyed or difficult to obtain later. According to the Article 58 of the New Arbitration Law, which stipulates the conditions and procedures for evidence preservation in domestic cases: where evidence might be destroyed or difficult to obtain later, a party may apply for evidence preservation; where a party applies for evidence preservation, the arbitration institution shall submit the party's application to the basic-level people's court at the location of the evidence, and the people's court shall handle it promptly according to law. For foreign-related cases, the competent court is designated as the intermediate people's court at the location of the evidence.

Paragraph 2 of Article 58 provides for pre-arbitration evidence preservation. Although Article 68 does not have a corresponding second paragraph, according to the residual clause in Article 78, where matters are not provided for in this Chapter, the other relevant provisions of this Law shall apply. Therefore, the provisions regarding pre-arbitration evidence preservation also apply to foreign-related arbitration. That is, due to urgent circumstances, a party to an arbitration agreement may, before applying for arbitration, apply for evidence preservation to the intermediate people's court at the location of the evidence in accordance with the relevant provisions of the Civil Procedure Law.

The designation of intermediate people's courts as the competent courts for evidence preservation is likely based on the following considerations:

A. ***Addressing the Complexity of Foreign-Related Cases***. Foreign-related arbitration cases often involve factors such as laws, cultures, and commercial practices of different countries, making them relatively complex. Intermediate people's courts generally possess more extensive experience and more professional capability in handling foreign-related cases. They are better equipped to understand and apply relevant international treaties, international practices, and domestic foreign-related legal provisions, thereby handling evidence preservation applications more appropriately.
B. ***Ensuring Judicial Quality and Uniformity***. Entrusting the review and ruling of evidence preservation in foreign-related arbitration to intermediate people's courts can better guarantee the quality of judicial decisions, ensuring accuracy and fairness in handling such matters. Simultaneously, it helps maintain uniformity in the judicial standard within a certain region, upholding judicial authority.
C. ***Facilitating International Alignment***. In the field of international commercial arbitration, procedural matters such as evidence preservation typically require review and handling by higher-level courts to ensure their fairness and authority. China's provision designating intermediate people's courts as responsible for evidence preservation in foreign-related arbitration is conducive to better aligning with international practices in this field, enhancing the international credibility and influence of China's foreign-related arbitration.

Article 10 of the Provisions of the SPC on Several Issues Concerning the People's Courts' Enforcement Work (For Trial Implementation) stipulates that during foreign-related arbitration proceedings, if a party applies for property preservation and the application is submitted by the arbitration institution to a people's court, the intermediate people's court at the domicile of the person against whom the application is made or at the location of the property to be preserved shall rule on and execute it; applications for evidence preservation shall be ruled on and executed by the intermediate people's court at the location of the evidence.[3] If two or more people's courts have jurisdiction, the party may apply to one of them for enforcement; if a party applies to two or more people's courts for enforcement, the court that first registers the case shall have jurisdiction. However, it also stipulates that for enforcement cases under the jurisdiction of basic-level or intermediate people's courts, if special circumstances require enforcement by a higher people's court, the matter may be referred to the higher people's court for enforcement.[4]

In applying this Article, it is necessary to determine whether the case is a foreign-related arbitration case. The criteria for determining foreign-related arbitration mentioned earlier apply here. If it is not a foreign-related arbitration case, the intermediate people's court will not accept the related evidence preservation application for filing. Even in foreign-related arbitration, if the court finds that the conditions for evidence preservation are not met, in other words, if there is no situation where the evidence might be destroyed or become difficult to obtain later, it will not grant the evidence preservation.

Generally, within the Chinese legal framework, the decision on interim measures, whether for evidence preservation or property preservation, is made by the court. However, in the realm of foreign-related or international commercial arbitration, the arbitral tribunal can also decide on interim measures. This introduces the possibility of an emergency arbitrator system. The emergency arbitrator procedure refers to the procedure applicable when, due to urgent circumstances, a party to the arbitration needs urgent interim relief before the constitution of the arbitral tribunal. In recent years, major Chinese arbitration institutions have incorporated provisions for the emergency arbitrator procedure in their rules. For example, Article 62 of the BAC Arbitration Rules stipulates that upon a party's application, the arbitral tribunal may decide to adopt interim measures it deems appropriate according to the relevant law. Decisions on interim measures can be made by a decision of the arbitral tribunal, an interim award, or in other forms recognized by the relevant law. If necessary, the arbitral tribunal has the power to require the party applying for interim measures to provide appropriate security. Article 63 stipulates that before the constitution of the arbitral tribunal, if a party needs to apply for interim measures, it may submit a written application to the BAC for the appointment of an emergency arbitrator according to the relevant law. Whether to approve the application is determined by the BAC. Article 26 of the SCIA Arbitration Rules states that, where permitted by the law applicable to the arbitration proceedings, from the commencement of the arbitration proceedings until the constitution of the arbitral tribunal, a party may apply to the SCIA Court for the appointment of an emergency

[3] See Article 10.

[4] See Article 15.

arbitrator in writing if interim measures are urgently needed due to emergency circumstances. Similar provisions regarding emergency arbitrators are found in Article 25 of the SHIAC Arbitration Rules and Article 80 of the CIETAC Arbitration Rules.

Decisions made by emergency arbitrators require enforcement by courts, but the issue of enforceability has not yet received uniform international recognition. Jurisdictions like Singapore, New Zealand, and Hong Kong SAR have provided for the enforceability of emergency arbitrator decisions in their arbitration laws. Currently, the New Arbitration Law does not contain explicit provisions on this matter. However, relevant cases involving decisions made by emergency arbitrators have already emerged in Chinese arbitration practice, and some decisions have been enforced by courts. This indicates that, for both property preservation and evidence preservation, and where permitted by the applicable law, interim measures can be obtained through the emergency arbitrator procedure in urgent situations.

Illustrative Cases

Case 1: *Beijing A Technology Company v. B Information Company*[5]

The case concerning the application for property preservation during arbitration by Beijing A Technology Company where a tribunal issued a decision on interim measures pursuant to the BAC Arbitration Rules, which was subsequently reviewed and granted by the court. A dispute arose between Beijing A Technology Company and B Information Company regarding the performance of the Technology Development and Service Integration Contract. Beijing A Technology Company filed for arbitration with the BAC and simultaneously applied for property preservation.

The arbitral tribunal rendered a decision on interim measures in accordance with the rules governing international commercial arbitration procedures. Upon the application of Beijing A Technology Company, the BAC submitted the relevant materials to Beijing No. 4 Intermediate People's Court.

The Beijing No.4 Intermediate People's Court held that, considering the possibility that B Information Company might lack the willingness or ability to fulfill its debt obligations, and to prevent the arbitral award from becoming unenforceable or difficult to enforce, the application for property preservation measures against B Information Company, which was filed by Beijing A Technology Company while providing sufficient security, should be supported. The scope of the measures requested did not exceed the claims asserted in the arbitration case. The Court particularly noted that the arbitral tribunal had heard both parties' statements and arguments regarding the property preservation request and had conducted a substantive review of the legitimacy, necessity, and appropriateness of the interim measures applied for by Beijing A Technology Company. The interim measures decision issued by the tribunal was well-reasoned and complied with the relevant rules of international commercial arbitration procedure. The people's court accorded due

[5] See the 10 Typical Cases published by the Beijing No.4 Intermediate People's Court in November 2024 to Support and Safeguard the Construction of an International Commercial Arbitration Center.

respect to this decision and treated it as a significant reference factor in its review of the property preservation application. Accordingly, the court ruled to grant the property preservation application.

This case demonstrated practical steps taken by the judiciary to actively incorporate advanced and internationally prevalent arbitration systems and concepts, promote the organic connection between arbitration and litigation, and support the construction of Beijing as an international commercial arbitration center.

Case 2: ***C Company v. H Company and others***[6]
On April 19, 2021, C Company initiated arbitration against H Company and Zhang before HKIAC. During the arbitration, to prevent the respondents from concealing or transferring assets, or encumbering them, and to ensure the eventual enforcement of the arbitral award, C Company applied to the Beijing Financial Court for property preservation. It requested the court to seize, freeze, or impound bank deposits of USD 14,784,384.42 (or other assets of equivalent value) held in the names of the respondents, H Company and Zhang. (Calculated using the USD to RMB central parity rate of 7.0992 published by the China Foreign Exchange Trade System on October 10, 2022, this amounted to approximately RMB 104,957,301.87).

This case was the first instance of a party in Hong Kong arbitration proceedings applying to a mainland court for property preservation accepted by the Beijing Financial Court. It was also the first case where the Beijing Financial Court applied the Arrangement Concerning Mutual Enforcement of Awards. The case involved a dispute over a securities repurchase agreement, characterized by both its foreign-related nature and its connection to Hong Kong arbitration proceedings. The preservation amount reached hundreds of millions of RMB, involved numerous and varied types of asset leads, including bank accounts, real estate, and equity interests, making the preservation process complex.

Upon receiving the application materials, the preservation review team promptly examined whether the documents were complete and whether preservation could be granted. After confirming jurisdiction, the court allowed the claimant to first submit electronic copies of the security materials and promptly accepted the case. After case filing, the collegial panel conducted preservation interviews via the "Nocturnal and Weekend Court" mechanism, promptly studied and deliberated on the case, achieving effective coordination between case filing, preservation, and enforcement to ensure timely and full preservation.

Concurrently, following the Arrangement Concerning Mutual Enforcement of Awards, the court promptly provided feedback on the preservation status to the HKIAC. This facilitated the orderly coordination between the arbitration proceedings and the preservation procedure, representing a significant measure in the financial judicial collaboration mechanism.

---

[6] See the 10 Typical Cases on Judicial Review of Financial Arbitration published by the Beijing Financial Court in October 2023.

Case 3: *G Company v. V Company*[7]
On April 10, 2017, G Company, registered in the Cayman Islands, and V Company signed a Loan Agreement, which stipulated that "either party has the right to submit any relevant dispute to the Hong Kong International Arbitration Centre (HKIAC) for arbitration." Subsequently, a dispute arose between the parties regarding the performance of the agreement. On May 18, 2022, G Company initiated arbitration against V Company and Su, a U.S. citizen, as respondents before the HKIAC, and simultaneously applied for preservation of assets. On June 9, 2022, G Company submitted the preservation application, the arbitration agreement, other relevant materials, and a scanned copy of a letter issued by the HKIAC to the Suzhou Intermediate People's Court of Jiangsu Province (hereinafter referred to as the Suzhou Intermediate Court), along with providing security for asset preservation. G Company stated that due to the pandemic, the HKIAC was unable to promptly forward the relevant materials by mail.

After accepting G Company's application for asset preservation, the Suzhou Intermediate Court sent an email to the HKIAC official email address to promptly verify the authenticity of the materials and the case. Upon confirmation via a reply email from the HKIAC, the Jiangsu Province Suzhou Intermediate People's Court issued a ruling on asset preservation on June 13, 2022. Based on this ruling, it seized the equity in a certain company held by the respondents, V Company and Su, on June 16, 2022.

On November 21, 2023, the HKIAC rendered its arbitral award on the dispute. Following this, G Company applied to the Jiangsu Province Suzhou Intermediate People's Court for recognition and enforcement of the arbitral award. After review, the Jiangsu Province Suzhou Intermediate People's Court determined that the arbitral award met the conditions for recognition and enforcement stipulated in the Arrangement Concerning Mutual Enforcement of Awards and the Supplemental Arrangement Concerning Mutual Enforcement of Awards. Accordingly, the Court ruled to recognize and enforce the arbitral award.

Article 80
A foreign-related arbitral tribunal may make a written record of the transcript or key points of the hearings. The written key points may be signed or sealed by the parties and other participants in the arbitration.

[7](2022) Su 05 Cai Bao 146; See the 6 Typical Cases published by the SPC on Supporting Hong Kong Arbitration in September 2024. This case is a model of a people's court providing assistance in arbitration preservation pursuant to the Arrangement Concerning Mutual Enforcement of Awards. The review occurred during the COVID-19 pandemic. The Jiangsu Province Suzhou Intermediate People's Court fully considered the urgency of the arbitration preservation need and the objective difficulties in transferring physical documents from Hong Kong SAR to the Chinese Mainland during the pandemic. It flexibly used email to verify the authenticity of the materials with the HKIAC and completed the entire process of review, ruling, and taking preservation measures within one week.

Notes

On the matter of hearing records, the New Arbitration Law stipulates different practices for domestic arbitration and international arbitration. According to Article 60 of the New Arbitration Law, in domestic arbitration hearings, the arbitral tribunal is obligated to prepare a full written record of the hearing proceedings. This includes all aspects of the hearing, such as the parties' statements, the cross-examination process, questions from the arbitrators, presentation of evidence, and the content of debates, to ensure the traceability of the arbitration procedure. The form of the record can be physical or electronic, but it must comply with the technical specifications of the arbitration rules. Simultaneously, the parties have the right to apply for corrections. If the parties or other arbitration participants discover omissions or errors in the record of their own statements, they have the right to apply to the arbitral tribunal for corrections. The scope of correction is limited to the record of one's own statements and does not include objections to others' statements. If the arbitral tribunal rejects the application for correction, it must clearly record this application in the transcript. Furthermore, the transcript needs to be signed or sealed by the arbitrators, recorder, parties, and other arbitration participants. All arbitrators must sign, the recorder must sign or seal, and the parties and other participants must sign or seal each page to confirm the accuracy of the recorded content. Once signed, the transcript becomes crucial evidence of the arbitration procedure and can serve as a basis for the award or material for subsequent review. Taking CIETAC and BAC as examples: Article 73 in Chapter 5 of the CIETAC Arbitration Rules, titled "Special Provisions for Domestic Arbitration," stipulates: (1) the arbitral tribunal shall keep a written record of the oral hearing. Any party or other participant in the arbitration may apply for correction of the record of its own statement if any omission or error is found in the record; if the application is refused by the arbitral tribunal, it shall be recorded in the file. (2) The written record of the oral hearing shall be signed or sealed by the arbitrator(s), the recorder, the parties and other participants in the arbitration. Article 41 of the BAC Arbitration Rules stipulates: (1) the arbitral tribunal shall prepare a written record of the hearing, except for mediation proceedings. (2) The arbitral tribunal may make audio or video recordings of the hearing. (3) Where a party or any other participant in the arbitration considers that there are omissions or errors in the record of its own statement, it shall have the right to apply for rectification thereof. If the arbitral tribunal decides not to make the rectification, the application shall be recorded in the written record. (4) The written record shall be signed or sealed by the arbitrators, the recorder, the parties, and other participants in the arbitration. For a hearing conducted online, the written record shall be confirmed in the manner determined by the arbitral tribunal. (5) Upon the joint application of the parties, or the application of one party, and with the consent of the BAC, the BAC may engage a stenographer to record the hearing, the costs of which shall be advanced by the parties.

In the CIETAC Arbitration Rules, unlike Article 73 mentioned above, which states the tribunal "shall" keep a record, Article 40 in Chapter 2 states that the tribunal "may" prepare a hearing transcript and/or audio-visual recording: (1) For an oral hearing, the arbitral tribunal may prepare a transcript and/or an audio-visual record of the hearing. The arbitral tribunal may, when it deems it necessary, prepare a summary of the hearing, and may require the parties and/or their representatives, witnesses and/or other persons involved to sign on or affix their seals to the transcript or the summary of the hearing. (2) Any party or other participant in the arbitration may apply for correction of the record of its own statement if any omission or error is found in the record; if the application is refused by the arbitral tribunal, it shall be recorded in the file. (3) The transcript, the summary and the audio-visual record of the hearing shall be available for the use of the arbitral tribunal. (4) Upon a party's application, the CIETAC may decide to engage a stenographer to take a transcript of the oral hearing, having regard to the specific circumstances of the case. The parties shall pay an advance for the costs incurred thereby.

This Article under the New Arbitration Law uses the term "may," vesting the discretion to choose the recording method with the arbitral tribunal. This enables the tribunal to determine the most appropriate form of record based on the specific circumstances of the case, such as the amount in dispute, complexity, whether the parties are represented, and the nature of the disputed issues. Whether it is "preparing a full written record" or "preparing a summary," the fundamental purpose is to create an objective account of the key proceedings of the hearing. This record is not intended to recreate every single word exchanged in detail, but rather to fix elements crucial for the progression of the procedure and the subsequent award. These include, for example: the appearance of the parties, confirmation or amendment of claims, key points from the cross-examination of evidence, facts acknowledged or undisputed by the parties, and new evidence submitted during the hearing. It is also important to note that in today's technological environment, both "preparing a full written record" and "preparing a summary" should be compatible with electronic methods to enhance efficiency and facilitate management. Electronic records confirmed via electronic signatures are equally viable.

Article 81

The parties may agree in writing on the seat of arbitration. Unless the parties have agreed otherwise on the applicable law for the arbitration procedure, the seat of arbitration shall serve as the basis for determining the applicable law for the arbitration procedure and the competent court with jurisdiction. The arbitral award is considered to be made at the seat of arbitration.

If the parties have not agreed on the seat of arbitration or the agreement is unclear, the seat of arbitration shall be determined according to the arbitration rules agreed upon by the parties; if the arbitration rules do not provide for it, the arbitral tribunal shall determine the seat of arbitration based on the circumstances of the case, in accordance with the principle of facilitating dispute resolution.

Notes

This Article is one of the key provisions of this revision, introducing the concept of the 'seat of arbitration' into Chinese arbitration legislation for the first time. The Arbitration Law (2017) stipulated the location of the arbitration commission and the location of the arbitration institution, but did not provide for the concept of the seat of arbitration. The acceptance and use of the concept of the seat of arbitration in China has gone through a developmental process. Article 283 of the Civil Procedure Law stipulates that the recognition and enforcement of foreign arbitral awards refers to awards made by foreign arbitration institutions, adopting the standard of the location of the arbitration institution to determine the nationality of an arbitral award. This has also been the traditional standard consistently used in China.

The Arbitration Law Interpretation first introduced the concept of the seat of arbitration. Its Article 16 states that the validity of a foreign-related arbitration agreement shall be governed by the law chosen by the parties; if the parties have not chosen the applicable law but have agreed on the seat of arbitration, the law of the seat of arbitration shall apply; if there is no choice of applicable law, no agreement on the seat of arbitration, or the agreement on the seat of arbitration is unclear, the law of the forum shall apply. The Law on Choice of Law first stipulated the seat of arbitration in legislation. Article 18 of the Law on Choice of Law states that the parties may choose by agreement the law applicable to the arbitration agreement; if the parties have not chosen, the law of the place where the arbitration institution is located or the law of the seat of arbitration shall apply.

In numerous judicial review cases of arbitration handled by Chinese courts, the seat of arbitration has, in fact, been gradually used to determine the procedural law applicable to the arbitration. For example, the case of ***X Machinery Company v. Y Technology Company*** was the first case involving an application to set aside an arbitral award rendered by a foreign arbitration institution with the Chinese Mainland as the seat of arbitration. It was also the first case to clarify the status and application of guiding principles commonly adopted in international commercial arbitration within the context of domestic judicial review of arbitration. The focal point of the dispute was the determination of the nationality of the arbitral award. In this case, the Beijing No.4 Intermediate People's Court held that the arbitral award was issued by the ICC International Court of Arbitration, with Beijing as the seat of arbitration. This constituted an arbitral award made by a foreign arbitration institution within the Chinese Mainland and should be regarded as a foreign-related arbitral award of China. Therefore, the relevant provisions of Chinese law governing foreign-related arbitration should be applied. When reviewing procedural issues, in addition to applying the relevant Chinese law on foreign-related arbitration and the arbitration rules of the foreign arbitration institution, this case explicitly established for the first time that the court may apply the procedural rules either chosen by the arbitral tribunal or unanimously agreed upon by the parties.

The seat of arbitration is the legal domicile or 'home' of the arbitration. Emphasizing the seat as the legal place aims to distinguish it from the physical locations where arbitration activities occur. Therefore, the seat is not merely a geographical concept determined by where activities happen, but a legal connecting factor. An arbitral tribunal's activities are not necessarily fixed to a single location. Proceedings often involve multiple jurisdictions. If a legal seat is not determined, it leads to uncertainty regarding the applicable law for the arbitration agreement, the arbitration procedure, the nationality of the award, and the competent court for judicial review. The seat of arbitration has the following four key legal implications:

A. ***Determining the governing law of the arbitration agreement***. The seat of arbitration usually coincides with the place where the award is made. Where the parties have not expressly chosen the law governing the arbitration agreement, the internationally common practice is to apply the law of the seat of arbitration as the governing law of the arbitration agreement.
B. ***Determining the law governing the arbitration procedure.*** The conduct of the arbitration relies both on the arbitration rules chosen by the parties and is subject to the law governing the arbitration procedure. The arbitration rules reflect the principle of party autonomy, whereas the law governing the arbitration procedure reflects the regulation of arbitration by a state's judicial sovereignty. The parties' agreements regarding procedure must not violate the mandatory legal provisions of the relevant country. Of course, the modern trend in arbitration development is a gradual reduction of restrictions on arbitration procedures by various countries.
C. ***Determining the nationality of the arbitral award.*** The key to distinguishing between domestic and foreign awards lies in determining the nationality of the award. In international practice, most countries adopt the territorial criterion, using the place where the award is made as the primary basis for determining nationality. A small number of jurisdictions use the criterion of the law governing the arbitration procedure. Although Chinese legislation does not explicitly stipulate the criteria for identifying foreign arbitral awards, judicial practice generally applies the criterion of the place where the award is made for foreign arbitral awards, meaning awards made outside the territory of China are regarded as foreign arbitral awards. However, traditionally, for Chinese arbitral awards, China used the criterion of the location of the arbitration institution, which created obstacles for awards made by Chinese arbitration institutions outside China. Similarly, the stance of Chinese judicial review regarding awards made by foreign arbitration institutions with China as the seat of arbitration has undergone a process from non-support to support.
D. ***Determining the Competent Court for Judicial Review***. Arbitration activities often involve cross-border elements. After an award is made, if a party applies to set aside the award, it is necessary to determine which country's court has jurisdiction. According to Article V of the New York Convention, the courts authorized to set aside an arbitral award include the courts of the country in which the award was made, or under the law of which the award was made. Therefore, the seat of arbitration is an important connecting factor for determining the court with jurisdiction to set aside an award.

Pursuant to this Article, the rules for determining the seat of arbitration are as follows, in order of priority: First, the principle of party autonomy prevails, which reflects the contractual nature of arbitration. Allowing parties to choose a legal jurisdiction they trust as the seat of arbitration is one of the most important procedural rights for international commercial entities and a core benchmark for measuring whether an arbitration law is open and advanced. Second, in the absence of party agreement, the arbitration rules apply. The rules of the vast majority of international arbitration institutions contain provisions for determining the seat of arbitration, which provides a quick and clear solution for most cases. Third, failing the above, the arbitral tribunal shall determine the seat based on the principle of facilitating dispute resolution. When the rules also lack provision, the arbitral tribunal is authorized to determine the seat according to the circumstances of the case and the principle of facilitating dispute resolution. This grants the arbitral tribunal ultimate authority over procedural management, ensuring that the proceedings can be initiated and advanced smoothly under any circumstances. The "principle of facilitating dispute resolution" provides valuable guidance for the tribunal's discretion, such as considering the place most closely connected to the dispute, the primary location of hearings, and the maturity of the legal environment, among other factors. Prior to the revision of the Arbitration Law, the arbitration rules of major domestic arbitration institutions had specific provisions regarding the seat of arbitration. For example, Article 7 of the CIETAC Arbitration Rules stipulates: (1) where the parties have agreed on the seat of arbitration, their agreement shall prevail. (2) Where the parties have not agreed on the seat of arbitration or their agreement is unclear, the seat of arbitration shall be the domicile of the CIETAC commission or its sub-commission/ arbitration center administering the case. CIETAC may also determine another location as the seat of arbitration having regard to the circumstances of the case. (3) The arbitral award shall be deemed as having been made at the seat of arbitration. Article 27 of the BAC Arbitration Rules and Article 4 of the SCIA Arbitration Rules contain similar provisions. Furthermore, Article 77 in the chapter on Special Provisions for Hong Kong Arbitration in the CIETAC Arbitration Rules specifically states that unless otherwise agreed by the parties, the seat of arbitration for cases administered by the CIETAC Hong Kong Arbitration Center shall be Hong Kong, the law applicable to the arbitration proceedings shall be the arbitration law of Hong Kong, and the arbitral award shall be a Hong Kong award. Article 4 of the Emergency Arbitrator Procedures states that unless otherwise agreed by the parties, the seat of arbitration for the case shall be the seat of the emergency arbitrator proceedings. The determination of the seat of arbitration for the case shall be governed by Article 7 of these Arbitration Rules.

According to this Article, the arbitral award is deemed to have been made at the seat of arbitration. This determines that the award is a "domestic award" of the country of the seat, and the procedure for setting aside such an award falls exclusively within the jurisdiction of the courts of the seat. Simultaneously, this constitutes the basis for its "nationality" when applying for recognition and enforcement worldwide under the New York Convention. The seat of arbitration is typically the place where the award is made. However, there are examples where the seat and the physical place of making the award differ. In the 1992 English case *Hiscox v. Outhwaite*, the award was considered made in France because it was signed there, even though the arbitration proceedings took place in London and had no connection to France. Section 100 of the English Arbitration Act 1996 provides that an award shall be treated as made at the seat of arbitration, regardless of where it was signed, dispatched, or delivered to the parties. This provision overturned the decision in *Hiscox v. Outhwaite* by the House of Lords. Where the parties have not expressly chosen the law governing the arbitration agreement, the internationally common practice is to apply the law of the seat of arbitration or the law of the place where the award is made as the governing law of the arbitration agreement.

Furthermore, pursuant to this Article, the primary roles of the seat of arbitration also include: firstly, unless otherwise agreed by the parties, the law governing the conduct of the arbitration proceedings (such as the constitution of the tribunal, service of documents, conduct of hearings, and the form of the award) is the arbitration law of the country of the seat, not the law of the country where physical hearings are held. Secondly, the seat of arbitration determines which country's courts have the authority to support the arbitration proceedings (e.g., appointing arbitrators, granting interim measures) and to exercise judicial supervision over them (e.g., setting aside the award).

Internationally, there exists a theory of delocalization or denationalization, which posits that international commercial arbitration procedures should float above the laws of any particular country, especially the procedural law of the seat of arbitration. Arbitration, according to this view, should free itself from the control of the law of the seat, or even from the laws of any specific country, and become a self-contained system. The delocalization theory initially emerged to address issues of state immunity in arbitration proceedings but has since expanded beyond cases where a state is a party. Proponents of delocalization argue that the choice of the seat of arbitration is often arbitrary; therefore, it is inappropriate for the laws of that country to influence the arbitration proceedings. They contend that arbitration procedures need only comply with the standards of international public policy.[8] Theoretical perspectives supporting and opposing the delocalization of arbitration procedures can be broadly divided into two schools: the jurisdictional theory and the contractual theory. The contractual theory holds that the foundation of arbitration lies in the agreement between the parties; thus, the arbitrators' powers and authority derive from this agreement. Supporters of this theory believe that the parties have the right to conduct arbitration in any manner they wish and can freely detach the procedure from domestic law, provided the procedure adheres to transnational minimum standards of justice. [Ibid.] The issue of delocalization typically arises in the context of enforcing arbitral awards. In simple terms, a delocalized arbitration procedure aims to shield the arbitral tribunal from the supervision of local courts. However, from a practical standpoint, no legal system has fully adopted the concept of completely delocalizing arbitration procedures.

The establishment of a "seat of arbitration" system aligned with international standards, connecting with globally accepted rules, represents a significant breakthrough in the new law's promotion of the internationalization of Chinese arbitration. In past practice, the absence of clear rules governing the seat of arbitration could affect the validity of arbitration agreements or the enforceability of arbitral awards, severely undermining the international credibility of arbitration in China. Under the New Arbitration Law, parties have the autonomy to agree on the seat of

---

[8] Mark Huleatt-James and Nicholas Gould, International Commercial Arbitration (LLP, 1996), 14–15.

arbitration. This means arbitral awards made in China can rely on the multilateral framework of the New York Convention, facilitating smoother recognition and enforcement in over 170 Contracting States worldwide. It also signifies that parties can more freely choose and utilize arbitration to resolve their disputes.

Article 82

In the case of foreign-related maritime disputes or foreign-related disputes arising between enterprises registered in the pilot free trade zones approved by the State Council, the Hainan Free Trade Port, and other areas stipulated by the state, where the parties have agreed in writing to arbitrate, they may choose either to submit the dispute to an arbitration institution; or to have the People's Republic of China as the seat of arbitration, with the arbitration conducted by an arbitral tribunal composed of personnel who meet the requirements of this Law according to the agreed arbitration rules. Such an arbitral tribunal shall, within three working days from the date of its constitution, file with the Arbitration Association a record containing the names of the parties, the seat of arbitration, the composition of the tribunal, and the arbitration rules.

Where one party applies for property preservation, evidence preservation, or requests the arbitral tribunal to order the other party to perform certain actions or prohibit them from performing certain actions, the arbitral tribunal shall submit the party's application to the people's court according to the law, and the people's court shall handle it in a timely manner according to the law.

Notes

One of the highlights of this revised Article is the introduction of *ad hoc* arbitration. In the field of commercial arbitration, ad hoc arbitration and institutional arbitration together form the important pillars of the commercial arbitration system. However, they differ in their operational logic and core characteristics, and these differences can impact the efficiency, cost control, and outcome stability of dispute resolution for the parties. Ad hoc arbitration is a dispute resolution path detached from the involvement of a fixed arbitration institution. Its core basis is the parties directly constituting an arbitral tribunal through their arbitration agreement to handle a specific commercial dispute. The tribunal is not a pre-established permanent organization but is specially formed for a particular case based entirely on the parties' agreement. Once the case is concluded and the award takes effect, the tribunal is dissolved and does not possess long-term continuity. Parties can autonomously agree upon key aspects of the arbitration procedure based on the industry characteristics of the dispute, its complexity, and commercial needs. This includes criteria for selecting arbitrators (e.g., specialized field, professional experience), setting the timeline for the proceedings, applying rules of evidence (e.g., allocation of burden of proof, requirements for evidence forms), and the format of hearings (online or offline), without being strictly bound by the standardized processes of a fixed institution. However, the limitations of ad hoc arbitration are also prominent. In practice, parties often find it difficult to comprehensively and meticulously predefine all procedural details for ad hoc arbitration in their arbitration agreement. If omissions occur in the initial procedures or disputes arise between the parties (for example, disagreements over arbitrator qualification criteria, or one party refusing to cooperate with the proceedings on the grounds of unclear procedural agreements), the subsequent hearing process can stall. This not only deviates from the original intention of "efficient dispute resolution" but may also give rise to new disputes over procedure, potentially leading to the arbitration agreement being deemed invalid or the arbitral award being set aside by a court, thereby increasing the uncertainty and additional costs of dispute resolution.

Institutional arbitration is a mode where parties submit their disputes to a specific permanent arbitration institution through a written agreement, with proceedings conducted strictly according to the institution's standardized arbitration rules. These permanent institutions typically possess a sound organizational structure and mature operational system, including a clear institutional name, established bylaws, fixed office premises, and professional case management teams. They pre-establish and publish unified arbitration rules, providing systematic and clear procedural guidance and an operational framework for the entire arbitration process. Compared to ad hoc arbitration, its core advantages lie in "professionalism" and "stability," offering multi-dimensional convenience and safeguards for both parties and arbitrators. For the parties, there is no need to design complex arbitration procedures; they simply need to specify the arbitration institution and applicable rules in their arbitration agreement to access the institution's full range of professional services. For arbitrators, the institutional rules clearly define their responsibilities, hearing timelines, procedural standards, and ethical requirements, effectively avoiding confusion arising from ambiguous procedural agreements. Additionally, the institution provides essential case support such as hearing transcripts, translation services, and compliance reminders, assisting arbitrators in handling cases efficiently and impartially while ensuring award quality. Furthermore, permanent arbitration institutions generally implement rigorous arbitrator selection and management systems, utilizing mechanisms like professional background checks, practical experience assessments, and ethical evaluations to form panels covering various sectors such as international trade, finance, intellectual property, and construction. This ensures appointed arbitrators possess solid legal expertise, extensive commercial practice experience, and high ethical standards, laying a solid foundation for professional and impartial case adjudication. Simultaneously, these institutions typically maintain comprehensive procedural management and supervision mechanisms that not only prevent prolonged procedures due to arbitrator delays but also reduce the risk of award invalidation from procedural defects or legal application errors through pre-issuance review of draft awards.

Traditionally, only institutional arbitration existed in China. All arbitrations conducted within China were administered by arbitration commissions. An arbitration agreement that did not designate a specific arbitration commission was invalid. However, even prior to this revision in 2025, China's judicial authorities and relevant institutions had already conditionally introduced elements related to ad hoc arbitration.

In December 2016, the SPC promulgated the Opinions on Providing Judicial Safeguards for the Construction of Pilot Free Trade Zones. Article 9 of these Opinions stipulated that an arbitration agreement could be found valid if it was made between enterprises registered within a Pilot Free Trade Zone, providing for arbitration of relevant disputes at a specific location within the mainland, in accordance with specific arbitration rules, and by specific personnel. Although the concept of "ad hoc arbitration" was not officially used here, this effectively constituted conditional ad hoc arbitration, and the stipulated "three specific elements" provided the basis for implementing *ad hoc* arbitration within the Pilot Free Trade Zones. The Shanghai Regulations on Promoting the Construction of an International Commercial Arbitration Centre, which took effect on December 1, 2023, stipulate in Article 20 that in accordance with national arrangements, this Municipality will explore allowing parties in commercial and maritime matters involving foreign-related elements to agree on *ad hoc* arbitration in Shanghai, conducted in accordance with specific arbitration rules and by specific personnel. In May 2024, the Several Provisions of Hainan Free Trade Port on the Development of International Commercial Arbitration, promulgated by the Hainan Provincial People's Congress and its Standing Committee, stated in Article 16 that commercial disputes between enterprises registered in the Hainan Free Trade Port, and between enterprises registered in the Hainan Free Trade Port and enterprises from foreign countries or the Hong Kong Special Administrative Region, Macao Special Administrative Region, and Taiwan region, may be resolved by ad hoc arbitration within the Hainan Free Trade Port; commercial disputes between enterprises from foreign countries or the Hong Kong Special Administrative Region, Macao Special Administrative Region, and Taiwan region that choose the Hainan Free Trade Port as the seat of arbitration may apply the preceding provision. On July 30, 2024, the Shanghai Arbitration Association released its "*Ad Hoc* Arbitration Rules." In fact, some cases have already tentatively included *ad hoc* arbitration agreements.

Article 82 of the New Arbitration Law, while granting the option for ad hoc arbitration for specific foreign-related disputes, also clarifies the conditions that must be simultaneously met to apply this ad hoc arbitration system:

A. ***Scope of application.*** The use of ad hoc arbitration is limited to two types of foreign-related disputes: Foreign-related maritime disputes, and Foreign-related disputes between enterprises in specific zones. The former refers to disputes in the field of maritime and commercial matters, such as disputes arising from contracts for the carriage of goods by sea, ship charter party disputes, and compensation disputes for damage caused by ship collisions, where one or both parties are foreign entities, the subject matter is located abroad, or the legal relationship was created or performed abroad. The latter must be foreign-related disputes occurring between enterprises registered and established in zones specifically approved by the State Council, such as Pilot Free Trade Zones, the Hainan Free Trade Port, and other zones stipulated by the state. The enterprises' place of registration must be within these special zones; enterprises registered elsewhere cannot apply.

B. ***Seat of arbitration.*** The seat of arbitration for the ad hoc arbitration must be the People's Republic of China. The seat determines the arbitration law governing the arbitration procedure. It must follow the judicial review procedures (such as setting aside and non-enforcement) prescribed by Chinese law. The courts at the seat of arbitration have jurisdiction over judicial assistance matters during the ad hoc arbitration proceedings (such as preservation measures and obtaining evidence).
C. ***Composition of the tribunal.*** The members of the ad hoc arbitral tribunal must satisfy the statutory requirements for arbitrators stipulated in the Arbitration Law. This is key to safeguarding the professionalism and impartiality of the ad hoc arbitration proceedings, including the previously mentioned qualification criteria for arbitrators, challenge requirements, etc.
D. ***Arbitration rules***. The ad hoc arbitration procedure must be conducted in accordance with agreed-upon arbitration rules. The parties may choose established domestic ad hoc arbitration rules, agree on internationally accepted ad hoc arbitration rules, or stipulate their own implementable rules.
E. ***Mandatory filing obligations.*** The ad hoc arbitral tribunal must fulfill the "mandatory filing obligation." This is a regulatory mechanism established by this Article for ad hoc arbitration. The filing materials required include the parties' names, the seat of arbitration, the composition of the arbitral tribunal, the arbitration rules, etc. This information must be true and complete, facilitating the arbitration association's grasp of the basic situation of ad hoc arbitrations and enabling appropriate supervision of the proceedings.

When parties choose ad hoc arbitration, they must simultaneously meet all the above conditions; the absence of any one condition may lead to the ad hoc arbitration procedure being invalid or the award being set aside by the court. Therefore, precise planning at the stage of concluding the arbitration agreement is necessary to ensure all conditions comply with the provisions of this Article.

Illustrative Case

A Trading Company v. B Freight Forwarding Company[9]

A Trading Company and B Freight Forwarding Company were registered in the China (Shanghai) Pilot Free Trade Zone and the Lingang New Area of the China (Shanghai) Pilot Free Trade Zone, respectively. In January 2024, the two companies

[9] (2024) Hu 72 Min Te 43; This case was selected as a typical case in the '2024 National Maritime Trial Typical Cases (2025)' published by the SPC. It was the first case accepted by a Shanghai court concerning the confirmation of the validity of an ad hoc arbitration agreement after the implementation of the Shanghai Regulations on Promoting the Construction of an International Commercial Arbitration Centre. The review in this case adhered to the principles of respecting party autonomy and supporting dispute resolution through arbitration. It provided fully reasoned explanations regarding the identification and criteria for recognizing the foreign-related elements required for ad hoc arbitration between enterprises registered in Pilot Free Trade Zones, and how to determine the agreed 'specific personnel' according to the arbitration rules when the parties have not selected arbitrators, based on whether the basic constituent elements of ad hoc arbitration were met.

signed the Transport Agreement, stipulating that B Freight Forwarding Company would handle customs clearance procedures for the imported goods for A Trading Company and transport the goods to A Trading Company's warehouse. During the performance of the agreement, a dispute arose between the parties concerning the transportation and customs declaration fees for a batch of goods imported from the Philippines.

In November 2024, the parties reached a written agreement on resolving the aforementioned fee dispute. They agreed to settle the dispute through arbitration, applying the Shanghai Arbitration Association Ad Hoc Arbitration Rules, with Shanghai as the seat of arbitration. The arbitration agreement was governed by the relevant laws of China, and the arbitral tribunal was to consist of a sole arbitrator. Subsequently, B Freight Forwarding Company contended that this arbitration agreement was legally invalid. A Trading Company then filed a lawsuit with the Shanghai Maritime Court, requesting confirmation of the validity of the ad hoc arbitration agreement.

The Shanghai Maritime Court held that, according to the arbitration agreement, the law of the People's Republic of China was the governing law for determining the validity of the arbitration agreement in dispute. The content of the Transport Agreement covered matters before and after the goods' customs entry, making it a contract with foreign-related elements. The claimants in this case and the designations of the seat of arbitration and the arbitration rules complied with the relevant provisions on *ad hoc* arbitration in the Shanghai Regulations on Promoting the Construction of an International Commercial Arbitration Centre. The arbitration rules chosen in the arbitration agreement provided a pathway for the selection of the arbitrator, effectively resolving potential deadlocks in the constitution of the arbitral tribunal. Therefore, it could be determined that the arbitration agreement in question had stipulated the "specific personnel." In conclusion, the Shanghai Maritime Court ruled that the *ad hoc* arbitration agreement was valid.

Article 83

Where a party presents evidence that proves that a foreign-related arbitral award involves one of the following circumstances, the people's court shall, after examination and verification by a collegial panel formed by the people's court, rule to set aside the award.

(1) **There is no arbitration agreement;**
(2) **The respondent was not notified of the appointment of an arbitrator or of the arbitration proceedings, or was unable to state its opinion for other reasons for which the respondent is not responsible;**
(3) **The composition of the arbitral tribunal or the arbitration procedure was not in accordance with the statutory procedure;**
(4) **The matters decided by arbitration exceed the scope of the arbitration agreement or the authority of the arbitration institution;**

Where the people's court determines that the award is contrary to public policy, it shall rule to set aside the award.

Notes

This Article concerns the setting aside of arbitral awards. Setting aside and non-enforcement of arbitral awards are the primary forms of judicial review provided for under the New Arbitration Law. Within the framework of the Arbitration Law, China implements a dual-track review system for foreign-related and domestic arbitral awards, with differing grounds for setting them aside. The grounds for setting aside a foreign-related arbitral award are enumerated under this Article. For both domestic and foreign-related arbitral awards, the public interest ground falls within the scope of the court's *ex officio* investigation, while the other grounds require the claimant to provide evidence.

Regarding the issue of the dual-track system for reviewing domestic and foreign-related arbitral awards, there are primarily two viewpoints within the industry. One view holds that granting a special status to foreign-related arbitration helps increase its appeal to foreign parties and maintains China's stable position in international arbitration. Simultaneously, limiting judicial supervision of foreign-related arbitral awards primarily to procedural matters helps preserve the stability and finality of arbitral awards. Courts do not re-examine the merits and should only serve to review and prevent major errors in the arbitration procedure; otherwise, the function of the arbitration system would be undermined. The other viewpoint argues that both foreign-related and domestic arbitration should be subject to supervision without differentiated treatment, and foreign-related arbitration should also be subject to comprehensive supervision. During the process of this law revision, a proposal to merge the tracks was also considered.

On an international level, examples exist of both dual-track review systems and single-track systems. For instance, Singapore employs a dual-track system for judicial supervision of arbitration: domestic arbitration is governed by the Arbitration Act, while international arbitration is governed by the International Arbitration Act. The Model Law does not distinguish between domestic and foreign-related awards and applies the same review content and rules. The United Kingdom applies a uniform standard for reviewing domestic and foreign awards, employing a relatively strict review system for arbitral awards in terms of judicial supervision.

A review of New Arbitration Law reveals that the scope of judicial review for domestic arbitral awards is broader and the standards are stricter compared to foreign-related arbitral awards. Regarding the judicial review grounds for setting aside foreign-related awards versus purely domestic awards, the primary distinctions, apart from public policy considerations, are as follows: The grounds for setting aside domestic awards include "forged evidence" and "concealment of evidence," both of which potentially involve substantive review, as well as "arbitrators committing embezzlement, accepting bribes, engaging in malpractice for personal benefit, or perverting the law." In contrast, the grounds for setting aside foreign-related awards do not involve substantive issues; besides public policy, they focus primarily on procedural aspects, examining whether the arbitration procedure violated legal procedures or the parties' agreed-upon arbitration rules. Chinese judicial review practice encompasses a substantial number of cases involving various defense arguments.

1. **There is no arbitration agreement**

The validity of the arbitration agreement directly affects the legality and enforceability of the award. The arbitration agreement must be in writing and clearly specify the matters for arbitration and the selected arbitration commission; otherwise, it may be deemed invalid. In arbitration practice, a significant number of cases involve issues concerning the invalidity of arbitration agreements. The determination of validity may differ between foreign-related and domestic arbitration agreements. For instance, the authority to sign the agreement, particularly when one party is a foreign company with specific requirements for executing agreements, may impact the validity of the arbitration agreement.

2. **The respondent was not notified of the appointment of an arbitrator or of the arbitration proceedings, or was unable to state its opinion for other reasons for which the respondent is not responsible**

This ground relates to procedural justice, ensuring parties have a fair opportunity to present their case in arbitration. In domestic arbitration, if the respondent was unable to present its case due to lack of notice or other reasons beyond its control, the court may set aside the award. This review may be combined with substantive grounds (e.g., concealment of evidence), potentially leading to stricter judicial intervention. For example, if the respondent failed to participate and the award was based on forged evidence, the court would be more inclined to set it aside. In foreign-related arbitration, pursuant to Article 70 of the New Arbitration Law and Article 274 of the Civil Procedure Law, this ground is purely procedural, focusing only on whether notice was timely and the procedure was fair, without involving substantive assessment. Foreign-related arbitration emphasizes procedural autonomy and efficiency to uphold the finality and predictability of international commercial arbitration. This distinction reflects strengthened protection of party rights in domestic arbitration, while foreign-related arbitration tends to minimize judicial intervention to facilitate the rapid resolution of international disputes. In practice, domestic courts might interpret "unable to present its case" more broadly, whereas in foreign-related arbitration, it is strictly confined to procedural defects, avoiding substantive review.

3. **The composition of the arbitral tribunal or the arbitration procedure was not in accordance with the statutory procedure**

The composition of the tribunal and procedural compliance are core to the legitimacy of arbitration. In domestic arbitration, if the tribunal's composition or the procedure violates the agreed arbitration rules or legal procedures, the court may set aside the award. This review may intertwine with other substantive grounds (e.g., arbitrators perverting the law), potentially leading to broader judicial scrutiny. For instance, if procedural violations affect substantive fairness, the court might directly set aside the award. In contrast, for setting aside foreign-related awards under Article 70 of the New Arbitration Law, review is limited to whether the procedure complied with the arbitration rules or legal requirements, without delving into substantive matters. Foreign-related arbitration places greater emphasis on procedural autonomy, respecting the parties' chosen rules (e.g., ICC Arbitration Rules, and UNCITRAL Arbitration Rules), ensuring the independence and consistency of international dispute resolution. This difference reflects a tendency in domestic arbitration towards mixed procedural and substantive review to prevent injustice, whereas foreign-related arbitration adheres to the principle of procedural priority to maintain the efficiency and credibility of international arbitration.

4. **The matters decided by arbitration exceed the scope of the arbitration agreement or the authority of the arbitration institution**

This ground concerns the jurisdictional boundaries of the arbitral tribunal, i.e., whether the award involves "ultra petita" or "excess of authority." In domestic arbitration, pursuant to Article 71 of the New Arbitration Law, if the award deals with matters beyond the scope of the arbitration agreement or addresses non-arbitrable matters as defined by law (e.g., disputes concerning personal rights, administrative disputes), the people's court shall rule to set it aside. During this review, to accurately define the tribunal's scope of adjudication, the court may inevitably touch upon substantive evidence to determine whether the facts ascertained by the tribunal align with the matters agreed in the arbitration agreement. This review method reflects the strict control over jurisdictional issues in domestic arbitration judicial supervision, aiming to maintain the uniformity and authority of the domestic legal order. In contrast, in setting aside proceedings for foreign-related awards, the court's review strictly adheres to principles of formal and procedural examination. The court primarily relies on the textual record of the arbitration agreement and prima facie evidence to determine excess of authority, typically without delving into the substantive content or merits of the award. This restrained approach to review fully respects party autonomy in international commercial transactions, aligns with mainstream international practice, and aims to safeguard the finality and international enforceability of foreign-related arbitral awards, providing stable and efficient dispute resolution expectations for cross-border commercial activities.

5. **Where the people's court determines that the award is contrary to public policy, it shall rule to set aside the award**

The public interest clause serves as an ultimate "safety valve" in the judicial review of arbitration, applicable to both domestic and foreign-related arbitral awards. Once triggered, the court shall rule to set aside the award. However, in specific judicial practice, its application standards differ significantly between domestic and foreign-related contexts. For domestic arbitral awards, people's courts tend to interpret and apply "social public interest" more proactively and broadly. Its connotation may extend to national economic security, social public order and good morals, protection of vulnerable groups, and even major local interests. When the award is substantively manifestly unfair, especially if coupled with other grounds like arbitrators perverting the law or parties forging evidence, courts are more inclined to find that it impinges upon fundamental societal concepts of good faith and justice, thus invoking the public interest clause to set it aside. Conversely, in the realm of foreign-related arbitration, guided by the principles of supporting international commercial arbitration and upholding the international reputation, courts maintain a highly deferential and cautious stance towards applying this clause. Its scope is typically strictly confined to extreme circumstances, such as violations of the most fundamental mandatory provisions of China's legal system, national sovereignty and security, or recognized international public order (e.g., involving core crimes like terrorism, piracy, or slave trading).

Furthermore, it is necessary to mention the reporting and approval system for setting aside foreign-related arbitral awards. This refers to the specific procedural mechanism that People's Courts must follow when handling cases involving applications to set aside China's foreign-related arbitral awards. According to the Notice on Issues Concerning Setting Aside of Foreign-Related Arbitral Award, if a party applies to a people's court to set aside a foreign-related arbitral award of China, and the people's court, upon examination, considers that the award falls under one of the circumstances specified in the relevant provisions of the Civil Procedure Law, it must, before ruling to set aside the award or notifying the arbitral tribunal to re-arbitrate, report the case to the high people's court within its jurisdiction for review. If the high people's court agrees to set aside the award or notify re-arbitration, it shall report its review opinion to the SPC. Only after receiving a reply from the SPC can the court then rule to set aside the award or notify of re-arbitration. The Provisions of the SPC on the Reporting and Approval of Issues in Arbitration Judicial Review Cases, issued on December 26, 2017, further stipulate that when Intermediate People's Courts or specialized courts handle arbitration judicial review cases involving foreign, Hong Kong, Macao, or Taiwan elements, and upon review intend to rule an arbitration agreement invalid, refuse enforcement, or set aside an arbitral award made by a Chinese mainland arbitration institution, they shall report to the high people's court within their jurisdiction for approval. If the high people's court, upon review, intends to agree with the proposed ruling, it shall report to the SPC for approval. Only after the SPC has reviewed the case can the ruling be made in accordance with the SPC's review opinion.

Illustrative Cases

Case 1: *KSHY Company v. RD Company*[10]

CIETAC accepted and awarded the dispute between KSHY Company and RD Company arising from the performance of the Sales Contract and rendered an award. KSHY Company applied to set aside the award.

The Court held that the respondent, RD Company in this case was a legal entity registered in the Hong Kong Special Administrative Region, making this a judicial review case involving Hong Kong-related arbitration. Pursuant to Article 70 of the Arbitration Law (2017), when a people's court reviews a foreign-related arbitral award, it should base its review on the matters stipulated in Article 281 of the Civil Procedure Law. The aforementioned clauses constitute the statutory grounds for a people's court to set aside a foreign-related arbitral award. Reasons raised by the

[10] (2023) Jing 04 Min Te No. 67.

parties that do not conform to the above provisions cannot serve as grounds for setting aside a foreign-related arbitral award. In this case, KSHY Company raised three grounds: first, that there was no written arbitration agreement between the parties; second, that the composition of the arbitral tribunal and the arbitration procedure were inconsistent with the arbitration rules; and third, that RD Company concealed and forged evidence sufficient to affect a fair award. As the third ground did not fall within the review matters stipulated above, the court did not accept it. The court analyzed the other two grounds separately as follows:

First, regarding whether there was a written arbitration agreement between the parties. According to Article 16(1) of the Arbitration Law (2017), an arbitration agreement shall include arbitration clauses stipulated in the contract and agreements of request for arbitration in writing concluded before or after the disputes arise. In this case, KSHY Company argued that there was no written arbitration agreement because the arbitral tribunal adopted the contract version provided by RD Company, which lacked KSHY Company's seal. Upon investigation, KSHY Company and RD Company each provided a different version of the Sales Contract. KSHY Company's version bore the seals of both parties, while RD Company's version lacked KSHY Company's seal. After thorough comparison, the arbitral tribunal found that the "only difference between the two versions of the Sales Contract lies in the quality standard for the blue isolation gowns," and thus both versions contained the same arbitration clause. Given that neither party objected to the arbitration clause itself, the court also had no objection. Since both parties had affixed their seals to the version of the Sales Contract provided by KSHY Company, it should be determined that the parties had concluded an arbitration clause in writing within the Sales Contract. Furthermore, since KSHY Company initiated arbitration based on the arbitration clause in its provided version of the Sales Contract, it could be determined that it recognized the arbitration clause in that contract version. Although the arbitral tribunal did not find the version of the Sales Contract provided by KSHY Company to be legally valid, according to Article 19 of the Arbitration Law (2017), which codified the principle of arbitration clause independence, the amendment, rescission, termination, or invalidity of a contract shall not affect the validity of the arbitration agreement. Therefore, a written arbitration agreement existed between the parties.

Second, regarding whether the composition of the arbitral tribunal and the arbitration procedure were inconsistent with the arbitration rules. "Violation of the legal procedure" referred to a violation of the arbitration procedure stipulated in the Arbitration Law (2017) or the arbitration rules chosen by the parties that could affect the correct adjudication of the case. KSHY Company claimed that the arbitration violated the legal procedure on the grounds that the summary procedure was applied, CIETAC failed to serve the Panel of Arbitrators, and the arbitration hearing failed to conduct cross-examination and verify the original evidence. Regarding this, the court held as follows: firstly, according to Article 56 of the CIETAC Arbitration Rules, the summary procedure was a hearing procedure established by CIETAC for cases where the amount in dispute did not exceed RMB five million. Its application itself did not affect a fair award. For cases where the amount in dispute did not exceed RMB five million, and in the absence of any separate agreement by the parties, the summary procedure shall apply. In this case, as the parties did not agree on the arbitration procedure and the amount in dispute did not exceed RMB five million, CIETAC's application of the summary procedure was not improper and did not violate the legal procedure. Secondly, according to Article 8(2) of the CIETAC Arbitration Rules, KSHY Company, as the arbitration claimant, provided CIETAC with its address for service. CIETAC sent the arbitration notice and attachments (including the CIETAC Arbitration Rules and the Panel of Arbitrators) to the service address provided by KSHY Company, and they were actually successfully delivered. Therefore, it could be determined that CIETAC had served the Panel of Arbitrators, the arbitrator recommendation form, and other arbitration documents to KSHY Company. CIETAC's service of the arbitration notice and attachments (including the Arbitration Rules and the Panel of Arbitrators) did not violate the legal procedure. KSHY Company's argument that it was unable to select an arbitrator or exercise its right to challenge due to CIETAC's failure to legally serve the Panel of Arbitrators was unfounded. Thirdly, according to the arbitration hearing transcript, the sole arbitrator fully protected the parties' rights to present and cross-examine evidence during the arbitration hearing. Regarding the failure to verify the original contract provided by KSHY Company, the sole arbitrator inquired about RD Company's opinion, and RD Company explicitly stated that verification was unnecessary. Furthermore, the sole arbitrator required KSHY Company to comment on whether the contract was the original. Therefore, the presentation and cross-examination of evidence during the arbitration hearing did not violate the legal procedure.

Case 2: ***EEI Company and others v. WY Company***[11]

On March 9, 2011, WY Company and A Technology Company signed the Procurement Contract, stipulating that WY Company would purchase 2.0 MW aerospace direct-drive wind turbine converters from A Technology Company, along with related technical documents, technical services, and technical training. Article 12.1 of the contract stated that all disputes relating to or arising from the performance of the contract should be settled through friendly negotiations between the parties; if settlement could not be reached through negotiation, the disputes shall be submitted for arbitration. Article 12.2 stipulated that the arbitration should be conducted in Beijing by the CIETAC in accordance with its arbitration rules and procedures. It was further agreed that the appendices of this contract were integral parts hereof and were equally authentic as the contract itself. Appendix VII of the contract was the format of a letter of guarantee. On the day the contract was signed, EEI Company did not sign or affix its seal to the letter of guarantee. On April 5, 2011, EEI Company signed the letter of guarantee in the format of Appendix VII, undertaking to guarantee the performance of the contract and assuming the same liabilities as A Technology Company.

[11] (2019) Zui Gao Fa Min Ta No. 14.

Subsequently, a dispute arose between WY Company and A Technology Company regarding the performance of the aforementioned contract. WY Company filed an arbitration application with CIETAC, naming A Technology Company and EEI Company as respondents. CIETAC accepted the arbitration application. On September 24, 2014, CIETAC sent the arbitration notice, arbitration rules, and the panel of arbitrators for this case to both parties, and also sent the arbitration application and its attachments submitted by WY Company to A Technology Company and EEI Company. On December 1, 2014, EEI Company submitted an application to CIETAC objecting to the arbitration jurisdiction. On April 30, 2015, CIETAC issued a jurisdictional decision, holding that: the arbitration clause in the contract was valid; the Arbitration Commission had jurisdiction over this case; EEI Company was bound by the arbitration clause in this case; and the arbitration proceedings should continue between WY Company, A Technology Company, and EEI Company. On May 12, 2017, CIETAC rendered the arbitral award.

EEI Company and A Technology Company applied to the Beijing No.4 Intermediate People's Court to set aside the award. They argued that there was a distinction between arbitration and litigation regarding the jurisdiction over principal and accessory contracts. In litigation, the jurisdiction over a supplementary contract could be determined based on the principal contract; however, this rule could not be simply applied by analogy in arbitration. If matters stipulated in an accessory contract were to be submitted to arbitration, the accessory contract itself must contain an expression of intent to arbitrate. In this case, the arbitration clause in the procurement contract could only bind the buyer and the seller, and could not bind EEI Company, which provided a guarantee for the performance of the seller, A Technology Company. Therefore, the arbitration clause was not binding on EEI Company.

After review, the Beijing No.4 Intermediate People's Court held that the award should be set aside. Subsequently, in accordance with Article 2(1) of the Provisions of the SPC on the Reporting and Approval of Issues in Arbitration Judicial Review Case, the court reported the case to the Beijing High People's Court for approval. The Beijing High People's Court, after review, agreed with the reporting opinion and, pursuant to the aforementioned judicial interpretation, reported the case to the SPC for approval.

The SPC, upon review, held that this case involved an application to set aside a foreign-related arbitral award rendered by a Chinese arbitration institution. Based on the facts described in the request for instructions, Article 12 of the procurement contract signed by the claimant A Technology Company and the respondent WY Company on March 9, 2011, constituted the arbitration clause, and Appendix VII of the procurement contract was the format of the letter of guarantee. The claimant EEI Company signed the letter of guarantee in the format of Appendix VII on April 5, 2011, and this letter of guarantee did not contain an arbitration clause. Resolution of disputes through arbitration requires a clear agreement by the parties; the arbitration clause in the principal contract cannot be presumed to bind the parties to the guarantee contract. Since EEI Company only signed the letter of guarantee format and did not sign the procurement contract, the arbitration clause in that contract was not binding on EEI Company. The arbitral tribunal's opinion that the arbitration clause in the procurement contract should also apply to the letter of guarantee lacked factual and legal basis. On June 26, 2019, pursuant to Items 1 and 4, Paragraph 1, Article 274 of the Civil Procedure Law and Article 70 of the Arbitration Law (2017), the SPC agreed with the opinion of the Beijing High People's Court that the involved arbitral award should be set aside. Subsequently, the Beijing No.4 Intermediate People's Court, based on this reply, ruled to set aside the arbitral award.

Case 3*: A Shipping Company v. Pei*[12]

In January 2022, A Shipping Company signed the Service Contract with Pei, stipulating that Pei would serve as the captain on the "Wanpeng 103" vessel managed by A Shipping Company. During his service, Pei caused losses to the shipowner due to his own error, and in May 2022, A Shipping Company notified Pei to take leave along with the vessel. In September 2022, Pei filed an arbitration application with the China Maritime Arbitration Commission regarding disputes under the Service Contract between him and A Shipping Company, requesting A Shipping Company to pay the salary difference, travel expenses to the vessel, repatriation travel expenses, wages during the pandemic quarantine period, social insurance, economic compensation, and other costs. The China Maritime Arbitration Commission rendered an award, ordering A Shipping Company to pay Pei wages during the quarantine period, travel expenses to the vessel, travel expenses off the vessel, and attorney fees, while dismissing Pei's claims for salary difference, social insurance, economic compensation, and other requests. In June 2023, Pei applied to the Qingdao Maritime Court to set aside the aforementioned arbitral award, on the grounds that the evidence on which the award was based was forged, the award lacked factual basis and incorrectly determined the legal relationship, the arbitrator had perverted the law during the arbitration, and the award violated public interest.

The Qingdao Maritime Court issued a civil ruling, dismissing Pei's application to set aside the award. This case involved a dispute over an application to set aside a maritime arbitral award. A Shipping Company was a Hong Kong company; according to Article 21 of the Arbitration Judicial Review Provisions, the provisions concerning judicial review of foreign-related arbitration cases applied by reference. Pursuant to Article 70 of the Arbitration Law (2017), the review should examine whether the foreign-related arbitral award involved any of the circumstances stipulated in Article 258 (1) (now Article 291) of the Civil Procedure Law. The grounds for setting aside raised by Pei all pertained to the arbitral tribunal's findings of fact and application of law, essentially requesting the court to overturn the arbitration institution's determinations on certain objective facts and to reassess those facts on their merits. These matters did not fall within the scope of review for setting aside an arbitral award under the aforementioned legal provisions, and therefore, the court did not review the issues raised by Pei.

---

[12] (2023) Lu 72 Min Te No. 221; See No.9 of the 10 Typical Cases for 2024 "World Oceans Day" published by the Qingdao Maritime Court.

Apart from the above reasons, Pei also claimed that the arbitrator had perverted the law during the arbitration. However, he failed to submit effective criminal legal documents or evidence of disciplinary sanctions proving that the arbitrator had engaged in perverting the law, which did not meet the requirements of Article 18 of the Arbitration Judicial Review Provisions. The arbitrator addressed all of Pei's arbitration claims in the award, and there was no evidence proving that the arbitrator intentionally rendered a wrong award based on special interests. Therefore, there was no situation where the arbitrator deliberately perverted the law contrary to facts and law.

Pei also argued that the arbitral award violated public interest. The Qingdao Maritime Court, upon review, held that public interest refers to the interests commonly enjoyed by all members of society, characterized by broad applicability and non-specificity, and is different from the rights between contracting parties. The arbitral award in this case addressed disputes arising from the performance of the contract between the parties, was binding only on the contracting parties, and did not involve public interest. Consequently, this ground raised by Pei was also unfounded.

Case 4: ***HQ Company v. TT Company, et al***[13]

HQ Company applied to set aside the award rendered by the CIETAC concerning its dispute with TT Company, DH Company, and HDM Company. The Beijing No. 4 Intermediate People's Court held that the claimant, HQ Company, was an enterprise legal person registered in the United Republic of Tanzania; therefore, the award was a foreign-related arbitral award. Summarizing HQ Company's grounds for applying to set aside the arbitral award in this case, there were two main points: on one hand, there was no arbitration agreement between the parties (HQ Company did not sign the Repayment Agreement containing the arbitration clause). On the other hand, it was not notified of the arbitration proceedings and was unable to present its case (the main facts focused on the service stage).

Regarding the service procedure during the arbitration period. The facts of the case were that during the arbitration, CIETAC first attempted service of the arbitration notice and other materials to HQ Company by express mail on July 28, 2016. However, the award did not record whether this express mail was effectively served or returned (although the award recorded that express mail sent to DH Company and HDM Company was returned due to "business termination"). Subsequently, CIETAC, "[i]n view of the special circumstances of HQ Company's communication address" (quoted from the award), applied the "deemed service" provision in Article 8 of the Arbitration Rules less than a month after the first attempt, and entrusted a notary institution to send the arbitration notice and other materials to HQ Company by ordinary mail for the second time on August 23, 2016. Thereafter, CIETAC used the same notarized service method to deliver relevant arbitration documents to HQ Company. However, evidence submitted by HQ Company during this court's review showed that it actually first received arbitration documents sent by CIETAC (the

13 (2017) Jing 04 Min Te No. 30.

express mail sent on July 28, 2016) on January 9, 2017. Upon this court's verification with CIETAC, CIETAC replied that the postal company had informed them that HQ Company's address "could not be served by express mail," hence they adopted notarized service. However, on one hand, the postmark date shown on the corresponding International Express Mail Inquiry Form was October 10, 2017, which was later than CIETAC's first notarized service on August 23, 2016 (in fact, the postmark date was also later than the award rendering date of February 14, 2017). On the other hand, the International Express Mail Inquiry Form did not state that HQ Company's address was "undeliverable," but rather that it "cannot be served by express mail; PO Box addresses are only available for mail sent by postal airmail," meaning service could be effected by sending postal airmail. Upon investigation, the "deemed service" provision in the Arbitration Rules relied upon by CIETAC should specifically be Article 8 "Service and Periods," Paragraph (3): "Any arbitration document to a party or its representative(s) may be served by hand-delivery, or sent by registered mail or express mail, or by any other means which can provide a record of delivery (including notarized service, entrusted service and retain service), to the addressee's place of business, registration place, domicile, habitual residence, or mailing address, or to the address agreed by the parties, or to the addressee's last known address. If none of these addresses can be found after reasonable inquiry by the other party, the arbitration document may be served at the addressee's last known place of business, registration place, domicile, habitual residence, or mailing address by the means stated above, which shall be deemed to have been served." This court held that Article 8(3) of the Arbitration Rules essentially prescribed three methods of service: ① Direct service ("hand-delivery to the addressee"), ② Postal service ("sent to the addressee's place of business, registration place, domicile, habitual residence, or mailing address," where "sent to" should be interpreted as actual receipt by the addressee), and ③ Deemed service ("if none of these addresses can be found after reasonable inquiry by the other party, the arbitration document may be served... to the addressee's last known... address... which shall be deemed to have been served"). The interpretation of the above provision in the Arbitration Rules should be based on the fundamental premise that the relevant arbitration documents can effectively reach the party. Only when actual service is difficult can other methods of deemed service be used as a supplement. In fact, based on a textual interpretation, Article 8(3) of the Arbitration Rules also stipulated that CIETAC could only use deemed service if, "after reasonable inquiry by the other party, none of these addresses... can be found." Specifically in this case, even disregarding the fact that it was later proven express mail could actually reach HQ Company, when the postal company explicitly stated that service could be effected by postal airmail, CIETAC did not attempt to use the corresponding postal method but directly concluded that the address was "undeliverable" and subsequently applied "deemed service" for follow-up arbitration documents. This did not comply with the relevant provisions on service in the Arbitration Rules.

Furthermore, the Court noted that the first hearing during the arbitration period was held on November 29, 2016, and CIETAC sent the hearing notice to HQ Company by notarized ordinary mail on November 1, 2016. Considering Article

37(1) of the Arbitration Rules, which stated, "For a case to be heard orally, the date of the first hearing shall be fixed by the arbitral tribunal and notified to the parties 20 days [prior to the hearing]," it could be calculated that CIETAC only allowed 8 days in transit for the hearing notice. Article 8(4) of the Arbitration Rules stipulated, "Any period referred to in these Rules shall start on the day following the day when the party receives or should have received the document, notice, or material sent by the [Court of Arbitration]." HQ Company's domicile was in the United Republic of Tanzania. As stated in the award, the company's communication address had "special circumstances." Based on common experience, allowing only 8 days for an ordinary mail sent from Beijing, PRC, to Tanzania was far from sufficient. Facts also proved that the mail did not reach HQ Company within 8 days. This court held that even when applying the "deemed service" rule, it should be done in a manner that strives to the greatest extent possible to deliver to the addressee. Since the Arbitration Rules stipulated that relevant periods should be calculated from the day after the party "should have received" the materials sent by CIETAC, allowing a reasonable transit time was inherently implied. Under the premise that CIETAC was clearly aware of the "special circumstances," the transit time allowed for the hearing notice was insufficient to complete normal service. It should be presumed that CIETAC's corresponding service work did not meet the procedural requirement of notifying the parties 20 days before the first hearing as stipulated in Article 37 of the Arbitration Rules. HQ Company first received the arbitration notice and other documents on January 9, 2017. According to Article 15(1) of the Arbitration Rules and CIETAC's notice, it was entitled to a 45-day defense period. However, CIETAC rendered Award No. 0059 on February 14, 2017, before HQ Company's defense period had expired.

Based on the above analysis, it could be determined that procedural errors occurred in CIETAC's service work during the arbitration period involved, resulting in HQ Company being unable to present its case for reasons not attributable to it. Therefore, the involved arbitral award should be set aside. Furthermore, as this Court had already determined that the involved arbitral award should be set aside, HQ Company's opinion regarding the non-existence of an arbitration agreement between the parties no longer required review in this case, and this court would not review it.

Case 5: ***LC Company v. ZF Company***[14]

The BAC rendered an award concerning the dispute between LC Company and ZF Company. LC Company applied to set aside this arbitral award. On November 22, 2019, the Xinyi People's Court issued a civil ruling, accepting the case for bankruptcy liquidation of LC Company. On November 26, 2019, the Xinyi People's Court issued a decision appointing Jiangsu LX Law Firm as the bankruptcy administrator. On December 17, 2020, ZF Company submitted an Arbitration Application to the BAC, requesting a ruling on the civil dispute between LC Company and ZF

[14] (2021) Jing 04 Min Te No. 719.

Company. After accepting the application, the BAC heard the dispute between the parties and rendered an arbitral award.

According to Article 21 of the Enterprise Bankruptcy Law, after a people's court accepts a bankruptcy application, any civil litigation concerning the debtor can only be initiated in the people's court that accepted the bankruptcy application. The BAC's arbitration of this case violated this provision. In summary, ZF Company could only file a lawsuit with the Xinyi People's Court regarding its civil dispute with LC Company, and could not apply for arbitration with the BAC. The BAC disregarded the legal provisions by arbitrating this case and ignored the defense opinion raised by LC Company's bankruptcy administrator regarding resolving the dispute through bankruptcy proceedings, which was contrary to law. Therefore, pursuant to Article 58(1)(2) of the Arbitration Law (2017), LC Company requested the court to set aside the arbitral award.

ZF Company argued that the parties had a signed arbitration clause, and the written arbitration agreement was legal and valid. Article 7 of the Settlement Agreement signed by the parties on January 4, 2011, clearly stipulated arbitration jurisdiction, stating that any dispute arising from or in connection with the performance of this Agreement shall be settled first through friendly negotiations. If the dispute could not be resolved through negotiation, either party could submit the dispute to the BAC for arbitration. The arbitral award shall be final." According to the law, the arbitration clause remained valid and did not apply to Article 21 of the Enterprise Bankruptcy Law. LC Company's claim that the arbitration institution lacked jurisdiction based on its bankruptcy was unfounded. Further, the issue of jurisdiction between the parties had already been determined by rulings from both the first and second-instance courts. The final court ruling explicitly confirmed that the BAC had jurisdiction. In June 2019, ZF Company filed a lawsuit with the Xinyi People's Court over this same dispute. During this period, in November 2019, the Xinyi People's Court accepted the bankruptcy application for LC Company. In December 2019, the Xinyi People's Court dismissed ZF Company's lawsuit on the grounds that an arbitration clause existed and the dispute should be resolved through arbitration. Subsequently, ZF Company appealed to the Jiangsu Province Xuzhou Intermediate People's Court. In November 2020, the Xuzhou Intermediate People's Court issued a ruling upholding the first-instance ruling. LC Company did not appeal the jurisdiction issue at that time. LC Company's current application to set aside the arbitral award, filed despite knowing that the Xinyi People's Court would not accept the case, violated the principle of good faith and was a malicious attempt to delay the enforcement process.

The Court opined that Article 21 of the Enterprise Bankruptcy Law stipulated that after a people's court accepted a bankruptcy application, any civil litigation concerning the debtor could only be initiated in the people's court that accepted the bankruptcy application. This restriction applied only to civil litigation and did not encompass arbitration cases where the parties had agreed upon an arbitration agreement. Article 8 of the Bankruptcy Law Interpretation (III) stated that if a debtor or creditor objected to a claim recorded in the schedule of claims, the reasons and legal basis for the objection shall be stated; If the objector remained dissatisfied after the administrator's explanation or adjustment, or if the administrator failed to provide an explanation or adjustment, the objector should file a lawsuit with the people's court for confirmation of the claim within fifteen days after the conclusion of the creditors' meeting's review; If the parties had concluded an arbitration clause or arbitration agreement before the bankruptcy application was accepted, they should apply to the chosen arbitration institution for confirmation of the creditor-debtor relationship. This demonstrated that arbitration was one method for confirming creditor-debtor relationships. If a valid and effective arbitration clause or agreement was concluded before the bankruptcy application was accepted, arbitration could still be used to resolve disputes after the enterprise enters bankruptcy proceedings. The arbitration institution designated in the Settlement Agreement was the BAC, and this arbitration case fell within its jurisdiction. In summary, LC Company's reason for applying to set aside the award did not conform to the legal provisions, and the court did not support its application.

Case 6*: M Machinery Company v. Swedish N Technology Company*[15]
In May 2009, M Machinery Company and Swedish N Technology Company signed the U-Tube Purchase Contract. The arbitration clause in the contract stipulated that any dispute arising from the contract should be finally settled by the ICC International Court of Arbitration in accordance with its Rules of Arbitration by one or more arbitrators appointed thereunder, with the seat of arbitration being Beijing, China. After the contract was signed, a dispute arose between the parties regarding its performance. M Machinery Company initiated arbitration against Swedish N Technology Company as the respondent before the ICC, which accepted the case. In this case, Swedish N Technology Company also filed a counterclaim against the Chinese M Machinery Company.

The parties jointly appointed Z as the sole arbitrator for the case. The arbitrator issued Procedural Order No. 1, Procedural Timetable No. 1, Procedural Order No. 3, and Procedural Order No. 4, among others, concerning the procedural arrangements and handling of the dispute. The arbitrator granted Swedish N Technology Company a 60-day extension to submit witness statements but dismissed M Machinery Company's application for a two-week extension to submit rebuttal witness statements and its application for leave to submit additional documents for disclosure out of time.

After the award was rendered in the case, M Machinery Company, dissatisfied with the award, believed that the arbitrator was biased towards the other party, treated the parties differently, and was unfair and non-neutral. It applied to the Beijing Fourth Intermediate People's Court to set aside the award. Some of the grounds raised by the claimant, M Machinery Company, were: First, the sole arbitrator and Swedish N Technology V Company violated Procedural Order No. 1 and Procedural Timetable No. 1, resulting in M Machinery Company being denied an equal opportunity to reply and defend against Swedish N Technology Company's counterclaim. Second, the sole arbitrator treated the parties differently when

[15] (2021) Jing 04 Min Te No. 726.

handling procedural issues, refusing its request for an extension, which lacked neutrality and impartiality, seriously violated the ICC Rules of Arbitration, and the award was clearly erroneous. Third, the sole arbitrator delayed submitting the award and, during the period when the award was being drafted, failed to disclose a personal friendship with the lawyer for Swedish N Technology Company. They had attended the same conference multiple times, and the arbitrator had published a book review for a book co-authored by that lawyer.

The Beijing No.4 Intermediate People's Court held, first, that the arbitral award in question was rendered by a foreign arbitration institution within the Chinese mainland and should be treated as a Chinese foreign-related arbitral award. Therefore, it should be reviewed according to the relevant provisions of the Arbitration Law and the Civil Procedure Law. Secondly, regarding the grounds raised by the claimant, the court found: First, concerning the alleged violations of Procedural Order No. 1 and Procedural Timetable No. 1 by the sole arbitrator and Swedish N Technology Company, the court noted that both parties and the sole arbitrator had accepted the IBA Rules on the Taking of Evidence in International Arbitration and were bound by them. No violation was found. Second, the Court held that the arbitral tribunal's refusal to grant M Machinery Company's application for a two-week extension did not violate the arbitration rules concerning fairness and neutrality, as M Machinery Company had not provided sufficient and reasonable grounds for the extension request. Third, the Court found that the existing evidence could not prove the existence of a personal friendship between the sole arbitrator and the representative of Swedish N Technology Company. Although the IBA Guidelines on Conflicts of Interest in International Arbitration were not mandatory law, they served as "soft law" with significant reference value. The fact that the sole arbitrator and the representative of Swedish N Technology Company had attended the same conference or lecture fell within the "Green List" of the IBA Guidelines on Conflicts of Interest in International Arbitration and did not require disclosure. Fourth, M Machinery Company never raised any objections during the arbitration proceedings and only raised them half a year later, which violated the principle of "estoppel" and should not be supported.

Article 84

Where the party against whom the enforcement is sought presents evidence which proves that the foreign-related arbitral award involves one of the circumstances set forth in paragraph 1 of Article 83 of this Law, the people's court shall, after examination and verification by a collegial panel formed by the people's court, rule to deny the enforcement.

Where the people's court finds that the enforcement of the award violates the public interest, it shall rule not to enforce it.

Notes

This provision concerns the non-enforcement of foreign-related arbitral awards, granting the respondent specific rights of defense during the enforcement stage. There are differences in the grounds for non-enforcement between domestic arbitral awards and foreign-related arbitral awards. Prior to the amendments of the Civil

Procedure Law, for domestic arbitral awards, non-enforcement was mandated if any of the following grounds existed: (1) the parties had neither an arbitration clause in their contract nor a written arbitration agreement reached afterwards; (2) the matters dealt with by the award fell outside the scope of the arbitration agreement or the arbitration institution lacked the authority to arbitrate; (3) the composition of the arbitral tribunal or the arbitration procedure violated statutory procedures; (4) the main evidence for finding the facts was insufficient; (5) there was indeed an error in the application of the law; (6) the arbitrator(s) committed embezzlement, accepted bribes, engaged in malpractice for personal gain, or perverted the law in the arbitration of the case. These grounds included both procedural and substantive reasons. The Civil Procedure Law, effective January 1, 2013, no longer includes "the main evidence for finding the facts was insufficient" and "there was indeed an error in the application of the law" as conditions for reviewing applications for non-enforcement of arbitral awards. Instead, it aligns with the standards under items (4) and (5) of the first paragraph of the original Article 58 of the Arbitration Law (2017) concerning grounds for applying to set aside an arbitral award, namely, "the evidence on which the award is based is forged" and "the opposing party has concealed evidence sufficient to affect the impartiality of the award.". This amendment restricted the scope of judicial review of arbitration and effectively curbed the situation in practice where the losing party would use different grounds to apply for non-enforcement and set aside the award in different courts, thereby delaying the enforcement of the arbitral award. However, the standards for reviewing applications for non-enforcement of foreign-related arbitral awards were not unified with those for non-enforcement of domestic arbitral awards. Consistent with the grounds for setting aside foreign-related arbitral awards, non-enforcement of a foreign-related arbitral award is only possible based on the five grounds mentioned in Article 83.

The judicial review procedure for foreign-related arbitral awards adopts a dual system combining the setting aside procedure and the non-enforcement procedure. This is based on a profound understanding of the particularities of the arbitral award enforcement procedure and the setting aside procedure, aiming to compensate for the shortcomings of a single objection system. Furthermore, the non-enforcement system can provide necessary relief for respondents who did not participate in the setting aside procedure. Applying to set aside an award is subject to strict statutory time limits, and the respondent might fail to apply within this period for various reasons (e.g., lack of timely knowledge of rights, strategic considerations, or objective obstacles). When the prevailing party applies for compulsory enforcement after the expiration of the period for setting aside or without initiating setting aside proceedings, the non-enforcement system provides the respondent with another crucial, and often final, opportunity for judicial review, ensuring that they do not lose the right to defend against fundamental flaws due to the passage of procedural deadlines.

The setting aside procedure is an independent procedure aimed at fundamentally negating the validity of the award. In contrast, the non-enforcement review is embedded within the enforcement procedure and is conducted only after the prevailing party initiates arbitration enforcement proceedings. Its direct concern is whether the award is "enforceable." The procedural nature, urgency, and focus of review differ between the two. Non-enforcement review directly concerns whether state coercive power should be used to intervene against the person or property of the party against whom enforcement is sought. For certain procedural defects that only become significant when resisting enforcement (such as the inability to present one's case), this system provides a more appropriate opportunity for objection.

Like the system for setting aside awards, the non-enforcement of foreign-related arbitral awards adheres to the principle of limited supervision over foreign-related arbitration. Article 84 clearly states that its review grounds are completely consistent with the setting aside grounds in Article 83. This, in fact, sends a clear and stable signal to both domestic and international markets: in China, whether challenging a foreign-related arbitral award through the setting aside procedure or the non-enforcement procedure, the courts will apply the same strict, internationally recognized standards limited to procedural issues and public policy.

Furthermore, cases concerning the non-enforcement of Chinese foreign-related arbitral awards must also follow the specific case reporting and approval system, requiring gradual reporting to the Higher People's Court of the relevant jurisdiction, and further reporting to the SPC for approval after the high people's court, upon review, intends to agree.

Illustrative Case

SD Company v. SJ Company[16]

CIETAC rendered an arbitral award concerning the dispute over an international sales contract between SD Company and SJ Company. SJ Company applied for non-enforcement of the award, citing as one of its grounds that there was no arbitration agreement between the parties. The contract submitted by SD Company to the arbitral tribunal was a copy, which could not serve as the basis for arbitration jurisdiction or the award. Even if the contract formation process as determined by the arbitral tribunal were accepted, wherein SJ Company sent the offer (contract text) to a specific third party (a Thai company), and SD Company returned the offer after modifying the name and address of the subject and other transaction terms to SJ Company, SD Company provided no evidence to prove the fact of its return, and SJ Company denied it. This meant that SD Company had not completed the expression of intent on a new offer, which could not yet be called a new offer; thus, the premise for the formation of the contract involved did not exist. Even though SD Company had evidence of returning a new offer, SJ Company did not provide a written acceptance of this new offer. This meant the parties did not reach a written arbitration clause, so there was no arbitration clause for the involved contract between the parties, and the arbitral tribunal also lacked jurisdiction. While there was actual performance and a single instance of order cancellation between the parties, this actual performance and order cancellation pertained to the parties performing a separate sales contract, not the performance of the contract involved. Furthermore, the

[16] (2013) Min Si Ta Zi No. 12.

separate contract contained no arbitration clause. Therefore, the arbitral tribunal also lacked jurisdiction over the dispute regarding the order cancellation between the parties.

SD Company argued that the contract involved was formed through actual performance, clearly contained an arbitration clause, and the arbitral tribunal had already rendered an award on the merits, which fell outside the court's purview to adjudicate. It did not acknowledge the relevance of the spot sales contract, considering it a substantive issue that the court should not review. Issues concerning investigation and appraisal were within the arbitral tribunal's authority, the procedure was legal, and the award should therefore be enforced.

After review, the Court ultimately ruled not to enforce the arbitral award. The SPC held that SD Company only submitted a copy of the contract containing the arbitration clause. SJ Company disputed the authenticity of this copy and denied the existence of a valid arbitration agreement between the parties. SD Company failed to submit other corroborating evidence and could not prove that it had reached a valid arbitration agreement with SJ Company. Furthermore, even if the authenticity of the contract copy was accepted, based on the contract formation process confirmed by the parties, after SJ Company faxed the offer to SD Company, SD Company made material modifications to the subject, quantity of goods, price, and other content stated in the offer, which constituted a new offer. SD Company also failed to provide evidence proving that SJ Company accepted this new offer; thus, the contract between the parties was not formed. Even if one were to infer the contract's formation from the parties' actual performance, according to the statutory requirement for a written form of arbitration agreements in Chinese law and the principle of the independence of arbitration agreements, this could not lead to the conclusion that the parties had reached an arbitration agreement on the method of dispute resolution. Moreover, based on the facts ascertained by the court of first instance, the contract actually performed by the parties was not the one submitted by SD Company containing the arbitration clause, but rather a separate sales contract, which did not contain an arbitration clause. Therefore, no valid written arbitration agreement existed between SD Company and SJ Company. In summary, the arbitral award fell under the circumstances stipulated in Article 258 of the Civil Procedure Law, and the people's court should not enforce it.

Article 85

Where a party applies for enforcement of a legally effective arbitral award made within the territory of the People's Republic of China, they shall directly apply to a competent foreign court for recognition and enforcement of the award if the party against whom the enforcement is sought or such party's property is not within the territory of the People's Republic of China.

Notes

This Article is amended on the basis of the original Article 72 of the Arbitration Law (2017). Compared with the original Arbitration Law (2017), this Article expands the scope of institutions, meaning it is no longer limited to foreign-related arbitration commissions. As long as it is a legally effective arbitral award made within the territory of China, regardless of whether it is made by a foreign-related arbitration commission, an institutional arbitral award, or an ad hoc arbitral award, if the person against whom enforcement is sought or their property is not within Chinese territory, the party may directly apply to a competent foreign court for recognition and enforcement. However, it simultaneously limits the territorial scope, applying only to legally effective arbitral awards made within the territory of China, and does not apply to awards made by Chinese arbitration institutions outside Chinese territory. Typically, the basis and pathways for enforcement of arbitral awards include international conventions, bilateral judicial assistance agreements, and the domestic law of the requested country.

1. **New York Convention**

As the most universal international convention in the field of cross-border enforcement of arbitral awards, the New York Convention currently covers 172 countries and regions globally. China formally acceded to this convention in 1987. If the country where the person against whom enforcement is sought is domiciled or where their property is located is a member state of the New York Convention, the party may directly apply to a competent court in that country (typically the court of the debtor's domicile or the court of the place where the property is located) for recognition and enforcement based on this Convention. The core advantage of the New York Convention lies in providing a unified framework for cross-border enforcement procedures: the court of the requested state reviews the award based on the principle of "formal review." The scope of review primarily includes the validity of the arbitration agreement, the compliance of the arbitration procedure, and whether the award exceeds the scope of the arbitration agreement, among others. The review standards are clear, and the procedure is relatively straightforward, making it the primary and most commonly used path for the cross-border enforcement of domestic awards. A considerable number of Chinese arbitral awards are enforced in other countries each year pursuant to the New York Convention.

2. **Bilateral or Multilateral Judicial Assistance Agreements**

If the country where the person against whom enforcement is sought or their property is located has not joined the New York Convention but has concluded a bilateral judicial assistance agreement with China that includes provisions for the "recognition and enforcement of arbitral awards," or if both countries are parties to other multilateral conventions involving arbitration enforcement, the party may apply to the court of the requested state for recognition and enforcement based on the aforementioned agreement or convention. The specific terms of different agreements or conventions may vary from the New York Convention. For instance, the length of the application period, specific requirements for application documents, and the breadth of the court's review scope may differ.

3. **Domestic Law**

If the country where the person against whom enforcement is sought or their property is located is neither a member state of the New York Convention nor has it concluded a relevant judicial assistance agreement with China, the party must proceed by applying based on the domestic law of the requested state. Typically, the requested state will characterize awards made by arbitration institutions within China as "foreign arbitral awards" and apply the specific provisions in its domestic law regarding the "recognition and enforcement of foreign arbitral awards." Due to significant differences in legal systems and judicial practices among different countries, the review standards, application procedures, time limit requirements, etc., for foreign awards under their domestic laws may vary considerably.

As it involves the enforcement of foreign arbitral awards, when advancing the process for the recognition and enforcement of a domestic award abroad, the party must strictly prepare the application documents in accordance with the specific agreement or convention's provisions. It is necessary to consult local lawyers in the requested country to ensure that the application materials and procedures fully comply with the requirements of the local court, avoiding any impact on the enforcement process due to procedural defects.

Illustrative Case

ChicV v. N&J[17]

On December 18, 2024, the United States District Court for the Central District of California ruled on the enforcement case of an arbitral award between Hong Kong company ChicV International Holding Limited ("**ChicV**") and U.S. company N&J USA, Inc. ("**N&J**"), confirming the arbitral award rendered by the Shenzhen Court of International Arbitration (SCIA) and ordering N&J USA, Inc. to fulfill its payment obligation under the award to ChicV.

The claimant, ChicV, was a Hong Kong company, and the respondent, N&J, was a U.S. marketing company. The parties entered into a cooperation agreement in September 2020, stipulating that N&J would conduct advertising campaigns in the United States on behalf of the claimant. The agreement provided that disputes would be submitted to the SCIA for arbitration. A dispute subsequently arose between the parties, and the claimant initiated arbitration with the SCIA on April 8, 2022.

The SCIA served the notice of arbitration to the respondent's last known business address on May 10, 2022. The respondent learned of the arbitration via email on July 7, 2022. The arbitration proceedings commenced on August 17, 2022, and both parties participated in the proceedings. On July 31, 2023, the SCIA issued an award upholding ChicV's claims. N&J subsequently applied to a Chinese court to set aside the arbitral award, but its application was dismissed.

After ChicV applied to the U.S. court for confirmation of the arbitral award pursuant to the New York Convention, N&J raised two defenses against enforcement:

[17] 5:24-cv-01720-SSS-SHKx.

first, that it did not receive adequate notice of the arbitration, and second, that the composition of the arbitral tribunal was inconsistent with the arbitration agreement.

Opinion of the U.S. Court: Regarding the first defense, the court noted that although N&J claimed its business address had changed and its phone number and email address were incorrect, the notice of arbitration was sent to its last known business address, and N&J ultimately received notice via email and actually participated in the arbitration proceedings. The court held that the notice of arbitration was reasonably sufficient and met the standard for proper notice under the New York Convention. Regarding the second defense, the court pointed out that N&J had explicitly stated during the arbitration that it had no objection to the composition of the arbitral tribunal and failed to provide any evidence proving that the tribunal's composition violated the parties' agreement or the relevant arbitration rules. Therefore, the court found N&J's defenses to be without merit.

The court ultimately confirmed the arbitral award rendered by the SCIA, requiring N&J to fulfill its obligation to pay the outstanding amount to ChicV in accordance with the award, with interest accruing from August 13, 2024, until the debt was fully satisfied.

Article 86

Arbitration institutions are supported in establishing operational entities outside the People's Republic of China and carry out arbitration activities.

According to the needs of economic and social development and reform and opening up, overseas arbitration institutions may be allowed to establish operational entities in pilot free trade pilot zones approved by the State Council, the Hainan Free Trade Port, and other designated areas, in accordance with relevant national regulations, to conduct foreign-related arbitration activities.

Notes

This Article, through a system design of two-way opening, encourages and supports the development of the arbitration industry, enhancing China's discourse power and influence in the global dispute resolution field. Supporting domestic institutions in establishing a presence overseas serves as a tangible platform for exporting Chinese arbitration concepts, rules, and practices, helping to build "Chinese Arbitration" into a globally recognized legal service brand. With the deepening development of the Belt and Road Initiative and the widespread global presence of Chinese enterprises, the cross-border commercial disputes they face are increasing. Supporting Chinese arbitration institutions in setting up operational branches overseas can provide these enterprises with close-at-hand arbitration services that are familiar with Chinese business culture and legal background, avoiding the high costs and risks they might face when resolving disputes in unfamiliar legal jurisdictions. Furthermore, it should be noted that globally, top arbitration institutions are actively expanding their international operations and competing for the dispute resolution market. If Chinese arbitration institutions remain solely within China, it will be difficult for them to occupy a significant position in the international arbitration landscape. Encouraging them to "go global" is the necessary path to participate in international competition and enhance their international reputation and brand influence.

Simultaneously, allowing well-known foreign arbitration institutions to "come in" demonstrates that China is proactively integrating into and participating in shaping the global arbitration governance system with a confident and open attitude. One hallmark of an international arbitration center is the clustering effect of top domestic and foreign arbitration institutions. By piloting the introduction of foreign arbitration institutions in open frontier zones such as Pilot Free Trade Zones and the Hainan Free Trade Port, the international standard of dispute resolution in these areas can be rapidly elevated, attracting more international commercial entities to designate them as the seat of arbitration in their contracts. This is of great significance for creating a genuinely market-oriented, law-based, and internationalized business environment. Additionally, it is important to note that the current market access for foreign institutions is limited to "Pilot Free Trade Zones, the Hainan Free Trade Port, and other areas," explicitly stipulating that they can only "conduct foreign-related arbitration activities," thereby separating their business scope from purely domestic disputes and avoiding potential complex coordination issues with the domestic judicial system.

In April 2015, the State Council proposed in the Plan for Further Deepening Reform and Opening Up of the China (Shanghai) Pilot Free Trade Zone to support internationally renowned commercial dispute resolution institutions in establishing a presence in the Shanghai Pilot Free Trade Zone, accelerating efforts to build a globally oriented Asia-Pacific arbitration center. In July 2019, the State Council's Overall Plan for the Lingang New Area of the China (Shanghai) Pilot Free Trade Zone further proposed allowing well-known foreign arbitration and dispute resolution institutions to set up operational entities within the Lingang New Area to conduct foreign-related arbitration business. The Shanghai Municipal Justice Bureau formulated the Measures for the Administration of Foreign Arbitration Institutions Establishing Operational Entities in the Lingang New Area of the China (Shanghai) Pilot Free Trade Zone. On April 22, 2025, the Shanghai Municipal Justice Bureau issued the revised Measures for the Administration of Foreign Arbitration Institutions Establishing Operational Entities in Shanghai, encouraging legally established non-profit arbitration institutions from foreign countries, the Hong Kong Special Administrative Region, the Macao Special Administrative Region, and the Taiwan region of China, as well as arbitration and dispute resolution institutions established by international organizations to which China is a party that conduct arbitration business, to set up operational entities in Shanghai to carry out foreign-related arbitration.

In August 2020, Article 8 of the State Council's Reply on the Work Plan for Deepening a New Round of Pilot Program for Expanding Opening-Up of the Service Sector in Beijing and Building a Comprehensive Demonstration Zone for Opening Up the National Service Sector stipulated that well-known foreign arbitration and dispute resolution institutions are permitted, upon registration with the Beijing judicial administrative department and filing with the Ministry of Justice, to establish operational entities in specific areas of Beijing to provide arbitration services for civil and commercial disputes arising in areas such as international commerce and investment. The application and enforcement of interim measures, including pre-arbitration and in-arbitration property preservation, evidence preservation, and conduct preservation, by Chinese and foreign parties shall be supported and safeguarded in accordance with the law.

On October 18, 2020, the General Office of the Central Committee of the Communist Party of China and the General Office of the State Council issued the First List of Authorized Matters for the Comprehensive Reform Pilot of Building Shenzhen into a Pioneer Demonstration Area of Socialism with Chinese Characteristics. Item 29 of this list requires that it is to build an International Arbitration Center for the Guangdong-Hong Kong-Macao Greater Bay Area based on the International Arbitration Institution of the Special Economic Zone, improve international legal services and dispute resolution mechanisms, support the International Arbitration Institution of the Special Economic Zone in taking the lead in building an International Investment Joint Arbitration Center, introduce relevant international organizations and world-renowned arbitration institutions through cooperative methods, and establish an exchange and cooperation mechanism for international mediation organizations and mediators. On September 6, 2021, the Central Committee of the Communist Party of China and the State Council issued the Plan for Comprehensively Deepening Reform and Opening Up of the Qianhai Shenzhen-Hong Kong Modern Service Industry Cooperation Zone. Section (10) states that well-known foreign arbitration and other dispute resolution institutions are permitted, upon registration with the judicial administrative department of the Guangdong Provincial Government and filing with the judicial administrative department of the State Council, to establish operational entities within the Qianhai Cooperation Zone to conduct arbitration business for civil and commercial disputes arising in foreign-related commercial, maritime, investment, and other fields.

Of course, allowing foreign institutions to operate in specific areas is not simply a concession of market share but, more importantly, aims to activate the domestic arbitration ecosystem through a "catfish effect," and by closely observing and learning from the operational models, management experience, and service standards of world-class institutions, force domestic arbitration institutions to deepen reforms and enhance their competitiveness. The introduction of foreign arbitration institutions will provide domestic and international commercial entities with more diverse and internationalized choices. This will create strong market competition pressure, compelling domestic arbitration institutions to continuously refine and improve the advancement of their rules, procedural efficiency, service professionalism, the caliber of arbitrators, and their level of internationalization.

Illustrative Case

Ennead Company v. R&F Company[18]

Ennead Company, a U.S. architectural design firm, and Chinese real estate developer R&F Company became involved in a dispute arising from two real estate design contracts, which were arbitrated at the CIETAC Hong Kong Center. The arbitral tribunal rendered an award. As required by the award, R&F Company paid design fees of RMB 6,407,640 and arbitration costs of RMB 299,476.50 to Ennead

[18] (2016) Su 01 Ren Gang No. 1.

Company on February 3, 2016, and March 16, 2016, respectively. Regarding the default interest, the parties reached a Settlement Agreement. According to the Settlement Agreement, Ennead Company agreed to accept a reduced amount of RMB 600,000 as default interest if R&F Company completed the payment by May 31, 2016. Otherwise, R&F Company would be liable for the full default interest amount of RMB 851,438.59. By May 31, 2016, R&F Company had failed to pay the interest as required.

Ennead Company applied to a Nanjing court for enforcement of the interest portion of the award against R&F Company and requested that R&F Company bear the application fee. The Nanjing court ruled to enforce the unpaid interest portion of the award. It explicitly cited Articles 1 and 7 of the Arrangement of the Mutual Enforcement of Awards. Article 1 of the Arrangement stipulated: "If a party fails to comply with an arbitral award made in the Mainland or in the Hong Kong Special Administrative Region, the other party may apply for enforcement to the relevant court in the place where the party against whom the application is made is domiciled or where the property of the said party is located." According to Article 7 of the Arrangement, the party against whom enforcement was sought could, after receiving notice, provide evidence proving the existence of any of the circumstances listed in that article to oppose enforcement. This Article referenced the provisions of Article V of the New York Convention. The Nanjing court noted that R&F Company did not attempt to prove the existence of any of the circumstances listed in Article 7. Furthermore, under Chinese law, the dispute involved was capable of settlement by arbitration, and enforcing the award did not violate the public interest of the Mainland, meaning there were no separate circumstances under Article 7 justifying refusal of enforcement. Therefore, the Nanjing court ruled to enforce the unpaid interest portion of the award against R&F Company and ordered R&F Company to bear the application fee.

Article 87

Parties to foreign-related arbitration are encouraged to choose arbitration institutions in the People's Republic of China (including special administrative regions) and to agree on the People's Republic of China (including special administrative regions) as the seat of arbitration.

Notes

Parties involved in foreign-related arbitration may choose to arbitrate either in China or in another country or region. This Article is a new addition to the New Arbitration Law and, together with Article 86, aims to achieve leapfrog development in China's arbitration cause through the organic combination of "going global" and "bringing in." These clauses are declaratory and guiding provisions based on China's arbitration opening-up and reform. For the first time, at the level of fundamental arbitration law and in the form of national legislation, they clearly express the stance of supporting and promoting China's foreign-related arbitration services. They represent a declaration to promote China's transition from a major arbitration country to a strong arbitration power and to enhance its discourse power and influence in the international dispute resolution landscape.

With the deepening of the Belt and Road Initiative and the construction of a higher-level open economy, China's economic and trade exchanges with the international market are becoming increasingly close, leading to a simultaneous growth in cross-border commercial disputes. However, a large number of high-end and complex international arbitration cases have long flowed to some traditional international arbitration centers. This situation does not match China's status as the world's second-largest economy. Therefore, clearly encouraging parties through legislation to choose Chinese arbitration institutions and seats of arbitration aims to proactively guide and shape the dispute resolution preferences of international commercial entities. It is an important measure to translate national economic strength into institutional soft power. The law, with its "encouraging" posture, sends a positive signal to global commercial entities that China's arbitration market is open, inclusive, and pursues excellence, aiming to change the international community's traditional perception of Chinese arbitration and enhance their confidence in considering China as a trustworthy seat of arbitration.

In recent years, the global arbitration landscape has also been reshaped. This clause intentionally includes "Special Administrative Regions," reflecting the intention, under the "one country, two systems" principle, to integrate the comprehensive advantages of the Chinese mainland, Hong Kong SAR, and Macao SAR in the field of arbitration, forming a complementary and interconnected Chinese arbitration ecosystem to jointly enhance overall competitiveness and cope with the fierce competition in the global arbitration market.

Of course, encouragement will not remain merely at the textual level; corresponding specific support policies and tangible improvements should follow. For example, various government-level supports for arbitration or conveniences and measures for the arbitration industry and practitioners. For arbitration institutions, they should internalize this legislative spirit as a driving force for their own development. By formulating more internationally competitive arbitration rules, building panels of arbitrators that include a large number of top foreign experts, and enhancing the professionalism and digitalization of case management, they can practically respond to the parties' expectations for fair and efficient arbitration services. For parties and their agent lawyers, this clause provides a clear policy guideline. When drafting international commercial contracts, they should more actively consider including Chinese arbitration institutions and seats of arbitration (including Beijing, Shanghai, Shenzhen, Hong Kong, etc.). This is not only a response to the national legislative direction but may also be the optimal choice, aligning with their commercial interests after full assessment.

In international commercial arbitration cases, the international recognition of Chinese arbitration needs improvement. Although China is a "major arbitration country," there is still significant room for improvement in its capacity to handle international arbitration cases. Purely international commercial disputes are seldom chosen to be arbitrated within China, and a considerable number of foreign-related arbitration cases related to China are also heard and adjudicated overseas. Part of the reason is that the construction of China's arbitration system itself may still fall short of international rules, and another reason relates to external factors such as history and culture. International commercial arbitration has long been centered in regions like Europe and America, and parties tend to prefer traditional international arbitration centers when choosing a seat. However, with China's economic and legal development, the development of international arbitration in China also holds considerable potential.

From the perspective of specific arbitration practice, one point this clause needs to remind parties drafting arbitration agreements is that if the potential case is non-foreign-related arbitration, such parties can choose arbitration institutions in the Chinese mainland, but in principle, they cannot choose arbitration institutions in the Hong Kong Special Administrative Region or the Macao Special Administrative Region, unless it falls under the following circumstances.

On February 10, 2025, the SPC and the Ministry of Justice jointly issued the Opinions on Giving Full Play to the Functions of Arbitration to Serve the High-Quality Development of the Guangdong-Hong Kong-Macao Greater Bay Area (the "Opinions").

On February 13, 2025, the SPC issued Judicial Interpretation No. 3 [2025], titled the Reply of the SPC on Issues Concerning the Validity of Agreements by Hong Kong and Macao Investment Enterprises Registered and Established in the Mainland of the Guangdong-Hong Kong-Macao Greater Bay Area to Choose Hong Kong or Macao Law as the Governing Law of the Contract or to Designate Hong Kong or Macao as the Seat of Arbitration (the "Reply").

These two documents primarily address matters related to the Guangdong-Hong Kong-Macao Greater Bay Area. As a major national development strategy, the Guangdong-Hong Kong-Macao Greater Bay Area requires the establishment of a dispute resolution mechanism aligned with international standards. The issuance of the Opinions constitutes a key measure in response to the increase in cross-border commercial disputes and the enhancement of the region's competitiveness in the rule of law. It contributes to creating a first-class business environment that is market-oriented, law-based, and internationalized, thereby facilitating the high-quality development of the Guangdong-Hong Kong-Macao Greater Bay Area.

Article 1 of the Opinions involves new provisions regarding the choice of the seat of arbitration by Hong Kong and Macao-funded enterprises. According to this article, Hong Kong and Macao-funded enterprises established in the nine Mainland cities of the Greater Bay Area can agree to resolve commercial disputes either with the Chinese Mainland or with Hong Kong or Macao as the seat of arbitration. The aforementioned Opinions and Reply, while limiting the subjects of the arbitration agreement, represent a "breakthrough" from the previous practice under Chinese law, where parties to purely domestic disputes were not allowed to choose arbitration in foreign arbitration institutions. By allowing Hong Kong and Macao-funded enterprises in the nine Chinese Mainland cities to freely choose the Chinese Mainland, Hong Kong, or Macao as the seat of arbitration, greater autonomy is granted to the parties. Enterprises can make flexible decisions based on factors such as preference (common law vs. civil law system) and the convenience of award enforcement.

In traditional Chinese arbitration practice, parties to foreign-related contracts could choose foreign arbitration institutions to resolve disputes, but purely domestic disputes could not choose arbitration in foreign arbitration institutions. Similarly, in judicial practice, courts generally do not recognize parties' choice of foreign law to govern contracts without foreign-related elements. The key to determining whether a commercial dispute case is foreign-related or purely domestic is to see if the case contains "foreign-related elements." Typically, cases without foreign-related elements cannot be submitted to extraterritorial arbitration institutions for arbitration, and the relevant arbitration clauses should be deemed invalid.

In recent years, Chinese judicial practice has adopted a more open and developmental attitude. After 2015, the judicial determination of foreign-related elements has shown a form of expansion. For example, in the case of ***Shanghai Gold Land Co., Ltd. v. Siemens International Trading (Shanghai) Co., Ltd.***,[19] the court held that although the parties were Chinese legal persons, they were wholly foreign-owned enterprises registered in the Pilot Free Trade Zone. The company's capital source, ultimate beneficial ownership, and operational decisions were closely related to foreign investors, thus such entities had relatively obvious foreign-related elements; additionally, the circulation process of the subject matter of the contract also had characteristics of international goods sales, therefore the case had foreign-related elements.

Another example is Article 9 of the Opinions of the SPC on Providing Judicial Safeguards for the Construction of Pilot Free Trade Zones issued in 2016, which stipulates that for commercial disputes between wholly foreign-owned enterprises registered within the Pilot Free Trade Zone that are agreed to be submitted to extraterritorial arbitration, the relevant arbitration agreement shall not be deemed invalid solely on the ground that the dispute lacks foreign-related elements. Where one or both parties are foreign-invested enterprises registered within the Pilot Free Trade Zone, and they agree to submit commercial disputes to extraterritorial arbitration, and after a dispute arises, the parties submit the dispute to extraterritorial arbitration, and after the relevant award is rendered, a party then claims refusal of recognition, recognition, or enforcement on the grounds that the arbitration agreement is invalid, the people's court shall not support it; if the other party did not raise an objection to the validity of the arbitration agreement during the arbitration proceedings, and after the relevant award is rendered, then claims that the arbitration agreement is invalid on the grounds that the dispute lacks foreign-related elements, and based on this claims refusal of recognition, recognition, or enforcement, the people's court shall not support it. Article 15 of the 2018 Opinions of the SPC on Providing Judicial Services and Safeguards for the Comprehensive Deepening of Reform and Opening Up in Hainan has similar provisions.

---

[19] See the 2nd batch of Typical Cases on the Development of the Belt and Road Initiative published by the SPC in 2017.

Illustrative Cases

Case 1: *H v. Y*[20]

Both Y and H were U.S. citizens. H entrusted Y to hold on his behalf the original shares of a company registered in the British Cayman Islands. The two parties signed the Share Escrow Agreement in Hangzhou, China, in February 2012. Article 9 of the agreement stipulated that disputes arising from the performance of this agreement shall be settled through friendly negotiation between the parties; if mediation through negotiation proved ineffective, both parties agreed to submit the dispute to the Hangzhou Arbitration Commission for arbitration; and the arbitration shall be final and binding upon both parties to the agreement. A dispute arose between the parties during the performance of the agreement. In April 2023, the Hangzhou Arbitration Commission accepted the case concerning the contract dispute between the claimant H and the respondent Y. Before the first hearing of the arbitral tribunal, Y applied to the Zhejiang Province Hangzhou Intermediate People's Court to confirm the invalidity of the arbitration agreement, on the grounds that the dispute involved lacked a substantial connection with the designated arbitration institution.

The Zhejiang Province Hangzhou Intermediate People's Court held that the arbitration agreement in question was a foreign-related arbitration agreement. As the parties had not chosen the law applicable to determining the validity of the foreign-related arbitration agreement, the law of the place of the agreed arbitration institution should apply. The Hangzhou Arbitration Commission was newly established after the implementation of the Arbitration Law (1994). Article 128 of the then-effective Contract Law stipulated that parties to a foreign-related contract may apply for arbitration to a Chinese arbitration institution or another arbitration institution in accordance with the arbitration agreement. The parties were permitted to enter into an arbitration agreement choosing a Chinese arbitration institution for resolving foreign-related disputes. Y's claim that the arbitration agreement was invalid because the designated arbitration institution was not one located in a place substantively connected to the dispute lacked legal basis. Consequently, the court ruled to dismiss Y's application.

Case 2: *T Company v. B Company*[21]

In the case concerning the application by claimant T Company for the recognition and enforcement of an arbitral award rendered by the International Court of Arbitration of the ICC, Article 20 of the Low-Sulfur Petroleum Coke Contract entered into by the parties stipulated that any disputes arising during the performance of the agreement shall be resolved through amicable negotiation between the

---

[20] (2023) Zhe 01 Min Te No. 453; See the 10 Typical Cases on Judicial Review of Commercial Arbitration published by the High People's Court of Zhejiang Province. Although the dispute in this case occurred outside China, where foreign parties voluntarily choose a Chinese arbitration institution for arbitration, the arbitration agreement shall be recognized as valid, provided no other circumstances invalidating the arbitration clause exist.

[21] See the Annual Report on Judicial Review of Commercial Arbitration published by the SPC in December 2025.

parties; if resolution cannot be achieved through negotiation, the dispute shall be finally settled by three arbitrators appointed in accordance with the ICC Mediation and Arbitration Rules. The parties unanimously agreed to conduct arbitration in Beijing, China. After accepting the case, the ICC rendered the award in Beijing, China.

The Court held that the arbitral award was an arbitral award rendered by a foreign arbitration institution within the territory of China. If the respondent B Company in the arbitral award fails to fulfill the award, T Company may, in accordance with Article 290 of the Civil Procedure Law, apply to the intermediate people's court in the place of B Company's domicile or where its property is located for enforcement. Given that the arbitral award did not fall within the scope of recognition and enforcement stipulated in Article 304 of the Civil Procedure Law, the case should not be reviewed as one involving the recognition and enforcement of a foreign arbitral award. As the claimant also amended its claims, the review should be terminated in accordance with the law. T Company may directly file an application for enforcement with the enforcement bureau of the Court in accordance with the law.

An arbitral award rendered by a foreign arbitration institution within the territory of China constitutes a foreign-related arbitral award and does not qualify as a foreign arbitral award.

Article 88
Arbitral awards made outside the territory of the People's Republic of China that have legal effect and require recognition and enforcement by the people's court, the party may directly apply to the intermediate people's court at the domicile of the person against whom enforcement was sought or the place of its property. If the domicile of the person against whom enforcement was sought or the place of its property is not within the territory of the People's Republic of China, the party may apply to the intermediate people's court at the domicile of the claimant or at a place which has an appropriate connection with the dispute arbitrated in. The people's court shall handle in accordance with international treaties concluded or acceded to by the People's Republic of China or under the principle of reciprocity.

Where a foreign arbitration institution restricts or discriminates against the legitimate rights and interests of citizens, legal persons, or other organizations of the People's Republic of China, the relevant authorities of the People's Republic of China shall have the right to apply the principle of reciprocity to citizens, enterprises, and other organizations of that country.

Notes
This first paragraph pertains to the enforcement within China of arbitral awards made outside the territory of China. Internationally, the recognition and enforcement of foreign arbitral awards can primarily be achieved through the following avenues: (1) recognition and enforcement under the New York Convention; (2) recognition and enforcement by invoking provisions on the recognition and enforcement of arbitral awards stipulated in bilateral or multilateral treaties; (3) recognition and enforcement based on the principle of reciprocity; and (4) recognition and

enforcement under domestic law. This first paragraph specifies two avenues: international treaties and the principle of reciprocity. The most important international treaty in the field of recognition and enforcement of foreign arbitral awards is the New York Convention. The New York Convention entered into force for China on April 22, 1987. According to Article 1 of the Notice on the Implementation of the New York Convention, China applies the Convention to the recognition and enforcement of arbitral awards made in the territory of another Contracting State. Where provisions of the Convention differ from those of the Civil Procedure Law, the provisions of the Convention prevail. For arbitral awards made in the territory of a non-Contracting State whose recognition and enforcement are sought from Chinese courts, the matter shall be handled in accordance with Article 204 of the Civil Procedure Law. Furthermore, following the handovers, the New York Convention was also extended to apply to Hong Kong and Macao. The enforcement of foreign arbitral awards in Hong Kong and Macao likewise proceeds under the provisions of the New York Convention.[22]

The first paragraph specifies the competent courts, which include: the intermediate people's courts at the place of the judgment debtor's domicile, the location of the property, the domicile of the claimant, or the place with connections to the dispute. In principle, the competent court is the intermediate people's court at the place of the judgment debtor's domicile or the location of its property. In accordance with the Notice on the Implementation of the New York Convention, an application filed by a party shall be accepted by the intermediate people's court at the following location: (1) for a judgment debtor who is a natural person, the court at the place of the debtor's domicile or place of residence; (2) for a judgment debtor that is a legal person, the court at the place of its principal place of business; (3) where the judgment debtor has no domicile, residence, or principal place of business within China but possesses property within China, the court at the location of such property.

With the increasing complexity of international commercial activities, the domicile of the person against whom enforcement is sought or the location of their property may be difficult to determine or located outside China. Where the domicile of the person against whom enforcement is sought or their property is not within the territory of the People's Republic of China, the party may apply to the Intermediate People's Court in the place of the claimant's domicile or a place having an appropriate connection with the dispute underlying the award. It is necessary to mention what constitutes a place with an appropriate connection.

According to the first paragraph, if there is no international treaty concluded or acceded to by China, the matter may be handled according to the principle of reciprocity. The principle of reciprocity is a concrete manifestation of the principle of equality and mutual benefit in private international law. However, Chinese law does not provide clear stipulations on how to ascertain reciprocity or how to apply the principle of reciprocity. Traditionally, China has adopted a stance of "*de facto*

[22] See Lin Yifei, *Essentials of Chinese Arbitration*, Sec. 7.5, Hong Kong Joint Publishing Company, 2025.

reciprocity," where the understanding and application of the reciprocity principle are based on whether the other country has previously recognized and enforced judgments or awards from Chinese courts. With China's expanding opening-up and the deepening implementation of the "Belt and Road" Initiative, the practical need for mutual recognition and enforcement of civil judgments between nations is growing. It is necessary to leverage the inherent incentive and support function of the reciprocity principle to actively foster reciprocal relationships. This also applies to the enforcement of foreign awards and foreign judgments within China. Case 1 below cites a case concerning an application for recognition of a UK civil judgment. This case established the principle and standard of "*de jure* reciprocity," differing from "*de facto* reciprocity." When a people's court reviews an application or request for recognition and enforcement of a foreign civil judgment or ruling to determine the existence of a reciprocal relationship, it shall not treat prior recognition and enforcement of civil judgments or rulings of the people's court by the relevant foreign court as a necessary condition. If, according to the law of the relevant country, civil judgments or rulings made by the people's court can be recognized and enforced by the courts of that country, and that country has no precedent of refusing recognition and enforcement of judgments or rulings of the people's court on the grounds of the absence of a reciprocal relationship, a reciprocal relationship between China and that country regarding the recognition and enforcement of civil judgments or rulings may be determined. The principle established in this case has vigorously promoted the new development of the reciprocity principle in China's judicial practice and holds significant guiding value for handling similar cases.

Illustrative Cases

Case 1: *S Shipping Company v. Hua Company*[23]

On March 5, 2010, S Shipping Company signed three charter contracts with Hua Company, chartering three vessels to Hua Company. On March 25, 2010, MH Logistics Company issued three letters of guarantee to S Shipping Company, providing guarantees for Hua Company's performance of the aforementioned charter parties. All three letters of guarantee stipulated that English law applied and that litigation should be submitted to the High Court of England and Wales in London. Due to Hua Company's delay in paying hire, S Shipping Company filed a lawsuit against MH Logistics Company in the High Court of England and Wales in accordance with the terms of the letters of guarantee. MH Logistics Company appeared in court to defend the action.

On March 18, 2015, the High Court of England and Wales rendered judgment [2015] EWHC 718 (Comm), upholding S Shipping Company's claims. Subsequently, the High Court quantified the claim amount and litigation costs, issuing orders on April 27, 2015, and October 3, 2016, a final costs certificate on November 1, 2016, and an amended order on May 17, 2018. MH Logistics Company appealed against the judgment to the Court of Appeal of England and Wales. On October 7, 2016, the Court of Appeal rendered judgment [2016] EWCA Civ 982, dismissing MH

[23] See the Guiding Case No. 235 of the SPC, published on November 25, 2024.

Logistics Company's appeal. The Court of Appeal subsequently issued orders on October 7, 2016, and May 8, 2017. MH Logistics Company failed to fulfill the obligations determined by the effective judgments. S Shipping Company then requested a Chinese court to rule on the recognition of the aforementioned judgments from the High Court and the Court of Appeal, as well as the related series of court orders. MH Logistics Company argued that China and the United Kingdom had neither concluded nor acceded to any international treaty concerning the mutual recognition and enforcement of court judgments and rulings, nor had they established a corresponding reciprocal relationship.

The Shanghai Maritime Court rendered Civil Ruling (2018) Hu 72 Xie Wai Ren No. 1 on March 17, 2022: recognizing the judgment [2015] EWHC 718 (Comm) rendered by the High Court of England and Wales on March 18, 2015, and the orders issued in that case on April 27, 2015, and October 3, 2016, the final costs certificate issued on November 1, 2016, and the amended order issued on May 17, 2018; recognizing the judgment [2016] EWCA Civ 982 rendered by the Court of Appeal of England and Wales on October 7, 2016, and the orders issued in that case on October 7, 2016, and May 8, 2017.

The Shanghai Maritime Court held as follows: this case involved an application for recognition of a foreign court's civil judgment. According to Article 289 of the Civil Procedure Law of the People's Republic of China (2021 Amendment), a people's court shall examine an application or request for recognition and enforcement of a legally effective judgment or ruling rendered by a foreign court in accordance with the international treaties concluded or acceded to by the People's Republic of China, or based on the principle of reciprocity. As there was no international treaty concluded or acceded to by China and the United Kingdom concerning the mutual recognition and enforcement of civil judgments and rulings of courts, the principle of reciprocity should serve as the basis for reviewing whether to recognize the judgments of the UK courts.

The principle of reciprocity is a concrete manifestation of the principle of equality and mutual benefit in private international law. China's Civil Procedure Law does not limit the principle of reciprocity to requiring that the relevant foreign court must have previously recognized and enforced civil judgments or rulings of Chinese courts. Certainly, if the relevant foreign court had precedents of recognizing and enforcing civil judgments or rulings of Chinese courts, a de facto reciprocal relationship regarding the recognition and enforcement of civil judgments and rulings between China and that country could naturally be established. However, even in the absence of precedents where that country recognized and enforced Chinese civil judgments or rulings, if, according to the law of the country where the judgment was rendered, the conditions for recognizing and enforcing judgments and rulings of foreign courts were substantially the same as or more lenient than those stipulated by Chinese law, it could be determined that civil judgments and rulings rendered by Chinese courts could be recognized and enforced by the courts of that country under the same circumstances. Under this premise, if there were no precedents where the courts of that country refused to recognize and enforce civil judgments or rulings of

Chinese courts on the grounds of the absence of a reciprocal relationship, a legal reciprocal relationship between China and that country could be established.

In this case, the claimant S Shipping Company did not provide evidence of precedents where UK courts had recognized and enforced civil judgments or rulings of Chinese courts, and thus failed to prove a *de facto* reciprocal relationship between China and the United Kingdom regarding the recognition and enforcement of civil judgments and rulings. However, based on the specific practices of UK courts, when foreign court judgments and rulings sought recognition and enforcement in the UK, a new lawsuit had to be initiated in a UK court based on the foreign judgment or ruling, following the common law rules of the UK. If the conditions for recognition and enforcement were met, the UK court would issue a judgment largely consistent with the original judgment, which would then be enforced according to the enforcement procedures prescribed by UK law. This was also the common practice in common law countries. According to UK law, the existence of a relevant treaty was not a necessary condition for recognizing and enforcing foreign court judgments and rulings. There was no evidence proving any legal obstacles to the recognition and enforcement of Chinese court judgments and rulings in UK courts, nor were there any instances found where UK courts refused to recognize and enforce Chinese court judgments and rulings on the grounds of the absence of a reciprocal relationship. Therefore, a legal reciprocal relationship between China and the United Kingdom could be established. The involved UK court judgments did not violate the basic principles of Chinese law or harm China's national sovereignty, security, or social public interests.

In summary, although China and the United Kingdom had not concluded or acceded to any international treaty concerning the mutual recognition and enforcement of civil judgments and rulings of courts, the involved UK court judgments could be recognized in this case based on the principle of reciprocity.

Case 2*: Italy L Company v. Ningbo S Company*[24]

In November 2005, Italy L Company and Ningbo S Company signed a contract concerning the establishment of a joint venture company. The contract stipulated that any disputes, controversies, or claims arising from the interpretation, performance, or related to the agreement should be submitted to the ICC International Court of Arbitration for arbitration in Paris, conducted in English according to its arbitration rules. After the joint venture company was established, Ningbo S Company transferred its shares in the joint venture to its affiliated fashion company. Subsequently, disputes arose among the parties regarding the distribution of company profits.

Upon the application of Italy L Company, the arbitral tribunal of the ICC International Court of Arbitration rendered an award in March 2018. The tribunal held that the fashion company had violated the provisions of the joint venture contract and ordered it to pay Italy L Company damages equivalent to RMB 3.2 million in US dollars, along with corresponding interest. In October 2019, Italy L Company

[24] (2019) Zhe 02 Xie Wai Ren No. 5.

applied to the Zhejiang Province Ningbo Intermediate People's Court for recognition and enforcement of this arbitral award.

Ningbo S Company argued that Italy L Company's claim, as a shareholder, for profit distribution from the joint venture company fell outside the scope of the arbitration agreement. It contended that the arbitral award exceeded the tribunal's authority and therefore should not be recognized or enforced.

The Zhejiang Province Ningbo Intermediate People's Court held that the arbitral award was rendered by the ICC International Court of Arbitration in Paris, France. Both China and France are contracting states to the New York Convention. Therefore, the case should be reviewed under the relevant provisions of the New York Convention. The Court found that the content of the arbitral award was an order for the Ningbo S Company to pay damages to Italy L Company for breach of contract, with the amount equivalent to the joint venture's profit distribution. It did not directly order the fashion company to distribute the joint venture's profits. Consequently, there was no scenario where the tribunal exceeded its authority. Furthermore, recognizing and enforcing the award did not harm the public interest of China. The arbitral award did not contain any circumstances specified in the New York Convention that would justify refusal of recognition and enforcement. The Court accordingly ruled to recognize and enforce the foreign arbitral award.

Case 3: *New Zealand A Hotel v. China B Group*[25]

China B Group signed a guarantee contract to provide a guarantee for the fit-out contract between its subsidiary in New Zealand and New Zealand A Hotel. After a dispute arose, New Zealand A Hotel initiated arbitration against China B Group before a New Zealand arbitration institution in accordance with the agreement, requesting China B Group to fulfill its guarantee obligations. The arbitral tribunal served the relevant arbitration documents to China B Group multiple times via electronic service and postal service, but China B Group did not participate in the arbitration. After hearing the case, the arbitral tribunal rendered a final award, ordering China B Group to pay New Zealand A Hotel the principal and interest of the debt, as well as costs incurred for protecting its rights. After the award became effective, New Zealand A Hotel applied to the Guangdong Province Shenzhen Intermediate People's Court for recognition and enforcement of the arbitral award.

The Guangdong Province Shenzhen Intermediate People's Court held that both China and New Zealand were contracting states to the New York Convention, and therefore, the application should be reviewed under the New York Convention. New Zealand A Hotel submitted the documents required by Article IV of the Convention, including the arbitral award and duly notarized and authenticated copies of the arbitration agreement between the parties, and also provided Chinese translations, which were confirmed. First, regarding the issue of the arbitration agreement. The arbitration clause involved in this case was stipulated within the guarantee contract, and the signature block of the contract contained the signature of China B Group's

[25] See the 10 Typical Cases for 2024 on Judicial Review of Arbitration published by the Guangdong Province Shenzhen Intermediate People's Court in July 2025.

legal representative at the time and was affixed with the company seal for confirmation. China B Group did not provide evidence proving that the company seal was forged, nor did it deny the authenticity and validity of its legal representative's signature. Therefore, the circumstance for non-recognition and enforcement under Article V(1)(a) of the Convention did not exist. Second, regarding the issue of proper notice. The procedural law applicable to the award was the English Arbitration Act 1996, and the review should be conducted according to the relevant provisions of that Act. The contact address retained by China B Group in the guarantee contract was its domestic registered address, and the email address provided for contact was also consistent with the contact information published on its official website. During the arbitration process, the arbitral tribunal had served the arbitration documents multiple times to the aforementioned agreed address of China B Group via electronic service and postal service, which did not violate the relevant provisions of the Arbitration Act 1996. Furthermore, New Zealand A Hotel submitted corresponding evidence such as EMS mailing receipts and logistics tracking information, which further proved the specific service process and the fact that the documents were signed for by an employee of China B Group. Thus, it should be determined that China B Group had been properly notified during the arbitration proceedings. Therefore, the circumstance for non-recognition and enforcement under Article V(1)(b) of the Convention did not exist. Third, regarding the issue of public policy. The matters decided in the arbitral award arose from disputes related to the performance of the fit-out contract and the guarantee agreement, falling within contractual commercial legal relationships between equal subjects. The parties had the right to choose arbitration to resolve their disputes, and recognizing and enforcing the arbitral award did not violate China's public policy. Consequently, the circumstance for non-recognition and enforcement under Article V(2) of the New York Convention also did not exist. The Court therefore ruled to recognize and enforce the arbitral award rendered by the New Zealand arbitration institution.

Case 4*: L Company and others v. Z Company*[26]

L Company and others signed the Investment Agreement with Z Company. During the performance of this agreement, a dispute arose between the parties. L Company and others, pursuant to the arbitration clause stipulated in the agreement, applied for arbitration to the Swiss Arbitration Centre, requesting Z Company to bear compensation liability. Although the Investment Agreement stipulated that the arbitral tribunal should be composed of three arbitrators, the parties agreed to submit the dispute to a tribunal composed of a sole arbitrator. The arbitral tribunal for the arbitration case was composed of a Chinese arbitrator jointly appointed by the parties as the sole arbitrator, and this appointment was confirmed. After hearing the case, the arbitral tribunal rendered a final award, ordering Z Company to pay corresponding compensation costs, interest, and other amounts to L Company and others. Z Company failed to fulfill the payment obligations stipulated in the effective arbitral award.

[26] See the 2nd batch of the 10 Typical Cases on Judicial Review of Arbitration published by the High People's Court of Guangdong Province in August 2025.

Consequently, L Company and others applied to the people's court for recognition and enforcement of this arbitral award.

The effective judgment held that this case involved an application for the recognition and enforcement of a foreign arbitral award. The involved arbitral award was rendered by the Swiss Arbitration Centre within the territory of Switzerland. Both China and the Switzerland are contracting states to the Convention on the New York Convention. Therefore, this case should be reviewed under the New York Convention. Article III of the New York Convention stipulates the mandatory obligation for each contracting state to recognize and enforce foreign arbitral awards, unless the party against whom the award is invoked can prove the existence of a circumstance set forth in Article V(1) or the competent authority in the country where recognition and enforcement is sought finds that a circumstance set forth in Article V(2) exists. Z Company did not raise during the court hearing that any statutory circumstances for non-recognition and enforcement of the arbitral award existed. The matters decided in the arbitral award arose from a dispute related to the performance of the Investment Agreement, which fell within a contractual commercial legal relationship between equal subjects. The parties had the right to choose arbitration as the method for resolving their disputes, and recognizing or enforcing this arbitral award did not violate China's public policy. The Court accordingly ruled to recognize and enforce the arbitral award.

Case 5: ***Hu v. Guangdong C Club***[27]

Hu (a Spanish professional coach) signed the Engagement Contract with Guangdong C Club, stipulating that the company would hire Hu as the head coach and that any disputes arising from the contract should be submitted to the Court of Arbitration for Sport (CAS), an international arbitration body under the International Olympic Committee, for a final and binding award. Subsequently, a dispute arose between the parties concerning contract termination and salary payments. Hu initiated arbitration based on the aforementioned arbitration agreement. The Court of Arbitration for Sport rendered a final award, ordering Guangdong C Club Company Limited to pay Hu wages, bonuses, interest, and other amounts. As Guangdong C Club Company Limited failed to fulfill its obligations, Hu applied to the People's Court for recognition of the award in accordance with the New York Convention and the relevant provisions of the Civil Procedure Law of the People's Republic of China.

The effective judgment held that the contract clearly stipulated submitting disputes to the Court of Arbitration for Sport for a final award, and this arbitration agreement was legal and valid. Furthermore, the contract differed from a standard, strongly subordinate labor contract; it substantively encompassed various

[27] See the 2nd batch of the 10 Typical Cases on Judicial Review of Arbitration published by the High People's Court of Guangdong Province in August 2025. The people's court accurately defined the nature of the arbitral award made by the Court of Arbitration for Sport concerning a dispute over a professional contract between a coach and a club, and recognized and enforced the award according to law, which is consistent with the commercial reservation declaration made by China upon its accession to the New York Convention.

contractual relationships such as the provision of services, payment of remuneration by the engaging unit, and shared benefits from cooperation, constituting a commercial contractual relationship between the parties. The involved arbitral award was rendered in the Swiss Confederation. Both China and the Swiss Confederation are contracting states to the New York Convention, therefore the provisions of the New York Convention were applicable for the review in this case. The composition of the CAS arbitral tribunal, the notice of hearing, and the service of the award all complied with the relevant rules. Although Guangdong C Club Company Limited had raised an objection to jurisdiction, it did not pursue further appeals and participated fully in the arbitration proceedings through its appointed legal counsel. Hu submitted the CAS award authenticated under the Hague Convention, along with a Chinese translation and notarized/certified materials, which met the formal requirements of the New York Convention. The award involved did not exhibit any grounds for refusal of recognition under Article V of the New York Convention. Consequently, the Court ruled to recognize the award.

Case 6: *A v. B*[28]
The submitted proof of identity and power of attorney from the claimant have not undergone the authentication procedures at the Embassy or Consulate of the PRC in Mauritania. Furthermore, although the Court requested the claimant to supplement the submission within a specified period, they failed to provide the required documents. The Court held that, in accordance with Article 275 of the Civil Procedure Law and Article 521 of the Civil Procedure Law Interpretation, the application of the foreign company did not meet the conditions for acceptance. Accordingly, the Court ruled to dismiss the claimant's request for recognition and enforcement of the award.

Where a party applies for the recognition and enforcement of a foreign arbitral award, and the country in which the arbitral award was made has not acceded to the Convention Abolishing the Requirement of Legalization for Foreign Public Documents, the arbitral award, proof of identity, and power of attorney formed outside the territory of China must be notarized by a notary authority of the country where they were formed and authenticated by the Embassy or Consulate of the PRC in that country. Otherwise, the application for recognition and enforcement shall be dismissed.

Case 7: *KOT v. Z and H Company*[29]
The respondent argued that the claimant had exceeded the statutory limitation period for applying for the recognition and enforcement of the arbitral award in question.

---

[28] See the Annual Report on Judicial Review of Commercial Arbitration published by the SPC in December 2025.

[29] See the Annual Report on Judicial Review of Commercial Arbitration published by the SPC in December 2025.

The Court held that, in accordance with Article 250 of the Civil Procedure Law and Article 545 of the Civil Procedure Law Interpretation, the time limit for applying for the recognition and enforcement of a foreign arbitral award was governed by the provision of the Civil Procedure Law, which stipulated a two-year period for applying for enforcement. The tolling and suspension of the limitation period for enforcement applications were governed by the relevant legal provisions concerning the suspension and interruption of limitation periods. If the legal instrument did not specify a time limit for performance, the calculation should commence from the date the legal instrument took effect. According to the arbitration rules, Z Company and H Company should have received the arbitral award in question at the earliest on December 28, 2017, and at the latest on December 31, 2017. The KOT claimed that it had sent DHL parcels to Z Company and H Company on December 20, 2018, notifying the respondents to fulfill the arbitral award in question, and provided proof of delivery. The delivery addresses corresponded to the business registration addresses of Z Company and H Company. Therefore, the respondents' defense that they did not receive the fulfillment notice could not be sustained, and the claim by the KOT that the limitation period had been interrupted was factually supported. In summary, the application by the KOT for the recognition of the arbitral award did not exceed the statutory limitation period.

Chapter 8
Supplementary Provisions

Article 89
The term arbitration institution, as referred to in this Law, shall include arbitration committees, arbitration courts, and other institutions established in accordance with the law.

Notes
This Article defines the scope of arbitration institutions and is a new addition introduced by the New Arbitration Law. From this revision, it can be observed that the term "arbitration commission" used in various articles of the Arbitration Law (2017) has been uniformly changed to "arbitration institution". Article 89 of the New Arbitration Law significantly expands the definition of an "arbitration institution". While on its face this appears to be merely a terminological update, a deeper understanding reveals that it is also an important step towards aligning the arbitration system with international standards and moving towards diversified development. This provision is located in the "Supplementary Provisions" section of the law, aiming to define core concepts. Through the use of a more inclusive umbrella concept, its scope has been substantially enlarged.

The use of the term "arbitration commission" in the Arbitration Law (1994) was consistent with the social context of that time. However, with continuous social development and deepening international exchange and cooperation, the term "arbitration commission" has revealed some shortcomings. For instance, it carries certain administrative connotations in nature, often being equated with public institution status (e.g., in terms of fiscal revenue and expenditure), deviating from the core attributes of the arbitration system: voluntary choice by the parties and the independence of the institution from administrative organs. But in the actual process of establishing institutions, the names of these arbitration commissions have also undergone changes, with common formulations being "arbitration court" or "arbitration center", such as the Shenzhen Court of International Arbitration, Beijing International Arbitration Centre, Shanghai International Arbitration Centre, etc.

Y. Lin, *New Arbitration Law in China*, China Arbitration Yearbook,
https://doi.org/10.1007/978-981-92-0642-1_8

The New Arbitration Law adopts the term "arbitration institution" and formulates this article with open-ended language, achieving, to a certain extent, a connection with the past and a vision for the future, clearly encompassing various organizational forms. Furthermore, within this terminological framework, entities including but not limited to domestic permanent arbitration institutions, business establishments set up by foreign arbitration institutions within China, and even international commercial arbitration institutions, are considered or may potentially be considered as subjects to which this Law applies.

According to Article 13 of the New Arbitration Law, arbitration institutions may be established in municipalities directly under the Central Government and in the cities where the people's governments of provinces and autonomous regions are located, and may also be established in other cities divided into districts as needed; they shall not be established level by level according to the administrative divisions. Arbitration institutions shall be established in a unified manner by the people's government of the city specified in the preceding paragraph, organizing relevant departments and chambers of commerce, and shall be public welfare non-profit legal persons. There are currently over 280 domestic arbitration institutions, mostly established in this way. While most use "Arbitration Commission" as their legal name, some use the designations "Arbitration Court" or "Arbitration Center". This category constitutes the apparent subjects of application for this article.

Meanwhile, according to Article 86 of the New Arbitration Law, based on the needs of economic and social development as well as reform and opening up, foreign arbitration institutions may be permitted to establish operational entities in areas such as pilot free trade zones and the Hainan Free Trade Port, as approved by the State Council, and conduct foreign-related arbitration activities in accordance with relevant state regulations. In April 2015, the State Council proposed in the Plan for Further Deepening Reform and Opening Up of the China (Shanghai) Pilot Free Trade Zone to support internationally renowned commercial dispute resolution institutions in establishing a presence in the Shanghai Pilot Free Trade Zone, accelerating efforts to build a globally oriented Asia-Pacific arbitration center. Subsequently, institutions such as the HKIAC and SIAC have successively set up representative offices in Shanghai.

Another category involves international commercial arbitration institutions established outside China conducting arbitration within China. We understand that, under the premise that the applicable governing law is Chinese arbitration law, such institutions might also be regarded as arbitration institutions under the Chinese arbitration law. Otherwise, the arbitration business they conduct would lack a legal basis, creating a dilemma. The Arbitration Law (1994) lacked provisions concerning foreign arbitration institutions, and the term "arbitration commission" could not cover foreign arbitration institutions. Furthermore, there were no relevant rules concerning the seat of arbitration, creating obstacles in areas such as determining the validity of arbitration agreements and the nationality of awards when foreign arbitration institutions handled individual arbitration cases within the Chinese mainland. Although this revision does not explicitly regulate the issue of foreign arbitration institutions arbitrating within China, judging from the relevant articles including those on the seat of arbitration and the establishment of arbitration institutions, and combined with the fact that the judiciary has already confirmed the legality of arbitration by foreign arbitration institutions within The Chinese mainland, it can be considered that courts will have more leeway in interpreting the term "arbitration institution" in the future. In fact, Chinese judicial practice has been consistently breaking away from a rigid literal interpretation of the Arbitration Law on this point.

The change from "arbitration commission" to "arbitration institution" will accelerate alignment with internationally accepted rules: "Arbitration institution" is the common terminology used in the international arbitration field. This change enhances the international compatibility of China's arbitration legal system and helps increase China's attractiveness as a destination for international arbitration. Due to the inconsistency with the common terminology used internationally, there was a discrepancy in the international community's understanding of the Chinese concept of "arbitration commission". The change in the new law helps boost the confidence of foreign parties in choosing China as a seat of arbitration. Efforts by China to attract international arbitration can also be seen from other articles, for example, by explicitly allowing foreign arbitration institutions to operate in specific zones and encouraging parties to choose China as the seat of arbitration, the new law aims to create a more market-oriented, law-based, and internationalized business environment, attracting more international commercial entities to choose China for arbitration. Simultaneously, recognizing diversified forms of arbitration organizations can provide parties with more diverse and flexible choices.

This change in the article will impact arbitration practice and also bring forth some issues requiring attention. Parties will have more choices; enterprises and individuals will have richer options when choosing arbitration methods, allowing them to select the most suitable arbitration institution or form (such as choosing a business establishment set up by a foreign arbitration institution within China) based on the nature of the dispute, its complexity, confidentiality needs, etc. Diversification will encourage all types of arbitration institutions and service providers to continuously improve their professional standards and service quality, and is also conducive to the formation of boutique, specialized arbitration services focusing on specific fields. However, challenges and regulatory issues also arise. How to implement effective and consistent supervision over arbitration activities of different organizational forms to ensure the fairness and quality of arbitration is a new subject; how courts uniformly apply standards when dealing with arbitral awards of different forms in judicial supervision procedures, such as enforcement and setting aside awards, requires subsequent judicial interpretation and practice to clarify.

Illustrative Case

Korea DC Company, an others v. PL Company[1]

In August 2012, Korea DC Company and PL Company, an enterprise established within the Shanghai Pilot Free Trade Zone, entered into the Purchase Agreement. Article 14.2 of the Purchase Agreement stipulated that for any dispute arising from or related to the agreement, if negotiation failed, both parties agreed to finally submit such dispute to the SIAC for arbitration in Shanghai in accordance with its arbitration rules. In February 2013, Korean DC Company, PL Company, and Guangzhou DC Company entered into the Supplemental Agreement (No. 1), transferring the rights and obligations of Korea DC Company under the Purchase Agreement to Guangzhou DC Company. Korea DC Company assumed joint and several guarantee liability for the performance of Guangzhou DC Company's obligations during the contract period of the Purchase Agreement. In March 2016, Korea DC Company and Guangzhou DC Company jointly filed an arbitration application with the SIAC, requesting the arbitral tribunal to determine that PL Company had breached the contract and to order it to fulfill its payment obligations, among other claims. During the arbitration proceedings at the SIAC, PL Company raised a jurisdictional objection to the arbitral tribunal. In July 2017, the arbitral tribunal issued a jurisdictional decision. The majority opinion held that the hearing location stipulated in the arbitration clause was Shanghai, China, while the seat of arbitration was Singapore. The governing law of the arbitration agreement was Singaporean law. The involved arbitration clause was valid under Singaporean law, and the tribunal therefore affirmed that it had jurisdiction over the dispute.

In August 2017, PL Company filed a lawsuit with the Singapore High Court, seeking a declaration that the arbitral tribunal lacked jurisdiction over the dispute. In the same month, the Singapore High Court ruled that the arbitration clause, which stipulated submitting disputes to the SIAC for arbitration in Shanghai, should be interpreted as having Singapore as the seat of arbitration. PL Company appealed to the Appellate Division of the Singapore Supreme Court. In October 2019, the Appellate Division of the Singapore Supreme Court rendered a second-instance judgment, determining that the phrase "arbitration in Shanghai" in Article 14.2 indicated Shanghai, not Singapore, as the seat of arbitration. However, it did not make a determination on other contested issues, including whether the arbitral tribunal had jurisdiction over the dispute. Consequently, the arbitral tribunal issued a Decision to Stay the Arbitration Proceeding, awaiting confirmation of the validity of the involved arbitration clause by a Chinese court. In January 2020, Korea DC Company and Guangzhou DC Company applied to the Shanghai No.1 Intermediate People's Court for confirmation of the validity of the arbitration clause.

The Shanghai No.1 Intermediate People's Court held that the dispute resolution clause in Article 14.2 of the Purchase Agreement represented the genuine intention of the parties and was contractually binding on them. Based on the context of the arbitration clause and an analysis of the interpretations provided by the parties, the seat of arbitration was Shanghai, China. The parties also confirmed that the

[1] See the 10 Typical Cases on Judicial Review of Arbitration published by the SPC in the early 2024.

governing law of the arbitration agreement was Chinese law. The arbitration clause in question contained an expression of the parties' intent to submit to arbitration, specified the matters for arbitration, and designated a clear and specific arbitration institution, i.e., SIAC. It thus complied with the requirements of Article 16 of the Arbitration Law (2017) and was deemed valid.

Article 90

Where the law provides for a limitation period for arbitration, such provisions shall apply; in the absence of such provisions, the limitation period for litigation shall apply.

Notes

This Article stipulates the limitation period for arbitration. Its purpose is to clarify the applicable rules for the arbitration limitation period and its relationship with the litigation limitation period, ensuring the smooth progress of arbitration proceedings and the effective protection of the rights and interests of the obligee. The content of this article has not changed significantly, with only minor revisions to some wording to align with Article 198 of the Civil Code. The arbitration limitation period, as the statutory period for an obligee to request an arbitration institution to protect their civil rights, holds significant practical value. Its suspension, interruption, extension, and the consequences of exceeding it profoundly impact the obligee's ability to assert their rights.

Although the substantive content of the relevant clause remains largely unchanged between the New Arbitration Law and the Arbitration Law (2017), the arbitration limitation period changed in 2021 with the implementation of the Civil Code on January 1, 2021. Prior to January 1, 2021, Article 135 of the General Principles of the Civil Law stipulated that "the statute of limitations for bringing a lawsuit in a people's court for the protection of civil rights is two years, except where the law provides otherwise." In contrast, according to Article 188 of the Civil Code concerning the ordinary statute of limitations and the maximum period for the protection of rights, the statute of limitations for bringing a lawsuit in a people's court for the protection of civil rights is three years, unless otherwise provided by law. Consequently, after 2021, unless otherwise provided by law, the statute of limitations for arbitration has changed from the original two years to three years. Regarding the duration of this limitation period, particular attention must be paid to the cut-off date of January 1, 2021. The applicable protection period for judging legal facts must be determined with reference to this date.

It is important to note specifically that the litigation or arbitration limitation period is not always three years; there are sometimes special provisions. Article 594 of the Civil Code provides an explicit exception for the limitation period for filing a lawsuit or applying for arbitration arising from disputes over international sales of goods contracts and technology import and export contracts, setting this limitation period at four years.[2] In commercial arbitration practice, arbitration cases arising from transactions such as international sales of goods and trade in services also

[2] This Article originates from Article 129 of the Contract Law, which was repealed upon the implementation of the Civil Code on January 1, 2021.

account for a certain proportion, especially in international commercial arbitration cases. These types of cases are generally more complex or involve cross-border parties, making a longer limitation period more reasonable.

The New Arbitration Law does not establish separate clauses for the duration, suspension, interruption, extension, or maximum protection period of the arbitration limitation period. According to the provisions of Article 90, and in conjunction with the relevant articles of the Civil Code, the following points regarding the arbitration limitation period require special attention:

A. ***Commencement and Maximum Period.*** In accordance with Article 188(2) of the Civil Code, the arbitration limitation period shall be calculated from the date the obligee knew or should have known that their right was harmed and who the obligor is. Where the law provides otherwise, such provisions shall prevail. However, if 20 years have passed since the date the right was harmed, the people's court shall not protect it, save under special circumstances where the people's court may decide to extend the period upon the application of the obligee. This provision ensures that parties exercise their arbitration rights within a reasonable time, preventing the loss of evidence or the obscuring of rights and obligations due to excessive delay. "The law does not protect those who sleep on their rights." Similar to the litigation limitation period, the arbitration limitation period is based on the same legal rationale – negligent failure to exercise rights is not protected by law.
B. ***Guarantee.*** Article 694 of the Civil Code also stipulates the limitation period for guarantees. "Where the creditor of a general guarantee files a lawsuit against the debtor or applies for arbitration before the expiry of the guarantee period, the limitation period for the guarantee obligation shall be calculated from the date when the guarantor's right to refuse to assume guarantee liability is extinguished. Where the creditor of a joint and several liability guarantee demands that the guarantor assume the guarantee obligation before the expiry of the guarantee period, the limitation period for the guarantee obligation shall be calculated from the date when the creditor demands that the guarantor assume the guarantee obligation." This article concerns the relationship between the guarantee period and the limitation period for the guarantee obligation. When a creditor requests a guarantor to perform the guarantee obligation, if the statutory limitation period has passed, the creditor loses the right to obtain a favorable judgment. This provision also applies to the arbitration limitation period.
C. ***Suspension and Interruption of Limitation Period.*** There are relatively clear distinctions between the suspension and interruption of the arbitration limitation period, differing in timing, triggering conditions, and legal consequences, requiring attention in practice. Suspension refers to the pausing of the arbitration limitation period during the last six months of the limitation period, if the obligee is unable to exercise their right to claim due to statutory obstacles such as force majeure, or the absence of a statutory agent for a person without or with limited capacity for civil conduct. (Suspension only occurs within the last six months of the limitation period; e.g., for an international sales contract dispute

subject to a 4-year period, suspension must occur within its last 6 months). The period of suspension is excluded from the calculation. Once the cause of suspension is eliminated, the calculation of the limitation period resumes. The suspended period is not counted within the arbitration limitation period; instead, the calculation accumulates further after the cause of suspension is eliminated. Interruption refers to the scenario where, during the progression of the arbitration limitation period, certain statutory events occur, such as the obligee demanding performance from the obligor, the obligor agreeing to perform, or the obligee filing a lawsuit or applying for arbitration, which renders the elapsed portion of the limitation period void. The period that elapsed before the interrupting event is disregarded. A new limitation period begins to calculate from the time the statutory interrupting event occurs.

D. ***Consequences.*** Regarding the consequences of exceeding the arbitration limitation period, if the obligee fails to file an arbitration application within the stipulated arbitration limitation period, and no circumstances for suspension or interruption exist, although the obligee's substantive right itself is not extinguished, their right to win the case (right to judicial relief) is affected. Once the statutory arbitration period has expired, and the obligee exercises their claim, if the obligor raises a defense, the arbitral tribunal will no longer provide protection.

Illustrative Case

Wang v. Wisdom Company[3]

Wang sought to set aside the arbitral award rendered by CIETAC. One of the grounds was that the case had exceeded the statutory time limit for arbitration, and the arbitral tribunal should not have accepted it. Wang received the Arbitration Notice for the Dispute over Settlement Agreement No. S20200647 at the end of April 2020, which was issued on April 16, 2020. Although the arbitration application submitted by Wisdom Company to the arbitral tribunal was dated November 8, 2019, the award stated that "the Claimant (Wisdom Company) completed the corresponding arbitration application procedures, including payment of fees, as required by the notice from the Court of Arbitration on November 26, 2019." Therefore, when the arbitral tribunal accepted the case, the statutory time limit for arbitration had already expired, and the case should not have been proceeded with. Wang argued that the arbitration procedure violated the provisions of the arbitration law and the award should be set aside.

Beijing No.4 Intermediate People's Court held that the statutory time limit for arbitration was the statutory period within which a right-holder might request an arbitration institution to protect their rights. If a right-holder failed to exercise their rights promptly within the statutory period, they could not obtain support for the protection of their substantive rights through arbitration. The statutory time limit for arbitration did not affect a party's right to file an application with the arbitration institution. The statutory time limit for arbitration fell within the scope of substantive issues to be examined by the arbitral tribunal during the proceedings and did not

[3] (2022) Jing 04 Min Te No. 130.

constitute a matter for the people's court to review when deciding whether to set aside an arbitral award. Although Wang claimed that the case had exceeded the statutory time limit when the arbitral tribunal accepted it, the specific reasons he raised did not pertain to the scope of the statutory time limit itself, but rather concerned whether CIETAC's process from receiving the party's arbitration application to the formal acceptance of the case complied with the Arbitration Law (2017) and the arbitration rules. In this regard, the award had already addressed the issue, stating that there was no scenario under Article 13(3) of the Arbitration Rules where Wisdom Company's arbitration application was deemed not to have been filed due to incomplete application procedures. Consequently, Wang's defense that the case had exceeded the statutory time limit for arbitration was unfounded.

Article 91
Arbitration institutions may formulate arbitration rules in accordance with this Law and the relevant provisions of the Civil Procedure Law of the People's Republic of China, with reference to the model arbitration rules established by the China Arbitration Association.

Notes
Article 75 of the Arbitration Law (2017) stipulated that before the China Arbitration Association formulates arbitration rules, arbitration commissions may formulate interim arbitration rules in accordance with the relevant provisions of this Law and the Civil Procedure Law. According to this article, arbitration rules were to be formulated by the China Arbitration Association, and prior to that, individual arbitration commissions could formulate interim rules. However, in practice, this provision was not strictly implemented. Some arbitration institutions formulated interim rules, while others did not use the designation "interim" in their rule names. Through this revision, Article 91 now formally grants arbitration institutions the power to formulate their own arbitration rules in the staturory text. According to Article 25 of the New Arbitration Law, the China Arbitration Association shall formulate model arbitration rules in accordance with the relevant provisions of this Law and the Civil Procedure Law. Article 91 of the New Arbitration Law corresponds with Article 25, requiring arbitration institutions to formulate their arbitration rules on the premise of legality and with reference to the model arbitration rules formulated by the China Arbitration Association. However, as this article also indicates, the model arbitration rules serve merely as a reference framework for formulating formal arbitration rules and are not mandatory.

Arbitration rules are the norms governing the conduct of arbitration proceedings, ensuring that arbitration activities comply with legal provisions or party agreements. Typically, arbitration rules can be a pre-established set of rules or rules temporarily agreed upon by the parties for the arbitration procedure. Therefore, arbitration rules are highly discretionary. Of course, arbitration rules must not violate mandatory provisions in the applicable arbitration law. Granting arbitration institutions the authority to formulate their own rules allows professional institutions to use specialized rules to resolve specialized disputes efficiently. A set of clear, stable, and publicly available arbitration rules provides a clear guide for all participants (parties, lawyers, arbitrators).

The authority of arbitration institutions to formulate their own arbitration rules is the keystone of their ability to resolve disputes independently, efficiently, and flexibly. The essence of arbitration is the voluntary submission of disputes by the parties to a third party (the arbitral tribunal) of their choice for adjudication. Parties can even explicitly agree in the arbitration agreement to apply a specific version of an institution's rules or to apply modified rules, which further reflects party autonomy. It is important to note that when an arbitration institution has multiple sets of rules, the correct set must be accurately applied.

Arbitration institutions may innovate and develop differently based on their own characteristics (such as specialization in maritime affairs, finance, intellectual property, etc.) and the needs of the parties. Different types of disputes have specific procedural requirements. A single set of rules, similar to civil procedure, may not meet these specialized needs. In practice, differences in international characteristics, specialized fields, procedural flexibility, and fee structures lead different arbitration institutions to focus their rule-making differently. For instance, some institutions' rules may focus more on procedural autonomy and high-end dispute resolution, while others may emphasize internationalization and financial specialization, or lean towards high levels of internationalization and innovative governance structures. Furthermore, commercial practices and technology are rapidly evolving (e.g., e-commerce, digital currencies), leading to the continuous emergence of new types of disputes. Arbitration institutions can revise their rules more swiftly than the legislature to adapt to these changes, ensuring modern and efficient procedures, particularly reserving flexibility for institutions to explore internationalization and modernization in areas like foreign-related arbitration and online arbitration. For example, in recent years, major arbitration institutions have promptly revised their rules to clarify the basis for electronic service, video hearings, etc., in their arbitration rules. Moreover, major institutions have also timely incorporated some of the latest international practices into their arbitration rules.

Article 92
Parties shall pay arbitration fees according to regulations.

The arbitration institution shall formulate measures for collecting arbitration fees in accordance with national regulations.

Notes
This Article introduces adjustments based on the original Article 76 of the Arbitration Law (2017). It removes the former requirement that "the measures for charging arbitration fees shall be submitted to the price administration department for approval" and adds the provision that "arbitration institutions shall formulate measures for charging arbitration fees according to relevant state regulations." This shift will help liberate arbitration fees from the framework of "administrative and institutional charges" that required approval from relevant government price administration departments. It acknowledges their market attributes as professional legal

services and represents a significant step towards the enhancement of their independence and professionalism.

In practice, Chinese arbitration institutions have traditionally adopted two primary methods for fee collection. One method, in accordance with the Measures for the Collection of Arbitration Fees by Arbitration Commissions, divides arbitration costs into a case acceptance fee and a case handling fee. The case acceptance fee is used to cover arbitrator remuneration and the necessary expenses for maintaining the normal operation of the arbitration commission. The specific standard for the case acceptance fee is determined by the arbitration commission within the range stipulated in its fee schedule and submitted to the price administration authorities of the provincial, autonomous regional, or municipal government where the commission is located for approval. The case handling fee includes expenses such as accommodation, travel, and other reasonable costs incurred by arbitrators for business trips and hearings related to handling the arbitration case. The other method involves charging a single fee under the name "arbitration fee," without distinguishing between an acceptance fee and a handling fee, although its primary purposes remain covering institutional expenses and arbitrator remuneration. The collection of arbitration fees ensures the normal operation of arbitration institutions and provides reasonable remuneration for arbitrators, forming the financial foundation for the independent and efficient functioning of the arbitration system.

To some extent, financial autonomy is a core pillar of institutional independence. When an arbitration institution can autonomously formulate its fee policies based on its business development and cost structure, it can truly break free from administrative dependence, achieve self-financing and sustainable development, thereby safeguarding its position of independent adjudication. Furthermore, this amendment also facilitates accelerated alignment with international practices regarding arbitration costs. One possibility is that arbitration institutions will separate fees into arbitrator remuneration and institutional administrative fees, and formally or on a larger scale introduce common models in international arbitration, such as hourly rates. The original Arbitration Law (2017) lacked unified standards for fees in foreign-related cases, and relevant regulations failed to provide detailed descriptions. In practice, fees for foreign-related cases were mostly determined by each arbitration commission independently within its Arbitration Rules. This regulatory model in the New Arbitration Law also serves as guidance and a delegation of authority concerning the methods for stipulating and collecting arbitration fees in practice.

Currently, the number of arbitration institutions in China is large. Whether over 280 arbitration institutions can each establish their own arbitration fee measures warrants careful consideration, especially for some smaller institutions. Whether the exploratory experiences of major arbitration institutions can be promoted nationwide remains unknown. Moreover, historically accumulated issues within arbitration institutions require a relatively long time to resolve. The more or less existing connections between various arbitration institutions under the Arbitration Law (2017) system and administrative institutions, especially financial relationships, may need to be redefined and clarified. Finally, establishing fairness and transparency in fee charging among arbitration institutions under the New Arbitration Law system, and preventing cutthroat competition or monopolistic pricing, requires industry self-discipline and appropriate macro-level guidance.

Illustrative Case

A Company v. Li[4]

Pursuant to the arbitration clause in the Real Estate Development Project Transfer Contract signed with Li, A Company applied for arbitration to the Shiyan Arbitration Commission. After the Shiyan Arbitration Commission rendered an award, A Company applied to set aside the arbitral award on the grounds of violation of statutory procedure. The Hubei Province Shiyan Intermediate People's Court set aside the award due to the violation of statutory procedure in the arbitral award. Subsequently, Li applied again to the Shiyan Arbitration Commission for arbitration regarding the Real Estate Development Project Transfer Contract. A Company applied to set aside this new arbitral award. The Hubei Province Shiyan Intermediate People's Court ruled to set aside the arbitral award, holding that after the previous award was set aside, the parties had not reached a new arbitration agreement, which should be regarded as a situation where no arbitration agreement existed.

After the arbitral award was set aside, Li filed a lawsuit with the court, claiming unjust enrichment and requesting an order for the Shiyan Arbitration Commission to return the arbitration fee of RMB 224,998.

Upon review, the court held that the civil law of China governs personal and property relationships between natural persons, legal persons, and unincorporated organizations as equal subjects. In this case, the relationship between Li and the Shiyan Arbitration Commission was that of an arbitration claimant and an arbitration institution. During the Shiyan Arbitration Commission's handling of the arbitration case concerning the real estate development transfer contract between Li and A Company, the two parties were not equal subjects. Secondly, a civil legal relationship refers to a social relationship, with civil rights and obligations as its content, that is governed by civil law. In this case, the Shiyan Arbitration Commission collected the arbitration fee according to the Measures for the Collection of Arbitration Fees by Arbitration Commissions. This act could be viewed as part of the arbitration process and was not based on a civil legal relationship. Regardless of whether the fee charged was reasonable, it did not fall within the scope of civil law. In summary, Li's lawsuit claiming restitution based on unjust enrichment under a civil legal relationship should be dismissed. Li subsequently appealed to the Hubei Province Shiyan Intermediate People's Court.

The Hubei Province Shiyan Intermediate People's Court held that, according to the law, civil law governed the personal and property relationships between natural persons, legal persons, and unincorporated organizations as equal subjects. However, during the arbitration process, the relationship between the parties and the arbitration commission was not a civil legal relationship between equal subjects. The arbitration commission handled civil disputes based on the parties' arbitration agreement

[4] (2017) E 03 Min Zhong No. 2210.

and did not create property or personal relationships with the parties. Furthermore, the arbitration commission's collection of fees during the arbitration in accordance with relevant regulations, and the reasonableness thereof, was not subject to litigation and did not fall within the scope of civil cases accepted by the People's Courts. The court of first instance's dismissal of Li's lawsuit on these grounds was not improper. The court of first instance cited relevant provisions of the General Principles of the Civil Law to illustrate the requirement of equal standing for civil litigation subjects. It cited the relevant legal provisions for dismissing the lawsuit and did not err in the application of the law. Given the limitless nature of social disputes and the limited nature of judicial resources, not all disputes could be resolved through litigation. The appellant Li's argument that disputes must be handled through civil litigation, excluding administrative and criminal litigation, lacked legal basis and was not accepted by this court.

Article 93

Disputes such as labor dispute arbitration, rural land contract management dispute arbitration, and sports arbitration shall be governed by the Law of the People's Republic of China on Mediation and Arbitration of Labor Disputes, the Law of the People's Republic of China on Mediation and Arbitration of Rural Land Contract Management Disputes, the Law of the People's Republic of China on Sports, and other relevant laws.

Notes

This Article addresses the application of law concerning special arbitration matters. It represents a further refinement based on the original Article 77 of the Arbitration Law (2017), which stated that arbitration of labor disputes and disputes over agricultural contract operations within agricultural collective economic organizations shall be provided for separately. The New Arbitration Law provides a more detailed elaboration on this foundation, explicitly stating that labor dispute arbitration, rural land contract management dispute arbitration, sports arbitration, etc., shall apply the provisions of relevant laws. It is not difficult to see that Article 93 of the New Arbitration Law, building upon the original labor arbitration and rural land contract management dispute mediation/arbitration, clarifies the phrase "provided for separately" by specifying "apply the provisions of... and other relevant laws," and adds the content "sports arbitration, etc." This enriches the connotation of arbitration exceptions while also expanding their scope, which is more conducive to guiding arbitration practice.

With continuous social development and progress, the forms and content of arbitration have been constantly changing and evolving. The New Arbitration Law excludes three types, i.e., labor dispute arbitration, rural land contract management dispute arbitration, and sports arbitration, from the scope of application of the Arbitration Law, primarily because these three types, despite bearing the name "arbitration," are not the commercial arbitration regulated by the New Arbitration Law.

1. **Labor Arbitration**

Labor arbitration differs from commercial arbitration. It does not require an arbitration agreement and is typically a mandatory procedure for resolving labor disputes. Article 5 of the Labor Dispute Mediation and Arbitration Law stipulates, "If a labor dispute occurs, the party may apply to a mediation organization for mediation if it is unwilling to negotiate, the negotiation fails, or after a settlement agreement is reached, it is not performed; if the party is unwilling to mediate, the mediation fails, or after a mediation agreement is reached, it is not performed, the party may apply to a labor dispute arbitration commission for arbitration; if the party is not satisfied with the arbitral award, it may bring a lawsuit in a people's court, unless otherwise provided by this Law." This legally defines the basic procedure for handling labor disputes and forms the foundation for distinguishing labor disputes from civil and commercial arbitration.

Simultaneously, the principle of "finality of award" generally does not apply to labor arbitration. In labor relations, workers are often in a relatively weaker position, and there may be significant disparities in litigation costs and capabilities compared to the employer. If the "finality of award" rule of civil and commercial arbitration were applied, workers dissatisfied with an unfavorable award would lose the opportunity to seek judicial relief from the court, which is not conducive to protecting the rights and interests of vulnerable workers. Setting labor arbitration as a mandatory pre-litigation procedure aims to provide workers with a relief channel that is faster, less costly, and procedurally simpler than litigation. Therefore, labor arbitration is a "process" of arbitration, but not the final procedure of arbitration. Whether the arbitration outcome is ultimately achieved depends on whether both parties fulfill the content of the arbitral award.

2. **Rural Land Contract Management Dispute Arbitration**

Similar to labor arbitration, rural land contract management disputes, due to their specific characteristics, cannot apply the relevant content of the Arbitration Law regarding the applicable law. The Rural Land Contract Management Mediation and Arbitration Law does not require an arbitration agreement. Article 4 clearly states, "If the parties fail in or are unwilling to engage in conciliation or mediation, they may apply to a rural land contract arbitration commission for arbitration, or may directly file a lawsuit in a people's court." Article 48 stipulates: "If a party is not satisfied with the arbitral award, it may file a lawsuit in a people's court within 30 days from the date of receiving the award. If no lawsuit is filed upon the expiration of this period, the award shall become legally effective." Thus, rural land contract management disputes share characteristics with labor arbitration, such as a non-consensual nature and pre-litigation procedure, and their arbitral awards are also not subject to finality. China is a major agricultural country, land is the most basic livelihood security for farmers, and disputes over rural land contract management concern the vital interests of Chinese farmers and relate to national policies and stability. There is a need to establish a specialized dispute resolution mechanism that is more protective and better suited to rural realities.

3. **Sports Arbitration**

Sports arbitration applies to the Sports Law and other relevant laws. Because sports arbitration emphasizes professionalism and efficiency, especially in specialized areas such as athlete eligibility and doping penalties, its awards often require a higher degree of finality to quickly stabilize sports competition. Therefore, specialized laws are needed for the application of law in sports arbitration. Article 92 of the Sports Law enumerates the relevant content of sports arbitration and explicitly states that arbitrable disputes under the New Arbitration Law and labor disputes under the Labor Dispute Mediation and Arbitration Law do not fall within the scope of sports arbitration. The content of Article 93 of the New Arbitration Law corresponds with Article 92 of the Sports Law. This adjustment actively responds to the global trend of the industrialization of sports and the specialization of dispute resolution, providing a clear superior law basis for establishing a professional and efficient sports arbitration system, and is a key step in improving China's sports legal system and aligning with international standards.

Notably, taking "sports" as an example, sports disputes often involve commercial, labor, and special rules of the sports industry simultaneously. How to clearly define the jurisdictional boundaries between sports arbitration, civil and commercial arbitration, and labor arbitration is a key issue. At the same time, there is an urgent need to break down the knowledge barriers between legal professionals and sports practitioners and cultivate more interdisciplinary arbitration talents. Other types of arbitration and commercial arbitration also face similar problems, requiring more practical and theoretical research in the future.

Illustrative Cases

Case 1: *A Company v. Huang*[5]

A Company signed the Professional Manager Economic Responsibility Agreement with Huang, which stipulated Huang's job responsibilities, compensation, annual operational targets, assessment management, and restraint mechanisms. If Huang caused losses to the Company by violating the Professional Manager Management Measures, the Professional Manager Assessment Rules, or resolutions of the board of directors, he would be liable for compensation. Any disputes arising from the execution of the Agreement could be submitted to the Guangzhou Arbitration Commission for arbitration. In 2022, A Company applied for labor dispute arbitration, claiming that Huang's violation of the Professional Manager Economic Responsibility Agreement had caused significant economic losses to the company. It requested an award ordering Huang to pay compensation for economic losses due to breach of contract during the appointment period, as well as losses from business suspension. The Lianping County Labor and Personnel Dispute Mediation and Arbitration Commission issued a Notice of Non-Acceptance, stating that the arbitration claims did not fall within the scope of labor dispute resolution. A Company then applied to the Guangdong Province Guangzhou Intermediate People's Court to confirm the validity of the arbitration clause in the Professional Manager Economic Responsibility Agreement.

---

[5] (2023) Yue 01 Min Te No. 185.

The Guangdong Province Guangzhou Intermediate People's Court held that the matters for arbitration agreed in the arbitration clause were "all disputes arising from the execution of this Agreement." As a professional manager of the Company, disputes arising from the execution of the Professional Manager Economic Responsibility Agreement included both labor disputes related to compensation and benefits, and disputes arising from losses caused to the company by Huang in the performance of his duties as a professional manager. Labor disputes did not fall within the scope of commercial arbitration. However, property disputes between the parties arising from non-labor dispute matters could be submitted to a commercial arbitration institution for arbitration. Therefore, the Court ruled to confirm that the part of the arbitration clause providing for submission of disputes over losses caused to the company by Huang's acts within his duties to the Guangzhou Arbitration Commission was valid.

Case 2: *SX Company v. SH Company and others*[6]
On February 20, 2019, SX Company and SH Company, along with their four players, signed identical Player Loan Agreements. The agreements primarily stipulated that SX Company would loan the players from SH Company and pay a loan fee, and specified that in case of breach by either party, the matter would be referred to the Chinese Football Association (CFA) for arbitration, with legal liability pursued if necessary. On February 25 of the same year, SH Company and SX Company signed a Training Cooperation Agreement, which stipulated the players' appearance rate and the calculation method for the reward payment SH Company would make to SX Company.

As the Chinese Football Association issued a decision not to accept SX Company's arbitration application on the grounds that SX Company had not registered in the CFA's registration system since 2020, SX Company filed a lawsuit with the Chongming Primary People's Court of Shanghai. It requested the court to order SH Company to pay the reward payment, penalty for breach of contract, attorney's fees, and other costs. During the defense period in the first instance, SH Company raised an objection to jurisdiction, arguing that the Player Loan Agreement and the Training Cooperation Agreement formed an organic whole, and the dispute over the reward payment arose from the player loan. Since the Player Loan Agreement stipulated that breaches should be submitted to the CFA for arbitration, SH Company contended that SX Company's lawsuit should be dismissed. The court of first instance ruled to dismiss SX Company's lawsuit on the grounds that the dispute fell

[6] (2023) Hu 0151 Min Chu No. 1673, (2023) Hu 02 Min Zhong No. 6825. This case is the first to clearly define the jurisdictional boundaries within the multi-level sports dispute resolution mechanism following the revision of the Sports Law and the establishment of the Chinese Sports Arbitration Commission. The people's court accurately defined the scope of cases accepted by the internal arbitration committee of a sports association and the Chinese Sports Arbitration Commission, promoting the development of a diversified sports dispute resolution mechanism. It reflects the encouragement of sports autonomy and leverages the advantages of specialized institutions in handling disputes with professionalism and timeliness.

within the scope of cases accepted by the CFA Arbitration Committee. SX Company appealed to the Shanghai No. 2 Intermediate People's Court.

The Shanghai No. 2 Intermediate People's Court held as follows: First, the scope of the agreement for CFA arbitration in the Player Loan Agreement did not extend to the Training Cooperation Agreement. The arbitration clause in the Player Loan Agreement clearly stipulated that the CFA Arbitration Committee accepted disputes arising from the performance of that agreement. The claims in this lawsuit pertained to SH Company's obligation to pay the reward payment after SX Company ensured the players' appearance rate and SX Company's right to receive the reward payment. These rights and obligations were governed solely by the Training Cooperation Agreement and did not fall within the content stipulated in the Player Loan Agreement. Therefore, the scope of the agreement for CFA arbitration did not include the dispute in this case. Second, the CFA Arbitration Committee, as a specialized branch of the CFA for handling internal disputes, was an internal self-governing body. Its adjudicative power derived from the collective authorization of its members, and the awards it rendered were internal decisions in nature, deriving their binding force and enforceability from internal rules. SX Company was not registered with the CFA, and thus, the enforceability of a CFA arbitral award was lacking. Third, the Sports Arbitration Commission could not accept this dispute. The Sports Arbitration Commission was a specialized arbitration institution established by the administrative department for sports under the State Council in accordance with the newly added Chapter IX of the Sports Law of the People's Republic of China (revised in 2022) to handle sports disputes. Its arbitral awards had legal effect. In this case, the parties involved in the dispute had not reached an agreement to arbitrate before the Sports Arbitration Commission; therefore, the Sports Arbitration Commission lacked the authority to accept this dispute. The court ruled to set aside the first-instance ruling and instructed the Chongming Primary People's Court of Shanghai to hear the case.

Case 3: *Ma v. SH J Football Club*[7]

Ma raised three grounds for setting aside the arbitration award: first, forgery of evidence; second, withholding of evidence; and third, that the chat records constituted evidence documenting the agreement between the parties, and that the arbitral tribunal's failure to admit them was improper.

The Court applied Article 98 of the Law of the People's Republic of China on Sports to review the case. It provides that under any of the following circumstances, a party may, within thirty days from the date of receiving the arbitration award, apply to the intermediate court in the location of the sports arbitration commission to set aside the award: (1) there is an error in the application of laws or regulations; (2) the matters ruled upon fall outside the scope of sports arbitration; (3) the composition of the arbitral tribunal or the arbitration procedure violates relevant provisions, which may affect the fairness of the award; (4) the evidence on which the

[7] See the Annual Report on Judicial Review of Commercial Arbitration published by the SPC in December 2025.

award is based is forged; (5) the opposing party has withheld evidence sufficient to affect the fairness of the award; or (6) an arbitrator has solicited or accepted bribes, engaged in malpractice for personal gain, or perverted the law in rendering the award. Where a court, upon review and verification by a collegiate panel, finds that the award falls under any of the circumstances specified in the preceding paragraph, or determines that the award violates public interests, it shall rule to set aside the award.

The Court held that: first, although Ma claimed that the content of Article 2 of the Training Agreement regarding the term of validity was filled in afterward by SH J Football Club and was forged, it failed to provide corresponding evidence, and thus this claim should not be sustained. Second, Ma claimed that SH J Football Club withheld the facts that the Training Agreement was its standardized template and that Article 2 thereof was filled in by SH J Football Club. This claim pertains to issues of fact, which may be determined by the arbitral tribunal in accordance with the law, and thus did not fall within the scope of withholding evidence. Third, whether the arbitral tribunal should admit the chat records falls within the scope of substantive review. In summary, the Court ruled to dismiss Ma's application to set aside the arbitration award.

Article 94

Arbitration institutions and arbitral tribunals may handle international investment arbitration cases in accordance with the provisions of relevant international investment treaties and agreements regarding the submission of investment disputes to arbitration, following the arbitration rules agreed upon by the parties in dispute.

Notes

This Article is a new addition, addressing international investment arbitration cases. International investment arbitration is a primary method for resolving investment disputes between investors and host states. International investment arbitration generally applies international rules such as the ICSID Convention, and its procedures differ significantly from traditional commercial arbitration. Although both are termed "arbitration," the mechanisms of international investment arbitration and ordinary international commercial arbitration differ in key aspects such as core purpose, the relationship between the parties, and the legal basis. China is a significant participant in international investment activities and should consequently be an important participant in international investment rules, including rules for resolving international investment disputes. Besides being a contracting state to the ICSID Convention, China has so far signed bilateral investment treaties with over 130 countries and regions. It is necessary for China to further improve its international investment arbitration system at the legislative level.

Article 94 of the New Arbitration Law does not stand alone. While authorizing arbitration institutions and tribunals to handle international investment disputes, it forms part of the overall layout for improving China's foreign-related arbitration system, together with other revised clauses in the New Arbitration Law. It provides a clear legal basis for Chinese arbitration institutions to handle foreign-related disputes, including international investment disputes, and is a key step in aligning China's arbitration system with international standards.

In recent years, traditional international commercial arbitration institutions have begun to venture into international investment arbitration. The SIAC and the SCC Arbitration Institute have also issued specific rules for investment arbitration. Major domestic arbitration institutions in China have started to include investment arbitration within their scope of accepted cases, some by adopting separate arbitration rules and others by adding provisions for international investment arbitration to their existing rules. The CIETAC implemented the CIETAC International Investment Arbitration Rules (for Trial Implementation) effective October 1, 2017. The BAC also released its 2019 edition of International Investment Arbitration Rules on September 13, 2019, effective October 1, 2019. SCIA explicitly stipulates in Article 2 (Scope of Acceptance), paragraph 2 of its Arbitration Rules that they accept arbitration cases concerning investment disputes between a government and an investor of another state."

As China has become a significant global capital importer and exporter, investment disputes between investors and host states have correspondingly increased. The legislative gap in the original Arbitration Law left Chinese arbitration institutions without a solid legal foundation when accepting such cases, which also affected parties' willingness to choose China as the seat for investment arbitration. Article 94 of the New Arbitration Law directly responds to this practical need, providing a source of legitimacy for related practices. This Article of the New Arbitration Law clearly states that matters may be handled "in accordance with the relevant international investment treaties and agreements" and "the arbitration rules agreed upon by both parties," reflecting full respect for the particularities of investment arbitration and helping to enhance China's attractiveness and credibility as a destination for investment arbitration.

Article 95
Where there is a violation of the provisions on the registration and administration of arbitration institutions, the matter shall be handled in accordance with the relevant laws and administrative regulations.

Notes
This Article establishes, for the first time, an independent legal liability clause specifically targeting violations of arbitration institution registration and administration requirements, thereby strengthening the supervision and management of arbitration institutions. Under the Arbitration Law (2017) framework, only the procedures for the establishment, alteration, and deregistration of arbitration institutions were stipulated in administrative regulations, such as the Interim Measures for the Registration of Arbitration Commissions, but there were no penalties for violations (e.g., false registration, failure to report changes). The New Arbitration Law first clarifies the procedures related to the registration and administration of arbitration institutions in Articles 14, 15, 16, and 17, and explicitly incorporates violations of registration and administration into the legal liability system in Article 95.

On June 14, 2016, the Ministry of Justice issued the Opinions on Regulating and Strengthening the Registration Administration of Arbitration Institutions to standardize and enhance the registration management of arbitration institutions. The main tasks and measures proposed in Article 3 are:

A. ***Further standardizing the registration of arbitration institutions.*** Registration work shall be carried out diligently in accordance with laws and regulations, such as the Administrative Licensing Law of the People's Republic of China, adhering to the principles of overall planning and rational layout. The conditions for establishing arbitration institutions shall be strictly reviewed in accordance with the law, strictly comply with the prescribed procedures for application and acceptance, review and decision, and registration time limits. Key examination areas include the composition of the arbitration commission and the proportion of experts, the panel of arbitrators, etc., to ensure the composition of the arbitration institution complies with legal provisions. The connection between the appointment of arbitrators (legal category) and the requirements of the national unified legal professional qualification system shall be ensured. The announcement and filing of arbitration institution registration shall be standardized. For approved registrations, the registration authority shall announce the establishment within 20 days after registration and file a report and the announcement text with the Ministry of Justice, simultaneously copying them to the people's court in the locality of the arbitration institution.
B. ***Further standardizing the filing of changes to arbitration institutions.*** Registered arbitration institutions that change their domicile or composition shall be required to proactively file the changes with the registration authority within 10 days of the change, submitting documents related to the changes. If the changes involve matters recorded on the Arbitration Commission Registration Certificate, the certificate shall be reissued. Failure to file as required or discrepancies found during filing that do not comply with laws and regulations shall be corrected according to law to ensure the legality of arbitration institutions.
C. ***Further strengthening the supervision and administration of arbitration institutions.*** The provisions of the Administrative Licensing Law of the People's Republic of China regarding the supervision and inspection of administrative licenses shall be implemented. Information concerning arbitration institutions shall be promptly understood and mastered, supervising them to strictly comply with laws, regulations, and rules. Key inspection areas include arbitration institutions operating beyond their scope of practice, illegally altering registered items, and improperly establishing branch agencies or service sites across regions. Non-compliant instances shall be promptly corrected according to law. Regulatory concepts shall be transformed, integrating service into management. Mid-event and post-event supervision measures shall be improved, utilizing methods such as material verification, planning guidance, random checks, and informed commitments to further enhance regulatory efficiency. Management methods shall be innovated, focusing on advancing the credit system construction for arbitration institutions. Gradually incorporating public disclosure of institutional personnel, disclosure of practice information, and handling of arbi-

tration complaints into credit management, and establishing integrity files for arbitration institutions shall promote their standardized operation.

D. ***Further improving the registration management system for arbitration institutions.*** Research and formulate measures for the registration administration of arbitration institutions to further standardize their establishment registration, change filing, and mid-event and post-event supervision. Various regions shall, based on local realities, establish and strengthen various work systems for the registration administration of arbitration institutions and guide arbitration institutions in strengthening their internal management system construction. Communication mechanisms between judicial administrative organs, government legal affairs agencies, people's courts, and other departments shall be strengthened and improved to promptly coordinate and resolve issues encountered in the registration administration of arbitration institutions and promote the standardized development of arbitration work.

Arbitration institutions often engage in ancillary or temporary activities such as accepting inquiries, transmitting arbitration materials, or holding hearings in different locations for the convenience of the parties. However, with the rapid development of arbitration, certain institutions, competing for case sources and expanding their business, have seen these temporary cross-regional activities evolve into establishing offices or case-handling sites in different locations with fixed premises and staff. These institutions conduct cross-regional arbitration business in a "grey area" manner without fulfilling the corresponding approval and registration procedures, and sometimes engage in non-standard practices, severely disrupting the normal competition order of arbitration and affecting its credibility. The following text provides two examples.

The addition of Article 95 in the New Arbitration Law, along with other revised clauses concerning the management of arbitration institutions in this revision, collectively provides clear legal authorization for judicial administrative departments to conduct full-cycle supervision. It is highly foreseeable that future regulations and systems will be formulated based on the authorization of the new Law to strengthen supervision. It is hoped and believed that all measures will be conducive to standardizing the operation of arbitration institutions and enhancing the overall credibility and international competitiveness of China's arbitration system.

Article 96
This Law shall come into effect as of March 1, 2026.

Notes
With a transition period of approximately five months between its passage in September 2025 and its formal implementation in March 2026, substantial preparatory work is required from all relevant parties due to the new systems and administrative arrangements introduced by this revision. During this period, for instance, the judicial administrative authorities need to formulate or revise a series of supporting administrative regulations and departmental rules, such as the measures for the administration of arbitration institution registration, under the authorization of the

new law, providing specific operational guidance for the new systems. Arbitration institutions nationwide must revise their own Arbitration Rules and constitutions, adjust their organizational structures, and conduct systematic training for arbitrators and staff in accordance with the new requirements of the law regarding institutional nature, internal governance, and information disclosure. People's courts need to adapt their internal workflows to the new provisions concerning arbitration preservation measures, setting aside of awards, and judicial review of foreign-related arbitration, ensuring they can handle various arbitration-related applications promptly and in accordance with the law. Market participants and legal practitioners require time to study and understand the new rules, such as those for online arbitration, *ad hoc* arbitration, and pre-arbitration preservation, in order to properly design arbitration clauses in future contracts and effectively protect their rights and interests when disputes arise.

Naturally, one of the core tasks during the transition period is to ensure a smooth transition between the old and new arbitration systems. This generally means that for arbitration cases already accepted prior to the effective date of the New Arbitration Law (March 1, 2026), the previous Arbitration Law and the arbitration rules chosen at that time shall generally apply to the procedures, namely the principle of non-retroactivity. For arbitration applications filed only after the new Law takes effect, the New Arbitration Law must be fully applied. If parties reach an arbitration agreement after the New Arbitration Law takes effect, they should also draft the clauses according to the requirements of the New Arbitration Law.

It is important to note that after the New Arbitration Law takes effect, it can be applied as the governing law for arbitration agreements, arbitration procedures, or other aspects through various means. For example, regarding the governing law of an arbitration agreement, it is generally determined in the following ways.

1. **Abiding by the Principle of Party Autonomy**

The principle of party autonomy is a fundamental principle in contract law. This principle is also recognized in international commercial arbitration. Since an arbitration agreement is a contract, the parties naturally have the right to choose its governing law. The principle of party autonomy serves as the primary rule for determining the governing law of an arbitration agreement. However, it is relatively rare for parties to separately agree on the governing law of the arbitration agreement. Article V(1)(a) of the New York Convention states that recognition and enforcement of an award may be refused if the parties to the agreement referred to in Article II were, under the law applicable to them, under some incapacity, or the said agreement is not valid under the law to which the parties have subjected it or, failing any indication thereon, under the law of the country where the award was made. The phrase "under the law to which the parties have subjected it" refers to the law chosen by the parties to govern the arbitration agreement. Just like the general principle for determining the governing law of a contract, the primary principle for determining the governing law of an arbitration agreement is the parties' agreement in the contract. Furthermore, it also clarifies the law of the country where the award was made as the second option for determining the law applicable to the validity of the arbitration agreement.

2. **Abiding by the Law of the Seat of Arbitration**

The seat of arbitration is typically the place where the award is made. When the parties have not explicitly chosen the governing law of the arbitration agreement, the internationally prevalent practice is to apply the law of the seat of arbitration or the place of the award as the governing law of the arbitration agreement. Article 2 of the Swedish Foreign Arbitration Act 1929 stipulated that if the arbitration agreement provides that the proceedings shall be conducted in a particular country, the law of that country shall apply to the arbitration agreement. The first part of Article 48 of the Swedish Arbitration Act 1999, which replaced it, states that if the arbitration agreement has an international connection, it shall be governed by the law agreed upon by the parties. Where no such agreement has been reached, the arbitration agreement shall be governed by the law of the state in which the proceedings have been or will be conducted. In practice, the seat of arbitration is indeed the most commonly used factor for legal choice. In the case of *Shandong Molong Petroleum Machinery Co., Ltd. v. High Sealed and Coupled S.A.L*,[8] the SPC held that the involved Exclusive Sales Agreement stipulated arbitration rules, namely the ICC Arbitration and Mediation Rules. Since the arbitration institution could be determined as the International Court of Arbitration of the ICC according to these rules, it should be deemed that the parties had agreed on a specific arbitration institution. The law of the seat of arbitration in this case was Swiss law. According to Swiss law, the arbitration clause agreed by the parties in this case was valid. Therefore, the Chinese courts had no jurisdiction over this case. In *Guangdong A Shipping Agency Co., Ltd. v. B (Hong Kong) Co., Ltd.*,[9] the Shanghai High People's Court held that the disputed arbitration clause was a foreign-related arbitration clause. The parties agreed: "The place of arbitration is Hong Kong, applying English law." According to the relevant provisions of English law, the disputed arbitration clause was valid. The substantive law applicable to the arbitration should be English law, the seat of arbitration was Hong Kong, and the procedural law applicable to the arbitration should be the law of the seat, i.e., Hong Kong law. According to the provisions of the Hong Kong Arbitration Ordinance, the disputed arbitration clause was also valid and enforceable.

3. **Abiding by the Principle of Closest Connection**

Like the principle of party autonomy, the principle of closest connection is widely used to determine the governing law of general civil and commercial contracts, but it is less commonly used to determine the governing law of arbitration agreements. However, in theory, it can also be used for this purpose. When applying the principle of closest connection, connecting factors to consider include: the place of

[8] [2010] Min Si Ta Zi No. 40.

[9] See the Latest Topics in Commercial Arbitration and Judicial Practice, Volume 10.

contracting, the location of the subject matter of the dispute, the domicile, nationality, habitual residence, place of business of the parties, etc.

4. **Abiding by the Principle of Favoring Validity**

An important principle in determining the validity of contracts is the principle of favoring validity. This principle is also adopted by some jurisdictions in determining the validity of arbitration agreements, such as Switzerland. For example, under the Swiss Federal Act on Private International Law, an arbitration agreement is substantively valid if it conforms to the law chosen by the parties, the law governing the subject matter of the dispute (particularly the law governing the main contract), or Swiss law. This approach provides multiple legal standards, and the agreement is valid if it meets any one of them, reflecting a supportive stance towards arbitration.

5. **Complying with the Governing Law of the Contract**

As mentioned earlier, applying the governing law of the underlying contract is also an option for determining the law applicable to the arbitration agreement. Explicitly agreeing on the law governing the arbitration agreement is rare. Usually, a contract will contain a governing law clause, but whether the law specified in that clause applies to all contents, including the dispute resolution clause, can be subject to different views. The general application theory holds that the arbitration clause, as part of the contract, should naturally be governed by the law applicable to the entire contract. The separate application theory, however, may argue that the arbitration clause, as a dispute resolution clause, is special, as it is designed to resolve disputes potentially arising from other parts of the contract, including the governing law clause itself, and thus should be excluded from the scope of the governing law clause.

6. **Other Methods**

The law of the forum, the law of the place of contracting, or mandatory application of the domestic law under certain circumstances are some methods that might be used when the parties have not chosen the applicable law. For instance, Italy and Austria apply the law of the place of contracting, and the European Convention on International Commercial Arbitration contains similar provisions. For example, under Swedish law, if the seat of arbitration is Sweden or if no seat is designated and at least one party was a resident of Sweden at the time of contracting, then Swedish law governs the arbitration agreement in the absence of party choice.[10]

Regarding the application of the law of the forum, it is the most convenient approach for courts in many countries. This approach is also reflected in a considerable number of recent judicial precedents in China. For example, in the case of *Wanhua Tourism Company v. RF Travel Service Company*,[11] the SPC held that when the arbitration clause does not stipulate the law governing its validity, and also does

[10] See The Stockholm Chamber of Commerce (ed), Arbitration in Sweden (1984), second (revised) edition, 23.

[11] [2003] Min Si Ta Zi No. 36.

not explicitly stipulate the seat of arbitration, its validity should be determined according to the relevant laws of China, which is the law of the forum.

The above discussion uses the applicable law of the arbitration agreement merely as an example. The approach to determining the applicable law for arbitration proceedings is largely similar. By the appropriate choice-of-law methodology, if it is ultimately determined that Chinese arbitration law should apply to resolve issues concerning the arbitration agreement, as well as matters related to arbitration proceedings, judicial review of arbitration, and other aspects, this forms the subject matter of this book, which I hope will be of benefit to all readers.

Table of Cases

Article 3

BO Company v. M Bureau and others, (2021) Zui Gao Fa Min Ta No. 97.
*B Company v. A Company and others, s*ee the 9 Typical Cases on Arbitration Judicial Review released by the Sichuan Province Chengdu Intermediate People's Court in May 2025.
*Zhejiang M Company v. Ninghai N Company, s*ee the 10 Typical Cases on Judicial Review of Commercial Arbitration published by Zhejiang Province Ningbo Intermediate People's Court in June 2024.
WMC v. Ruisu Company, see the 10 Typical Cases on the Construction of Pilot Free Trade Zones published by the SPC.
Shanghai M Company v. Guangzhou B Company and others, see the 10 Typical Cases on Judicial Review of Commercial Arbitration published by the Zhejiang Province Ningbo Intermediate People's Court.
FY Company v. CPC Company, HD Company and others, (2022) Zhe 09 Min Chu No. 47;(2022) Zhe Min Zhong No. 1415.

Article 4

Sun, Sunfei Company v. Shengke Company, (2022) Gui 71 Min Te No. 21; see also the 10 Typical Cases of Judicial Review of Arbitration published by the SPC in January 2024.
A Company v. B; See the Typical Cases of Judicial Review of Arbitration published by the Zhejiang Province Hangzhou Intermediate Court in March 2024.
Leidi Company v. Germany IBG Company, (2021) Su 01 Min Chu No. 321, (2021) Su Min Zhong No. 606.
Fanhai Company v. Guo, (2022) Jing 74 Min Te No. 13.
A Company and others, v. Luo, see the 9 Typical Cases of Judicial Review of Arbitration released by the Sichuan Province Chengdu Intermediate People's Court in May 2025.
Fan v. M Entertainment Company, see the 2nd batch of 10 Typical Cases on Judicial Review of Arbitration published by the High People's Court of Guangdong Province.
X Communications Company v. Y Bank, see the 10 Typical Cases of Judicial Review Involving Financial Arbitration published by the Beijing Financial Court in October 2023.

Y. Lin, *New Arbitration Law in China*, China Arbitration Yearbook,
https://doi.org/10.1007/978-981-92-0642-1

Ningbo N Company v. Zhou, see the 10 Typical Cases on Judicial Review of Commercial Arbitration published by the Zhejiang Province Ningbo Intermediate People's Court in June 2024.
Yu v. Li and others, see the 2nd batch of 10 typical cases of judicial review of arbitration released by the Guangdong Provincial High People's Court in August 2025.

Article 5

X Capital Management Company v. Y Securities Company and others, see the 10 typical cases on judicial review of financial arbitration released by the Beijing Financial Court in October 2023.

Article 6

Party A v. Party B, see the Typical Cases of Judicial Review of Arbitration published by the Zhejiang Province Hangzhou Intermediate People's Court in March 2024.

Article 8

Henglong Company v. Yixiangyuan Company, (2022) Lu 04 Min Te No. 9.
Zhang Lan and others v. La Dolce Vita Fine Dining Group Holdings Limited, (2019) Zui Gao Fa Min Te No. 5.

Article 9

Company A v. Company B and others, see typical cases of judicial review of arbitration released by the Hangzhou Intermediate People's Court On 15 March 2024.

Article 10

Funing X Bureau v. Yaxin Company, (2021) Su 09 Min Te No. 22.
SIPC v. UNI-TOP, (2017) Jing 04 Min Te No. 39.

Article 11

Hairun Company v. Song, (2023) Jing 74 Min Te No. 37.

Shenzhen M Construction Company v. Zhuhai M Technology Company; see the 2nd batch of the Typical Cases on Judicial Review of Arbitration publsihed by the High People's Court of Guangdong Province in 2025.

Article 27

Svensk Company v. Changli Company, (2018) Su 01 Xie Wai Ren No. 8.

M Securities Company v. N Company, One of the 10 Typical Cases on Judicial Review Involving Financial Arbitration published by the Beijing Financial Court in October 2023.

Wu v. A Fund Sales Company, see the 10 Typical Cases on Judicial Review of Commercial Arbitration published by the Zhejiang Province Ningbo Intermediate People's Court in June 2024.

W Company v. Ningde M Company and others, (2018) Min 07 Ren Gang No. 1.

Article 28

Lianping A Company v. Huang, (2023) Yue 01 Min Te No. 185.

Li v. A Culture Company, see the Ten Typical Cases on Domestic Arbitration Judicial Review in 2022 issued by the Beijing No. 4 Intermediate People's Court.

Wang v. Huya Company, (2020) Chuan 13 Min Te No. 34.

Qu v. Zhai, Annual Report on Judicial Review of Commercial Arbitration by the SPC (2024), released in December 2025.

Fang v. B Education Company, see the 10 Typical Cases on Judicial Review of Domestic Arbitration Judicial Review published by Beijing No. 4 Intermediate People's Court's in July 2022. T

Article 29

Baoyuan Trading Company v. Yu, (2007) Min Si Ta Zi No. 38.

Rongcheng Company v. Li and others, (2021) Zhe 06 Min Te No. 47.

Chen v. Hong Company, see the 1st batch of Typical Cases on Judicial Review of Arbitration published by the Guangdong High People's Court in February 2024.

A Logistics Company v. B Shipping Company, see the Typical Cases on Judicial Review of Arbitration from 2020–2024 published by the Shanghai High People's Court.

Shan Company v. Niu Company, see the 2nd batch of the 10 Typical Cases on Judicial Review of Arbitration published by the Guangdong High People's Court in August 2025.

Tianjin A Hotel Management Company v. Hong Kong B Company, (2021) Jin 01 Min Te No. 1; see the 6 Typical Cases Supporting Hong Kong Arbitration published by the SPC in September 2024.

Liu v. Long, (2022) Yue 03 Min Chu No. 7444; see the 10 Typical Cases on Judicial Review of Arbitration for 2024 published by the Guangdong Province Shenzhen Intermediate People's Court in July 2025.

Article 30

Yunyu Company v. Zhongyuan Company, Guiding Case No. 196.
Ningbo X Biotechnology Company et al. v. Shanghai Y Technology Company, see the 10 Typical Cases on the Judicial Review of Arbitration from 2020-2024 published by the High People's Court of Shanghai in July 2025.
J Company v. P Insurance Company; see the Typical Cases on Judicial Review of Financial Arbitration published by the Shanghai Financial Court in November 2024.
H Securities Company v. L Bank, see the 10 Typical Cases on Judicial Review of Financial Arbitration published by the Shanghai Financial Court in October 2024.

Article 31

Hui A Company, Yang v. Hua B Bank, see the 10 Typical Cases on the Judicial Review of Arbitration published by the High People's Court of Guangdong Province in February 2024.
Lin v. X Education Technology Company, see the 2nd batch of the 10 Typical Cases on the Judicial Review of Arbitration published by the High People's Court of Guangdong Province in August 2025.

Article 34

Singapore M Company v. Ningbo N Company, see the 10 Typical Cases on Judicial Review of Arbitration published by the Zhejiang Province Ningbo Intermediate People's Court in June 2024.

Article 37

Hydraulic Company v. Technology Company, (2009) Da Min Chu Zi No. 3868.
Technology Company v. Catering Management Company, (2009) Feng Min Chu Zi No. 04471.
Huang v. G Company, (2009) Hai Min Chu Zi No. 10243.
Lin v. F Company, (2009) Yuan Min Yi Chu Zi No. 52.
Linying G Company v. Pingdingshan H Company, (2009) Ping Min Chu Zi No. 82.
LH Transport Company v. J Property Insurance Company, (2009) Yuan Min San Chu Zi No. 42.
Wang v. K Property Insurance Company, (2009) Tai Min Chu Zi No. 1348.
Guangxi L Company v. Beijing M Company, (2009) Da Min Chu Zi No. 8125.
Beijing N Company v. O Bank, (2009) Xi Min Chu Zi No. 4851.
Yang v. P Insurance Company, (2009) Xuan Min Chu Zi No. 8327.
Q Bank v. Cheng and others, (2009) Da Min Chu Zi No. 10645.
Henan R Company v. Huangchuan S Company, (2009) Xing Min Er Chu Zi No. 461.
H Company v. B, (2009) Min Si Ta Zi No. 1.
N Bank v. Wen and others, (2009) Dong Min Chu Zi No. 794.
Henan X Bureau v. Y Company, (2009) Yu Fa Min Yi Zhong Zi No. 5.
W School v. Huang, (2009) Min Yi Zhong Zi No. 359.
Deng v. X Insurance Company, (2009) Bei Min Yi Chu Zi No. 836.
Liu v. Y Property Insurance Company, (2009) Zhan Min Chu Zi No. 669.

Dai v. Z Property Insurance Company, (2009) Nei Min Chu Zi No. 248. (2009) An Min San Zhong Zi No. 239

GY Company v. S Transportation Bureau, SPC Guiding Case No. 197.

A Holding Company and others v. C Company and others, (2018) Zui Gao Fa Min Xia Zhong No. 453.

Article 39

A Resources Company v. B Industrial Company, see the 10 Typical Cases on Judicial Review of Arbitration published by the Beijing No.4 Intermediate People's Court in November 2024.

Shenzhen A Company v. Zhuhai B Company, see the 10 Typical Cases on Judicial Review of Arbitration Published by the High People's Court of Guangdong Province in August 2025.

UK M Company v. Hong Kong N Company and others, see the 10 Typical Cases on Judicial Review of Arbitration published by the Zhejiang Province Hangzhou Intermediate People's Court in March 2024.

Article 40

Singapore A Company v. Ningbo B Company, see the 10 Typical Cases on Judicial Review of Arbitration published by the Zhejiang Province Ningbo Intermediate People's Court in June 2024.

Article 41

Wu v. X Investment Company, see the 10 Typical Cases on Judicial Review of Commercial Arbitration published by the Zhejiang Province Ningbo Intermediate People's Court in June 2024.

B Trading Company v. C Import & Export Company, see the 10 Typical Cases on Judicial Review of Domestic Arbitration published by the Beijing No. 4 Intermediate People's Court in July 2024.

TH Company v. JZ Company, (2021) Su 03 Min Te No. 51-2.

SVM Company v. Wansheng Company, (2019) Su 05 Xie Wai Ren No. 6.

WRE Company v. APM Company, (2019) Su 02 Zhi Yi No. 49.

Indian D Company v. Shanghai E Company, see the Typical Cases on Judicial Review of Arbitration published by the High People's Court of Shanghai in July 2025.

A Company v. B Company, see the Typical Cases on Judicial Review of Arbitration published by the Zhejiang Province Hangzhou Intermediate People's Court in March 2024.

Article 42

A International Logistics Company v. Singapore B Shipping Company, see the Typical Cases from 202-2024 on Judicial Review of Arbitration published by the Shanghai High People's Court in July 2025.

C Finance Company v. D Salt Company, (2020) Chuan 03 Ren Gang No. 1.
German SE Company and others v. J Company, see the 6 Typical Cases Supporting Hong Kong Arbitration published by the SPC in September 2024.

Article 43

A Company v. J, see the Typical Cases on Judicial Review of Arbitration published by the Zhejiang Province Hangzhou Intermediate Court in March 2024.

Article 45

A Engineering Company v. TB Company, (2018) Zhe 03 Min Te No. 63; see the 10 Typical Cases on Judicial Review of Arbitration published by the SPC in January 2024
Wang v. B Bank, see the Typical Cases on Judicial Review of Arbitration published by the Guangdong Province Shenzhen Intermediate People's Court in July 2025.

Article 46

A Office v. B Company, see the 9 Typical Cases on Judicial Review of Arbitration published by the Sichuan Province Chengdu Intermediate People's Court in May 2025.
M Company v. N Company, (2023) Su 06 Min Te No. 34.

Article 47

Li vs A Fund and others, see the Typical Cases from 2020–2024 on Judicial Review of Arbitration published by the Shanghai High People's Court in July 2025.

Article 49

Chongqing A Company v. HT Company, (2024) Yu 03 Zhi Yi No. 2.
Shandong B Company v. Jinan C Company, (2023) Lu 01 Min Te No. 154.

Article 51

Chen v. Y Trust Company and others, see the 10 Typical Cases on Judicial Review of Financial Arbitration published by the Shanghai Financial Court in October 2024.

Article 52

A Airlines v. B Aircraft Leasing Company, see the 10 Typical Cases on Judicial Review of Arbitration published by the Beijing No.4 Intermediate People's Court in November 2024.

Article 53

Du v. SH Company, (2020) Su 11 Zhi Yi No. 21.

Article 54

Sun v. Lu, see the 10 Typical Cases for 2024 on Judicial Review of Arbitration published by the Guangdong Province Shenzhen Intermediate People's Court in July 2025.

Article 55

Hong Kong A Company v. B Company and others, see the Typical Cases from 2020–2024 on Judicial Review of Arbitration published by the Shanghai High People's Court in July 2025.
A v. B, see the 2nd batch of the 10 Typical Cases on Judicial Review of Arbitration published by the High People's Court of Guangdong Province in August 2025a.

Article 56

X Fire Protection Company v. Y Engineering Company, see the Typical Cases for 2024 on Judicial Review of Arbitration published by the Guangdong Province Shenzhen Intermediate People's Court in July 2025.

Article 57

Yantai A Company v. Shandong B Company, see the Typical Cases on Judicial Review of Commercial Arbitration published by the Shandong Province Qingdao Intermediate People's Court in 2018–2021.

Article 58

HC Company v. JL Company, (2023) Jing 04 Min Te No. 298.
Lin v. Zhuang, (2017) Yue 03 Min Te No. 465.

Article 59

Hua Company v. Guang Company, see the 1st batch of the Typical Cases on Judicial Review of Arbitration published by the High People's Court of Guangdong Province in February 2024.
ZT Company v. JG Company, (2022) Zhe 01 Min Te No. 226.
Zhang v. HX Company, (2022) Min 02 Min Te No. 273.

Article 61

A Asset Management Company v. B Industrial Development Company, see the 9 Typical Cases on Judicial Review of Arbitration published by the Sichuan Province Chengdu Intermediate People's Court May 2025.
HS Company v. HD Company and others, (2020) Su 09 Zhi Yi No. 11; (2021) Su Zhi Fu No. 83.

Article 62

CM Company v. Chen, (2018) Jin 02 Min Chu No. 1050.

Article 64

EL Company v. KH Travel Agency, see the 10 Typical Cases on Judicial Review of People's Courts Serving and Guaranteeing the Construction of Pilot Free Trade Zones published by the SPC in February 2022.
A Bank v. B Fund Company, see the 10 Typical Cases on Judicial Review of Financial Arbitration published by the Beijing Financial Court in October 2023.

Article 65

Guangzhou A Investment Company and others v. Liu, see the 2nd batch of the 10 Typical Cases on Judicial Review of Arbitration published by the High People's Court of Guangdong Province in August 2025.
Zhao vs. Chongqing A College, see the 10 Typical Cases for 2016–2020 on Judicial Review of Commercial Arbitration published by the High People's Court of Chongqing.

Article 66

TH Company v. XD Company, (2023) Yu 03 Min Te No. 60.

Article 69

Chen v. Kuang and others, (2021) Zui Gao Fa Min Ta No. 404.
Electric Power Company v. Construction Company, (2023) Gan 01 Min Te No. 44.

Article 71

JQ Company and others v. JK Company and others, (2018) Jing 04 Min Te No. 23.
TZ Company v. WX Company, (2019) Wan 06 Min Te No. 12.
Jiang v. JD Company, (2019) Xiang 12 Min Te No. 1
C Company v. D Company, see the 10 Typical Cases on Judicial Review of Financial Arbitration published by the Beijing Financial Court in October 2023.
F Company v. G Management Committee, (2024) Jing 04 Min Te No. 287.
H Company v. I Company, see the 10 Typical Cases on Judicial Review of Domestic Arbitration published by the Beijing No.4 Intermediate People's Court in July 2023.
Sun v. Lyu, see the 10 Typical Cases on Judicial Review of Arbitration published by the Guangdong Province Shenzhen Intermediate People's Court in July 2025.
J Company v. Fu and others, see the 10 Typical Cases for 2022 on Judicial Review of Domestic Arbitration published by the Beijing No. 4 Intermediate People's Court in July 2023.
K Company v. Jiang, see the 10 Typical Cases on Judicial Review of Financial Arbitration published by the Beijing Financial Court in October 2023.
Zhang v. Nanchang L Culture Company, see the 10 Typical Cases on Judicial Review of Arbitration published by the Fujian Province Xiamen International Commercial Court in November 2023.
LY Hotel v. JH Administration, (2023) Zhe 07 Min Te No. 58.
Li v. Wang, (2023) Qian 01 Min Te No. 54.
A Company v. B Company and others, see the 9 Typical Cases on Judicial Review of Arbitration published by the Sichuan Province Chengdu Intermediate People's Court in May 2025.
Lai v. O Real Estate Company, see the 10 Typical Cases on Judicial Review of Domestic Arbitration published by the Beijing No. 4 Intermediate People's Court in July 2023.
AC Company v. BC Company, see the 9 Typical Cases on Judicial Review of Arbitration published by the Sichuan Province Chengdu Intermediate People's Court in May 2025.
R Technology Company v. S Electronics Company, see the 10 Typical Cases for 2022 on Judicial Review of Domestic Arbitration published by the Beijing No.4 Intermediate People's Court in July 2023.

Article 72

Li and others v. Ma and others, (2025) Jing 74 Min Te No. 104.

Article 73

YH Company v. ZH Company and others, (2022) Yu 01 Min Te No. 104.

Article 74

BJ Company v. Zhou and others, (2022) Su 01 Min Te No. 212.

Article 76

WS Company v. YSG Company, (2019) Su 02 Zhi Yi 49.
Zhang v. C Company.
TH Company and others v. ZH Company, (2021) Su 05 Zhi Yi 150.
D Bank v. Wang, (2023) Zui Gao Fa Zhi Jian 427.
YM Company v. XMD Company, see the Ten Typical Cases on Arbitration Judicial Review released by the Xiamen International Commercial Tribunal in 2023.

Article 77

ZG Shipbuilding Company v. YY Shipping Company, (2016) Min 72 Min Chu No. 565.

Article 78

Wang v. SZA Investment Company, (2021) Jing 04 Min Te 667.
HR V Company. ZX Company, (2021) Zui Gao Fa Zhi Min Xia Zhong 90.

Article 79

Beijing A Technology Company v. B Information Company, see the 10 Typical Cases published by the Beijing No.4 Intermediate People's Court in November 2024 to Support and Safeguard the Construction of an International Commercial Arbitration Center.
C Company v. H Company and others, see the 10 Typical Cases on Judicial Review of Financial Arbitration published by the Beijing Financial Court in October 2023.
G Company v. V Company, (2022) Su 05 Cai Bao 146.

Article 82

A Trading Company v. B Freight Forwarding Company, (2024) Hu 72 Min Te 43.

Article 83

KSHY Company v. RD Company, (2023) Jing 04 Min Te No. 67.
EEI Company and others v. WY Company, (2019) Zui Gao Fa Min Ta No. 14.
A Shipping Company v. Pei, (2023) Lu 72 Min Te No. 221.
HQ Company v. TT Company, at al., (2017) Jing 04 Min Te No. 30.
LC Company v. ZF Company, (2021) Jing 04 Min Te No. 719.
M Machinery Company v. Swedish N Technology Company, (2021) Jing 04 Min Te No. 726.

Article 84

SD Company v. SJ Company, (2013) Min Si Ta Zi No. 12.

Article 85

ChicV v. N&J, 5:24-cv-01720-SSS-SHKx.

Article 86

Ennead Company v. R&F Company, (2016). Su 01 Ren Gang No. 1.

Article 87

Shanghai Gold Land Co., Ltd. v. Siemens International Trading (Shanghai) Co., Ltd., see the Second Group of Model Cases Involving the Development of the Belt and Road Initiative Released by the SPC in 2017.
H v. Y, (2023) Zhe 01 Min Te No. 453.
T Company v. B Company, Annual Report on Judicial Review of Commercial Arbitration by the SPC (2024), released in December 2025.

Article 88

S Shipping Company v. Hua Company, see the Guiding Case No. 235 of the SPC, published on November 25, 2024.
Italy L Company v. Ningbo S Company, (2019) Zhe 02 Xie Wai Ren No. 5.
New Zealand A Hotel v. China B Group, see the 10 Typical Cases for 2024 on Judicial Review of Arbitration published by the Guangdong Province Shenzhen Intermediate People's Court in July 2025.
L Company and others v. Z Company, see the 2nd batch of the 10 Typical Cases on Judicial Review of Arbitration published by the High People's Court of Guangdong Province in August 2025.

Hu v. Guangdong C Club, see the 2nd batch of the 10 Typical Cases on Judicial Review of Arbitration published by the High People's Court of Guangdong Province in August 2025.
A v. B, Annual Report on Judicial Review of Commercial Arbitration by the SPC (2024), released in December 2025b.
KOT v. Z and others, Annual Report on Judicial Review of Commercial Arbitration by the SPC (2024), released in December 2025.

Article 89

Korea DC Company and others v. PL Company, see the 10 Typical Cases on Judicial Review of Arbitration published by the SPC in early 2024.

Article 90

Wang v. Wisdom Company, (2022) Jing 04 Min Te No. 130.

Article 92

A Company v. Li, (2017) E 03 Min Zhong No. 2210.

Article 93

A Company v. Huang, (2023) Yue 01 Min Te No. 185.
SX Company v. SH Company and others, (2023) Hu 0151 Min Chu No. 1673, (2023) Hu 02 Min Zhong No. 6825.
Ma v. SH J Football Club, Annual Report on Judicial Review of Commercial Arbitration by the SPC (2024), released in December 2025.

Article 96

Shandong Molong Petroleum Machinery Co., Ltd. v. High Sealed and Coupled S.A.L, (2010) Min Si Ta Zi No. 40.
Guangdong A Shipping Agency Co., Ltd. v. B (Hong Kong) Co., Ltd., see the Latest Topics in Commercial Arbitration and Judicial Practice, Volume 10.
Wanhua Tourism Company v. RF Travel Service Company, (2003) Min Si Ta Zi No. 36.

GPSR Compliance
The European Union's (EU) General Product Safety Regulation (GPSR) is a set of rules that requires consumer products to be safe and our obligations to ensure this.

If you have any concerns about our products, you can contact us on

ProductSafety@springernature.com

In case Publisher is established outside the EU, the EU authorized representative is:

Springer Nature Customer Service Center GmbH
Europaplatz 3
69115 Heidelberg, Germany

www.ingramcontent.com/pod-product-compliance
Ingram Content Group UK Ltd.
Pitfield, Milton Keynes, MK11 3LW, UK
UKHW020633260926
475829UK00003BA/64
9789819206414